"I have watched with much interest the developments in Christian counseling over the past forty years. The issues discussed here are still very important, and this book is a good introduction to them. Even readers already familiar with this movement will learn new things. David's book is entirely judicious, careful, and balanced in its treatment of Adams, his opponents, and the events affecting the biblical counseling movement. I hope the book attracts a large readership."

John M. Frame, D.D.
Professor of Systematic Theology, Reformed Theological Seminary; author of *The Doctrine of the Christian Life*

"Powlison is provocative and delightful: provocative because he addresses fault lines within pastoral care; delightful because he does it with honesty and kindness. Thank you, David, for showing us where we need to be heading!"

D. Clair Davis, Dr. Théol.
Professor of Church History and Chaplain, Redeemer Seminary

"David Powlison and I share a deep commitment to biblical counseling and to church history. Dr. Powlison unites these twin themes in his excellent work, *The Biblical Counseling Movement: History and Context*. Everyone interested in the modern biblical counseling movement over the past generation needs to read this well-researched and well-written book. This is a fair and balanced presentation of one of the most important movements in the evangelical church over the past forty years. Readers will be equipped not only with historical insight but, more importantly, with wisdom for how to speak the truth in love."

Bob Kellemen, Ph.D.
Author of *Soul Physicians*, *Spiritual Friends*, *Beyond the Suffering*, and *Sacred Friendships*

"It is diffi ... this book. The counseling wars of the past half century have ignited passions often characterized by labels rather than by careful analytic thought. This is the first broadly comprehensive history of these developments. Although Powlison is one of the important players, he takes extraordinary pains not to misrepresent those with whom he disagrees. Above all, while trying to be open to truth and insight whatever their source (after all, the reaches of common grace are vast), Powlison faithfully argues that the Christian faith must play a constitutive role in building a robust model of Christian counseling. Amen and Amen."

D. A. Carson, Ph.D.
Research Professor of New Testament, Trinity Evangelical Divinity School; author of *The Gagging of God, Christ and Culture Revisited,* and *An Introduction to the New Testament*

"David Powlison has written the definitive account of a biblical counseling movement that arose in the 1960s and continues to influence the field of Christian counseling today. The reader is taken on a journey through the historical development of nouthetic counseling, its origins, influences, theological content, organizational fault lines, and key figures. Powlison is not a dispassionate outsider. He is clear in what he believes, but he approaches his subject with such a thoroughness and fairness in his research and assessment that he will leave readers from all sides of the Christian counseling field with a new comprehension of the theological, philosophical, personal, social, and cultural components of the movement. This book is a must-read for anyone interested in understanding the rapid and turbulent growth occurring in faith-based counseling in the latter part of the twentieth century."

Ian F. Jones, Ph.D.
Director, Baptist Marriage and Family Counseling Center; Professor of Psychology and Counseling, Southwestern Baptist Theological Seminary; author of *The Counsel of Heaven on Earth*

THE BIBLICAL COUNSELING MOVEMENT

THE BIBLICAL COUNSELING MOVEMENT
HISTORY AND CONTEXT

David Powlison

www.newgrowthpress.com

New Growth Press, Greensboro, NC 27404
Copyright © 2010 by David Arthur Cameron Powlison. All rights reserved.
Published 2010.

Cover Design: The DesignWorks Group, Nate Salciccioli and Jeff Miller, www.designworksgroup.com

Typesetting: Lisa Parnell

ISBN-13: 978-1-935273-13-4
ISBN-10: 1-935273-13-2

Library of Congress Cataloging-in-Publication Data

Powlison, David, 1949–
    The biblical counseling movement : history and context / David A. Powlison.
        p. cm.
    Includes bibliographical references and index.
    ISBN-13: 978-1-935273-13-4 (alk. paper)
    ISBN-10: 1-935273-13-2 (alk. paper)
    1. Counseling—Religious aspects—Christianity. 2. Bible—Psychology. 3. Bible—Use.
    4. Christianity—Psychology. 5. Christian life—Biblical teaching. I. Title.
    BR110.P725 2010
    253.509'045—dc22
                                                                            2009036560

26 25 24 23 22 21 20 19   13 14 15 16 17

This book is dedicated to the memory of

PETER ANDREWS POWLISON (1922–1987).

He would have found great pleasure in this day.

Contents

List of Tables

Preface

It delights me that this book has been read by so many readers and has been so well received. It is, after all, a "dissertation." That genre does not usually promise a stimulating read—more an Esther 6:1 soporific for sleepless nights than a spine-tingling page turner!

This new edition makes two changes from the original dissertation. The first is minor but significant. The second is more substantial. We have also corrected many small errors of spelling, punctuation, fact, and format.

The minor alteration is a title change from the original. It is now, as you have seen, *The Biblical Counseling Movement: History and Context*. This accurately describes both the topic: biblical counseling; and the intellectual task: to trace the history and to set that history in its sociocultural context, both ecclesiastical and professional.

Why the change? It is a matter of intended audience, in order to clear up a common misunderstanding. The original title was *Competent to Counsel?: The History of a Conservative Protestant Anti-Psychiatry Movement*. This PhD dissertation completed my studies in the history of science and medicine at the University of Pennsylvania in 1996. Like all dissertations, it was written primarily for practitioners in its particular field. To an audience of historians of medicine, "anti-psychiatry movement" describes a well-known genre. Under that label come studies of various proposed alternatives to the reigning psychiatric orthodoxy. These have included feminist, Marxist, Szaszian, and liberal Protestant alternatives to the ideas and professional assumptions of the mental health establishment. Historically, biblical counseling is one of many proposals to reconfigure psychiatric thought and practice (and it is one of the few that generated a significant social movement). As an historian, I was able to justify and to locate my topic by portraying the biblical counseling movement as one more alternative to mainstream psychiatry and psychotherapy. So "conservative Protestant" parallels "feminist" or "Marxist" as an adjective, and "anti-psychiatry movement" is the genre that each adjective describes.

What communicated well to professional historians too easily miscommunicates to counseling practitioners trying to sort out the history of a movement in which they are actively involved or about which they are curious. "Anti-psychiatry" tends to be read as a defining characteristic of the biblical counseling movement, as if a negative rhetoric of attack is the leading edge. But, as both the dissertation and a reading of relevant literature make clear, the biblical counseling movement has never been "anti-psychiatry" in the way that adjective tends to be heard by nonhistorians. Negative rhetoric appears on occasion (see chap. 7), but the movement essentially voiced a positive and practical intention: to enrich the practical theology and ministry of the church of Jesus Christ (for example, see chaps. 4–6). Regarding psychiatry, it has tried to redefine how a properly reconfigured psychiatric profession would go about useful medical business, while not trespassing into the work and theology of the church. Chapters 1 and 6 of this dissertation (and the citations therein) orient the reader to this question.

You will find a discussion of the technical definition of "anti-psychiatry" on pages 9–10. Chapter 7 (p. 143) will discuss what Jay Adams said about psychiatry in 1975, answering questions often posed by his critics:

> *Are you saying that psychology and psychiatry are illegitimate disciplines? Do you think that they have no place at all?*
> No, you misunderstand me. It is exactly not that. . . . My problem with them is that they refuse to stay on their own property. . . .
> If [the psychiatrist] were to use his medical training to find medical solutions to the truly organic difficulties that affect attitudes and behavior, the pastor would be excited about his work.

Given this fundamentally positive vision, it is no accident that many Christians with mental health credentials—psychiatrists, neurologists, psychiatric nurses, social workers, psychotherapists—embraced biblical counseling, believing that it offered a truer understanding of people and a better cure for troubled souls.

The second change is more substantive. I have added several appendices not included in the original dissertation. In a personal note on page 15, I commented on the challenge of writing dispassionate history when one is a passionate participant in the events described: "I hold views on many of the issues that will be described. . . . I have written some of mine down." What was true in 1996 is even truer by 2009. I think readers have appreciated that this book is written from the standpoint of a professional historian, seeking above all else to be accurate, comprehensive, and fair minded. But for this new edition I've added three articles that show explicitly where I stand. "Cure of Souls (and the Modern Psychotherapies)" (2007) updates the history but in a way that openly reveals my commitments and hopes. "Crucial Issues in Contemporary Biblical Counseling" (1988) outlines my assessment of balances and imbalances in Jay Adams's model. "Biological Psychiatry" (1999) updates the discussion of what constitute "truly organic difficulties" in the light of developments in psychiatry decades after Adams wrote his views.

Given these additions, you may want to consider your reading strategy as you begin. My preference is for readers to plunge into the history first, later going on to the appendices where I give my point of view. I suspect that this preference expresses my instincts as a counselor—listen carefully to people and to all that's going on, then seek to make sense of it all! But some readers may want to start with the appendices, then double back to ponder the historical flow. Either way, I trust you will gain a vivid sense for the challenge of embodying two things simultaneously. A *scholar* and *historian* aims to be self-critical, observant, and evenhanded in describing persons, ideas, and events. An *advocate* and *counselor* should embody those same strengths but also care deeply about what happens, applauding or lamenting at every turn, always hoping to influence what happens next. By instinct, I'm an advocate and counselor. I care deeply about the outcome of this story. But the discipline of learning to be a fair-minded historian brought incalculable benefits. I hope that you, too, benefit from the combination.

Wise ministry is always "occasional" and particular, rather than timeless and general. It takes place with reference to the particulars of person, place, time, and current challenges. Locating ourselves in history is extremely valuable. I hope that you find *The Biblical Counseling Movement: History and Context* both informative and helpful. I hope that one fruit of your reading will be to further the development of counseling ministries that worthily glorify Jesus Christ. After all, Christian faith and practice is the original "cure of the soul"—the pastoral phrase which supplied the Greek etymology for both "psychiatry" and "psychotherapy." The reinvigoration of cure of souls in our time and in our varied places is one great challenge that currently faces each of us and all of us together.

Now may the God of peace who brought again from the dead our Lord Jesus, the great shepherd of the sheep, by the blood of the eternal covenant, equip you with everything good that you may do his will, working in us that which is pleasing in his sight, through Jesus Christ, to whom be glory forever and ever. Amen.

— Hebrews 13:20–21 ESV

David Powlison
February, 2009
Glenside, Pennsylvania

Acknowledgments

I would like to thank the people who helped in various ways to bring this project to completion. Charles Rosenberg, my advisor, modeled for me what it means to be an historian. My readers, Ronald Numbers, Riki Kuklick, and Clair Davis offered not only their comments but also their encouragement. Charles Bosk told me to prepare to be changed by participant research. He was right in more ways than I could have imagined; in fact, the history itself was changed in some small way by becoming subject to participant research.

Jay Adams, my prime subject, and Betty Jane Adams generously gave their time and hospitality, for which I am very thankful. I owe thanks also to many others who appear in these pages, with whom I conversed or corresponded over the years, in particular Donald Capps, John Carter, John Coe, Gary Collins, Larry Crabb, Howard Eyrich, Bill Goode, Vernon Grounds, Lloyd Jonas, Stan Jones, Wayne Mack, Bruce Narramore, Robert Roberts, George Scipione, Bob Smith, and Richard Winter, along with numerous attenders at AACC, CAPS, and NANC. Of those listed, George Scipione's diligence and insight were particularly helpful.

Edmund Clowney first suggested I study history. John Bettler suggested the specific topic and contributed in many other tangible and intangible ways. Paul Tripp, Ed Welch, and my other colleagues managed to know when and when not to ask how the dissertation was going. Barb Bradley provided invaluable help on CCEF's client database. Brad Beavers and Bill Smith helped to find sources. Librarians at the University of Pennsylvania, Westminster Theological Seminary, Fuller Theological Seminary, and Biola University patiently assisted and guided me.

Others provided moral and material support along the way. Without Bob Kramer's steady and practical encouragement, this project could not have happened. The encouragement of many other friends—the Blakemans, Covingtons, DeHarts, Groves, Millers, Yenchkos, and others—carried me along. Maryanne Soper tidied up countless details at the proofreading stage. Jane Burns's hospitality at St. Clare's and St. Julian's came at a crucial point in the writing process. My mother, Dora Powlison, quietly but persistently encouraged me, as did my parents-in-law, Frank and Eloise Gardner. I would like to thank Peter, Gwenyth, and Hannah, who grew up with "Dad's dissertation" as a somewhat mysterious backdrop throughout their lives. Finally, I would like to thank my wife, Nan: it is not without reason that "love is patient" heads the list.

Abstract

In 1970 Jay Adams, a Presbyterian minister, launched an anti-psychiatry movement among American, conservative Protestants. Partly inspired by O. H. Mowrer and Thomas Szasz, Adams made a threefold claim. First, modern psychological theories were bad theology, misinterpreting functional problems in living. Second, psychotherapeutic professions were a false pastorate, interlopers on tasks that properly belonged to pastors. Third, the Bible, as interpreted by Reformed Protestants, taught pastors the matters necessary to counsel competently. Adams's "nouthetic counseling" rapidly developed the institutional forms that typically signal a profession. But it was environed by three powerful professional neighbors. Secular psychological professions dominated twentieth-century discourse and practice regarding problems in living. The mainline Protestant pastoral counseling movement had shaped religious counseling from the 1940s. A rapidly professionalizing community of evangelical psychotherapists shared Adams's conservative Protestant faith but looked to integrate that faith with modern psychologies. A conflict over professional jurisdiction ensued between Adams and evangelical psychotherapists. This conflict has never been documented historically. I studied it almost exclusively from primary sources: interviews, publications, case records. Adams's intellectual system contained six main parts. First, his epistemology arose from Reformed Protestantism and featured the Bible. Second, he defined problems in living morally as expressions of sin. Third, he treated physiological and social constraints as the context of personal problems, not their cause. Fourth, he proclaimed the grace of Christ as the comprehensive solution to life's problems. Fifth, he defined counseling as pastoral and church-based. Sixth, he subjected secular psychologies to a program of suspicion, debunking their intellectual and professional claims. Adams gained followers among pastors and their parishioners but largely lost the interprofessional conflict. In the 1980s evangelical psychotherapists successfully asserted their claim to cultural authority over problems in living, extending their institutional power in higher education, publishing, and the provision of care. The nouthetic counseling movement became isolated from the mainstream of conservative Protestantism; its institutions languished; fault lines emerged internally. But in the 1990s, nouthetic counseling again began to prosper.

CHAPTER 1

Introduction

I am convinced about you, my brothers, that you are competent to counsel one another.
— Paul to the Roman church, c. AD 60[1]

Nearly all the wisdom we possess, that is to say, true and sound wisdom,
consists of two parts: the knowledge of God and of ourselves. . . . [A] veritable world of miseries
is to be found in humankind. . . . Accordingly, the knowledge of ourselves not only arouses us
to seek God, but also, as it were, leads us by the hand to find him.
— John Calvin, 1559[2]

Has Evangelical religion sold its birthright for a mess of psychological pottage?
—O. Hobart Mowrer, 1961[3]

A good seminary education rather than medical school or a degree in clinical psychology
is the most fitting background for a counselor.
—Jay Adams, 1970[4]

In 1970 Jay Adams, a forty-one-year-old Presbyterian pastor and seminary professor, published an inflammatory book about counseling. Written for an audience of theologically conservative Protestants—chiefly pastors and seminary students, but including laypeople and mental health professionals—*Competent to Counsel (CtC)* attacked the hegemony of the psychiatric establishment over the church's thinking and practice in the area of problems in living. Stimulated by the anti-psychiatries of O. Hobart Mowrer, William Glasser, Perry London, and Thomas Szasz, Adams intended a particularized revolution: he wanted conservative Protestants to take care of their own, to defer and refer to psychiatric authority no longer.[5] The agitator succeeded in the way that agitators often do, gaining both loyal converts and resolute foes.

Adams and the movement he created present the historian with an unusually discrete case study in jurisdictional conflict. Both the intellectual and the institutional boundaries between Adams and his opponents were remarkably clear. Unlike, for example, the conflicts between doctors and nurses in medical settings, this is not a story of infighting to reallocate privileges and responsibilities within a set of shared cognitive and institutional assumptions. In this story, an intellectual and institutional paradigm attacked the dominant paradigm and created a parallel world of practice. At the same time, the fiercest conflicts in this story occurred between people who apparently had a great deal in common:

1

Adams and the rapidly professionalizing community of conservative Protestant psychotherapists. *The Biblical Counseling Movement: History and Context* traces the historical, intellectual, and social dimensions of this jurisdictional conflict.

Adams's dispute with the mainstream understanding of personal problems was organized around a knowledge system framed in explicitly theological terms. He objected to the prevailing notions of mental illness and mental health. In his view, the medical model, as an interpretive schema mapped onto troubled emotions or troubling behavior, excised human life of its fundamentally moral character. It defined men and women as basically nonresponsible, both for themselves and to God. Corresponding to this presumed misdiagnosis of the human condition, the medical model misinterpreted the therapeutic ideal, contenting itself with producing untroubled emotions and untroubling behavior. Adams did not think that either peace of mind or socially acceptable behavior prescribed an adequate goal for the "cure of souls." He asserted instead that the church should understand the vast majority of problems in living in terms of an explicitly moral model.

Given this diagnostic framework, he established goals for the church's counseling that employed the ingredients of the traditional Christian message. First, because "man's greatest need is forgiveness,"[6] the forgiving grace of Jesus Christ was essential to solving problems in living. Adams believed that God worked within the human personality, and that those who were forgiven would also be helped by the Holy Spirit to alter patterns of thinking, feeling, and behavior. Second, as thankful recipients of such grace, "human beings should look like Jesus Christ."[7] Thus Adams defined the change process, again in frankly theological terms, as "progressive sanctification." Both normal- and extreme-range sin and misery would find progressive resolution as

people began to live according to the pattern of "faith and practice" taught in the Bible.[8]

Given his redefinition of both the human dilemma and its solution, Adams logically objected to the institutions of the psychiatric and psychotherapeutic professions. In Adams's eyes, the systems of education, training, and licensing; the instruments of publication and public relations; the agencies that delivered services—all these were enemies, not friends, because they were prejudiced against the beliefs and purposes of the conservative Protestant churches. Adams's redefinition of the counseling task as explicitly "pastoral" brought with it a number of institutional ramifications. Expert authority in the personal problems jurisdiction needed to be reallocated to pastors and pastoral theologians—away from mental health professionals who did not interpret or address problems in living in terms that Adams found acceptable. He claimed that people needed a pastoral cure-of-souls, not the ersatz of psychotherapy or psychiatry. Such counseling practice needed to be relocated into local churches—away from hospitals and professional offices.

Predictably, Adams suspected those fellow conservative Protestants who sought to acquire secular credentials and to replicate professional mental health structures, ideas, and practices within the Christian community. Their growing control over higher education, publication, and counseling services during the time period of our story seemed to Adams simply to cloak the wolf in sheep's clothing. Pastor and church were the primary institutions in Adams's proposed reconstruction of counseling practice, intended to replace the characteristic institutions of America's twentieth-century mental health system. Adams, however, did pour a great deal of energy into creating secondary institutions that paralleled the forms of the established mental health system: programs to provide various levels of training and education, a professional journal, an association for accrediting counselors, links with publishing houses willing to print his books.[9]

Given the theological and institutional assumptions that Adams brought to interpreting personal problems, he logically objected to prevailing therapeutic methods. In his view, such methods were predicated on commitments regarding human nature, God, and the role of the human community inimical to conservative Protestant beliefs. Central to his vision was the notion that human life is meant to be lived under benign authority—parental, pastoral, ecclesiastical, and, ultimately, immediate theocratic authority as articulated in the Bible—whose purposes were to transform human nature, not actualize it. In particular, he excoriated the notion that the counselor's stance should be detached, nonevaluative, nondirective, and all-accepting in the attempt to elicit healing forces from within the troubled individual. Such a stance only pretended to neutrality in Adams's view. It obscured the value-laden character of the counselor's covert commitment to a notion—"the solution to man's problems lies in the man himself"[10]—that Adams deemed unacceptable, given that Christianity believed in an external Savior and in a necessary conversion from those evils presumed to operate deep within human nature. He conceived of the counselor's role as activistic—even intrusive. He believed that counselors needed to become caring mentors: advisory, consultive, didactic, informative, confrontive, guiding. In a phrase, Adams called on counselors to be "lovingly frank" or "irenically direct" in impressing a biblical worldview on counselees.[11] Adams coined a name for his approach: "nouthetic counseling."[12]

Adams's system sought to apply conservative, Reformed Protestantism to counseling. The adjective "Reformed" highlights the distinctives of Adams's theological position within Protestantism. He was heir to that particular tradition of the Reformation deriving from John Calvin. Within the Reformed tradition he was most influenced by nineteenth-century American Presbyterianism and by certain elements of twentieth-century Dutch Calvinist philosophy. Adams presented his system as a comprehensive worldview, explicitly denying that it was "scientific," or could be validated or invalidated scientifically:

> The conclusions in this book are not based upon scientific findings. My method is presuppositional. I avowedly accept the inerrant Bible as the Standard of all faith and practice. The Scriptures, therefore, are the basis, and contain the criteria by which I have sought to make every judgment. Two precautions must be suggested. First, I am aware that my interpretations and applications of Scripture are not infallible. Second, I do not wish to disregard science, but rather I welcome it as a useful adjunct for the purposes of illustrating, filling in generalizations with specifics, and challenging wrong human interpretations of Scripture, thereby forcing the student to restudy the Scriptures. However, in the area of psychiatry, science largely has given way to humanistic philosophy and gross speculation.[13]

As a worldview, Adams's counseling had totalitarian qualities, like other comprehensive worldviews.[14] It thus entailed a sweeping critique of systems founded on other assumptions. In *CtC* and subsequent books Adams repeatedly attacked the three major schools of personality theory (psychodynamic, humanistic, behavioral), along with medical model psychiatry and all forms of secular psychotherapy, for misconstruing the human dilemma. He expressed guarded appreciation only for experimental psychology, for strictly somatic psychiatry, and for anti-psychiatrists such as O. H. Mowrer, William Glasser, Perry London, and Thomas Szasz.[15]

Mowrer was particularly catalytic. Adams read his works and studied with him during the summer of 1965. Adams subsequently wrote:

> Reading Mowrer's book *The Crisis in Psychiatry and Religion* . . . was an earth-shaking experience. In this book Mowrer, a noted research psychologist who had been honored with the Presidency of the American Psychological Association for his breakthrough in learning theory, challenged the entire field of psychiatry, declaring it a failure, and sought to refute its fundamental Freudian presuppositions. Boldly he threw down the gauntlet to conservative Christians as well. He asked: "Has Evangelical religion sold its birthright for a mess of psychological pottage?"[16]

Adams answered yes to Mowrer's question, picked up the gauntlet, and called on his fellow conservative pastors to join him in reclaiming their birthright. He urged ministers to retake the personal problems domain for those people under their pastoral care.

The precision with which Adams defined both his program and his audience contributes unique features to this case study in interprofessional relations and intellectual conflict. For example, Adams evidenced little interest in suggesting public policy for a pluralistic society; he intentionally constructed a sectarian counseling system for a limited audience. He showed no interest in contributing to forms of counseling that could be tailored to the diverse worldviews of people who did not share his belief system. He thought others should come to share his beliefs, hence he was explicitly evangelistic in counseling. He had no interest in simply gaining an increased role for pastoral counselors within the existing mental health system; he intended to build a parallel, alternative system.

Another noteworthy feature is that little direct confrontation occurred between Adams and those theoreticians and institutions he opposed. He had little interaction with mental health professionals. His reiterated opposition to "Freud, Rogers, and Skinner" served in large part as a symbolic resource for his ongoing feud with other Christians who more or less embraced the theories and practices of secular psychologists. He collided with the two groups wielding cultural authority over the personal problems sphere within Protestant churches, groups claiming authority in the same jurisdiction as Adams. First, Adams occasionally criticized theoreticians of the "pastoral counseling movement," who had defined pastoral counseling for both liberal and conservative seminaries. The pastoral counseling movement had been extremely influential in the 1950s and 1960s, mediating Carl Rogers, Alfred Adler, Carl Jung, Sigmund Freud, and others—packaged in liberal theologies—to liberal pastors, and to those few conservative pastors who thought at all about counseling. Second, Adams more frequently argued with evangelical psychotherapists who, beginning in the mid-1950s, articulated a nonpastoral psychotherapy to explain and address the personal problems of conservative Protestants.[17] The nascent psychotherapy movement among theologically conservative Protestants—who called their program the "integration" of psychology and theology—mediated the same set of secular psychologists to a community increasingly interested in thinking about and practicing counseling.[18]

If *CtC* had simply offered one more attack from the borderlands of the disaffected and disenfranchised, Adams would merit only a minor footnote in the history of his generation's anti-psychiatric writings. But he was only secondarily disaffected from the mental health establishment in which he had received a fair bit of instruction, and under whose intellectual and institutional hegemony he had chafed. He was primarily an entrepreneurial system builder, with aspirations to retake turf for a particular constituency. Attacks on psychiatry, psychotherapy, theoretical psychology, and the mental health system[19] served defensive functions for Adams's positive intentions. He sought to offer—in particular to conservative Protestants—an intellectual, methodological, and institutional alternative to the mental health system.

Adams possessed two resources lacking in most anti-psychiatries. First, he could draw on a well-developed body of articulated belief and practice, the vast intellectual resources of classic Protestantism. To the extent that Adams was an innovator, it was in suggesting a new range of contemporary implications and applications of traditional Calvinist beliefs. Second, Adams belonged to a community that found those beliefs compelling, and had a teaching position at one of the leading educational institutions, Westminster Theological Seminary.[20] His social location within conservative Protestantism gave him a ready—if, as we shall see, ambivalent—constituency for institution building. Many anti-psychiatrists must content themselves to play the role of intellectual guerrilla or gadfly; Adams was able to establish a homeland.[21]

The Genesis and Development of This Project

In conceptualizing this project, I have been chiefly influenced by two writings: Charles Rosenberg's "The Crisis in Psychiatric Legitimacy" and Andrew Abbott's *System of Professions*.[22] Let me briefly indicate the impact of these two pieces on the definition and framing of my topic. Rosenberg's analysis of the status of psychiatry prompted the questions I asked. Abbott's systematic analysis of jurisdictional disputes—particularly his chapter on how psychiatry replaced the pastorate's jurisdiction over personal problems—suggested the lineaments of an historical narrative.

Rosenberg noted how psychiatry's social legitimacy depended on its maintaining a distinctly medical identity. Promises of rationality and efficacy—a science and technology of human dysfunction and dysphoria, as it were—define psychiatry's badge of authority. Yet the profession has been unable to provide "either understanding or relief consistent with the pretentiousness of such demands" for cognitive and therapeutic authority.[23] The truth contents are often dubitable assertions of faith: "We still debate the fundamental basis of the most common psychiatric diagnoses and their relationship to belief systems and the realities of social structure."[24] Therapeutics are equally problematic. Only the "hard medicines"—psychotropic medication, electroconvulsive therapy, lobotomy—and physical care of the chronically disabled are easy to categorize as medicine. Professional claims to possess effective psychotherapeutic methods only too easily wobble in the face of both dubitable efficacy and the intrinsic difficulty of staking sustainable claims to the methods and contents of talking cure.[25] Psychiatry's identity as a distinctly medical specialty is sometimes tenuous.

A further complication arises because those affiliated with psychiatry's most overtly "medical" institutions and clientele—mental hospitals treating people with chronic organic syndromes—have occupied the lowest status within the profession. The high-status activities of psychiatrists have been those least distinguishable from philosophy, theology, and pastoral care: "much of our century's most influential psychiatric writing has consisted of general statements about the human condition."[26] Such high-status activities—to teach the meaning of life and to cure the soul's ailments—contribute a great deal to psychiatry's status as more than a custodial profession. But the meaning of life is difficult property over which to sustain a professional claim.[27]

Rosenberg noted that psychiatry has been assigned an immense social role in secular

America. This profession has assumed responsibility for the varied ills, dysfunctions, and pains of the human soul. Yet the profession's knowledge and efficacy lag seriously behind its responsibility to provide aid. The call to love and help overwhelms the resources of truth and power. The "embittering gap" between social expectation and professional performance continually threatens the profession's legitimacy.[28]

Within this general framework, Rosenberg made two specific comments that catalyzed this project. First, "We are no more willing, many of us, to suffer the pain of depression or anxiety than that of some more readily localized and meliorable physical ailment; in our society neither stoicism nor traditional religious viewpoints seem ordinarily to provide a context of meaningfulness for such ills of the soul."[29] Psychiatry not only must deal with society's most intractable problems: the demented or behaviorally deviant. It also must deal with the gamut of Everyman's troubles in life, a responsibility inescapably mirroring in reverse the fortunes of religion in modern society. Rosenberg's description of the usual—the modern failure of both stoicism and traditional religion—invited an exploration of the unusual. Jay Adams wrote within a cultural context that frequently still found traditional religious viewpoints meaningful in addressing the soul's ills.

Second, Rosenberg observed, "Because the specialty of psychiatry has so diffuse a responsibility and possesses so little limit-defining knowledge, it is prone to border disputes."[30] That last phrase turned on lights. There are many possible configurations of jurisdictional conflict. For example, the institutional politics within inpatient psychiatric facilities often find psychiatrists, psychologists, and social workers contending for the territory of psychotherapeutic intervention (with nursing staff—psychiatric nurses and mental health workers—occasionally thrown into the mix).[31]

This is "normal" politics. But the biblical counseling movement presents a case study of a different sort of border dispute: "secessionist" politics. The case study before us is no contest for relative allocations of power and responsibility within psychiatry's heartland; it is a breakaway republic. Theologically conservative Protestants never fit easily into a mental health system that claimed to explain and treat the wanderings and woes of the soul as a medical ailment. Jay Adams experienced and capitalized on such unease and turned it into an intellectual and institutional program.

Rosenberg concluded that psychiatry's legitimacy is tenuous but sustainable within the medical profession, mainstream American society, and public policy. But Adams found an eddy of society within which psychiatric claims could be fiercely and—given the presuppositions of his constituency—persuasively opposed. Few anti-psychiatry programs have had a social and institutional base from which their claims might be sustained with relative success and turned into the legitimating basis for an alternative institutional structure. Jay Adams was able to make a case both for his anti-psychiatry polemic and for his biblical counseling agenda within the institutions of conservative Protestantism. His success was modest, for he was opposed more often than embraced, especially among the cultural gatekeepers of his natural constituency. But he won a hearing and adherents to his program in certain local churches, conservative theological seminaries and Bible colleges, mission agencies, and publishing houses.

If Rosenberg suggested the broad contours of my project, Andrew Abbott suggested many particulars. He asserted that "it is the history of jurisdictional disputes that is the real, the determining history of the professions."[32] *The Biblical Counseling Movement* will trace a multifaceted conflict between professional groups for authority—both intellectual dominance and control over tasks.

Abbott gave a nuanced set of categories for understanding this conflict.

For example, Abbott emphasized the significance of knowledge systems, rather than trivializing cognitive content as the cost of recognizing the importance of economics, politics, professional organization, and rhetoric. "Knowledge is the currency of competition."[33] This proved very illuminating for my project, in part because it fit so well the self-conscious beliefs and practices of my subjects, people who taught, wrote, and preached because they never doubted that structured knowledge mattered supremely.

In Abbott's terms, a profession's ability to control a jurisdiction hinges on the viability of its system of abstract knowledge. "Only a knowledge system governed by abstractions can redefine its problems and tasks, defend them from interlopers, and seize new problems—as medicine has recently seized alcoholism, mental illness, hyperactivity in children, obesity, and numerous other things."[34] Jay Adams would have read that list and accused medicine of trespassing into functional problems in living. He attempted to seize back what he would call drunkenness, flight from responsibility, willfulness, gluttony, and numerous other things also in need of relabeling.[35]

Abbott's chapter tracing the modern history of the personal problems jurisdiction in America proved fruitful for my purposes. He described how "legitimate psychotherapy was to be an official, public monopoly of the medical profession" from the 1930s into the 1970s.[36] During this period of relative professional peace, "'neurologists' gave organic treatments to patients who had diseases with organic etiology, and 'psychiatrists' gave psychic treatments to patients who had diseases with psychic etiologies," including those who were "anxious, depressed, and upset with their everyday life."[37] Abbott, following the trail of the professional fortunes of psychiatry, noted that in the 1970s and subsequently competition from psychologists and social workers prompted a "rebiologizing" of personal problems by psychiatrists.

We will follow the fortunes of the other professional group that figures prominently in Abbott's story: the clergy. Abbott describes the clergy's historical decline this way. In the nineteenth century "clergy analysis remained primitive. . . . The clergy's failure to provide any academic foundation for their practice with personal problems ultimately proved their undoing."[38] The absence of a compelling knowledge system—to explain and treat problems in living, to interact critically with newly ascendant systems—accelerated marginalization. "By the 1920s the clergy had lost any vestige of cultural jurisdiction over personal problems."[39] They had clearly lost such jurisdiction over high culture; and even in their own self-image and among their own religious constituency, the authoritative voices increasingly spoke *to* the church from the outside, not *from* the church. Abbott summarized the eclipse of the clergy in these words: "There emerged in this period [the 1920s] a clinical pastoral training movement aiming to give young clergymen direct experience with the newly defined personal problems. Seminarians would learn the rudiments of human nature from psychiatrists, psychologists, and social workers who 'knew' those rudiments, that is, from the professionals who currently controlled the definitions of them."[40] Abbott cited the career of Anton Boisen as an object lesson in the fate of those who fail in conflicts for jurisdiction. Boisen "became a guerrilla in the psychiatric heartland. . . . But few rallied to the flag Boisen raised."[41] Jay Adams agreed with Boisen that problems in living had a moral-spiritual explanation, but he eschewed both the psychiatric heartland and the mainline Protestant churches that Boisen had sought to address.[42] Adams averred that the controllers of knowledge, who claimed to know the rudiments of human nature, had brokered error not truth, and he proposed a different set of definitions. He raised his flag in a different country, and there won converts.

Abbott concluded his discussion by noting the "drift of pastoral counseling towards secular psychotherapy."[43] Pastoral counseling was supplanted by secular psychotherapy in large part; it also drifted toward secular psychotherapy even where it continued to claim a distinct identity. This dual phenomenon provoked Adams's anti-psychiatry. He launched his jurisdictional offensive by seeking to redefine both personal problems and the counseling task in opposition to secular psychotherapy. He sought to debunk both secular professionals (psychiatrists, psychologists, social workers) and religious professionals (pastoral counselors and evangelical psychotherapists) who drifted toward a secular and medicalized psychotherapy.[44]

In many other ways, Abbott's paradigm helped me both to understand and to tell my story. For example, his discussion of the different ways claims may be settled was provocative—even prescient. He thought that a "jurisdictional reconstruction seems to be imminent in psychotherapy," as he described that form of settlement in which a jurisdiction is divided along the lines of different client constituencies.[45] He observed that such client differentiation is crucial to the success of a group that invades the jurisdiction of another group. "The pattern of attacking groups emerging from the paraprofessional periphery, serving ignored clienteles, and urging reform is the most common."[46] This is exactly what happened as Jay Adams and the biblical counseling movement identified and engaged conservative Protestants as a client type.

All this is of interest historically. On the one hand, the most frequently studied religious counseling movements—for example, the Emmanuel movement, clinical pastoral education, and the pastoral counseling movement—tell stories of thorough-going psychiatric dominance. In each case mainline clergy attempted to retake at least a significant portion of the jurisdiction of everyday life problems. But in each case religious practitioners ended up in a distinctly subordinate role: they were either dismissed or assimilated, or they consciously placed themselves in the student role. On the other hand, the most frequently studied influences of religion on secular counseling—for example the influence of "positive thinkers" on twentieth-century American systems of counsel—trace themes characteristic of optimistic, mainline, liberal Protestantism.[47] The biblical counseling movement yields a different kind of story. Its anti-psychiatric obstinacy continued into the 1990s. The pessimism of its view of human nature assailed optimistic liberalism in both its religious and secular forms. To the historian's gaze, this movement presents a coherent set of culture-, time-, place-, and people-specific ideas and practices. Jay Adams articulated a distinctive knowledge system that a particular kind of people believed. He built an alternative institutional structure that those same people chose to inhabit.

Relevant Literatures

The Biblical Counseling Movement: History and Context is based on primary sources.[48] No secondary literature exists because the events and ideas described have thus far existed under conditions of invisibility to the wider culture. But the story told is related to other stories. Many bodies of literature have proved helpful for understanding my topic; I hope this project might also contribute to a number of different scholarly discussions.

History of medicine naturally frames my story, particularly the history of psychiatry and the numerous discussions of the "medicalization" of problems in living since the late nineteenth century. If the ailments of the human body provide "raw material for the imprinting of cultural messages,"[49] how much more transparently do problems in living carry messages. Matters of value and philosophy appear in the problems of living domain explicitly rather than covertly. The intellectual constructs, therapies, and institutions of medicine respond to the physical constraints of the human condition. We might say, analogously, that psychotherapy, broadly defined, responds to the psychosocial constraints of the human condition. Psychotherapy has its origins in the social response to timeless realities: dysphoric emotion, interpersonal conflict, the search for meaning, decision making, the varied psychological and behavioral responses to suffering, child-rearing, uncertainty about the criteria of truth and goodness, disorders of the conscience, and those habitual behaviors variously (and tellingly) labeled either sin, vice, deviancy, or addiction. Hence the history of psychotherapy is the history of attempts to explain and ameliorate the "moral" drama of the human condition.

The *anti-psychiatry* literature also frames our story. A diverse literature of criticism has arisen in the broad wake of such pioneer critics of institutional psychiatry as Foucault, Goffman, and Szasz. Psychiatry's attempts at asserting normativity and eternality have been assailed from many directions for many different reasons. Some revolutionaries made sweeping policy suggestions. For example, Szasz suggested the dismantling of coercive institutions in service of a libertarian social agenda. Marxist historians, such as Scull, made the same suggestion based on a different analysis and aiming for a different social effect. Other critics have weighed in with intentions more reformist than revolutionary. Mowrer wished to displace the dominant psychodynamic therapies and explanations in favor of a moral behavior model. Showalter pursued a psychiatry sensitive to feminist per-

spectives. Other more moderate reformers have suggested modifications of emphasis in public and professional policy. For example, Gerald Grob urged that psychiatry vigorously assume a caring and custodial role, as an act of social compassion toward some of the most helpless members of our society.[50]

Like many other anti-psychiatries, the biblical counseling movement arose in the 1960s. But unlike them, it has not had its chroniclers. This was most likely due to the relative invisibility of the conservative Protestant subculture until recently, a product of scholarly inattentiveness on the one hand and cultural separatism on the other. Adams is a different sort of revolutionary or reformer: the builder of a sectarian, parallel system of thought and practice. His most noteworthy accomplishment—as I have suggested—is having succeeded in developing a constituency so that his alternative to the mental health assumptions of modern American culture has become institutionalized. But both Adams's accomplishment and the turf battle between him and conservative Protestant psychotherapists have been invisible to the wider culture.

As a member of a separatist subculture, Adams's social vision was very different from that of other anti-psychiatrists. He focused his attention almost exclusively on local churches and on sectarian schools and seminaries, intending that they should provide an alternative to public therapeutic institutions. In his few comments on public policy he contended that well-defined organic problems constitute psychiatry's legitimate sphere.[51] He added to this a further rationalization for psychiatric hospitals. They might serve as protective and disciplinary social consequences. People whose behavior became so unacceptable that they threatened themselves, others, or the social order faced the psychiatric hospital as a freedom-limiting consequence.[52] The social agenda Adams proposed was not liberationist—like Szasz, Rothman, or Showalter—but conservative, like Mowrer. He did not see people as slaves of coercive mechanisms of social control, needing freedom in order to act autonomously. He saw people as slaves of their sins, needing freedom to act responsibly. But even my description is culled from stray comments, for Adams only rarely alluded to a general social vision. Unusual among anti-psychiatrists, Adams spoke only to his well-defined constituency.

I have found the literature on *alternative medicine and science* in America during the nineteenth and twentieth centuries stimulating. This body of work suggests numerous parallels—and contrasts—and helps to frame my story.[53] Biblical counseling was clearly deviant, an alien amid the dominant psychotherapeutic culture. It replayed many of the themes of disenfranchised medical therapies. For example, the often-noted linkage between religious interests and alternative therapeutic schemas explicitly appears in my narrative. The history of nouthetic counseling offers a case study that both complements and contrasts with Ronald Numbers's *The Creationists*.[54]

Studies of alternative medicine have provided a window on cultural meanings embedded in both diagnosis and treatment. Alternative systems appear to incarnate their worldview "obviously"; they enable a backward glance that reveals less obvious worldviews incarnated in dominant medical philosophies. As mentioned earlier, even more dramatically than with somatic misery and dysfunction, problems of living lend themselves to a great variety of constructions which reflect the views of practitioners and constituencies. The medicalization and moralization of life play tug-of-war, as do competing moralizations.

Biblical counseling not only sought to "seize back" behavioral problems that had been medicalized in the relatively recent past; it also sought to reach into areas long a part of standard medical practice. One subtheme of this history will be the extensive writing on psychosomatics and lifestyle diseases published by medically trained nouthetic counselors. Medical doctors contributed about one-fifth of the articles in the *Journal of Pastoral Practice* and addressed the physical effects of poor dietary habits (gluttony or self-starvation); sleep loss; sexual promiscuity; use of cigarettes, alcohol, and both prescription and street drugs; worry and unresolved anger; and so forth. Articles targeted not only presumed moral causes of physical problems but also moral responses to unavoidable physical problems such as illness, pain, disability, menstrual cycle dysfunction, and aging.[55]

Like many alternative medical philosophies and practices, a populist strand ran strongly through the biblical counseling movement. Adams's writing exhibited a tension between the well-trained pastor as "God's professional" and the traditional Protestant theme of the priesthood of all believers, defining anyone with life wisdom as "competent to counsel." It provides a case of relatively deprofessionalized knowledge and practice, offering truths and techniques that the common person was intended to grasp and apply in self-care and care for family, friends, and neighbors.

The biblical counseling movement was also striking in its differences from most alternative therapies that have been studied by historians. For example, in contrast to spiritual psychotherapies—the Emmanuel movement, Christian Science, and contemporary "inner healing" movements—biblical counseling did not pursue "healing" as the goal of face-to-face resolution of emotional and behavioral problems. Adams saw healing only as a metaphor when it came to problems in living, and he contended that the metaphor had lost virtually all utility because of the medicalization of human moral existence.[56] Adams did not view problems in living as dysfunctions to be diagnosed, nor did he conceive of counseling as therapeutic treatment.

Rather he claimed to offer a rational assessment of problems, and then counsel, things meant to be believed and acted upon. Adams was distinctly nonmystical and decidedly hardheaded: "I don't have a mystical bone in my body."[57] Even when he spoke of the Holy Spirit as the power of God to change sinful beliefs, attitudes, and behaviors—and he reiterated this at the beginning of nearly every book—he meant "Holy Spirit" as a reference to an enabling person, the third person of the Trinity in historic Christian belief, who intended to enact a rational agenda for cognitive, behavioral, and motivational renovation. Similarly, the "Word of God" for Adams contained a rational message, and prayer was meant to be focused toward specific, describable goals.[58]

As already mentioned above in discussing Andrew Abbott, *histories of the professions* also bear on the story of biblical counseling. The clergy is one of the classic professions, and the degrading of their status in the modern age has been repeatedly noted. An eddy against the historical flow, in which clergy take the offensive intellectually and institutionally, merits notice.[59]

Histories of pastoral care also frame my story. For example, Holifield traced the development of pastoral care in America from the eighteenth century to the 1960s. His major thesis is that a theocentric concern for "salvation" was replaced by an anthropocentric concern for "self-realization." Holifield significantly breaks off his story with this comment: "My narrative comes to its conclusion at the end of the 1960s. . . . I would argue that the end of that decade did mark a turning point."[60] The story of pastoral care and counseling evidenced a marked "liberalizing" drift for most of two centuries. But at the end of the 1960s a number of more conservative tendencies emerged: from theological self-criticism by liberal pastoral counselors, to the evangelical psychotherapy movement, to Adams's biblical counseling movement. Pastoral counseling in the twentieth century was generally a story of religionists making derivative adaptations of the dominant paradigms.[61] But from 1970, theological liberals and conservatives alike increasingly sought to ground their counseling practice more explicitly in their (various) conceptions of the faith.

The rapidly growing body of literature on *American conservative Protestantism* proved very helpful for setting and interpreting my story.[62] American evangelical religion is notoriously fluid. Semantic precision in describing religious groups is notoriously difficult to attain. A rather extensive literature has grown up in recent years attempting to map contemporary conservative Protestantism. Adjectives such as conservative, evangelical, Reformed, separatist, fundamentalist, and Bible-believing express a wide range of denotative and connotative meanings. I ran through the gamut in considering the original title of this book before settling on perhaps the most generic term: "conservative protestant."[63]

Already I have used a variety of terms to locate Jay Adams: conservative Protestant, Calvinist, Presbyterian, Reformed. To this list other terms might be added. Some terms are relatively precise but obscure to the general reader: the scholarly Calvinism of "Old Princeton" Seminary, Old School Presbyterianism, the presuppositional apologetics of Westminster Seminary. Other terms are more popular but less precise: evangelical, fundamentalist, separatist, Bible-believing. Each of these terms helps to a degree to locate Adams theologically, ecclesiastically, and sociologically. But many of them, unfortunately, bear a freight of meanings that varies substantially from reader to reader.

Adams is easiest to describe precisely in terms of his theological commitments. He was a thoroughgoing Calvinist, self-consciously Reformed theologically.[64] For Adams, God sovereignly controlled everything, and that assumption saturated his counseling system both in theory and practice.[65] The "Five Points of Calvinism" described his view of how God's grace works.[66] Adams also held more particular theological positions within generic Calvinism: for example, the children of believers should be baptized as members of the covenant community; the mode of baptism is pouring or sprinkling, not immersion;[67] the proper form of church government is rule by elders—Presbyterian—rather than by bishops or by the congregation;[68] the millennium is currently realized in the reign of Christ spreading his kingdom worldwide—amillennialism—rather than occurring in the future as postmillennialists and premillennialists believe;[69] epistemology and apologetics must be presuppositional, in the way of Calvinistic philosopher Cornelius Van Til, not positivistic and evidential.[70]

Adams's ecclesiastical affiliations occurred within a series of small conservative Presbyterian denominations, several of which had splintered from the northern Presbyterian Church in the 1930s during the modernist-fundamentalist controversies. His academic career as a professor of practical theology took place at Westminster Theological Seminary, which had broken off from Princeton Seminary during those same controversies, and was also generally Presbyterian in orientation. But locating Adams ecclesiastically is complicated by the wider impact he had. He found respondents across a wide spectrum of conservative denominations: various Presbyterians; Dutch Christian Reformed; fundamentalist and independent Baptists; the milder sorts of charismatics and Assembly of God Pentecostals; inner-city, black independent churches; Brethren churches; Mennonites; Episcopalians and Congregationalists involved in conservative "renewal" movements in their mainline denominations; and even an occasional "renewed" Roman Catholic. He also found opponents—for many different reasons—in the same circles.

Historical analyses of conservative Protestant phenomena illuminate many of the themes and subthemes that play out in and around the history of Adams's nouthetic counseling. The movement was a hybrid, combining intellectual and practical features of both the Reformed tradition and the fundamentalist tradition. It hatched within Reformed circles but found its widest reception in fundamentalist audiences. Adams himself combined Reformed commitments with certain fundamentalist tendencies that made him acceptable to some moderate fundamentalists. These moderate fundamentalists who received Adams often were criticized by more militant fundamentalists for deemphasizing the significance of traditional distinctives: premillennial eschatological preoccupation, believer's baptism, sectarian separatism, instant experiential sanctification, exclusive use of the King James Version of the Bible, and biblicistic proof-texting. Moderates were willing to embrace an amillennial, paedobaptist Presbyterian who taught a more painstaking progressive sanctification and employed Reformed biblical scholarship.

Yet Adams also stressed traditional fundamentalist themes: the authority and scope of Scripture; the antithesis between Christian and secular thought; a relatively uncomplicated counseling method promising relatively rapid progress; an activistic call to arms and action, rather than to reflective or scholarly concern; a populist, grassroots emphasis; a separatist style of disengagement from both the wider Christian counseling community and the culture at large; a communication style that emphasized rhetorical abilities and public speaking rather than measured scholarly subtleties. What Noll terms "fundamentalist Manichaeism"[71]—construing the world as an immediate battleground between Christian forces of light and demonized forces of darkness—finds articulation in Adams, yet with Reformed subtleties that his followers sometimes did not retain.

Lastly, my small story is naturally embedded in one of the largest of historical narratives: the *secularization of the West,* a story whose further telling and analysis preoccupied so much of twentieth-century scholarly work. The biblical counseling movement envisioned itself as a counterculture. But to what degree its pretensions to swim against the current will succeed is a story for a future historian. It can at this point in history be considered a reactionary eddy, or perhaps a small ripple in an upstream direction. Rearguard action, reactionary retreat, accommodation, reconstructive engagement, and aggressive debunking have typically been the themes of churchly reactions to modernity. Strands of defense, flight, surrender, engagement, and offense can be seen—in varying proportions—in the story of nouthetic counseling that follows.

I hope to contribute in some small way to each of these bodies of literature. Though my story is small and self-contained, it is also a story worth pondering in other communities of historians. It bears on the histories of medicine, alternative medicine, anti-psychiatry, and the professions; it bears on histories of pastoral care and conservative Protestantism; and, finally, it bears on histories of secularization and resacralization.

The Historian's Stance

How will I parcel out my attention and purposes between the descriptive, the explanatory, and the evaluative? I have sought to stand chiefly in the role of historian-as-narrator. This study plows in previously unbroken soil; therefore, my chief purposes will be descriptive. There is a story to be told and positions to be explicated. It is a story worth entering the repertoire of contemporary historians of medicine, psychiatry, psychology, and religion. I have labored to establish basic facts—both narrative and intellectual—

and to provide an extensive bibliography of primary sources.

I will offer my explanations with a cautious hand. There are two reasons for this. First, my subject matter is contemporary, and in good conscience I can only be tentative in offering historical explanations for a movement that is still rapidly developing. To extend the apt metaphor of warfare for professional territory, at times I have felt like a war correspondent dropped near the front lines of a fluid battle. Events have swirled before my eyes. But to probe cause and significance demands more historical distance. Second, I admit to a certain agnosticism when it comes to determining the weight of the numerous forces presumably contributing to historical causality. I am sure that my story happened; I am less sure of why it happened.

Nouthetic counseling was only conceived in the mind and practice of its founder during the summer of 1965. Rudimentary courses in a theological seminary were developed during the late 1960s. The first book was published in 1970, and other institutional forms were created in the late 1970s. As a social movement, nouthetic counseling enjoyed an initial spurt of popularity in the decade after 1970, leveled off through the 1980s, and then has become resurgent since about 1990. My initial intention, at the point I chose this book topic (1988), was to cover the history of a movement that seemed to have peaked historically, leveled off, and even stagnated. I intended to concentrate on the initial trajectory of the movement, cutting things off at the mid-1980s. But at present biblical counseling is in an expansive mode. Books by new authors are being published, conference attendance and course enrollments are swelling, fresh conflicts are occurring both outside and inside the movement, and institutions are being developed or redeveloped. My story will sketch events into the 1990s. The movement is less than fifty years old;

many of the principals are still active; interesting things are happening as news, not history. The contemporaneity of my subject matter demands that the purposes of narrative predominate over purposes of explanation. I will avoid evaluative commentary, neither indicting nor extolling my subjects. Neither will I speculate on the trajectory of a movement that currently appears to be in early adolescence: headstrong, with signs of greater institutional and cognitive maturity collocating with certain conflicts and uncertainties about identity.

Here is the place for an autobiographical aside. Let me say outright that I am a sympathetic critic of my subjects. My sympathies arise from sharing similar Christian convictions, of a Reformed persuasion, nurtured through master of divinity studies at Westminster Theological Seminary. My sympathies are also nurtured by my participation and friendship with many of the individuals and institutions studied. To a minor degree, I am even an actor in the later phases of my story. I teach pastoral counseling at Westminster Theological Seminary and succeeded Adams as editor of the *Journal of Pastoral Practice* in 1992 (an appointment that both slowed and enriched this book).

My criticisms of nouthetic counseling also arise from Christian convictions: the critical, historical gaze is extremely valuable. Most of life is lived within the self-justifications of parochial and partisan bias. But the glimpse from afar can reveal the ambiguities, contradictions, and rationalizations endemic in human affairs. George Marsden described his work as an historian in words I cannot improve on.

> Inevitably one's point of view will shape one's work. Since it is impossible to be objective, it is imperative to be fair. One way of being fair is to say something about one's point of view so that others can take it into account and discount it if they wish. . . . [H]istorians . . . can provide critical perspectives, especially on traditions that they take seriously. Partisanship, then, although to some degree inevitable, is to be suppressed for the purposes of such historical understanding.
>
> This approach will not entirely please those who see Christian history as adequately understood only as a battle in which it is perfectly clear who stands with the forces of light and who with the forces of darkness.[72]

I also see many ways where my own thinking has been shaped by that relativizing of self and society that an historical and cross-cultural consciousness produces. I grew up in a place that was as Asiacentric as Eurocentric—Honolulu—and most of my schoolmates were Amer-Asians. My father taught Asian history, and our dinner guests were as often as not from South or East Asia. Subsequent educational and practical experience—a degree in social relations at Harvard College, '60s-style alienation from capitalist and nationalist values, three years of work on the wards of McLean Psychiatric Hospital, and doctoral studies at the University of Pennsylvania—have reinforced habits of critical disenculturation and dislike of Whiggish triumphalism. As an adult convert to Christianity, and as a participant in a sometimes triumphalist and parochial movement, I can still find myself a stranger in the sometimes strange land of conservative Protestant Christianity.

Both debunking and apotheosizing one's subjects shape myths. In both actions the really interesting things about history are lost in the interests of self-justification. I don't believe that either angels or demons determine human affairs. My intent is to put both relative sympathy and relative reserve to work, to the end of being a good historian. The reader will have to weigh the cumulative effect of both my sympathetic and critical biases.

Let me mention three effects of which I am immediately aware.

First, I differ in many ways from "fundamentalists"—theologically, culturally, politically, ecclesiastically, temperamentally—but I respect them. When fundamentalists and other conservative Protestants appear in my story, I will make none of the disparaging and caricaturing remarks that one frequently reads when scholars discuss those who believe in a living, speaking, authoritative God.

Second, I have sought to write this history as a relatively detached observer, but I hold views on many of the issues that will be described. Doubtless my opinions have shaped both the selection of data and the manner of presentation. Though every historian of psychology and theology has his or her opinions about both the human and the divine, unlike most, I have written some of mine down. In a number of articles I have articulated criticisms of both biblical counseling and its critics, and I welcome the reader becoming informed of ways I am not simply a dispassionate historian. The appendices of this book include three articles expressing my personal views in a context of historical analysis.

Third, in doing research for this project I have developed friendships with my interlocutors—on both sides of the jurisdictional conflict that will be portrayed. My reactions to written words have often been tempered by personal experience. I have come to know the people I discuss in many modes: published writings, interviews, correspondence, public lectures and debates, counseling transcripts and case studies, casual personal hospitality. This has undeniably affected my "reading" of what I have read and, hence, what I write. Familiarity may breed contempt on occasion, but it can as easily breed sympathy.

For example, some of Jay Adams's written statements sound dogmatic, harsh, polemical, trium-phalistic, simplistic, legalistic, impudent, reductionistic. Many readers have reacted to this, sometimes with violent antipathy. But I found my reaction tempered by a number of things. First, I read Adams both widely and thoroughly, which exposed me to many nuances and balances in his thought. Matters that other readers have described as seriously lopsided after reading one or two books by Adams, I often tended to see as understated or overstated matters of emphasis. Second, Adams discussed his rhetorical strategy freely. Blunt overstatement sounds different when understood as a conscious strategy rather than as the summary of a person's position. In person he offered a rationale for conscious overstatement: as a populist strategy for engaging in turf warfare, it pushed people to decide either for or against. He then criticized scholarly understatement as ineffective strategically, and frequently pusillanimous. He went on to acknowledge lacunae, nuances, qualifications, and debatable and vexing questions in the counseling field and in his own writings. Third, I found Adams in person to be engaging and humorous, even riotously so. His generosity with time and materials, his genuine kindness on the occasion of my father's death, his evident love for those he counseled and taught—these things could not help but make an impression.

My hope is that the reader will also reserve judgment, and enter into the life and logic of the narrative. Adams's views (and those of his leading critics, as well) may seem inconceivable from the standpoint of modern culture's absolutes; and from within the deeply internalized relativism of postmodern culture, he may seem sinfully absolutist. In the modern or postmodern West, the gods of traditional faith are dead, and truth and morals relative. Yet for Jay Adams, God is alive, and truth and morals are absolute and revealed. He was self-consciously premodern, which at the very least should enable us to see prevailing assumptions and their implications more clearly.

For a number of reasons, Adams makes an intriguing case study. First, he thought and practiced with remarkable consistency to his premises. To enter a full-blown alternative, intellectual and professional culture cannot help but make us see our dominant intellectual and professional culture in new ways. Second, Adams was an unusually self-conscious turf-warrior. What sociologists of professional competition say people do, he did, intentionally and out loud. And, as with any case study, nuances and variations emerge that enrich accepted models of interprofessional relations. Third, Adams was unusual among alternative psychiatries, psychologies, and psychotherapies because he emerged from a community that was once culturally dominant—conservative, Reformed Protestant orthodoxy. The voice of this community, though variously muffled, still catches the ear and arouses the passions of modern Americans. Adams offered "religious" counseling but from a perspective that derived neither from sentimental Protestant modernism (e.g., Emmanuel movement, strands in the mental hygiene movement, clinical pastoral education, positive thinking), nor from a religious fringe movement (e.g., Christian Science, New Age), nor from pietistic conservative Protestantism (e.g., demon exorcism, mystical subjective experience, moralizing). He represented a religious tradition that valued rational, hardheaded, and systematic thought, just as it valued principled action. Each of these factors—consistency, boldness, and historical memory—makes this case study unusual.

An Outline of the Narrative

Chapters 2 and 3 trace the history of Jay Adams's development of "nouthetic" counseling and its leading institutions through 1979. His historical context included three professional competitors: the secular mental health system, mainline Protes-

tant pastoral counseling, and evangelical psychotherapists. He emerged out of a sectarian religious community that had long stressed the epistemological antithesis between secular and biblical systems for interpreting human experience. He and his cohorts founded institutions to provide counseling services and education.

Chapter 4 explores Adams's success as an aspirant for jurisdictional authority by analyzing the counselee population of CCEF. Numerous would-be counselees chose or were referred to nouthetic counseling when seeking help for their personal problems.

Chapters 5, 6, and 7 look at Adams's cognitive system. The first two chapters examine the positive system by which he defined problems and solutions in frankly theological, ecclesiastical, and pastoral terms. Then chapter 7 considers Adams's polemics, tracing the nuances of his position and rhetoric regarding secular psychologies. The biblical counseling movement arose into a context of well-institutionalized alternatives, and its authors rarely ventured far without doing battle.

Chapter 8 considers the various opponents of nouthetic counseling. Interprofessional conflicts occurred occasionally with secular mental health professionals and with the liberal pastoral counseling movement, and continually with evangelical Christian psychotherapists. Opposition from the last group was particularly fierce, as they directly competed with nouthetic counselors both for cultural authority among conservative Protestants and for clientele.

Chapter 9 will briefly trace the story of Adams's nouthetic counseling through the 1980s and into the 1990s. It will describe the lines of tension and conflict that arose within the biblical counseling movement, and the results of the jurisdictional conflict between that movement and the evangelical psychotherapists.

Chapter 1 Notes

1. Excerpted from Romans 15:14, as translated in Jay E. Adams, *The Christian Counselor's New Testament: A New Translation in Everyday English with Notations* (USA: Presbyterian & Reformed, 1977), 437.

2. John Calvin, *Institutes of the Christian Religion,* trans. Ford Lewis Battles, ed. John T. McNeill, The Library of Christian Classics (Philadelphia: The Westminster Press, 1960), 35–37.

3. O. Hobart Mowrer, *The Crisis in Psychiatry and Religion* (Princeton: Van Nostrand, 1961), 60.

4. Jay E. Adams, *Competent to Counsel* (USA: Presbyterian & Reformed, 1970), 61.

5. Ibid., 18.

6. Jay E. Adams, *More Than Redemption: A Theology of Christian Counseling* (Phillipsburg, N.J.: Presbyterian & Reformed, 1979), 184.

7. Jay E. Adams, *Change Them?. . . into What?: Counseling in America Today* (Laverock, Pa.: Christian Counseling and Educational Foundation, 1977), 12.

8. Chapters 5–7 will explore in greater depth Adams's intellectual system, but this brief summary gives some sense of how he performed an explicit theologization of problems in living.

9. Chapter 3 will trace the founding and initial development of the alternative set of institutions created by Adams and his confreres.

10. Adams, *Competent to Counsel,* 81; cf., 78–82.

11. Ibid., 62; Jay E. Adams, *The Christian Counselor's Manual* (USA: Presbyterian & Reformed, 1973), 59.

12. For a summary of the distinctives of such "nouthetic" counseling, see Adams, *Competent to Counsel,* 41–56. We will discuss it in detail in chapter 6. Adams derived "nouthetic" from the Greek word *noutheteo,* which underlies the quotation at the head of this chapter, "competent to *counsel.*" Adams commented, "I have no great zeal for the label 'nouthetic' beyond its obvious advantages. However, since every school of thought eventually must be identified by an adjective, I should prefer to choose that adjective for myself" (*infra,* 52). In New Testament usage, the Greek word *noutheteo*—literally "to place in mind"—meant reproof, admonition, or other pointedly personal, constructive conversation. The word was often paired with expressions of intense love: for example, Paul's "admonishing with tears" (Acts 20:31) and his "as my beloved sons I admonish you" (1 Corinthians 4:14). It served as a summary word for wise and constructive conversation: whether as a general description of mutual counsel ("competent to counsel one another," Romans 15:14) or as counsel delivered with pastoral authority (1 Thessalonians 5:12). It also summarized the verbal aspects of a parent raising children (e.g., "bring them up in the admonition of the Lord"; Ephesians 6:4). *Noutheteo* in New Testament usage presumed objective criteria for the message presented: according to Colossians 3:16, the "word of Christ" was to be spoken to others both publicly ("teaching") and personally (*noutheteo*). Adams's intention as a biblicist was to replicate these sorts of activities in a twentieth-century context.

Adams believed that the Bible's objective authority mandated a style of counseling that was direct and directive. This emphasis

was prominent in the ways both Adams and his critics characterized his system. But it is worth noting that Adams qualified this directiveness in three ways. First, he noted that the bias of assumptions in any system creates at least a covert directiveness; hence, he only made explicit what he believed was concealed by duplicity in professedly nondirective systems. Second, he declared that nouthetic counselors could operate in other modes than the directive and gave examples of such. He chose to emphasize the directive in order to highlight one significant contrast between his approach and the counseling ethos that prevailed since the 1940s (deriving from Carl Rogers's nonintrusive, client-centered therapy: Carl R. Rogers, *Counseling and Psychotherapy* [Boston: Houghton Mifflin, 1942]; Carl R. Rogers, *On Becoming a Person: A Therapist's View of Psychotherapy* [Boston: Houghton Mifflin, 1961]). Third, though emphasizing more problem-centered, remedial counseling, he frequently alluded to "preventive" counseling that partook of other modes of human discourse. For example, he mentioned or alluded to all three of these qualifiers in the following quotation. After citing Carl Rogers's list of differences between directive and nondirective counseling, Adams commented: "Rogers . . . fails to recognize the subtle directiveness that even his method must employ. Yet, no nouthetic counselor would consider his activity limited to the items Rogers describes as 'directive.' He does all those things that Rogers calls directive but also does many of those things that Rogers calls nondirective. The fact is that the whole range of appropriate Christian responses is available to the nouthetic counselor. He does not force every case into one limited role. Rather, in responding appropriately to each client and each problem, the entire gamut of possible Christian responses may be used in nouthetic counseling." Adams, *Competent to Counsel,* 89.

13. Adams, *Competent to Counsel,* xxi.

14. On the totalitarian interpretive qualities of nonscientific conceptual systems, note Michael Polanyi's skeptical comments about Freud, how believers "regarded the all-embracing interpretive powers of this framework as evidence of its truth; only when losing faith in it did they feel that its powers were excessive and specious." Michael Polanyi, *Personal Knowledge: Towards a Post-Critical Philosophy* (Chicago: University of Chicago Press, 1958), 288. Adams's system made its faith assumptions overt, and he never lost faith in its interpretive powers.

Similar to Polanyi, Karl Popper described the "apparent explanatory power" of Freud and Adler as akin to myth not science because their systems were "able to explain practically everything that happened within the fields to which they referred. The study of them seemed to have the effect of an intellectual conversion or revelation, opening your eyes to a new truth hidden from those not yet initiated. Once your eyes were thus opened you saw confirming instances everywhere: the world was full of *verifications* of the theory. Whatever happened always confirmed it. Thus its truth appeared manifest." Freud's and Adler's theories "describe some facts, but in the manner of myths." Karl R. Popper, *Conjectures and Refutations: The Growth of Scientific Knowledge* (New York: Harper & Row, 1963, 1965), 34–38. Adams's system was self-consciously "mythical," in Popper's terms, rather than pretending to validation as "science." He literally called for conversion on the basis of a revelation.

15. William Glasser, *Reality Therapy: A New Approach to Psychiatry* (New York: Harper and Row, 1965); Perry London, *The Modes and Morals of Psychotherapy* (New York: Holt, Rinehart and Winston, 1964); Mowrer, *The Crisis in Psychiatry and Religion*; Thomas Szasz, *The Myth of Mental Illness: Foundations of a Theory of Personal Conduct* (New York: Harper & Row, 1961). I will delineate the nuances in Adams's view of psychology-related fields in chapter 7.

16. Adams, *Competent to Counsel*, xvi. Citation of Mowrer is from Mowrer, *The Crisis in Psychiatry and Religion*, 61.

17. "Evangelical" is perhaps the broadest term for nonfundamentalist conservative Protestants. See George M. Marsden, "The Evangelical Denomination," in *Evangelicalism and Modern America*, ed. George M. Marsden (Grand Rapids: William B. Eerdmans, 1984), vii–xix; George M. Marsden, *Reforming Fundamentalism: Fuller Seminary and the New Evangelicalism* (Grand Rapids: William B. Eerdmans, 1987), 1–11; George M. Marsden, *Understanding Fundamentalism and Evangelicalism* (Grand Rapids: William B. Eerdmans Publishing Company, 1991), 1–6. See the discussion of terminology later in this chapter and a sketch of the history of the evangelical psychotherapy establishment in chapters 2, 3, and 9. A full history of the evangelical psychotherapists, the "integrationists" who squared off against Adams, remains to be written.

18. Chapter 8 will treat the criticisms of Adams emerging from the pastoral counseling and evangelical psychotherapy movements. For an intellectual history of the pastoral counseling movement, see E. Brooks Holifield, *A History of Pastoral Care in America: From Salvation to Self-Realization* (Nashville: Abingdon Press, 1983). Pages 231–69 trace the development of the clinical education movement from the 1920s until World War II. Pages 269–348 trace the resurgence of postwar pastoral psychology. Holifield cuts off his story in the mid-1960s. For a sketch of developments subsequent to 1965, see Donald Capps, "The Bible's Role in Pastoral Care and Counseling: Four Basic Principles," in *The Church and Pastoral Care*, ed. Leroy Aden and J. Harold Ellens (Grand Rapids: Baker Book House, 1988), 41–55; and Donald Capps, *Reframing: A New Method in Pastoral Care* (Minneapolis: Fortress Press, 1990).

19. Rather than continually repeating these four variously overlapping terms—referring respectively to a profession, a protean form of practice employed by several adjoining professions, protean intellectual constructs, and a complex institutional arrangement—I will vary my terms depending on the primary referent. But typically I will intend loose, mutually inclusive meanings, rather than precise differentiation.

Anti-psychiatry—as used, for example, in my original subtitle—usefully provides a historiographic reference, connecting my subject to other anti-psychiatries and my work to other histories of anti-psychiatry. Though even Szasz has distanced himself from the term—see Thomas Szasz, "Mental Illness Is Still a Myth," *Society* 31, no. 4 (1995): 34–39—I think the appellation still usefully applies to Szasz, et al., who have generally opposed attaching medicalistic labels to human behavior.

Anti-psychology is ambiguous and potentially misleading but may serve as a synecdoche with appropriate qualifications. Adams was frequently termed an "anti-psychologist" or "psychology basher" by the conservative Protestant psychotherapists who occupied the immediate jurisdiction for which Adams aspired. Yet Adams often expressed high regard for psychology as a discipline that studied psychological, psychophysiological, and psychosocial topics. His explicit objections were to psychologists acting in what he saw as the proper role of theologians and pastors: as theoreticians and therapists of the human condition.

Anti-psychotherapist is probably the most accurate description of Adams's central concern. The term captures his opposition to both the intellectual systems and practical methods operating in secularized versions of generically "pastoral" activities. But even that term doesn't capture Adams's objections to psychotropic medications being given to redress functional problems in living.

Some of Adams's critics eventually even labeled him the founder of an "anti-counseling" movement. In fact he was an energetic promoter of counseling—a certain kind of counseling—into a community that was often resistant to and suspicious of counseling activities under any guise. His polemics were directed toward secular counseling and toward what he perceived as secularizing tendencies in those conservative Protestants he criticized.

Strictly speaking, then, he is the founder of an "anti-secular-psychotherapy-and-psychiatry" movement, in the interests of his own system of personal, pastoral counsel. Adams primarily objected to attempts to minister secularized explanations and solutions—whether psychological or medical—to people experiencing problems in living. This footnote ought to be borne in mind when for concision I employ various shorthand terms in the pages that follow. It also ought to be borne in mind when I seek to disentangle the rhetoric of attack and counterattack in chapters 7 and 8.

20. Westminster's founder, J. Gresham Machen, authored *Christianity and Liberalism*, one of the defining works in the religious controversies of the 1920s. He is the subject of a recent critical biography, D. G. Hart, *Defending the Faith: J. Gresham Machen and the Crisis of Conservative Protestantism in Modern America* (Baltimore: The Johns Hopkins University Press, 1994).

21. Chapters 3, 4, and 9 will look at the ground Adams's biblical counseling movement gained—and lost.

22. Charles E. Rosenberg, "The Crisis in Psychiatric Legitimacy: Reflections on Psychiatry, Medicine, and Public Policy," in *American Psychiatry Past, Present, and Future*, ed. George Kriegman et al. (Charlottesville, Va.: University Press of Virginia, 1975), 135–48 (reprinted in Charles Rosenberg, *Explaining Epidemics and Other Studies in the History of Medicine* [New York: Cambridge University Press, 1992], 245–57); Andrew Abbott, *The System of Professions: An Essay on the Division of Expert Labor* (Chicago: University of Chicago Press, 1988).

23. Rosenberg, *Explaining Epidemics*, 140.

24. Ibid., 137.

25. The literature debating psychotherapeutic efficacy is vast. During the 1960s, two influential works were H. J. Eysenk, "The Effects of Psychotherapy," in *Handbook of Abnormal Psychology*, ed. H. J. Eysenk (New York: Basic Books, 1961); and Charles B. Truax and Robert R. Carkhuff, *Toward Effective Counseling and Psychotherapy: Training and Practice* (Chicago: Aldine Publishing, 1967). Jay Adams would cite Eysenk (Adams, *Competent to Counsel*, 2f.) to the effect that patients did not get better under psychotherapy. Evangelical psychotherapists frequently cited Truax

and Carkhuff's description of the conditions for successful therapy (e.g., Andre Bustanoby, "Without These, Don't Start," *Christianity Today* [August 1973]: 38f.; William T. Kirwan, *Biblical Concepts for Christian Counseling: A Case for Integrating Psychology and Theology* [Grand Rapids: Baker Book House, 1984]).

26. Rosenberg, *Explaining Epidemics,* 142. For example, Carl Jung's *Modern Man in Search of a Soul,* Alfred Adler's *Understanding Human Nature,* along with Sigmund Freud's *Introductory Lectures on Psychoanalysis* are texts of enduring influence that illustrate Rosenberg's thesis. Psychologists have written similar works: e.g., B. F. Skinner's *Beyond Freedom and Dignity,* Carl Rogers's *On Becoming a Person,* Rollo May's *Man's Search for Himself,* and Abraham Maslow's *Toward a Psychology of Being.*

27. Similar observations underlie Thomas Kuhn's claim that most aspects of the social sciences are prescientific and function more like the arts, being "still characterized by fundamental disagreements about the definition of the field, its paradigm achievements, and its problems." Thomas S. Kuhn, *The Essential Tension: Selected Studies in Scientific Tradition and Change* (Chicago: University of Chicago Press, 1977), 222; cf., 118, 228–32.

28. Rosenberg, *Explaining Epidemics,* 144.

29. Ibid., 139.

30. Ibid.

31. My own experiences as a mental health worker at McLean Psychiatric Hospital (Belmont, Mass.) during 1973–1976 bear this out. I remember a sharp dispute between psychiatrists and social workers over the appropriateness of the latter doing "psychotherapy." And in the professional ecology of that hospital at that time, clinical psychologists did no counseling but were restricted to diagnostic testing. Nursing staff who talked too often and too long with patients were occasionally reproved for attempting to do therapy.

32. Abbott, *System of Professions,* 2.

33. Ibid., 102.

34. Ibid., 9; cf., 30.

35. Jay E. Adams, *The Language of Counseling* (Phillipsburg, N.J.: Presbyterian & Reformed, 1981) illustrates the degree to which Adams was scrupulous to give away as little terminological ground as possible.

36. Abbott, *System of Professions,* 302.

37. Ibid., 303.

38. Ibid., 286. Adams had commented in similar fashion: "With notable exceptions, there has been a general failure of the church since apostolic times to enter into the study and pursuit of personal counseling with the enthusiasm and vigor that must characterize any serious endeavor. No large body of theoretical thought or case study data has been accumulated. The meager amount of discussion concerning the work of counseling that has been preserved seems to view counseling as little more than a subhead of Church Discipline. As a result, personal counseling was carried on largely in unsystematic ways. It is no surprise, then, that personal counseling by ministers so readily was supplanted by psychiatrists." Jay E. Adams, *Shepherding God's Flock: A Handbook on Pastoral Ministry, Counseling, and Leadership* (Grand Rapids: Zondervan, 1974–75), 168.

39. Abbott, *System of Professions,* 308.

40. Ibid., 309.

41. Ibid., 309f.

42. See chapters 2, 7, and 8 for further discussion of mainline pastoral counseling and its relationship to Jay Adams.

43. Abbott, *System of Professions,* 310.

44. Adams hoped to foster a sharp-edged division. "[The] incursions of psychiatry and clinical psychology into areas that require one to determine ethical norms as the basis for the alteration of attitudes and behavior, therefore, should have been met by a significant response from the church. . . . O. Hobart Mowrer, William Glasser, E. Fuller Torrey, and others have been exposing the fundamentally nonmedical nature of the psychiatric enterprise for more than a decade and have awakened even many sleeping members of the church to the reasons for the growing disenchantment and disillusionment with psychiatry. Increasingly, the basically ethical nature of psychiatric activities has become apparent and has resulted in a growing concern over the attendant dangers involved in an uncritical acceptance of these activities. . . . The future of the relationship between the mental health movement and conservative biblical Christianity . . . can hardly be predicted. But it would seem that in the period immediately ahead the antithesis between clinical psychologies and psychiatries that are based upon non-Christian presuppositions and biblical Protestant Christianity will come into sharper focus, thus separating the two into distinct camps in which the issues that divide them and the discussions that shall ensue will center about the ethical question." Adams, *Shepherding God's Flock,* 167–70.

45. Abbott, *System of Professions,* 77f.

46. Ibid., 95.

47. Donald Meyer, *The Positive Thinkers: Popular Religious Psychology from Mary Baker Eddy to Norman Vincent Peale and Ronald Reagan* (Middletown, Conn.: Wesleyan University Press, 1988).

48. See the Note on Sources that precedes the bibliography.

49. Rosenberg, *Explaining Epidemics,* 4.

50. Michel Foucault, *Madness and Civilization: A History of Insanity in the Age of Reason,* trans. Richard Howard (New York: Pantheon Books, 1965); Erving Goffman, *Asylums: Essays on the Social Situation of Mental Patients and Other Inmates* (Garden City, N.Y.: Anchor Books, 1961); Gerald N. Grob, *Mental Illness and American Society, 1875–1940* (Princeton: Princeton University Press, 1983); Mowrer, *The Crisis in Psychiatry and Religion*; Andrew Scull, *Museums of Madness: The Social Organization of Insanity in Nineteenth-Century England* (New York: St. Martin's Press, 1979); Andrew Scull, ed., *Madhouses, Mad-Doctors, and Madmen: The Social History of Psychiatry in the Victorian Era* (Philadelphia: University of Pennsylvania Press, 1981); Elaine Showalter, *The Female Malady: Women, Madness, and English Culture, 1830–1980* (New York: Penguin Books, 1985); Szasz, *The Myth of Mental Illness.*

51. His view of the social role of psychiatry resembled Gerald Grob's on this point (see previous footnote for reference).

52. Adams was not averse to using the mental hospital as a threat to recalcitrant counselees exhibiting bizarre behavior or as a protection for suicidal counselees. Interview, December 4–5, 1990. Cf., Jay E. Adams, "The Christian Approach to Schizophrenia," in *The Construction of Madness: Emerging Conceptions and*

Interventions into the Psychotic Process, ed. Peter A. Magaro (New York: Pergamon Press, 1976), 143.

53. See, for example, Norman Gevitz, ed., *Other Healers: Unorthodox Medicine in America* (Baltimore: Johns Hopkins University Press, 1988); Steven C. Martin, "The Only Truly Scientific Method of Healing: Chiropractic and American Science, 1895–1990," *Isis* 85, no. 2 (1994): 206–27; John Harley Warner, "Medical Sectarianism, Therapeutic Conflict, and the Shaping of Orthodox Professional Identity in Antebellum American Medicine," in *Medical Fringe and Medical Orthodoxy, 1750–1850,* ed. W. F. Bynum and Roy Porter (London: Croom Helm, 1987), 234–60. The references in Gevitz (pp. 265–91) provide a thorough bibliography of this literature—both primary and secondary sources—as of 1988.

54. Ronald L. Numbers, *The Creationists* (New York: Alfred A. Knopf, 1992).

55. Adams respected medical doctors and gained a significant following among physicians. Chapter 5 will explore Adams's views of medicine and the body, and his interactions with conservative Protestant doctors.

56. Interview, October 7, 1991, Lafayette, Indiana. In biblicist fashion, Adams cited chapter and verse to support his view: "The metaphor has been detached from its referent. Jesus said, 'It is not those who are healthy who need a physician, but those who are sick; I did not come to call the righteous, but sinners.' People take the first half of that and read into it any meaning they want."

57. Interview, October 5, 1994, Lafayette, Indiana.

58. Consistent with this, biblical counseling was highly skeptical of mystical religious approaches to healing physical ailments, for example, the ministrations of healer-evangelists such as Oral Roberts.

59. Joseph Ben-David, "Professions in the Class System of Present Day Societies," *Current Sociology* 12 (1963): 247–98; Eliot Freidson, *Professional Powers: A Study of the Institutionalization of Formal Knowledge* (Chicago: University of Chicago Press, 1986); Everett C. Hughes and Agostino DeBaggis, "Systems of Theological Education in the United States," in *Education for the Professions of Medicine, Law, Theology, and Social Welfare,* ed. Everett C. Hughes et al. (New York: McGraw-Hill, 1973), 169–200.

60. Holifield, *A History of Pastoral Care in America,* 12f.

61. Abbott, *System of Professions,* 309f. Howard Clinebell is exemplary in this regard. Anton Boisen's co-opted revolution was a "sport" that found no ecological niche. Some mainline Protestant pastoral counselors were hostile to the modern therapeutic paradigms: e.g., Thomas Oden assailed the practice of "aping ineffective psychotherapies" by "secularized, hedonically oriented, fee-basis 'pastoral psychotherapists.'" Thomas C. Oden, *Pastoral Theology: Essentials of Ministry* (San Francisco: HarperCollins, 1982), 4f, 8f.

62. Martin Marty and R. Scott Appleby, eds., "Fundamentalisms Observed," *The Fundamentalism Project* (Chicago: University of Chicago Press, 1991); Martin Marty and R. Scott Appleby, eds., *Fundamentalisms and Society: Reclaiming the Sciences, the Family, and Education* (Chicago: University of Chicago Press, 1993); Richard T. Hughes, ed., *The American Quest for the Primitive Church* (Urbana, Ill.: University of Illinois Press, 1988); Marsden,

Reforming Fundamentalism; George M. Marsden, *Fundamentalism and American Culture: The Shaping of Twentieth-Century Evangelicalism, 1870–1925* (New York: Oxford University Press, 1980); Marsden, ed., *Evangelicalism and Modern America*; Marsden, *Understanding Fundamentalism and Evangelicalism*; Martin Marty, *Modern American Religion* (Chicago: University of Chicago Press, 1986ff); Mark A. Noll, *The Scandal of the Evangelical Mind* (Grand Rapids: William B. Eerdmans, 1994).

63. Cf., preface for discussion of the change in title for this edition.

64. Adams described his approach to the tasks of counseling this way: "I can speak only from my conservative, Calvinistic viewpoint as a Christian" (Jay E. Adams, "Grief as a Counseling Opportunity," in *The Big Umbrella and Other Essays and Addresses on Christian Counseling* [USA: Presbyterian & Reformed, 1972], 68). Similarly, "What has been going on in the practical theology department at Westminster [Theological Seminary] in the area of counseling has issued from a tight theological commitment. The position that has been developed and articulated is the direct result of Reformed thinking." (Jay E. Adams, "Counseling and the Sovereignty of God," in *Lectures on Counseling* [Grand Rapids: Zondervan, 1975–77], 72).

65. Jay E. Adams, *Counseling and the Sovereignty of God* (Philadelphia: Westminster Theological Seminary, 1975); Jay E. Adams, *How to Overcome Evil* (Nutley, N.J.: Presbyterian & Reformed, 1977); Jay E. Adams, *How to Handle Trouble: God's Way.* Phillipsburg, N.J.: Presbyterian & Reformed, 1982); Jay E. Adams, *The Grand Demonstration: A Biblical Study of the So-Called Problem of Evil* (Santa Barbara, Calif.: EastGate, 1991).

66. In Jay E. Adams, *Counseling and the Five Points of Calvinism* (Phillipsburg, N.J.: Presbyterian & Reformed, 1981). He applied these traditional Reformed emphases to counseling issues. The Calvinistic "TULIP" consists in the following:

Total depravity: though people are never as bad as they could be, every part of human nature—intellect, volition, emotions, passions, body, conscience, memory, and so forth—is affected by sin in some way;

Unconditional election: God saves people from sin based on his choice, not because of any good or anticipated good in them;

Limited atonement: the death of Christ was personal and effective, forgiving the sins of those whom God chose unto eternal life;

Irresistible grace: God makes the dead alive, and those in whom he works will come to faith;

Perseverance of the saints: all whom God makes alive will continue in faith unto death and the fulfillment of their hopes at the return of Christ.

67. Jay E. Adams, *The Meaning and Mode of Baptism* (Phillipsburg, N.J.: Presbyterian & Reformed, 1975).

68. Adams, *Shepherding God's Flock,* 167–70.

69. Jay E. Adams, *The Time Is at Hand* (Greenville, S.C.: A Press, 1966).

70. Adams, *Competent to Counsel,* xxi.

71. Noll, *Scandal of the Evangelical Mind, infra.*

72. Marsden, *Reforming Fundamentalism,* xi.

CHAPTER 2

The Making of a Conservative Protestant Counselor

[In colonial America] clerical counselors envisioned the cure of souls primarily as a remedy for sin. Despite the vast scope of pastoral counsel . . . the aim was always to allay the doubts resulting from sinfulness, or to temper the passions disordered by sinfulness, or to correct the vision clouded by sinfulness. The aim was to overcome the sinful temptations and undermine sinful resolves, to arouse the conscience against sin and to calm anxiety about sin.
— E. Brooks Holifield[1]

[Twentieth-century America] has evidenced a singular preoccupation with psychological modes of thinking— modes which have tended to refashion the entire religious life of Protestants into the image of the therapeutic.
— E. Brooks Holifield[2]

Like many other pastors, I learned little about counseling in seminary, so I began with virtually no knowledge of what to do.
— Jay Adams[3]

How did a middle-aged, theologically conservative, Presbyterian pastor come to develop an institutionalized anti-psychiatry? In this chapter and the next I will trace this historical development through the 1970s, establishing the chronology of key events, introducing the leading actors, and describing the central institutions. This story has not previously been told, so I will seek to ascertain and fix basic historical facts. This chapter will first set the historical context and then will pick up Adams's story through 1969. I will divide that story into two periods: (1) the years before 1965 and his catalytic encounter with O. H. Mowrer and (2) the crystallization of Adams's distinctive system, 1965–69.

The following chapter will carry the story on through the 1970s, when Adams initiated a fierce jurisdictional conflict by launching his nouthetic counseling movement.

With respect to the counseling field, Jay Adams was the classic outsider or "marginal man." He had been socialized into the intellectual and practical habits of a conservative Bible exegete, a local church pastor, and a contender for the faith in ecclesiastical wars—hardly characteristics typical of twentieth-century psychotherapists. Coming from the periphery, he did not share the near-instinctive assumptions of those within the field. He was well suited to play the role of prophetic innovator in the eyes of those who would come to embrace the paradigm shift he proposed; he was well suited to appear impudent and opinionated, even demagogic, in the eyes of those offended both by the matter of his propositions and by the manner in which he stated them.

What were the professional contours of that field into which Jay Adams attempted to insert himself? Many voices clamor for the right to explain and treat troubled and troublesome people. The "counseling" field—that vast realm of "functional" woes, disorders, malaise, interpersonal conflicts, vice, angst—is untidy both professionally and intellectually. Three professional communities provided the social environment for Jay Adams's career as a psychotherapeutic renegade in late-twentieth-century America: secular psychotherapists, mainline Protestant pastoral counselors, and conservative Protestant psychotherapists. The secular mental health professions achieved intellectual and professional dominance over the sphere of personal problems during the twentieth century, but from the late-1950s that establishment had been troubled by various critics who either commented on the immorality of current arrangements or suggested an overt remoralization of the "therapeutic" task. The mainline pastoral counselors variously accommodated to and argued with the modern psychologies throughout the twentieth century, but their dominant mode was acquiescence to the intellectual and professional program of the surrounding mental health professions. Evangelical psychotherapists only came into existence in the late-1950s, but rapidly professionalized, laying claim both to a knowledge program and to authority to provide psychotherapeutic services with a distinctively conservative Protestant theological twist.

We will look briefly at developments in each of these environing groups, touching lightly on the secular mental health system and the mainline Protestants but treating Adams's fellow conservative Protestants somewhat more fully both in this and subsequent chapters. Nouthetic counseling was a small, restive sect within a far larger counseling movement that began among evangelicals in the 1950s. A comprehensive, critical history of these co-religionists who were Adams's immediate professional neighbors remains to be written; in fact, no internalist histories exist, besides stage-setting sections of books and articles by practitioners. To fill such a gap is beyond the scope of this project, but some of that background is necessary in order to locate nouthetic counseling.

The Secular Mental Health Professions

In the century after the Civil War, the professional roles of asylum superintendent, psychological research scientist, and charity worker transmuted into a new secular psychotherapeutic pastorate. Professional jurisdiction over Americans' problems in living gradually passed from the religious pastorate to various medical and quasi-medical professions: psychiatry, neurology, social work, and clinical psychology. Pastoral retreat and subordination mirrored the advancing authority of those secular professions offering and administering psychotherapy, psychotropic medication, and psychiatric institutions.

The "therapeutic" was triumphant. Psychiatry and psychotherapy displaced the cure of souls, reifying the medical metaphor and so ordaining "secular pastoral workers" to take up the task.[4] Emotional and behavioral ills of the soul that once registered dislocations in a moral agent's relationships to God and neighbor were reenvisioned as symptomatic of a patient's mental and emotional illness. Worry, grumbling, unbelief, lovelessness, strife, vicious habit, and deceit came to be seen through different eyes, as neurotic anxiety, depression, inferiority complex, alienation, social maladjustment, addiction, and unconscious ego defense. Hospital, clinic, and office displaced church and community as the locus of cure.

By the mid-twentieth century, the dominant psychotherapeutic ethos in the United States combined two broad tendencies: (1) generically psychodynamic insight into unconscious neurotic conflicts within the individual (a pessimistic, diagnostic, "Freudian" strand), and (2) permissive, nondirective counseling methods to elicit healing forces from within the psyche (an optimistic, curative, "Rogerian" strand).[5] The medicalization of problems in living and the creation of a benign secular pastorate set the background for Adams's reactionary response. But two particular developments within the mental health world during the 1950s and early-1960s played an immediate catalytic role in the development of Adams's nouthetic counseling.

First, numerous overtly directive-interventive psychotherapies were created midcentury: rational-emotive therapy (Albert Ellis), transactional analysis (Eric Berne), integrity therapy (O. Hobart Mowrer), reality therapy (William Glasser), structural family therapy (Salvador Minuchin), and other marriage and family therapies. These therapies reacted against the notion of a medicalized, encapsulated psyche; they sought instead to define and treat problems in living within a social-moral nexus. They reacted to the passivity and disengagement enjoined on therapists and urged that therapy look more like counseling: active, intrusive, problem-solving, didactic, hortatory. They urged a revolution against the medicalization of personal and interpersonal problems.

Of course, moralization, suggestion, and call to commitment are timeless components of any psychotherapeutic intervention; one moralization or other informs every social interaction, and suggestion, however covert, gives expression to particular moralizations, inviting commitment.

But these new therapies made overt imposition of moral standards the instrumentality and pivot for change. Different as these approaches were from one another in details, they had much in common. Each traced its lineage to Alfred Adler and bore at least a familial resemblance to the ideas and practices of Harry Stack Sullivan.[6] They all tended to focus on present events rather than past history. Instead of probing unconscious processes and complex emotional states, they were concerned with consciousness and behavior. Instead of viewing problems in living as symptomatic of personal illness, they put responsibility for cognitive and behavioral change on the person. They were explicitly educational. Except for Ellis and Berne (who replicated the individualism of the prevailing therapeutic ethos), the new directive therapies also stressed the social nature of problems in living, and they often worked with groups of people rather than individuals. They offered short-term, educative counseling—"brief, direct, action-oriented intervention procedures"[7]—rather than a long-term, exploratory relationship.

The rise of moralistic therapies corresponded to a second, somewhat overlapping development. A spate of influential "anti-psychiatric" works called attention to various supposed failings of the prevailing therapeutic professions. These failings—whether exposed for political, intellectual, or professional purposes—had presumably been masked by the tidy functionalist assumptions that legitimized extant professional arrangements. In the eyes of critics, the match between social needs and those professions currently claiming to meet the needs was dubious. For example, psychiatrist Thomas Szasz argued that those processes by which diagnoses were made and patients committed to psychiatric institutions bore the malign stamp of ideology and political oppression, rather than fulfilling the benign purposes usually claimed for scientific knowledge and medical practice.[8]

Sociologist Erving Goffman analyzed psychiatric hospitals as "totalitarian" institutions, tracing the impact of institutionalization and stigmatization on the identity and career of inmates.[9] Psychotherapists O. Hobart Mowrer, William Glasser, and Perry London attacked the dominant psychodynamic therapies for ineffectualness and for neglecting the moral dimension inherent in problems in living.[10]

This was the wider cultural context in which Jay Adams's intellectual and professional formation occurred. He would spend a year studying with a Freudian psychiatrist; he assiduously attempted to apply Rogerian methods in his pastoral counseling; he would be radicalized by contact with Mowrer.

The Mainline Protestant Pastoral Counseling Movement

The history of mainline Protestantism—"liberal," "modernist," or "ecumenical" in orientation (in contrast with "conservative," "fundamentalist," or "sectarian" Protestantism)—is closely tied to the rise of modern psychological theories and professions. Modernist Protestantism and its approaches to pastoral counseling were both creature and cocreator of "the triumph of the therapeutic" in modern America. From the late nineteenth century on, popular social movements, influential pastors, and leading psychologists, neurologists, and psychiatrists met at the interface between liberal religion and the modern psychologies: William James, G. Stanley Hall, James Jackson Putnam, Elwood Worcester's Emmanuel movement, the mental hygiene movement, Harry Emerson Fosdick, Richard Cabot, Anton Boisen, clinical pastoral education, Harry Stack Sullivan, Carl Rogers, Rollo May, Seward Hiltner, Norman Vincent Peale, O. Hobart Mowrer, and Karl Menninger.[11]

The influences worked both ways. Liberal Protestants flavored American psychology with an optimism both about human nature and about the potential to offer salvific cures for what ailed people and relationships.[12] The psychologists in turn gave modern Protestantism a strongly psychotherapeutic cast. The assimilation of the modern psychologies into liberal theology created the "first crucial turning point in the history of American pastoral theology,"[13] as concern for a transcendent salvation receded into the background, and the urgencies attending individual adjustment and self-realization advanced into the foreground. "One can trace a massive shift in clerical consciousness—a transition from salvation to self-fulfillment—which reveals some of the forces that helped to ensure the 'triumph of the therapeutic' in American culture."[14]

In theory, an alliance existed between mainline pastoral counseling and the psychotherapeutic professions. Both sought to sustain and restore clients' mental health, and in theory their efforts were complementary and cooperative. But what transpired was largely a history of the church's subordination to the modern psychologies' intellectual contents and professional arrangements, with clerics hard pressed to define their distinctive intellectual and professional ground. Habits of deferring to the modern psychologies' understandings of human nature became well-established. Mainline Protestant pastors typically asserted their jurisdictional rights only by claiming that their religious resources could help solve those problems for which the modern psychologies had provided the diagnostic categories, a strategy that "concedes too much to be effective,"[15] and left pastoral counselors in a vulnerable professional position. Invariably, pastoral counseling drifted toward a junior version of psychotherapy.[16] Seward Hiltner dominated pastoral care in the 1950s, mediating "Rogers with a dash of Freud," as Howard Clinebell half-appreciatively and half-critically summarized it in 1965.[17] A kindly, largely nonintrusive methodology combined with a Freudian analysis of human depravity to become a standard feature of mainline pastoral care.

Similarly, the rationale and mechanisms for referring troubled parishioners to the expertise of mental health professionals became well established in mainline churches. Hiltner called pastoral counselors to provide short-term spiritual encouragement. They lacked the time and training to provide anything more substantial or searching. As a matter of course they ought to refer seriously troubled people to mental health professionals for long-term psychotherapy.[18]

Though the subordination of pastoral counseling to psychology has been often noted, mainline pastoral counselors never entirely capitulated to the psychologies. Discontent with the terms of the current jurisdictional settlement repeatedly surfaced; however, programs to institutionalize such discontent quickly aborted intellectually and institutionally. For example, the Emmanuel movement failed in part because its pastoral self-assertion threatened doctors; a successful backlash in the 1910s put pastors back in their place. Anton Boisen had claimed in 1936 that mental breakdowns were fundamentally religious events and had to be understood and resolved in such terms[19]; but the clinical pastoral education movement he inspired was soon trimmed of radicalism. In the mid-1950s, Albert Outler gave lucid voice to a sentiment common even at the height of Hiltner's influence:

The work of the psychotherapist involves the well-being of the whole person in a way which goes beyond the customary medical treatment—and thus requires a more explicit estimate of "the human condition." Nor can the Christian borrow and use the practical wisdom of psychotherapy without testing its presuppositions about human

nature and existence. Christianity and psychotherapy are both wisdoms-about-life, and it is by no means clear that they are the same wisdom.[20]

Outler observed that "the *cura animarium* has always had to depend, for its psychological categories, upon the prevailing doctrines of each particular age" and criticized the deficiencies in those prevailing doctrines, going so far as to say that the psychotherapies proclaimed an "anti-Christian gospel."[21] Nonetheless, "Rogers with a dash of Freud" still claimed the field.

After the mid-1960s mainline Protestants, influenced by anti-psychiatric writing, directive-interventive therapies, and Thomas Kuhn's history and philosophy of science, again went on the offensive to distinguish themselves from psychotherapists. Pastoral theologians such as Donald Browning and Donald Capps reinjected theology and the Bible into the counseling task and engaged in a program of suspicion toward the presuppositions of the modern psychologies: "secular therapists assume a moral context . . . even though it may not be directly invoked," therefore their stance of moral neutrality was a pretense; psychotherapies could take on "quasi-religious" meanings and "become competitors with established religious orientations"; the minister had a "direct professional responsibility to help shape this moral universe of values and meanings," instead of maintaining a stance of nonintrusive neutrality.[22] But the results of mainline Protestant opposition to secular psychology continued to be notoriously ambiguous: "Pastoral counseling [is repeatedly criticized] for its vaguely defined boundaries with psychology, namely that it tends not to have much of a life of its own independent of secular psychology from which it draws a great deal if not most of its vocabulary, content, and techniques. . . . [P]astoral counseling continues to be in search of its own soul."[23]

The mainline pastoral counselors proved influential even among conservative Protestants in the midcentury. When Jay Adams sought to improve his counseling as a young pastor in the 1950s, he read and sought to apply Hiltner. Conservative Protestants had few alternatives, having abandoned the counseling task over the previous century. Conservative pastors might disagree with the formal theology mediated by mainline pastoral theologians such as Hiltner, but their options were either to accept his counseling methodology or to revert to the primitive means that characterized their own versions of pastoral care: "prayer-and-Bible-verse prescriptions," rationalistic persuasion, moral condemnation, or casting out demons.[24]

The Beginnings of the Evangelical Mental Health Establishment

The counseling movement among mainline Protestant pastors antedated that among conservative Protestants by half a century. When conservative Protestants discovered the psychologies and psychotherapies during the late 1950s, the discoverers were not pastors, however. The immediate backdrop of this study of Adams's nouthetic counseling was a different professional group, evangelical psychotherapists. The prototypes arrived on the professional scene while Adams was still a young pastor, some fifteen years before his attempt at a counseling revolution.

The 1950s and 60s witnessed the beginnings of an evangelical psychotherapy profession and professoriate. Before then conservative Protestants in the United States had neither organized counseling services, nor counseling professionals, nor counseling models, nor any seeming inclination to develop these things. Though "the therapeutic" seemed to be triumphing in the wider culture, conservative Protestants were largely untouched. They continued to evangelize, to go to

"Higher Life" or prophecy conferences, to enter into "Christian service," and to "read the Bible, pray, and obey." In this community authority over problems in living had historically resided with the pastorate—and with various paraecclesiastical, charismatic leaders who gained influence through their books, radio programs, conferences, and evangelistic crusades. But the intellectual, methodological, and institutional resources remained threadbare. Fundamentalist-revivalist pastoral care regressed into what might be termed an anti-counseling mode. Problems in living were addressed by a hybrid of highly rationalistic, moralistic, mystical, and emotionalistic persuasion that aimed to accomplish a miraculous, instantaneous, absolute change.[25] The dropouts, failures, or burnouts either suffered in silence or covertly found their way into the secular mental health system. Beyond the traditional resources of piety (effective as those may have been in preventing or resolving some problems in living), the community provided no further organized resources for the counseling task.

The mainstream of American conservative Protestants traced their roots back to the Puritans and Jonathan Edwards, who had been notable for their conscientious empiricism and case-wise pastoral practice. But no conservative Protestant had set forth a systematic counseling model since Ichabod Spencer in the 1850s.[26] By the turn of the twentieth century, conservative Protestants retained some elements of Jonathan Edwards's formal theology, but William James was heir to Edwards's style of careful observation and rational reflection on human experience. The anti-intellectualism, cultural retreat, social disengagement, millennarian preoccupation, pietism, and subculture clannishness of emerging fundamentalism—the "paranoid style"—all contributed to a neglect of the problems in living and the counseling practices that might redress them.[27] The pockets of scholarly activity and ability that remained devoted most of their energies to battles for the "fundamentals": biblical authority and other traditional tenets of Protestant orthodoxy.[28] After the Civil War and into the twentieth century, the secular psychologies and the liberal Protestant theologies were ascendant. Stimulating and shaping one another to a large degree, both defined themselves as empirical and practical, in counterpoint to the old scholastic orthodoxies of conservative Protestantism.

The first conservative Protestant institutional initiatives to take on the care of troubled people did not arise in the mainstream of evangelical-fundamentalist-revivalist religion, but among small Dutch and Mennonite ethnic denominations. The (Dutch) Christian Reformed Church had begun the first psychiatric services by and for conservative Protestants—largely their own constituents—earlier in the century. The Christian Psychopathic Hospital and Pine Rest Sanitarium (Grand Rapids, Mich.) had been founded in 1910.[29] The first association of conservative Protestant mental health professionals also arose in this same Dutch community. The Christian Association for Psychological Studies (CAPS) was founded in 1952 among a small group of predominantly Christian Reformed psychiatrists and psychologists.

Around the midcentury, Mennonites also began to institutionalize psychiatric services. Some 1,500 Mennonite conscientious objectors had worked in state mental hospitals performing alternative service during World War II. That experience catalyzed the formation of Mennonite Mental Health Services in 1947. The Mennonites were initially interested in "serving chronically ill, former hospital patients, in a homelike atmosphere for long periods of time," as a corrective to the impersonality and overcrowding witnessed in state hospitals. But plans shifted to "treating acutely ill patients for a shorter time in an active treatment facility," and a medical and psychiatric model was adopted.[30]

Over the next seven years four psychiatric hospitals were opened.[31]

But Christian Reformed and Mennonite groups lay outside the mainstream of indigenous, American conservative Protestantism. In that mainstream, monolithic fundamentalist suspicion of counseling practice per se did not begin to crack until the 1950s. The "new evangelicalism" of the 1940s, signaled by Carl Henry's *The Uneasy Conscience of Modern Fundamentalism*, had articulated a vision for reengagement in long-ignored cultural and social tasks.[32] Problems in living, the modern psychologies, and mental illness gradually emerged into the evangelical purview. Though conservative Protestant seminaries and pastors continued to neglect counseling, other conservative Protestants began to acquire graduate education and became licensed mental health professionals.

In the late 1950s Clyde Narramore became the first well-known author, speaker, and counseling practitioner who was certifiably both a psychologist and a conservative Protestant.[33] He packaged a popularized Freudianism with evangelical terminology and morality, and gained a nationwide reputation among conservative Protestants. His Narramore Christian Foundation provided a vehicle for publicizing mental health needs, distributing self-help literature, training pastors and other Christian workers, and offering counseling services.

During the 1960s the institutional foundations for an evangelical psychotherapy community were laid. Fuller Theological Seminary started its Graduate School of Psychology in 1965. The program was under the leadership of Lee Edward Travis, a well-known experimental psychologist at the University of Southern California, who had become a professing evangelical in 1961.[34] Its theoretical mandate was to "integrate" conservative Protestant faith with modern psychology's insights and therapies. In so doing, Fuller sought to fill a perceived intellectual and social vacuum in conservative Protestantism. Its professors intended to engage—and profit from—the modern psychologies, which fundamentalists had simply ignored or disdained. They intended that their students replicate the mental health professions, whose role and activities had been almost wholly neglected by conservative Protestants, a neglect that presumably extended to people in need of help. Fuller's was the first graduate program to train evangelicals, those "reforming fundamentalists," to become mental health professionals.

These psychologists and religionists set out "to integrate the evangelical understanding of biblical doctrine with scientific and applied aspects of psychology . . . to reconceptualize psychology in such a way as to be consistent with the tenets of an orthodox, Protestant cosmology and anthropology."[35] That agenda was intended to produce intellectual goods that psychotherapeutic professionals might bring to an evangelical public struggling with life's problems. The catchword "integration" typically served to represent both the intellectual and professional tasks.[36] Though the definition of "integration" was much controverted, its common denominator could be found in the emergence of a new kind of professional, new both in ecclesiastical and mental health circles: a conservative Protestant psychotherapist who intended to take both halves of that designation with equal seriousness.

They professionalized rapidly and successfully over the decades that followed. They had stepped into a professional vacuum. Even by the late 1960s, though they often felt that they had a hard time persuading their church communities of the legitimacy of psychotherapy, they had gained a growing measure of recognition as the church's experts in the personal problems sphere. That a group of evangelical psychotherapists, not pastoral theologians, would be called in to evaluate Adams's *Competent to Counsel (CtC)* in 1969 indicates the professional success they had achieved by that time. Among conservative Protestants there were simply no pastors, preachers, or pastoral counselors recognized as intellectually or professionally competent in the personal problems sphere. The psychotherapists would be the professionals with whom Adams came into immediate and continual conflict throughout the 1970s. Through the 1970s and 1980s psychology-related academic programs would proliferate among evangelicals; psychotherapy professions experienced tremendous growth; and the popular authority of psychologists soared. Evangelical psychotherapists would prove to be the agents of a belated triumph of the therapeutic within their subculture during the 1980s. By the 1990s one of their leaders could justly speak of "the Christian mental health establishment."[37]

Prior to 1965: The Prehistory of an Anti-Psychiatrist

Jay Adams was a conscientiously biblicistic, local church pastor. His intellectual and professional formation occurred largely in a context shaped by the battles between Presbyterian separatism and liberal Protestantism fought by the generation that preceded him. Born on January 30, 1929, Jay Edward Adams grew up in the Windsor Hills suburb of Baltimore as the only child in a working-class family; his father was a policeman, his mother a secretary. He graduated from high school at sixteen years old, in 1945, having accelerated a year. He described his childhood as happy and active, unexceptional, characterized by neighborhood play, sports, hanging on the street corner. He had "always liked to organize things" and had participated in a "Leaders Club" for boys but had no evident intellectual interests. He claimed never to have read a book through until his senior year in high school when he read the New Testament for the first time.[38]

Adams was brought up in a nonreligious family. Neither parent attended church before their son was converted, though he had been "dragged to a liberal Methodist Sunday school" for several years. His chief memory of that experience was of a teacher throwing the Bible across the room on the first day of class, saying he knew nothing about it and did not intend to refer to it; the class spent the following months talking about sports, dating, and whatever else happened on the minds of class members.

When Adams was fifteen years old a neighborhood friend initiated a discussion on the street corner about whether the Bible was true.[39] Adams's interest was sparked; from a pile of old books in his pantry, he dug out a khaki New Testament that his father had been given during World War I. For the next two months he carried the book around "surreptitiously" and read it wherever he went, "devouring the New Testament." Over that two months he "came to understand and believe the gospel." His was a conversion apparently unmediated by social or emotional inducements; the Word of God had spoken and the human creature had believed. The unadorned biblicism of this conversion established a characteristic theme; the way Adams himself had changed would reappear in the emphases he would bring to the tasks of counseling twenty years later.

Adams's chief interest in school had been cartooning. Previously uninterested in reading, "suddenly I became voracious, I couldn't get enough." He began to attend a conservative Presbyterian church. Through the pastor's influence the sixteen-year-old Adams decided to attend Reformed Episcopal Seminary (RE) in Philadelphia the fall after his conversion.[40] As a largely ignorant new Christian, "I didn't even know who Moses, Jonah, and Noah were when I went to seminary." But he

proved to be an indefatigable worker, researcher, and debater and quickly absorbed the Bible and Calvinist theology. Adams credited RE with a profound influence on both his basic convictions and his intellectual style. "The chairman of the faculty . . . asked me the standard question, as he did (individually) to every incoming student: 'Are you willing to test every question by the Scriptures?' In the fifty years that followed, to do so has been my avowed goal."[41] The head of the Systematic Theology Department, Robert Rudolph, had a profound influence on Adams's beliefs and style.[42] Rudolph was noted for his zeal for conservative Protestant orthodoxy, the adversarial atmosphere of his classroom, and his passionate conviction that true believers needed to separate from error rather than engage in cool discussion. Adams's recollection was that "the whole of the teaching methodology at RE was you've got to prove everything you believe. Every class was an argument. It taught you to think, and it taught you to think on your own, not just parrot back." The debater's style, the constant recourse to biblical evidence, hard work and constant study, and an iconoclastic instinct would characterize his subsequent endeavors.

He went on to do a double undergraduate degree, completing a two-year bachelor of divinity at RE (BD, 1951) and a four-year bachelor of arts in Greek at Johns Hopkins (AB, 1951).[43] At Hopkins he carved his own path: "The entire undergraduate classics department at Hopkins existed for me alone for two years. Then the last two years they threw me in with graduate students." A tutorial on *koine* Greek was particularly influential. That the New Testament had been written to plain people in rough, fish-market, gutter Greek contributed to Adams's lifelong aversion to forms of theological writing and religious expression that were primarily abstract, sentimental, pietistic, or aesthetic, rather than "practical" and "direct."[44]

Adams received minimal exposure to psychology during his extended undergraduate education: RE offered no counseling courses, and Adams took only an introductory psychology course at Hopkins. There the professor's opening act made quite an impression:

On the first day of an elementary psychology course at Johns Hopkins University some twenty years ago, a professor sat on his desk silently reading the morning newspaper. The bell rang, but he didn't seem to notice it. Then audibly he began to read the headlines of the front page articles. They captioned difficult world problems, spoke of inhuman acts of man to his fellow man, and, in general, painted the typical sensational front page picture one may read every day. Presently, he looked up and said, "The world is in a mess." He spent the rest of the hour explaining how psychology is the world's one hope for straightening out that mess.[45]

The pastor-to-be, believing in a different Savior, had his doubts, but they were as yet inarticulate. Adams's intellectual formation, heavy on theological science, was almost entirely innocent of social and behavioral science. His practical formation, heavy on proclamation and debate, was nearly innocent of the all-tolerant probing and affirmation that typified the midcentury psychotherapeutic ethos.

The preacher and organizer did not waste time before getting involved in ministry after his graduation.[46] Adams demonstrated a take-charge ability early on. In 1951–52 he served as director of Youth for Christ in Baltimore, organizing evangelistic rallies and doing follow-up work with young people.[47] Adams went on to serve in a series of small conservative Presbyterian denominations during the 1950s and 1960s. He was ordained in the United Presbyterian Church as a twenty-three-year-old on October 10, 1952.[48]

His first pastorate was at Mount Prospect United Presbyterian Church outside Pittsburgh (1952–54). "I couldn't find a single person who understood the gospel. I started to preach the gospel and we had a mini-revival the first year with maybe sixty people saved. The youth group grew from about four to over a hundred." But while the congregation swelled in size, Adams's ineptitude in counseling was driven home to him.

Early in my first pastorate, following an evening service, a man lingered after everyone else had left. I chatted with him awkwardly, wondering what he wanted. He broke into tears, but could not speak. I simply did not know what to do. I was helpless. He went home that night without unburdening his heart or receiving any genuine help from his pastor. Less than one month later he died. I now suspect that his doctor had told him of his impending death and that he had come for counsel. But I had failed him. That night I asked God to help me to become an effective counselor.[49]

Adams characteristically followed up prayers with action. The inadequacy of his training and skill led him to begin to study counseling informally in attempts to improve himself.

Over the next decade, Adams read widely in the counseling field: representative secular psychologists, the mainline pastoral counselors who dominated the religious counseling field, and the first generation evangelical psychologists (e.g., Clyde Narramore). The message to which he was consistently exposed was some form of depth psychology (generically "Freudian," in Mowrer's term that Adams later adopted); the methodology was typically Carl Rogers's style of benign, nonintrusive affirmation. Adams also attended the workshops that mental health professionals offered to pastors, workshops which, while teaching a few rudimentary interpersonal skills, carefully reinforced the pastor's awareness of his limitations and encouraged referrals.

Local church counseling problems were not the only difficulties Adams faced. Theologically conservative Presbyterians in the 1950s agonized in the latest round of an issue "that had plagued Protestant reformers in America since the first Puritans set foot on Plymouth Rock: Must they separate from corrupted denominations?"[50] In the 1930s, Presbyterian separatists had left the mainline PCUSA because of its "modernism and indifferentism" and formed splinter denominations.[51] In the 1950s, the United Presbyterians were contemplating a merger into that perceivedly corrupt PCUSA. Adams strongly opposed the merger and became a spokesman for this cause in 1954.

Adams had continued to pursue formal education throughout this time. During 1952–54 he completed most of the course work for a master's in theology at Pittsburgh-Xenia Seminary, but he quit without doing his thesis. His stand against the denominational merger had jeopardized his relations with the faculty at Pittsburgh-Xenia Seminary, who largely favored the merger, and he withdrew from the program.

In 1954 the Mount Prospect church split in a backlash over the stir produced there by Adams's aggressive and successful evangelism and by his stand in the wider ecclesiastical controversy. Adams and the new converts left and founded Viewcrest Community Church in Eighty-Four, Pennsylvania (1954–56). Adams was never sentimental about preserving unity at all costs or about working within existing institutions. He operated with the instincts of a revolutionary, not a reformer. Without a backward glance he was willing to lead like-minded people to separate from existing institutions and to form new institutions.

Adams's next pastorate was in Covenant Bible Presbyterian Church in Haddonfield, New Jersey (1956–58).[52] This congregation was embroiled in a different ecclesiastical war, between varying degrees of separatists. It had split from the congregation pastored by extreme fundamentalist Carl McIntire shortly before calling Adams to become their first full-time pastor. McIntire was also becoming persona non grata in the wider Bible Presbyterian Church for his dictatorial tendencies and political extremism.[53] When Adams entered the denomination, he immediately became part of a group working to oust Carl McIntire from influence.[54]

Back in the Philadelphia area, Adams completed his master's in sacred theology at Temple University School of Theology (1958), studying under well-known homiletician Andrew Blackwood. During this time Adams took a year-long psychotherapy course under a Freudian psychiatrist at Temple University, an experience he subsequently recalled in *The Power of Error*. In a case study presented for the class, Adams described counseling a man fruitlessly for that year, presuming he suffered from a "psychoneurosis." The professor had annotated Adams's case records with comments and suggestions reinforcing such an interpretation. In retrospect, Adams attacked the psychiatrist's comments as "unsubstantiated dicta" and "gross speculation."[55] But his most withering remarks were reserved for himself, a would-be pastoral counselor in the psychotherapeutic mode:

Robert [the counselee] made a great number of attempts to discuss the issue of his sin. Not once did the pastor-counselor [i.e., Adams] take up the invitation. You may wonder why the counselor didn't do so. The sad fact is that he *would* have if he had been following the Scriptures and if he had not been indoctrinated against doing so by psychological and psychiatric dogma and propaganda. Strange, how he refuses to accept pagan theory and practice altogether (his methods are directive and his faith surfaces now and again), but it is most interesting to discover how at every crucial point the pagan viewpoint takes ascendancy over all else. . . .

The counselee has given him proper direction and permission to become personal—"look at my sin," he begs; but the counselor refuses to follow his direction. Why? He thinks, "The problem can't be anything so simple as sin. Indeed, the very fact that Robert talks in such an unusual way about himself is indicative of some fairly serious mental illness." So pagan dogma steers him from the true course to look for a label denoting something more complex.

Once labeled, the counselee's problem can be dealt with more comfortably under the rubrics appropriate to that "illness." Eventually he finds it: Robert is suffering from psychoneurosis. Thereafter, all that the counselor does is governed by the definitions and theory surrounding that concept. He will read all of Robert's actions and judge all of his words through the grid. . . .

What was [Robert]'s sin? We never find out because the counselor's bias blinds him and doesn't allow his biblical training to override his psychological orientation. Sad! . . .

Pastors galore have not helped Robert. Presumably they have tried giving him prayer-and-Bible-verse prescription. . . . One tried to cast a demon out of him. . . . The pastor-counselor who brings this report *wants* to understand, but . . . clearly he doesn't.[56]

Adams dutifully attempted to become socialized, even as he tried to avoid the evident pitfalls of pietistic, moralistic, or exorcistic pastoral counsel

typical within conservative Protestant churches. But his "biblical training" and his "psychological orientation" made restless bedmates.

In 1958 Adams's energetic and successful work in the ministry was recognized with a call to become executive secretary of Home Missions for the Bible Presbyterian Church. He moved out to St. Louis, and from there traveled the country, meeting with groups interested in starting churches, assessing pastoral candidates, raising money, exploring potential properties, and troubleshooting church problems. Adams was first and foremost a "churchman." His counseling interests were never primary but represented a subset of an overarching preoccupation with the gamut of problems faced by churches and pastors. And his churchmanship did not play out primarily at the level of denominational politics. He had the instincts, sympathies, and antipathies of a local churchman, the pastor of a flock he knew by name, a flock that he would evangelize, baptize, teach, lead, visit in the hospital, marry, advise, reconcile, and bury. The social, institutional, and professional habits he would bring to the counseling task were decidedly not those of the autonomous mental health professional.

Though opposing McIntire's extreme separatistic stance, Adams frankly advocated that ministers and their congregations separate from denominations tainted with liberalism. When the merger of the old United Presbyterians with the Presbyterian Church USA finally occurred in 1958, it occasioned a frank statement of Adams's separatist views. He called dissident pastors to come out of their now compromised ecclesiastical situation. Articulating standard separatist arguments, he invited them to consider the Bible Presbyterians as a new home. The enterprising home missions' director would build his denomination by recruiting shepherds to come out of apostasy with their flocks just as he had.[57]

In 1959 Adams wrote his first book, on a subject far removed from counseling. In a denomination that was largely premillennial in eschatology, he bluntly advocated the amillennial view.[58] This generated heated debate across the denomination. Adams was widely perceived as a "militant" amillenialist.[59] Though the issue was resolved at the 1960 synod in Adams's favor, allowing liberty of conscience, he quit his job in the Home Missions Department that same summer because the controversy seemed likely to prove detrimental to funding for church planting. It would not be the last time that Adams's militance proved as provocative as the content of his views. He was a controversialist, out to define and magnify differences, not a diplomat out to blur or reconcile differences.

If RE Seminary had honed the instincts of the biblicist debater, Adams's tumultuous church experiences during the 1950s produced two other things that would one day prove significant in his counseling revolution. First, by the time he was thirty, he was a veteran of the widely varied joys and strains of pastoring local churches. He felt with and for the pastor. When he subsequently spoke to conservative pastors about counseling, they knew they were hearing one of their own. That same voice, those same sensibilities, those institutional habits, would sound discordant to mental health professionals, even when they subscribed to the same basic theological system as Adams. But pastors heard a pastor, and his counseling model would be a model for them. The pastor would be defined as the "counseling professional," and the local church would provide the setting for most counseling activities. "Counseling," far from being esoteric, would overtly cohere with the content and goals of preaching, sacraments, discipleship, small groups, and church discipline. The Bible would serve as the sourcebook for counseling content and methods, and those methods would be frankly didactic and conversional in intent.

Even the anticipated trajectory of the counseling process—six to twelve weeks of highly structured and interventive counseling—would fit within the time constraints on a busy pastor.

Second, by the time he was thirty, Adams was a veteran of ecclesiastical wars. He had become well aware of the intense conflicts generated by matters of theology, church practice, and personality—and he was willing to participate. "No one *likes* conflict, unless he's proud and divisive, but sometimes you've got to take a stand. And when you do take a stand, you need the hide of a rhinoceros." Adams was not one to shrink from a fight where he thought the true and the right were at stake in a contest with compromisers. He took a hard-boiled attitude toward existing institutions and was willing to separate in order to start something new. A decade later, Adams's *CtC* and nouthetic counseling movement would be intended—as a matter of principle—to stir up trouble for the compromisers he perceived running the dominant counseling institutions. He would aim to create a church-based counseling practice separate from and parallel to extant counseling worlds, whether secular or religious. Adams would present his pastor-led endeavor as a theologically pure and ecclesiastically separate alternative, in sharp contrast with professions tainted by the forms and ideas of secular psychology.

But Adams eventually launched his counseling revolution neither as a local church pastor nor as a denominational administrator. His eventual platform proved to be a theological seminary. He had become increasingly interested in teaching other pastors how to do their job better. But a call to teach would not come for several more years and after yet another stint in higher education. On leaving the Home Missions office in 1960, Adams entered a PhD program in speech at the University of Missouri. He studied there until 1963, focusing, naturally enough, on preaching not counseling.

Again he was distinctively the pastor, interested in proclamation, persuasion, and conversion.

Adams, in fact, completed two dissertations. The first examined audience adaptation in the speeches of the apostle Paul. The tailoring of message to audience—based on detailed, first-hand knowledge of the listeners—was a lifelong preoccupation. This emphasis would eventually appear in Adams's approach to counseling in the attention he paid to detailed "data gathering."[60] Adams was forced to abandon the dissertation when his conservative assumptions about the Bible's integrity were challenged by a member of his committee who was "a theological liberal."[61] This experience reinforced a conviction that had arisen out of experiences in the ecclesiastical wars at Pittsburgh-Xenia a decade earlier, that "liberals play dirty pool."

Adams completed his second dissertation in 1965. It addressed a less controversial subject: the homiletical distinctives of his former mentor at Temple, Andrew Blackwood.[62] Blackwood's emphasis on reconstructing the seminary around the tasks of practical theology, particularly preaching, rather than around formal scholarship, resonated with the quintessential local church pastor. Though Adams would spend almost twenty years teaching in seminaries, he endured rather than adopted the institutional habits of academia. He was always the activist, the iconoclast, the popularizer, the *practical* theologue. He would later propose a revolution in the seminary curriculum that bore a strong resemblance to Blackwood's, seeking to remake seminary study to serve pastoral practice not academic interests.[63]

After completing his course work at University of Missouri, Adams and his family moved back East to accept another pastoral call. From 1963 to 1966 he served as pastor of Grace Orthodox Presbyterian Church in Westfield, New Jersey. Upon this move back into the local church setting,

the issues of pastoral counseling again presented themselves full force: "I'd always had an interest in counseling from the beginning—because of people. As a pastor I was trying to help people, and I'd always be thrust into the middle of their problems." But Adams was doubly intimidated. In his own attempts at counseling, he "muddled along, with no coherent alternative to the secular stuff." And he continued to attend periodic workshops for pastors sponsored by mental health agencies in which it was reiterated that the pastor should not attempt much but should "defer and refer" to secular mental health experts. "The bottom line message to pastors was, 'Leave things to the professionals. There is little you can do besides provide an accepting atmosphere for people. Troubled people are not violators of conscience, but morally neutral victims of an accusing conscience. They need professional help.' I couldn't see my way through the propaganda."[64]

The catalyst for the preacher and generalist pastor to concentrate on counseling came when Adams was assigned to teach pastoral counseling in a seminary curriculum. At the time he took over the pastorate of Grace OPC, Adams had been asked to come to Philadelphia one day a week to teach remedial speech at Westminster Theological Seminary. In 1963 the successful preacher, trained speaker, and PhD candidate gained his first opportunity to train other preachers in public speaking techniques. The next year he was appointed special lecturer in Practical Theology, assigned to teach courses in public speaking, preaching, and poimenics.[65] The poimenics course contained a unit on counseling:

What would I teach? I was stuck, and I didn't know the answers. So I started digging. I read everything I could find on counseling in two or three seminary libraries, as well as other books on psychology. I got immersed in Freudianism because that was the thing that both the pagan books and the Christian books taught. I threw something together for a course; it was horrible. But at least I had started to wrestle with the issues.

Over the next five years, Adams's views on counseling theory and practice would dramatically change. This outsider to the well-developed sociocultural world of professional counseling would lay the foundation for developing his own separate world of counseling practice.

1965–69: The Crystallization of Adams's Bible-Oriented and Pastor-Oriented System of Counseling

Adams had heard the name O. Hobart Mowrer from a Christian psychologist friend who thought Adams might be interested in Mowrer's work. In the early 1960s, Mowrer[66] had begun to challenge Freudian theory, to describe people as morally responsible, and to call troubled and troublesome human behavior "sin." In the winter of 1965, Mowrer gave a lecture at Beaver College, one mile down the road from Westminster Seminary in the suburbs just north of Philadelphia. Adams went to hear him. Afterward Adams spoke with Mowrer, who invited him to apply to a summer fellowship program for clergy sponsored by the Eli Lilly Foundation. Adams was accepted, and the six-week intensive course proved to be a dramatic turning point. Adams and the other five religionists "virtually lived with Mowrer." They spent the days working in therapy groups that Mowrer conducted in state mental hospitals in Galesburg and Kankakee, Illinois. Over meals, commuting, and in the evenings, they talked with Mowrer.

Adams witnessed Mowrer dealing with the moral failings of psychiatric patients, rather than treating them as mentally ill.[67] Four aspects of Mowrer's work made a profound impression on

Adams. First, the "sins" Mowrer uncovered in people were eye-opening to a pastor who took the Ten Commandments seriously: adultery, theft, lying, shirking responsibility, laziness, bitterness, fear, false beliefs, rebelliousness, substance abuse, and the like. The vast majority of the so-called "mentally ill," those with functional rather than organic etiologies, looked strikingly normal once Mowrer cut through the bizarre symptoms. Their guilt was real, not false. They were violators of conscience and avoiders of honesty, not victims of an overactive and diseased conscience.

Second, the "repentance" Mowrer taught people was no less striking to a pastor whose professional life had been dedicated to persuading people to convert. Mowrer called for confession of failings and for making restitution by marking out appropriate concrete behavioral changes. Those who had done wrong could own up and make things right. Mowrer emphasized hope that long-standing patterns of behavior and attitude could be broken if matters were faced and dealt with honestly. He emphasized responsibility—that people could choose to act in new, more constructive ways.

Third, Mowrer's counseling methodology was a revelation to an authoritative pulpit proclaimer. Adams had chafed at the passivity, patience, and professional reserve enjoined by the reigning counseling authorities. Therapeutic passivity had made little sense to someone whose life mission was to proclaim a message intended to change people's "faith and practice." Mowrer was direct and directive. The sedate pace of modern psychotherapy made little sense amid the demands on a busy pastor. Mowrer aimed to identify and solve problems quickly. Professional reserve did not square with life in the small community of the local church, the "family" where people unavoidably knew their pastor, where he knew them, and where all avowedly needed grace for common sins. Mowrer was assertive, no-nonsense, honest about his own failings, and dealt practically with objectively discoverable failings. "He was rough on people in the psychiatric hospitals. He would tackle the impossible cases, and in groups would go after someone until a breakthrough occurred. And he would tell his own story freely." For Adams, Mowrer blew apart the mystique attached to the therapeutic process, to diagnostic and explanatory categories, and to the counselor's identity.

Lastly, Mowrer's withering attack on generic Freudianism brought a message of liberation to a would-be student of modern therapies who could never quite get it right. It simultaneously sounded the alarm to a religionist whose theological tradition featured an analysis of the presuppositional antithesis between biblical religion and the "world's" lies and whose ecclesiastical tradition featured militant separation from errorists. And it bluntly challenged the pastor and pastoral theologian, maintaining that clergymen and theologians were "more heavily under the sway of Freudian ideology than any other comparable group, including psychologists and, quite possibly, even psychiatrists."[68] Mowrer had demonstrated to Adams that the "irresponsibility ethic" woven into the medical model of neuroses and psychoses was bankrupt, a "mess of pottage" contradictory to church's "birthright."[69] The counseling world—secular psychiatrists, mainline pastoral counselors, and evangelical psychologists—had been broadly deceived. Mowrer and like-minded therapists such as Perry London and William Glasser, actively prosecuted the medical model in favor of a moral model. Mowrer's message was both a call to arms and a call to repentance. Adams leapt to join the debunkers, these "young, vigorous individuals who have begun to challenge the traditional Freudian and Rogerian ideas."[70]

The speech at Beaver College, Mowrer's book, *The Crisis in Psychiatry and Religion,* and that summer of study had a catalytic effect. Adams was duly appreciative of what Mowrer had given him.

Mowrer did two things for me. First, he *destroyed* the Freudian system in my mind. He knew it inside out; he'd been a part of it; he'd come out of it and rejected it, and he knew why he'd rejected it. That was the reigning system then. Second, at the same time, he shook my faith in the mental health professionals. Previously I was still caught up in the idea that we preachers shouldn't be doing counseling. Mowrer cleared the field of rubble for me. He gave me the confidence to go forward.

Mowrer's moral framework, conversional intent, direct manner, and polemic against the dominant models dovetailed with many of Adams's existing commitments, discontents, successes, failures, and gropings.

Four major influences played a part in Adams's counseling revolution. First, his intellectual formation had occurred in terms of Reformed-Calvinist orthodoxy's view of truth, God, human nature, and the church. Second, Adams's professional life was shaped around the exigencies of local church pastoral ministry. He encountered people's problems in living in a social context that included many other activities besides "counseling." Third, his social style and ecclesiastical vision had been forged in the tumults that attended militant, separatist Presbyterianism. Mowrer provided the fourth and final ingredient in the formation of Adams's anti-psychiatry: a counseling vision. He gave a view of history: the church had capitulated to modern psychological theory and therapy. He provided the genre in which problems in living were to be understood: human beings were responsible for their behavior. He modeled a solution to such problems that encouraged pastoral assertion. He provided a catalyst to action as the founder of an anti-psychiatry movement of his own. Mowrer's approach to the field fell on fertile soil.

Adams strongly insisted that he was not a disciple of Mowrer's.[71] He criticized many particulars of Mowrer's positive system.

His own system, integrity therapy, like Glasser's reality therapy, was totally unbiblical. People got help in the sense that took responsibility. But there had to be something more. Mowrer had no objective standard, and he could offer no real forgiveness. The graduates of his counseling didn't graduate; they became dependent on the group. He didn't give me much positive. During the evenings that summer I'd study Scriptures; I did a major study of conscience, thinking it through biblically. I began to do biblical work which gave me something positive to offer.

Adams particularly disagreed with the pervasive effects of Mowrer's atheism. "Mowrer once said to me that the Bible would be fine if you could take out the vertical dimension." Mowrer had also fiercely attacked Calvinism—even linking it genetically to the pessimism and fatalism of "Freudianism"—because Calvinism spoke of sinners needing salvation by grace rather than salvation by vigorous self-effort.[72] The Calvinist Adams believed that Christ forgave and changed sinners, and that Mowrer's moralism was an old heresy updated.

Adams's criticism of Mowrer included an *ad hominem* strand. He thought that Mowrer's public confessions had an obsessive, self-torturing quality because he did not know the Savior who had died to forgive sinners and who could enable grateful, energetic efforts by his Holy Spirit.

Mowrer uses words like religion, sin, and guilt, but he drains them of biblical meaning and then fills them with humanistic content. . . . Confession, restitution,

and atonement, remember, are strictly horizontal; they have dimensions only on the level of man to man. Atonement is not through Christ (with Bonhoeffer, Mowrer calls Christian grace "cheap grace"); it is achieved by the suffering of confession and restitution.

But because he has no Savior, Mowrer is like the priest that stands daily ministering the same sacrifice that can never take away sin. . . . Mowrer, the secular priest, stands daily making atonement. . . . Mowrer's own personal unrest and that of his counselees grows from this fact.[73]

In Adams's view, Mowrer's subsequent suicide (1982) arose from the ineffectiveness of his confessional methods for dealing with the sins of his youth that haunted him.[74] Mowrer would tell his story over and over while working to help people but, in Adams's opinion, could neither find nor grant lasting relief.

But Mowrer had given Adams the contours of a counseling model and had set him in motion. Adams set out to build a system that would be "biblical," the catchword for his movement, just as "integration" became the catchword for his professional opponents. During 1965–66 Adams began to implement what he had discovered from Mowrer and what he was discovering in the Bible. He did counseling in his own church, experimenting with more intentional probing of counselee's lives and more directive methods of addressing the problems discovered.[75]

On June 1, 1966, Jay Adams was appointed assistant professor of Practical Theology at Westminster. He stepped down from pastoring his local church (the instinctive local church pastor would not return to that role until 1990, for the next quarter century becoming a pastor of pastors and of pastors-to-be). He was hired to teach all aspects of pastoral care, counseling, and preaching.

Adams described the content of his first counseling course this way: "For the first couple of years that course was a mess, rough. I spent night and day counseling and studying: studying people, studying counseling books, studying the Bible. I was counseling and I didn't have answers, counseling by the seat of the pants. I'd see problems as they were thrown at me, and I'd study and try to come out with biblical answers. My teaching, like my books later, came out in an ad hoc manner; it was a question of what questions I was confronting." The first rough outline of his nouthetic counseling began to emerge in 1966 in a small segment of the poimenics course (renamed Pastoral Theology): "At first it was little more than 'Sin is the problem and the Bible has the answers,' illustrated with a few case studies." Adams initially was influenced by Mowrer's use of groups as the context to conduct counseling, but he soon became a foe of such groups for their practice of "promiscuous confession."[76] By 1967 Adams's thinking about counseling was jelling into a system. In 1968, the third time he taught his emerging version of pastoral counseling, the counseling segment was expanded into an entire course.

Meanwhile, Adams also began to think in terms of a counseling and training center where other pastors could learn his style of frank pastoral conversation, the approach he came to label "nouthetic."[77] While the seminary could train future pastors, Adams's first loyalty lay with those already in the pastorate. Late in 1965 he had met Gardner McBride, the pastor of a neighboring church in northern New Jersey, while both attended a mental health meeting for pastors held at Marlboro State Hospital (New Jersey). Adams, stimulated by the experience with Mowrer and his fledgling Bible study and counseling practice, was highly critical of the presentation. He discovered that McBride was thinking along similar lines.

They decided to start a counseling center based in McBride's church, White Oak Ridge Community Chapel (Short Hills, N.J.), and incorporated it as the Christian Counseling and Educational Center (CCEC) in 1966.

Adams and McBride started counseling one day a week, simultaneously training other pastors to counsel through participant observation. Adams's counseling sessions frequently involved team counseling in the 1960s.[78] And they were pointedly training sessions. Typically two observers sat in on each case. Adams would involve trainees in the session, inviting them to comment or pray. He was renowned among his students for getting up and walking out in the middle of a session at some point in the training process, leaving a student to carry on as lead counselor.[79] Counselors were pointedly interchangeable, something Adams considered beneficial both for counselees—they would learn in the process to depend on God, not their counselor—and for trainees.

Adams was no advocate of the secrecies and securities that obtain in private, one-on-one counseling. His counseling came close to being a public affair. Sessions might even become crowded. Along with the counselee[s], counselor[s], and two participant observers, he liked to bring in family members, or friends who might prove helpful, as well as the counselee's pastor. He would train that pastor to counsel, too, along the way. "Multiple counseling is to be preferred as the rule rather than the exception. . . . The number of participants who ought to be included seems to be as great as the number of individuals who are intimately involved in the problem."[80] Problems in living were social by definition, failures to love God and neighbor; their solution would be social as well. These were goal-oriented work sessions. Adams did everything he could to break the mystique of the expert counselor on whom a counselee depended.[81] He negotiated and assigned homework (e.g., a log to track occasions when a problem arose; study of a Bible passage or other appropriate book; an assigned task, such as to look for a job) that was intended to carry the conversation of the session out into daily life; a counselee repentant for adultery might be asked to make a phone call on the spot to break off the relationship; a counselee who had not taken time to complete homework might be sent back to the waiting room to work on it; family members who had been arguing might be asked to seek forgiveness and reconcile on the spot.

At the time of his full-time appointment at Westminster in 1966, Adams and his family moved down to the Philadelphia area. He began attending Trinity Orthodox Presbyterian Church (Hatboro, Pa.), pastored by John Bettler. Bettler (b. January 4, 1940) was a recent Westminster graduate who had been one of Adams's preaching students but had never studied counseling under him in seminary.[82] Bettler had taken poimenics in 1965 under Adams's predecessor. He commented later: "I remember, as a student at Westminster Seminary in the mid-sixties, leaving a class in Apologetics in which Cornelius Van Til railed against the incorporation of unbelieving thought into a consistent Christian world-view and then walking to a class on pastoral care where Rogerian methods were taught and practiced uncritically—and nobody blinked. One year later Jay Adams began teaching that course and the counseling revolution began."[83] With Jay Adams as his parishioner, Bettler would learn to blink—and would play a significant role in the revolution that ensued.

In years to come, Bettler became second only to Adams in influence upon the nouthetic counseling movement. He brought an organizational vision to nouthetic counseling and was instrumental in founding and developing many of its leading institutions. Bettler was the first pastor trained under Adams at CCEC, traveling weekly up to northern New Jersey with Adams during 1967. Both men

retained vivid memories of their conversation in the car after the first day Bettler had observed Adams counsel:

Jay Adams: "We had a couple hours drive each way, and I had spent about ten hours counseling that day with John observing. John was driving me home. I was dead tired. I noticed John started shaking his head, not even saying anything. Then about five or ten minutes later he said, 'You can't talk to people that way.' I was too tired to argue, so I just sat there and didn't say anything. Then about five or ten minutes later he said, 'Well, maybe *you* can talk to people that way, but *I* can't.' I didn't say a word. But eventually John found out you can talk to people in whatever way helps them. Someone who really wants help wants a counselor who can be tough with him in the right way."

John Bettler: "I remember that. And I even remember the woman's face in the case I was referring to. You were sitting behind the desk. A cocounselor was in one corner. I was the trainee in the other corner. Here is this woman in her sixties—and you were talking *loudly*. You were trying to give her encouragement. You were also labeling her sin. And when you gave encouragement, you'd get excited and stand up sometimes! It looked overwhelming to me."

Jay Adams: "But she responded well."

John Bettler: "She did. But the only training I'd had up until then was of a Rogerian strain where you didn't say anything direct, and what you said you said nicely and softly. But you guys came on like gangbusters. There was a period of time after that when I thought of confrontation as being loud. That was a downside, that in order to counsel you had to be loud and exuberant. It's not that at all. You have to operate within the context of truth and who the counselee is, and also within the context of how God in his providence has made you. If you aren't an exuberant person, counseling won't work if you start shouting."

Jay Adams: "Also, as you sat in on enough cases over that year, you saw *every* kind of emotion exhibited. The circumstances and the person determined the manner of approach. That woman said, 'I haven't got any hope.' She needed hope, and I got a little exuberant at how much good God had for her. 'Look what the Scripture says here!' About all she'd been hearing from people was, 'Yeah, I know, life is tough, then you die.'"[84]

That anecdote signals themes that characterized their relationship over the decades that followed.

Their personal differences were marked. Bettler was as restrained as Adams was boisterous; he was as intensely private as Adams was a loquacious, larger-than-life public presence. Bettler was the skeptic and devil's advocate, looking for exceptions and complications. Adams was the evangelist, urging hearers to uncomplicated faith and action. Where Adams might walk out of a counseling session, turning it over to a trainee, Bettler did not even like observers to sit in.

Their intellectual differences were equally marked. Bettler was preoccupied with questions of what went on inside people to produce behavior—motive, belief, identity, self-image. He was wary of superficial behavioral alteration. Adams largely focused on behavior and was wary of speculating about what could not be seen. Bettler thought that life's hardships affected people significantly and that counselors who failed to attend to such risked harshness; Adams was wary that attending to such things might easily encourage evasion of moral

responsibility and blame shifting. Bettler was concerned to identify potentially useful contributions of psychologists; Adams highlighted their errors. As Adams had been prodded by Mowrer, so Bettler had been prodded by Alfred Adler.

Marked differences in institutional vision existed between them. Bettler's interest in and respect for scholarship and higher education was as habitual as Adams's interest in and respect for local church pastors. Bettler worked to open doors for women to train and to counsel; Adams worked to establish a male-dominated model of counseling training and practice. Bettler had been raised fundamentalist and reacted against it, coming to embrace a version of Reformed theology with a broad vision for social and intellectual engagement. Adams had been a-religious and had embraced separatist Presbyterianism. Bettler reacted strongly against separatist, sectarian, and anti-intellectual tendencies; he enjoyed the stimulus of dialogue with intellectuals to his "left" who differed with him. Adams reacted strongly against those to his "left" theologically and ecclesiastically and was comfortable with pastors from separatist traditions. Largely alluding to Bettler, Adams wrote, "The nouthetic counseling group differs significantly from the psychoanalytic coterie with which Freud surrounded himself. For them to differ with the Master was heresy and it was necessary either to recant of anti-Freudian dogma or be excommunicated. No such relationship exists among nouthetic thinkers, all of whom are thinkers and theologians in their own right. They are yes *and* no men; and I learn continually from their nos."[85]

For all their differences, Adams and Bettler were best friends from the mid-1960s on and were cocreators of the major institutions of the biblical counseling movement. Both were instinctive iconoclasts; both valued reason above emotion and experience; both were effective public speakers; both were ordained pastors in the Orthodox

Presbyterian Church. And both were convinced that the Bible was about counseling and that the psychologies and psychotherapies had gotten things fundamentally wrong. They were "the yin and yang of biblical counseling—and it's clear who's the yang," in the words of a longtime associate.[86] Adams would dedicate his book on laycounseling this way: "To John Bettler, a warm friend and trusted colleague: the hidden force behind nouthetic counseling."[87] Over the next twenty years Bettler would play a leading role in developing the institutional framework for Adams's ideas. He would also play a leading role in bringing competing intellectual and practical emphases into the nouthetic counseling movement. Most of the major fault lines in the movement would map onto the differences between Adams and Bettler.

CCEC was a minuscule operation, operating one day a week out of a church in northern New Jersey, with two counselors and a handful of trainees. But by 1968 Adams and his fellows had hatched bigger plans. They reincorporated as the Christian Counseling and Educational Foundation (CCEF), envisioning a far wider scope of potential activities: counseling services, education and training of counselors, publication and mass media, and diversified institutions of care.

First, they intended to provide pastoral counseling for the gamut of "personal and social difficulties, family and domestic conflicts, marital difficulties," along with vocational guidance and pre- and postmarital counseling. CCEF was to function as an auxiliary to churches in the mid-Atlantic region, a place where experienced pastoral counselors could supplement the work of local church pastors. Second, they intended to "educate ministers and missionaries and any other member of the religious community" in "the use of biblical principles of pastoral counseling." In Adams's mind, the fulfillment of this second purpose would eventually make the first purpose extraneous.

Third, to accomplish their wider goals, CCEF was chartered to produce "publications, manuals, pamphlets, learned journals and treatises, educational material, books and literary articles . . . and [to] utilize radio, television and any other available form of public communications in order to effectively present to the general public" their view of counseling. Lastly, CCEF was chartered to "own and operate nursing and convalescent homes, extended care hospitals, hospitals and homes for the aged" in order to combine medical and religious objectives. Similar counseling purposes obtained in a provision to "own and operate camping and recreational facilities."[88] The last named item arose from Adams's hope—never fulfilled—that entire families might be counseled together during summer camping trips, something he saw as an ideal example of doing "multiple counseling" with all involved parties.[89]

That same year, 1968, CCEF moved most of its operations to the northern suburbs of Philadelphia, maintaining limited counseling services in northern New Jersey but doing most counseling and all of the training out of Bettler's Trinity OPC (Hatboro, Pa.). Within the first year of CCEF's existence, marked philosophical differences arose on the board of trustees. Two of the five original board members were counseling psychologists, and tensions arose between them and Adams. The issue, not surprisingly, turned on professionalism. Increasingly they did not see eye-to-eye about what was coalescing at the heart of Adams's counseling revolution: "Is the pastor 'competent to counsel,' or does graduate training in psychology prepare one to counsel?"[90] The difficulties in establishing cooperation between evangelical psychologists and Adams's nouthetic pastoral counseling played out within the first year of nouthetic counseling's first institution. The board was reconstituted with members favorable to Adams's vision. At the same time, by 1970 all operations shifted to Hatboro.

Bettler, Trinity OPC's pastor between 1967 and 1970, became increasingly involved, first as a trainee at CCEC, then as a counselor at CCEF. Eventually he was groomed to take over as director. With the move to Philadelphia, CCEF began to train students at Westminster Seminary as well as pastors already serving in local churches. The symbiosis between CCEF and Westminster became a significant feature in the institutional landscape of nouthetic counseling.

Meanwhile Adams worked assiduously to produce the first writings from his nouthetic counseling perspective. In 1968 he published his first counseling article in *The Presbyterian Guardian,* a small denominational magazine. "Behind the Study Door" considered a case study of a depressed woman. His opening sentence, "How about your ironing?," as well as the article that followed, sounded a note of "practicality" not often heard in his theological and ecclesiastical circles. His counselee's depression

> had developed from guilt arising out of a long-standing inner feud she had been carrying on between herself and her mother-in-law. This had recently erupted into open hostilities. By neglecting her ironing and other duties (because she rightly felt guilt-depression over her sin) Sharon had turned a bad depression into a severe one.
>
> The depression would lift slightly when she began to reassume her responsibilities as a homemaker and mother, but she would find complete relief only when she finally confessed her sinful ways to God and asked her mother-in-law's forgiveness. Beyond that, Sharon had to set about building a new Christian relationship between herself and her mother-in-law. . . .
>
> Since the problem of resentment extended to many areas of her life, she found it necessary to straighten out some matters in

> her church. These efforts went a long way toward healing a grievous division among the women of the congregation.[91]

This brief article broached themes that became characteristic of Adams's system of directive, interventive, optimistic counseling. He aimed to produce rapid, tangible changes in a counselee's relationships to God and to neighbors. He worked to get people to act on defined right and wrong, true and false. This brief article even included a typical cautionary note about organic causes: "Not all problems have an interpersonal base. Some, of course, develop from organic causes: e.g., brain damage, glandular or other chemical imbalances. There is also a gray area of problems which are of uncertain etiology."[92] In this article, as throughout his subsequent corpus, Adams sought to write about counseling issues in layman's language, addressing the daily problems of church people in a direct manner using specific terminology from the Bible.

Adams had a book in the works through the late 1960s. Part testimonial, part polemic, part Bible study, part introductory counseling textbook, *CtC* was rough hewn even in the final version. But it sounded Adams's call for a revolt by conservative pastors, calling them back to the counseling task that he believed was theirs. Adams thought pastoral jurisdiction over personal problems had been abandoned and forfeited by diffident, inept pastors and had been seized by expansionist mental health professionals. *CtC* intended to remedy both ineptitude and diffidence. In so doing, it simultaneously stepped on the toes of those Adams viewed as "self-styled [or] self-proclaimed 'professionals'": they lacked valid education and ordination for the task of curing souls.[93] Even prior to publication, *CtC* engendered sharp criticism from those whose professional lives were jeopardized by Adams's proposals.

Adams received some financial aid in the final stages of the writing process from the National

Liberty Foundation, a charitable foundation interested at the time in developing an approach to counseling and psychology that would cohere with conservative Protestantism. When Adams completed the rough draft of *CtC,* the foundation sponsored a meeting between leading evangelical psychologists and Adams for the purpose of evaluating Adams's work. On March 20–21, 1969, a dozen men met at the International Airport Motel in Philadelphia. Representatives from the chief institutions practicing and teaching evangelical psychotherapy—Narramore Christian Foundation (Rosemead, Calif.), The Evangelical Counseling Center (Atlanta), Fuller Theological Seminary (Pasadena, Calif.), and Conservative Baptist Theological Seminary (Denver)—presented informal and formal critiques of the rough draft of Adams's book.[94]

Adams was buoyed by the outcome of the meeting. He had been commended for the consistency of his attempt to anchor counseling in the Bible and conservative Protestant orthodoxy. He had also been criticized, at times sharply, by some of the psychotherapists. They charged him with diverse and serious failings. His version of presuppositionally biblical counseling tended to be "biblicistic" and failed various particular tests of both Scripture and science. His model was superficial and simplistic in addressing the complexities of both the human psyche and the counseling task. They thought Adams guilty of at least an incipient legalism-moralism that compromised the graciousness of God's acceptance of people. He neglected motivational issues in the interests of stressing behavioral change. His ideal counselor projected an aggressive, impatient, and businesslike stance toward counselees, rather than communicating a caring and patient presence. His discussion failed to comprehend other theoretical positions, and so misrepresented those he attacked. He failed to recognize the extent of Mowrer's heritage implicit in nouthetic counseling. His arguments were framed too polemically, and he had oversold the success of nouthetic counseling by making unsubstantiated claims.[95]

But Adams thought that he could answer each of the objections. He felt that his critics had not been able to shake his central thesis that the Bible could equip Christians to become competent to counsel, that it was intended to do so, and that the church had in this respect neglected its birthright. His assessment of the weekend was that the participants' most sustained objections had been to his blunt polemics against psychiatric psychotherapy:

> To a man, in effect they all said, "Even if it's right, it's too rough. Don't publish it like that; smooth it off. People will be upset. Take the edge off it." You know, that troubled me. I went home and thought and prayed about what they said and I became concerned about that matter. And I thought about their writings, and reread some of them. I concluded, "They're too soft. They don't have *enough* rough edges. Maybe that's why they haven't done anything earthshaking in this field." So I went home and I sharpened it up more![96]

The warrior for counseling turf had been blooded.

This meeting established the initial trajectory of both nouthetic counseling and its critics. Jay Adams's emphases were "sharpened"; he determined to raise his volume level and he went his own way. He pointedly did not rebalance his system, temper his tone of voice, or seek to establish cordial, cooperative relationships with the evangelical psychotherapy community. It would be a decade before he and his critics again sat down to discuss their differences.

The specific criticisms of Adams made at "the airport meeting" would be repeated and elaborated from many quarters during the following decades. Yet through it all, Adams would be viewed ambivalently by the community most at odds with him.

On the one hand, he was attacked as the *enfant terrible* of the conservative Protestant counseling world. His perceived narrowness, shallowness, and polemicism became the foil against which evangelical psychotherapists defined their intellectual, methodological, and institutional program. On the other hand, many of the leading psychologists appreciated Adams as the biblical conscience of the evangelical counseling world, a somewhat curmudgeonly conscience who held conservative Protestant psychotherapists to their alleged commitments. He was even granted public honors some twenty years after *CtC*. At the First International Congress on Christian Counseling in 1988 (Atlanta), a convocation of several thousand evangelical psychotherapists, Adams was one of three men honored as a "father of Christian counseling."[97] Adams's agenda was shockingly and comprehensively wrong, but there was something to what he said.

The relationship would prove markedly asymmetrical. Adams's critics grudgingly appreciated him in a way he certainly did not appreciate them. To Adams, the psychotherapists essentially acted as false teachers leading the church astray, however admirable some might be in their personal faith and life and however well-intended their work. His acceptance speech at Atlanta in 1988 would bluntly criticize his hosts and audience.[98]

Neither Adams nor his critics would budge. The next twenty-five years came close to a stalemate both socially and intellectually. Positions hardened; both sides created stereotypes of the other. The evangelical psychotherapists would become compromisers perpetrating heresy in the church; the nouthetic counselors would become sectarian, anti-intellectual incompetents. This was, after all, a conflict for professional jurisdiction over the problems in living, and a conflict between "psychological" and "biblical" knowledge systems.

The substance of the criticisms first voiced did not disappear. John Bettler would raise most of the same substantive issues in his running, cordial debate with Adams through the years. Not surprisingly, however, Adams's friends would draw reformist rather than dismissive implications from the shortcomings they would come to perceive in the original articulation of nouthetic counseling.

One other evangelical psychotherapist also read the manuscript of *CtC* prior to publication. Gary Collins, who would subsequently become a leader in the "integration" movement, reflected many years later on what he had thought at the time.

I liked some of what I read. My friend[99] stressed that the Bible says much about counseling people with their personal problems. He stressed the importance of the Holy Spirit in counseling and argued that pastors could and should do counseling, instead of referring most of their counselees to psychiatrists or to other mental-health professionals. . . .

But in his writing, my friend insisted that except for biologically based difficulties, all problems result from the counselee's own sin. . . .

I still can remember my reaction to the manuscript. "I am glad for the clear recognition of the role of sin in human problems," I said only to myself, "but the author's approach is so confrontational, so directive, so insensitive, so simplistic and bombastic, that there is never any possibility that this book will ever get published, much less read."

I was wrong.

Jay Adams' *Competent to Counsel* became a best-seller that stirred considerable controversy and did much to stimulate interest in Christian counseling among theologically conservative believers who, to that point, had tended to ignore or resist counseling issues.

I suspect that Dr. Adams intended to be provocative with his book—and he was. Despite some of its debatable conclusions, the book boldly focused attention on the role of sin in causing problems and the author proclaimed that Christian counseling has to consider and deal with sin.[100]

As Collins noted, the book was published, and it *was* read.

Chapter 2 Notes

1. E. Brooks Holifield, *A History of Pastoral Care in America: From Salvation to Self-Realization* (Nashville: Abingdon Press, 1983), 17f.

2. Ibid., 355f.

3. Jay E. Adams, *Competent to Counsel* (USA: Presbyterian & Reformed, 1970), xi.

4. Sigmund Freud's provocative term simultaneously took the psychotherapeutic task away from clerics and medical doctors. Sigmund Freud, *The Question of Lay Analysis,* ed. and trans., James Strachey (New York: W. W. Norton, 1927, 1959), 93.

5. This sentence obviously makes a sweeping generalization, ignoring countless theoretical details and debates and numerous psychotherapeutic sects. But it does capture the tendencies in the Americanization of Freud: generic rather than purist in theorizing, optimistic and curative rather than rigorously analytical in methodology.

6. Many of the moralistic therapists directly credited Adler. See William Glasser, "Reality Therapy" (p. 306), Albert Ellis, "Rational-Emotive Therapy" (p. 190), and Vincent Foley, "Family Therapy" (p. 463), in Raymond J. Corsini and contributors, *Current Psychotherapies* (Itasca, Ill.: F. E. Peacock, 1973). Harry Stack Sullivan was another earlier psychologist whose theory of personal problems was, like Adler's, markedly social and whose therapeutic interventions were directive. For a comment on Adlerian and Sullivanian themes in transactional analysis, see Joel Kovel, *A Complete Guide to Therapy: From Psychoanalysis to Behavior Modification* (New York: Pantheon Books, 1976), 175.

7. Irene Goldenberg and Herbert Goldenberg, *Family Therapy: An Overview* (Pacific Grove, Calif.: Brooks/Cole Publishing, 1985), 177.

8. Thomas Szasz, *The Myth of Mental Illness: Foundations of a Theory of Personal Conduct* (New York: Harper & Row, 1961).

9. Erving Goffman, *Asylums: Essays on the Social Situation of Mental Patients and Other Inmates* (Garden City, N.Y.: Anchor Books, 1961); Erving Goffman, *Stigma* (Englewood Cliffs, N.J.: Prentice-Hall, 1963).

10. William Glasser, *Reality Therapy: A New Approach to Psychiatry* (New York: Harper and Row, 1965); Perry London, *The Modes and Morals of Psychotherapy* (New York: Holt, Rinehart and Winston, 1964); O. Hobart Mowrer, *The Crisis in Psychiatry and Religion* (Princeton: Van Nostrand, 1961).

11. Holifield, *History of Pastoral Care, infra,* provides a useful summary and an entry point into the extensive secondary literature on these personages and movements.

12. Cf., Rieff's analysis of the salvific elements in Jung's and Adler's psychologies—also derived from liberal Protestantism but in the European context—in comparison with the irreligious rectitude of Freud's analytic stance. Philip Rieff, *The Triumph of the Therapeutic: Uses of Faith after Freud* (Chicago: University of Chicago Press, 1987). Adler converted to liberal Protestantism, embracing its hope for social renewal. Jung had grown up in it and spent his life trying to find a personal myth to replace the failed Christian myth.

13. Holifield, *History of Pastoral Care,* 161.

14. Ibid., 16.

15. Andrew Abbott, *The System of Professions: An Essay on the Division of Expert Labor* (Chicago: University of Chicago Press, 1988), 100.

16. Ibid., 310.

17. Howard Clinebell, *Basic Types of Pastoral Counseling* (Nashville: Abingdon Press, 1966), 28.

18. Kenneth R. Mitchell, "Shepherds of the Needy," in *Turning Points in Pastoral Care: The Legacy of Anton Boisen and Seward Hiltner,* eds. Leroy Aden and Harold Ellens (Grand Rapids: Baker Book House, 1990), 178f.

19. Anton T. Boisen, *The Exploration of the Inner World: A Study of Mental Disorder and Religious Experience* (New York: Harper, 1936).

20. Albert Outler, *Psychotherapy and the Christian Message* (New York: Harper & Row, 1954), 8.

21. Ibid., 18, 40f.

22. Don S. Browning, *The Moral Context of Pastoral Care* (Philadelphia: Westminster Press, 1976), 11–13. Cf., Don S. Browning, *Religious Thought and the Modern Psychologies: A Critical Conversation in the Theology of Culture* (Philadelphia: Fortress Press, 1987); Donald Capps, "The Bible's Role in Pastoral Care and Counseling: Four Basic Principles," in *The Church and Pastoral Care,* eds. Leroy Aden and J. Harold Ellens (Grand Rapids: Baker Book House, 1988), 41–55.

23. William Hunter, "Review of *Clinical Handbook of Pastoral Counseling,*" *Journal of Psychology and Theology* 21, no. 4 (1993): 329.

24. Jay E. Adams, *The Power of Error: Demonstrated in an Actual Counseling Case* (USA: Presbyterian & Reformed, 1978), 2, 21.

25. Thomas Oden noted how the ancient church fathers had "argued for the primary importance of the smallest quantum of behavior modification. This goes contrary to caricatures of Christian conversion and behavioral change that imagine that total transformations should occur in an instant (which later became a special problem of Protestant revivalism)." Thomas C. Oden, *Classical Pastoral Care,* vol. 3, *Pastoral Counsel* (Grand Rapids: Baker Books, 1987), 236. Holifield briefly discussed the rationalistic tendencies of modern fundamentalism in Holifield, *History of Pastoral Care,* 161–64.

26. Holifield, *History of Pastoral Care*, 107–58. Adams would give this observation a polemical thrust. In presenting a case study from Ichabod Spencer, he commented, "[The case study] is a sample of one sort of pastoral counseling that was done by a Presbyterian preacher prior to the near capitulation of the Christian ministry to psychiatry." Jay E. Adams, *The Christian Counselor's Manual* (USA: Presbyterian & Reformed, 1973), 130.

27. Richard Hofstadter, *Anti-intellectualism in American Life* (New York: Random House, 1962); Richard Hofstadter, *The Paranoid Style in American Politics, and Other Essays* (New York: Random House); George M. Marsden, *Fundamentalism and American Culture: The Shaping of Twentieth-Century Evangelicalism, 1870–1925* (New York: Oxford University Press, 1980); Martin Marty and R. Scott Appleby, eds., "Fundamentalisms Observed," in *The Fundamentalism Project* (Chicago: University of Chicago Press, 1991).

28. For example, the works of B. B. Warfield and J. Gresham Machen of Princeton Theological Seminary.

29. Other small hospitals were subsequently founded and operated by the Christian Reformed Church in Wyckoff, New Jersey, and Denver, Colorado.

30. Vernon H. Neufeld, *If We Can Love: The Mennonite Mental Health Story* (Newton, Kans.: Faith and Life Press, 1983), 39f. This shift occasioned an ongoing tension between the "Christian" motives of the founders and the "humanistic outlook" of the psychiatrists, a tension that threads through Neufeld's institutional history (e.g., pp. 43, 252–56).

31. Ibid., 26–37.

32. Carl Henry, *The Uneasy Conscience of Modern Fundamentalism* (Grand Rapids: William B. Eerdmans, 1947). George Marsden's numerous articles and books have traced the modern history of both fundamentalism and those "reforming fundamentalists" who, decrying the anti-intellectualism and cultural isolationism of their tradition's recent history, became "new evangelicals."

33. Narramore was an educational psychologist (EdD from Columbia University) and published numerous books on marriage, child-rearing, teenagers, and mental health in the late 1950s.

34. Travis narrated his story in Maloney H. Newton, ed., *Psychology and Faith: The Christian Experience of Eighteen Psychologists* (Washington, D.C.: University Press of America, 1978), 72–83. Cf., George M. Marsden, *Reforming Fundamentalism: Fuller Seminary and the New Evangelicalism* (Grand Rapids: William B. Eerdmans, 1987), 233–39, for a sketch of the founding of the Fuller Theological Seminary Graduate School of Psychology and comments on how vexing the "task of integrating the largely opposed assumptions of modern psychology and evangelical theology" proved.

35. Randy Timpe, "Christian Psychology," in *Baker Encyclopedia of Psychology*, ed. David G. Benner (Grand Rapids: Baker Book House, 1985), 166.

36. See the numerous programmatic articles in the *Journal of Psychology and Theology* for a sampler of the debates and proposals. The following works provide entry points into the literature: John D. Carter and Bruce Narramore, *The Integration of Psychology and Theology* (Grand Rapids: Zondervan, 1979); Gary R. Collins, "Moving Through the Jungle: A Decade of Integration," *Journal of Psychology and Theology* 11, no. 1 (1983): 2–7; James D. Foster and Scot A. Bolsinger, "Prominent Themes in Evangelical Integration Literature," *Journal of Psychology and Theology* 18, no. 1 (1990): 3–12; James D. Foster, Debra A. Horn, and Steve Watson, "The Popularity of Integration Models, 1980–1985," *Journal of Psychology and Theology* 16, no. 1 (1988): 3–14. A landmark project that brought together most of the leading integrationists was David G. Benner, ed., *Baker Encyclopedia of Psychology* (Grand Rapids: Baker Book House, 1985).

37. Stanton Jones and Richard Butman, *Modern Psychotherapies: A Comprehensive Christian Appraisal* (Downers Grove, Ill.: InterVarsity Press, 1991), 414.

38. Many of the bits of biographical information in this and succeeding paragraphs were gained from extensive interviews with Jay Adams and Betty Jane Adams, his wife, on December 4–5, 1990. It was possible to corroborate many dates and the objective elements in Adams's vita from other sources (and to establish others when memory did not serve). But many of the reminiscences are obviously impossible to verify from other sources. Memory is selective, constructed, and ambiguous, but it is also significant. It reveals the rememberer by its very selectivity (even with prevaricators, which I had no reason to think Adams was). In the course of the interviews I often had the experience, "Aha, now I understand better why Adams wrote *x*, emphasized *y*, or did *z*." Adams's personal "myth" shed light on his career and intellectual emphases.

I have treated Adams's anecdotes as self-revealing reminiscences, not as purportedly "objective facts" according to some imaginary canon of videographic realism. The pages that follow represent a second-order construction. Both the narrative flow and the transitional, interpretive comments are my own. I have selected and organized material from what I heard according to my own construction of my subject. My interpretive framework is summarized at the head of this paragraph and was stated in somewhat different form at the beginning of this chapter: Adams "had been socialized into the intellectual and practical habits of a conservative Bible exegete, a local church pastor, and a contender for the faith in ecclesiastical wars." The reminiscences that follow "fit" this construction, even as they contributed to its articulation.

39. This friend, Milton Fisher, went on to become a professor at Reformed Episcopal Seminary and edited the missions section of Adams's *Journal of Pastoral Practice* from 1977–82.

40. The Reformed Episcopal Church was a tiny denomination that had separated from the mainline Episcopal Church in the nineteenth century over the issue of theological liberalism. The seminary was noted for its Calvinist, biblicist, and separatist orientation.

41. Jay E. Adams, *The Christian Counselor's Commentary: Hebrews, James, I & II Peter, and Jude* (Woodruff, S.C.: Timeless Texts, 1996), 268.

42. One pastor who had sat under both men commented, "Many times, listening to Jay Adams speak, I overhear Robert Rudolph." Conversation with Paul Tripp, July 29, 1996.

43. The work at RE was completed in 1947, but in the RE system the divinity degree was awarded contingent upon the student acquiring a liberal arts degree at a college.

44. See the preface to Jay E. Adams, *The Christian Counselor's New Testament: A New Translation in Everyday English with*

Notations (USA: Presbyterian & Reformed, 1977) for Adams's philosophy of Bible translation.

45. Adams, *Competent to Counsel*, 1.

46. In his personal life, Adams married Betty Jane Whitlock in 1951. They eventually adopted four children.

47. About five years earlier, evangelist Billy Graham also got his start in ministry working with Youth for Christ.

48. The various alignments, splits, realignments, and mergers of the Presbyterian denominations ("the split Ps") are difficult to follow. The following provides a scorecard of the various splits and mergers relevant to our story. Adams's successive denominational affiliations are italicized. Current denominational alignments are bracketed for reference. I am indebted to George P. Hutchinson, *The History Behind the Reformed Presbyterian Church, Evangelical Synod* (Cherry Hill, N.J.: Mack Publishing, 1974); cf., Gaius J. Slosser, ed., *They Seek a Country: The American Presbyterians, Some Aspects* (New York: MacMillan, 1955).

The "old" *United Presbyterian Church*, into which Adams was ordained, merged with the Presbyterian Church USA ("old" PCUSA) in 1958 to form the "new" United Presbyterian Church USA (UPC), the mainline Presbyterian denomination in the northern United States. [In 1983 the UPC merged with the southern mainline Presbyterian Church United States (PCUS) to form the current Presbyterian Church USA ("new" PCUSA).]

Adams served in the *Bible Presbyterian Church* from 1956–63. It had been founded in 1937. The dominant personality in the BPC had been Carl McIntire, who was squeezed out in 1956, forming his own denomination, the Bible Presbyterian Church (Collingswood Synod). Partly because of the name confusion, the original BPC changed its name to the *Evangelical Presbyterian Church* in 1961. [In 1965 the EPC joined with the Reformed Presbyterian Church to become the Reformed Presbyterian Church, Evangelical Synod (RPCES). In 1982 the RPCES joined the Presbyterian Church in America (PCA), a group of southern Presbyterians disaffected by theological liberalism in the southern PCUS.]

The Bible Presbyterian Church had originally split from the *Orthodox Presbyterian Church* (OPC), which had split from the old PCUSA in 1936 at the peak of the wars between separatistic and liberal Protestantism. The OPC was particularly associated with Westminster Theological Seminary. Adams pastored in the OPC during 1963–66, and taught at Westminster 1963–76 and 1982–89. Both institutions were founded by J. Gresham Machen.

The *Associate Reformed Presbyterian Church*, into which Adams was received when he reentered the pastorate in 1990, was a tiny denomination that had its roots in church splits of the eighteenth and early nineteenth centuries.

49. Adams, *Competent to Counsel*, xi.

50. Marsden, *Reforming Fundamentalism*, 6.

51. Hutchinson, *History Behind the Reformed Presbyterian Church*, chapters 5 and 6.

52. By his own description this was Adams's second church, not his third. He viewed his first pastorate as with that "flock" that had been part of both the Mount Prospect and the Viewcrest churches.

53. It appeared that "in Carl McIntire's mind the Bible Presbyterian Church was simply another part of his empire," and "McIntire more and more directed his energies toward preaching American-ism and combating Communism." Hutchinson, *History Behind the Reformed Presbyterian Church*, 269, 267.

54. McIntire preempted the attempt to discipline him by leaving the denomination.

55. Adams, *The Power of Error*, 46–48.

56. Ibid., 20f.

57. Jay E. Adams, "An Open Letter to Former United Presbyterians," *Bible Presbyterian Record* (January 1959), 15. Arguments summarized in Hutchinson, *History Behind the Reformed Presbyterian Church*, 309.

58. Jay E. Adams, *Realized Millennialism: A Study in Biblical Eschatology* (Saint Louis, Mo.: Jay Edward Adams, 1959). The four major eschatological positions differ over what they expect to precede the second coming of Jesus Christ. The first three were common among conservative Presbyterians.

(1) Amillennialists believe that the "millennium" is metaphorical for Christ's present reign as the king of his people, and that when he returns he will bring the day of judgment. Historically, it has been the most common view within Christendom.

(2) Postmillennialists believe that a thousand-year golden age of Christian civilization will precede the return of Christ for the last judgment. Many optimistic seventeenth-century English Puritans, taken with the possibilities of ecclesiastical, political, economic, technological, and scientific progress, were postmillennialists. It has enjoyed a resurgence in America in recent decades with the political growth of the "Christian right."

(3) "Historic" premillennialists believe that Christ will return to set up a visible millennial kingdom before the final judgment. This view was the most common in Adams's BP denomination.

(4) "Dispensational" premillennialists are as pessimistic as postmillennialists are optimistic. They believe in visible decay, not visible progress, and that the Gentile church will be "raptured" before the Messiah establishes a Jewish-Israeli millennium, which will precede the last judgment. Most American fundamentalists have characteristically been "dispensationalists."

The postmillennial and dispensational positions have tended to be held most passionately; Jay Adams was an unusually vigorous and tenacious amillennialist.

59. Hutchinson, *History Behind the Reformed Presbyterian Church*, 310, 329f.

60. See Adams, *Competent to Counsel* and Adams, *The Christian Counselor's Manual, infra*. Many of the reasons that Adams cited for counseling failure turn on the counselor's defective knowledge of counselees and their situations: e.g., Adams, *The Christian Counselor's Manual*, 469–71.

61. Adams subsequently published a digest of this dissertation: Jay E. Adams, *Studies in Preaching*, vol. 2, *Audience Adaptation in the Sermons and Speeches of Paul* (USA: Presbyterian & Reformed, 1976).

62. Published as Jay E. Adams, *Studies in Preaching*, vol. 3, *The Homiletical Innovations of Andrew W. Blackwood* (USA: Presbyterian & Reformed, 1975).

63. Jay E. Adams, "Design for a Theological Seminary," *Journal of Pastoral Practice* 3, no. 2 (1979): 1–10.

64. From interview. Cf., the more extended statement of this in Adams, *Competent to Counsel*, 9.

65. Poimenics means "shepherding," the overall work of the pastor.

66. Mowrer, a professor of psychology at the University of Illinois, had gained renown within experimental psychology for reconciling the functionalist and associationist paradigms in learning theory, an achievement which led to his serving as president of the American Psychological Association in 1953–54. He also had practical interests in counseling and, particularly, counseling by religious professionals, who were presumably predisposed to Mowrer's emphasis on human responsibility.

67. The place of markedly somatic ailments in Adams's system will be discussed later. Like Mowrer he came to believe that most psychiatric patients were not "ill" but were morally troubled. For those with unambiguously somatic problems—tumors, senile dementias, brain injuries, sleep loss, drug and alcohol effects—Adams proposed that pastors work alongside medical personnel.

68. Mowrer, *Crisis in Psychiatry and Religion,* 134. Adams's use of the terms "Freud" and "Freudian" was mediated through Mowrer. These terms stood for (1) generically psychodynamic theories and therapies, not only Freud's psychoanalytic theory, but also the theories of Jung, Rogers, et al., and (2) the "Freudian Ethic" or "Freudian ideology" as a "broad social ideology and personal philosophy" that viewed people as ill and not responsible, rather than as immoral and responsible. Mowrer here borrowed the work of David Bakan (*Sigmund Freud and the Jewish Mystical Tradition,* 1958) and Richard LaPiere (*The Freudian Ethic,* 1959); see ibid., 133–36, 238. Mowrer's "Freud" would serve Adams, as it did Mowrer, as shorthand for all that was wrong with modern counseling and, even, modern life.

69. Ibid., 60.

70. Adams, *Competent to Counsel,* 13. Adams's enthusiasm for the secular moralizers and for their potential to significantly affect the wider mental health system was short-lived. By 1973 (*The Christian Counselor's Manual*) his verbalized approbation for them extended only to their debunking of mainstream psychiatry, not to their positive accomplishments either intellectually or practically.

71. Jay E. Adams, *What About Nouthetic Counseling?* (Grand Rapids: Baker, 1976), 84. Numerous critics of Adams would dispute this, noting significant structural resemblances between Adams's theory and Mowrer's. See chapter 8.

72. Mowrer, *Crisis in Psychiatry and Religion,* 159f.

73. Adams, *Christian Counselor's Manual,* 86ff.

74. Mowrer wrote openly of being haunted by adolescent involvement in "an ugly sexual perversion" (O. Hobart Mowrer, *Abnormal Reactions or Actions?: An Autobiographical Answer* [Dubuque: William C. Brown Co., 1966], 18). Adams discussed at length his response to Mowrer's self-revelations: Adams, *Competent to Counsel,* 180ff; and Adams, *Christian Counselor's Manual,* 86–89.

75. The poimenics course was taught by another professor in 1965–66, so Adams had a year to develop his system before he again taught counseling.

76. Jay E. Adams, "Group Therapy—or Slander?," *The Presbyterian Guardian* (February 1971): 25–27; and Adams, *Christian Counselor's Manual,* 86ff.

77. Adams wrote in 1976, "I prefer the words 'biblical' or 'Christian' but reluctantly have used the word 'nouthetic' . . . as a con-

venience by which the biblical system of counseling that has been developed in such books as *Competent to Counsel* and *The Christian Counselor's Manual* might be identified more easily. The reason why the title Nouthetic Confrontation is not to be preferred is because while admirably embracing the major biblical concepts of counseling, the use of *nouthesia* is not universal. It appears almost exclusively in Paul. Other terms are employed by other writers." Adams, *What About Nouthetic Counseling?,* 1.

78. Adams advocated team counseling as desirable whenever possible, another mark of his distance from the habits of the psychotherapeutic and his orientation toward conditions that might more easily obtain in local church communities, as they had obtained during his internship with Mowrer. Adams, *Competent to Counsel,* 204–08.

79. In conversation many of Adams's former students recollected the combination of terror and confidence-building that this practice induced in them.

80. Adams, *Competent to Counsel,* 237.

81. Adams, *The Christian Counselor's Manual,* 304–06.

82. Bettler received his BS from Philadelphia College of Bible in 1963, and a BD from Westminster in 1967. He pastored in the Orthodox Presbyterian Church from 1967–70 at Trinity OPC (Hatboro, Pa.) and 1970–73 at Bethel OPC (Wheaton, Ill.). He received his DMin from Chicago Theological Seminary in 1974.

83. John F. Bettler, "CCEF: The Beginning," *Journal of Pastoral Practice* 9, no. 3 (1988): 47.

84. Interview with Adams and Bettler, June 10, 1993.

85. Adams, *What About Nouthetic Counseling?,* 6. In chapter 9 we will look in greater depth at the fault lines within the nouthetic counseling movement. The differences of emphases and lines of conflict or potential conflict mapped strikingly onto the differences between Adams and Bettler.

86. Interview with George Scipione, October 6, 1991.

87. Jay E. Adams, *Ready to Restore: The Layman's Guide to Christian Counseling* (Phillipsburg, N.J.: Presbyterian & Reformed, 1981), 3.

88. The quotations in this paragraph are from the Certificate of Incorporation of the Christian Counseling and Educational Foundation, filed with the State of New Jersey on February 21, 1968. The institutional diversification allowed in the last point of the charter was never implemented. Adams discussed his hopes for family counseling in Adams, *Competent to Counsel,* 244.

89. Ibid., 244.

90. Bettler, "CCEF: The Beginning," 50.

91. Jay E. Adams, "Behind the Study Door, Part 1," *The Presbyterian Guardian* (April, 1968): 39f.

92. Ibid., 39, n. 2.

93. Adams, *What About Nouthetic Counseling?,* 45; Jay E. Adams, *More Than Redemption: A Theology of Christian Counseling* (Phillipsburg, N.J.: Presbyterian & Reformed, 1979), 13.

94. Bruce Narramore and Maurice Wagner represented the Narramore Christian Foundation. William Donaldson, Fred Donehoo, and Paul Walder represented the Evangelical Counseling Center. Donald Tweedie came from Fuller Theological Seminary's Graduate School of Psychology. Vernon Grounds came from Conservative Baptist Theological Seminary.

Henry Brandt, a psychologist with an independent speaking, teaching, and writing ministry, was an unaffiliated commentator. Brandt was the only participant who might be presumed to be immediately sympathetic to Adams. Though he had a PhD in psychology, he was a forerunner of Adams, having adopted a didactic, moralistic, biblicistic, short-term approach to counseling in the early 1950s. See Henry Brandt, "My Journey as a Christian Psychologist," in *What to Do When,* ed. Howard Eyrich (Phillipsburg, N.J.: Presbyterian & Reformed, 1978), 5–36. He had written numerous self-help books, though, unlike Adams, he wrote nothing programmatic, ideological, or polemical, and he was not a pastor. Brandt had been the keynote speaker at CCEF's founding in 1968. He would be involved with CCEF on several other occasions in the 1970s.

95. This summary derives largely from Bruce Narramore's "Critique of *Competent to Counsel*" and Fred Donehoo's "Critique of Jay Adams' *Competent to Counsel*," unpublished manuscripts distributed at meeting. Vernon Grounds also communicated similar objections to Adams's model in personal correspondence (August 28, 1995). Tweedie, Narramore, and Grounds were the most critical; Brandt, Donaldson, and Donehoo the most positive. Chapter 8 will look in detail at specific criticisms of Adams made by these evangelical psychotherapists and other subsequent critics.

96. Jay E. Adams, "On Writing," *The New Testament Student and Bible Translation,* ed. John Skilton (Phillipsburg, N.J.: Presbyterian & Reformed, 1978), 216.

97. The others were pioneering evangelical psychologist Clyde Narramore and H. Norman Wright, an influential marriage counselor.

98. Jay E. Adams, "Jay Adams Response to the Congress on Christian Counseling," *Journal of Pastoral Practice* 10, no. 1 (1989): 2–4.

99. At the time Collins lived near Adams in the northern suburbs of Philadelphia, and they had developed a cordial acquaintance. Adams particularly respected Collins as a Christian gentleman.

100. Gary R. Collins, *The Biblical Basis of Christian Counseling for People Helpers* (Colorado Springs: NavPress, 1993), 96.

"Your Place in the Counseling Revolution"[1]: The Emergence of a Biblical Counseling Movement

Competent to Counsel is not a great book by any means. But it was a war cry for people. If you throw anything into an empty barrel it makes a racket. A lot of people said, "This is what I was waiting for." It hit a nerve.
— Jay Adams[2]

The word nouthetic *comes from the Greek word* nouthesia *and is translated "counsel," "admonish," "exhort" and various other ways in the New Testament Scriptures. It is one of the biblical words for pastoral counseling, and it is included in the title of this organization to indicate the commitment of its membership to counseling that is thoroughly grounded in the Scriptures as the only rule of faith and practice.*
— Constitution of the National Association of Nouthetic Counselors[3]

The publication of *Competent to Counsel (CtC)* in 1970 marked the inception of a discernible nouthetic counseling movement and triggered lively controversy in the evangelical community. Adams sought to mobilize pastors against what he perceived as a fourfold foe: their own ineptitude in and evasion of the counseling task, the secular mental health system, the liberal pastoral theologians, and the evangelical psychotherapists. Adams's offensive well illustrates Andrew Abbott's description of the "pattern of attacking groups emerging from the paraprofessional periphery, serving ignored clienteles, and urging reform."[4] But in this particular case, two professional groups competed for that ignored clientele, one bearing mental health credentials, the other bearing ecclesiastical credentials. Conservative Protestant pastors had lacked any articulated rationale for counseling, either as paraprofessionals within the mental health system or as competitors outside it. Similarly, troubled members of their flocks had lacked any rationale for pursuing help. Adams offered such a rationale, along with intellectual, methodological, and institutional resources—which he claimed derived from the Bible—so that pastors might take on a task that had long been the prerogative of other groups.

What had previously been disseminated among a handful of conservative pastors and seminarians (mostly Presbyterian) in the mid-Atlantic region rapidly gained national, even international, influence.[5] *CtC* sold more than a quarter of a million copies in the United States during the first ten years.[6] It was reviewed in numerous theological journals and Christian magazines and commented on in the introductory paragraphs and chapters of numerous works by evangelical counselors. *CtC* received dramatically contradictory reviews, hailed in some quarters, pilloried in others.[7] After a brief look at what was occurring among the psychotherapists, this chapter will trace the first decade of the nouthetic movement, 1970–79.

Evangelicals continued to embrace the psychologies and psychotherapies somewhat nervously. Evangelicals knew they needed to do something to solve counseling problems; psychologists who held to the tenets of Bible-believing faith promised help that no one else could offer. The 1970s proved to be a decade of significant professional advance for them—growing popular influence, increasing presence in seminaries and other higher education, an expanding professional association, and new journals.

In 1969 Trinity Evangelical Divinity School (Deerfield, Ill.) hired its first psychologist, Gary Collins, as a professor of pastoral psychology.[8] Collins later noted wryly how he had been shunted off into a basement office and his courses little publicized during that first year because of institutional nervousness about his presence.[9] He would become perhaps the major actor in the evangelical psychotherapy movement over the next twenty-five years. Collins had been greatly influenced by Paul Tournier, a Swiss Christian psychiatrist who had combined broadly evangelical beliefs with a gentle mentoring style, the polar opposite of Adams's brisk, didactic approach to counseling. In 1977 Collins wrote *The Rebuilding of Psychol-ogy,* which became one of several programmatic texts for the integration movement.[10]

Meanwhile in 1968 the Narramore Christian Foundation began to explore the possibility of starting a graduate school of psychology. They intended a school whose theology would be more conservative than Fuller Seminary's and whose emphasis would be on practitioners rather than theoreticians. Clinical psychologist Bruce Narramore, Clyde Narramore's nephew, became the founding dean of the Rosemead Graduate School of Professional Psychology, which opened in 1970 (separate from Narramore Christian Foundation, which continued in its former more populist role).[11] Rosemead was one of the first free-standing schools of psychology in the United States; its PsyD and PhD programs gained hard-won regional accreditation in 1975 and APA accreditation in 1980. In 1977 Rosemead became a graduate school within Biola University (La Mirada, Calif.). Narramore was joined in 1973 by John Carter, who gained a reputation as a theoretician of integrationism and as one of the most systematic critics of Jay Adams.[12] At the end of the decade Carter and Narramore, like Collins, wrote a programmatic text on the integration of psychology and theology.[13]

In 1973 the integration movement gained its first journal, with Bruce Narramore as founding editor. The *Journal of Psychology and Theology* aimed to "serve as a forum for the integration and application of psychological and biblical information."[14] Narramore's opening, programmatic editorial noted many of the same historical themes that Jay Adams had sounded, though the implications Narramore drew were distinctly different:

> In many quarters the whole process of "curing sick souls" is moving from the church to the doorsteps of psychologists and other mental health professionals. Increasingly, our society is looking to

psychology to shed new light on the basic issues of human existence. . . .

Most of us view this trend with mixed emotions. On the one hand we sense the great potential in a scientific study of man. . . . We are also aware that the church has sometimes failed to minister to the emotional needs of its constituents. . . .

On the other hand, the rapid growth of the psychological sciences and professions may also be viewed as an encroachment on the ministry of the church. We sense a veiled threat (or sometimes obvious) to the authority of the Scriptures, the reality of the supernatural, and the role of the Christian ministry.[15]

Narramore went on to defend the potential of the psychological disciplines to redress things long neglected by fundamentalism: a penetrating understanding into human nature and the provision of skillful counsel.

From its tiny beginnings among members of the Christian Reformed community, the Christian Association for Psychological Studies (CAPS) expanded significantly after the mid-1970s under Harold Ellens's assertive leadership. By the early 1980s it grew to more than one thousand members and held a large national conference each year. In 1975 Ellens began the *Bulletin of CAPS* to provide both news and articles. In 1982 this was upgraded to become the second integrationist journal, *The Journal of Psychology and Christianity*.

Nonaffiliated psychologists also became increasingly influential and played a significant role in making evangelical psychotherapy acceptable. By giving the evangelical public usable advice, popular books by psychologists contributed significantly to creating a climate of favorable public opinion toward psychology. For example, in 1970 evangelical child psychologist James Dobson wrote a hugely successful book on par-

enting.[16] *Dare to Discipline* sold more than two million copies in the next twenty years. It combined folksy warmth, common sense, behavioral psychology's benign climate of positive rewards, a stress on self-esteem deriving from humanistic psychology, carefully circumscribed spankings, and uncomplicated evangelical faith. Dobson rarely took part in the intellectual or professional life of the wider integration movement, but his genial manner and message made the "integration" of psychology and the faith seem as natural as breathing to millions of conservative Protestants. He was suitably critical of the scientific pretensions of Watson, Freud, and Spock; he was openly evangelical and "traditional" in his values: "Perhaps this will sound like heresy coming from a man who spent ten years of his life in behavioral and medical research, but I don't believe the scientific community is the best source of information on proper parenting techniques. . . . The best source of guidance for parents can be found in the wisdom of the Judeo-Christian ethic."[17] But Dobson could as easily draw on Thorndike, Glasser, and self-esteem theory as on the Bible. His Focus on the Family provided popular resources to help resolve everyday problems in living. What Narramore Christian Foundation was in the 1950s and 60s, Focus on the Family became on a huge scale in the 1970s and 80s: a clearinghouse for mental health information, advice on child-rearing or school difficulties, self-help for common life problems such as low self-esteem and marital unhappiness, counselor referrals, evaluations of TV and movies, and information on drug abuse.[18]

If Dobson focused on how-to advice for popular markets, clinical psychologist Larry Crabb[19] concentrated on giving skills to lay- and master-level counselors. Crabb offered an easily digestible psychodynamic model, grafting familiar evangelical themes—sin, the love of Jesus, practical obedience, church friendships—onto an acknowledgment of the darker feelings and drives in the human heart. He targeted the dysphorias of daily life—anxiety, irritability, mild depression—but also more major problems: eating disorders, marital breakdown, sexual perversions, recovery from the effects of abuse. His books were primarily intended to give self-conscious counselors a working philosophy. But many of his books were also accessible to readers looking for self-help. Crabb counseled in private practice through the 1970s; his writings sold tens of thousands of copies (in the 1980s, hundreds of thousands), bringing him wide influence.

In 1975 Dallas Theological Seminary invited two psychiatrists, Frank Minirth and Paul Meier, to teach counseling in the practical theology department. They, like most of the men mentioned above, combined an impeccable profession of evangelical faith with professional credentials. This hiring signaled a significant institutional defeat for Adams, as he had presented a major lecture series at Dallas Seminary in 1973 entitled "The Use of the Scriptures in Counseling." Dallas Seminary had seen the need to remedy a gap in practical ministry, but evangelical psychotherapy proved to be the successful candidate. The most significant impact made by Minirth and Meier would not occur in the seminary classroom, however. In 1976 they founded the first Minirth-Meier Clinic, an outpatient psychiatric clinic. In the 1980s Minirth-Meier would pioneer proprietary inpatient psychiatric services by and for evangelicals.

The institutions of the evangelical psychotherapy movement were themselves nascent in 1970, when Adams wrote *CtC*. Clyde Narramore had been on the scene for less than fifteen years. Fuller Seminary's school of psychology was only five years old. Other institutions were just being formed or were only beginning to hire psychotherapeutically minded personnel. Neither programmatic nor popular self-help books existed.

The psychotherapy movement lacked any journal or widely recognized professional organization. They perceived themselves in a somewhat uncertain position with regard to the evangelical mainstream. Adams's militant position appeared as an immediate and major threat at the very time they were getting established.

It was into this context that Adams dropped *CtC*. He himself was aware that the book was crudely fashioned. But it hit a nerve.

> In the counseling field, when you read counseling books—whether by pagans, or Evangelical Christians, or Roman Catholics—they all said the same thing. Certainly a lot of pastors were uneasy. They'd send people off to psychiatrists or so-called Christian psychologists and they'd come back worse—or saying things they shouldn't say. And multitudes of pastors were being convinced in seminary that they had no way to help their people, because the people brought in to train pastors were psychologists and psychiatrists. I saw biblically oriented men respond enthusiastically to *Competent to Counsel*—and at the same time saw the growth of strong reactions against it, as the church continued to be inundated with psychology.[20]

Conservative Protestant pastors had been intimidated by the seeming confidence and competence of the mental health system; yet many shared Adams's unease about psychological paradigms that did not square with the Bible. Biblicistic religion and secularistic psychology have always seemed dissonant, and Adams tapped a widespread, previously inarticulate discontent.

Among pastors who subsequently became leaders in the movement, the following reactions were typical:

> I had my theological education in hand from Faith and Dallas [Seminaries] and had

been taking graduate work in counseling at Millersville State in 1970. Wrestling the counseling issues through, I had come to many of Jay's conclusions before reading *CtC*. When I read it I told my wife, "This guy has systematized what I've been working on. I want to study with him."[21]

At first in the pastorate I did little counseling because I was scared to death. I began to read the Christian-flavored things, such as Clyde Narramore, but they didn't seem right. And people would come back from their counselors with counsel I'd *never* preach. I struggled, but who was I? In 1970 I read *Competent to Counsel* and said, "*This* is what I believe!" It reinforced what I was beginning to think already. It gave me confidence and courage to believe God would have me get involved. Everything I'd read and heard up 'til then warned that I could hurt people, not help people with the Bible.[22]

In 1956 I had taken an M.Div. from Fuller Theological Seminary with a concentration in counseling. The model was basically Carl Rogers via Seward Hiltner. Over the years, I tried to be a Christian Rogerian, but anything really helpful to people—and to me with my own problems—seemed to come from the Bible: commitment and faith in the Lord, prayer, practical obedience. In the late 1960s, before Jay Adams, I had gotten from Bill Gothard [a popular evangelical teacher][23] a basic way to use the Bible practically. I was no longer counseling as a wallowing Rogerian. I had a system, but it was primitive. Fortuitously, I picked up *Competent to Counsel* off the senior pastor's desk. "This is it!" Lights went on. I blitzed through it, then read it again carefully.[24]

In their self-conception, many of those who embraced Adams's vision had been primed by a set of experiences remarkably similar to Adams's own.

CtC caught the ear of conservative Protestants with a stake in the counseling field, both pastors and psychotherapists. It became something of a defining document during the 1970s because its radical views and militant tone forced conservative Protestants to declare themselves either for or against Jay Adams. A decade later Gary Collins would note that despite the imbalances in Adams's system and the abrasiveness of his manner, "More than anyone else he has attempted to develop an approach to counseling which is consistent with the truths of Scripture."[25] That attempt carried unavoidable weight with conservative Protestants.

On July 1, 1970, Adams was appointed associate professor of Practical Theology at Westminster Seminary. That same year John Bettler left the Philadelphia area to pursue a doctor of ministry degree at the University of Chicago Divinity School, with the intention that he would return to direct CCEF. Meanwhile, George Scipione, a Westminster graduate, served as part-time administrator of CCEF from 1970–74.[26] CCEF remained small during those years. By 1974 Adams, Scipione, and another pastor from the area each counseled one day a week in the Hatboro church, seeing some twenty-five clients per week. They taught their thirteen-week introductory pastoral counseling course three times that year, to fifteen to twenty pastors and seminarians each time.[27]

During his years of doctoral study in Illinois, Bettler also pastored an OPC church and began, in 1972, to edit the first publication of the nouthetic movement, an occasional newsletter from CCEF entitled *Nouthetic Confrontation*. In addition to notices and news, *Nouthetic Confrontation* published brief articles and case studies. The title reinforced the aggressive image of the nascent movement. Nouthetic counseling presented itself as the pointed alternative to the benign, tolerant, nonintrusive ethos that dominated the psychotherapy and pastoral counseling of the era.

During the mid-1970s, Presbyterians Adams, Bettler, and Scipione, each with Westminster Seminary connections, were joined by an ecclesiastically diverse group of other individuals to form the first generation leadership of the nouthetic counseling movement. Adams's main goal was to reform extant institutions, the hundreds of thousands of "Bible-believing" local churches. But with Bettler, he also developed the other institutions characteristic of modern American professions. As the movement proliferated, it attracted interest from a wide range of conservative Protestants, drawing from fundamentalist, evangelical, and Reformed traditions, along with a few Lutherans and Pentecostals/charismatics.[28]

Adams generated a great deal of interest and controversy, while winning few adherents, in institutions of higher education. The sites of Adams's formal lectureships between 1973 and 1976 provide some indication of the scope of his impact within conservative Protestant circles. In giving the 1973 W. H. Griffith Thomas Memorial Lectures at Dallas Theological Seminary, Adams addressed the apex of the conservative, dispensational wing of evangelicalism. In his 1975 Staley Lectures at Cedarville College, Adams spoke in one of the most respected institutions among fundamentalists. Later that year he delivered the Lyman Stewart Lectures at Talbot Theological Seminary, another leading evangelical seminary. Also in 1975, in his inaugural address upon becoming Professor of Practical Theology at Westminster Theological Seminary, Adams spoke in the most respected conservative Reformed seminary. Finally, in 1976 he lectured at Concordia Theo-logical Seminary, which represented theologically conservative Lutherans.[29]

In no place—even Westminster—was Adams embraced without reservations. That his position had become a force to be reckoned with opened doors for him in conservative Protestant academia. But Adams's proposals seemed radical and alien. On the one hand, his counseling model was so theological that it manifested little continuity with models of counseling familiar in the American mental health culture; on the other hand, his theology was so oriented toward counseling processes that it evidenced little continuity with common styles of theological thinking. That alien quality, combined with his polemicism and the uncompromising tenor of his position, typically closed those same doors, except at Westminster and Biblical Theological Seminaries in the northern suburbs of Philadelphia. Adams refused to moderate or conciliate. For example, after giving his lecture series at Biola University's Talbot Seminary, he gave a guest lecture at the Rosemead Graduate School of Psychology. There his words to students and faculty created significant and memorable alienation. His message to these psychologists-to-be and their professors pulled no punches: "This program has no reason for existence. Not only can you not integrate pagan thought and biblical teaching, but what you are trying to do is to train people to attempt the work of the church without ordination, outside the church. That is distorting God's order of things. Counseling may not be set up as a life calling on a free-lance basis; all such counseling ought to be done as a function of the church, utilizing its authority and resources."[30] His hearers were repelled by the implications for their professional existence.[31] Adams professed surprise at the reaction, "To my amazement, I discovered that to many students this was virtually new material. . . . It seemed as if they were encountering the thought for the first time."[32]

Disagreement—whether about the matter or the manner—heavily outweighed agreement in many settings. Adams won an initial hearing in educational settings that spanned American conservative Protestantism. But his program and language were styled either to win immediate converts or to put people off; they created few curious sympathizers and built no bridges for future conversation. But local church pastors in the traditions represented by those institutions often did listen. Nouthetic counseling took root, consistent with the tendencies and intentions of its founder, in local churches, not in graduate schools.

For those who wanted more, Adams kept writing, eventually producing a prodigious corpus. In 1973 he published his second major book, *The Christian Counselor's Manual (CCM)*. *CtC* had been "largely polemic . . . [seeking] to grapple with the problem and place of Christian counseling in today's world."[33] But in *CCM* Adams sought to systematize his approach to counseling methodology. In places he spoke of his work as still in a formative stage: "No one has a foundation and methodology that is totally scriptural. Such work has only been begun. My foundation surely has planks that are rotten and some that are missing. The reader must watch where he walks. There may be planks that have been nailed in backwards or upside down. But of one thing I am certain: there are a number of biblical planks that are solidly nailed down."[34] But *CCM* was hardly a tentative book. Adams boldly exhorted his readers to walk onto the planks he had nailed down: "If . . . I should at places seem brash or appear to take too much for granted, it is probably because I have tried to use bold strokes and vivid colors. After all, I am writing this book for my friends; for those who so enthusiastically responded to my previous efforts. I am not trying to sell anyone here; this is an instruction manual intended principally for those who have already bought the product and

wish to make the most effective use of it."[35] *CCM* also proved to be a best-seller, selling more than 125,000 copies in its first ten years (about half the rate of *CtC*). The two books gave the nouthetic counseling movement its programmatic documents, setting the characteristic content, tone, and social strategy of the movement's first decade.

With its call to arms ringing out and its procedural manual in hand, the institutional landscape of nouthetic counseling began to fill out during the 1970s. A number of new institutions joined Westminster and CCEF during the initial expansion of nouthetic counseling. Characteristically, the movement did not build links with existing institutions but created separate ones. We will look at the most significant developments: Faith Baptist Counseling Ministries (1973); the development of a doctor of ministry program at Westminster Seminary in conjunction with CCEF's expansion (1975); Adams's prolific writing during this period; the Biblical Counseling Foundation (1977); the National Association of Nouthetic Counselors (NANC, 1976); the *Journal of Pastoral Practice* (1977); and, finally, a defining interaction between Adams and his closest professional neighbors, the evangelical psychotherapists, that occurred in 1979.

Faith Baptist Counseling Ministry

In 1972 Bill Goode, a Baptist pastor in Gary, Indiana, and Bob Smith, a physician and member of Goode's congregation, spent an intensive week with Adams at a training conference in pastoral counseling. Both were former believers in psychotherapy whose disillusionment had followed the typical trajectory. In 1970, after Goode had encountered counseling cases that he found too difficult, his church had sent him for a month of training with Clyde Narramore. There he had been socialized into the predominant contemporary counseling model: a Freudian view of the conscience, Rogerian methodology, the requisite referral of difficult cases to psychotherapeutic professionals.[36] He found his counseling no more effectual after his training than before, and his sense of the incompatibility of the two belief systems increased. Smith had strongly considered pursuing psychiatry when in medical school because "Freudian psychiatry seemed to have the answers; it seemed to describe problems in detail, and gave a structure to knowledge for diagnostic purposes." But several unsettling cases had rattled his confidence in psychiatry, and he spent a number of years as a general practitioner "trying to mix the Bible and Freud—unsuccessfully" in the informal counseling that came his way.[37] Reading the works of evangelical psychotherapists—Clyde Narramore, Gary Collins, Quentin Hyder—in the late 1960s only increased his dissatisfaction. *CtC* found a ready response from both men.

Goode and Smith became instant converts to Adams's alternative model. When they returned from the week with Adams, they arranged for John Bettler to come down from Chicago weekly during 1973 to help them found a church-based counseling and training center. In 1977 they moved their base of operations to Faith Baptist Church in Lafayette, Indiana, and named their counseling center Faith Baptist Counseling Ministries (FBCM). Smith, Goode, and other FBCM staff would go on to train more than one thousand pastors and missionaries between 1973 and the early 1990s, as well as conducting scores of seminars throughout the United States.

Goode and his fellows were members of the General Association of Regular Baptist Churches (GARBC), a classically fundamentalist denomination that had arisen in the ecclesiastical wars of the 1930s, breaking off from the mainline American Baptist Church. FBCM's greatest influence was into the fundamentalist heartland in the Midwest: to GARBC pastors and missionaries and in numerous Baptist Bible colleges. The GARBC's historical commitments to dispensational eschatology, adult baptism, and the "separated life" (e.g., abstinence from alcohol, tobacco, and "worldly" entertainment) made FBCM's relationship with Jay Adams interesting. By rights he should have been suspect: a Reformed, amillennialist seminary professor; assertively in favor of baptizing babies; bearded and casually dressed (he foreswore ties with loud good humor), from a denomination and seminary known for defending the liberty to drink, smoke, and participate in entertainments; an expert in Greek whose Bible translation not only departed from the conventional language of the King James Version but also followed critical scholars by dispensing with Mark 16:9–20 and John 7:53–8:11 as spurious. But as prickly as Adams could be with evangelical psychologists to his left, he was winsome with fundamentalist pastors to his right.[38] To an audience of hundreds of fundamentalist Baptists at Faith Baptist Church, including scores of pastors, Adams disarmed and delighted his hearers with these opening words:

Faith Baptist Church is a lighthouse. What they've done with counseling is *the* navigational aid, among all the churches I know in the world! It's true they aren't Presbyterians yet. They still believe in all this paraphernalia about ties! But they've taken all the things that are in the books and put them into practice. Take their model back to your churches. When I heard Bill Goode speak earlier I felt like shouting! Of course, we Presbyterians must be judicious in Baptist circles, otherwise we'll get thrown into the swimming pool back there behind me.[39]

Goode and others embraced Adams, let him preach in their churches—without a dunking—and were willing to take criticism from more extreme separatists to their right.

Adams had "hit a nerve among biblically oriented men," earned a respect that allowed his nouthetic counseling to cross many ecclesiastical barriers to the right of his Presbyterianism (even as his biblicism triggered warning bells against fundamentalism in those to the left of his Presbyterianism). He offered such pastors a model that seemed practical, comprehensible, case wise, and consistent with their understanding of the Bible and Christian doctrine. Their own previous approach to counseling had often consisted in "prayer-and-Bible-verse prescription," in anxious avoidance of troubled people, and in reluctant referral to the secular mental health system—approaches that Adams assailed as sharply as he assailed the secular psychotherapies.

As the quotation two paragraphs above indicates, Adams viewed FBCM as the institutional paradigm that he most approved: "More and more, the idea of counseling as the work of the organized church (in general) and the pastor and elders (in particular) has begun to emerge."[40] Counseling ministry and training were to be housed squarely within a local church; the pastors of the church not only preached but counseled and wove their counseling practices into the entire life of the church. The counseling ministry could take advantage of its local church setting to offer counseling services for a nominal fee or—to parishioners, to the indigent, and to non-Christians—gratuitously.[41] They also sought out and trained other pastors in the area for a minimal tuition, drawing trainees from a several hundred-mile radius. Faith Baptist Church did the things Adams wanted to see done.

Developments with Adams and at Westminster and CCEF

Meanwhile, nouthetic counseling's first specialized degree program for pastors was initiated at Westminster Seminary in 1975. Westminster's doctor of ministry program offered an opportunity for pastors to return to seminary for graduate studies and to write their projects on biblical counseling topics if they so chose. John Bettler had returned to Philadelphia in 1974, becoming CCEF's director, a counselor on staff, and the first full-time employee. He was also hired by Westminster to direct the new DMin program. This program proved to be a significant source of the future leaders in nouthetic counseling. In the 1990s, of the eleven NANC board members besides Adams, six had been affiliated with Westminster's DMin. Despite the stir that Adams's publications and grassroots speaking had produced, through the 1970s Westminster remained the only theological seminary philosophically committed to Adams's radical biblical counseling.[42] Other leading Reformed and evangelical seminaries—Covenant (St. Louis, Mo.), Reformed (Jackson, Miss.), Dallas, Talbot, Trinity Evangelical (Deerfield, Ill.), Gordon-Conwell (Hamilton, Mass.), and Fuller—embraced the integrationist agenda, seeking to wed their orthodoxy and the modern psychologies in a manner that would preserve the former and profit from the latter.

During 1975 Adams decided to leave Westminster Seminary and CCEF. An indefatigable worker, he had published fifteen books and some forty articles and pamphlets during a six-year period. He had traveled extensively to give lectures and conferences about counseling, crisscrossing the United States and Canada, along with travels to Europe, Australia, South and Central America, and east Asia. He counseled and trained counselors one thirteen-hour day a week at CCEF. All this extracurricular activity occurred alongside his seminary teaching. Interest in nouthetic counseling was exploding, and Adams decided to devote himself to further writing and to the occasional teaching of his travels, spreading the message of his counseling revolution rather than wearing the harness of seminary routines. Adams had often chafed in academia.[43] Health problems sealed the decision. He was burning himself out physically at age forty-six; a recurrent heart problem produced incidents of blacking out. He decided to move to a rural setting in order to write, to reduce physical stress, and to spend more time with his teenaged children.[44]

Adams was appointed Professor of Practical Theology at Westminster on May 27, 1975; the announcement that he would step down one year later came simultaneously.[45] In 1976 he moved to Macon, Georgia, to devote himself to writing and speaking. He became a Visiting Professor of Practical Theology at Westminster and dean of the Institute of Pastoral Studies (providing continuing education workshops for pastors) at CCEF, responsibilities that brought him back to Philadelphia several times a year to teach one- or two-week courses. The bulk of his energies went into writing. Adams's literary output was stupendous during this time, if somewhat uneven in quality and sometimes repetitious. Between 1976 and 1982 he published thirty books and at least as many pamphlets and articles.[46] These included a translation of the New Testament, half a dozen books on preaching, and a score of counseling books variously intended to serve the interests of either counselors or counselees.

Toward the end of the decade Adams published two books that completed what he considered to be his four basic texts. *Lectures on Counseling* (1977) printed lightly edited transcripts of his major lectureships in the middle of the decade. It dealt with crisis counseling situations frequently encountered by pastors, taught how to use the Bible practically, and succinctly restated his call for a counseling revolution based upon his conservative Protestant assumptions.[47] Finally, in *More Than Redemption* (1979) Adams sketched what he saw to be the counseling implications of key biblical doctrines,

the standard beliefs held by his potential converts (e.g., God, the image of God in man, the nature of sin, forgiveness, sanctification, the role of the church, etc.).[48] Such beliefs had rarely been given a "counseling" spin in the theological education his hearers had received; by giving them such a spin Adams intended to build upon his hearers familiar, traditional, and cherished convictions in order to move them to embrace his innovative applications.

Adams was gone from CCEF and Westminster by the middle of the decade, though he remained on the CCEF board and returned for conferences. Adams had viewed the counseling role of CCEF as distinctly subordinate to the training needs of pastors; he envisioned the primary purpose of CCEF's counseling caseload as providing a site where experienced pastor-counselors could train other pastors to become "the professionals" in counseling. In 1975 it was pointed that "the counseling staff of the Christian Counseling and Educational Foundation is composed of men who, in addition to extensive supervised training in counseling, are also ordained ministers, [and] have professional theological training, or are in the process of procuring such training."[49] But as Bettler went to work developing the institutions, they increasingly became an extension of his vision for specialized education in counseling and for specialized pastoral counseling practice by nonpastors as well as pastors. Adams had initially communicated a certain ambiguity about who should counsel, though it was clear that his own primary loyalties lay with the pastor. He had concluded *CtC* with these words: "In this volume I have tried to show that the minister, Christian workers, and indeed every Christian, may consider himself at least potentially competent to counsel. . . . That the work of counseling should be carried on preeminently by ministers and other Christians whose gifts, training, and calling especially qualify and require them to pursue the work, I do not doubt." Bettler built CCEF to teach those "other Christian workers" and "every" Christian as well as the pastor. He broadened CCEF's hiring policy, continuing to hire ordained ministers, but also beginning to hire nonordained men and, in the 1980s, women. He created a "professional laity" to counsel alongside the "professional pastorate."[50]

The trajectory for CCEF's expansion was set. George Scipione (who had been interim director while Bettler was in Chicago and a longtime CCEF board member) commented, "Jay Adams always said for effect, 'CCEF's goal is to put itself out of business because it will get pastors doing the job of counseling.' John Bettler would never say that."[51] Bettler would get pastors doing the job as well as lots of other people, some highly specialized. Previously operating out of borrowed rooms in a local church—the "counseling center" was stored in a small closet at Trinity OPC except for the two days a week it operated—in 1975 CCEF purchased a mansion across the street from Westminster Seminary.[52] This became the site of rapid expansion during the late 1970s; the location conveniently reinforced the bond between CCEF and Westminster Seminary. Both the staff and counseling load expanded steadily during the late 1970s. In 1974 counselors conducted slightly more than one thousand hours of counseling. By 1978 CCEF conducted about two thousand hours of counseling; by 1980, three thousand hours.

Bettler also envisioned CCEF's educational role quite differently from Adams. Adams wanted grassroots continuing education for pastors. Even his ideal seminary would become significantly more church-based, intended to equip practicing pastors rather than acting as a graduate school to train scholars.[53] At CCEF, nonpastors interested in nouthetic counseling might pick what they could alongside, but Adams rarely deviated from his emphasis on pastors. But Bettler wanted a CCEF that was "both the Harvard and Moody of biblical counseling"[54] As the "Harvard," it would provide intellectual leadership and scholarly education, interacting with the wider culture, and it would train a small number of graduate students to become pastoral counselors with specialized scholarly and practical skills. As the "Moody" (alluding to Moody Bible Institute in Chicago), CCEF would train numerous pastors, missionaries, other practitioners, and laypeople to get the job done with struggling people. In effect Bettler envisioned both a professoriate and an army of other practitioners, formal and informal, who would complement the pastor's counseling ministry. His CCEF would train all three groups. Adams had established a broad charter for CCEF; it rapidly began to develop aspects of that charter that left it somewhat at odds with the founder's animating vision.

Biblical Counseling Foundation

The tension between a "professional pastorate" and a "professional laity" was not the only difference of perspective that emerged as the first generation of practitioners developed their institutions. And Bettler, Goode, and Smith were not the only men with abilities in building institutions. John Broger envisioned biblical counseling for the "lay laity"—the Christian in the pew—and founded the Biblical Counseling Foundation to carry it out.[55] At the time he met Adams, Broger (b. 1913) served as the director of Information for the Armed Forces, working in the Pentagon as the military's highest-ranking civilian employee. As director of Information he ran a vast communications network: Armed Forces radio, television, newspapers, publications, and motion pictures. Broger was also an evangelical layman, a pioneer in radio broadcasting for missionary purposes, and an influential member of the National Association of Evangelicals. He had been active in informal, peer counseling for many years. In the course of this, he had felt his own version of the tensions Adams had experienced.

> [Broger would deal] with people's personal problems . . . [by doing] what most Christians would do in a similar situation: he encouraged individuals from Scripture, asked them to hold steady and remain constant, and advised them to read the Bible, have Christian fellowship, pray, and place their trust and confidence in God. . . . He did not know what else to give them other than normal, traditional Christian encouragement. They would leave with hope, but no further practical guidance on how to deal with their problems using Scripture. . . .
>
> Broger remained dissatisfied with the less-than-adequate counsel he was giving. He began to investigate secular therapies to see if he could gain insight into better ways to handle life's problems.
>
> As he studied books on psychiatry and psychology . . . it became obvious that these approaches had very different ideas of the origin and nature of man than found in Scripture. It was equally clear that they held little hope for dealing with the underlying cause of man's problems.[56]

Jay Adams's nouthetic counseling could find no better prepared soil. The threefold tension Broger experienced—a commitment to the Bible, an inability to handle people's deep problems, an unease with the secular psychologies—repeated a pattern that appeared countless times in those who came to embrace Adams's model.

Broger first heard Adams in 1973. He responded enthusiastically and, being both a committed evangelical and a communications magnate, quickly saw the possibilities for inserting a frankly Bible-based counseling curriculum into the military context. He arranged with the chiefs of chaplains of the U.S. Armed Forces to sponsor Adams for a training course in peer counseling that would "train military lay men and women to counsel others in need of help."[57] Adams gave a series of lectures outside Washington, D.C., in 1974, speaking under Pentagon auspices to military chaplains. Broger had the lecture series transcribed, and he worked it into a two-part syllabus. *Self-Confrontation* adapted Adams into a workbook intended to foster self-examination and personal growth; *Biblical Counseling* then trained people to help others.

Broger rapidly set about putting his enormous influence within the military to work in further spreading the nouthetic counseling message. The chiefs of chaplains made Broger's training materials available to military chaplains worldwide. Broger prepared "a series of Armed Forces radio and TV spots to be aired over 1,100 stations worldwide. The plan also called for radio spot announcements and written material for 1,900 troop newspapers to support the counseling 'hot-lines' planned at various U.S. military bases around the world. The theme for the radio and TV spots and troop newspapers was 'IT'S IN THE BIBLE.'" Broger overplayed his hand, however. Adams's model was too biblicistic for the multi-denominational military chaplaincy to tolerate as the official peer counseling substratum of its ministries. A backlash developed, leading to a *Washington Post* exposé by columnist Jack Anderson. Anderson charged Broger with conflict of interest and administrative malfeasance for using his Pentagon office to promote evangelical Christianity and right-wing politics.[58] The training course Broger and Adams had developed ended up being marketed by the National Association of Evangelicals, rather than distributed through the United States military.

Though stymied within the military context, Broger had found his new calling. In 1977 he retired from government service and founded the Biblical Counseling Foundation (BCF) to implement his adaptation of Adams to self-counseling and to "discipleship" for laity and pastors alike. His *Self-Confrontation* manual consisted in a twenty-four-week course of detailed Bible studies on common life problems. Its format bore the stamp of Broger's expertise in writing technical, procedural manuals. *Self-Confrontation* went through a half dozen self-published versions over the next fifteen years and was used as an instrument to train thousands of people. More than 100,000 copies were sold or distributed to students who went through its contents either in week-long intensive courses sponsored by BCF or in weekly courses over six months in their local churches.[59]

Broger's major emphases—self-counseling, training laypeople, a rigorous and highly structured program of transferable concepts, detailed study of individual Bible verses, scrupulous avoidance of polemics—usually complemented, but sometimes crossed, Jay Adams's emphases. Adams stressed counseling done by men in the role of pastor; Broger emphasized self-help for all. Adams trained pastors to do their job in face-to-face ministry; Broger wanted to disciple laypeople, as well as pastors, to trust and obey Christ in their personal lives. Adams argued for adaptation of counseling methods based on audience awareness, a flexibility based on numerous variables of the person, the problem, the counselor[60]; Broger produced a tightly structured workbook, a programmatic curriculum for counseling. Adams was very willing to become didactic with those he counseled, and he stressed pastoral teaching authority to communicate how to understand and apply biblical passages in their context; Broger preferred to get people reading and personally responding to Bible verses and was wary of abuses of pasto-

ral authority. Adams freely engaged in polemics against opponents; Broger sought to promulgate what he saw as the Bible's positive alternative to other systems.

Many of these differences in perspective and emphasis are understandable in the light of Adams and Broger's differing ecclesiastical backgrounds and social location. Broger was a layman from a Brethren background. The Brethren were a conservative, anti-clerical tradition that stressed lay leadership rather than the pastorate and pastoral authority. Broger had been active in the National Association of Evangelicals, which specifically distanced itself from fundamentalist polemicism a generation before Adams. Broger had been involved in informal laycounseling and discipleship for many years. He saw the potential in what Adams was saying, but he read it with different eyes than the Presbyterian pastor from the ecclesiastical wars of the 1950s who wanted to rehabilitate the pastorate. But both Adams and Broger agreed that the Bible's message of specific faith in Christ and practical obedience to Christ provided the solution to people's difficulties in living. Broger served on the boards of both CCEF and the National Association of Nouthetic Counselors (see next section). And his BCF proved quite successful at the grassroots level. BCF was able to take advantage of Broger's longstanding contacts throughout the evangelical world, both in the United States and abroad, to spread his adaptation of Adams's message.

National Association of Nouthetic Counselors

While Broger was discovering Jay Adams as the answer to his desire to provide self-help and informal counseling for laypeople, a very different sort of development took place in Adams's immediate circle. Bettler proposed that there was a need for a professional organization to ensure the quality of nouthetic counseling.[61] In 1974 the CCEF board "agreed that the director [Bettler] should proceed with the formation of a proposed National Association of Nouthetic Counselors to be kept under the control of CCEF."[62] Bettler's intention was to form an accrediting body to set standards both for training programs and for the individual practice of those who would claim to be nouthetic counselors.[63] It took two years to hammer out the details, and in 1976 the CCEF board adopted Bettler's proposal for NANC.

NANC initially reflected Bettler's concern for quality control, his fears of incompetence among those who would use the Bible in counseling, and the threat of malpractice suits as pastoral counselors attempted to move back into turf well monitored by secular professionals. NANC as initially constituted sought to fulfill a number of roles: (1) to set standards for training programs; (2) to certify the competency of individual counseling practitioners, whether clergy or lay; (3) to certify pastoral counseling centers; (4) to develop constructive relationships with other schools and agencies involved in training counselors; (5) to promote research into Christian counseling; (6) to provide opportunities for fellowship among like-minded practitioners.[64] NANC would hold members and member institutions to standards of Bible commitment, quality counseling, and ethics, so that they might be certified, might be disciplined in the breach, and might receive protection from lawsuits.

Though the founding group was small (ten men) and all were loyal to and appreciative of Adams as their pioneer, the particular shape NANC would take remained to be hammered out. From the start the distinctive emphases of Adams, Bettler, and Broger contended for dominance. The fledgling association debated three main questions in seeking to define its functional identity: Who should be the target population? How high should standards of education and competency be set? How should nouthetic counselors treat evangelical psychotherapists? Jay Adams wanted to put NANC's major emphasis on pastors of local churches; he wanted standards that the average hard-working pastor, a generalist committed to nouthetic counseling, could meet; he was willing to name names in polemics with psychotherapists. John Bettler wanted to put a greater emphasis on scholarship and on producing highly trained and specialized counselors; he wanted to raise standards that defined professional competency; he thought that nouthetic counselors ought to engage psychotherapists in cordial dialogue rather than savaging them. John Broger wanted an informal association of like-minded laymen and pastors, rather than a professional accreditation organization for pastors; he thought the notion of professional standards suspect because it would squelch lay involvement, and he did not like Adams's heavy emphasis on pastoral authority; he thought that the greatest effort should be put into positive teaching of biblical counseling, rather than either polemics against or dialogue with psychotherapists.

NANC's bylaws ended up combining Adams's emphasis on pastors with Bettler's on higher education. They established four levels of membership. The lowest level was for certifiable "clergymen and laymen who have demonstrated competence in Christian counseling" but who did not have a seminary degree. The second level was for "ordained clergymen" who demonstrated the same competence with a seminary degree in theology. The next level, Fellows, were "ordained clergymen who demonstrate[d] a unique ability to counsel in a parish or counseling center to serve as a supervisor of counselors in training" and who held an advanced degree beyond the primary theological degree. Finally, Members of the Academy were "ordained clergymen . . . involved in teaching and/or training college students, seminarians, or pastors for a counseling ministry . . . [who] made a significant contribution to the development of nouthetic counseling."[65] The intended effect was the creation of a professoriate to guide and supervise the biblical counseling movement. NANC had established itself on paper, but growth was slow. It held its first annual conference in 1976 with about 50 in attendance. The following year 120 attended, and the proceedings were published.[66] Annual conferences during the next decade averaged about 150 attendees.

During the first several years NANC was run by CCEF and volunteer labor. But by 1978 Bettler concluded that it was irregular for the accrediting organization to be subordinate to the chief educational institution, and CCEF severed control over NANC.[67] Though officially separated from CCEF, NANC only gradually developed its own identity. Until 1983, CCEF's business manager functioned as the volunteer executive director for NANC, handling daily details. High hopes had translated into fewer members than anticipated and little money to publicize NANC. All the men involved were busy doing other ministries, so no managerial hand guided the association.

The accreditation process was not particularly taxing by secular standards. It entailed taking a recognized course of study in nouthetic counseling that covered four basic areas: an introductory course, marriage and family counseling, counseling case studies, and critique of psychological theories (essentially, the Westminster counseling curriculum that Adams had created). In addition, applicants needed to pass written examinations in counseling and theology and to have fifty hours of counseling supervised by a NANC fellow.

But this process—a screening process on top of ordination exams, an accountability to be supervised outside of normal ecclesiastical oversight—was not something most pastors seemed to have

the time, inclination, or commitment to pursue, however committed they were to nouthetic counseling itself. The legal protections NANC had carefully crafted seemed largely irrelevant to pastors sheltered by the long-standing legal protections that had attended pastoral care.[68] They were busy and pragmatic and simply wanted to learn how to counsel their people better. Only a committed core embraced the NANC vision; its professionally certified pastor-counselor did not fit within long-standing conventions of pastoral ordination and church government. Though *CtC* sold a quarter of a million copies in the 1970s, NANC would not reach one hundred members until the early 1980s.

The Journal of Pastoral Practice

In 1977 Bettler and Adams created the final piece of the first generation of nouthetic counseling institutions, founding the *Journal of Pastoral Practice* under CCEF's auspices. Adams served as overall editor and Bettler as publisher. The title was chosen to reflect wider interests than counseling, to embed counseling within the entire range of pastoral work. Adams's stated hope was to rehabilitate pastoral ministry in general—from counseling to preaching, from doctrine to higher salaries. His opening statement came with high hopes of what his new journal might accomplish:

The *Journal of Pastoral Practice* is a new venture in the history of American Christianity. Unthinkable as it may seem, the oldest institutionalized profession in the United States—the ministry—has no professional journal! It is our purpose to remedy this situation.

"But there are many theological seminary journals," someone may object. . . . While a number of these theological journals are excellent, and serve an important place, nevertheless they are quite different from a professional journal. More often than not, in both style and content, articles in these magazines are highly academic, better suited to satisfy the interests of other scholars than to meet the needs of men serving in the pastoral ministry.

In the *Journal of Pastoral Practice,* while adhering to scholarly standards, authors will be encouraged to make every effort to be intensely practical. They also will be urged to write in everyday English, leaving the esoteric jargon of their disciplines for other endeavors."[69]

The *JPP* would not be a highbrow theological or biblical studies journal; it would not be a narrowly focused preaching or pastoral counseling journal; it would not be a popular magazine. Rather it would focus on any and all aspects of pastoral life in the local church. Adamsian distinctives are obvious, as he wrote for "the most neglected guy in the world, the pastor in the trenches."[70] *JPP* was created with nine subdivisions, each independently edited by friends of Adams. He provided final oversight. Counseling articles predominated, in a section edited by Howard Eyrich; Adams edited, and usually wrote, a regular preaching section; Bob Smith did the same for medical subjects of relevance to counselors. Other subdivisions—Christian education, missions, church finances, evangelism, the cults, and pastoral work—appeared more or less regularly, depending on the industry, enthusiasm, and busyness of the particular editor. The *JPP* thrived initially. By 1980 it had grown to more than 1,000 subscribers, including 250 seminary, Bible college, and university libraries, spanning the spectrum from Bob Jones University to Harvard Divinity School. After publishing biannually during 1977 and 1978, it stepped up to four issues a year, and the size of each issue swelled to more than two hundred pages.

Adams's revolution seemed to be succeeding. Though seminaries had not come aboard en masse, though minor in-house tensions existed between competing visions of professionalization, and though the national association had sputtered, the books were selling well, education was thriving, and the pastors who had flocked to buy the product were putting it to work. Through its first decade, nouthetic counseling had operated largely in self-conscious isolation from other species of counselor. But during that same decade, the evangelical psychotherapy professions had greatly expanded their institutional base and their cultural authority within conservative Protestantism. The two groups could not help but acknowledge and debate one another, usually from afar in books, articles, classrooms, and pulpits.

The Krisheim Symposium

At the end of the decade Bettler initiated a face-to-face meeting not unlike the airport meeting of 1969, persuading Adams again to meet with a group of evangelical psychotherapists. This time the intention was to hammer out differences that had become highly visible. On March 7–8, 1979, CCEF sponsored a two-day symposium at Krisheim, a mansion in the Chestnut Hill section of Philadelphia, then being used as a Presbyterian retreat center.[71] Adams and Henry Brandt represented the biblicistic point of view.[72] Four leading evangelical psychologists were invited: Bruce Narramore and John Carter from Rosemead, Gary Collins from Trinity, and Larry Crabb. John Bettler moderated the meeting. The purpose was to debate the question, "What is biblical counseling?" Subquestions included the relationships between psychopathology and sin, between secular psychology and biblical theology, between psychotherapists and pastors as counselors, and between supportive and directive counseling relationships.

All attenders stayed at Krisheim in hopes that informal conversations would also occur and constructive relationships develop.

All participants were conservative Protestants, with a stated commitment to standard tenets regarding God, sin, Christ, and the authority of the Bible. Similarly, all shared a stated commitment that those tenets ought to consistently inform the tasks of counseling. Overarching agreements aside, they obviously differed markedly in how they implemented those commitments for the counseling task. Bettler hoped to bridge the rift between nouthetic counselors and evangelical psychotherapists for the sake of mutually constructive dialogue.

The rift had been produced by and had generated much polemicizing and misunderstanding, sometimes seemingly willful, as both sides sought to delegitimize the other. On the one hand, nouthetic counseling had often been ridiculed by psychologists, and effectively excluded from serious consideration in the lecture halls of higher education and pastoral training; on the other hand, the evangelical psychotherapists had often been attacked by populist nouthetic counselors. Bettler was concerned that nouthetic counseling had become and would continue to be marginalized within the wider body of conservative Protestants concerned about counseling matters. He feared that the nouthetic counseling movement—partly by its own insular tendencies, partly by exclusion at the hands of sociocultural gatekeepers—would end up without a platform to speak into the wider church. Bettler was content with something less than the immediate conversion of those with whom he differed: "I believe in defining differences in a way that fences off positions clearly. But there's a difference between a fence and a chasm. You can talk over a fence. You have to shout over a chasm. Over a fence you can listen, you can learn, and others can listen and learn from you."[73] Each attender

presented a paper, followed by a lengthy period of discussion and debate. Over the two days, the conversation ranged widely. But three topics recurred, leading to consensus in the first case, rather muddied disagreement in the second, and sharp and wholly unpredictable division in the third.

The first vexed issue concerned the nature of sin, what was summarized by one participant as the relationship between "sins" (discrete behaviors) and "sin" (complex intrapsychic distortions of belief and motive). The discussants raised many questions about each other: Did Adams and Brandt ignore "sin" in favor of "sins"? Was Crabb too exclusively cognitive in his view of "sin"? Did the psychotherapists ignore "sins" to focus on "psychological problems and needs," only paying lip service to the Bible when they occasionally termed the latter "sin"? But in the end the participants seemed to find their differences more apparent than substantive and reached a significant measure of consensus.

On the second topic marked differences arose, but even a satisfactory definition of those differences proved highly elusive. The question turned on the relationship between secular psychology and the Bible. On the one hand, all participants affirmed the final authority of Scripture over psychology; on the other hand, all affirmed that there was something to be gained from studying the secular psychologies. But what the exact contribution of each source looked like in practice proved highly controversial and difficult to articulate. It was evident that Narramore, Carter, and Collins gave psychology far greater weight than Adams, Brandt, and Crabb. Bettler, acting as moderator, provided perhaps the most telling summary of the sticking point. The former were relatively "optimistic" about what secularism could discover about human nature and therapeutic method; they thought that the Bible did not provide significant detail about the issues of counseling; they believed that multiple models of counseling might comport with a generally biblical worldview. The latter were relatively "pessimistic" about secular systems because of the distorting intellectual effects of sin; they thought the Bible spoke comprehensively to the issues of counseling; they believed that a specific, coherent approach to the cure of souls might be derived from the Bible. Though this difference repeatedly surfaced, discussion often bogged down or became disjointed.

The third controverted topic concerned the nature of the counseling relationship. Here differences did not remain murky and inarticulate. The issue had been raised the first day by the Rosemead psychologists, who criticized Crabb for overemphasizing cognitive change at the expense of the counselor-counselee relationship. Late on the second day a vigorous debate began. It concluded in a startling realignment that provided the symposium's defining moment. Initially, the discussion found Crabb and Adams lining up against Carter and Narramore, while Collins tried to synthesize the positions and Brandt listened in. Crabb challenged Narramore's (and Carter's) view that the psychotherapeutic relationship was more important than the content of counsel. The Rosemead psychologists argued with Crabb for the validity of their psychoanalytic style: long-term psychotherapy, from one to three years, several times per week, whose goals were more relationship-building than directive. The Bible gave no more warrant for short-term counseling, like Adams's, than for long-term counseling, like theirs, and the biblical emphasis on human relationships provided a significant rationale for their extended psychotherapy. They identified themselves as heavily influenced by psychoanalytic thought and practice and defended analysis as "greatly misunderstood overall, and perhaps even more so in the Christian community," making a pointed allusion to Adams's writings. They argued that most clients needed a "curative relationship [more] than new scriptural insights" and, thus, "The most helpful part of my counseling is not the content that I offer, but my relationship with a hurting person." Narramore commented that his choice of long-term psychotherapeutic relationships rather than directive, didactic problem solving was ultimately a matter of personal preference, not biblical mandate. He launched straight at Adams, Brandt, and Crabb: "This is one of the single largest weaknesses in the evangelical church; we have somehow made spiritual growth a cognitive and a willful process much more than an interpersonal one."

A string of concerns were raised. Crabb led off in disputing Narramore, "The care is not the cure.... Is the relationship corrective or does relationship provide a vehicle for correction? . . . Shouldn't the church be doing this? . . . Shouldn't our energies be focused on helping the church to do its job better rather than replacing the church by offering long-term analysis?" Collins joined in with a temporizing statement that the church was meant to be a deprofessionalized community of people helpers (acknowledging Crabb) and yet affirmed that there were different kinds of valid counseling relationships (acknowledging Narramore). Finally Adams began to question Narramore closely about the connection between his views and distinctives of "Freudian" analysis: lengthy therapy without concretely defined moral goals, the couch, free association, catharsis, transference, supportive nondirective relationships. They sparred over these, and, briefly, over whether Adams was equally indebted to Mowrer for his model of short-term counseling.

Henry Brandt had been silent, except for one comment, early in the conversation, to the effect that Narramore's lengthy counseling process reminded him that Jesus spent three years intensively working with his twelve disciples. But in the middle of Narramore's lengthy defense of psychoanalysis to Adams, Brandt suddenly interjected a frank commendation. The effect was electrifying. Adams, seemingly stung at the sudden switch of allegiance, again challenged Narramore about the "Freudian" content that operated in his system. Then he turned to Brandt, "Henry, I think you've had the wool pulled over your eyes." He attempted to argue Brandt back to his side. Virtually ignoring the rest of the group, Adams appealed to Brandt alone. He attempted to describe "an antithesis, an utter antithesis . . . rather than a synthesis" between what Narramore had been saying and Brandt's earlier presentation. But Brandt was adamant, eventually affirming that there were indeed many different possible configurations of counseling. As long as Narramore could affirm that what he was "doing was discipling . . . acting as a mirror and leading the [counselee] in the Word and helping him to deal with his sin," then he had no problem with it. He might even refer someone to Narramore, "who was prepared to spend more time with a few people." Brandt considered that his own choice for relatively brief counsel was also only a matter of personal preference and was tailored to people in immediate crises.

Adams again tried to convince Brandt that his own counseling over the years had dealt with the gamut of personal problems in a rapid, directive, and hortatory manner. But Brandt was not going to be told what he had really meant: "I've got to admit that—even if you want to call it the wool being pulled over my eyes—there are different relationships." Brandt was satisfied with Narramore's use of the Bible, and he dismissed the murky issue about the Bible and psychology: "What I like about [Narramore's] presentation, he's finally telling me how he uses the Word rather than me and him arguing over whether to use extra-biblical stuff or not."

Adams's only presumed ally among the participants had dramatically switched his allegiance.

Adams had loudly voiced his grievance and his conviction that the psychologists had duped Brandt. Adams sat silent during the final few minutes of the symposium as Brandt, Narramore, and Collins discussed a newfound consensus regarding the legitimacy of variety in counseling models. Distinctly pastoral, church-based, "anti-Freudian" counseling had come up short in the exchange.

The attempt at dialogue had chiefly succeeded in delineating stark differences between Adams and the evangelical psychotherapists. Though they shared numerous commitments in common, the implications they drew had proved strikingly incompatible. The attempt at cordial dialogue and at building bridges for future conversation had disintegrated in the dramatic events of the final fifteen minutes. Bettler closed the meeting with an attempt to salvage something. He talked of publishing the proceedings[74] and asserted that "our areas of agreement are larger than our differences." But the differences over counseling had carried the day.

Bettler had come with high hopes. But his hope for a nouthetic counseling come into its intellectual maturity, engaging the wider evangelical counseling world, a party in significant dialogue, able to be both sharpened and to sharpen others, was dashed. Adams was a proclaimer of truth who endured but did not enjoy forums such as Krisheim. He was one to convert others, not one to converse with them. He was not one to listen quietly to those he suspected of using Bible words to pull secular wool over the eyes of the church. The Krisheim conference confirmed in Adams's mind that the evangelical psychologists promoted serious conceptual, methodological, and institutional errors dressed up in Bible words. He had come to Krisheim at Bettler's urging, having previously stated that he had no interest in dialogue with "the self-styled 'professionals'": "I could debate, argue and try to persuade them. . . . That, I am convinced, would in most cases be useless. So I don't. . . . Others, with perhaps a different mission, may want to engage in dialogue with the 'professionals.' God bless them; but it is not for me."[75] He would never again dialogue with them.

The conference also confirmed Adams's identity to the psychologists. They largely gave up on Adams as irascible and sectarian. A year later, John Carter wrote CCEF a pessimistic summary of nouthetic counseling while commenting on a proposed new journal:

> If CCEF and Jay seriously want to influence and relate to the larger Christian Counseling Community, you will have to move from a stance of hostile elite isolation into a position of dialogue and discussion. The spirit of the symposium a year ago was a beginning but I fear a new journal will appear as competitive isolationism which characterized Jay's earlier writings. . . . What you call "distinctively Christian counseling" will perish shortly after Jay's passing if you do not develop a perspective which is broader than the thoughts of one scholar and which has some root in the Christian Counseling Community outside Westminster and CCEF.[76]

Bruce Narramore reported that he was willing to talk again with Bettler, but he did not care to interact with Adams. Larry Crabb, whose denunciations of nouthetic counseling had always exhibited the sharpest edge, wrote even more sharply against Adams and his fellows in years to come.[77] Henry Brandt, who had been the most favorable to Adams in the airport meeting a decade earlier, who had spoken at CCEF's inaugural conference in 1968 and at NANC in 1977, had little more to do with Adams and the nouthetic counseling movement.[78] The ever-diplomatic Gary Collins kept trying, in his own way, but the two only met briefly on one further occasion.

The intellectual and institutional rift had been ratified interpersonally. The evangelical psychotherapists, those committed to integrate their faith with psychology and psychotherapy, and the nouthetic counselors, those committed to find a counseling model from the Bible itself, ceased to communicate. Each movement's writing about the other largely consisted of polemics. The psychologists had convinced Adams that they were indeed false prophets who would persuasively twist Bible words to mean unbiblical things; Adams had convinced the psychologists that he was indeed too cantankerous and intransigent to be worth talking to. The 1980s would prove to be a decade of almost wholly autonomous development for both movements. Neither side had regrets, Bettler and Collins, perhaps excepted.

Nouthetic counseling had become a presence. Thousands of pastors found Adams persuasive. Other counseling professionals were taking notice and had been put on the defensive. By the late 1970s, the rudimentary institutional pieces were in place, intended to nourish a movement of pastors—and interested laypeople—who would enter the counseling field as competitors to the existing system, not subordinates within it. Intellectually, the corpus of writings, predominantly penned by the founder, rapidly grew.[79] Institutionally, Jay Adams and his first trainee and best friend, John Bettler, had pioneered the first generation of settings where biblical counseling was the modus operandi and agenda. Adams had deeply involved himself in four institutions meant to disseminate his vision for a counseling revolution: a theological seminary program, a counseling and training center, a professional association, and a professional journal. And Adams had significantly influenced the founders of several other institutions that would play significant roles in years to come: Bill Goode and Bob Smith's Faith Baptist Counseling Ministry and John Broger's Biblical Counseling

Foundation. Though differences of perspective existed—Adams's orientation to the generalist pastor in the local church, Bettler's to academia and specialized pastoral counseling, Broger's to laypeople—there was a high degree of harmony and cooperation. The boards of directors in the key institutions interlocked. The leaders knew one another well, trusted one another, and were unified by a common loyalty to Jay Adams who had introduced each of them to nouthetic counseling.

Most significantly, in Adams's mind:

> By making pastors fully aware of the property given to them in a clear deed from God, I have been trying to persuade pastors to so utilize and cultivate their own backyards that such encroachments from [psychology and psychiatry] would become unnecessary and, indeed, highly embarrassing to those who make them.
>
> This approach I believe is succeeding. The self-styled "professionals" (I say *self-styled* because I believe that the Bible teaches that God has called the pastor to be the professional counselor) have felt the impact of thousands of pastors who have themselves begun to take seriously the work to which God called them and for which they are well equipped by their knowledge of the Scriptures.[80]

The counseling revolution among conservative pastors seemed to be happening.

Chapter 3 Notes

1. This title is borrowed from Staley Lectures that Adams delivered at Cedarville College (Cedarville, Ohio) in January 1975. Jay E. Adams, *Lectures on Counseling* (Grand Rapids: Zondervan, 1975–77), 13–53.

2. Interview, December 4, 1990.

3. Adopted October 16, 1978.

4. Andrew Abbott, *The System of Professions: An Essay on the Division of Expert Labor* (Chicago: University of Chicago Press, 1988), 95.

5. *Competent to Counsel* was translated into about fifteen languages during the next decade. Records of translation of this and others of Adams's books are spotty: he typically negotiated rights and kept few records. Many of his books, including *CtC*, were translated into German, Spanish, Portuguese, Chinese, and Korean. In another dozen languages one or two books were translated, usually *CtC* and/or *The Christian Counselor's Manual*. The international aspect of the nouthetic counseling movement is beyond the scope of this book, but during the 1970s organized biblical counseling movements arose in Germany, South Africa, Great Britain, and Brazil.

6. *Competent to Counsel* has remained in print. It continued to sell five thousand to ten thousand copies per year during the first half of the 1990s.

7. Chapter 8 portrays both the commendation and criticism.

8. Gary Collins received both an MA (University of Toronto, 1958) and PhD (Purdue University, 1963) in psychology. He was one of the first psychologists to teach at an evangelical seminary. He was a prolific writer and served on the boards of the leading institutions of evangelical psychology.

9. Conversation with Gary Collins, March 11, 1995.

10. Gary R. Collins, *The Rebuilding of Psychology: An Integration of Psychology and Christianity* (Wheaton, Ill.: Tyndale House, 1977).

11. Bruce Narramore took his MA in psychology from Pepperdine University (1964) and his PhD in psychology from the University of Kentucky (1967). He subsequently took a master's in theology from Fuller Theological Seminary (1978). He wrote extensively, both academic pieces and self-help books.

12. John Carter held an MA and PhD from the New School for Social Research and a BD from Conservative Baptist Theological Seminary (Denver). His critiques of Adams included John Carter, "Nouthetic Counseling," in *Baker Encyclopedia of Psychology*, ed. David Benner (Grand Rapids: Baker Book House, 1985), 762–65; John D. Carter, "Adams' Theory of Nouthetic Counseling," *Journal of Psychology and Theology* 3, no. 3 (1975): 143–55; John D. Carter, "Nouthetic Counseling Defended: A Reply to Ganz," *Journal of Psychology and Theology* 4, no. 4 (1976): 206–16; John D. Carter, "Towards a Biblical Model of Counseling," *Journal of Psychology and Theology* 8, no. 1 (1980): 45–52; John D. Carter and Bruce Narramore, *The Integration of Psychology and Theology* (Grand Rapids: Zondervan, 1979).

13. John D. Carter and Bruce Narramore, *The Integration of Psychology and Theology* (Grand Rapids: Zondervan, 1979).

14. Bruce Narramore, "Perspectives on the Integration of Psychology and Theology," *Journal of Psychology and Theology* 1, no. 1 (1973): 3f.

15. Ibid., 3.

16. He held a PhD in child development from the University of Southern California.

17. James Dobson, *The New Dare to Discipline* (Wheaton, Ill.: Tyndale House, 1992), 16f.

18. By the 1990s, Focus on the Family had more than seven hundred employees, and Dobson's daily radio show aired on more than 1,800 radio stations.

19. Crabb held an MA and PhD in clinical psychology from the University of Illinois.

20. Interview with Jay Adams, December 4, 1990.

21. From questionnaire and interview with Howard Eyrich: October 2, 1990 (Lafayette, Ind.). Eyrich (b. 1939) was a Presbyterian minister who worked at the Christian Counseling and Educational Foundation (1974–76), founded counseling centers in Atlanta and Macon, Georgia (1976–81), was on the board of the National Association of Nouthetic Counselors for many years, serving as its director from 1983 to 1988, and taught at Covenant Theological Seminary (1985–92). After 1992 he taught at Trinity Theological Seminary.

22. From interview with Wayne Mack, February 21, 1993 (Los Angeles). Mack was a Conservative Baptist minister who received a DMin in counseling from Westminster Seminary in 1978. He founded a counseling center in Lake Charles, Louisiana (1976–78), worked at the Christian Counseling and Educational Foundation (1978–92), and taught at Westminster Theological Seminary (1978–87). After 1992 he was on the board of the National Association of Nouthetic Counselors and directed the Biblical Counseling Department at The Master's College in Newhall, California.

23. Bill Gothard, like Henry Brandt (who had been part of the "airport meeting" in 1969), was a popular layman teacher. Both addressed "counseling issues" for conservative Protestants, how to solve life's problems, with straightforward calls to biblical faith and obedience. Though neither directly influenced Adams's own development, they might well be considered forerunners of Adams. They were similarly biblicistic and helped prepare the ground in some sectors of conservative Protestantism. Both offered simpler, less-systematic models than Adams; neither was a pastor; both wrote only "practical" rather than theoretical and programmatic books; neither engaged in developing institutions or in a polemical contest for professional turf. Adams interacted with both of them after his model had taken shape.

24. Interview with Lloyd Jonas, October 20, 1990. Jonas was a Baptist minister and on the board of the National Association of Nouthetic Counselors for many years. He had founded church-based counseling and training centers in Loudonville, New York (1974–81) and Forestdale, Massachusetts (1981–95).

25. Gary R. Collins, ed., *Helping People Grow: Practical Approaches to Christian Counseling* (Santa Ana, Calif.: Vision House, 1980), 16.

26. Scipione had obtained an MDiv and ThM from Westminster and an MA in psychology from Temple University. In Scipione's self-assessment, he was "a Jay Adams clone." During 1974–82 he became an OPC pastor in Phillipsburg, New Jersey, and served on CCEF's board. In 1982 he founded CCEF West in San Diego and began teaching nouthetic counseling part time at Westminster Theological Seminary's new campus in Escondido, California. CCEF West became independent of CCEF in 1991, still under Scipione's directorship.

27. CCEF was chiefly affiliated with Westminster Theological Seminary, but a significant number of students from Biblical Theological Seminary (Hatfield, Pa.) also took CCEF courses during the 1970s and early 1980s. In 1984 Biblical Seminary would start its own degree program in biblical counseling, using CCEF faculty as adjunct instructors.

28. The largest mass of American conservative Protestants had roughly divided into "evangelicals" and "fundamentalists" during the 1940s and 1950s. The evangelical movement had been triggered by the formation of the National Association of Evangelicals in 1942. Bellwether evangelical institutions also included the Billy Graham Evangelistic Association, Fuller Theological Seminary, Wheaton College, and *Christianity Today*. The core theological beliefs of both groups were similar, but they differed markedly in their theological emphases and their sociocultural strategies. Evangelicals tended to value intellectual life and engagement with wider culture; they were more committed to dialogue and cooperation with other Christians. Fundamentalists tended to suspect the corruptions of modern intellectual life ("secular humanism") and to separate themselves both from other Christians and from the culture in the interests of maintaining purity. See the works of George Marsden for further discussion.

Theologically conservative Reformed and Lutheran Christians often stood somewhat apart from developments in the larger mass of conservative Protestants, though some (such as Adams) exhibited more fundamentalist tendencies while others (such as Bettler) tended more toward evangelical emphases. In the 1980s an increasing number of charismatic and Pentecostal Christians began to embrace Adams's approach to counseling, but in its first decade the nouthetic movement tended to oppose, not to include, members of those movements.

29. These lecture series were collected in Adams, *Lectures on Counseling*.

30. Jay E. Adams, *More Than Redemption: A Theology of Christian Counseling* (Phillipsburg, N.J.: Presbyterian & Reformed, 1979), 276.

31. In the early 1980s, before the genesis of this project, I talked with several evangelical psychotherapists who had been present while pursuing their graduate studies at Rosemead. I cannot remember the names of my interlocutors but remember vividly the hostility generated by Adams's idea that their graduate studies were both illegitimate and a waste of time.

32. Adams, *More Than Redemption,* 276.

33. Jay E. Adams, *The Christian Counselor's Manual* (USA: Presbyterian & Reformed, 1973), xi.

34. Ibid., 92.

35. Ibid., xiii.

36. Steve Viars, "Counseling in the Local Church—A Working Model," DMin, Westminster Theological Seminary (1988), 32f.

37. Interview with Robert Smith, October 3, 1990 (Lafayette, Ind.).

38. Adams genuinely enjoyed and respected fundamentalists. He separated from "liberals" in characteristically fundamentalist style, but he was an ecumenical force in bringing fundamentalists together with an otherwise disparate group of conservative Protestants. In contrast, John Bettler got along cordially with those to his left that he largely disagreed with but tended to be suspicious of separatist and anti-intellectual tendencies of those to his right. Adams and Bettler's differing social styles, their contrasting repugnancies and comfortabilities, were another one of many individual idiosyncrasies that mapped onto subsequent fault lines in the movement.

39. Jay Adams, plenary address, "Biblical Forgiveness," at annual conference of National Association of Nouthetic Counselors, Lafayette, Indiana, October 2, 1990.

40. Adams, *More Than Redemption,* 277.

41. In contrast with FBCM, CCEF, as a freestanding counseling and educational institution, remained largely dependent on counseling and educational fees. CCEF's counseling and education was expensive by comparison. And CCEF's close affiliation with seminary academics eventually generated questions about whether its approach to counseling had become overly intellectual, perhaps even compromising the basic nouthetic gospel by its willingness to interact with the psychologists. The issue of whether to charge for pastoral counseling became a tension point in the movement in the 1980s, as did the intellectual experimentation at CCEF. See chapter 9.

42. In 1980 Westminster further specialized its doctor of ministry program by creating a specialized pastoral counseling track that drew six to ten students a year. It was a year-long residency program, followed by seven hundred hours of supervised counseling and a DMin project.

43. A few years later Adams wrote up his objections to the kind of preparation seminarians received. Predictably, he wanted more hands-on, "practical" training. Jay E. Adams, "Design for a Theological Seminary," *Journal of Pastoral Practice* 3, no. 2 (1979): 1–10.

44. The information in this paragraph derived from interviews with Jay Adams, December 4–5, 1990.

45. *Bulletin of Westminster Theological Seminary* 14, no. 3 (Fall 1975), 3.

46. In 1982 Adams would return to seminary teaching. Ever the pastor's pastor, with counseling only a subset of his larger preoccupation, he became director of a DMin program in preaching at Westminster Theological Seminary West (Escondido, Calif.).

47. Adams, *Lectures on Counseling.*

48. Adams, *More Than Redemption.*

49. "Proposal for the Institute of Pastoral Studies," unpublished document prepared and presented by the Christian Counseling and Educational Foundation (1975), 2–3.

50. The last quoted phrases derive from an interview with George Scipione, October 6, 1991 (Lafayette, Ind.), as does the phrase "lay laity" in the next section.

51. Interview with George Scipione, October 6, 1991 (Lafayette, Ind.).

52. *Nouthetic Confrontation* (March 1975).

53. Adams, "Design for a Theological Seminary." Cf., John M. Frame, "Proposal for a New Seminary," *Journal of Pastoral Practice* 2, no. 1 (1978): 10–17.

54. Conversations with Bettler in the 1980s.

55. Broger had an engineering background. He had written the Navy's radar training manuals during World War II. After the war he founded the Far East Broadcasting Company, one of the first conservative Protestant radio ministries. From 1954 Broger worked as a consultant to the Joint Chiefs of Staff, and from 1960 to 1977 he worked as the director of Information for the Armed Forces. Information in this section comes from *Early Days of the Biblical Counseling Foundation: A Brief History* (Rancho Mirage, Calif.: Biblical

Counseling Foundation, 1993); John Broger, *Self-Confrontation: A Manual for In-Depth Discipleship* (Nashville: Thomas Nelson, 1994); and interview with Broger, February 26, 1993.

56. *Early Days of the Biblical Counseling Foundation: A Brief History* (Rancho Mirage, Calif.: Biblical Counseling Foundation, 1993), 1. This was a brief institutional history of BCF for publicity purposes.

57. Ibid., 2.

58. Jack Anderson and Les Whitten, "Military Radio Mismanagement Cited," *The Washington (D.C.) Post,* January 13, 1977.

59. In 1994 a major evangelical publisher brought it out: John Broger, *Self-Confrontation: A Manual for In-Depth Discipleship* (Nashville: Thomas Nelson, 1994). Meanwhile, it had been translated into half a dozen languages. In the 1990s BCF's weeklong training conferences each drew hundreds of people in the United States and in a number of other countries, especially India, Nigeria, Korea, and Hong Kong.

60. Adams warned of the dangers of "rigid and mechanical approaches" whereby people were "crammed into molds" in Jay E. Adams, *Insight & Creativity in Christian Counseling: An Antidote to Rigid and Mechanical Approaches* (Grand Rapids: Zondervan, 1982), ix.

61. In contrast, the professional organizations among evangelical psychotherapists served only fellowship purposes. Such practitioners pursued licensing and oversight with state boards and the bodies of the mental health professions, a fact that aroused Adams's ire. NANC's structure was intended to parallel licensing and oversight boards, not associations for professional fellowship.

62. Minutes of the board meeting of the Christian Counseling and Educational Foundation, September 19, 1974.

63. *Nouthetic Confrontation,* 1, no. 8 & no. 9: 6.

64. National Association of Nouthetic Counselors Constitution, October 16, 1978, p. 3.

65. National Association of Nouthetic Counselors Bylaws, adopted October 16, 1978, pp. 5–7.

66. Howard Eyrich, ed., *What to Do When* (Phillipsburg, N.J.: Presbyterian & Reformed, 1978).

67. Minutes of the annual meeting of the board of the Christian Counseling and Educational Foundation, October 18, 1978.

68. John Broger had even arranged the services of Pentagon lawyers on behalf of the fledgling NANC to ensure that its Constitution, Bylaws, Standards of Conduct, and Code of Ethics could stand up to potential legal challenges.

69. Jay E. Adams, editorial. *Journal of Pastoral Practice* 1, no. 1 (1977): 1.

70. Interview with Jay Adams, December 4, 1990.

71. Information for this section comes largely from a transcript of the proceedings; secondary sources include interviews with Adams, Bettler, and Narramore, and from my own notes and recollections. I was one of several students from Westminster Seminary who were invited to observe.

72. Brandt's counseling style was even brisker and more directive than Adams's. Brandt was a PhD psychologist who had become disillusioned with the supportive listener role and opted for bluntness instead. He had become a writer of popular books on marriage, family, and personal problems in the early 1960s.

He typically saw people a maximum of three or four times, confronting the typical client's focus on situational difficulties with a "kindly, firm pressure" to acknowledge personal failings and to resolve them by repentance, faith, and obedience to God.

73. Conversation with John Bettler, c. 1980. Bettler frequently voiced to his best friend, Adams, his objection to the way Adams treated opposing views. Bettler thought that Adams was unfair, creating and attacking caricatures. On one occasion Bettler put these concerns in print: John Bettler, "Biblical Counseling: The Next Generation," *Journal of Pastoral Practice* 8, no. 4 (1987): 3–10.

74. Over the next year a great deal of work went into transcribing and editing the proceedings, but the project was never finished.

75. Jay E. Adams, *What About Nouthetic Counseling?* (Grand Rapids: Baker, 1976), 45.

76. Correspondence, November 4, 1980.

77. The relationship between Crabb and Adams is difficult to categorize. They lined up on the same side of each major issue discussed at the Krisheim symposium. Crabb, too, believed that the Bible addressed all nonorganic problems in living and wanted to create a counseling model that emerged distinctively from the Bible. But other differences created a chasm between them. There was no doubt that when the debate with Narramore grew hot, Adams viewed only Brandt in the category of (now apparently erstwhile) ally. See chapter 8 for further discussion of Crabb's views.

78. This was not entirely personal. Brandt was aging and went into semiretirement. Brandt never had become institutionally involved in the movement that grew up around Adams. At the airport meeting, while he had been the most favorable, he had objected to Adams's polemicism and had questioned whether Adams had oversold nouthetic counseling's success and competency.

79. Adams's ideas and productivity overwhelmingly dominated the movement he started. The only books by other nouthetic authors during that time were workbooks: Wayne A. Mack, *How to Develop Deep Unity in the Marriage Relationship: A How To Manual for Christian Growth and Development* (USA: Presbyterian & Reformed, 1977a); Wayne A. Mack, *How to Pray Effectively: A How To Manual for Christian Growth and Development* (USA: Presbyterian & Reformed, 1977b); Wayne A. Mack, *How to Read the Bible: A How To Manual for Christian Growth and Development* (USA: Presbyterian & Reformed, 1977c); George C. Scipione, *Timothy, Titus, and You: A Workbook for Church Leaders* (Phillipsburg, N.J.: Pilgrim Publishing Co., 1975); Robert B. Somerville, *Help for Hotliners: A Manual for Christian Telephone Crisis Counselors* (USA: Presbyterian & Reformed, 1978). Even in 1995, Adams's books filled as many feet of shelf space as all other authors in the movement combined.

80. Adams, *What About Nouthetic Counseling?*, 45.

CHAPTER 4

Ground Taken: Adams's Clientele

Help us (with the help of God) to find out what is causing the problem.
I want to be told how I can deal with the problems I am having with my daughter.
— CCEF counselee, File #142

I accepted Christ as Savior eighteen months ago but recently have felt very separated and alone.
Help me learn how to obey God's will for me. I really need some biblical answers
to help me get back in touch with God again.
— CCEF counselee, File #184

By having my Christian ideals strengthened and educated,
I can overcome loneliness and boredom so I won't want to sniff glue.
— CCEF counselee, File #206

I didn't think God was loving, and I was afraid he would hurt me. But I came to one mind,
and God showed me tremendous love. I'm completely tired of secular input to my having multiple
personality disorder. I need to learn about hate, anger, jealousy, and forgiveness.
— CCEF counselee, File #406

Practice lies at the heart of professional life, and practice demands a clientele. Adams's anti-psychiatry is best understood not as animated by political or intellectual goals, as with Szasz, Foucault, and Goffman. It was instead animated by professional goals, a pastoral analogue to those behaviorists and reality therapists who partly inspired Adams. Just as Mowrer and Glasser bid for rights of practice with selected client groups—psychiatric patients and delinquent youths, respectively—so Adams bid for rights of practice with conservative Protestants.

The success of Adams's institutional program depended on catching the ear of conservative Prot-estants, both the "pastor in the trenches" and those church people experiencing difficulties in living. He had tailored his model of counseling practice to the intellectual loyalties, Bible education, and daily experience of conservative Protestant pastors, and to the religious beliefs common to both them and their parishioners. Many of those pastors sought training from Adams, so that in their own counseling ministries they might learn to interpret and treat problems in living in terms of his particular theological and moral framework. Many of them in the Philadelphia region, and beyond, also referred parishioners to Adams and CCEF, or even came themselves to seek counsel. This chapter will examine one segment of Adams's constituency: counselees at the Christian Counseling and Educational Foundation.

During the 1970s and 80s, presumably hundreds of thousands of people either sought help from nouthetic counselors or sought to help themselves utilizing some self-help booklet authored by Adams. The vast majority of counseling encounters were informal, for Adams's biblical counseling was intentionally counseling for the pastor's study, the church foyer, the telephone, or breakfast at a restaurant. Self-help activities are similarly unquantifiable, though publishing figures provide some indication of scope. For example, in the early to mid-1970s Adams wrote a series of pamphlets on basic life problems: hopelessness in the face of problems, self-discipline, anger, worry, fear, marital conflict, depression, addiction. Each sold between 200,000 and 400,000 copies, a total of more than 2.5 million copies.[1] The deprofessionalized, pastoral, and popular nature of nouthetic counseling meant that most of what took place was never documented. In the vast majority of cases, there was no need to seek third-party reimbursement or to satisfy medical or social service examiners; therefore, there was no repository of records. But documented counseling did take place at CCEF from 1968 on.

Who were CCEF's counselees? Who were these individuals, couples, and families who hoped that they might find a resolution to their personal and interpersonal ills through a form of counseling that claimed to operate in opposition to the prevailing psychotherapeutic and psychotropic ethos? How did they come to choose CCEF? What were their identified problems and expectations? Many of the answers to these questions confirmed intuitive expectations. Unsurprisingly, the religious outlook, practice, and affiliation of counselees largely fit conservative Protestant patterns. But there were surprises in the data too. For example, though conservative Protestants are evangelistic and though American religious affiliations are notoriously fluid, I was surprised at the percentage of counselees who had changed their religious affiliation. In addition, even the explicitness of Adams's antipsychiatric agenda and the predictable religious bias to the clientele did not prepare me to expect the degree to which CCEF existed in a counseling subculture discrete from and invisible to the surrounding mental health system. I also could not have predicted the dramatic changes that occurred in counselees' occupational and educational backgrounds during the twenty years studied.

Since beginning counseling practice in 1968, CCEF accumulated well more than ten thousand files, to which I was given access.[2] My purposes were chiefly demographic, to identify characteristics of the clientele. My total sample consisted of 602 cases, culled randomly. Each person who came to CCEF filled out an extensive questionnaire, the Personal Data Inventory (PDI).[3] This inventory elicited information about family and marital history; education and occupation; religious affiliation, beliefs, and practices; referral source; and medical conditions. It also asked the counselee to write out a description of the presenting problems, what he or she had previously sought to do about these problems, and expectations of counseling. These 602 case files represented a total of 879 individuals who each completed a PDI. My primary purpose in analyzing the counselee case records was to determine characteristics of the people who thought CCEF's nouthetic counseling might be what they needed to help resolve their personal problems.

I was not only interested in ascertaining the overall demographics of the CCEF client group but also in noting changes in the population over time. To this end, I selected my population from three time periods: c. 1970, c. 1980, and c. 1990. In this chapter I will discuss the client group as an aggregate and then disaggregate it into the three time periods for those categories where significant diachronic differences emerged.[4]

Before getting to the data, one further introductory observation is appropriate. Obviously, many general characteristics of this population cannot be considered typical of the recipients of nouthetic counseling in other places and other institutional settings. These were people who came to a particular counseling center in the northern suburbs of Philadelphia. That location had numerous socio-economic, ethnic, and ecclesiastical implications. For example, the composition of the client group differed markedly from that at other places even in the Philadelphia area where nouthetic counseling institutionalized: e.g., Christian Stronghold Baptist Church in the black community of west Philadelphia; Whosoever Gospel Mission, a "rescue mission" to addicted men in north Philadelphia; the Esperanza Health Center that served the Hispanic community in Kensington; and the numerous Korean churches in and around Philadelphia whose pastors had received their pastoral counseling training from CCEF teachers at Westminster Seminary. CCEF was located on the southern edge of Montgomery County, the wealthiest county in Pennsylvania, and only one mile from Chestnut Hill, one of the wealthiest neighborhoods in Philadelphia. As a freestanding counseling center, it offered fee-for-service counseling, unlike the institutions mentioned above and unlike the churches in which pastors and laycounselors trained at CCEF worked.[5] Also CCEF's association with Westminster Theological Seminary and its historical links with Presbyterians, who were strong in the mid-Atlantic region, shaped the clientele.[6] In sum, CCEF drew a clientele that was unusually Caucasian, unusually Presbyterian, and both willing and able to spend money for counseling. But though these factors affected the general demographic picture, CCEF's particular cli-

ent group still tells us a great deal about who was drawn to seek what Jay Adams and his fellows had to offer. Certain features clearly generalized to other locations.

This chapter will answer four questions regarding the client group. First, how were counselees referred to CCEF, and what was the geographical range from which they were drawn? The question of referral identifies the social network of counselees relevant to their choice to seek nouthetic counseling. The geographical range offers circumstantial evidence along the same lines. Both questions testify to the outworking of Jay Adams's sectarian strategy. Second, what was the religious orientation of CCEF's counselees? Many different indicators point to what I will term a conservative Protestant profile. Third, what general demographic features characterized these counselees? We will look at matters such as age, gender, educational level, and occupation. Fourth, why did they come and what did they want? Counselees came in various configurations—as individuals, married couples, or families—and typically identified the gamut of standard "problems in living," both interpersonal conflicts and personal troubles. Their stated expectations of the counseling usually included desires for practical advice with a religious orientation.

1. Lines of referral and geographical distribution

CCEF stood outside that modern social system whose lines of referral routinely link mental health professionals both to one another and to various other institutions: educational, medical, judicial, social service, business, and, frequently, ecclesiastical. It also stood outside any local church or denominational structure that might have directly channeled troubled or troublesome church members into counseling. Nonetheless, CCEF developed an informal referral network and drew clients from a wide geographical radius.

At the time CCEF was founded, almost no recognizable counseling services were organized within conservative Protestant churches, a vacuum that Adams—like the nascent movement of evangelical psychotherapists—hoped to fill. His overarching goal was to organize such services within local congregations. But one of CCEF's stated purposes was to provide a place where particularly difficult cases could be referred, as an auxiliary service to churches, mission agencies, and schools. This purpose, along with training and publication, formed Adams's rationalization for CCEF's existence as a freestanding counseling center whose counseling services were organized along the model of an outpatient clinic and professional training center, rather than like a church. Jay Adams's activities in each of three areas—writing, education, and counseling practice—built a wide reputation for CCEF among pastors and others and had the effect of generating a client and referral pool.

What lines of referral brought counselees to seek nouthetic counseling and to seek it specifically at CCEF? The PDI asked this question directly, and the data is summarized in table 1.

This pattern of referrals reveals the well-demarcated social network from which CCEF drew its counselee constituency. It also registers both the scope and the limitations of the kind of success that Adams achieved: this was a personal network, not an institutionalized professional and interprofessional network. Those routinized interconnections and inertias of the mental health system of referrals were not replicated or replaced. The data hints at the significance of Jay Adams's personal reputation—and, subsequently, the reputations of his successors—as the cause of referrals. People were not going to "see a psychiatrist" or to "see a counselor"; in a well-institutionalized network, such a social role or professional title is self-validating. CCEF's clients, on the other hand, were going to see someone whom they or someone they trusted knew by name. They were going to "see Jay Adams" or to "see a biblical counselor at CCEF." The data allows us to draw both a positive and a negative conclusion.

Positively, the overwhelming majority of counselees came to CCEF at the suggestion of either their pastor or someone else in an informal network of friends, relatives, and students. The significant institutional loci were local churches and families. One half of CCEF's counselees came at the specific recommendation of their pastor. The other leading sources of referral similarly located CCEF and its counselees in the conservative Protestant community: friends and relatives generated one quarter of the referrals; one-sixth more came from knowing either a CCEF staff member or student. Less than 10 percent of the clients came from CCEF-minded sources in educational, medical, judicial, or social service institutions.

TABLE 1

Referral Sources for CCEF Counselees
(n=473)[7]

Pastors and parachurch leaders[8] (n=236)	50%
Friends[9] (n=90)	19%
Know CCEF counselor personally[10] (n=49)	10%
CCEF students[11] (n=34)	7%
Relatives (n=30)	6%
Christian school[12] (n=12)	3%
Medical doctors (n=9)	2%
Evangelical mental health professionals (n=5)	1%
Social services[13] (n=3)	1%
Telephone book and radio ads (n=3)	1%
Court referral[14] (n=2)	—

Negatively, the isolation of CCEF from the mental health establishment is equally demonstrated by these figures. Not a single referral came from secular mental health professionals.[15] The only two court-referred cases came to CCEF at the client's initiative. Only 1 percent of the referrals came from evangelical mental health professionals. These five cases of atypical referral—from two psychologists, one psychiatrist, one college psychology professor, and one Mennonite-run psychiatric hospital—are the rare exceptions that prove the rule. CCEF was invisible to and incommunicado with the mental health system.

The PDI also yielded one other piece of information that indirectly indicated how CCEF drew counselees based on personal relationships, word-of-mouth, and reputation, rather than by embedment in a local institutional system. A significant number of counselees drove an hour or more—or even flew in from out of state. CCEF's location in the suburbs north and slightly west of Philadelphia sits almost dead center in the geographical area termed southeastern Pennsylvania. That area, comprising Philadelphia, Bucks, Montgomery, Delaware, and Chester Counties, is served by the postal codes 189xx, 190xx, 191xx, 193xx, and 194xx. Counselees from adjoining postal codes (as well as those on the western end of 189xx, 193xx, and 194xx) would have had to drive close to an hour, or longer, to get to CCEF. Table 2 indicates the geographical distribution of the client population.

This data shows that CCEF did not function only as a local or even a regional counseling center. It became a Mecca, of sorts, for conservative Protestants struggling with life problems. Only half the clients, those from Philadelphia and eastern Montgomery County (190xx and 191xx), lived locally, within a half-hour drive. Another quarter drove between thirty minutes and an hour. And fully one-quarter of CCEF's constituents came

TABLE 2

Postal Codes of CCEF Counselees
(n=584)

Southeastern Pennsylvania (n=430)	74%
190xx and 191xx (n=295; 51%)	
189xx, 193xx, and 194xx (n=135; 23%)	
New Jersey (n=78)	13%
Central and Northeastern Pennsylvania (n=42)	7%
Delaware (n=13)	2%
New York and Maryland (n=10)	2%
Remote (n=11)[16]	2%

from outside the region to seek out Adams's distinctive form of counseling.

In sum, CCEF occupied a highly insulated niche of professional practice, one whose lines of referral were distinctively personal, ecclesiastical, and wide-reaching. Counselees or their acquaintances knew of CCEF by name. Adams's "grassroots revolution" to call conservative Protestants to counsel their own in a manner consistent with their conservative Protestant beliefs won adherents. Winning adherents, it captured, or created, a clientele.[17]

2. Religious orientation

The most obvious factor distinguishing this counselee population was its particular religious orientation. A major section of the PDI explored the religious life of CCEF clients from a variety of perspectives. The vast majority fit a profile of conservative Protestant characteristics.

One series of questions explored religious beliefs at the level of general religiosity and theism. Only 2 of 858 respondents wrote that they did not believe in God. Sixteen stated that they were uncertain of God's existence, and most of these indicated that religious doubts were part of the reason they sought counseling. Thus 98 percent claimed to believe in God, and most of the rest were troubled over the matter. While such questions cannot uncover dissembling to please presumed expectations of counselor, parents, or other parties, it is at least clear that CCEF's religious perspective did not overtly impose on the stated beliefs of most counselees.

The question *Are you saved? (Yes__ No__ Unsure__Not sure what you mean__)* utilized distinctively conservative Protestant jargon whose meaning would be significant among those who stressed individual conversion and a "personal relationship" with the Christ who died to "save" sinners from the wrath of God. It further revealed the contours of a client's belief system, as well as eliciting estrangement from, doubts about, or ignorance of evangelical distinctives. Eighty-six percent believed that they were "saved." The remaining answers were scattered evenly: 4 percent said No; 5 percent answered Unsure; 5 percent were uncertain what the question meant. For most of CCEF's clientele, the conservative Protestant[18] outlook would sit comfortably. And in one out of seven cases, the answer to this question revealed something nouthetic counselors would take very seriously: either conscious estrangement from Christ's gospel, religious doubts, or ignorance, any of which might give the counseling an evangelistic thrust.

Another series of questions probed religious behavior. *How often do you read the Bible?* and *How often do you pray?* invited a concrete description of those private religious practices traditionally so important to "Bible-believing" Protestants. Most of these counselees prayed: 81 percent said that they prayed often; 17 percent offered occasional prayer; 2 percent never prayed. Counselees listened somewhat less frequently than they talked: 61 percent claimed to read the Bible often;

32 percent read it occasionally; 7 percent said never. They would encounter a counseling model that made prayer and the Bible central to problem solving:

As one regular homework assignment, the counselee may be told to set up regular family (or personal) devotions. I have prepared a devotional workbook for counselees, entitled *Four Weeks with God and Your Neighbor* . . . [that] focuses on prayer, Bible study, and the practical application of the Scriptures to life. . . . From the start, counselees should be taught their dependence upon God for the changes desired. It is the Word and the power of His Spirit that brings these changes, not the counselor (or the counselee). . . .

At times, too, the counselee will be *invited* (no strong pressures should be exerted; some counselees, however, require, and indeed appreciate, gentle, well-timed pressure) to pray in a particular counseling session.[19]

The religious element in Adams's counseling practices would not seem alien to most of this counselee population, given the typical behaviors by which conservative Protestants defined their "relationship" to God.

Other questions probed corporate religious practices: 78 percent of the counselees attended church regularly, with half of these attending two or more services each week. In fact, 23 percent of CCEF's clientele claimed to attend church ten or more times per month. On the other end of the spectrum, 8 percent were sporadic attenders (once or twice a month), and 14 percent did not currently attend church at all. The questions *Member?* and *Baptized?* probed formal alliance with a local church with its authority structure and sacrament of entry. Counselees attended more often than joined: 60 percent were members; 17 percent said that they were not members; 23 percent left the question blank (and, presumably, most of these were not members). Adams believed so strongly in church membership that he treated persons not affiliated with local churches as functionally non-Christian, whatever their professed personal beliefs.[20] His counseling placed a high value on the community activities characteristic of conservative Protestant piety, and one of the invariable goals of his counseling was to get counselees involved in church membership and activities.

A third series of questions probed current and childhood ecclesiastical affiliation and revealed whether significant shifts of allegiance had occurred: 95 percent of CCEF's clientele identified a denominational preference for some species of Christian church. As table 3 indicates, counselees' preferred church affiliations came largely from the numerous conservative Protestant denominations and associations of independent congregations. Almost four-fifths of CCEF's clientele came from conservative Protestant denominations. There were exceptions, but this was an audience that on the surface of things might be presumed to listen to appeals to the Bible.

A comparison between childhood religion and current religious affiliation brought out several further aspects of the religious orientation of this clientele. Three-quarters of the sample had switched their religious affiliation at some point in their lives. Approximately one-third of the counselees were converts to evangelical religion from some other religious type. They were currently conservative Protestants but had been raised Roman Catholic, mainline Protestant, or a-religious.

For example, twenty-six of twenty-eight current Roman Catholics who sought CCEF counseling had been raised Roman Catholic. None had converted to Roman Catholicism from conservative Protestantism; one had been raised mainline Protestant, and one had no religious upbringing.[37]

TABLE 3

Religious Affiliation of CCEF Counselees
(n=855)

Conservative baptistic churches (n=360)	42%
Fundamentalist[21] (n=185; 22%)	
Unspecified Baptist[22] (n=112; 13%)	
Reformed or Conservative Baptist (n=34; 4%)	
Other conservative, baptistic churches (n=29; 3%)[23]	
Conservative paedobaptistic churches (n=179)	21%
Conservative Presbyterian denominations[24] (n=131; 15%)	
Unspecified Presbyterian[25] (n=31; 4%)	
Other Reformed paedobaptist churches[26] (n=17; 2%)	
Other evangelical churches (n=101)	12%
Unspecified evangelical[27] (n=54; 6%)	
Mennonite and Moravian (n=23; 3%)	
Calvary Chapel[28] (n=17; 2%)	
Evangelical Free Church (n=7; 1%)	
Charismatic and Pentecostal churches (n=36)	4%
Assemblies of God (n=17; 2%)	
Unspecified Pentecostal (n=13; 2%)	
Unspecified charismatic[29] (n=6; 1/2%)	
Mainline churches[30] (n=104)	12%
United Presbyterian (n=25; 3%)[31]	
United Methodist (n=22; 3%)	
Episcopalian (n=19; 2%)	
Lutheran[32] (n=15; 2%)	
United Church of Christ (n=5; 1/2%)	
Generic mainline, Protestant, or Christian (n=18, 2%)[33]	
Roman Catholic Church[34] (n=30)	4%
Other responses (n=45)	5%
None[35] (n=34; 4%)	
Undecided, not sure, no preference[36] (n=6; 1/2%)	
Specific non-Christian beliefs (n=5; 1/2%)	
Unitarian (n=2)	
Jewish (n=1)	
Agnostic (n=1)	
Atheist (n=1)	

But 115 counselees had been raised Roman Catholic and no longer identified themselves as such. Of these former Roman Catholics, eighty-six were converts to some conservative Protestant ecclesiastical group; fifteen answered "None" for current religion; and fourteen had become mainline Protestants (six of these showed conservative

Protestant characteristics on other questions). Thus, more than 10 percent of CCEF's counselees were converts from Roman Catholicism to evangelical religion; none had converted the other way.

CCEF counselees raised in mainline Protestant denominations exhibited the same pattern, only slightly less marked. Of ninety-four current mainline Protestants who sought CCEF counseling,[38] sixty-three had grown up in their own denomination or had moved from other mainline churches, fourteen had been raised Catholic, eleven had been nonspecifically Baptist, two had had no religious upbringing, and one had been a Christian Scientist.[39] Three mainline Protestants had become such by shifting their allegiance from an evangelical denomination. But of 125 former mainline Protestants who sought counseling, 120 had reaffiliated with a conservative Protestant church, one had become a Catholic, and four professed no religion. This was a population with many converts, and the tide had flowed largely in one direction. Over 15 percent of CCEF's adult counselees had been raised in mainline churches but had subsequently become evangelicals.

The twenty-nine counselees who listed "None" under current religious commitment included fifteen from Roman Catholic backgrounds, four former mainline Protestants, four nonspecific Presbyterians, three nonspecific Baptists, and three with no religious upbringing. But of those twenty-six counselees listing "None" under childhood religion, twenty-four had become conservative Protestants (eleven fundamentalists, and a scattering of others), one had become Roman Catholic, and one a Lutheran. None of CCEF's religiously disaffected clients were identifiably former evangelicals; almost all who had been raised a-religious had become evangelical.[40]

The fluidity of religious affiliations is a feature of life in modern America that has been frequently noticed by sociologists. CCEF's clientele proved to be no exception to that observation: only one-quarter of the adults were involved in the same religious group in which they had been raised. The pattern in their shifts of allegiance meant that Adams was most often addressing people like himself, converts to a worldview they held in common.

Who then were CCEF's counselees? About four-fifths are easily identifiable as fitting a conservative Protestant type. Even members of largely liberal, mainline Protestant churches (12 percent of the sample) fit a conservative Protestant profile of theological commitment and religious practice almost half the time—unsurprising, since they and those who referred them chose CCEF-style counseling. A number made a point to mention their participation in "biblical witness," "good news," or "renewal" movements within their generally more liberal denominations. Their statements of belief and patterns of practice were frequently indistinguishable from counselees in nominally more conservative denominations. An Episcopalian who wrote, "Assure me of a Scriptural approach to my problem," and a Methodist who wrote, "I have been more committed and submitted to Christ in the past year," did not sound like liberal Protestants but like Jay Adams. Even a significant percentage of Roman Catholics arrived in CCEF offices having written such conservative Protestant statements as, "I asked Jesus into my heart and have a personal relationship with him," or "I was saved last Saturday," or, somewhat more cryptically, "I've joined a group at a Presbyterian church and it has brought a big change in my life." Though a certain imprecision in both data and categories is inevitable, matters are clear enough in the broad strokes to reveal that about 85 percent of CCEF's counselees fit a conservative Protestant profile.

The other end of the spectrum was just as easy to identify as not fitting in with conservative

Protestantism. The other 15 percent of the client pool was evenly divided among liberal members of mainline Protestant denominations, traditional Roman Catholics, and unchurched persons.[41] This last segment of the population, 5 percent of the counselees, stood distinctly outside any Christian affiliation, belief, and practice. They usually wrote "None" regarding religious commitment, a statement reinforced by no church attendance or Bible reading. A handful identified themselves with a particular non-Christian belief system, as Unitarian, Jewish, atheist, or agnostic. Typically such counselees were referred to CCEF by friends and family rather than by a pastor. Their orientation indicated that they were evident misfits—or, rather, candidates for conversion—to the counseling system offered by biblical counselors.

The religious orientation of the typical CCEF counselee confirms intuitive expectations. These were counselees whose religious concerns often provided the interpretive framework they themselves already overlaid upon the problems that drove them to seek counsel. Jay Adams offered a counseling system that interpreted problems in living as fundamentally and precisely religious; the vast majority of his counselees already had tendencies to think the same way.

3. General characteristics of the client population

The PDI provided a great deal of general background information about the counselee population. I analyzed the following factors: age, gender, education, and occupation. We will examine these in turn. Some of the information is simply of general interest; other items shed light on the thesis that drives this project and on changes that occurred at CCEF over the years.

CCEF's counselees ranged in age from seven to eighty years old. The vast majority were young

and middle-aged adults, sometimes with their children. Very few of those who sought counsel were elderly.[42] Children and youths made up 10 percent of those counseled; 58 percent of the counselees were between the ages of twenty and thirty-nine, and 29 percent were between forty and fifty-nine. Table 4 portrays the age distribution.

TABLE 4

Age of CCEF Counselees
(n=873)

7–19 (n=86)	10%
20–29 (n=232)	26%
30–39 (n=280)	32%
40–49 (n=164)	19%
50–59 (n=86)	10%
60–69 (n=20)	2%
over 70 (n=5)	1%

Females outnumbered males by a slight margin (54 percent female; 46 percent male). Among children, males predominated, as parents typically sought help either for school difficulties among preteens or for behavior problems among teens. In all other age groups females outnumbered males. There were no significant variations over time. See table 5.

The ethnic background of counselees was not recorded. From interviews with CCEF staff—all of whom have been Caucasian—it is clear that their clientele was also overwhelmingly Caucasian. They estimated that perhaps 2 to 3 percent of the counselees were black, 1 percent Asian, and almost none were Hispanic. Though several large black communities (Cheltenham, Mt. Airy, North Hills, Crestmont) and a rapidly growing Korean community (West Oak Lane) were within ten

TABLE 5

Proportions of Females and Males
(n=873)

Age	Female	Male
7–19	43% (n=37)	57% (n=49)
20–29	58% (n=135)	42% (n=97)
30–39	52% (n=145)	48% (n=135)
40–49	54% (n=88)	46% (n=76)
50–59	58% (n=50)	42% (n=36)
60+	52% (n=13)	48% (n=12)
Total	54% (n=468)	46% (n=405)

TABLE 6

Educational Levels
(n=748)[43]

Less than a bachelor's degree (n=482)	64%
Less than high school (n=77; 10%)	
Completed high school (n=197; 26%)	
Less than college degree (n=208; 28%)[44]	
At least a bachelor's degree (n=266)	36%
Bachelor's (n=191; 26%)[45]	
Advanced degree (n=75; 10%)[46]	

minutes drive of CCEF, they contributed little to the counseling caseload. A number of factors might be speculated regarding relative absence of people of color among the CCEF clientele: the fee for counseling was an economic disincentive; different social habits regarding seeking as well as paying for counseling services; the provision of pastoral counseling by pastors in local ethnic churches (many of whom received CCEF training); the uniformly Caucasian racial composition of CCEF's counseling staff; the institution's location in a mansion in an upper middle-class neighborhood relatively inaccessible to public transportation. CCEF's courses, on the other hand, drew much more widely from pastors, pastors-to-be, and layworkers from black, Asian, and Hispanic churches. Asians, in particular, were heavily represented at Westminster Seminary.

Analysis of the educational background of counselees (tables 6, 7, 8) demonstrates that on the whole they were a fairly well-educated group, and that the educational level rose markedly over time. Educational levels changed dramatically over the twenty years, and the change greatly accelerated in the 1980s. The percentage of those with

a high-school education or less dropped from 41 percent to 23 percent. College graduates doubled from 26 percent to 53 percent, while counselees holding graduate degrees rose from 5 percent to 21 percent.

Differences emerged in educational levels between men and women, both overall and over time. On the whole, men averaged about a year more education than women. And quite striking changes occurred between 1970 and 1990, especially for men. The proportion of male college graduates rose from 30 percent to 67 percent over twenty years. By 1990, only 1 percent of CCEF's adult male counselees had failed to complete high school (down from 14 percent and 13 percent in the earlier cohorts). The number of male counselees with graduate degrees evidenced a particularly striking increase: in 1970, 10 percent of the men held an advanced degree; by 1990 fully 40 percent of the men had advanced degrees. The pattern with women was not as dramatic, but the same trend was evident. The percentage of college graduates rose from 25 percent to 48 percent. The percentage of those who had not completed high school fell from 12 percent in 1970 and 1980 to 4 percent in 1990. By 1990 8 percent of the women held graduate degrees, up from 2 percent twenty years earlier. In effect, CCEF increasingly became a counseling center for the educated.

Occupational backgrounds were consistent with educational levels. Occupations also consistently expressed traditional differences between women and men's occupational roles. I have broken the data down into an analysis between women and men's occupations.

The women generally filled traditional women's roles. Almost one half of the adult women defined their work life in terms of homemaking. When they entered the paid workforce, they worked in traditionally female jobs, as subordinates in business and medicine, or as teachers. One in five did office work in a support job (secretary, clerk, receptionist, bookkeeper). Subordinate medical personnel (nurse, medical technician, dental assistant), schoolteachers, and other providers of social services comprised another 13 percent of the population. Very few of CCEF's female clients worked as unskilled laborers. Housewives tended to be less educated (average education=12.8 years) than non-housewives (average education=14.4 years).

Men's jobs equally fit traditional cultural patterns of men's work, with a skewing toward religious professionals. Over one in four worked in skilled or semi-skilled labor (e.g., mechanic, building trades, technician, programmer, foreman, driver). One in five was a businessman, filling a role that could be described as managerial (administrator, supervisor, owner) or as autonomous (e.g., salesman, broker), rather than subordinate. Eight percent were adult students (a significant number of these in seminary). That one in fourteen men seeking help proved to be a religious professional (not counting seminarians) is perhaps not surprising, given the pastoral audience that Jay Adams sought to address and CCEF's affiliation with Westminster Seminary.

Large changes in occupational patterns occurred between 1970 and 1990 for both women and men. Women moved from the home into the workforce. Women identifying their occupation in terms of

TABLE 7
Occupations

Women's Occupations (n=410)[47]

Homemaker/housewife (n=189)	46%
Office subordinates (n=83)	20%
Teachers & social services (n=29)[48]	7%
Medical subordinates (n=24)[49]	6%
Unskilled labor (n=18)[50]	4%
Business (n=14)	3%
Students in college or graduate school (n=10)	2%
Other skilled & semiskilled labor (n=9)[51]	2%
Secular professions (n=5)[52]	1%
Religious professions (n=5)[53]	1%
Not working (n=24)[54] (unemployed, disabled, retired)	6%

Men's Occupations (n=365)

Skilled & semiskilled labor (n=104)[55]	28%
Business (n=70)[56]	19%
Unskilled labor (n=33)[57]	9%
Students in college or graduate school (n=30)	8%
Religious professionals (n=25)[58]	7%
Engineers (n=20)	5%
Secular professionals (n=18)[59]	5%
Office subordinates (n=17)[60]	5%
Teachers & social services (n=13)	4%
Public service (n=7) (fire, police, military)	2%
Media (n=6) (producer, editor, broadcaster, reporter)	2%
Not working (n=22)[61] (unemployed, disabled, retired)	6%

wife and home—"housewife" or "homemaker"—constituted 58 percent of the adult women in 1970. This dropped to 43 percent by 1980, and by 1990, though still the largest category, it further dropped to 29 percent.[62]

In the pattern of men's occupations, there was an equally dramatic shift from blue-collar to white-collar work. I categorized men's occupations roughly into people who accomplished a task with their hands and people who accomplished something through manipulating and communicating knowledge. In the former category I included unskilled, semiskilled, and skilled workers, office subordinates, and public services. In the latter category I included workers in business, religious and secular professions, education, engineering, and the mass media. In 1970 the percentage of hand workers to knowledge workers was 61 to 39; in 1980 it was 48 to 52; by 1990 it was 29 to 71. This, of course, accords with the changes in educational level discussed previously and with larger demographic shifts in modern American culture. It also accords with the increases in CCEF's counseling fees during the decade—from fourteen dollars to fifty dollars per session. CCEF served an increasingly educated clientele of white-collar males and working women.

4. Stated problems in living and expectations of solutions

No one was ever remanded to counseling at CCEF; they chose to come.[63] The reasons for that choice were accessible from several directions. We will look first at the particular social configuration of each case and then at the answers to questions that elicited clients' definitions of their problems and expectations: *What is your problem?* and *What do you want us to do about it?*

I analyzed each case in terms of its "constellation," i.e., the social configuration of the person or

persons who sought counsel: individual, married or premarried couple, family. I also identified the marital and family status of each individual person who sought counseling. This clientele divided in half between those seeking counseling as individuals and those pairs or trios seeking to solve marriage and family problems. Single adults constituted 29 percent of the sample.

TABLE 8

Constellation of CCEF Cases
(n=602)

Individuals (n=308)	51%
Married (n=132; 22%)[64]	
Never married (n=123; 20%)	
Separated (n=25; 4%)	
Divorced (n=22; 4%)	
Widowed (n=6; 1%)	
Marital or familial groups (n=294)	49%
Marital (n=177; 29%)	
Family (n=108; 18%)[65]	
Premarital (n=9; 2%)[66]	

The client constellation revealed some significant variation over the years. The percentage of family cases stayed relatively steady, but the number of cases with a marital configuration dropped in half, from 38 percent in 1970 to 20 percent in 1990. Correspondingly, the number of individuals seeking counseling for themselves increased from 44 percent to 60 percent over the twenty years. We noted earlier how Adams's own counseling was nearly a public affair, with a crowd of counselees, counselors, and trainees present. In 1970 cases averaged 1.8 counselees present. But by 1980 this had dropped to 1.4; by 1990 it had dropped to 1.2. On average, then, a third fewer clients were present in the room; put more starkly, the average case involved one person not two.

How did counselees perceive and define their need? CCEF's counselees came with the gamut of garden variety "problems in living." They bickered with their spouse, got upset about their children, were financially irresponsible, struggled with anxiety, felt guilty over the use of pornography, felt hopeless about their likelihood of finding a spouse. Their varied answers to the question *What is your problem?* as much as restate commonsense definitions of problems in living. That variety of answers—and the fact that CCEF forswore Diagnostic and Statistical Manual codes as a matter of principle—makes quantification impossible. But several generalizations are possible.

Those counselees who came in groups—marital, familial, premarital—brought the most predictable problems. While not quantifiable, unmistakable patterns emerged. Counselees' expectations of counseling significantly registered the way they viewed their problems and the means of resolving them. The half of the clientele that came in groups tended to define its problems and desires for aid in social and pragmatic terms: "Give us advice on how to quit arguing and improve our marital communication so that our marriage can honor God." or "Help us deal the right way with our rebellious teenager." These were people whose agenda included things Jay Adams's directive counseling was designed to provide. They wanted practical advice about changes they could implement, advice consonant with their religious values.

The married people almost invariably sought help for a breakdown in their relationship: either interpersonal conflict (the majority of cases; see Appendix 1: "An Annotated Case Study of Adams's Model") or the aftermath of infidelity. In either case, issues of reconciliation and communication predominated:

- "My adultery and masturbation has caused us great problems, along with noncommunication. Explain why I can't express myself. Show us things we can't see about our lives which will help us do better together."

- "I've been cold and unreceptive. Evaluate if our marriage is salvageable."
- "My wife is critical and resentful. Help my wife forgive me and quit bringing my sins up."
- "Our arguments have been increasing in intensity and frequency. Help us see the root of our problems and find a biblical approach. There must be root attitudes that we need to find, examine, and change."
- "Marital breakdown. Tell me whether I want the wrong things out of life."

The issues in premarital counseling were also predictable. Couples wanted either to prepare for marriage and prevent future problems, to solve a communication problem, or to deal with the turmoil caused by their relationship becoming sexualized. Several nouthetic counselors wrote premarital counseling books that structured such counseling.[67] Families similarly sought help for a narrow band of problems: family conflicts or the difficulties their children were having in school. A stubborn child typically occasioned counseling; the course of counseling might eventually address a domineering or neglectful parent as well:

- "My oldest son is fighting with his brothers and is rebellious at times. We want guidelines for family behavior. We need better relationships as a family with boys, and help to build those."
- "Our daughter is having problems in school, struggles with depression, and made a suicide attempt. She's also been in rebellion against her parents. I don't know what you can do to help."

Counselees might not know what could be done to help, but Adams came to such cases with a standard repertoire of tools to work on communication and reconciliation (a "family conference table") and to define family responsibilities along with the consequences for success or failure (a "code of conduct").[68]

Individual counselees, whether married or single, brought the greatest variety of problems into CCEF offices. The problems can be divided into four rough categories: relational problems, religious problems, moderate personal problems, severe personal problems. We will look briefly at each of the kinds of problems that counselees believed they suffered from.

A significant number of those individuals who sought counseling explicitly defined their problems in interpersonal terms. Many of those who had never been married came for help coping with disappointment, loneliness, sexual incontinence, or anger that arose in the context of their desire to be married. Conservative Protestants were a client group that greatly valued marriage and whose ideal of singleness entailed celibacy, and single adults often sought counsel for the "sin and misery" that appeared in the light of those ideals. Many of those married persons who sought counseling individually came in order to discuss their marital difficulties. For many of the formerly married, their separation, divorce, or widowhood occasioned the dysphorias that prompted seeking nouthetic counseling.[69]

In the process of counseling Adams would turn all problems in living into fundamentally religious problems, but even prior to that process some clients presented themselves with narrowly "religious" problems: doubts about their relationship with God, fears of going to hell, difficulties with prayer or Bible reading, conflicts with their church:

- "My faith is confused. I've been frustrated and rebellious. I had grown in faith in college but recently have been assailed with doubts and arguments against Christianity. I've read books on knowing what you believe. Answer my questions, help me get straightened out, to figure out why I doubt and how to stop."

- "I'm troubled about my Christian life, where I fail too often: spiritual disciplines, overeating, doubt my faith. Memories of the past plague me. Help me understand myself and the way I act."

Such clients had done some of the nouthetic counselors' diagnostic work ahead of time.

Many CCEF clients identified themselves as suffering personal problems, either moderate or severe. They typically defined these in behavioral, emotional, or attitudinal terms and frequently stated or implied some moral evaluation of themselves:

- "I've been willful toward authority, not submissive. Help me discover my personal problems so I can change."

- "I got messed up on drugs and 'New Morality' and I'm getting back on my feet now. I still struggle with temptations to use drugs and alcohol. Help me set life goals to be a productive person. Listen and give me advice."

- "I've been unable to hold jobs or stay committed. I've been deceitful, lazy, and done petty theft. I've had pride in seeking status, popularity, and money. Show me my errors through Scripture and bring me to repentance of sinful patterns; help me see how and where I have gone wrong and counsel me for the future."

- "I'm struggling with homosexual tendencies. Give me practical suggestions on how my life can be reordered away from homosexuality and reliant on the Holy Spirit. Help me gain a better idea of what my future will be like (e.g., satisfied as single unmarried)."

- "I can't adjust to this world; I'm an impatient, selfish, miserable person."

- "Compulsive eating; guilt, especially false guilt; fear; pride; legalistic view of God. Give me a detailed analysis of trouble spots and solutions to attempt. Help pinpoint problems and sin beneath this food pattern, along with solutions to deal with it realistically."

- "I think the worst of people and fear people will hurt me. Give me counsel and guidance and understanding. I want to learn how to handle my problems with God's help."
- "I get extreme anxiety reactions during PMS. I feel inadequate and tend to be a perfectionist. Help me know I am loved and have friends. I spoke with my minister, but I need something more practical. Help me find methods to deal with my feelings."

Like other moral models, Adams's diagnostic categories mapped easily onto such concrete descriptions of troubles in living.

A significant number of CCEF's counselees had experienced problems severe enough to give them experience in the mental health system. The PDI inquired after previous experiences of counseling and psychiatric care, as well as use of psychotropic medications. Adams had prominently featured instances of extreme bizarre behavior in his *Competent to Counsel*, dramatically offering hope that even the most troubled people could change under nouthetic counseling. Families, pastors, and churches—and troubled people themselves—reached for what he promised. Particularly in the early 1970s, CCEF drew a significant number of such counselees. In c. 1970, 25 percent of the cases revealed a history of severe problems and extensive involvement with the mental health system: years of psychotherapy, multiple therapists, longtime use of psychotropic medications. Over half of these cases (14 percent of the total population) cited one or more previous major breakdowns that had led to psychiatric hospitalization, a suicide attempt, or both. Given that CCEF was an ambulatory, suburban counseling center located in an Orthodox Presbyterian Church, presumably such cases would not have normally walked through

the door. But CCEF's founder elicited a clientele through his writing and teaching.[70] The labels schizophrenia, manic-depression, multiple personality disorder, or clinical depression occasionally appear in the case record. But even these psychiatrically experienced clients rarely employed psychiatric labels in their self-description of troubles that they or others found crippling, dangerous, or bizarre. Like other counselees, they spoke about how they felt and acted, about their disappointments and their interpersonal conflicts, about their hopes to feel better, to act better, to relate better, to change circumstances, to find religiously toned help. In subsequent years, the percentages of CCEF counselees with long psychiatric histories dropped markedly. By c. 1980, only 10 percent had experienced some long-term involvement in the mental health system (8 percent had been hospitalized or attempted suicide). By c. 1990, these percentages had dropped further: 8 percent had extensive mental health involvement (3 percent included a suicide attempt or hospitalization).[71]

Over 40 percent of CCEF's clientele (including those discussed above) had some previous experience with modern mental health practices, having come under either psychiatric or psychotherapeutic care. Almost half of CCEF's counselees had never before sought formal counseling.

TABLE 9

Previous Counseling Experience
(n=557)

First-time seekers of counseling (n=259)	46%
Previous counseling or psychiatry (n=298)	54%
Previous nouthetic counseling (n=13; 2%)	
Pastor only (n=27; 5%)[72]	
Both pastor and psychotherapy (n=16; 3%)	
Evangelical psychotherapy (n=15; 3%)	
Secular psychotherapy or psychiatry (n=188; 34%)	
Details missing or obscure (n=39; 7%)	

There was some variation over time in counseling experience. In 1970, 58 percent of the cases contained a record of previous formal counseling, but by 1990 that percentage had dropped to 41 percent. I suspect that this change registers the successful institutionalization of nouthetic counseling within the conservative Protestant community: it became the court of first resort for a growing constituency. Most of the case records were silent regarding how counselees viewed their previous counseling experiences. A few put into print sentiments that made them ideal candidates for Adams's counseling:

- "It helped a little, but didn't really change anything; we talked about my problems but not how God could help me solve my problems."
- "I didn't like the counseling leaving God out; he was not a Christian and couldn't relate to me."
- "I terminated therapy after a year and a half because I got frustrated; I got descriptive insight but no answers because the Bible was not used."
- "It was nonbelieving advice."

But others were more sanguine about their experiences of psychotherapies that Adams attacked in his books:

- "It helped me see things, and I learned a lot about myself."
- "Very helpful."
- "I felt a lot better about things."
- "Greater self-acceptance and direction by internal motivation rather than other people."

At the grassroots level, Adams's "counseling revolution" reasonably often encountered people who had experienced the alternatives. We will look next at the cognitive framework by which he interpreted and interacted with their problems.

Chapter 4 Notes

1. Adams's pamphlets included "Christ and Your Problems" (1971), "Godliness through Discipline" (1972), "What Do You Do When Anger Gets the Upper Hand?" (1975a), "What Do You Do When Fear Overcomes You?" (1975b), "What Do You Do When You Become Depressed?" (1975c), "What Do You Do When You Know That You're Hooked?" (1975d), "What Do You Do When You Worry All the Time?" (1975e), "What Do You Do When Your Marriage Goes Sour?" (1975f), all published by Presbyterian & Reformed. Though these pamphlets each sold several hundred thousand copies, their use was not universal among nouthetic counselors, especially after 1980 as the movement broadened out, as other authors wrote their own self-help materials, and as differences of emphasis emerged between nouthetic counselors. Some of Adams's self-help books were also popular: *Christian Living in the Home* (Phillipsburg, N.J.: Presbyterian & Reformed, 1972) sold more than a quarter-million copies.

2. The number of counseling cases per year rose from about 200 in the early 1970s to nearly 600 in the early 1980s to around 800 in the early 1990s. That caseload translated into an expansion of hours counseled from about 1,000/year to 4,000/year to 10,000/year, respectively.

3. The PDI evolved somewhat over the years, but for an example of the basic form, see Jay E. Adams, *The Christian Counselor's Manual* (USA: Presbyterian & Reformed, 1973), 433–35.

4. My data is not strictly decadal, however. My organizing principle represented a hybrid of two different, and not always congruent, purposes. First, as mentioned, I wanted to assess overall client demographics and, along the way, to analyze changes over time. Second, I wanted to explore differences between successive generations of counselors (i.e., changes in CCEF, not changes in CCEF's clientele). The c. 1970 sample clusters between 1968 and 1974, but I sampled a few cases from later in the 1970s. In so doing I sought to represent the entire first generation of CCEF counselors hired by Adams himself, some of whom began practicing in the mid-1970s. The c. 1980 sample is tighter, taking cases from 1979–81 and representing a second generation of counselors, almost wholly discrete from the first and hired by John Bettler. The c. 1990 sample is also tight, taking counselees from 1988–92, and representing a staff that had undergone further significant shifts. I will discuss changes in the staff and their practices in chapter 9.

My sampling procedures introduced some distortion into diachronic comparisons. In particular, the characteristics of the c. 1970 group shift slightly in the direction of the c. 1980 group. In three categories there were significant changes over time: educational level, occupation, and the average number of counseling sessions. In each category, the c.1980 group stood in the middle of each trend (i.e., no trends reversed themselves). The net effect of the distortion is that differences between the c. 1970 group and the later groups were presumably dampened.

My sampling procedures and the nature of the sample introduced several other minor anomalies. The number of cases and counselees was not the same between the three cohorts: in c. 1970, 175 cases involved 308 individuals; in c. 1980, 248 cases involved

352 individuals; in c. 1990, 179 cases involved 218 individuals. One anomaly arose because I sampled a disproportionate number of cases from c. 1980. Thus aggregate statistics at the *case* level reflect the 1980 group disproportionately—though the net effect of this is minimized because that group stood in the middle of every category that I examined. A second anomaly arose because the number of individuals per case dropped markedly over the years, from 1.8 counselees/case to 1.4 counselees/case to 1.2 counselees/case. Thus aggregate statistics at the *individual* level reflect the two earlier periods disproportionately because so many more individuals were represented. The net effect of this, however, is minimal because I disaggregated demographic categories for which significant differences arose over time.

5. The base fee typically ran about one-half of standard psychotherapy fees in the region. It averaged twelve to twenty dollars between 1968 and 1981, when it was raised to thirty-two dollars. It went to forty dollars in the mid-80s and to fifty dollars in 1990. CCEF employed a number of different arrangements over the years to help clients who could not pay: asking the deacons' fund of a local church to assist, offering a negotiable sliding fee scale, using a scholarship program, exchanging work (e.g., odd jobs or other services) for counseling. Sometimes CCEF counseling was eligible for insurance reimbursements—from the mid-1980s the director of counseling was a state-licensed psychologist as well as a nouthetic counselor.

Still, CCEF's counseling was always expensive in comparison to most nouthetic counseling and other pastoral counseling, which was usually offered as a free service rather than on a fee-for-service basis. Counselees' concerns about the expense of counseling recur within the case records. In contrast to CCEF, Faith Baptist Counseling Ministry (FBCM), the other leading nouthetic institution that combined counseling with training, was based in a local church, rather than freestanding. FBCM offered its counseling free of charge to its members, the indigent, and non-Christians, and charged a nominal fee to others from the community. The question of the ethics of charging fees for pastoral counseling created tensions within the biblical counseling movement after the late 1980s. Adams rationalized it in cases where training and education were provided but opposed "hanging out a shingle" as an autonomous professional. See chapter 9.

6. In contrast to CCEF, FBCM, located in the Bible belt of Indiana where there are few conservative Presbyterian churches, drew heavily from fundamentalist churches.

7. Of 602 total cases, 129 either left this blank or listed "self" as the source of the referral. Obviously, those who came "self-referred" knew about CCEF from somewhere, but they interpreted the question in a way that did not allow identification of the linkage.

8. Forty-six percent of the referrals specifically listed the pastor. The other 4 percent included elders, staff members on mission agencies, and pastors' wives.

9. These included former counselees, roommates, and members of Bible study groups. When someone simply listed a name whose role I could not identify, I included it in this category. Hence, this figure likely includes people from other categories, such as pastors or students at CCEF.

10. These included people either who cited one of Jay Adams's books (he often listed CCEF's address in his writings) or who knew a CCEF counselor, perhaps as their pastor or as a member of their local church or perhaps from hearing a counselor speak at a conference.

11. These included students at Westminster Theological Seminary, as well as those taking nondegree course work through CCEF. Presumably many of the pastors who referred parishioners to CCEF had once been students there or had read Adams's books.

12. These included teachers, guidance counselors, and principals of secondary and elementary schools. In the 1970s Adams had been a frequent keynote speaker at conventions of Christian school personnel.

13. These three referrals came from evangelicals who worked in social services: a youth center worker, a public assistance counselor, and a group home supervisor. Only the last was a formal referral, coming from a Christian agency that ran homes for emotionally disturbed youths. The others were personal, informal referrals.

14. In one case a divorce court mandated three sessions of counseling in an attempt to reconcile the marriage; one of the parties knew of and chose CCEF. In the other, a delinquency court suggested a family get counseling, and they chose CCEF. In neither case was CCEF selected by the legal system; it was approved as an acceptable option.

15. This isolation was also evident both during the process of a case and afterward. I did not find a single referral to secular mental health professionals from CCEF, nor did I discover any subsequent request for records addressed to CCEF from a secular agency. The contacts that occurred during a case were rare and formal. I found no evidence of partnership on a treatment team. Occasionally the files contained a "release of medical/psychological records" form and the report of a psychologist's earlier assessment; occasionally they contained medical, personnel, or school records that the CCEF counselor had requested. Occasionally the files noted a conversation between a CCEF counselor and either a psychiatrist monitoring psychotropic medication or a school guidance counselor. Occasionally the files contained a case evaluation written up for a school or court.

Relations between CCEF and the mental health system were generally nonexistent or remote and formal. The only sign of overt hostility I found appeared in a letter from an evangelical psychotherapist whose testy refusal to release requested patient records cited the CCEF counselor's lack of state licensure.

16. In my particular sample, these people came from Arkansas, California, Florida, Georgia, Hawaii, Maine, Montana, Rhode Island, Virginia, and Pittsburgh, Pennsylvania. They might fly in for several days or a week of intensive counseling, perhaps followed up with counseling over the telephone in subsequent weeks or months.

17. In one sense, of course, utilizing CCEF represented only a halfway revolution in terms of Adams's stated goals. Pastors and other church people who referred others to CCEF for presumably competent, and distinctively nouthetic, counseling were referring to "professionals" rather than doing the counseling themselves as "competent" counselors. Such referral sources had apparently appropriated enough of Adams's model to wish to send parishioners, friends, and family to pastoral counselors whom they thought would follow Adams's ideas and methods. But they apparently

were either unwilling or did not think themselves competent to do the counseling themselves.

18. In this section I will use the adjectives "conservative" and "liberal" as sweeping generalizations to describe Protestants. "Conservative" Protestants tended to believe the Bible was a true revelation from God, and hence they held to those doctrinal and moral views traditionally characteristic of Christianity. "Liberal" Protestants tended to believe the Bible was a record of religious experience, and hence they were open to innovations in teaching and morals.

19. Jay E. Adams, *More Than Redemption: A Theology of Christian Counseling* (Phillipsburg, N.J.: Presbyterian & Reformed, 1979), 64.

20. Jay E. Adams, *Handbook of Church Discipline* (Grand Rapids: Zondervan, 1986), 81.

21. I coded as "fundamentalist" the following responses: fundamentalist, independent Bible, Bible Baptist, General Association of Regular Baptist, Independent Fundamental Churches of America, born-again Baptist, Bible chapels, and variants on these.

22. No respondents specifically indicated the mainline American Baptist Church, but presumably a small percentage of Baptists may better fit into the mainline category. Based on other answers, the vast majority were clearly from fundamentalist, Reformed, or evangelical Baptist churches; only a handful gave typically liberal or undecided sorts of answers.

23. Includes Southern Baptist, Nazarene, Holiness, Christian and Missionary Alliance, and various Brethren churches. Some of these might be classed as "Fundamentalist" or as "Other Evangelical."

24. Orthodox Presbyterian Church (6 percent), Presbyterian Church in America (5 percent), Reformed Presbyterian Church (1 percent), and unspecified conservative or Bible-believing Presbyterian (3 percent).

25. I have listed unspecified Presbyterian churches among conservative Presbyterian denominations, though some of these may have belonged to the mainline denomination. About two thirds of the counselees in this category gave a pattern of conservative Protestant answers to other questions, though precise identification of their denominational affiliation was impossible. Cf., note 37.

26. Includes Christian Reformed Church, Reformed Church in America, and Reformed Episcopal.

27. I included in this type nondenominational evangelical churches that did not appear to be distinctively baptistic. I also included other miscellaneous types that only had a few entries, such as conservative Congregational, Wesleyan, Messianic Jewish, and Chinese churches.

28. Calvary Chapels were a national movement of nondenominational Bible churches that began in the 1970s and were popular with people in their twenties and thirties. During the 1980s a large congregation in northeast Philadelphia worked closely with CCEF and referred many counselees.

29. Some charismatics might have come from mainline, Roman Catholic, or evangelical churches as members of "renewal" movements. Probably none were fundamentalist or Presbyterian.

30. More than 40 percent of the individuals included in this category made a point of expressing conservative Protestant sentiments. More than half of United Methodists and United Pres-

byterians fit a conservative Protestant profile. A third or less of Episcopalians and Lutherans fit that profile. At the other end of the spectrum, one-third of the mainline church members gave answers that indicated they were distinctly outside conservative patterns of faith and practice. They read the Bible and prayed infrequently; they answered "Uncertain" or "No" to the question about being "saved."

31. Only half of these counselees gave answers to other questions that identified them as mainline, liberal Protestants. The other half gave explicit evidence of conservative Protestant orientation. Several local UP congregations regularly referred people to CCEF. Tenth Presbyterian Church (Philadelphia) and Oreland Presbyterian Church (less than a mile from CCEF's building), from whom many counselees came to CCEF, were known as theologically conservative churches within their more liberal denomination.

32. Some of these Lutherans may have been from conservative Lutheran denominations such as Missouri Synod (from which a number of leaders had been favorable to nouthetic counseling). But Philadelphia area Lutheran churches tended to be part of the mainline denomination, and only three of these counselees gave an indication of a conservative Protestant orientation.

33. Most of these respondents had somewhat ill-defined commitments both religiously and ecclesiastically. Many commented on their current attempts to find a church. A third of them either fit the conservative Protestant profile or seemed to be moving in that direction: e.g., "My wife has become a born again Christian, and I am trying to learn how to become a born again Christian too."

34. Seven Catholics made conservative Protestant sounding statements. See later discussion. Many of the Catholics were evidently nonpracticing: for example, ten (of n=23, because of forms lacking data) attended church once a month or never. Four of the Catholics came as spouses of conservative Protestants.

35. Almost all of these also answered "0" to the question about how many times per month they attended church, and most gave other evidences of disaffection from Christianity.

36. These included one person who sporadically (1/month) attended "any" church. Others made comments such as "I just started back to church," "I'm unsure about salvation," and "I only go to church when I'm forced to, but I feel guilty when I don't go."

37. Two case records lacked data on childhood religious upbringing. In the paragraphs that follow, similar discrepancies in the total numbers cited arise for the same reason.

38. Ten forms lacked information.

39. Footnote 22 commented that counselees who were currently "Baptist" without specification were almost all conservative according to other indications; therefore, I included them among conservative Baptists. Of the eleven who had been raised "Baptist" and were now mainline Protestants, only three gave typically conservative answers to other questions. I suspect that most of these eleven moved from one mainline church (American Baptist) to another because so few other counselees moved from conservative Protestantism in the direction of liberal, mainline Protestantism. This places me in the awkward position of having reasons to think that current "Baptists" were largely conservative, while making an untestable assumption that former "Baptists" were largely liberal.

In fact, the matter is indifferent because the general tendency of the data is unaffected.

40. Predictably, the pattern of those raised in conservative Protestant denominations was the opposite of what we have just seen. For example, all the former fundamentalists and conservative Presbyterians who sought counseling were still involved in some other conservative Protestant denomination.

41. A few of these came as spouses of conservative Protestants.

42. Only five counselees were over seventy, and only one of these came more than one time (three times).

43. Of 879 counselees, 24 did not list educational level; 82 were currently primary or secondary school students; 25 were college students.

44. Of these, 86 (12 percent) completed vocational or technical training and 122 (16 percent) had begun but not completed college.

45. Of these, 148 (20 percent) had a bachelor's and 43 (6 percent) had studied or were currently studying beyond a bachelor's.

46. Of these, 61 (8 percent) had master's and 14 (2 percent) doctorate's; 18 of these master's and 1 doctorate were in religious fields and largely held by pastors and missionaries. The other degrees covered the spectrum of graduate study: education (11), medicine (10), business (8), engineering (6), psychology and social work (4), science (4), law (3), humanities (3), and architecture (2); (6 could not be determined from the data).

47. In the figures that follow, school children are excluded, and information was unavailable on a number of the PDIs.

48. Includes guidance counselor, recreational therapist, and social worker. School teachers preponderated.

49. RNs, LPNs, medical technicians, physical therapists, and dental assistants.

50. Includes waitresses, hostesses, and other food-service workers, along with factory workers.

51. This is a miscellaneous category and includes artists (n=4), computer technicians (n=2), and beauticians (n=3).

52. These included two medical doctors, two scientists, and a psychologist.

53. All of these women were missionaries. The conservative Protestant churches from which CCEF generally drew its clientele did not ordain women to the pastorate.

54. Four percent of the women were unemployed.

55. Includes mechanics, building trades, foremen, and technicians.

56. Includes managers, administrators, storeowners, brokers, and salesmen.

57. Includes laborers, guards, janitors, and shipping clerks.

58. Includes ministers, missionaries, and parachurch workers.

59. Includes doctors, lawyers, professors, architects, dentists, and psychologists.

60. Includes clerks and dispatchers.

61. Four percent of the men were unemployed.

62. These changes are accentuated by the increase in the number of unmarried women who sought counseling. In 1970, 81 percent of the adult women were married; by 1990 that figure had dropped to 65 percent. The percentages of divorced women and women who had never married both doubled (the former from 3 percent to 7 percent; the latter from 13 percent to 27 percent). Among married female counselees, the percentage of homemakers dropped significantly but not precipitously: from 68 percent to 47 percent. Conservative Protestants traditionally valued the homemaking role, but such values did not insulate them from wider social trends toward singleness and toward women in the workplace.

63. This is not to say that a truculent teen or reluctant spouse might not appear alongside the party who initiated counseling, or that a counselee might not have been given some sort of ultimatum by church leaders or family members as part of pressuring him or her into counseling.

64. Many of these cases (and those of individuals separated from their spouse) might be considered marital, though only one party sought counseling initially. In one-fourth of these cases (and those of separated individuals) some notation was made that the spouse came in subsequently, participating in some part of the counseling process. Such participation raised the overall percentage of cases of group counseling to 55 percent. In numerous other cases, such participation was sought as one of the goals of counseling without success.

Balancing this, on the other hand, some undetermined number of the cases labeled marital (see the next section of chart)—because a husband and wife came in together—were occasioned by the individual problems of only one of the members. In my data, a husband suffering from anxiety attacks who came in with his wife was considered a "marital" constellation. Despite these ambiguities, for the purposes of this study more discriminating analysis is not necessary because the broad tendencies of the client group are readily apparent.

65. These cases typically involved parents either in conflict with teenagers in conflict or anguished over younger children experiencing behavioral and emotional problems in school or home.

66. CCEF counselors occasionally filled one of the traditional pastoral roles of providing premarital counseling to couples considering counseling.

67. Howard A. Eyrich, *Three to Get Ready: A Christian Premarital Counselor's Manual* (Grand Rapids: Baker Books, 1978, 1991); Wayne A. Mack and Nathan A. Mack, *Preparing for Marriage God's Way* (Tulsa, Okla: Virgil W. Hensley, 1986).

68. Jay E. Adams, *Competent to Counsel* (USA: Presbyterian & Reformed, 1970), 188–92, 231–36.

69. The PDI inquired about previous marriages. The divorce rate for this population of counsel seekers was 21 percent. Overall, this sample had constituted a total of 537 current or previous marriages, of which 108 had ended in divorce. The divorce rate rose slightly over the time period studied: 18 percent in 1970, 21 percent in 1980, and 23 percent in 1990.

70. I did not attempt any version of outcome study, as that did not fit with my historical purposes. But my subjective impression of the case records is that such people did not usually do well at CCEF. Almost a quarter of them came to CCEF only once, and two-thirds came five times or less. These figures were identical to those of all counselees during Adams's tenure. Most of these case records reveal such counselees dropping out without any evidence of change. The one-third of counselees who got established tended to come longer than counselees with other

problems. Almost 20 percent of the "psychiatric" counselees came ten or more times, whereas only 7 percent of other clients came that long. (See chap. 9 for diachronic comparisons of length of counseling.) Some in this latter group of cases contain evidence of some sort of positive change in mood and lifestyle. As an ambulatory counseling center offering fee-for-service counseling of a directive sort, CCEF did not replicate the peculiar social circumstances in which Adams had witnessed Mowrer working: lengthy small-group meetings with patients confined to a totalitarian institution.

71. CCEF did not draw many with hard-core addictions to drugs and alcohol. Addicts might typically find religion at Alcoholics Anonymous or in residential treatment programs run by evangelical Protestants. A number of the latter in the Philadelphia area adopted nouthetic counseling and adapted it to their clientele: the Colony of Mercy at America's Keswick (in Whiting, N.J.; the oldest residential "rescue mission," founded in the 1890s); Whosoever Gospel Mission (north Philadelphia), some Teen Challenge centers. CCEF's outpatient structure offered none of the consistent accountability and structure that typically characterized both secular and religious approaches to substance abuse.

72. People tended to interpret the question in terms of formal counseling/psychotherapy, so many others had "talked with" their pastor but did not list it as an experience of counseling.

CHAPTER 5

God, Sin, and Misery: Adams's Positive System
(Part 1)

[The] moralistic function [of psychotherapists] is that of a secular priesthood. . . . For psychotherapists must finally appeal to science to justify their activity, just as ministers appeal to revelation. . . . Religion, in most of its modern institutional forms, is so unimpassioned in objectives and impoverished in ideology as to have little current claim to the loyalties of good minds and men. Science is our sacred cow, and psychotherapists, with their apparent roots in scientific knowledge and method, can lay their claims to preach whatever codes they do, not merely on the grounds of great truth, or on the assurances across guilds that they will not compete for the same pulpits, but also on the apparent facts that the clergy have tended to abdicate their claim to moral competence in favor of psychology and that the congregations have, by and large, resigned from their clergy.

— Perry London, 1964[1]

All of life is sacred; none is secular. All life is God-related; none is neutral. Systems, methods, actions, values, attitudes, concepts are all either God-oriented or sinful. None are neutral.

— Jay Adams[2]

Personal sin [is] the root and cause of most of the day-by-day counseling problems that arise.

— Jay Adams[3]

A great purpose (and use) of suffering is growth through testing.

— Jay Adams[4]

What was Adams's theory of counseling, and how did it inform the jurisdictional offensive he conducted? How did Adams appeal cognitively to the people he sought to win? He made an impassioned appeal to their core loyalties and suspicions; he offered them a comprehensive counseling ideology framed in terms of conservative Protestant orthodoxy. The next three chapters will present the knowledge system by which nouthetic counseling defined problems, tasks, and competency in the personal problems domain for its constituency of prospective counselors and counselees.

Adams prosecuted his claim that conservative Protestant pastors—as experts in the Bible with hands-on knowledge of the solution to sin and misery—had both truth and title from the Bible to work with troubled people. He taught a positive counseling system that was framed in theological terms familiar to his intended constituents. It was a system whose innovations appeared primarily to be matters of application, not matters of substantive belief. Adams both reassured and challenged his constituents by appealing to their most fundamental loyalties. Chapters 5 and 6 will explore this positive system.

Similarly, Adams appealed to his constituents' fundamental suspicions of secular intellectual and institutional systems. Psychological systems of thought seemed alien to those who adhered to a different metaphysic, epistemology, ethic, history, and eschatology. Adams attacked the competing systems, and he charged as interlopers the psychotherapeutic professionals who preached such ideas. They were false prophets, in that idiom for interprofessional rivalry provided in the Bible: "Advocating, allowing, and practicing psychiatric and psychoanalytic dogmas within the church is every bit as pagan and heretical (and therefore perilous) as propagating the teachings of some of the most bizarre cults."[5] To a constituency that habitually viewed itself as a sociocultural counterpoise to the secular establishment, both Adams's positive and negative assertions carried weight. Chapter 7 will examine his polemic toward psychology.[6]

Intellectual systems prove their adequacy by "their abstracting ability to redefine old problems in new ways," serving as expert witnesses in the trial between competing professional claims.[7] The knowledge system's plausibility hinges on a fourfold ability: to diagnose problems persuasively, to map out coherent explanations of problems, to formulate plausibly effective plans for treatment, and, all the while, to debunk competing systems.[8] Abstract knowledge represents the "currency of competition" between professions, and attacking groups seek to "expand their cog-

nitive dominion by using abstract knowledge to annex new areas, to define them as their own proper work."[9] Adams labored hard to produce a coherent body of nouthetic counseling principles, tools, insights, and strategies both for counseling practice and apologetics.

An abstract knowledge system rarely functions abstractly where rights and reputations, both personal and corporate, are at stake. Rhetorical and polemical purposes shape the emphases within any articulated counseling system; these effects were magnified in nouthetic counseling, which at times appeared to critics to be more interested in polemics than in helping troubled people. Both the matter and manner of presentation were greatly influenced by the perceived needs of persuasion. Adams was a rhetorician by training, an orator who had written a doctoral dissertation on audience analysis for the purposes of persuasion.[10] Much of his prolific written output consisted of lightly edited transcriptions of lecture series or other public addresses. What he wrote was almost always more ad hoc than systematic. He wrote tracts meant to persuade and to equip for action, not disquisitions meant to demonstrate a dispassionate grasp of nuances in the relevant literature. Nouthetic counseling was always embattled. It was always a minority position and, in many quarters, a despised position. The marks of battle appear at every turn in nouthetic counseling literature. In the chapters that follow, I will extract a coherent system. But it is worth noting the fact that Adams himself never did such. The occasional nature of his literary production is best understood in the context of the needs of interprofessional conflict: intended audiences, identified foes, and immediate problems to be redressed.

A more extended discussion of Adams's audience is in order. As has been mentioned, Adams made little effort to appeal either to mental health professionals or to academics. He selected a grassroots constituency, pastors of local churches, and he tenaciously pursued them. These were men who had pragmatic concerns on their minds.[11] They had a weekly sermon to prepare and too many other responsibilities filling too little time. They fretted and prayed over pastoral problems: the disintegrating marriage, the rebellious teenager, the depressed thirty-five-year-old single person, the fornicator caught out by pregnancy, the young mother dying of cancer, the new Christian visited by Mormon missionaries. The only higher education such pastors would ever have lay in the past: Bible college for many, a liberal arts BA followed by theological seminary for others. Their training in modern psychology was frequently limited to introductory psychology, if that.

Such pastors had typically been convinced, perhaps by their own fears and failures in the face of counseling problems, perhaps by the "brainwashing" of mental health "propaganda,"[12] that serious counseling was beyond them. Though Adams thought that "there are so many incompetent ministers, and in particular, ministers who are incompetent counselors,"[13] he hoped to provide them the books and training to create competency. Adams's model sought to overcome the well-socialized diffidence of a constituency that had been marginalized with reference to the socially legitimated helping professions. Adams wrote to capture practitioners whose conscious goals were effectiveness in ministry within a parochial setting; he wrote to give this clientele confidence that they had the goods on human nature, despite their lack of what the dominant cultural surround deemed prerequisite for that task. His intellectual choices and emphases are best understood in the light of such rhetorical purposes, his consistent choice to speak to the concerns and in the language of his intended converts. By design, his was a counseling approach for pastors, trafficking in the realities that constrained them.[14]

Adams believed that the Bible—understood by literal, grammatico-historical exegesis, and partly systematized in the creeds of the Reformation—provided three things needed to alter this state of affairs. First, it taught a comprehensive intellectual system, defining the truth about people, their problems in living, and the processes of change. Adams's distinctive view of normative human functioning informed his categories for analyzing problems in living, hence his approach to the change process.[15] His particular interpretation of the Bible's theology was shaped by his commitment to a Calvinistic epistemology that stressed, positively, the comprehensive scope of biblical revelation and, negatively, the presuppositional antithesis between theistic and a-theistic thought. From that standpoint, he opposed the major twentieth-century personality theories and their attendant therapies, believing that modern psychologists had fundamentally and systematically misconstrued the human dilemma. He sought to expose their misconstructions and replace such with an interpretation of problems in living consistent with his Calvinistic worldview.

Second, Adams believed that the Bible defined and exemplified a methodology for the cure of souls, a methodology that complemented and implemented its interpretive system. He thought that the older creeds had not covered the methods of practical theology adequately.[16]

Truths that the church does not treat systematically (i.e., theologically) it has a tendency to lose.

The pressures that had a part in compressing and shrinking the church's counseling role were able to make headway (and indeed, all but succeeded in totally supplanting it) because, even though counseling by its nature was theological through and through, it had been carried on in an unsystematic, atheological manner.

When doctrine becomes creedal (e.g., the Athanasian Creed), it becomes defensible against (Arians and other) heretics. Heresy, as well as truth, becomes identifiable. Before it takes creedal form, however, almost any sort of heresy can claim a place. . . . To date, no serious theological (let alone creedal) statements have been made about the place or task of counseling in the Christian church.

One of Adams's theological innovations was to extend the scope of his Calvinistic presuppositions to cover tasks of personal counseling. In his view, psychotherapeutic methods were as theory- and value-laden as the propositional contents of the contemporary personality theories. He opposed the therapeutic methods of the psychotherapies and psychiatries, and sought to replicate modes of conversation he thought prescribed by and illustrated in the Bible.[17]

Third, Adams believed that the Bible prescribed a particular institutional and professional locus for helping people: the church and the pastoral role. This had been assumed in the Reformed creeds, but he thought creedal development was also needed here. He opposed the institutional and professional arrangements of the mental health system and deplored the subordination of church and pastor to the authority of psychiatric and psychotherapeutic establishment.

In sum, Adams aimed at a cognitive, methodological, and institutional revolution among conservative Protestant pastors. Few secondary sources summarize Adams's system.[18] I will organize the leading emphases of nouthetic counseling under six heads: (1) God, (2) sin, (3) trials and temptations, (4) gospel, (5) church ministry, and (6) apologetics against unbelief. As unexceptional as these headings might have seemed in colonial or antebellum America, they sounded revolutionary—or bizarre, atavistic, and obscurantist—when injected into the context of the therapeutic secular society that held sway in late twentieth-century America. We will consider each of these six headings in turn. The first three deal with Adams's interpretation of the human dilemma and will be the subject of this chapter. The next two deal with changing people and will be the subject of the next chapter.[19] The last heading will be the subject of a chapter of its own.

1. God was at the center of Adams's explanation of the human condition and his proposal for addressing it through counseling activity

Perhaps the single key to understanding Adams's view of problems in living and their redress through counseling is this: for Adams, the God of classic Protestantism actually existed. The entire nouthetic counseling system intended to unfold twentieth-century implications of the God described in John Calvin's *Institutes of the Christian Religion*. The following characteristics of this God appeared and reappeared within Adams's counseling system, providing backdrop—and frequently foreground—for what he said and did about troubled people.

First, God is. Adams viewed God as a person with whom all created persons had to do: "A counselee can no more avoid and ignore God than he can live without air."[20] His God was the classic "living" God of the biblical covenants: "I AM THAT I AM." Adams's assumption that God was an objectively self-existent person—not the product of human social experience, psychological wish fulfillment, or philosophical abstraction—provided the reference point for his entire system of counseling. "God is man's environment" summarized the basic assumption of his model.[21] Adams followed Calvin in predicating that all valid knowledge of self and others hinged on knowing God.[22]

Not surprisingly, the resultant counseling system was explicitly didactic, directive, and hortatory. Adams taught, proselytized, and exhorted counselees, seeking to inculcate acknowledgment of this God. Consistent with this, Adams's polemic against various psychologies and psychotherapies turned on their atheism, and his view that such secularity corrupted human self-knowledge by substituting myths for realities.

Second, God controls. There were no accidents or random events in Adams's world because God was the primary cause of all things. A personal will stood behind all secondary causes.[23] The God who made all things controlled all things by his inscrutable—but trustworthy—providence. God acted in history; God answered prayers. This providence predictably operated to accomplish purposes of character formation and reformation. Adams's counseling engaged people facing the varied trials of the human condition as if these trials occurred within a context of knowable and significant meaningfulness.[24]

Third, God knows. There were no secrets in Adams's world, because his God knew all things about all people at all times: "God knows your counselee (and you) inside out. . . . If God knows us and can reveal something of the wickedness of our hearts to us, then we ought to remember that it cannot and will not escape His notice."[25] God saw into the crevices of human belief, craving, feeling, fantasy, self-deception, conscience, word, and deed—and whatever else constituted the inward and outward existence of the soul. Moral suasion within Adams's system hinged on the "fear of the LORD," on convincing counselees to live as before the eyes of an all-seeing God—*coram Deo* in a favorite phrase of those sixteenth- and seventeenth-century Protestants whose heir Adams sought to be.

Fourth, God speaks. Adams was relentlessly biblicistic. The Bible was the literal word of authoritative truth from the living, powerful, knowing God in whom Adams believed. As a Protestant operating in a premodern theological style, Adams believed that God had spoken directly to human beings to reveal who he is, who we are, what his will is, and what he has done and will do. On Adams's interpretation, what God had to say defined human existence as an historical and moral drama down to the details of each individual life. What people were about—hence what counseling and true psychological insight were about—was a pervasive conflict between good and evil, truth and lie, love and hate, trust and fear, faith and idolatry, obedience and rebellion, wisdom and folly. The issue at stake in "personal problems" was the issue of the "kingdom of God," whether the individual soul would be autonomous or theonomous, self-ruled or God-ruled. Because Adams's Bible cast human life, both ultimately and immediately, in moral and theological terms, he interpreted human life in such terms.[26] The authority of Scripture—and, derivatively, the authority of counseling that promulgated biblical doctrine and directives—found frequent iteration both in Adams's writing and in pastoral conversations within the counseling office.

Finally, God recompenses. Adams's God-saturated world was consequence-laden. Because human life inescapably played out a moral drama, the stakes were life or death, joy or misery, blessing or curse, justification or condemnation, both here and hereafter. Adams did not hesitate to hold out the theocentric carrot and to wield the theocentric stick to those he counseled. He used the Bible's promises to encourage people to embrace his counsel: "There is no temptation that has overtaken you that is not common to all. God is faithful, and will not let you be tempted beyond what you can endure."[27] God's mercy, aid, and protection were offered to those who would believe. Similarly, Adams addressed warnings to the wayward in doctrine or life who might shrug off or disagree with his counsel: "The way of the transgressor is hard."[28] Trouble would dog the steps of those who preferred some different way than that Adams's Bible prescribed.

To enter into the assumptions of Adams's counseling system is to enter a preskeptical world, a world where God did not die, but kept on speaking and acting. The world in which Adams and his pastoral audience lived—the world into which they would plunge their counselees—was a world lived in terms of God. Adams's frank insertion of religious values and beliefs seems unethical to a culture whose psychotherapeutic ethos usually recoils at the intrusion of the counselor's values into the counseling process.[29] But to a subculture whose heroes were those most fervent in evangelistic and missionary activity, such insertions were marks of fidelity not deviance.

Even those who disagree with all Adams believed can sympathize with at least one thing. When Adams averred that all counseling systems were value-laden, covertly if not overtly, and argued that counselors should have the integrity to spell out their values, rather than pretending to neutrality, thoughtful moderns nod assent. Adams was highly self-conscious about his assumptions, set them forth without equivocation, and thought and practiced with remarkable consistency to first principles. He was highly critical of scientistic pretensions to neutrality when social scientists or medical doctors sought to extend their competency to psychotherapeutic "attempts to change values and beliefs."[30]

Adams's view of God churned out counseling implications, some of which we have alluded to, and others that we will explore in the sections that follow. But under this heading, I will further develop one central implication of Adams's commitment to the God of the Bible. He believed that what the Bible said, God said. Biblicism was the signal element in Adams's model. The social and behavioral sciences might provide illustrative material for a system of counseling derived from the Bible, but the sciences could never align or constitute a system of truth and morals, of faith and practice. Their attempt to do so was a sinful usurpation and presumption in Adams's view.[31]

Adams asserted repeatedly that the Bible was God's "textbook" on counseling[32]: "The Bible is the basis for a Christian's counseling because it deals with the same issues that all counseling does . . . because of what counseling is all about (changing lives by changing values, beliefs, relationships, attitudes, behavior)."[33] He was, in the more generic, less pejorative sense of the word, a fundamentalist about the Bible, an "old-fashioned Bible-believer" in the intellectual tradition of high Calvinism. For Adams, the Bible was true, God-breathed, inerrant, useful; it was an infallible "guide to faith and practice," in words of the creed to which Adams subscribed as a traditional Presbyterian. Adams's intellectual and methodological program was to construct a system of counseling defensible as exegetically emergent from the Bible.

Adams's commitment to a premodern hearing of the Bible was revealed everywhere in his writings. Most obviously, the titles of his books often derived from Bible passages: *Competent to Counsel* (Rom. 15:14); *Godliness through Discipline* (1 Tim. 4:7); *Ready to Restore* (Gal. 6:1). More pointedly, he claimed that the contents of his books were shaped in large measure by Bible texts, interpreted in a very concrete manner. When Adams read that Jesus said, "Sanctify them by the truth; your word is truth" (John 17:17), he took it literally, seeking proof texts for each major proposition and for many minor propositions in his approach to human problems.

In Adams's world, the speaking God was not adjunct to the human psychological drama either as a projection of psychic conflicts or as a comforting resource to resolve life's struggles. He was, rather, the rightful King to whom every person owed allegiance—and he had published his identity, will, actions, and promises in the Bible. Human life, by definition, revolved around the conservative Protestant God, both in the large issues of ultimate meaning and in the minuscule details of life's problems. This theocentric preoccupation generated Adams's definition of what went wrong with people.

The appropriateness of this starting point for his audience is unmistakable. These were people whose core beliefs centered on who they believed God to be, and whose central aspiration, at least in theory, was to live faithfully in a God-saturated world. Adams provided a rationale for explicitly approaching the tasks of counseling in terms of such fundamental beliefs and aspirations. These were also people for whom the central failings of human nature were defined with respect to this living God. Adams's organizing diagnostic category lay on the surface of the Bible that he and his fellows believed.

2. Sin is the problem

"Biblical counseling, in contrast [to Sigmund Freud and Carl Rogers], assumes that problems stem from sin."[34] Sin provided a comprehensive and concrete diagnostic category for Adams. It included specific wrong behavior, distorted thinking, and bad attitudes, whether conscious or unconscious, all organized around a compulsion to live for one's own desires—the pervasive depravity captured in an Augustinian-Calvinistic view of human nature. Sin as a diagnostic category logically followed from the centrality of the Bible's God in Adams's system. Problems in living did not occur in a psychological, psychosomatic, psychosocial, or psycho-socio-somatic

universe; they were not self-existent, abstracted from God. Rather, problems in living, accurately defined, were God-referential. Adams therefore believed that

There is really *no new problem.* . . . No one is going to present to you a unique problem tomorrow or next week. Of course the specific features of each problem are unique: the way that it comes, the configuration that it takes, the intensity with which it appears, the rapidity with which it grows, naturally all of these things vary. And there are hundreds of subtle little details that differ, so that no two cases are ever exactly the same. But at bottom, when you boil off all of the fat, when you get down to the bones and meat, the problem is precisely the same as the problems that you must face, or that anybody else has to face, or anybody in the future will ever have to face.[35]

This fundamental leveling of individual, cultural, and historical differences was calculated to make a tremendous impression on listeners, giving them hope that the Bible truths they most cherished had a universal relevance to the tasks of counseling. If his hearers were simultaneously convicted of their ineptitude or ignorance, it was only a relative failure of their own understanding or application, not the absolute failure of their core commitments. The basic truths of conservative Protestantism might have been understood superficially or used ineffectively, but they were still sufficient for the task as Adams spelled it out.

That sin was the problem derived from Adams's definition of normative human functioning. Rather than defining a model of mental-emotional health, social adjustment, or self-actualization, Adams posited a frankly theological ideal: the image of God or the imitation of Christ. Any defection from that image and model entailed sin. In defining righteousness as the goal and sin as the problem, Adams translated old-fashioned Protestant theology into a counseling idiom. The yardstick Adams chose served a double function intellectually. It measured what was wrong with counselees, and it prescribed the goals of counseling. The Law of God revealed the character of God and was perfectly embodied in the life of Jesus Christ. It served first as a mirror to reveal sin in order to bring people to embrace Christ as their merciful Savior; it served second as a lamp to guide such believers into holiness under Christ as their effective Master. Such notions defined counseling as the province of pastors who understood their calling as the redemption of sinners. Instead of being condescended to, intimidated, or belittled, they were affirmed.

For Adams, then, the gamut of problems in living found their cause—remote, proximate, and immediate—in human sin. This included not only the normal range of life's difficulties but also those extremes of personality disintegration that could not be correlated to an identifiable physiological substrate such as brain injury, alcohol psychosis, or dementias associated with aging. I will briefly describe six representative problem areas to illustrate the ramifications of Adams's diagnostic system: relational difficulties, troubling emotions, troublesome behaviors, faulty beliefs, morally freighted responses to suffering, and bizarre behavior.

First, Adams devoted a great deal of attention to marital, familial, and other interpersonal conflicts. Human beings were inescapably social, a fact to which their "longings and strivings" for social contact and love gave evidence, however distorted such longings might become.[36] Adams frequently asserted that all problems were ultimately relationship problems, having to do with failures to love God and neighbor: "Love for God and one's neighbor constitutes the sum of God's requirements for the Christian. The man who loves needs no counseling."[37] He even interpreted seemingly "victimless" problems—e.g., experiences of anxiety or depression, acts of social withdrawal, or habits of masturbation—as interpersonal in that they involved sins of unbelief to God and omission of love to neighbor. He wrote extensively, for both counselors and counselees, explaining and offering solutions to behaviors that jeopardized loving social relationships: hostility, shyness, manipulation, avoidance, jealousy, fear of betrayal, gossip, lying, betrayal, and so forth.[38]

Second, bad feelings frequently constituted the "presenting problems" that led people to seek counseling. Adams interpreted dysphorias on a case-by-case basis, as either sins, or consequences of sin, or natural responses to suffering. Adams addressed the typical range of felt misery: despair and depression; fear and anxiety; confusion; anger and bitterness; guilt.[39] He consistently emphasized feelings as a point of contact with people but deemphasized feelings as a guide for where counseling should proceed. He often reiterated a slogan from William Glasser's *Reality Therapy*—"Act right, feel right"—that subordinated feeling to what he saw as more significant behavioral causes, and treated feeling as symptomatic or epiphenomenal to action.[40] Adams did not trust that people's feelings were reliable gauges of reality. He frequently inveighed against the assumptions of much contemporary psychotherapy that feelings were the major focus of counseling, to be "gotten in touch with," to be viewed as "neutral" rather than morally colored, to be trusted as reliable guides for faith and practice.[41] Adams did believe that all emotions were potentially constructive—anger, fear, desire, guilt, sorrow, happiness, and the rest.[42] But his counseling subordinated feeling and experience—like cognition and volition—to the call to "obedience to God's commands."[43] He explored feelings as information to know and to identify as either sinful or righteous for the purposes of changing people.

Third, Adams naturally had a great deal to say about "bad" behaviors. He promulgated an overtly moral model as we have seen. His nouthetic counseling spoke of behavior in explicitly, not implicitly, evaluative language: good or bad, obedient or sinful. Adams avoided and criticized language that cast human behavior into less morally freighted terms. He refused to speak of alcoholism, extramarital affairs, emotional problems, kleptomania, or schizophrenia, except as dubious labels, euphemisms, for the phenomena to which they pointed.[44] He did not speak of mistakes, maladjustment, failings, bad habits, vices, or behaviors that might create social disrepute and personal unhappiness. He intended to up the ante to the highest possible level. In his world, sinners lived before the eyes of their Judge.

Adams's catalogue of behavioral sins was traditional: the Ten Commandments, the seven deadly sins, and their ramifying fellows, as portrayed in the extensive sin lists in New Testament epistles and historical theology.[45] Adams catalogued various aspects of interpersonal conflict as sin: anger, lying, fears, manipulation. He identified the various escapist pleasures as sin: drunkenness, drug use, laziness, gambling, and the like.[46] He listed the conventional varieties of immorality, all non-marital sexuality, as sin: adultery, fornication, masturbation, homosexuality, pornography, pedophilia, and so forth.[47] He and his followers interpreted numerous behaviors as sin, even when no explicit biblical proof text could be adduced for the particular phenomenon. For example, the modern "eating disorders" ("food addiction, anorexia, bulimia") were interpreted into moral-theological language by such terms as gluttony, service to varied cravings of the flesh, self-serving asceticism, love of pleasure, worship of idolatrous images of beauty, desire for Godlike control, fear of death,

self-atonement, and the like.[48] Adams's diagnostic model provided cognitive tools for reasoning about problems that pastors had often been hard-pressed to account for as sin.

Much of Adams's attention in counseling was devoted to carefully identifying behavioral habit patterns, and then defining alternative behaviors that counselees could implement. He gathered extensive, detailed data about the what, when, and where of his counselees' behavior. Then he and they hammered out the appropriate alternatives, setting equally detailed goals. One characteristic nouthetic phrase was "the put off and put on." Sinful, problem behaviors would be "put off" and godly behaviors "put on" with God's aid. Adams described this process, borrowing language from Mowrer, as a process of "dehabituation" and "rehabituation." One set of definably sinful behaviors, often habitual, would be replaced by another set of behaviors, definably righteous and loving, that might with time become a fresh set of habits.[49]

Adams's emphatic and detailed discussion of behavioral habituation represented a theological innovation and was closely linked to another idiosyncrasy in his views on sin and "the flesh." He gave great emphasis to the physical body as the locus of sins that needed to be changed through counseling. Sinful habits had been "programmed" into the human body (the brain and the bodily "members") by the mind: "The body [is] plunged into sinful practices and habits. . . . The body 'wants' to do [sinful things] because it has been programmed to do them automatically, unconsciously, and with ease."[50] Adams believed that under the influence of the Bible and the Holy Spirit the mind could "reprogram the brain and, through it, the members of the body" to operate the body differently.[51] He envisioned counseling as furthering "a battle for self-conquest. . . . The body is still too much in control of me; *I* should be in control of *it*."[52] Adams's preoccupation with neurologically programmed habits distinctively colored his answers to ancient theological questions. For example, his version of the nature of "indwelling sin" and of Calvinism's traditional moral strenuousness featured behavioral habituation: "Your whole life ought to be disciplined (i.e., structured, set up, organized, and running day by day) toward the goal of godliness. . . . Jesus insisted that Christians must deny *the self* within them. By the self, He meant the old desires, the old ways, the old practices, the old habit patterns that were acquired before conversion."[53] The body programmed to sin could be reprogrammed.[54]

Fourth, Adams also defined faulty cognitions and false beliefs as sinful. He interpreted these as doctrinal errors, as false views of God, self, circumstances, and the purpose of life. In counseling practice, he particularly challenged the specific verbalizations by which counselees revealed their worldview: "The repetition of what Margaret Mead once called 'pickled clichés' is an element for which every counselor searches diligently in the speech of his counselees. . . . The counselor looks for inaccurate and biased words and language constructions that, when repeatedly spoken by him, may influence the counselee's thinking and behavior."[55] For example, Adams assiduously listened for when counselees talked about their felt "needs." He would confront such word choice on the spot: "The counselor will soon find it necessary to explain to him that what he persists in calling a 'need,' God actually calls a 'desire,' or, sometimes, 'lust.'"[56] Adams listened for many sorts of definably deviant language: psychiatric jargon, terms that shifted blame onto someone else, exaggerations or overgeneralizations, stiff formality, vagueness. Regarding counselees who

spoke in global negatives ("can't," "impossible") or catastrophic language ("hopeless," "ruined"), Adams noted that such language revealed "that his *working* view of God (not the theoretically articulated one that he would give you if you asked, but the one that emerges in a crisis) at best is deistic."[57] Such functional deism was yet another of the sins that truth was meant to confront in love. In his manual on counseling method, Adams included an appendix of possible counselor comebacks to typical counselee remarks. A portion of that is reproduced in table 10 (see p. 105).[58]

Fifth, Adams and his fellow nouthetic counselors repeatedly addressed the presumably sinful ways people tended to respond to their varied sufferings. A voluminous literature, much of it intended for use by counselees experiencing hardships, treated both daily hardships and major tragedies.[60] Consistent with Adams's Calvinistic belief in the sovereignty of God, he embedded such events within a framework of ultimate meaningfulness: sufferings tested people, bringing out what needed to change, and provided a context to make significant changes.

I will say more about Adams's view of suffering in the next section, but a comment on his approach to sufferers is apposite. The moral strenuousness of Adams's system of counseling emerges clearly in his treatments of suffering. He was not averse to offering a certain amount of consolation and comfort. Indeed, he made "giving hope" a central activity in all his counseling, and people who had "suffered life-shattering experiences" stood in particular need because "hope in grief is the antidote to despair."[61] His definition of hope in the midst of intractable circumstances strongly emphasized the potentiality for personal change in the midst of hardship, not simply consolations to be nursed.[62]

TABLE 10

Counselor Responses to Counselee Remarks[59]

Typical Counselee Remarks	Typical Counselor Responses
"I can't!"	"Do you mean can't or won't?"
"I have done everything that I could."	"Everything? What about . . . ?"
"I've tried that, but it didn't work."	"Precisely, what *did* you do?"
"*No one* believes me."	"I believe you."
"If I had the time, I'd do it."	"You do. We all have twenty-four hours each day; it all depends on how you slice the pie. Now let's work on drawing up a schedule that honors God."
"I guess so."	"Are you guessing, or is that what you believe?"
"You know how it is."	"No, I don't know; can you explain it more fully?"
"But I've *prayed* about it."	"Fine! Then what did you *do?*" or "What exactly did you pray?"
"I'm at the end of my rope."	"Which end? Perhaps you are beginning to uncoil your problem for the first time."
"That is impossible."	"What you mean, of course, is that it is very difficult."
"I'll never forgive him!"	"If you are a child of God, as you claim, you will. You are going to live with him for eternity; why don't you forgive him and begin to get used to it now?"
"Everything [one] is against me."	"No, you are wrong. If you are a Christian the Bible says the opposite: 'If God be for us, who can be against us?'"
"How do you feel about . . . ?"	"May I tell you what I think, or may I only discuss my emotions?"

Adams sharply reacted against the historical "restriction" of the pastoral role to consolatory functions.[63] He tended to define compassion in action terms: meeting practical, material needs of counselees or teaching them biblical doctrine that gave a framework for hope. In talking about sympathy, he said:

> By concern, I mean something more than sympathy. Concern is not *only* weeping with those who weep—as essential as that may be—but also the willingness to help another to do something about his problems. Sympathy, too often, means "sympathetic *agreement*." But that sort of expression of solidarity with the sufferer goes too far, since seeing a crisis only as the counselee does, in fact, precludes that possibility of helping him. . . .
>
> Scriptural concern, therefore, is not the expression of sympathetic agreement; rather it is the expression of sympathetic *disagreement*. It is only by *countering* perplexity, and hopelessness, and depression, and temper, and fear with biblical alternatives that the counselor maintains his integrity as such.[64]

He moved rapidly through consolation and on to the pursuit of change. Suffering was an "evil," but his counselees were not to "return evil for evil." In a typical statement he noted, that "suffering, rightly handled, brings about growth."[65] Even in suffering, sin was the major problem in living. The anger, fear, depression, or escapism that so typically attend experiences of suffering were viewed as occasions to learn varied Christian graces: to forgive, to love one's enemies, to confront evil courageously, to endure, and so forth.

As we have seen, Adams considered the diagnosis "sin" appropriate for the gamut of normal problems in living: interpersonal conflict, unhappy emotions, bad behavior, faulty beliefs, and typical reactions to suffering. But he also believed it applied to the most extreme problems in living: "schizophrenia" and other forms of bizarre behavior.[66] The extremes of bizarre behavior—the "mentally ill"—played a significant part in Adams's articulation and defense of his system. He believed that most "mental illnesses" could be unmasked as instances of things the Bible treated under the category of sin. Just as he reacted to defining the pastor as one who offered consoling promises to sufferers, so he reacted to defining the pastor as one who should deal with nothing "more serious than a psychic scratch," referring more difficult problems to mental health professionals.[67]

He commenced *Competent to Counsel* by discussing extreme cases—inmates of psychiatric hospitals—rather than arguing for jurisdiction over garden-variety problems. This was a striking rhetorical choice. It defined his pastoral audience as the counselors-of-choice for the toughest functional problems. This cut directly across the grain of the standard view of the role of religious personnel in the treatment of mental patients. Adams pointedly criticized the conventional wisdom that he had heard espoused in a talk given by a mental hospital chaplain to a group of pastors:

A summary of his address is as follows: "First of all, there is little you can do as ministers for people in a mental hospital. Secondly, what you can do is support the patient's right to feel injured by others. Thirdly, it is important to understand that in a mental institution people with guilt are no longer subjected to rebuke from others outside, the pressure is off, and in this way they quietly lose their guilt and get well. Fourthly, we must consider people in mental hospitals not as violators of conscience but as victims of their conscience. Finally when we look at their erratic behavior, it seems to be sin, but it isn't; the patient is not really responsible for his actions. He can't help what he's doing; he's sick. Often he blames himself for what he can't help, for what isn't his fault, and this is a cause of his problems. Consequently bad behavior as blameworthy is taboo in a mental hospital. The usual religious approach of responsibility, guilt, confession and forgiveness is no good here. The patients' consciences are already too severe. These people are morally neutral persons, and all we can do is be ventilators for them." This verbatim summary of the chaplain's speech, about as succinctly as any other, sets forth the institutionalized view of our time. Every point he made will be challenged in this book.[68]

Adams was not about to agree that pastors should be domesticated.

Adams's fundamental thesis about bizarre behavior was simple: "Apart from organically generated difficulties, the 'mentally ill' are really *people with unsolved personal problems.*"[69] In other words, "There may be several things wrong with the so-called 'mentally ill,' but the one cause which must be excluded in most cases is mental illness itself."[70] He thus staked a claim for pastors to treat the entire field of "functional" problems. In *CtC*, he detailed cases where garden-variety sins were discovered to underlie extremely bizarre behavior.[71] Adams described three (often interlinking) causes that contributed to psychiatric diagnoses. First, cultural perception labeled certain behaviors as deviant, whether or not these merited definition as problems of sin. Second, chronic or acute biological malfunctions (e.g., tumors or senility in the former case; sleep loss or drug effects in the latter) could cause patterns or incidents of bizarre thinking and action. But, third and most significant, habitual sinful responses to life generated most of the behaviors that led to a psychiatric label and to varieties of treatment ranging from incarceration to psychotropic medications to psychotherapy.[72] Adams described a range of particular discernible sins that might be encountered in so-called schizophrenics: avoidance of responsibility or of suffering, resentment, fears, guilt, false beliefs, self-pity, adultery, grandiose fantasizing, mishandling of disappointment, camouflage, manipulation, and so forth.

Adams did not mean that such extreme problems were always, or even usually, cases of malingering and dissembling. He wrote frequently about unconscious sinful patterns of thinking, belief, attitude, and behavior. He thought that people had a "basic personality 'set'" that was "usually unconscious."[73] Much sin occurred without awareness because sin by its very nature was both self-deceiving and habitual.[74] That sin was often instinctive, automatic, and unwitting compounded rather than lessened human responsibility according to the Calvinistic schema to which Adams subscribed. Nouthetic counseling set as one of its goals to awaken the sense of sin in people who did not know what they were doing or why.

Adams set forth a simple labeling theory that made two points. First, labels acted as signpoints to solutions congruent with the assumptions of the label: "Wrong labels point in wrong directions. . . . *Schizophrenia* is a psychological or psychiatric label which leads toward psychological or psychiatric solutions. . . . If [investigation] indicates that the problem comes from sinful living, the term 'sin' points in the direction of a theological solution."[75] Second, labels created powerful expectations and could influence the production of confirmatory symptoms. He wrote that the power of language "may be performative; it shapes and thereby brings about the fact that it describes. In some instances this may be true of people who have been labeled according to psychiatric categories."[76] Adams discussed labels with the charm and crudity of a successful popularizer:

I shall, therefore, use the word "schizophrenia" throughout the remainder of this article merely for the sake of present convenience—I cannot argue here for the use of different nomenclature. But I do so reluctantly and with great reservation. The sooner we can adopt new terminology, the better. Whenever the word "schizophrenia" appears I shall be referring not to any definable, diagnostic category representing a specific illness or behavior. Rather, I shall view it solely as a broad collective term having no one clear-cut referent, but rather pointing to bizarre behavior that is the result of any cause—contrived or otherwise—or any complex of causes that may lead to severe inability to function in society. I, therefore, consider the words "red nose" to be on precisely the same communicational level with the word "schizophrenia." To observe that one has a red nose is to say nothing more than that; the statement carries no necessary causal implications. The words refer to an observable effect, not to etiology. That is to say (whatever its cause), the observation refers to an effect that may have any number of different and widely diverse causes. Thus, the statement, "You have a red nose," does not necessarily carry with it the insinuation (for instance) that the person addressed has been boozing. It would be wrong to infer that from the simple statement itself. Indeed, he may have fallen asleep under a sun lamp, his wife may have punched him in it, he may be growing a pimple on it, etc. Similarly, to say that one is schizophrenic is merely to observe that his behavior has become so bizarre that he is unable to function (or is not allowed by others to function) in society.[77]

In Adams's practice, the ambiguity of "schizophrenia" was no barrier to the energetic pursuit of moral causes that could be addressed through nouthetic confrontation.

Moral causes of bizarre behavior might be mingled with physiological factors. Adams was interested in ostensible organic concomitants to bizarre behavior: "Not all peculiar behavior, of course, stems from specific acts of sin; there are people who have toxic problems, tumors on the brain, brain damage, etc., who because of physical damage or chemical malfunction perform badly."[78] Such organic problems, external to moral responsibility, might come into play and modify the counselee's capabilities to some undetermined degree. Adams never got more specific than saying "to the extent that it is possible to do so" organically impaired patients were responsible to obey God.[79] In Adams's view, physiological impairment was an indirect consequence of the problem of sin, one component in that comprehensive impairment characteristic of the "fallen" state of humankind:

> That man may be subject to (or may subject himself to) internal and external forces that may impair his ability to function, that he is capable of intentionally and unintentionally stimulating and simulating such impairment in order to mislead, and that over a period of time (or suddenly) he can develop such faulty responses to stress situations that he loses a grip on reality (i.e., he may misread it) is to picture him at once as a frail, a conniving, a self-deceptive and a foolish being. That is to say, as Christians look at it, man is a sinner. . . .[80]

In treating people whose behavior was peculiar, Adams was amenable to cooperation with physicians, and to a cautious use of both medical treatments and medical research in seeking to disentangle vexing cases.[81] Adams's discussion of organic components to bizarre behavior was typically hedged and tentative, a contrast to his typical style. For example, while he generally opposed psychotropic medications, finding "the excessive use of pills among psychiatrists and physicians alarming," he granted that "not all medication is unnecessary."[82] When he wrote regarding depression that "the physician might uncover some of the infrequent cases of chemically caused depression and in very serious cases may help the pastor to engage in meaningful counseling by temporarily administering antidepressants,"[83] he did not seek to resolve either the ambiguities of "chemically caused" or to define the parameters of "serious."

In Adams's proposed reconfiguration of the professional landscape, he reassigned psychiatrists to explore such organic problems and not to intrude into the functional problems. "That there is much for the psychiatrist to do *medically* to help persons suffering from problems in living whose etiology is organic cannot be questioned."[84] He never gave a more specific answer to the question of disentangling organic from moral etiologies.

But Adams was clear about the relative numbers of people to be expected in each category. By comparison, the number of people "whose problems are organic in origin (as over against those who are simply not 'making it' in life because they are not solving life's problems biblically) is negligible." Adams thus defined the great bulk of severely troubled people as candidates for his nouthetic counseling. In fact, even those patients whose problems demonstrated a marked organic component were not outside the pastor's purview and care. Wherever *counseling* took place, Adams would have his biblically competent counselors do the job, joining their efforts with medical doctors.

> The psychiatrist has reason for existence when he specializes as a physician to treat

medically those persons whose problems have an organic etiology. Even then, most likely there will be need for twofold help. While the physician treats the physical problem, the Christian counselor should pedal in tandem. . . . The pastor's task will be to help him to alter sinful life patterns that may have developed in response to chemical disorder. These may include bad human relationships resulting from suspicion, withdrawal from others, etc.[85]

Troubled people would find the aid they needed in the combination of medical care and nouthetic counseling.

Only infrequently did Adams allude to any contribution from social causes to bizarre behavior. In one case study he discussed a "schizophrenic" young woman with whom he had worked at CCEF. She had a history of multiple psychiatric hospitalizations and had barely spoken during the previous two years. Her parents had been missionaries. They had sent her to boarding school from a young age, leading to "many years of deprivation apart from her parents." In counseling the parents came to see "that their conduct toward her in many ways had been sinful. They became deeply repentant." In that context the young woman was encouraged to "face her problems rather than running from them," and she was able to "break through the barrier and [tell] her parents (as she had been urged to do) about her resentments." In the reconciliation that followed, the parents faced up to their well-rationalized neglect ("They believed that they had been 'doing the Lord's work' and that this justified their behavior toward their child."), and the woman faced up to her years of bitterness. The mutual repentance led to a reconstituted relationship, the disappearance of bizarre symptoms, and the woman's reentry into normal human society.[86] Such an interweaving of social context and moral response was atypi-

cal, however. Both Adams's discussions and case studies focused heavily on personal sin and physiological complications.

As the paragraphs above indicate, Adams concluded from his time with Mowrer and his own counseling experience that most people diagnosed as mentally ill and, consequently, subjected to psychiatric care were chiefly suffering from a "failure to meet life's problems. To put it simply, they were there because of their unforgiven and unaltered sinful behavior."[87] Adams concluded that if the real problem was sin, then "many of the 'mentally ill' are people who can be helped by the ministry of God's Word."[88]

Identifying *the* fundamental problem in living as sin, in specific detail, generated numerous counseling implications. Adams believed that counselors should deal with others' sin candidly, lovingly, and humbly—even as they dealt with their own sin. The candor would come because hard truth could only help when spoken of in the light of the grace of God for sinners, both to forgive sinners and to help them change. The love would come because Christ had loved sinners and suffered to redeem them; counselors who ministered in Christ's name could do no less for others as recipients of that love themselves. The humility would come because counselors were no different than those they counseled, equally prone to sin, equally recipients of divine mercy, equally in need of counsel.[89]

Identifying how the fundamental problems in living were sin served Adams's cause well in the task of persuading his hearers. They were people who already believed much of what he said, at least in principle if not in the details. If the secular psychologies had used their case-wise empirical detail to sell the culture their diagnostic models, then Adams might equally use empirical detail to convince people that those seemingly exotic problems really were sin after all.

3. Trials, temptations, and misery

God was the invisible environment within which human life played out a struggle with sin and the consequences of sin. But the immediately tangible, visible environment was suffering. Adams interpreted the circumstances surrounding morally freighted responses in terms familiar from classic theological formulas: "trials and temptations" might incite a counselee to sin; "misery" might register the consequences of a counselee's sin, or simply reflect the tough circumstances of life in a fallen and cursed world. All in all, the varied hardships and beguilements that attended human life found their interpretation within the cosmic moral drama that anchored the belief system of Adams and his hearers. Hearers would be struck by the familiarity of both his concepts and the features of life to which he applied those concepts. They would be equally struck by the unfamiliar degree of detail in his gaze and by the unusual concreteness with which he applied those concepts. "Sickness"—traditionally to be prayed for, endured, and treated medically—became the occasion for lengthy discussion of the interplay between moral response and various medical problems. "Enemies" who treated one with "evil"—traditionally to be forgiven and loved—prompted entire books that sought to describe and redress the reactions to interpersonal betrayal. The "world"—traditionally to be resisted—occasioned a close look at the impact of companions, upbringing, role models, reading material, TV habits, and other occasions of sociocultural conditioning. "Reaping what you sow"—traditionally a rather general warning about the consequences of sin—occasioned a close look at the varied somatic, psychosomatic, social, psychological, and financial woes (or blessings) that might attend lifestyle choices against (or for) God's revealed will. Adams would certainly urge his hearers to pray, endure, forgive, love, resist, and heed in the face of the varied factors that impinge on moral actors—but he extended the scope and magnified the detail of such activities.

Adams described a common pattern in the many factors that contributed to problems in living. In each case he located sinners in a sin-inducing and sin-produced context, but that context was never sin-causing. Difficult circumstances compelled some sort of response, but never predicted or constrained the particular response. Adams considered that the various exigencies of social circumstance and physical illness provided occasions in which sinfulness or faithfulness would be revealed. A full treatment of Adams's views would need to consider his assessment of the range of factors that act to significantly shape human behavior, but his treatment is unsystematic and uneven. Somatic factors were mentioned often, as were those social events in which people were immediately wronged by others. He never discussed more general social factors that contributed to problems in living: socialization and enculturation, the impact of political, economic, racial, class, and gender issues. Adams occasionally mentioned another factor not typical of twentieth-century secular counseling models, the role of the devil and demonic agencies as "social" actors in the situations that evoke moral choices and responses—one could never say "the devil made me do it." Though Adams's discussion was spotty, a common pattern emerged whenever situational factors were discussed: such things provided the significant context, not the cause, of morally freighted responses.

Though the general pattern was the same (a pattern characteristic of any moral model of human behavior), Adams granted somatic events a far more significant impact than social events. When writing about physiological influences, he called his nonmedical readers to recognize that somatic variables created significant ambiguities for their counseling, to do further study, and to work closely with doctors:

> That the body affects the soul and the soul the body in so many obvious, as well as subtle, ways is a fact that the Christian counselor must always remember. His work, therefore, constantly involves the organic dimension. . . . He should take the time and trouble, therefore, to study the fundamental functions of the human body. Because the problem of the dividing line between problems caused by organic factors and nonorganic factors is often fuzzy, the best solution to this problem . . . seems to be for the counselor to cultivate a close alliance with a Christian physician with whom he can work closely.[90]

When writing about social influences Adams took a different tack. He acknowledged the pervasiveness of socialization effects, but his sole concern was to warn against excuse-making and to exhort to moral responsibility. "That others have done much to shape our lives, no one can deny. However, each individual must bear personal responsibility for how he has allowed others to influence his conduct. No one can blame another for his bad behavior, even when he has been taught that behavior from childhood. What he learned may be unlearned. Since we may reshape ourselves, we are responsible for the shape we are in."[91] Adams never detailed what he meant by this undeniable shaping and gave no indication of how pastors ought to weigh such influences. He never exhorted nouthetic counselors to study secular disciplines that studied environmental influences on the individual: psychology, social psychology, anthropology, sociology, or analyses of contemporary culture. He was typically concerned to get at the generic "human nature" presumed to operate within social, cultural, and historical variability. Such variability merely represented the

varied "styles" of sinning and consisted in "secondary dimensions—the variations on the common themes."[92] Adams's recurrent concern was to exclude any possibility of social determinism for sin. He thought such determinism came readily enough to mind as counselees made excuses for themselves, and it dominated the various social scientific theories.[93]

In this section, after a brief discussion of Adams's rather sketchy view of social factors, I will focus largely on his view of somatic factors and the role of medicine. Adams's interpretation of the social milieu must be extrapolated from stray comments and anecdotes. It was weighted in two directions. First, he often wrote about the anguish and temptations that come with being overtly wronged by others.[94] He would seek to give such victims hope in the form of Bible promises to trust, help in the form of whatever tangible assistance others might offer, and a practical strategy for responding constructively to ill treatment. Second, he was particularly interested in the impact of modeling. As the second quotation in the paragraph above illustrates, he typically identified the responsibility of those he counseled to assess the models that had influenced them and to choose proper models, i.e., Jesus Christ and godly people currently in their circles.[95]

Adams pressed the notion of human responsibility on his hearers, even when speaking of children. Even the child "who has been berated time and again by his parents; who has been told in a hundred ways that he is worthless; who is constantly criticized and condemned" was entirely responsible for the depression or rebellion that typically followed: "If he believes what he is told, then that is what he is—a weak person dependent upon others for self-evaluation."[96]

The question, therefore, is not *whether* the sinful lifestyles developed by children with sinful natures in response to sinful influences or even acts of abuse against them are wrong or not. They are. Sin is sin, whether the sinner is young or old. Nor is it a matter of whether they are responsible. Again, they are. The very fact that children are not considered to be morally neutral in the sight of God means that they may be held responsible for making whatever righteous responses that it is possible for a child to make at any given age. As unredeemed sinners, children will fail to respond *as they should*. For this they are accountable. As they grow in age, their responsibility grows as capability for response enlarges. . . . At any given point in life, therefore, a child is held responsible for doing whatever he ought to be able to do at that age. That is to say, the child is held accountable for doing what a sinless child might have done were the fall not to have occurred. "Man's responsibility goes far beyond his ability," wrote R. B. Kuiper [a Reformed theologian] in an excellent clear discussion of this point.[97]

In Adams's view, "sinful influences" and "acts of abuse" only gained purchase in the human soul because of the susceptibility of sinful hearts to embrace sin or to react to sin sinfully.[98]

In his concern to forestall "blameshifting" and not allow any reasons for bad behavior external to the individual, Adams quickly inserted the theological perspective into any discussion of the impact people have on each other. Adams's characteristic response to interpersonal distress or social shaping was to say, "God is sovereign over the situation, God is in the situation, God is up to something good, therefore trust him and obey him in ways specifically appropriate to this situation."[99] Consistent with the weight Adams assigned to situational and moral factors, his practice of counseling spent relatively little time

exploring or addressing situational factors. Locating counselees *coram Deo* was more significant than locating them *in situ*. The past or present situation would be studied chiefly to discover sinful responses and to determine what responses would now be timely and appropriate.

Adams was slower to insert his theological perspective into discussions of medical factors. His view of medicine is particularly accessible because he and his fellows wrote extensively and systematically about the body's ailments. His interaction with doctors is also of particular interest for understanding the pattern of jurisdictional conflicts and alliances that attended nouthetic counseling. Adams maintained a high degree of respect for the physiological component in behavioral and emotional problems, and hence reiterated to his readers and trainees the need to work "back to back" and "side-by-side" with physicians.[100]

Adams typically advised counselees early in the counseling process to get a complete physical examination in order to rule out somatic causes for their problems in living. The prominence of somatic issues for Adams was signaled when in his list of "Twenty-Five Basic Principles" of counseling he placed this as the very first principle:

Check out possible organic causes of problems. While laymen are not supposed to be physicians or diagnosticians, it is important to be aware of the possibility of organic causes of behavioral problems. Whenever there is the slightest suspicion that the difficulty may have organic roots, refer your counselee to a physician (not a psychiatrist) for a medical checkup. In *The Journal of Pastoral Practice* . . . Bob Smith, M.D., has been describing various signs and symptoms, in laymen's language, to help Christian counselors detect such difficulties so that they may know when to refer a counselee to a physician. . . . Be

sure you refer to a physician—a man who
does *body* work—not a psychiatrist.[101]

Two of the other twenty-four basic principles similarly dealt with somatic issues: (1) counselees on drugs (either street or prescription) needed special care, so "Counsel only sober persons," and "Learn something about drugs so you will know whether you are talking to a pill or a person"; (2) sleep loss might lead to perceptual problems, so "Don't try to counsel hallucinating persons who haven't been sleeping; put them to bed!"[102] The concern to inform nouthetic counselors of basic medical facts led to numerous journal articles by medical doctors for medical laymen. Topics covered everything from rheumatism to menopause, from irritable bowel syndrome to headaches, from sleep disorders to psychopharmacology.[103]

In addition to utilizing doctors' somatic expertise, Adams admired doctors for their rationality, thoroughness, and practicality. He thought pastors were all too often sentimental, shoddy, and ineffectual in comparison. Adams sought to model pastoral counseling activities on the style of professional competency he saw evidenced in doctors. That Adams valued medical expertise and respected doctors won him a hearing among many conservative Protestant doctors sympathetic to his suspicions of psychiatry.[104] Doctors came to play an active role in nouthetic counseling. Between 1977 and 1994, about 20 percent of the some five hundred articles in the *Journal of Pastoral Practice* were written by medical doctors and treated topics at the interface of counseling and medicine.[105] Medical doctors also figured prominently as speakers at nouthetic counseling conferences. They were second only to pastors in influence, and often used their prestige as medical professionals to enhance the case they made for nouthetic counseling. At NANC national conventions typically about 20 percent of the speakers were MDs.

In typical biblicistic manner, Adams warranted his respectful view of medicine and the conjoining of nouthetic counseling with medical treatment by appealing to Bible texts. He observed that "from the days of Paul and Luke, pastors have found kinship with medical personnel."[106] James 5:14–16 served as an often-cited proof text:

Is anybody among you sick? Let him call for the elders of the church and let them pray for him, rubbing him with oil in the Name of the Lord, and the believing prayer will deliver the one who is sick, and the Lord will raise him up. And if he has committed sins, he will be forgiven. So confess your sins to one another and pray for one another so that you may be healed. The petition of a righteous person has very powerful effects. . . . My brothers, if anybody among you errs from the truth and somebody brings him back, you should know that the one who brings back a sinner from the error of his way will save his soul from death and will cover a lot of sins. [107]

Adams interpreted the confession of sins, prayer, and restoration from the error of one's ways as shorthand for a counseling consultation in which honest talk had taken place. He interpreted the particular sicknesses in view as specifically psychosomatic or lifestyle induced—sin-engendered ailments in other words—hence the significance of the counseling remedy enjoined. He did not interpret anointing with oil (the standard translation) either as a ceremonial act or as possessing mystical, sacramental efficacy. It was an act of rational medical care, rubbing in oil-based medicaments.[108] Thus in Adams's view, the elders about whom James had written operated as both spiritual leaders and medical personnel (according to the common premodern pattern), who would apply both cure of soul and cure of body to the sick person. Adams believed that the modern application of this involved cooperative work, with the counselee being under the "overall care of the pastor and the elders of his church. This is a care that must be exercised prior to, *during*, and after the care of the attending physician."[109]

Though Adams and his medical allies respected what medicine could contribute to counseling, they voiced misgivings about the expansion of medicine into those realms of life that they thought contained a significant moral component. Bob Smith, who did a great deal of counseling at Faith Baptist Counseling Ministries and wrote most of the medical articles in the *Journal of Pastoral Practice*, said, "The fact that I am an M.D. matters about twice a year in my counseling."[110] As part of his particular definition of the counseling task, Adams assailed what he saw as medicalistic presumption. Nouthetic counseling, and the doctors who subscribed to it, attempted four deep forays into medical territory. They sought to stake out a pastoral role and an alternative perspective regarding psychosomatic problems, lifestyle diseases, the medicalization of moral issues, and medical ethics. In a fifth area—the response of sufferers to their own disease, disability, pain, or imminent death, and the response of those bereaved or coping with another's ailment—Adams and his colleagues did not so much seek to invade medical turf as to reclaim and extend a traditional domain in which the pastoral role had become truncated. The response to pain and bereavement had long been the pastor's province but had suffered significant invasion from psychotherapists. Pastors needed to take action in each of these five areas to regain and protect ground that had been illegitimately appropriated, misconstrued, or threatened by the secular medical profession. We will consider the views of nouthetic counselors in each area.

First, psychosomatic problems, almost by definition, are contested ground. The ambiguity of psychosomatic ailments makes them an intellectual *tabula rasa*, a screen onto which various interpretive systems project meanings. Such problems stand between strictly somatic medicine and the rabble of competing definitions of problems in living. In interprofessional politics, psychosomatic ailments are ripe prizes, a natural location for border disputes to recur between medicine and its many neighbors. Psychosomatics stand outside the heartland of medicine's strictly somatic expertise: "Doctors themselves were quoted as to the varying, but usually high, proportion of their patients whom they diagnosed as suffering for psychological causes," hence "jurisdictional haziness" was a given.[111] Psychosomatic ailments attract other groups, and are perennially subject to depredations by non-MDs. The writing of books on psychosomatics has been a profitable industry since the nineteenth century, with perspectives ranging from health cultists to mainline physicians, from positive thinkers to fundamentalists.[112]

From the inception of nouthetic counseling, Adams and his medical colleagues—particularly Bob Smith—sought to incorporate psychosomatic phenomena within the purview of nouthetic counseling.[113] Over the first five years of the *Journal of Pastoral Practice* references to psychosomatic processes appeared in almost every issue. Typical of the rhetorical strategy of the movement, Smith suggested a relabeling—"spiritual-physiological reactions" or "hamartiagenic [sin-engendered] symptoms"—to capture the dynamic thought to underlie psychogenic symptoms.[114] He asserted that identifiable "spiritual issues"—false beliefs, a wrong fundamental orientation to life, distorted motives, and sinful behaviors and emotions—led people to mishandle life's stresses. He proposed that sufferers of physical illnesses ask themselves a sequence of questions that would prompt moral self-examination: "A Christian should look at all illness from two perspectives. First, he should ask, "Does God want to change something; is there some sin in my life that is producing this illness?" Once he has closely examined his life and found nothing there, then he can turn to the second principle. He may ask, "How does God want to glorify Himself through this illness?"[115] Smith's interpretation of the significance of illness captures well the tone of religious earnestness that characterized nouthetic counseling. Sickness occurred within a context of God's sovereign will. Hence it demanded self-examination regarding possible moral causes of psychosomatic (or lifestyle-induced) illness and then a determination of the proper moral response to physical affliction, however caused. In the nouthetic response to suffering one witnesses the seventeenth-century Puritan ethos revived.

Second, lifestyle diseases drew a great deal of attention from nouthetic counselors. In the mid-1980s, after a busy decade of writing occasional pieces on medical issues, Bob Smith summarized his philosophy of medicine in a four-part series.[116] The third article focused on health problems consequential to a wide range of particular lifestyle choices: sedentary habits, use of alcohol and tobacco, poor dietary choices, bad hygiene, sexual promiscuity, failure to use seat belts, unresolved sinful emotions and attitudes, and sleep loss.

Nouthetic counselors were not shy about engaging in moral exhortation to address matters of sinful belief and behavior that contributed to physical ills (or to other consequences, financial, social, and so forth). But they were not "positive thinkers," offering keys to health, wealth, or friendship. Consistent with their Calvinistic commitment to God's sovereignty, proper choices in these areas were no formulaic guarantee of a healthy, happy life: "Counselors must, therefore, warn counselees not to make the gifts, blessings, and good health their fundamental goal. Obeying and worshiping God to please and serve Him for what He is produces good health and long life as a by-product. But He does not guarantee good health and long life."[117] The inscrutability of God's ways with humankind amid the vicissitudes of life did not seem to perplex an MD who made "glorifying God and enjoying Him forever" the goal of his counsel to his patients/counselees.[118] The reversal of lifestyles was primary; the amelioration or prevention of lifestyle diseases was a consequential good, perhaps likely to occur, but distinctly secondary.

Nouthetic counseling's third foray into the medical heartland involved an attack on the widespread medicalization of problems in living. We have already noted how Adams considered most "mental illness" a misnomer for failures to handle life properly. He was similarly exercised about the medicalization or biologization of drunkenness, sexual immorality, cowardice, anger, and the like. Explanations of such behaviors and emotions that invoked heredity, hormones, or temperament drew his fire. Adams appreciated that biological psychiatry might discover brain correlates to states of mind and volition but spoke of the body as typically habituated in sin, not as victimized by nonmoral factors. Adams was concerned to carefully circumscribe doctors and psychologists to what he considered to be the proper domains of "medicine" and "science." Psychological and medical research and psychiatric practice could be "legitimate and very useful neighbors" to pastoral counselors if only they would mind their own business.[119]

Medical ethics was the fourth area into which nouthetic counselors occasionally pressed onto medical ground, claiming that the Bible needed to guide the decisions that doctors and patients made. The principles by which ethical decisions were made were seen as outside the sphere of medicine proper and needing theological oversight. Pastors continually encountered parishioners facing ethical dilemmas occasioned by medical problems and by the capabilities of modern medicine. Nouthetic counselors wanted a say about the questions of right and wrong that their parishioners and counselees faced. Adams wrote occasionally about medical ethics, and, more significantly, served as theological consultant for a group of conservative Protestant doctors who organized the *Journal of Biblical Ethics in Medicine* in 1987.[120] These doctors argued positions reflecting their political conservatism and traditional morality across the range of ethical issues in medicine: artificial insemination by donor, birth control prescriptions for single women, abortion, government-funded health care, fetal experimentation, active euthanasia, use of psychotropic medications, animal experimentation, transsexual surgery, identification and quarantine of AIDS sufferers, and so forth. Adams considered that, since pastors frequently had to advise parishioners about such ethical issues, conservative Protestants needed to articulate their positions. Such positions would become part of the casuistic resources that nouthetic pastors might use in counseling to help guide parishioners.

Fifth, helping sufferers cope with grief and pain had long been a recognized role of clergy in medical settings. Pastors and chaplains had traditionally acted as providers of meaning and consolation, engaging the moral response of patients to their experience of physical affliction. But Adams thought that pastors needed to redefine this area for several reasons. First, their own ineptitude caused pastors to miss counseling opportunities; he thought consolation should be only the initial step in a goal-oriented counseling process, not the full extent of what was offered. Second, Adams opposed the incursion of psychiatric theories of grief. In particular, he opposed stage theories (e.g., Elizabeth Kübler-Ross) and spiritism (e.g., Kübler-Ross and Raymond Moody) that had become popular ways to conceptualize the psychology of grief.[121] He thought stage theories converted descriptions—what happens sometimes to some people in some cultures—into a normative theory, and he thought that both stage theory and spiritism ignored Christian realities.[122] Third,

the mental health professions were increasingly aggressive in claiming the turf of death, dying, bereavement, and medical suffering. The merely consolatory pastor would quickly become incidental to the care of sufferers.

In discussing the pastor's role in the grief process, Adams had this to say about the counselor's role in the initial stages of shock:

The pastor during this period sometimes may be more present than active. This is something that you hear all of the time, of course. I hesitate ever to say that about a pastor, and yet this seems to be the one place where we have to say it. The pastor normally ought to be far more active as a counselor than many believe he should. But here is one of those rare occasions where frequently there simply is not too much that he can say or do."[123]

This comment captures Adams's instinctive activism. He chafed at the notion that the pastoral counselor should chiefly provide a caring presence and words of comfort. He did not emphasize using the Bible—for example the Psalms—in the consolatory manner of much traditional pastoral care. While he spoke often of suffering and of God's sovereign care for suffering people,[124] he rarely talked about counselees as "hurting people." Adams believed that sin and misery appeared together, pervading the human condition,[125] but he tended to speak less often of anguish than of the depravity presumed to cause misery. He was keen to help people move through grief into rebuilding lives of activity; in his view suffering was dignified as an opportunity to glorify God.[126]

Adams treated reactions to physical loss or hardship in the same way he treated bereavement. Whether counselees faced physical disabilities, premenstrual syndrome, the debilitations of old age, or chronic pain, each difficulty in its own way provided an opportunity to live by faith and in obedience to the God who promised to remove all suffering when Jesus Christ returned. One of Adams's first trainees was a pastor with wooden legs. Adams frequently spoke with approval of how this man would let a new counselee complain for a while about tough circumstances, and then he would wheel his chair out from behind the desk, pull up his pants leg, and say "Let's talk about what it's like to experience hardship."[127]

Adams's message to his constituents was clear and consistent: life's pressures and hardships tempted people to react sinfully. His formulation was consistent with their most basic commitments. In a culture whose psychologies often grounded personal and relational problems in traumatic experiences, in environmental contingencies of reinforcement, in the failures of caregivers to meet psychological needs, or in some form of biological determinism, he found a hearing. Adams spoke into a subculture whose commitments already induced them to read problems as emergent from a sinful heart, whatever the pressures produced by various "trials and temptations."

Adams's views of God, sin, and suffering found their logical correlate in his view of the evangelical solution to sin and suffering: the traditional Protestant "gospel" as a message peculiarly appropriate to the work of a pastor in the church. In the next chapter we will look at the nouthetic solution to the dilemmas of sin and misery within God' world.

Chapter 5 Notes

1. Perry London, *The Modes and Morals of Psychotherapy* (New York: Holt, Rinehart and Winston, 1964), 156, 163, 172.

2. Jay E. Adams, *More Than Redemption: A Theology of Christian Counseling* (Phillipsburg, N.J.: Presbyterian & Reformed, 1979), 43.

3. Jay E. Adams, *The Christian Counselor's Manual* (USA: Presbyterian & Reformed, 1973), 136.

4. Adams, *More Than Redemption,* 275.

5. Ibid., xi.

6. In expositing the knowledge system offered by nouthetic counseling, we must also ask what intellectual influences contributed to that system. Adams naturally claimed that the Bible itself played the leading role, with constitutive ingredients emerging out of the tradition of Reformed Protestant orthodoxy. But his counseling system did not emerge in a vacuum. His relationship to the secular psychologies is more intricate than appears on the surface; this will be explored in chapter 6.

7. Andrew Abbott, *The System of Professions: An Essay on the Division of Expert Labor* (Chicago: University of Chicago Press, 1988), 30.

8. I have adapted Andrew Abbott's comment that professional knowledge "claims to classify a problem, to reason about it, and to take action on it: in more formal terms, to diagnose, to infer, and to treat. Theoretically, these are the three acts of professional practice." Ibid., 40. I have added a fourth typical act: to dispute competitors. Professional knowledge typically conducts a running apologetic against real or potential intellectual and/or practical opponents. This apologetic can be either edificational (continuing to reinforce the faith of the faithful), defensive (answering the attacks of outsiders), or offensive (claiming fresh ground).

9. Ibid., 102.

10. Jay E. Adams, *Studies in Preaching,* vol. 2: *Audience Adaptation in the Sermons and Speeches of Paul* (USA: Presbyterian & Reformed, 1976).

11. The conservative denominations to which Adams appealed rarely allowed the ordination of women to the pastorate. Through the 1970s the biblical counseling movement had a distinctly male flavor, though pastors trained were expected to train both men and women in their local churches. The numbers of women enrolled in formal courses, attending conferences, practicing in church or paraecclesiastical counseling ministries, and writing or teaching dramatically increased in the 1980s. By the mid-1980s at CCEF and Westminster, pastors accounted for less than one quarter of the student body, and women more than half. But leadership in the movement remained male.

12. Jay E. Adams, *The Big Umbrella and Other Essays and Addresses on Christian Counseling* (USA: Presbyterian & Reformed, 1972), 27.

13. Adams, *The Christian Counselor's Manual,* 441.

14. The single-mindedness with which Adams thought in terms of the pastor is perhaps best revealed indirectly, by his one book ostensibly written for lay counselors, *Ready to Restore: The Layman's Guide to Christian Counseling* (Phillipsburg, N.J.: Presbyterian & Reformed, 1981). The model of counseling suggested is highly formalized and directive, making few adjustments for the give-and-take of those informal "counseling" situations that arise in the daily course of friendship, family life, work, school, and church.

15. In my choice of terms within this sentence, I seek to reflect Adams's world of thought and practice. I might have said, "Adams's distinctive view of healthy human functioning informed his psychopathological categories, hence his approach to the therapeutic process." But this would do violence to his conceptualization, by interpreting him from the standpoint of the very things he explicitly opposed. In Adams's view, the medical model had "ruined a good

metaphor" (interview, October 8, 1991, Lafayette, Indiana). Jesus, the Great Physician of the sin-sick soul, had been replaced by healers of sick psyches in the twentieth century.

16. Adams, *More Than Redemption,* xi.

17. Jay E. Adams, *What About Nouthetic Counseling?* (Grand Rapids: Baker, 1976), 73–75.

18. The three encyclopedia articles were written by critics, and gave the barest sketch of Adams's views before assailing them: John Carter, "Nouthetic Counseling," in *Baker Encyclopedia of Psychology,* ed. David Benner (Grand Rapids: Baker Book House, 1985), 762–65; Steven D. King, "Fundamentalist Pastoral Care," in *Dictionary of Pastoral Care and Counseling,* ed. Rodney J. Hunter (Nashville: Abingdon Press, 1990), 448–50; Chris Wigglesworth, "Bible: Pastoral Use," in *A Dictionary of Pastoral Care,* ed. Alastair V. Campbell (New York: Crossroad, 1987), 25f. Perhaps the most dispassionate summary of Adams, still relatively brief, was written by a British psychiatrist Roger Hurding, *The Tree of Healing* (Grand Rapids: Zondervan, 1985), 276–90.

19. In order to give readers a firsthand feel for Adams, the appendix contains a lengthy, annotated excerpt from his writings.

20. Adams, *More Than Redemption,* 49. Cf., pp. 118–35 for Adams's discussion of human beings as in the image of God.

21. Adams, *More Than Redemption,* 39; quoting Calvinistic philosopher Cornelius Van Til.

22. See the well-known opening paragraphs of Calvin's *Institutes of the Christian Religion.*

23. Jay E. Adams, *Counseling and the Sovereignty of God* (Philadelphia: Westminster Theological Seminary, 1975). Reprinted in Adams, *What About Nouthetic Counseling?,* 7–20; and as Jay E. Adams, "Counseling and the Sovereignty of God," *Journal of Biblical Counseling* 11, no. 2 (1993): 4–9.

24. Jay E. Adams, *How to Handle Trouble: God's Way* (Phillipsburg, N.J.: Presbyterian & Reformed, 1982); Adams, *More Than Redemption,* 271–75.

25. Jay E. Adams, *The Christian Counselor's Commentary: Hebrews, James, I & II Peter, and Jude* (Woodruff, S.C.: Timeless Texts, 1996), 32. Cf., Adams, *More Than Redemption,* 40.

26. The word "moral" bears numerous meanings. In this book I employ it as a way of summarizing the view that human life turns on "moral" issues: good and evil, true and false, faith and unbelief, God and false gods, and so forth. In Adams's own theological tradition, this would have been termed a "covenantal" or "spiritual" view of life that human existence inescapably played out—even in problematic psychological states—the themes of the "Two Great Commandments" to love God and neighbor.

The word "moralistic" will also appear in these pages, particularly from Adams's critics, to refer to acting in an authoritarian manner, appealing to willpower and rationality, nagging, perhaps acting unmercifully and speaking censoriously, focused on outward behavior to the neglect of the complexities of a counselee's personal history and emotions, ignoring the grace and patience of the Christian message.

I realize that this definition of terms will not eliminate all ambiguity. For example, when Perry London used the word "moralistic" in the quotation at the beginning of this chapter, he meant something analogous to how I am using "moral."

27. Adams's favorite promise came from 1 Corinthians 10:13. Adams expounded it in a self-help pamphlet, *Christ and Your Problems* (Phillipsburg, N.J.: Presbyterian & Reformed, 1971), which he typically handed out early in the counseling process with new counselees.

28. Adams's favorite warning came from Proverbs 13:15. When Adams encountered counselee resistance—particularly if it became apparent that the current counseling session would likely be the last—Adams tried to "weave [this verse] in twenty times and even write it down on a piece of paper . . . that he can carry with him. I try to indelibly impress it upon him so that he'll never forget it." Adams, *More Than Redemption,* 326. Failing with the carrot, he made the stick memorable.

29. The "directive" psychotherapies are an obvious exception to this generalization.

30. Adams, *What About Nouthetic Counseling?,* 18f.

31. Ibid., 16–19; Adams, *More Than Redemption,* ix–xiv.

32. Jay E. Adams, *Lectures on Counseling* (Grand Rapids: Zondervan, 1975–77), 24; Adams, *Counseling and the Sovereignty of God,* 13.

33. Adams, *More Than Redemption,* xiii.

34. Adams, *The Big Umbrella,* 109. Cf., Adams, *The Christian Counselor's Manual,* chap. 14.

35. Adams, *The Big Umbrella,* 30. Cf., Adams, *The Christian Counselor's Manual,* 124.

36. Adams, *More Than Redemption,* 126f.

37. Adams, *The Christian Counselor's Manual,* 141.

38. Jay E. Adams, *Christian Living in the Home* (Phillipsburg, N.J.: Presbyterian & Reformed, 1972); Jay E. Adams, *What Do You Do When Your Marriage Goes Sour?* (Phillipsburg, N.J.: Presbyterian & Reformed, 1975); Jay E. Adams, *Solving Marriage Problems: Biblical Solutions for Christian Counselors* (Phillipsburg, N.J.: Presbyterian & Reformed, 1983). Other books treated interpersonal conflict and estrangement in general: Jay E. Adams, *Sibling Rivalry in the Household of God* (Denver, Colo.: Accent, 1988); Jay E. Adams, *From Forgiven to Forgiving: Discover the Path to Biblical Forgiveness* (USA: Victor Books [Scripture Press], 1989). In all these, Adams typically focused on the call to identify sins, to forgive others and seek forgiveness from others, and to actively show love—even toward "enemies." Still another book treated a vexed casuistic issue among evangelical counselors: Jay E. Adams, *Marriage, Divorce, and Remarriage in the Bible* (Grand Rapids: Zondervan, 1980). Adams took the classic Presbyterian stance on this, a middle position between those who forbade divorce and remarriage under any circumstances and those who allowed no-fault divorce. He argued that adultery and desertion constituted grounds that allowed the victimized party to pursue a divorce.

Other nouthetic writers often wrote on the same issues. For example, Wayne Mack, the second most prolific author within the biblical counseling movement, specialized in self-help books treating marriage and family issues: Wayne A. Mack, *How to Develop Deep Unity in the Marriage Relationship: A How-To Manual for Christian Growth and Development* (USA: Presbyterian & Reformed, 1977); Wayne A. Mack, *Homework Manual for Biblical Living,* vol. 2, *Family and Marital Problems* (USA: Presbyterian & Reformed, 1980); Wayne A. Mack, *Your Family God's*

Way: Developing and Sustaining Relationships in the Home (USA: Presbyterian & Reformed, 1991); Wayne A. Mack and Nathan A. Mack, *Preparing for Marriage God's Way* (Tulsa, Okla.: Virgil W. Hensley, 1986).

39. Adams, *The Christian Counselor's Manual*, 375–83 and 413–28; Jay E. Adams, *What Do You Do When Fear Overcomes You?* (Phillipsburg, N.J.: Presbyterian & Reformed, 1975a); Jay E. Adams, *What Do You Do When You Become Depressed?* (Phillipsburg, N.J.: Presbyterian & Reformed, 1975b); Jay E. Adams, *What Do You Do When You Worry All the Time?* (Phillipsburg, N.J.: Presbyterian & Reformed, 1975c); Jay E. Adams, *What to Do About Worry* (Phillipsburg, N.J.: Presbyterian & Reformed, 1980); Adams, *More Than Redemption*, 187–232.

40. The influence of William Glasser (*Reality Therapy*) and O. Hobart Mowrer (*Integrity Therapy*) on Adams's construction of the relationship between feeling and behavior will be discussed later. Many of Adams's critics would signal this affinity between his system and those secular moral models promulgated by Glasser and Mowrer (see chap. 8).

41. Adams, *What About Nouthetic Counseling?*, 23f; Adams, *The Christian Counselor's Manual*, 112–15, 135f.

42. E.g., "Jealousy is not bad per se any more than any other emotion that God gave us. But all may be perverted," Jay E. Adams, *The Christian Counselor's New Testament: A New Translation in Everyday English with Notations* (USA: Presbyterian & Reformed, 1977), 497. Cf., Jay E. Adams, *The Christian Counselor's Wordbook: A Primer of Nouthetic Counseling* (Phillipsburg, N.J.: Presbyterian & Reformed, 1981), *infra*, under respective emotions.

43. Adams, *The Christian Counselor's Manual*, 135.

44. Ibid., 109f.

45. Adams, *More Than Redemption*, 139–73, presented his view of sin in some detail.

46. Jay E. Adams, *What Do You Do When You Know That You're Hooked?* (Phillipsburg, N.J.: Presbyterian & Reformed, 1975). Cf., general discussion of the topic in Adams, *The Christian Counselor's Manual*, 206. As a Presbyterian Adams came from a temperance tradition, not an abstinence tradition, regarding intoxicating beverages. But he predictably inveighed against abuse.

47. Adams, *The Christian Counselor's Manual, infra.*

48. See, for example, the series on eating problems by a staff member at CCEF. Elyse Fitzpatrick, "Helping Overeaters," *Journal of Pastoral Practice* 11, no. 1 (1992): 51–56; Elyse Fitzpatrick, "Disorderly Eating . . . for the Rest of Us," *Journal of Biblical Counseling* 12, no. 1 (1993a): 20–23; Elyse Fitzpatrick, "Helping Anorexics," *Journal of Biblical Counseling* 11, no. 3 (1993b): 19–23; Elyse Fitzpatrick, "Helping Bulimics," *Journal of Biblical Counseling* 11, no. 2 (1993c): 16–20.

49. Adams, *The Christian Counselor's Manual*, chapters 18–19. I have included discussion of habit—and the two-sided dehabituation and rehabituation process—under the heading of behavior. Adams himself usually described *behavioral* habits, but he also viewed thoughts, desires, and attitudes as habitual and liable to transformation by this same dynamic.

50. Adams, *More Than Redemption*, 160, 163. Cf., Jay E. Adams, *The Christian Counselor's Commentary: Romans, Philippians, and I & II Thessalonians* (Hackettstown, N.J.: Timeless Texts, 1995), 62.

51. Jay E. Adams, foreword to John Vandegriff, *In the Arena of the Mind: Philippians 4:8* (Howell, N.J.: Ask, Seek, and Knock Publishing, 1992), 1. Adams intended "no ultimate mind/body . . . dualism here, but only a tension in believers occasioned by the regeneration of the inner man and the indwelling of the Spirit in a body habituated to do evil. This leads to an inner/outer struggle."

52. Jay E. Adams, *The War Within: A Biblical Strategy for Spiritual Warfare* (Eugene, Ore.: Harvest House, 1989), 60.

53. Jay E. Adams, *Godliness through Discipline* (Phillipsburg, N.J.: Presbyterian & Reformed, 1972), 2, 4. Cf., Adams, *The War Within*, 60–69. "Self-denial" had anchored John Calvin's view of the Christian life, but it lacked Adams's emphases on neurology and behavioral habituation: John Calvin, *Institutes of the Christian Religion*, trans. Ford Lewis Battles, ed. John T. McNeill, The Library of Christian Classics (Philadelphia: The Westminster Press, 1960), vi-x.

54. Adams discussed the issues in the preceding two paragraphs repeatedly and at great length: e.g., Adams, *The Christian Counselor's Manual*, 171–216; Adams, *Lectures on Counseling*, 231–38; Adams, *More Than Redemption*, 160–64; Adams, *The War Within*, 60–69.

55. Jay E. Adams, *The Language of Counseling* (Phillipsburg, N.J.: Presbyterian & Reformed, 1981), 20.

56. Ibid.

57. Ibid., 69.

58. The examples in table 10 also communicate something of Adams's brisk style.

This style of bluntly confronting a counselee's language and beliefs reminded many critics of aggressive cognitive psychotherapies such as Albert Ellis's Rational-Emotive Therapy. His emphasis on retooling specific behaviors and cognitions, to the neglect of feelings and more "psychodynamic" issues, prompted critics to conclude that he represented a Christianized cognitive-behavioral psychotherapy, contrary to his claim to be "radically biblical." See lengthy discussion of Adams's critics in chapter 8.

59. Adams, *The Christian Counselor's Manual*, excerpted from pp. 451f.

60. Adams, "Grief as a Counseling Opportunity," in *The Big Umbrella*, 63–94; Adams, *Counseling and the Sovereignty of God*; Jay E. Adams, *How to Overcome Evil* (Nutley, N.J.: Presbyterian & Reformed, 1977); Jay E. Adams, *What to Do About Worry* (Phillipsburg, N.J.: Presbyterian & Reformed, 1980); Adams, *How to Handle Trouble*; Jay E. Adams, *The Grand Demonstration: A Biblical Study of the So-Called Problem of Evil* (Santa Barbara, Calif.: EastGate, 1991); Adams, *Christ and Your Problems*; Jay E. Adams, *Coping with Counseling Crises: First Aid for Christian Counselors* (USA: Presbyterian & Reformed, 1976); Jay E. Adams, *Prayers for Troubled Times* (Grand Rapids: Baker, 1979); Jay E. Adams, *From Forgiven to Forgiving: Discover the Path to Biblical Forgiveness* (USA: Victor Books [Scripture Press], 1989).

61. Adams, *The Christian Counselor's Manual*, 45. "Giving hope" was a standard emphasis in addressing all sorts of problems. See the next note for reference, and the next chapter for further discussion.

62. Ibid., 39–48.

63. Adams, *The Big Umbrella*, 63–94.

64. Adams, *Coping with Counseling Crises*, 7.

65. Adams, *The Christian Counselor's New Testament*, 413.

66. Jay E. Adams, "The Christian Approach to Schizophrenia," in *The Construction of Madness: Emerging Conceptions and Interventions into the Psychotic Process*, ed. Peter A. Magaro (New York: Pergamon Press, 1976), 133–50; Adams, *What About Nouthetic Counseling?*, 27f; Adams, *The Big Umbrella*, 3–61; Adams, *Competent to Counsel*, 26–40; Adams, *The Christian Counselor's Manual*, 25–28; 384–90.

67. Adams, *The Christian Counselor's Manual*, 441.

68. Adams, *Competent to Counsel*, 9f.

69. Ibid., 29 (emphasis his).

70. Ibid., 40.

71. Ibid., 26–34.

72. Adams occasionally alluded to demon possession as another possible cause of bizarre behavior. But he believed on theological grounds that the power of Satan had been curtailed, that most supposed possession phenomena were spurious, arising either from the power of suggestion or from misreading what was occurring, and that even if demonic forces were present there was no need to do exorcisms. "A heavy burden of proof belongs to the one who retreats to demon possession as the cause of bizarre behavior." Adams, *The Big Umbrella*, 120.

73. E.g., Adams, *The Big Umbrella*, 165; Adams, *The Christian Counselor's Manual*, 111, 115, 180–82, 199f; Adams, *More Than Redemption*, 161; Adams, *Godliness through Discipline*, 6f.

74. Adams, *The Christian Counselor's Wordbook*, 23, 49; Adams, *The Christian Counselor's Manual*, 199f.

75. Adams, "The Christian Approach to Schizophrenia," in Magaro, *The Construction of Madness*, 138. This article was Adams's lone written contribution to the secular academic and professional world.

76. Adams, *The Christian Counselor's Manual*, 103, note 1. Cf., Adams, *The Language of Counseling*, for a fuller expression of Adams's views on labeling.

77. Adams, "The Christian Approach to Schizophrenia" in Magaro, *The Construction of Madness*, 134.

78. Adams, *Christ and Your Problems*, 11f.

79. Adams, *Competent to Counsel*, 40.

80. Adams, "The Christian Approach to Schizophrenia" in Magaro, *The Construction of Madness*, 136.

81. For example, in *Competent to Counsel* Adams flirted with the short-lived Osmond-Hoffer theory that some cases of schizophrenia might derive from an adenochrome deficit and prove treatable with massive doses of niacinamide. He hedged his curiosity with cautions and qualifiers and did not mention the theory in later books. Adams, *Competent to Counsel*, 36–40.

82. Adams, *Competent to Counsel*, 142.

83. Jay E. Adams, "Depression," in *The Encyclopedia of Christianity*, ed. Philip Hughes, The Foundation for Christian Education (Marshallton, Del., 1972), 362f.

84. Adams, *The Christian Counselor's Manual*, 10. Cf., Adams, *Counseling and the Sovereignty of God*. See the following section of this chapter that treats Adams's views of medicine more extensively.

85. Adams, *The Christian Counselor's Manual*, 11. Cf., Adams, *Competent to Counsel*, 39f, note 2.

It is worth remembering that Adams's proposal here was explicitly sectarian and separatistic; it was not a prescription for a theocratic reordering of society. "We shall not stop unbelievers from setting up their own counseling systems and from doing counseling that competes with the Scriptures; that is a given. But Christian counseling itself must be free from eclectic borrowings and influences *in order to set forth a genuine and viable alternative*." Adams, *More Than Redemption*, 22.

86. Adams, *The Christian Counselor's Manual*, 25–28.

87. Adams, *Competent to Counsel*, xvi.

88. Ibid., xvii.

89. Adams, *Lectures on Counseling*, 44, 48; Adams, *The Big Umbrella*, 30; Adams, *Ready to Restore*, 7; Adams, *The Christian Counselor's Manual*, 21, 25. The last citation is particularly interesting: "[One] can know a lot about others by looking into his own heart. . . . Every young pastor should spend much time carefully exegeting the Bible and *at the same time* looking at his own wicked and deceitful heart as it is laid bare by the Word." Chapter 6 will treat Adams's counseling style and methodology in more detail.

90. Adams, *The Christian Counselor's Manual*, 438f.

91. Adams, *Competent to Counsel*, 214.

92. Adams, *The Christian Counselor's Manual*, 124.

93. Critics would comment on the asymmetry in Adams's appropriation of secular disciplines. He and medically minded nouthetic counselors appeared able to tolerate the somatic determinism of modern medical science, to appropriate usable information while sifting out deterministic theory. They did not treat the social sciences the same way. John D. Carter, "Nouthetic Counseling Defended: A Reply to Ganz," *Journal of Psychology and Theology* 4, no. 4 (1976): 206–16. See chapter 8.

Adams's view of the demonological, to mention those other occupants of the social universe he envisioned, was similar to his view of the impact of human society. Adams's book on warfare with the devil was chiefly about how to battle one's own inner tendencies, where the devil played the role of tempter to morally responsible humans: Adams, *The War Within*. He often spoke of Satan as arch-liar and arch-enemy who stood behind the lies and sufferings that the social context presented and inflicted: Adams, *More Than Redemption*, 4ff. But Adams believed that supposed instances of demonic possession were chiefly artifacts of the worldviews of those exhibiting symptoms and those observing them. "A heavy burden of proof belongs to the one who retreats to demon possession as the cause of bizarre behavior. Counselors, in this present era, have every reason to expect that the cause of the problems with which they will deal in counseling will be other than demonic possession." Adams, *The Big Umbrella*, 120.

94. See, for example, Adams, *How to Overcome Evil*; Adams, *How to Handle Trouble*.

95. E.g., Adams, *Competent to Counsel*, 177–82; Adams, *The Christian Counselor's Manual*, 332–37; annotations in Adams, *The Christian Counselor's New Testament*, *infra*, under "Association" and "Example." In this emphasis Adams's critics would find yet another instance of the influence of Mowrer's learning theory.

96. Adams, *The Christian Counselor's Manual*, 149. Cf., Jay E. Adams, "What About Emotional Abuse?," *Journal of Pastoral Practice* 8, no. 3 (1986): 1–10. Adams's critics often thought that such statements communicated a callous disregard for human suffering. Even John Bettler, who rarely wrote, was moved to dispute Adams's emphatic deemphasis of the impact of being sinned against. Regarding abused counselees, Bettler thought that biblical warnings about how parents might provoke their children to anger and despair had to be given their appropriate weight. To acknowledge the impact of such things was not necessarily to encourage hopelessness or blameshifting in Bettler's view. John Bettler, "Biblical Counseling: The Next Generation," *Journal of Pastoral Practice* 8, no. 4 (1987): 3–10. See chapter 9.

97. Adams, *The Christian Counselor's Manual*, 138f.

98. See the exchange between Adams and Bettler: Adams, "What About Emotional Abuse?," 1–10; Jay E. Adams, "A Reply to the Response," *Journal of Pastoral Practice* 9, no. 1 (1987): 1–5; Bettler, "Biblical Counseling: The Next Generation."

99. Adams, *How to Handle Trouble*.

100. Adams, *Competent to Counsel*, 37; Adams, *What About Nouthetic Counseling?*, 19.

101. Adams, *Ready to Restore*, 32.

102. Ibid., 36, numbers 18 and 19 in the list.

103. Nouthetic counselors did little, if any, strictly scholarly writing or academic research. Even medically oriented pieces were written to inform medical laymen. This was a practitioner's movement, all about jurisdiction. Therefore the literature consists almost exclusively of "practical" pieces—training for counselors, aids for counselees, programmatic statements, polemics.

104. The spread of nouthetic counseling internationally is generally beyond the scope of this project, but a brief cross-cultural comparison is of interest regarding the involvement of physicians. In England nouthetic counseling was slow to institutionalize, being often viewed, along with other forms of counseling, as an American enthusiasm. But the leaders in the Association for Biblical Counseling founded in the late 1970s were all medical professionals: two neurologists and a dentist. In England the movement generally tended to attract laypeople, including doctors, rather than pastors.

105. This journal was renamed *Journal of Biblical Counseling* in 1992.

106. Adams, *What About Nouthetic Counseling?*, 19. Luke was "the beloved physician" in the words of Colossians 4:14.

107. Adams's translation of James 5:14–16, 19f, Adams, *The Christian Counselor's New Testament*, infra.

108. Adams, *Competent to Counsel*, 105–10.

109. Adams, *The Christian Counselor's Manual*, 438. As an aside, Adams's hostility to pietism and faith healing is also evident in this positive evaluation of modern medicine. He took the view of classic Calvinistic orthodoxy regarding the cessation of those miracles described in the Bible. He thought that faith healers and exorcists preyed on human suggestibility, and distracted people from a rational analysis of the problems of both body and soul.

110. Interview, October 3, 1990 (Lafayette, Indiana).

111. Donald Meyer, *The Positive Thinkers: Popular Religious Psychology from Mary Baker Eddy to Norman Vincent Peale and Ronald Reagan* (Middletown, Conn.: Wesleyan University Press, 1988), 254–55.

112. Adams referred favorably to a book on psychosomatics (and other topics) written for fundamentalist laypeople: S. I. McMillen, *None of These Diseases* (Westwood: Spire Books, 1963). In a biblicistic style, McMillen, a college physician at Houghton College (Houghton, New York), extolled the medical prescience of the Bible regarding quarantine, sanitation, circumcision, and diseases with a psychosomatic or lifestyle etiology.

113. In the first two issues of the *Journal of Pastoral Practice* Bob Smith wrote no less than five articles addressing themes pertinent to reclaiming psychosomatics for nouthetic counseling: Robert D. Smith, "Illness and a Life View," *Journal of Pastoral Practice* 1, no. 1 (1977a): 80–84; Robert D. Smith, "A Look at Psychosomatic Relationships," *Journal of Pastoral Practice* 1, no. 2 (1977b): 81–87; Robert D. Smith, "A Physician Looks at Counseling: Depression," *Journal of Pastoral Practice* 1, no. 1 (1977c): 85–87; Robert D. Smith, "A Physician Looks at Counseling: Symptoms," *Journal of Pastoral Practice* 1, no. 1 (1977d): 88–90; Robert D. Smith, "Psychosomatics in the Bible," *Journal of Pastoral Practice* 1, no. 2 (1977e): 88f.

114. Robert D. Smith, "Physician Looks at Counseling: Depression," *Journal of Pastoral Practice* 1, no. 1 (1977): 86.

115. Robert D. Smith, "Illness and a Life View," *Journal of Pastoral Practice* 1, no. 1 (1977): 83.

116. Robert D. Smith, "It's Not What You Eat, It's What Eats You," *Journal of Pastoral Practice* 8, no. 1 (1985): 1–10; Robert D. Smith, "Fearfully and Wonderfully Made," *Journal of Pastoral Practice* 8, no. 2 (1986a): 2–12; Robert D. Smith, "God's Word and Your Health," *Journal of Pastoral Practice* 8, no. 3 (1986b): 11–27; Robert D. Smith, "What to Do When Illness Strikes," *Journal of Pastoral Practice* 8, no. 4 (1987): 11–18.

117. Robert D. Smith, "God's Word and Your Health," *Journal of Pastoral Practice* 8, no. 3 (1986): 26.

118. The quote paraphrases the famous answer to the first question of the Westminster Shorter Catechism, "What is the chief end of man?"

119. Further discussion in chapter 7.

120. The founders were two conservative Presbyterians who professionally were family practice physicians and medical professors. Franklin E. Payne worked at the Medical College of Georgia (Augusta, Ga.) and Hilton Terrell at the McLeod Regional Medical Center (Florence, S.C.). Adams spoke at medical ethics conferences they sponsored and wrote for the *JBEM*: e.g., Jay E. Adams, "What Are/Is Christian Ethics?," *Journal of Biblical Ethics in Medicine* 1, no. 2 (1987): 20f; Jay E. Adams, "The Physician, The Pastor, Psychotherapy, and Counseling," *Journal of Biblical Ethics in Medicine* 3, no. 2 (1989): 21–26. CCEF West (San Diego) sponsored three medical ethics conferences in the 1990s, bringing together medical doctors and pastors.

121. Elizabeth Kübler-Ross, *On Death and Dying* (New York: Macmillan, 1968); Raymond Moody, *Life after Life* (New York: Bantam Books, 1975).

122. Adams, *The Big Umbrella*, 63–94; Jay E. Adams, *Shepherding God's Flock*, vol. 1, *The Pastoral Life* (USA: Presbyterian & Reformed, 1974), 126–34; Adams, *Coping with Counseling Crises*; Adams, *More Than Redemption*, 297–300.

123. Adams, *The Big Umbrella,* 79.

124. Adams, *What About Nouthetic Counseling?,* 7–14.

125. Ibid., 11.

126. The moral strenuousness of Adams's discussion of suffering caused many of the most impassioned outcries against his model of counseling. Many critics thought that he sounded heartless to afflicted people and passed too quickly over their suffering. Adams rebutted that such criticisms did not arise because nouthetic counseling was unconcerned with suffering, but because the critics lacked optimism about the power of the Bible's hope to encourage sufferers.

127. Interview, December 4, 1990.

CHAPTER 6

Good News and the Pastoral Task: Adams's Positive System
(Part 2)

Karl Menninger [in Whatever Became of Sin?*] thinks that there are many persons who are wrongly labeled sick or criminal. If these people were to be rightly labeled and treated as "sinners," they would be capable of being forgiven and thus healed of various disorders. . . . Labels are important not only as signs of the thing they signify but also as signposts that point to solutions to the problems they categorize.*
— Jay E. Adams, 1989[1]

There is great hope in calling sin "sin." Every Christian knows that God sent Christ to deal with sin.
— Jay E. Adams, 1972[2]

Jesus guided, instructed, rebuked, encouraged, and taught His disciples. He was truly their Counselor. . . . As Jesus was about to leave His disciples, He graciously calmed their fears by informing them that He would send "another" Counselor like Himself to be with them. . . . He identified this Counselor as the Holy Spirit. . . . If counseling is in essence one aspect of the work of sanctification, then the Holy Spirit, whose principal work in the regenerated man is to sanctify him, must be considered the most important Person in the counseling context.
— Jay E. Adams, 1973[3]

All Christians may (indeed, must) do counseling. Yet, not all Christians have been solemnly set aside to the work of "nouthetically confronting every man and teaching every man" (Col. 1:28), as the Christian minister is.
— Jay E. Adams, 1973[4]

As we have seen, Jay Adams summarized those human dilemmas out of which the need for counseling arose as sin and misery before the face of God—as each of those terms had been understood in traditional Calvinistic Protestantism. Such diagnostic categories presumed the set of answers prescribed by that same theological system. The "Good News of Jesus Christ" and the "grace of God" were intended to redress what was definably wrong. Adams's counseling model is impossible to comprehend in abstraction from his belief that the things the Bible said about Jesus Christ were verities that provided a meaningful context for the ills of the soul. Sinners could be first forgiven by Christ's self-sacrifice, and then progressively changed by Christ's present aid.

Sufferers could be given a threefold framework of meaning and hope through which to interpret their hardships: Christ's own experience of suffering on their behalf, Christ's purposes in remaking them, Christ's return to deliver them from all sin and misery.

Both the diagnosis and the cure also signaled the institutional locus for counseling practice. The church, particularly in its pastoral task of "speaking the truth in love," was the institution intended to accomplish the cure for what ailed souls. And the pastors of those churches stood front and center in the performance of that curative task. The content of Adams's message would have been very familiar to his constituency; they heard or spoke these things every Sunday morning, and read them every time they opened their Bibles. But the scope of application he gave to that message struck his hearers as revolutionary, variously delighting and threatening those who grasped its implications.

This chapter will consider the cognitive and institutional solutions that Adams's knowledge system proposed as solutions to the problems it had defined.

1. Counselors offered the "grace of God in Jesus Christ" as the answer to transform sinners and sustain sufferers

Jay Adams's writing focused on what he believed the Bible prescribed regarding the message, methods, and goals of the counselor. Biblical writers had taught and exemplified what should be said to troubled people, the way to go about saying it, and the way hearers should respond. This cognitive content and intended counselee response both arose out of Adams's belief in the "grace of God." We will examine each in turn.

The message of the nouthetic counselor centered around three things that God was supposed to offer troubled people: forgiveness for the sins identified in counseling, power to make the requisite constructive changes, and hope that every misery and trial along the way would ultimately come to a happy ending. If counselors did their diagnostic work well, then the gospel message would be seen as immediately applicable to the varied problems in living.

These themes are readily seen in Adams's pamphlet *Christ and Your Problems* (*CYP*). He routinely gave this piece to his counselees during their first session together, intending that they study it before the second session.[5] His intent was twofold: to challenge people to take "personal responsibility before God" for their problems, and to assure them of God's help.[6] *CYP* directly exhorted readers in sermonic style, combining Bible exposition with homely illustrations and concrete applications. Adams constructed this pamphlet around a Bible passage that was a particular favorite of his: "No trial has taken hold of you except that which other people have experienced; but God is faithful Who will not allow you to be tried beyond what you are able to bear, but rather, will provide together with the trial the way out so that you may be able to endure it."[7] Adams took Paul's words touting God's faithfulness in life's struggles as reason to remove any excuse for despair, fear, improper action, or inaction on the part of counselees: "So, Christian, throw off excuses, stop shifting blame to others, and instead, by the power of God's Spirit, 'walk in a manner worthy of the calling wherewith you have been called.'"[8]

In *CYP* Adams appealed to his readers first by presenting a sampler of typical life pressures: the selfishness or harshness of a spouse, angry customers, unfair parents, sexual temptations, an intractable illness, bereavement, financial pressures. He went on to argue that beneath the differences of time, place, language, culture, and historical circumstance all human beings were fundamentally alike in how they tended to respond to difficulties: "Beneath [the unique] features you will find that the problems of the Jews in the wilderness, the temptations of the Corinthians in the Roman empire, and the frustrations of modern day Americans are not significantly different. God has not changed; His commandments have not been altered; and sinful man below his modern sophisticated exterior is still the same."[9] Since personal problems (i.e., "sins") typically correlated with pressures of life (i.e., "trials and temptations"), struggling counselees would presumably hear Adams speaking to them. Those readers persuaded that their personal problems arose from or consisted in sin were then assured that both the sins and the pressures had an answer deriving from three distinctively Calvinistic understandings of the Bible's message.

First, the death and resurrection of Jesus Christ were presumed to offer forgiveness to objectively guilty people on whom God had set his love.[10] Those things that Protestant theology had summarized under the heading "justification by faith" are mentioned a dozen times in *CYP:* "The saving grace of Jesus Christ . . . [was expressed] in dying on the cross for the sins of those whom the Father had given Him that they might have forgiveness and life."[11] Adams felt no qualms in prosecuting the case with counselees that their problems arose from identifiable sins because he believed that the Bible's message was specifically about the forgiveness of such sins. He often stated that "forgiveness is man's greatest need"[12] and thought counselors ought to do their job in such a way that the need became evident. If Christ had died in the place of counselees to forgive them, then in the counseling context they ought to be willing to look frankly at their sins. Counselees who looked honestly at their failings would consider these failings in the light of the Bible's promise that Christ died to forgive sins and would presumably be thankful to God.

Such gratitude provided one of the prime motivations for change in Adams's system.[13]

Second, Adams believed that the presence of the Holy Spirit as the agent of Christ's immediate rule offered counselees the possibility of divine power to aid them in making requisite, concrete changes in belief and behavior. Those things that Protestant theology had termed "progressive sanctification" recur throughout *CYP* and can be considered a centerpiece of Adams's thought and interests. Adams was optimistic that counselees could develop different ways of handling life, if only they would rely on God's truth (the Bible), power (the Holy Spirit), and people (those who had become "competent to counsel").

Adams began most of his major books with a discussion of his belief that God's personal presence would help people replace sin with obedience. He averred that there were "always more than two" persons involved in the counseling relationship:

> It is by no means self-evident that the persons involved in pastoral counseling are, as Seward Hiltner has written, "the parishioner and the pastor" or, as nearly every book on counseling assumes, the counselor and the counselee. . . . In truly biblical counseling, therefore, where a counselor and counselee meet in the name of Jesus Christ, they may expect the very presence of Christ as Counselor-in-charge. . . . Jesus Christ now dwells invisibly in His church in the person of the Holy Spirit.[14]

Adams wove together the empowering Holy Spirit and those things that Protestants had traditionally called the "means of grace": the Bible, prayer, the sacraments, and the counsel of other believers. He understood the Holy Spirit as a rational, moral person, whose agency stood behind the biblical authors, and who enabled obedience in faith and practice in the lives of those who heeded the Bible. The net effect was that Adams treated as functionally interchangeable the presence of Christ, the presence of the Holy Spirit, the directives and promises of the Bible, and the ministry of that Bible to others by people who had become competent to counsel by dealing with their own problems.

Third, the sanctifying purposes of God in current hardships, the presence of Christ after death, and the eventual return of Christ to destroy all sin, hurt, and misery were presumed to offer hope in the midst of any struggle, however painful and unrelenting. In CYP Adams reiterated this Calvinistic view of both present and future circumstances. In the present, hardships were presumed to be purposeful: "Even though the trials we face are not unique in their basic designs, the detailed form they take, the intensity with which they come, and the point in life at which we must face them, are all tailor-made to each individual child of God, and, don't forget, God is the tailor!"[15] In Adams's hands the fatherly tailor's present purposes were not as inscrutable as religious people often portrayed them: God was always teaching his children how to know him, love him, and become like him, whatever else might seem baffling.

In the future, all hardships were presumed to come to a happy end: "Whatever way of escape God may provide, even if it is the very best of all (i.e., to take you to be with Himself), if you have been saved by grace through faith in Jesus Christ, you may be certain that the way out will come just as surely as the problem itself."[16] Adams's pastoral counselors brought heavy artillery to bear on those counselees sensitive to such appeals. Even if they died, they had hope and so could live in a responsible manner.[17]

Of these three ingredients—Christ's mercy, the Holy Spirit's present power, God's ultimate purposes[18]—the second received by far the largest share of his attention. At every turn in his writing, Adams sounds the note of change. He never stressed the comforts of the first and third ingredients alone. He viewed such messages, common as they were within conservative Protestantism, as encouraging pietism where the first stood alone and resignation where the third stood alone. Adams intended that piety and patience should get people moving in a change process. He thought pastoral counseling ought to aim at progressive sanctification, the renovation of lives to "look like" Jesus: in morals, beliefs, intentions, attitudes, and behavior. "Nouthetic counseling in its fullest sense, then, is simply an application of the means of sanctification."[19]

By setting such a goal, Adams frankly dissociated himself from other common goals that had been posited for psychotherapeutic change processes and had become common both in secular and religious counseling models: exploration of one's inner world, behavioral engineering to accomplish the will of either client or therapist, emotional healing, self-actualization, learning to get psychological or social needs met, producing cathartic relief from the feelings attached to repressed memories, building ego strength, cultivating self-confidence, releasing inner forces of health, breaking undesirable habits, getting in touch with inner divine energies, learning to cope with the disease of addiction, becoming better adjusted socially, constructing a personal myth, learning to assert one's own will, and so forth. He similarly dissociated his agenda from the goal of symptomatic relief produced by such tools of medical psychiatry as psychotropic medications and electroconvulsive therapy.[20]

In Adams's definition, such sanctification described a particular form of personality and behavioral change: into the likeness of Jesus. If Jesus could love his enemies, counselees could learn not to be bitter or fearful. If Jesus could trust God, then depressed counselees could learn not to believe that God hated them or didn't care about them. If Jesus could face betrayal and pain with resolute hope, then malcontents could learn not to grumble. If Jesus could devote his life to giving to the needs of others, then self-seeking counselees could learn to do likewise in some measure. If Jesus could eat and drink in a thankful, self-controlled manner, then counselees need not be either anorexic or gluttonous. If Jesus had hope when he faced death, then counselees need not fall into despair over life's hardships.[21] In all this, Adams's message sounded notes familiar to traditional Reformed Protestantism.

In a phrase, his counselees were supposed to "repent, trust, and obey": "The task of the Christian counselor is to call for repentance, which is a call for *change*—a change of mind leading to a change of life."[22] Counselees would turn away from their instinctive, socially conditioned, and well-habituated ways of living, thinking, choosing, and feeling—a lifestyle produced by "the world, the flesh, and the devil." They would turn to God and his grace, and so to God's way of living, thinking, choosing, and feeling. Again, Adams again touched the chords of his hearers' basic assumptions.[23] But this is not to say that he did not strike readers as innovative in his views on progressive sanctification. The way Adams developed his idea of repentance as the goal of counseling was novel in at least two major ways: the first appealing to one of his hearers' typical frustrations, the second appealing to one of their deepest commitments.

First, conservative Protestants had lacked any systematic, detailed approaches to problems in living, anything that defined a rational counseling process. Adams's pragmatic, rational, troubleshooting approach was far removed from common habits of most conservative Protestants, habits Adams considered pietistic or moralistic, and useless for helping people concretely change. Many of his hearers came to agree. Over the previous century, popular conservative Protestant views of sanctification had tended in two directions: either toward dramatic, once-for-all experiences, or toward diligence in definably religious activities. The more pietistic tended in the first direction: yield oneself to God in prayer to "let go and let God in dying to the flesh," or cast out the demon that held someone in bondage to sinful habits and unbelief. They treated sanctification as an instantaneous act, not a process. The more moralistic tended the other way, exhorting faithful use of the means of grace—Bible reading, prayer, church attendance—or urging involvement in some form of ministry activity. They tended to treat sanctification as a matter of increased religious activity, not making detailed changes to redress the problems of daily life. Adams's practice of defining in minute, concrete detail what needed to change and what change would look like was a revelation to many of his readers. His definition of a process by which habits might be broken and rebuilt was no less a revelation.

Adams put heavy emphasis on having his counselors and counselees get specific about intended behavioral changes. He railed against speaking platitudes and generalities: "Don't just tell counselees what to do; tell them how to do it. Don't just tell a husband to love his wife better; have him take her out for dinner. Don't just tell a couple they need to communicate better; help them set up a regular conference table with ground rules. Don't just tell a woman she needs to read the Bible; show her how to do it. Don't just tell a man to stop buying pornography; help him plan what he'll do instead."[24] Adams's counseling was oriented toward producing specific action, toward building new skills and habits in his counselees. His counseling was a training program in problem-solving, a "how-to" course in godly living. He exhorted his readers, "Problems must be viewed as *projects,* not *topics.*"[25] It is no accident that more than a dozen of his titles contain the words "How to" or "What to Do" or "What Do You Do When." In one of his common metaphors, the counselor was a coach who taught, modeled, cheered, warned, and encouraged others: "The counselor does not do their work for them. He coaches them; he is a shepherd who *leads* sheep. Yet *they* do the work."[26]

As the coach of those he counseled, Adams was concerned to break old habits and build new habits. He believed that motivated counselees could change relatively rapidly but not instantly. He thought most discrete problems could be significantly remedied in six to twelve weeks if both counselor and counselees stayed on task.[27] That the Holy Spirit's life-changing activities might typically occur by a rationally describable process— rather than by an instantaneous and mysterious act—caught the ear of pastors frustrated with their failure to experience instant transformation either in their own lives or in those they ministered to. That significant change could be expedited over a period of weeks and months—rather than through an interminable psychotherapeutic process with indeterminate results—kept busy, pragmatic pastors listening.

Adams's methods were straightforward. He would first seek to discover the problem patterns, then the specific alternatives that the Bible prescribed. He would give counselees hope with the promises of God's help. Upon repentance and commitment, counselees could pray for God's mercy and aid and bend energetic efforts toward clearly defined goals for change: "It is by willing, prayerful, and persistent obedience to the requirements of the Scriptures that godly patterns are developed and come to be part of us."[28] Adams labored to defend himself against the charge that by this he was proposing a system of strenuous self-effort:

It takes nothing less than the power
of the Spirit to replace sinful habits with

righteous ones. . . . Now the work of the Spirit is not mystical. . . . The Holy Spirit Himself has plainly told us how He works. He says *in* the Scriptures that He ordinarily works *through* the Scriptures. The Bible is the Holy Spirit's book. . . . The Holy Spirit gives help when His people read His Word and then step out by faith to do as He says. He does not promise to strengthen unless they do so; the power often comes *in the doing.*[29]

But there is no doubt that Adams's writing was strongly flavored with the language and metaphor of habit: habituation, dehabituation, rehabituation, discipline, practice, pattern, repatterning, reprogramming. Patterns of sin, practiced until they had become second nature, needed to be dug up and replaced with new patterns. Counselees committed to this struggle to change Adams's way would learn "godliness through discipline," as he titled a pamphlet he frequently handed out during the second counseling session as he sought to elicit commitment to tackle their problems in an energetic and disciplined fashion.[30]

Adams's piety and pastoral counsel were alike rational, pragmatic, disciplined, and hard-working. This "coach" would offer none of the sentimental "support," "unconditional positive regard," or "bolstering to self-esteem" of the prevailing psychotherapeutic ethos.[31] There was work to be done, problems to be diagnosed, solutions to be hammered out and implemented by the grace of God.

Adams frequently lamented the vacuum of practical instruction on the basics of marriage, child-rearing, communication, peacemaking, handling sexual temptations, solving problems with anger or anxiety, setting goals in the midst of suffering, and so forth. "When I graduated from seminary, you could go into a religious bookstore and all you'd find would be Bible study aids and books on doctrine, piety, and eschatology. There just weren't any practical books."[32] Adams wrote extensively about such "practical" matters. That, too, touched a chord in his hearers. His step-by-step detailing of a change process for daily life problems appealed across a wide spectrum of conservative Protestantism. His model of *progressive* sanctification became a rallying point for otherwise disparate conservative Protestants. He exposed the weakness of their pietism and moralism, and he gave them a practical method to facilitate progressive sanctification.

The second distinctive implication of Adams's view of change emerged in his approach to non-Christian counselees. The pervasively religious coloration of his counseling model has been obvious; he treated non-Christians in a manner consistent with his presuppositions. If counseling was a "ministry of the Word of God's grace," then the goal of his counseling with non-Christians was to bring them to know, trust, love, and obey Jesus Christ. When counseling those who did not profess faith or whose profession seemed dubious, Adams did "problem-oriented evangelism" or "precounseling," as he variously termed it.[33] The former term captured something of the fact that he did not open counseling with a call to faith. In the opening stages of counseling, his methods of working with non-Christian counselees were the same as with Christians. He sought to discover their problems in detail and to identify and label their sins; by so doing, he would presumably demonstrate the relevance of Christ's love and power to the counselee's specific need. Adams described his position this way:

> Nouthetic confrontation requires the deepest involvement; deep enough to take people seriously when they mention their sin, even when they fail to identify it as sin. . . . Because of the radical nature of man's problem, radical measures are required. The diagnosis leading to radical surgery must be open, frank, honest, and to the point—man has sinned and needs a Savior. Nothing less than death to the past and resurrection to a brand new way of life can really solve one's problems. Consequently, proper concept of nouthetic counseling must have deeply embedded in it the premise that man cannot be helped in any fundamental sense apart from the gospel of Jesus Christ.[34]

At the point where he deemed confrontation appropriate, he would attempt to "present biblical answers to man's physical, social, intellectual, and psychological needs."[35]

The term "precounseling" was Adams's way of reminding counselors that counselees were not ready for the sanctification process (the goal of *noutheteo*) until they had been first reconciled to God. Though what he did looked like "counseling," Adams pointedly labeled it precounseling until the counselee became a believer in Christ. Adams was, however, not averse to helping non-Christians make constructive changes in their lives, short of them becoming believers: "To help unbelievers solve their problems, to help them change habit patterns from less correct to more correct patterns, to get them to do formally what the Word of God says about certain aspects of their lives, is to honor God and to do that which is of good use, both to the unbeliever and to others. There is warrant, in conjunction with evangelism, to help unbelievers . . . though evangelism be unsuccessful."[36] In characteristic biblicist fashion, Adams cited chapter and verse: Jesus himself had healed ten lepers, but only one returned to give him thanks.[37]

Adams's overt evangelistic thrust communicates how his counseling model was counseling for conservative Protestants, and preeminently for the pastor commissioned to be a minister of the conservative Protestant gospel. Adams was happy to report, "In the avowedly evangelistic milieu within which I work, there have been conversions in counseling sessions."[38] He took on the question of whether a counselor should impose his values on a counselee head on:

> Some object to evangelism in counseling because they say that counselors must not impose their standards and values upon another. But that, of course, is precisely what evangelism is all about. Evangelism imposes new standards and new values. . . . The answer to the objection to evangelism in counseling is simply that the counselor does not impose his own standards upon the counselee, but that he seeks to impose God's standards."[39]

He added that even a supposedly "nondirective" approach to counseling such as Carl Rogers's "fails to recognize the subtle directiveness that even his method must employ."[40] Adams believed that counseling methods were bearers of the presuppositions of those who used them. Counselors who failed to impose God's values had two choices: either they inculcated their own values, however covertly, or they flattered and pandered to counselees by reinforcing their extant values, "confirm[ing] sinful man's belief that he is autonomous and has no need of God."[41] In Adams's eyes, overt evangelism was simply more honest than the covert evangelism of those who pretended to objectivity and neutrality.

Such an emphasis was hardly off-putting to many of Adams's hearers. Indeed, it squared with and reinforced their deepest convictions, convictions that the psychotherapeutic ethos had always opposed. The competency in counseling that Adams promoted was consistent with evangelism aiming at conversion, and conservative Protestants defined their faith as evangelistic. Even while appealing to such core beliefs, however, Adams challenged conservative Protestants to be less for-mulaic in their approach to evangelism. He thought that counseling provided a unique opportunity to tailor-make God's Good News to the individual. Counselors were encouraged to take time to get to know non-Christians as people with struggles and needs, to seek to express love in tangible ways, creating a context through such "problem-oriented evangelism" where the message of God's grace would perhaps strike receptive hearers as immediately relevant.

Again, Adams's intellectual choices had striking rhetorical implications. He was appealing to a body of people who defined themselves as believers in God's Good News in Jesus Christ. They believed in classic Protestant doctrines: justification, sanctification, and glorification. They felt the vacuum in their ability to practically apply what they claimed to hold most dear. They were committed to view Jesus Christ as the answer to the problems in living both for themselves and for those still outside the faith. His model was tailored both to their faith and to their failures.

2. Counseling is fundamentally a pastoral activity and must be church-based

The counseling methods and institutional locale Adams advocated cohered with the message. I have spoken so far of the message that Adams sought to communicate to his counselees. But he also believed that the Bible taught a distinctive counseling methodology and ordained the church as the community in which both message and method would be implemented. That methodology naturally sustained formal parallels to other systems of counseling. All counselors presumably apply their system to their own lives; all seek to communicate benign intentions; all ask questions, listen, and observe in order to get to know their counselees; all offer interpretive remarks of some sort; all aim to bring about some sort of change in how counselees feel, think, and act.[42] But Adams believed that methodologies grew out of the beliefs and purposes of the cognitive system which they expressed, and on close inspection proved distinctive.[43] The distinctive methods and institutional structure he proposed involved the professional, paraprofessional, and lay ministries of the church that existed to promulgate the Good News of Jesus Christ to sinners and sufferers. It is no surprise, then, that Adams proposed the pastor and the church as, respectively, the therapeutic agent and institution of choice. Three features of Adams's model are germane to understanding its primary location within local church pastoral ministry.

First, Adams was not uninterested in counseling done by people other than the pastor. Indeed, his nouthetic counseling was also intended to be the *modus operandi* in other formal and informal helping relationships: "All that has been said thus far concerning Christian counseling is applicable to nearly *every* form of relationship in which Christians come together."[44] The nouthetic counseling movement is best understood sociologically as a case study both in interprofessional conflict and in the deprofessionalization of tasks claimed by professionals. Adams intended that his form of constructive candor characterize every relationship. For example, school teachers in Christian schools could use his methods to structure their classrooms as constructive, problem-solving communities.[45] Parents would learn to nouthetically counsel their children, as the key proof text on child-rearing instructed them.[46] Married couples could learn to counsel each other effectively, becoming "assistant counselors" in any formal counseling processes.[47] They could also learn skills in setting up a "conference table"—one of Adams's most common assignments to aid feuding couples and families—that would enable

them to solve their interpersonal problems on a daily basis by learning to communicate both honestly and constructively.[48] Individuals could apply his model to address and redress their own previously unresolved personal problems.[49] Adams alluded to "preventive" counseling as the daily complement to more narrowly "remedial" (pointedly nouthetic) counseling.[50] The "mutual ministry" of one Christian to another was meant to include: " . . . exhortation, encouragement, restoration, admonition, rebuke and the giving of other sorts of counsel. What is of greatest importance to note is that all of them are concerned not with the ministry of someone who is called to counseling as a life calling, but with the ministry of individual, every-day-man-in-the-pew Christians to one another."[51] What such people were called to give, they were also exhorted to receive: "Mutual ministry means more than merely helping others; it also means willingness to ask for and to receive help from others when needed. There is no one of us who at some time or another does not need the counsel of his brother. We must not become too proud or too embarrassed (which is only another way of saying the same thing) to seek help when we recognize that we are at the end of our own resources."[52] Adams believed that the church's failure to practice such things had robbed it of plausibility and power. He believed that if conservative Protestants heeded his call, their churches would become places where once troubled people came to live "shining lives," and "the effect on the surrounding society might even occasion another Great Awakening."[53] Adams little developed what the counseling of these lay Christians might look like, but he issued the rhetorical call.

What Adams did develop was predictable, and this is the second implication of Adams's definition of a churchly location for counseling practice. The lead person was the pastor, whose call Adams described in glowing terms: to reconcile suffering sinners to God through Christ's grace was the only way to really change people:

> Pastors have often been told (and their parishioners have often thought), "This person's problem is *much too deep* for a pastor to handle. He will need professional help. I'll have to send him to a psychiatrist." My friends, it ought to be the other way around. The only person who can really operate at a level of *depth* is the person who knows how to go to the *heart* of a man's problem. That's because the heart *is* the man's problem. The only way to go to the heart of a man's problem is through the gospel of Jesus Christ. . . . And—never forget this—in such work the *pastor* is the professional—*God's* professional.[54]

All other claimants were interlopers. The pastor had title to the job; the pastor had gifts for the job (if not, he had no right to his title); the pastor could develop competency in the job. Adams's counseling was first and foremost "pastoral" counseling, in the strict sense: the work of the ordained pastor.

Adams sought to create many inducements for pastors and potential pastors to assume the mantle of a pastoral counseling calling. He discussed in detail how aspects of pastoral work that frequently drew a pastor's attention away from working with people to help them solve their problems could in fact be reinvigorated by giving them a counseling slant. Preaching, church administration, and visitation needed to be reorganized around the tasks of pastoral work and solving problems in living. In "Your Place in the Counseling Revolution," Adams laid out his comprehensive vision for church-based, pastor-led counseling.[55]

Preaching, and other teaching occasions, offered pastors a prime opportunity to do "preventive" counseling, to reach scores or hundreds of people at the same time with practical aid from the Bible. The same message that Adams's counseling model promulgated in a counseling context was intended to inform and revitalize preaching as well. "Preaching, among other things, is preventive counseling."[56] Adams never tired of talking about how counseling and preaching could mutually reinforce each other. He rued "the divorce between preaching and counseling [that] took place when counseling came to be identified with psychotherapy rather than with the ministry of the Word."[57] He thought that "the counselor who preaches each week will grow as a counselor . . . [and] the preacher who does not counsel makes a grave mistake." The former was forced to develop "biblical underpinnings"; the latter lost touch with real people and how the Bible met their needs.[58]

Preventive work demanded access to people, and a pastor's organizational activities were meant to facilitate such access, not prevent it. Visitation ought to be organized and ought to have a pastoral counseling purpose. Visiting, in Adams's hands, was no formality for clerical functionaries: "as a pastor you have the opportunity and the right to initiate counseling. Nipping problems in the bud, before they ever get so large that the person might think about consulting a counselor, is a significant part of true pastoral concern (which, incidentally, is what the word visitation means in the Bible)."[59] Adams thought that pastoral visitation rightly conceptualized and properly organized could keep parishioners out of difficulties in the first place and prevent the need for remedial counseling later. Adams thought that most pastors wasted far too much time doing things around the office that they had no business doing. He wanted them to be "pastors," out in the fields doing their job as shepherds to their sheep.

Adams was eloquent about the possibility that his church-based counseling model could offer things other institutional arrangements could barely dream of. He thought his hearers ought to be thrilled to become nouthetic counselors. Not only could their preaching, teaching, and visiting help people before they developed serious problems. His model had other advantages that would stimulate pastors to join his revolution and draw talented men to consider the pastorate, rather than entering psychotherapeutic professions.

He anticipated that his model of pastor-counselor could draw upon an entire congregation to help him. Others in the community might pray for his counseling, might aid counselees financially or medically, might take a troubled person into their home or shelter a battered spouse, might provide a job for a counselee or financial counsel or friendship or modeling. Adams sought to wed his counseling not only to such formal activities as preaching and worship but also to the informal community activities of friendship, hospitality, generosity.

He thought that the ministers to whom he wrote would be as excited as he was about the fact that "the pastor can counsel with authority—the authority of the living God himself." Adams reveled in the notion of authoritative counseling. If the Word of God were true and binding on faith and practice, then a pastoral counselor could and should offer far more than tentative observations and suggestions and his own occasional caring presence: he offered God's truth and wisdom and the promise of God's continual presence. The note of authority extended to the power of church discipline, as well. Adams's counselors were enjoined not to sit passively by if sinning counselees refused to change their ways. The adulterer, the drunk, the slanderous gossip, the violent, the irreconcilable, and others could be pursued through a process that gradually escalated the scope and pointedness of confrontation. Adams wrote extensively about how church discipline properly done—in pursuit of repentance, forgiveness, reconcilia-

tion and constructive change—logically extended and strengthened the effectiveness of counseling ministry.[60] Adams viewed church discipline as an essential component in the biblical counseling endeavor.

This point underscores the finally "public" nature of Adams's counseling model. It began with the "fear of the LORD"—the notion that a person's life contained no ultimate secrets. It sought to solve problems by involving as small a circle of people as possible and as large a circle of people as necessary. When an individual refused to change in order to resolve problems, Adams gradually brought larger community resources to bear. This point also underscores how far Adams's model deviated from the habits of modern, voluntary, fee-for-service model of professional activity. It took on elements of that model when institutionalized in a freestanding counseling center like CCEF, but Adams's basic model was constructed along premodern communitarian lines. His counseling "professional" had a responsibility to God's honor in a community of faith, and he could draw on the resources of that community. Adams's counseling was not essentially an activity in which a professional consulted with a private client who might take or leave the suggestions with impunity.[61] If he did his pastoral job well, the nouthetic pastor might often be the initiator of counseling, and his counseling contained an authoritative element: take it for your well-being, leave it at your peril. While Adams did not believe that church authority was coercive or punitive, it could involve public declarations with the intent to bring about repentance and change. For example, a man who continued to beat and curse his family ought to be pointedly warned that "the way of the transgressor is hard," should then be cut off from "good standing" in the church, and might then become subject to criminal charges.[62] Nouthetic counseling deviated from secular psychotherapeutic ethics regarding the issue of "confidentiality." It promised no absolute confidentiality. Exceptions to a general atmosphere of confidentiality arose because such churchly counseling demanded the latitude to bring in other parties in order to fulfill the responsibilities of church discipline. For the sake of the community, it could not allow certain problems to remain private.[63]

In sum, Jay Adams taught that the church-based pastoral counselor had the opportunity to "provide *total* care for the counselee; not merely care that extends to one hour one day a week. He can follow up his counseling as no other counselor is able to do."[64] The parish and community location of pastoral counsel, its organic link to preaching, small groups, friendship, diaconal assistance, and the rest, seemed in Adams's mind to be the Bible's way to go about things.[65]

Adams was suspicious of counseling centers, even though he had founded one with a comprehensive charter. He rationalized his creation of and participation in the Christian Counseling and Educational Foundation by the education promised in its name—its training of pastors and pastors-to-be adjunct to Westminster Seminary's programs, its publishing arm—and by its employment of ordained pastors on a part-time basis.[66] But any institution that might weaken the links between counseling and local church ministry carried potential danger. A parachurch organization was inherently anomalous in Adams's vision, but it could serve certain auxiliary functions—education, publishing, promoting the cause—that would be difficult to accomplish at a local church level.

It is not accidental or coincidental that Adams wrote numerous volumes on various aspects of the pastor's task. He wrote more than a dozen books on preaching, as well as books on pastoral leadership, pastoral life, and church discipline. In Adams's vision preaching and counseling shared a common conceptual body, common goals, and even a cer-

tain commonality in method. His often-repeated stress on the "authoritative" nature of Christian counseling flowed out of his conception of the task of ministry to proclaim God's Word. It is not accidental or coincidental that Adams named his journal the *Journal of Pastoral Practice*. Adams intended that nouthetic counseling practice would occur as one function within a multifaceted role quite different from the private practice psychotherapist; counseling was but one function within a community structured and functioning very differently from a psychotherapist's office.

How did Adams propose to train such pastors? Certainly they did not need training and accreditation in the mental health professions. But Adams also expressed a marked ambivalence about what was available in theological education. On the one hand, he said:

> The place to study for a counseling ministry is in a good theological seminary, because *that* is the only place where an adequate education for counseling as a life calling can be obtained. I am not referring primarily to the counseling courses in such institutions. Rather I am thinking of the Greek, and of the Hebrew, and of the theology, and of the exegesis courses, and so forth; those studies that enable one to become intimately and accurately acquainted with the Bible. That is what a counselor needs above all.[67]

But on the other hand, he often evidenced a marked frustration when he considered seminary education and its preparation of pastors. He commented on the "sterility of past training (or lack of training) in counseling" that pastors had received and the lack of role models; "seminary curricula are heavily weighted toward other concerns, and counseling courses are eclectically conditioned"; "there is little systematic scholarly biblical pastoral material on counseling available."[68] He spent two stints as a professor of practical theology (1964–77 and 1982–90), but he had reservations regarding the ability of seminaries to prepare pastors. For example, his comments on how scholars approached Bible translation are equally applicable to how he viewed most pastoral preparation in seminary settings:

> Many important counseling nuances have been missed by other translators, who didn't have a counseling (or often even a pastoral) orientation when translating. . . . Something of the pastoral concern inherent in the original writings has been lost. . . .
>
> Men, sequestered in ivy-covered halls, who find their closest friends among the formless and faceless authors of stuffy tomes, who rarely mix with the common man in the supermarket, often will find it difficult to locate the everyday idiom that approximates the fish-market Greek in which the New Testament was written. They must be in touch with the reader.[69]

These same professors might as easily be out of touch with the strugglers whose problems in living would soon besiege the pastor-in-training.

Adams thought that pastors were often poor at counseling—largely as a result of poor training—and that they had justly earned the derogatory and dismissive attitudes expressed toward them both in the wider culture and in the church. His own approach to remedying the situation was to propose a redesigned seminary that would construct its education around the tasks of pastoral ministry.[70] Some of these ideas he attempted to build into his own teaching: participant observation, profuse use of case studies, a relentless drive to identify in each case the appropriate concrete applications of general principles, throwing students into the fray of actual ministry, largely abandoning the grading system ("What we want are competent ministers; what we get are test whizzers"[71]), ensuring that professors were also practitioners.

As mentioned in the introductory chapter, Adams showed no interest in commenting on how society at large should address its ills. It is worth repeating that point in this context. Adams clearly did not wish to define a counseling methodology that would be suitable for counselors operating autonomously of conservative Protestant doctrine and ecclesiastical contexts. "We shall not stop unbelievers from setting up their own counseling systems and from doing counseling that competes with the Scriptures; that is a given."[72] Other systems of redressing problems in living were the equivalent of mosques or Mormon churches. Similarly, he did not intend a counseling methodology suitable for counselees who had no interest in considering the implications of the Christian faith for explaining and addressing their problems. As we saw previously, when Adams encountered a non-Christian counselee, his goal was evangelistic, to bring such a person into the fold of Bible belief and pastoral care.

We have seen that the ecclesiastical locus of nouthetic counseling had implications first for the counseling that all Christians did and second for the pastor. The third implication of Adams's local church orientation was that his counseling methodology was particularly tailored to the exigencies, constraints, and advantages that came with the role of pastor within a community. He self-consciously attempted to replicate what the Bible narrated about the ways that Jesus and Paul communicated with their intimates, with the disciples in the former example, with the churches he had founded in the latter. The give and take of the community location for counseling lent a number of distinctive emphases to the methods enjoined on nouthetic counselors.

Candor about oneself and to others about themselves was a natural part of caring relationships as has been mentioned previously. But Adams proposed numerous other ways by which the counseling relationship could be demystified and made an extension of daily-life community relationships. Diverse forms of hospitality could be given and received—those counseled might even be taken in to live with the pastor or with someone else in the church—rather than counselors maintaining professional distance.[73] This created several marked differences between nouthetic counseling and secular psychotherapy. First, secular therapy tended to view "dual relationships" as a serious ethical violation, but nouthetic counseling encouraged an embedding of formal counseling within informal, communitarian relationships. Second, nouthetic counseling made no attempt to elicit the heightened "transference" effects that appear when a counselor appears essentially mysterious to a counselee. Team counseling also served as a "deterrent to the evils of transference."[74] Adams pilloried the eliciting of both negative and positive transference effects as "encouraging clients to perpetuate and multiply their sin and guilt . . . [and] one more faulty pattern which clients develop instead of squarely facing the actual people involved in their problem."[75]

Nouthetic counseling invited and encouraged its counselors to a wide gamut of emotional responses—grief, concern, outrage, enthusiasm. Counselors might appropriately weep ("with those who weep") or rejoice ("with those who rejoice"): "Perhaps it is sufficient to note here that biblical counseling frequently gets so exciting that nouthetic counselors might get up and walk around the room, shout, laugh uproariously, and on occasion even shed tears."[76] Adams was an opponent of cool, "clinical" detachment in counseling:

There are times to plead as Paul did here [2 Cor. 6]. There are times to spill your gut as he is doing throughout this very personal letter. But you must be careful

not to do so in wrong ways and at wrong times. . . . Few counseling sessions of any length and consequence will be free of emotional moments. Nor should they be. Don't become a white-coated, unemotional automaton; in counseling bring all you are and feel into the sessions. . . .[77]

He envisioned an intensity of distinctly pastoral love and concern that would have his counselors replicate Paul's "for three years, night and day . . . I didn't stop counseling [noutheteo] each one of you with tears."[78]

Adams also freely brought into his sessions those actions that communicated a belief that God was present and powerful as the agent of change in people's lives. Frank prayer arising out of the flow of a session was typical: "As a matter of practice, under ordinary circumstances, prayer always ought to be offered at least at the close of the session. At other times, during a session prayer may be appropriate. It may be the natural outcome of a decision or commitment. It may be the fervent cry of the counselee for forgiveness as the Word that was ministered brought conviction of sin and repentance."[79] At the end of a session, as necessary changes for the upcoming week had been mapped out, counselees would be encouraged to ask God for aid. Adams himself penned a book of his prayers that, typically, bore the marks of his frankness and bent toward life's practical problems:

That temper of mine! Forgive me, Lord—I let it get the better of me again. When will I ever learn to wait until I've heard the whole story, to respond under pressure as Christ would, to meet evil with good? . . . ("Anger," p. 9)

Caught myself: I've been complaining again instead of thanking You. How often I find myself joining the chorus of those who can see nothing more than the skin of life's trials. . . . ("Complaint," p. 11)

Lord, I can almost taste the bitterness of disappointment; my shattered expectations and dreams are like gravel in my mouth. So help me—my strength fails. . . . Teach me in this disappointment to empty my mouth of grit and to savor instead the delicacies You have prepared for me. That I may honor Christ. ("Disappointment," p. 17)

I am so afraid that I am almost shivering; I dread what may happen next. Lord, that is because I have been looking away from Your face and at the stormy waves. . . . Teach me to fear You, Lord, so that I need never fear what waves—or wavemakers—can do to me. ("Fear," p. 22)

"Unbearable," did I say? I take it back, Lord; forgive me for staining my lips with the world's language. What I mean is it hurts—it hurts a lot, and I am having difficulty bearing up. . . . Help me also to remember that others have endured successfully among whom, principally, was my Savior Himself, Who bore all I am undergoing—and much more. It is He who sets pain's limits. . . . ("Pain," pp. 34f)

I have said the words "I love you" to You and to my neighbor—but do I really love? Do I really put first others or self? Am I patient and kind? Or am I jealous, proud, ugly, irritable, bitter? . . . You know too that it is because You first loved me that I love at all and that I want to love as I have been loved. ("Love," pp. 26f)[80]

Such blunt, problem-solution prayers would be a revelation to those whose piety had been shaped by vague generalities, by the phraseology and cadence of religious language, or by the search for elevated religious feelings.

Even worship was not unknown in counseling sessions—some nouthetic counselors sang with counselees on occasion or played music, an application of the methodology for doing *noutheteo* enjoined by Paul in Colossians 3:16.[81] And, of course, the Bible was typically open and referred to pointedly, and Adams sought to teach counselees how to use it well on their own.[82] In all these, Adams focused on how to handle problems in living in a way that took the traditional resources of Bible-believing Protestantism but innovated in the way he employed them.

Adams wanted to know facts, to "gather data." In the local church setting, knowledge of a counselee's life was typically based on observation in daily life situations and on the comments of other involved parties (often present in counseling), as well as on the counselee's self-report. One common homework assignment at CCEF sought to compensate for the fact that the institution and its counselors stood more remote from the counselee's daily life. Counselors would have the counselee enlist a half-dozen people—friends, family members, employer—to write up a frank assessment of strengths and shortcomings. Adams spent a great deal of energy teaching his counselors how to get the facts they needed in order to be able to give reasonable counsel.[83] He was convinced that much of the failure of conservative Protestant methods of pastoral care lay in a failure to know how to probe people's lives intentionally.

Adams's counseling demonstrated a marked didactic component. The preacher and teacher who taught crowds each Sunday how to know God and please the one who had loved them would hardly stop teaching those same things when face-to-face in an office or living room. Adams did not believe that people had the answers to solve their problems within themselves; he thought they needed the "ministry of the Word" to renovate what they believed and did in the tests of daily life.[84] Counseling was intentionally directive, just as the Bible was directive about both faith and practice. Instructional homework assignments were a staple of nouthetic counseling. Assignments might include Bible study on a particular topic, a study pointedly made complete by posing application questions to oneself and acting on one's answers. Homework also might include reading and pondering a pamphlet or book; Adams's numerous popular writings about varied problems in living sought to address the need.[85]

Nouthetic counselors were encouraged to speak frankly and authoritatively when communicating the promises and commands of God: "You must stop committing adultery. God will forgive you and will give you a fresh start; Christ died for that. Confess your sin. Ask for help. You must learn to love your wife, and by God's grace you can." Adams placed a great deal of emphasis on "giving hope" to people in the midst of their problems, hope based on promises in the Bible regarding God's love, power, and purposes.[86] Adams intended that the counseling room would be charged with the counselor's enthusiasm for God's loving power, and that such buoyant confidence would be infectious. He believed that counselors had "good news" to give, however tough people's circumstances and however tangled their sins.

Adams similarly placed great emphasis on the specific commands of God. As indicated above, he did not shrink from giving pointed advice, and giving it energetically. Pastors and their counselees might then explore tentatively the varied options for how something from the Bible might be implemented, what change would look like in any particular person's case. But their common framework for faith and practice was a God-given command. Adams distinguished between the authority of God, communicated by the pastor-counselor, and a tentativeness appropriate to working out how to apply God's will. A counselor could say, "You must learn to love your wife." He could not say, "You must take her out for dinner Friday night and quit spending so much money on your hobbies." Such con-

crete items might be possibilities subject to negotiation by all concerned parties—husband, wife, counselor—regarding what love would look like.[87]

Another characteristic of Adams's methodology, mentioned previously, was the use of "homework." He wanted counselees to tackle their problems all week, not simply during the "magic hour" of counseling; he wanted them to engage "life as it is lived" rather than become dependent on their counselor.[88] He used homework in numerous ways to facilitate the change process. It could be part of data-gathering or Bible study, as mentioned above. He was committed to have people actually change what they did in life. When a necessary, constructive action had been determined—to look for a job, to ask someone's forgiveness, to become accountable to a friend not to buy pornography, to set up a family conference table—that became the content of homework. Counselees were to ask God for help, commit themselves, and do it. Adams noted that his conservative Protestant counselees frequently answered the intake question, "What have you done about your problem?" with one word, "Prayed." He said, "The counselor must make the point that the biblical answer is different. Instead it is *ora et labora*, 'pray and work.'"[89]

Finally, Adams's model emphasized a brief, goal-oriented series of brisk counseling sessions. He frequently stated that the work that needed to get done could typically be accomplished in six to twelve weeks. If counselees "meant business" and set about facing, tackling, and solving their problems in order to build new patterns of thinking and behavior, "Certainly by eight or ten weeks counseling ought to be well on its way toward reaching solutions to specific problems."[90] He vigorously opposed simply talking about problems and the notion that airing troubles was inherently therapeutic. Cathartic relief was temporary relief in Adams's view and proved detrimental in the long run because it took the pressure off, pressure intended by God to press people to solve the underlying issues:

> It is never adequate merely to talk about problems. All talk in counseling must be oriented toward biblical solutions. That is why it is essential to direct the entire session toward its climax—the commitment of the counselee to his homework task(s) for the next week. . . . It is important to orient the entire counseling session toward commitment to biblical change as its climax. This change may be a change of knowledge, belief, or action. Almost always the former two will lead to the latter.[91]

Adams intended homework to solve problems. Along the way it served to flush out those who simply wanted to enlist the counselor in a "pity party" rather than doing something constructive about their lives. He brought in other actors from the counselee's social network to hear all sides of every story: to help those who wanted to change, to expose those who sought only to vindicate themselves by making a case for how wronged they had been by others. He had no patience with the "Professional Counselee," who turned sessions into a "chess game" and simply wanted to talk rather than work.[92]

His counseling offered people a remedial consultation, and he would not spend time on those who wanted to continue in their problems and ignore good advice. The busy pastors to whom Adams appealed might want to do more than offer token prayers and Bible verses, but they could hardly fill their schedules with interminable counseling cases. Nouthetic counseling fit within a pastor's schedule. It taught them to say no—with a good conscience—to people who absorbed time and energy. It taught them how to accomplish something with people who wanted to be taught, wanted accountability, wanted help. Nouthetic counseling worked the way pastors worked.

In sum, "The pastor who is nouthetically oriented will tend to become lovingly frank with his people. Counseling principles carry over into every area of the pastoral ministry. . . . He will be specific about personal problems and straightforwardly attempt to correct them."[93] In the consultation between parishioner and pastor about life's problems, Adams was not content to restrict his role to passive empathy and support or to fulfilling symbolic religious functions.[94] His was the counseling model of an activistic pastor, and he appealed directly to the pastoral leaders of his subculture to share his activism. His was the counseling model of a local church pastor, infused with the habits, constraints, and opportunities attendant to that role.

We have examined the leading features of Jay Adams's reconstruction of the counseling task.[95] Conservative Protestant pastors had been given a model of counseling that mapped onto many of their beliefs, habits, and institutions. But the field was not clear. A crowd of "interlopers, compromisers, syncretizers, collaborators and integrationists" had already staked out their claims to cultural, social, and pragmatic authority—to truth, love, and power—in the counseling realm. Adams took the offensive from the start, and the tasks of apologetics consumed a great deal of the attention of nouthetic counselors.

Chapter 6 Notes

1. Jay E. Adams, *From Forgiven to Forgiving: Discover the Path to Biblical Forgiveness* (USA: Victor Books [Scripture Press], 1989), 121f.

2. Jay E. Adams, *The Big Umbrella and Other Essays and Addresses on Christian Counseling* (USA: Presbyterian & Reformed, 1972), 33.

3. Jay E. Adams, *The Christian Counselor's Manual* (USA: Presbyterian & Reformed, 1973), 5f.

4. Ibid., 12.

5. Jay E. Adams, *Christ and Your Problems* (Nutley, N.J.: Presbyterian & Reformed, 1971).

6. Adams, *The Christian Counselor's Manual* 46, n. 17.

7. Adams's translation of 1 Corinthians 10:13; Jay E. Adams, *The Christian Counselor's New Testament: A New Translation in Everyday English with Notations* (USA: Presbyterian & Reformed, 1977), *infra*. The entire book of 1 Corinthians was favorite of Adams. He chose to begin his Christian Counselor's Commentary series with 1 Corinthians. Jay E. Adams, *The Christian Counselor's Commentary: I & II Corinthians* (Hackettstown, N.J.: Timeless Texts, 1994). He saw 1 Corinthians as "the epistle of church problems" (p. xi), and liked the orderly way that Paul sorted through and addressed a string of problems one after the other. He also viewed this entire letter as an exemplar for "nouthetic" counseling, as Paul himself had described his letter in these words, "I am not writing these things to shame you, but to counsel [*noutheteo*] you as my dear children" (1 Cor. 4:14). Adams aspired to replicate Paul's manner—brisk, familial, hortatory, optimistic about God's power and love, organized, blunt about issues to be tackled, frank about one's own feelings and failings.

8. Adams, *Christ and Your Problems*, 3.

9. Ibid., 1. Adams was obviously not a relativist about human nature. His system was predicated on the belief that a "human nature" transcended differences of culture, gender, ethnicity, and historical situation.

One implication of this leveling of human nature and abandonment of the medical model for problems in living was that Adams did not consider himself well and his clients sick: "A counselor knows that in his own sinful heart is the tendency to succumb to every failure which he observes in his clients. Counselors may let clients know that they understand by narrating an incident or giving an example. . . ." Jay E. Adams, *Competent to Counsel* (USA: Presbyterian & Reformed, 1970), 137. Adams wrote that the proper attitude to approach counseling "comes from keeping in mind one's own inabilities and sinfulness, and from remembering that any wisdom, knowledge, skill, or righteousness that he has is the result of God's grace" and that "[this] attitude is expressed most fully when [it] says, 'I'm helping you today, but who knows whether I may need your help next week?'" Jay E. Adams, *Ready to Restore: The Layman's Guide to Christian Counseling* (Phillipsburg, N.J.: Presbyterian & Reformed, 1981), 7.

10. Adams frequently registered his complaint against the post-Freudian therapeutic ethos that it had substituted concern for guilt feelings for the problem of objective guilt: "It is important . . . to distinguish between *guilt* and *a sense of guilt*." Jay E. Adams, *More Than Redemption: A Theology of Christian Counseling* (Phillipsburg, N.J.: Presbyterian & Reformed, 1979), 144; cf., pp. 143–46 and chap. 13. Cf., Adams, *From Forgiven to Forgiving*, 160f.

11. Adams, *Christ and Your Problems*, 9, 11. Adams typically wove Calvinistic distinctives into his writings, a subtext intended to work covertly on those many Protestant readers who were not Calvinists. Here he alludes to the "L" in TULIP, limited atonement.

12. Adams, *More Than Redemption*, 184; Adams, *From Forgiven to Forgiving*, 12.

13. For example, Adams, *From Forgiven to Forgiving*, was about how bitter people could resolve their problems with those who had wronged them. Knowing that their own wrongs were forgiven would create a dynamic enabling them to forgive others.

14. Adams, *The Christian Counselor's Manual*, 3–5.

15. Adams, *Christ and Your Problems*, 15.

16. Ibid., 18f.

17. Adams wrote frequently on these subjects when he wrote self-help pieces for counselees. See e.g., Jay E. Adams, *How to Overcome Evil* (Nutley, N.J.: Presbyterian & Reformed, 1977); Jay E. Adams, *How to Handle Trouble: God's Way* (Phillipsburg, N.J.: Presbyterian & Reformed, 1982).

18. Adams's choice of these ingredients simply clothes leading categories from his systematic theology in concrete rather than abstract language. These three items arise from the *ordo salutis* (order of salvation) that he had learned in seminary: justification, sanctification, glorification.

19. Adams, *Competent to Counsel*, 73.

20. As we saw in the previous chapter, Adams made a place, albeit small, for medical intervention in problems in living. But he was wary of offering symptomatic relief that might undermine his counseling goals: "Pills may remove much motivation by lessening pain and depression. . . . There may be cases in which the counselor must refuse to work with the client until the use of drugs has been moderated or eliminated." Adams, *Competent to Counsel*, 142. In such cases Adams believed that experiences of pain, anxiety, and unhappiness were linked with God's sovereign purposes, were meant to be attended to in the interests of changing beliefs and lifestyle, not blunted by medication.

21. Adams's speech to Austrian psychiatrists (Jay E. Adams, *Change Them? . . . into What?: Counseling in America Today* [Laverock, Pa.: Christian Counseling and Educational Foundation, 1977]) turned on this question of the goal of counseling.

22. Adams, *The Christian Counselor's Manual*, 173.

23. E.g., John Calvin, *Institutes of the Christian Religion*, trans. Ford Lewis Battles, ed. John T. McNeill, The Library of Christian Classics (Philadelphia: The Westminster Press, 1960), 587. "The Christian life is a race of repentance."

24. My quotation here is a composite from many sources, both written and oral.

25. Adams, *The Christian Counselor's Manual*, 44.

26. Ibid., 305f.

27. In the early years of CCEF 96 percent of the counseling cases lasted twelve sessions or less; only 1 percent extended to more than twenty sessions.

28. Ibid., 187.

29. Ibid., 184, 186–87. Charges that Adams was overly strenuous and "legalistic" had first surfaced during the "airport meeting" and would continue to appear. *Competent to Counsel* had struck almost all commentators as so emphasizing human responsibility to obey God that it seriously neglected God's provision of acceptance, mercy, and a relationship of love through Jesus Christ.

30. Jay E. Adams, *Godliness through Discipline* (Phillipsburg, N.J.: Presbyterian & Reformed, 1972).

31. Adams, *The Christian Counselor's Manual*, 141–60.

32. Interview, December 4, 1990.

33. Adams, *More Than Redemption*, 320. He discussed this topic extensively and repeatedly: Jay E. Adams, *What About Nouthetic Counseling?* (Grand Rapids: Baker Book House, 1976), 65–68; Adams, *The Big Umbrella*, 97–112; Adams, *Competent to Counsel*, 67–73.

34. Adams, *Competent to Counsel,* 67f.

35. Ibid., 71.

36. Ibid., 73.

37. Ibid.

38. Ibid., xix.

39. Ibid., 68f.

40. Ibid., 89.

41. Ibid., 82.

42. In Adams's view, such formal parallels were inconsequential, and to be expected in "counterfeits." They did not point to some deeper truth that unified any and all therapies but to the fact that even deceivers could not escape living in God's world. He interpreted such parallels in the same way he would interpret the fact that various religions, by definition, talk about God, encourage people to pray, and, like any worldview, by definition entail a cosmology, an epistemology, an ethic, a hamartiology, a soteriology, and an eschatology.

43. Ibid., 100–104; Adams, *What About Nouthetic Counseling?,* 73-75.

44. Adams, *Competent to Counsel,* 252.

45. Ibid., 252–67.

46. Ephesians 6:4; Jay E. Adams, *Christian Living in the Home* (Phillipsburg, N.J.: Presbyterian & Reformed, 1972), 121f.

47. Adams, *Competent to Counsel,* 241.

48. Ibid., 231–36.

49. Jay E. Adams, *Lectures on Counseling* (Grand Rapids: Zondervan, 1975–77), 44; Jay E. Adams, *Four Weeks with God and Your Neighbor: A Devotional Workbook for Counselees and Others* (USA: Presbyterian & Reformed, 1978).

50. Adams, *Ready to Restore,* 10; Jay E. Adams, *Handbook of Church Discipline* (Grand Rapids: Zondervan, 1986), 25f.

51. Adams, *Lectures on Counseling,* 47.

52. Ibid., 48.

53. Ibid., 38–40.

54. Adams, *More Than Redemption,* 310.

55. Adams, *Lectures on Counseling,* 50–53. The paragraphs that follow are largely drawn from these pages even where there is no specific quotation.

56. Ibid., 50.

57. Jay E. Adams, *Preaching with Purpose: A Comprehensive Textbook on Biblical Preaching* (Phillipsburg, N.J.: Presbyterian & Reformed, 1982), 114f.

58. Ibid., 36–38.

59. Adams, *Lectures on Counseling,* 51.

60. Adams's *Handbook of Church Discipline* summarized discussions of candor, mercy, reconciliation, and church discipline that had appeared in many of his earlier books.

61. This made Adams's anti-psychiatry markedly different from Szasz's anti-psychiatry. The latter sought to remove the coercive element out of psychiatry in order to establish a therapeutic laissez-faire, free-market economy, where troubled people would seek the help they wanted and needed. Szasz viewed the state church's historical "coercive" role as paradigmatic for the coercions institutionalized by the twentieth-century state. Adams, arguing from the point of view of disestablished churches, believed that pastoral authority ought to make the implications of people's choices clear to them, while pursuing their repentance from what he saw as ultimately fatal life choices.

62. Adams proposed to solve many problems within the church that might eventually have a legal dimension if unsolved. He favored appeal to secular authorities only after the resources of church and community discipline, mediation, and reconciliation had been exhausted. Some followers who were lawyers worked to develop mediation and conciliation services and protocols within churches: e.g., Ken Sande, *The Peacemaker: A Biblical Guide to Resolving Personal Conflict* (Grand Rapids: Baker Book House, 1991).

63. Adams, *Handbook of Church Discipline,* 30–33; George C. Scipione, "The Limits of Confidentiality in Counseling," *Journal of Pastoral Practice* 7, no. 2 (1984): 29–34; Larry Spalink, "Warning: This Office Bugged by the Holy Spirit," *Journal of Biblical Counseling* 3, no. 3 (1979): 56–62.

64. Adams, *Lectures on Counseling,* 52.

65. Most of the discussion in the previous paragraphs, where a quotation is not cited, derives from the chapter, "Your Part in the Counseling Revolution" in Adams, *Lectures on Counseling,* 46–53.

66. When in future years Bettler expanded CCEF's counseling activities beyond the needs of training; began hiring nonpastors, both male and female; reoriented CCEF's educational offerings to increase the proportion of courses that interacted with the secular psychologies; reoriented CCEF's target audience to educate laypeople equally with pastors; and reduced the role of participant-observation in the training process; it created tensions between CCEF's emphases and the heart of Adams's vision for pastors. The differences generally proved negotiable because of the proviso for "other Christian workers/counselors" in Adams's vision. The female counselors at CCEF almost exclusively counseled other women and children. CCEF counselors would cooperate with local church pastors in church discipline—even encouraging them in those tasks. Pastors always continued to make up about half of CCEF's staff, and a significant percentage of its students. See chapter 9.

67. Ibid., 53.

68. Ibid., 7f.

69. Adams, *The Christian Counselor's New Testament,* ix-x.

70. Jay E. Adams, "Design for a Theological Seminary," *Journal of Pastoral Practice* 3, no. 2 (1979): 1–10.

71. Ibid., 9.

72. Adams, *More Than Redemption,* 22.

73. Many of the nouthetic counselors I interviewed had counselees live with their families at various times.

74. Adams, *Competent to Counsel,* 207.

75. Ibid., 101.

76. Ibid., 54. This comment tells much about Adams's boisterous personality; Bettler was far more restrained.

77. Adams, *The Christian Counselor's Commentary: I & II Corinthians,* 143.

78. Adams, *The Christian Counselor's New Testament, infra,* Acts 20:31.

79. Adams, *The Christian Counselor's Manual,* 49f. Cf., Adams, *More Than Redemption,* 61–87.

80. Jay E. Adams, *Prayers for Troubled Times* (Grand Rapids: Baker Book House, 1979).

81. Ronald T. Harris, "Entering Zion with Singing," *Journal of Pastoral Practice* 9, no. 2 (1988): 35–57.

82. Adams, *Four Weeks with God and Your Neighbor;* Jay E. Adams, *What to Do on Thursday: A Layman's Guide to the Practical Use of the Scriptures* (Phillipsburg, N.J.: Presbyterian & Reformed, 1982). As an aside, Adams opposed the widespread use of the King James Version among his constituency. He thought it—and other translations—often obscured practical biblical truth and missed the everyday idiom in which pastoral concern ought to engage everyday problems. See Adams, *The Christian Counselor's New Testament,* viii–x.

83. Adams, *The Christian Counselor's Manual,* 252–93.

84. Adams, *Competent to Counsel,* 78–104. He fiercely opposed "nondirective" counseling that presumed that all the resources people needed to solve their problems were innate or provided by the nurturing atmosphere of therapeutic kindness.

85. See bibliography. Another nouthetic author who was notably prolific in the self-help genre was Wayne Mack.

86. Adams, *The Christian Counselor's Manual,* 39–48.

87. Ibid., 15–17; Adams, *More Than Redemption,* 18–20.

88. Adams, *The Christian Counselor's Manual,* 305.

89. Ibid., 50f.

90. Ibid., 234.

91. Ibid., 242f; see context, 243–47.

92. Ibid., 298f.

93. Adams, *Competent to Counsel,* 63.

94. Adams, *The Christian Counselor's Manual,* 154–60.

95. What did it look like in action? Adams was not well known outside of those conservative Protestant circles in which both his adherents and opponents were to be found. The world of such "religious" counseling (a designation Adams would fiercely oppose, averring repeatedly that all counseling was fundamentally "religious" in that it addressed matters of belief, value, attitude, behavior, and desire; the real issue was whether any particular model promulgated true or false religion) tended to be generally invisible in the wider culture. In an appendix I have reprinted the contents of a brochure Adams would hand out to couples undergoing marriage counseling with him.

CHAPTER 7

Adams's Interaction
with the Modern Psychologies

It isn't those who are well who need a doctor, but those who are sick. . . .
I didn't come to call righteous people, but sinners.

— Jesus, c. AD 30[1]

Psychotherapists are not really doctors because the people they treat are not really sick.

— Perry London, 1964[2]

A new practitioner, part physician (a very small part) and part secular priest (a very large part),
came into being to serve the host of persons who previously were counseled by ministers but now
had been snatched away from them and placed beneath the broad umbrella of "mental illness." . . .
The psychiatrist should return to the practice of medicine, which is his only legitimate sphere
of activity; the minister should return to the God-given work from which he was ousted
(and which, in many instances, he too willingly abandoned).   — Jay Adams, 1973[3]

Knowledge systems claim totalitarian interpretive powers over their field of view.[4] Such systems not only proffer positive meanings and practices that invite faith; they also assail competing systems, inviting committed disbelief. Ways of seeing claim the ability to identify the astigmatism in other ways of seeing. In the final analysis, debunking transmutes other systems into instances of false consciousness and myth, follies that can be seen from the standpoint of wisdom and truth that one's own system uniquely provides. This is simply to say that attack and defense—polemics and apologetics—are intrinsic to prosecuting any claim to knowledge.

The personal problems jurisdiction provides particularly fertile soil for claimants to spring up. All manner of religions, psychologies, medicines, political ideologies, and popular philosophies present themselves as the cure for at least a significant piece of what ails humanity. Authority to interpret and solve the problems in living is endlessly contested, and debunking counterclaimants is a critical activity in sustaining a jurisdictional claim. In the previous chapters we examined the positive system Adams offered potential converts. In this chapter we will look at the conceptual resources he employed to debunk competitors.

In 1975 Adams opened "Your Place in the Counseling Revolution" with these revealing, programmatic words:

> I am sending these lectures forth to the Christian public, hoping that in some measure God will use this humble effort as one small contribution to bringing about the revolution in counseling that may in time spark a new revival of the Christian faith in this country. . . .
>
> If at first the word *revolution* sounds too sweeping and belligerent, let me urge you to reserve your judgment. . . .
>
> *Revolt* . . . signifies originally a warring or turning against the power to which one has been subject; but *revolt* is mostly taken either in an indifferent or a good sense for resisting a foreign dominion which has been imposed by force of arms.
>
> That definition in every way is *apropos* of the situation that until recently has prevailed. If "force of arms" may be considered figuratively referring to the warnings by which pastors and Christians have been intimidated, the picture is complete. A power, foreign to the Christian Church, has held her tightly in its grips for a long while. There have been many collaborators. But, at long last, tired of the failure, convinced that within the Church itself there are resources that have been virtually untapped, many are awakening to the need and to the opportunities and are beginning to throw off the yoke of oppression. The collaborators, understandably, are not happy. Hopefully, some of them can be won to the cause. But largely, the revolution—as indeed most revolutions are—has begun as a grass-roots struggle.[5]

That quotation sounds the leading notes of Adams's polemical strategy as a turf warrior: identify the foreign power and its local collaborators, and call loyal citizens to join the resistance.

Adams, like many other observers before and since, noted that the secular psychologies had largely replaced the church as the culture-wide authority in the personal problems domain. Within the mainline churches, that displacement had created an extensive intellectual and practical subordination of pastoral practice to secular authority when it came to addressing people experiencing problems in living. Adams noted, further, that the historical insulation of the conservative Protestant community from the influence of psychology and psychiatry had recently broken down. He saw, as others were seeing (and describing in less prejudicial terms), a growing community of "collaborators"—evangelical psychiatrists, psychotherapists, and pastoral counselors influenced by the modern psychologies. That they were "not happy" with what Adams proposed had become obvious in the conflicts that immediately ensued upon his publishing *Competent to Counsel*.

The quotation above also alludes to Adams's sources of both ordnance and soldiery, to "virtually untapped" theological and institutional resources and to a "grass-roots" constituency in the "Christian public."[6] Adams largely bypassed the leaders and the leading institutions in conservative Protestant counseling. Though a few might be "won to the cause" of his revolution, most were committed to a nonpastoral, relatively a-theological counseling practice predicated on a distinction between those "psychological-emotional-behavioral" problems addressed in counseling and those "spiritual" problems addressed in the Bible. The former were the province of the psychotherapist; the latter belonged to the pastor. By reducing all functional problems to the theological category, Adams thereby eliminated the mental health professional's province.[7]

A declaration of war could hardly be more explicit: Adams called for a "revolution." In particular he wanted to undermine confidence in the foreign power's "propaganda," which had sapped pastoral confidence in ideas and methods that he believed lay on the surface of the Bible. By building his hearers' confidence that they already had the goods needed for competency in counseling, Adams then wanted them to repel the "collaborationist" incursion into the conservative Protestant church.

This chapter will examine the rhetorical and apologetic strategies and resources Adams employed. In his treatment of psychology, Adams is best understood as a rhetorician. His intentions were partisan, with no pretense of scholarly dispassion. He wrote polemically, to persuade groups of people to act: to inform, to convince, to motivate hearers to do something about what he proclaimed.[8]

Rhetoric, polemics, and apologetics often carry derogatory implications, as if they are synonymous with something at least vaguely unethical or intellectually disreputable, with sophistry, manipulation, prejudice, obscurantism, or bigotry. But I mean these words in their straightforward sense. Commitment to any reasoned position involves argument and persuasion, exposing a positive position, attacking other positions, and answering objections. Adams's critics thought that his arguments verged on the argumentative and that his polemics crossed the line into ranting. But in this chapter I will simply examine the content of Adams's controversy with psychology. Chapters 8 and 9 will treat reactions to the tone and balance, as well as the content, of his polemics.

Adams designed the bulk of his rhetoric to catch the ear of the conservative pastor, anticipating that ministry-minded laypeople would listen in. But he did engage two other audiences occasionally, and discernibly altered his strategies of persuasion when he addressed them. First, as an occasional, secondary audience, conservative Protestant psychotherapists were objects of Adams's suspicion and came in for unalleviated criticism. The sectarian tendency manifest in the Krisheim symposium was characteristic. Adams consistently stressed the illegitimacy of both the psychotherapy professions and the intellectual agenda of the evangelicals who integrated psychology with their faith. When invited to receive an award as a pioneer in Christian counseling before a gathering of several thousand evangelical psychotherapists, Adams noted:

I have been a source of irritation to many of you. I know also that I can't consider myself one of you, except as we are brothers and sisters in Christ. . . .

Contrary to what you may think, I have not spent the last fifteen or twenty years trying to refute (or even irritate) so called Christian professionals (psychiatrists, psychologists, sociologists) like yourselves. Had I intended to do so, I assure you I would have done a better job of it! My efforts solely have been to help pastors who, according to 2 Timothy 3:17, are God's professionals. That's why the approaches and arguments in my writings are not tailored to you. Rather I designed them to expose to pastors the futility and dangers of attempting to integrate pagan thought and biblical truth.

Moreover, while these negative measures are necessary to alert and inform pastors, my work is fundamentally positive. I am more at home with the construction gang than with the wrecking crew. . . .

With all that is within me I urge you to give up the fruitless task to which I alluded: the attempt to integrate pagan thought and biblical truth. . . .

God doesn't bless His competition. That's why integration won't work.

I invite you to abandon this useless endeavor. Instead, come, join the growing number of those who are discovering that the way to construct a truly Christian counseling system is to begin with biblical blueprints, use biblical bricks and mortar, and find Christian workmen to construct it from the ground up.[9]

With his closest professional foes, Adams bluntly—irritatingly, perhaps—drew the intellectual and professional lines and invited repentance.

Second, non-Christian mental health professionals provided a rare, tertiary audience. As indicated in the previous paragraph, most of Adams's polemic never actually intended psychiatrists, other psychotherapists, or personality theorists as the audience; it was framed for the benefit of his primary audience of pastors, warning them off from mental health ideology and institutions.[10] In Adams's few actual interactions with secular mental health professionals he was typically courteous, giving information about nouthetic counseling and its benefits, noting its spreading popularity, and posing provocative questions.[11] Of the three purposes of rhetoric—to inform, to convince, to motivate—he chiefly sought to inform.

What specific rhetorical resources did Adams employ to motivate his primary readers to commitment and action? I will identify six characteristic elements in his anti-psychological polemic. First, he often conducted his attack in testimonial form. *CtC* commenced in the "I once was lost but now am found" genre. With sophisticated audiences, this genre often arouses suspicion, but for Adams's intended audience it was a natural choice. Those who themselves "had a testimony" and who pursued converts overtly were engaged, not offended, by his references to firsthand experience.[12] Second, he took advantage of the disarray and internal criticisms within psychology-related fields. Both the fragmentation of psychological theory and the work of other anti-psychiatrists played into his purposes. Third, Adams proposed a normative sociology of the professions radically at odds from current historical reality. His idealized restructuring of the prerogatives of pastors, psychologists, and psychiatrists both reproved pastors for their ineptitude and identified various psychotherapists as interlopers who had wrongly expanded their legitimate spheres of activity.

Fourth, Adams offered carefully delimited commendations of psychology, noting his own intellectual debts to psychologists. Defining what he found acceptable and useful served strategically in several ways. It distanced him from obscurantist anti-intellectualism and let him describe the faults in psychology as abuses or errors within potentially valid fields. Qualified commendation also served a negative function, restricting psychologists from precisely the turf to which he aspired. Fifth, he set forth highly schematized and simplified versions of the leading theoretical schools within modern psychology, and then criticized these for being antithetical to Christian presuppositions. By identifying how core features of the major psychologies contradicted elementary theological positions, Adams sought to debunk their claims to truth, goodness, and efficacy. Sixth, he criticized the prominence of secular psychological concepts and practices in the writings of both pastoral counselors and evangelical psychotherapists. If the first five points were true, then pastors were foolish to embrace recycled psychological materials, even when offered by psychotherapists who shared their conservative Protestant faith. We will consider in turn each of these elements in Adams's apologetic.

1. Adams spoke in the first person of what he had seen, thought, and experienced

The evangelist is typically the convert. The first dozen pages of *CtC* are largely autobiographical. Adams's opening words—"Like many other pastors, I learned little about counseling in seminary, so I began with virtually no knowledge of what to do"—acknowledged both personal and educational failure. He went on to speak of his inability to help struggling people and of how inarticulate discomfort with psychotherapeutic ideas and methods led to disillusionment with extant counseling systems. He then discussed his catalytic encounter with O. Hobart Mowrer. Adams portrayed himself as one who had come to embrace the "psychiatric heresy" that a "Moral Model of responsibility" must replace the "Medical Model."[13] By a circuitous pilgrimage, Adams had become a heretic from heresy; he offered this newfound orthodoxy to his hearers.

By using the testimonial form, Adams also highlighted the fact that he himself was a pastor, speaking to pastors. The first page of *CtC* resonated with allusions to common pastoral experiences. In that opening sentence cited above, Adams frankly identified himself with the experiences of seminarians and neophyte ministers. He went on to speak of an incident "in my first pastorate" following "an evening service"; he spoke of how he "asked God to help me become an effective counselor," of a certain queasiness at translating "what seemed to be sin, as 'sickness,'" of the schedule of a "busy pastor" that could never allow the months or years of weekly counseling sessions spoken of in the books on counseling. Adams was one with his auditors. Just as their past experience had also been his, so his present experience might now become theirs. Thus Adams's assault on the psychological professions began with a frank statement that he was a pastor with a story to tell, not a psychological professional. He had "found little help" in the things nonpastors had told him about counseling.[14] Instead, he claimed that real help had come from the manual that all pastors already possessed: "Gradually I drifted into hit-or-miss patterns of counseling growing out of on-the-spot applications of scriptural exhortations as I remembered them. . . . I could not help but notice that the more directive I became . . . , the more people were helped. Spelling out and getting commitments to biblical patterns of behavior after an acknowledgment of and repentance for sin seemed to bring relief and results."[15] The pastor had drifted onto distinctively pastoral shores.

Adams's "testimony" adopted a standard evangelical genre. After a period of "lostness" and confusion, the seeker was brought to a crisis through a series of apparently fortuitous events. In the crisis, truth from God was discovered and appropriated. Such a story allowed the evangelist to bear witness to his hearers, combining humility (he had been lost in darkness) and confidence (he had been found by the light). The persuasions of story constituted the first ingredient in Adams's anti-psychiatric polemic.

2. The conflicts within psychology itself offered Adams another rhetorical resource

In a number of ways, Adams took advantage of the cognitive disarray within the counseling field. At the simplest level, he was fond of citing a report that "there are at least 230 distinct schools of psychotherapy and counseling in the United States at the present time" as evidence that the field was unscientific and woefully divided against itself.[16] Similarly, Gregory Zilboorg's assessment of the history of psychotherapy proved to be highly and repeatedly quotable: "Psychotherapy is today in a state of disarray almost exactly as it was 200 years ago."[17] The lack of consensus among diverse psychologies, each claiming to be the right way to explain and treat human woe, made good copy among conservative pastors.

Adams also availed himself of anti-psychiatry writers, especially during the formative years of nouthetic counseling. Different as his positive program was from theirs, he could cite them as reputable cobelligerents in his attack on the reigning paradigm. O. Hobart Mowrer, William Glasser, and Perry London provided the most significant resources for Adams. They constituted reputable opposition to the dominant psychodynamic paradigm and reputable advocacy for a moral model. Adams's purposes were well served by Perry London's description of the psychotherapist as a "secular priest" and by his comment that "medical training and license is largely irrelevant to its proper practice."[18] These secular anti-psychiatrists were part of a "revolution [that] has been brewing" against the "institutionalized system." The essence of this "new movement" was, like Adams's nouthetic counseling, its opposition to "the Freudian irresponsibility formulation" that had defined problems in living as illnesses.[19]

Adams drew on numerous other anti-psychiatric and anti-psychotherapeutic writers. Thomas Szasz was frequently cited. He provided Adams with three things. First, his call to treat all people "seriously, as responsible human beings" fit well with Adams's purposes and added one more voice to the arguments made by Mowrer and others.[20] Adams also picked up Szasz's labeling theory to argue that "the term mental illness is nothing more than a figure of speech, and in most cases a poor one."[21] Adams's theocentric concept of human moral agency might have differed radically from Szasz's concept of agency, but they agreed that people who experienced problems in living were not in fact victims of disease processes. Finally,

Szasz served as Adams's historian for how the notion of mental illness had gained currency in the twentieth century. Adams recommended that his hearers read the first two chapters of Szasz's *The Myth of Mental Illness* to understand how "Charcot and Freud . . . stretched the concept of illness until it pertained to nearly any and every sort of difficulty in life."[22]

Other writers offered Adams bits and pieces that contributed to the goal of discrediting the mental health system and thereby encouraging his auditors to consider nouthetic counseling's definitions of human nature and the tasks of counseling. As proof that the psychological professions were ineffectual, despite their pretentious claims, Adams quoted Hans Eysenk's negative assessment of the effectiveness of psychotherapy.[23] When psychiatrist E. Fuller Torrey commented that the techniques of "witch doctors" and psychotherapists employed the same mechanisms and operated "on exactly the same scientific plane," Adams found it a useful argument to buttress his point that the "esoteric expertise" of psychiatrists (their diagnostic categories, fanciful interpretations of dreams, etc.) had substituted for telling a counselee that "he is a sinner who needs to be forgiven."[24] The Rosenhan Experiment—where graduate students had posed as vaguely troubled persons and sought admission to mental hospitals—also made good copy for Adams.[25] It seemed to demonstrate the arbitrariness and insubstantiality of psychiatric diagnoses. He chortled that "other patients in the institution proved to be more able diagnosticians than psychiatrists!"[26] When Karl Menninger, whom Adams identified as "perhaps . . . our most loved psychiatrist in America," said, "Schizophrenia? That to me is just a nice Greek word," it served debunking purposes. Whether Menninger's words created dissonance or resonance in Adams's hearers, they might become susceptible to his arguments for nouthetic counseling as a viable and desirable alternative.

That psychotherapy was ostensibly neither "scientific" nor "medical," that it was neither unified nor efficacious, that its categories were illegitimate and unstable, all this provided an important resource to Adams in prosecuting his case. The stage-setting chapters of a number of Adams's major books were sprinkled with quotations from anti-psychiatrists.[27] His was no dispassionate survey of the range of anti-psychiatric opinion.[28] But pastors who accepted Adams's arguments would be encouraged—as he himself had been—that to oppose psychotherapy did not entail the intellectual discredit that accrues to mere reactionaries. The anti-psychiatric moralists were an energetic and respected—if controversial—avant-garde. For a short while, nouthetic counseling portrayed itself as part of what was happening in the culture—only better.

3. Adams advocated a normative sociology of professional jurisdictions

Adams proposed a tidy reconfiguration of professional rights and responsibilities among those who studied and serviced people experiencing problems in living. He claimed counseling for the pastorate, while delegating scientific research to psychologists and strictly medical practice to psychiatrists. This strategy struck to the very heart of the jurisdictional conflict, attempting to shut down the referral pipeline from the conservative Protestant churches into the mental health system by delegitimizing all nonpastoral psychotherapeutic activity.

The history and current ecology of the psychological professions told a moral tale in Adams's hands: "I am concerned here to make but two observations only: (1) the psychiatrist should return to the practice of medicine, which is his only legitimate sphere of activity; (2) the minister should return to the God-given work from which he was ousted (and which, in many instances, too willingly abandoned)."[29] The contemporary professional landscape had acquired its shape by a process of usurpation and abdication; therefore, something *should* be done about that state of affairs. Like any historical relativizing, Adams's description served to debunk the presumption of givenness that tended to accrue to current arrangements. The pastor who accepted Adams's argument could not help but become simultaneously humbled at his own failings, hostile toward those he had now learned to see as interlopers and confident that he could learn to do the job that he had been called to by God. Adams intended that pastors would be aroused to do something about the situation. By improving their skills and shutting down the lines of referral they might dislodge mental health professionals and repossess the turf on which the cure of souls proceeded.

Historians, sociologists, and culture critics might describe and analyze in cool terms the clergy's "desertion of its traditional work," the cure of souls that sought to help "people who were anxious, depressed, and upset with their everyday life."[30] Academics might describe both how pastoral counseling had lost compelling intellectual authority and how the residuum of churchly counseling steadily drifted toward psychotherapy as pastoral counselors, under the intellectual jurisdiction of psychodynamic psychiatry, became foot soldiers in the army of personal problems workers. But what academics described, Jay Adams decried.

Adams's analysis of recent professional history contained two chief elements, each calculated to arouse a strong response in his intended readers. In the first place, he argued that pastors themselves, with himself as a case in point, had seriously failed, and needed to repent. *CtC* opened with an anecdote of his own ineptitude in the counseling task, as noted previously. Pastoral failure correlated with educational defects of seminaries that had left pastors ill-prepared.[31] These failures of preparation and performance occurred specifically in the personal problems sphere, a sphere Adams believed was coterminous with the sphere the Bible gave to pastoral activity. "To what task does the pastoral counselor address himself? In counseling, does he handle a very narrow band of 'spiritual' or 'ecclesiastical' problems, or is his field of legitimate activity substantially larger? Is his counseling activity bordered (and thereby limited) by others from clearly distinct disciplines, namely psychologists and psychiatrists (whose titles, curiously enough, might be translated—not too freely—as 'soul specialists' and 'soul healers')?"[32] He concluded that the pastor's field of activity was as broad as the problems in living, whether situational, relational, behavioral, or intrapsychic. They had failed to do their job.

In the second place, Adams argued that invaders had transgressed divinely ordained boundaries by inserting themselves into the professional counseling role proper only to the pastor. Pastoral failure had first created the vacuum that other professionals had presumed to fill; the success of those other professionals in laying claim to a difficult task had then made it easy for pastors to refer to them. In *CtC* he launched out at the mental health professionals early and often:

> One of the purposes of this book is to show that psychiatry is a usurpation of the work of the Christian minister. Their goal is personality and behavior change, and their method is value alteration. This usurpation has been achieved by declaring a host of people "sick" who are not, and thus taking them under the pale of medicine. Freud himself anticipated this usurpation

of the minister's work. He . . . predicted that "the cure of souls [the term used for pastoral care] will one day be a recognized non-ecclesiastical and even non-religious calling."[33]

Adams framed his attack in frankly jurisdictional language. His perspective on the jurisdictional battle, phrased in literal "turf" terms, is well captured in the following quotation:

> Are you saying that psychology and psychiatry are illegitimate disciplines? Do you think that they have no place at all?
>
> No, you misunderstand me. It is exactly not that. Remember, I said clearly that they live next door to the pastor. My problem with them is that they refuse to stay on their own property. I have been trying to get the pastor to mow his lawn to the very borders on his plot.
>
> Psychology should be a legitimate and very useful neighbor to the pastor. Psychologists may make many helpful studies of man (e.g., on the effects of sleep loss). But psychologists—with neither warrant nor standard from God by which to do so—should get out of the business of trying to change persons. It can tell us many things about what man does, but not about what he should do.
>
> Similarly, the neighbor who lives on the other side of the pastor's lot could be a most welcome one with whom the pastor could live in real harmony were he satisfied to play croquet in his own yard. . . .
>
> The pastor recognizes the effects of Adam's sin upon the body; he, therefore, has no problem working side by side with a physician who treats the counselee's body as he counsels him about its proper use. From the days of Paul and Luke, pastors have found kinship with medical personnel.

Why, then, does the psychiatrist present a problem? Certainly it is not because of his medical background. The problem is that he will not stay in his own backyard. He keeps setting up his lawn chairs and moving his picnic table onto the pastor's property.

If he were to use his medical training to find medical solutions to the truly organic difficulties that affect attitudes and behavior, the pastor would be excited about his work. But the difficulty arises as the psychiatrist—under the guise of medicine—attempts to change values and beliefs. That is not medicine. The pastor is disturbed at having residents from the adjoining lots digging up his backyard to plant corn and tomatoes. He does not object to—but rather encourages—all such activity in the yards next door.[34]

Doctors and psychologists were carefully circumscribed to the domains of "science" and "medicine." There, psychological and medical research, along with psychiatric practice, could be "legitimate and very useful neighbors." Adams would eject psychology and psychiatry from the counseling and psychotherapy business entirely and get them to mind their own business.

In sum, Jay Adams sought to fence psychology in to only one social role: a descriptive science studying human functioning. He similarly sought to fence psychiatry into a strictly medical role, as doctors to the ailments of the body. Neither profession had title to the functional troubles of the soul, which belonged to the pastor by divine right. Adams's normative sociology—couched in terms of literal, God-ordained, "backyard" turf—neatly reallocated professional responsibilities in a way that many conservative pastors found appealing.

4. Adams frequently sought to articulate, and thereby delimit, the good in psychology and psychiatry

If psychology and psychiatry had a legitimate social role, then they had an identifiable positive contribution to make. Identifying these potential benefits was another characteristic feature of Adams's polemic. When the practitioners of knowledge systems collide, domesticating one's opponents is standard procedure. To reduce another profession's utility to a subset of one's own is a powerful strategy.

What good, if any, did Adams see in psychology? This subject demands a multifaceted answer. His chief critics heard his loudest notes: they interpreted him as the prototypical "psychology basher," the forerunner of even more strident critics in an "anti-psychology" movement that arose among fundamentalists in the 1980s.[35] But Adams's epistemology and rhetoric were more subtle and complex, and were interwoven with his proposed normative sociology of the professions. He made two chief arguments: a contribution could be made to pastoral counseling both by "science" and by the "element of truth" in theories that were fundamentally wrong-headed. We will consider these in turn.

First, as alluded to in the previous section, Adams touted the positive contributions that could be made by the more descriptive and "scientific" forms of psychology and medicine. Psychology and psychiatry, rightly conceived, had the potential to do several things as a "useful adjunct" to pastoral counseling. They might play a provocative role, challenging pat answers and "wrong human interpretations of Scripture," and posing questions that needed answers.[36] To the degree they were descriptively acute, the psychology-oriented disciplines could stimulate pastoral ministry, just as

Mowrer had been catalytic in helping Adams discover gaping holes in his practical theology. They might also play an illustrational role, "filling in generalizations with specifics."[37]

The community he appealed to valued classic, positivistic science, and Adams generally shared that view.[38] By commending the most stereotypically "scientific" features of psychology (and "medical" features of psychiatry), Adams allied nouthetic counseling with the prestige of scientific epistemology and sought to avoid the taint of anti-intellectualism and obscurantism. He also sought to ensure that his attack would be understood as a turf war against speculative, antiscientific tendencies that masqueraded as psychological and medical science, not as an attack on science itself. The "legitimate" work of psychology, as delineated in his reallocation of professional turf, defined the good that psychologists might do:

> Question: Don't you think that we can learn something from psychologists?
> Answer: Yes, we can learn a lot; I certainly have. That answer surprised you, didn't it? If it did, you have been led to believe, no doubt, that nouthetic counselors are obscurantists who see no good in psychology. . . .
>
> While I can understand how the idea that I am opposed to psychology and psychologists could have gotten abroad because of my strong statements about the failures of psychologists *as counselors*, a *careful* reading of my materials will make it clear that I do not object to psychology or to psychologists as such. . . . That I deplore psychology's venture into the realms of value, behavior and attitudinal change because it is an intrusion upon the work of the minister, in no way lessens my interest, support and encouragement of the legitimate work of psychology.[39]

Adams went on to mention how he had profited from work done at Harvard sleep labs on the effects of sleep deprivation on bizarre behavior. Psychology as a descriptive and exploratory science stood in sharp contrast to psychology as normative theory and prescriptive therapy. The latter invaded theological and pastoral turf. The former was a potentially useful adjunct discipline for pastoral counselors, as long as it did not become constitutive of the counseling methodology, and findings were handled tentatively and seen "with Christian eyes."[40] The relationship between Adams's form of Christian counseling and "legitimate" psychology was "occasional and expediential." The information "garnered by legitimate psychological activities" might fruitfully prove helpful, but "Christian counseling [does not bear] a *necessary, dependent* relationship to psychology."[41]

Similarly, the "legitimate" work of psychiatrists defined the goods they could contribute to the amelioration of sin and misery. They should "do the important medical work that it is necessary to do to help people whose behavior is adversely affected by organic causes."[42] Adams asserted that:

> The Christian pastor would rejoice to see psychiatry leave the area of the non-organic to become what . . . it falsely claimed to be, a medical specialty. . . . Of course, in returning to the medical aspects of behavioral problems, psychiatrists will have to do much more than they have done already for "real progress has been near zero in establishing a biochemical basis for mental illness" [from *Readings in Sociology*]. Since this is true, medical psychiatry at first will be restricted to grosser problems like brain damage, tumor, etc.

Despite his skepticism, Adams publicly entertained hopes that psychiatry might also contribute regarding toxic problems, chemical imbalances, and the medical component in drug abuse and sleep loss.[43]

Adams was not sanguine about the possibility he would be heeded. In general, psychiatrists came in for harder blows than psychologists—although this comment must be qualified because at the time he wrote his programmatic books in the early 1970s the rapid growth of clinical psychology had just begun. He believed that "in the area of psychiatry, science largely has given way to humanistic philosophy and gross speculation."[44]

In sum, psychologists and psychiatrists could legitimize themselves by cultivating their own relatively scientific backyards. But Adams also identified a second kind of good—a relative good, laced with dangers for the unwary, hence prompting a marked ambivalence. Psychotherapists and personality theorists were pervasively wrong when they made general pronouncements about the human condition and attempted to resolve problems of belief, value, relationship, and behavior without reference to God. But they could also be somehow perceptive and right at the same time. Noting this ambiguity had been a longstanding feature of Calvinistic epistemology.[45]

In this way, Adams described a place for the relative insightfulness of theories and counseling models that he fiercely opposed. He stated that "elements of truth" intermixed with error in the more theoretical and therapeutic forms of psychology.[46] Such elements of truth were dim and distorted, "as reflected in a dented bronze mirror," because of the intellectual effects of sin. These provocative and insightful semitruths had to be approached from several angles. In the first place, they had to be noted because they were the very things that made other views "plausible, and therefore dangerous."[47] At the same time, "nuggets" might be "reclaimed" with some profit and, like more scientific activities, might serve nouthetic counselors provocatively and illustratively.[48]

That "element of truth" could be turned to profitable use if it were teased from its context and reworked into the context of conservative Protestant faith. For example: "Mowrer and Glasser have shown us that many of the old views were wrong. They have exposed Freud's opposition to responsibility and have challenged us (if we read their message with Christian eyes) to return to the Bible for our answers."[49] As critics of the dominant mental health illness model and as proponents of a moral model, Mowrer and his cohort could prove stimulating and informative. At the same time, however, Adams made a sweeping indictment of their particular version of a moral model. Since they had no final standard (lacking "Christian eyes"), Mowrer and Glasser fell into "subjectivism" and moral relativism.[50]

Adams sought to give his conservative Protestant readers a way of making sense of the paradox that each modern psychology seemed, in its own way, simultaneously astute and misguided. He did not want his readers to be led astray by systems that were fundamentally skewed; at the same time he acknowledged the influence Mowrer, Glasser, Szasz, and others had had on him, and he recognized strands of insight even in theorists less to his taste. The line dividing "science" from personality theory and psychotherapy was hardly fixed. "Christian eyes" should approach the psychologies with extreme caution, for the strands of insight lent plausibility to theories that markedly deviated from biblical faith. At the same time those same eyes could profit in some manner from the encounter with theorists with whom they fundamentally differed.[51]

Adams described the following pattern in the various secular psychological schools: "usually there is an element of truth reflected by every false position."[52] Particular psychologists noticed things that were important and true but embedded their insights in a faulty interpretive framework, hence their attempts to redress perceived problems were misguided. Adams would have nouthetic counselors learn facts about people and be stimulated by the questions raised, just as he had been by Mowrer, but he wanted to ensure that they maintained the "vantage point" of their conservative Protestant faith. His general attitude was captured in the following statement (occurring in a context where he sharply criticized theories of the grief process, while noting their occasional observational acuity): "Although we may learn much that is valuable and useful from others (if we know how to evaluate their work by the standard of biblical principle) we must not be intimidated by them into conforming our ideas to theirs. What we do and say must not conflict with the Scriptures."[53]

Whether perfunctory or profuse in his approbation, Adams always qualified it by noting the failures of secular psychologists to get matters right.[54] This was because "in the common grace of God, unbelievers stumble over aspects of truth in God's creation. They always distort these by their sin and from their non-Christian stance toward life."[55] Adams's treatment of Victor Frankl's logotherapy was typical and, standing in the midrange between grudging and heartier commendation, provided a clear example of Adams's method. He was unequivocal in affirming Frankl: "Frankl is correct in observing that meaning (or perhaps a better word would be 'purpose') is fundamental not only to a full and productive life, but also to the well being and, in some instances, the continued existence of a human being. . . . Frankl rightly has observed that man cannot live without at least such day-to-day goals and purposes."[56] But Adams immediately went on to say that without the message of the God of the Bible,

> Frankl and other existential psychiatrists can offer nothing . . . ; for them the future is but a long dark tunnel.
>
> Apart from meaning related to God, the apparent meaning that one finds in the

pleasures of this life soon evaporates. This is the disconcerting message of the book of Ecclesiastes; all temporal activity is meaningless ("vanity," or "emptiness") apart from the God of meaning.[57]

The existentialists, and those psychologists and psychiatrists who are influenced by them, have described this awareness [of fundamental discomfort registering in the human psyche] as *alienation* and an undifferentiated *angst*. . . . But the very thing that creates the problem—his separation from God—also makes it impossible to conceptualize the issues in those terms.[58]

The dynamics of turf warfare are nicely captured in all of this. Adams was "friendly" toward Frankl in the same way Frankl had been "friendly" toward religious faith. Each was courteous and commendatory, but each pointedly turned his subject's leading commitment into an instance within his embracing model. In Frankl's case, religious faith had represented one significant way that "man's search for meaning" might be fulfilled. For Adams the logic was reversed. The anguish of meaninglessness and the evanescence of life's satisfactions stood as evidence of the human need for what only biblical faith offered. Adams saw Frankl's system as "fundamentally non-Christian" because it refused to adopt normative Christian values and meanings and failed to introduce these as essentials in the counseling process.[59] If Adams had seen Frankl in counseling, doubtless he would have spoken the gospel to him and invited him to faith.

Adams's hearers received an unambiguous message. They were not to become "integrationists" who sought to meld their faith with one or more of the modern psychologies; but they were not to become obscurantists who refused to engage—from the standpoint of their faith—the observations, theories, and questions raised by their surrounding culture. Under Adams's tutelage conservative Protestants were given a faith purportedly superior to modern psychology; they were given the realities that the psychologies had only "dimly" perceived and had systematically misperceived. That was the message of a polemicist, and it served as one more significant ingredient in Adams's bid for the loyalty of conservative Protestants.

Though Adams spoke of how *"from the vantage point of his biblical foundation* the Christian counselor may take note of, evaluate, and reclaim the truth dimly reflected," in practice, very little of such appropriation took place within nouthetic circles.[60] The note of antagonism predominated. Nouthetic counseling was always embattled with the evangelical psychotherapists whose leading note was the integration of the psychologies with their faith, what Adams saw as an "eclectic viewpoint" that compromised the faith.[61] So Adams's rationale for such "recasting" or "reclaiming" activities stood primarily as a rhetorical point.[62]

Identifying the good in his opponents not only advanced the matter of Adams's argument. It also accrued benefits to him as a speaker who aimed to persuade. Naming—and delimiting—the strengths of one's opponents is as effective rhetorically as identifying one's own weaknesses and calling for repentance. Like Adams's testimony, qualified commendations contributed *ethos* and *pathos* to the *logos* of his formal model.

These first four rhetorical elements—giving personal testimony, citing disarray in the field and competent internal critics, reallocating professional turf, and identifying the strengths of opponents—only supplemented Adams's fundamental and most characteristic argument against psychology. Personal testimony, after all, cuts both ways. The evangelical psychologists also had stories to tell, typically of how their encounter with psychology had freed them from fundamentalist legalism and anti-intellectualism without costing them their

faith. And citing somewhat questionable cobelligerents—Mowrer and Szasz, after all, had savaged Calvinism—hardly provided a banner under which conservative Protestants could be rallied to intellectual and practical activism. Similarly, for Adams to state how nice it would be if psychological workers minded to their proper business and got out of the mental health field hardly would sustain action in a world unlikely to cooperate. In fact, strictly considered, these second and third arguments actually contradicted each other, as long as Adams held out hopes for those "young, vigorous individuals" who were rattling the psychodynamic establishment. The fact that Mowrer, Glasser, and Szasz were clearly in the business of tinkering with client's beliefs, values, and behavior—and no Christian reference deemed necessary—made the anti-psychiatrists just as intrusive into the pastor's realm as any other less acceptable brand of psychologist. Finally, mentioning the scientific status of some psychological activities, and the nuggets of truth in deviant psychological models, if left to itself had potential to threaten the claim to be "radically biblical" and to make nouthetic counseling indistinguishable from "integrationist" evangelical psychology. In fact, these four arguments did not stand alone, but, rather, buttressed a fifth argument that anchored Adams's polemic in what were presumably the core theological commitments of his hearers.

5. Adams's prime argument detailed *theological* faults in psychological theories and psychotherapeutic practices

As previously indicated, Adams did not interact with the contents of psychiatric and psychological theory in the mode of the relatively dispassionate scholar. He was the populist turf warrior seeking to rally supporters, careless of nuance in expositing other positions, unconcerned about making carefully qualified criticisms. He painted with extremely broad strokes, isolating a few presumably defining tendencies of each theory. His interests were polemical and propagandistic, hence he was reductionistic, pouncing on what he perceived as objectionable core ideas and methods. When he proclaimed these objections, he was speaking to an audience that in some cases was learning its psychological theories from Adams, in rough fashion, at the same time those theories were being assailed for egregious failings.[63]

The heart of Adams's analysis of the defects in modern psychological theory and practice lay in his assertion that any and all approaches to interpreting problems in living and to redressing them entailed theological commitments that were subject to theological scrutiny and evaluation: "All counseling, by its very nature . . . implies theological commitments by the counselor. He simply cannot become involved in the attempt to change beliefs, values, attitudes, relationships and behavior without wading neck deep in theological waters. . . . These theological commitments may be conscious or unconscious, biblical or heretical, good theology or bad, but—either way—they surely are theological."[64] Hence Adams interpreted Freud, Rogers, Skinner, Mowrer—and the evangelical psychotherapists who mediated such theorists and practitioners into the conservative Protestant church—as theologians first and foremost. Despite the fact that psychologists rarely used overtly theological language, they trafficked in realities that had to do with "how to live a human life in this fallen world that God made for His glory," something that "*requires* theological responses."[65] Psychologists made such responses willy-nilly: "Whether he knows this or not is irrelevant. One doesn't need to know that he is breathing air to do so!"[66] Adams's hearers would come to understand the psychologists specifically as

heretical theologians, as well as ersatz pastors. As propagators of bad theology, they would be discredited. The intellectual deference conservative Protestants often granted such "scientists" would be withdrawn. The mess of psychological pottage would compare unfavorably to the biblical birthright, and Adams's nouthetic counseling would score a coup in legitimating itself.

Countless particular criticisms of psychological theory are scattered through Adams's corpus. But for our purposes, an understanding of the broad contours of that criticism will prove sufficient. Adams arranged his criticisms under two different taxonomies of the personality theories. One taxonomy he derived from Mowrer and London. It described two families of theories, one reprehensible, one relatively admirable: (1) broadly psychodynamic theories portrayed people as victims of intrapsychic and social forces; (2) broadly moral-behavioral theories portrayed people as responsible actors capable of significant choice.[67] Adams followed Mowrer in describing a generic "Freudianism" as the reigning and malign paradigm for psychotherapeutic practice. It served as shorthand for all generically psychodynamic psychologies: from Sigmund Freud's classic psychoanalysis to Carl Rogers's humanistic psychology to Alfred Adler's individual psychology to Jung's psychological religion of archetypal myths.[68] On Mowrer's authority, Adams comfortably alluded to "Rogerians and other Freudians."[69] "Freud" was an icon, a symbolic figure for the major ailment that afflicted the twentieth-century psychologies and psychotherapies. It was shorthand for a bogy: the generic psychotherapy that located the cause of personal problems in intrapsychic conflicts generated in the crucible of childhood experience.[70]

On Adams's reading, the moralistic theories were relatively good in comparison to psychodynamic theories. The "responsibility ethic" of the former was at least formally analogous to something he as a conservative Protestant pastor wished to assert to his counselees.[71] When Mowrer asked, "Has Evangelical religion sold its birthright for a mess of psychological pottage?"[72] Adams commented, "Every conservative counselor must consider Mowrer's question to be an implied challenge. Nearly all recent counseling books for ministers, even conservative ones, are written from the Freudian perspective in the sense that they rest largely upon the presuppositions of the Freudian ethic of non-responsibility."[73] Psychological determinism was the key. The notion that the significant springs of behavior were amoral, rooting in the collision between unconscious drives, however variously defined, and infantile trauma or social constraint, was anathema to Adams.

More commonly Adams used a second taxonomy, a common tripartite division of the personality theories into psychodynamic, humanistic, and behavioristic theories.[74] He criticized each for signal failings. The triumvirate of "Freud, Rogers, and Skinner" appeared repeatedly and stereotypically in Adams's polemic. Each symbolized both a particular intellectual error and a corresponding failure in counseling methodology.[75]

"Freud" stood for making people irresponsible victims of childhood trauma and mental illness; hence the characteristic therapy mode was the "shovel," the archaeologist's spade that probed the historical layers of what lay buried in the unconscious. Freud himself "was a great writer (largely of fiction). He was *not* a scientist. Actually, above all else, he was a master inventor of labels."[76] The labels generated by the Freudian heresy chiefly had the effect of anesthetizing counselor and counseled alike to the moral dilemmas that Adams believed inhered in problems in living; victims of conscience, poor socialization, or trauma needed no repentance. Sinners who violated divine law, as well as their own conscience, needed repentance, faith, and obedience.

"Rogers" stood for man's basic goodness, a rosy view of human nature that located the resources for change in the counselee; hence the characteristic therapy mode was the "mirror" that revealed and drew out the good from within. Carl Rogers had perpetrated a compelling fraud on twentieth-century counselors:

It has been only in quite modern times that the concept of counseling did an about-face so that for some the word came to mean *listening* rather than speaking. . . . *Non-directive counseling* [represents] a contradiction of terms. Of all the terms that Carl Rogers might have chosen, this combination is at once the most strategic and the most tragic. The Rogerian title is like that ingenious combination of *Christian Science,* in which respected words are misused to designate their opposites. The Rogerian title, however, unlike that used by Mrs. Eddy, has found such wide acceptance that (against all history) vast numbers of intelligent people today equate counseling with something other than giving direction and advice.[77]

The Rogerian heresy, by numbing its believers to human sinfulness and the consequent need for the Christian salvation, took the counsel out of counseling.[78]

"Skinner" stood for reducing humans to trainable animals; his characteristic therapy mode was the "biscuit" that manipulated outward behavioral renovation. B. F. Skinner's intellectual and social program embodied the cult of the expert who dehumanized his subjects: "starting with genetic manipulation and then setting up the desired environmental contingencies. . . . The only fly in the ointment is this: when you get two Skinnerians together to decide what kind of sausage they want to come out of the meat grinder, they can't. There is no value, no standard; all is relative. Christians alone can say *what* a man should be, for they alone have that Standard in God's written and living Word."[79] The Skinnerian heretics denied the moral freedom and dignity of responsible humanity created in the image of God, things of creedal importance to conservative Protestants.

Thus, in Adams's hands, the three major psychological schools each evidenced marked theological deficiencies.[80] Each in its own way denied human depravity and responsibility to God, the need for repentance and faith, the truth of the Bible and power of the Holy Spirit, the necessity of Christ. They offended against cardinal doctrines of that conservative Protestant faith held by both Adams and his hearers. And the psychologies were deficient specifically in their "practical theology." Their characteristic methods expressed their characteristic beliefs, and both came up short next to nouthetic counseling. Their reconstruction of counseling as a professional, technical activity, pretending to value-neutral efficacy in a fee-for-service context, came up short next to the churchly context of nouthetic pastoral counseling. Adams hoped that nouthetic counseling would reinvigorate practical theology conceptually, methodologically, institutionally. His agenda demanded the overthrow of the "self-appointed professionals" by "a new generation of conservative Protestant ministers, unimpressed by psychiatric pretensions, . . . who have determined that it is *they* who are (or must become) the 'professionals.'"[81]

In sum, Adams created an anti-psychotherapy rhetoric that could be easily encapsulated. "Freud, Rogers, and Skinner" formed the authoritative triumvirate whose theories and practices contradicted the Bible. Human beings were either irresponsible victims, good at heart, or animals, which contradicted doctrines of accountability to God, human sinfulness, and creation in the image of God. Problems in living could be resolved by use of "the Spade, the Mirror, or the Biscuit," which

contradicted the need for salvation in Christ and the ministry of the Word.

This theological criticism anchored Adams's polemic. His personal testimony of theological conversion and discovery might add zest to his rhetoric. The well-documented fact that the triumvirate and their successors were incurably factious, and that credible secular critics discredited the whole lot, further buttressed nouthetic counseling's legitimacy. The image of a society where science and faith colabored to the glory of God, and where focused psychological research, diligent medical activity, and competent pastoral care might mutually reinforce one another, as each tended to business, made for an appealing ideal. But the chief argument was that the alternatives to nouthetic counseling were simply wrong when Adams compared them to his Bible and theological tradition. The psychotherapists were heretics, not applied scientists. It is no surprise that such a polemic could be spectacularly successful with its intended audience.

6. The incursion of psychological theory into the church represented a compromise fatal both to Christian truth and to pastoral practice

The final ingredient of Adams's anti-psychiatry polemic was his explicit identification of "compromisers" and "collaborators." He raised the stakes to the highest level: "The church . . . either has been deceived by Satan's counsel or has found itself in conflict with it. There is no neutral ground. *Compromise* or *conflict* are the only two alternatives. We are (hopefully) now beginning to emerge from an era of compromise. . . . For a long time Satan's deceitful counsel has prevailed in the church; only during the 70s has a successful challenge been mounted."[82] Adams had almost nothing good to say about the various psychotherapy movements within the Protestant churches. He attacked both the pastoral counseling movement (established in mainline churches) and the evangelical psychotherapists (emerging in conservative churches). Here the turf warfare again became explicit. The mental health system, from which Adams's normative sociology proposed the church secede, was not the only enemy. Psychologized foes operated inside the camp. Mainline Protestant pastoral counselors had long dominated seminary curricula, hence the training of pastors. They modeled and inculcated an intellectual subordination to psychologists' doctrines. An emerging evangelical mental health establishment was aggressively bidding for cultural authority and rights of practice. To Adams's eyes, they imported the same set of faulty doctrines, as well as importing the institutional habits of the mental health system into the conservative Protestant community.

One natural implication of this model is that Adams frequently railed against the autonomous professional who "hung up a shingle" and practiced detached from the structures of the church community. Though an evangelical psychotherapist might be an individual whose personal beliefs and ethics were orthodox, such a practitioner was in a highly irregular and dangerous position. Such counselors were uneducated in the things that mattered most and too educated in things that were dubious:

> Typically, the self-appointed Christian "professional" has spent years studying psychology at the graduate level, but has little more than a Sunday School (or, at best a Bible school) knowledge of the Bible. . . .
>
> I am not saying that they are ill-intentioned; to the contrary, there are even some examples of valiant attempts to use what little understanding exists in proper ways— but these attempts simply fall apart from

the outset because of the frightful exegetical and theological inadequacy. . . . One of the saddest failures of all is to appoint such psychologists as professors in theological institutions to teach prospective ministers of the Word. In the end, they teach them how not to use their Bibles in counseling.[83]

"Marinated with clinical psychologically," theologically shallow, and biblically ignorant, such practitioners, though they had "assumed places of leadership in Christian counseling," almost invariably tended toward syncretism and compromise.[84] In addition, such counselors were unordained— "self-appointed." They were untested by church authorities regarding the content and manner of their counsel. Similarly, they remained unaccountable to those same ordaining and overseeing presbyteries, bishops, pastors, or elders that kept the nouthetic counselor within the fences of orthodoxy. Instead, the psychotherapists' training, credentials, and accountability rested with the secular mental system that was the church's great competitor.

Adams viewed both liberal pastors and conservative psychotherapists as compromisers who undermined the pastorate and orthodox theology. He evaluated the perceived collaboration of such "integrationists" with the dominant psychotherapeutic culture in various terms. Criticism at its mildest defined integrationists as well-meaning folk. Their good intentions, however, inevitably miscarried. Somewhat stronger, they were presumptuous: lacking both the imprimatur and ongoing oversight of the church, their claims to professional status and authority were "self-styled" and "self-appointed." Most pointedly, their expertise in the modern psychologies coexisted with a telling theological and exegetical ineptitude that caused them to broker falsehoods to the church.

Adams dealt the leading pastoral theologians of the twentieth century severe and virtually unmitigated condemnation. Only Anton Boisen, the founder of the modern pastoral counseling movement in the 1920s and 1930s, came in for commendation. Adams noted that despite Boisen's "liberal" theology, he "saw clearly" that mental disorders ought to be "retrieved [from psychiatrists] and made the object of theological discussion. He was right in claiming that counseling about life problems was the province of the church." Adams quoted with approval Boisen's statement that "in mental disorders we are dealing with a problem which is essentially spiritual" and, with similar approbation, noted that Boisen had argued against Freud, claiming that "mental disorders arise from a bad conscience occasioned by real guilt rather than inner conflict over 'false guilt.'"[85]

However, Boisen's efforts failed historically. Instead, "the pastoral counseling movement—even among Bible-believing churches—soon was redirected into Freudian channels and early succumbed to the idea that the pastor's major task is to defer and refer to the psychiatrist."[86] The leading pastoral theologians were each criticized for returning to psychodynamic models and nonintrusive methods. Seward Hiltner, for example, was "essentially humanistic" in his approach. He mediated Carl Rogers's methods to pastors, teaching them to pursue a nondirective counseling relationship, without any essential place for God and interventive truth.[87] Adams believed that the popular success of the Rogerian methodology with pastors lay in the fact that it was "simple, easy to learn, runs little risk, and is so immediately usable."[88] He similarly criticized Carroll Wise, James Dittes, Rollo May, William Hulme, and other leading pastoral counselors who taught ministers to offer their clients Rogerian, noninterventive empathy, not to let their convictions control the interview, and to refuse to give advice.[89]

Adams believed, on the contrary, that convictions must control the interview, and that Rogerian benignity only masked its directiveness, a directiveness committed to a worldview at odds with the Bible. He stated that the "basic point of contention" between him and the Rogerian pastoral counselors was that "nouthetic counseling assumes that the feelings are not the most profound level of human relationship with which one must be concerned in counseling. God speaks of love in attitudinal and behavioral forms when he defines it as keeping his commandments."[90] This component of Adams's polemic was tailored for an audience of pastors. Those who had studied counseling in seminary would have read the mainline pastoral counselors because conservative Protestants had been largely silent on the subject for a century. Adams partly debunked the previous training that many of his auditors had received.

Adams cited the mainline pastoral counselors in his early books because they had largely dominated the church-based counseling field and had markedly influenced conservative Protestant pastors. But he soon stopped citing pastoral counselors. The evangelical psychotherapists moved much more prominently into his purview. The 1970s had been a decade of rapid professional growth for Adams's most immediate competitors for intellectual and professional rights. He had offered scattered criticisms of them in his early books, but he began to focus much more extensively on them. *CtC* (1970) had only briefly mentioned evangelicals (Clyde Narramore and Vernon Grounds), focusing instead on "Freudian" psychiatry, to which pastors were to refer and defer, and on "Rogerian" pastoral counseling, which narrowly prescribed the limits of what pastors could do. *The Christian Counselor's Manual* (1973) began to alter the balance, criticizing the Narramores, James Dobson, and Gary Collins more extensively and only briefly noting mainline pastoral counselors.

More Than Redemption (1979) focused largely on the evangelical psychotherapists. In general terms, they were the center of attention throughout the introduction and first two chapters. And Adams eventually named names: Bruce Narramore and Bill Counts (a chapter was devoted to refuting their recent book), Larry Crabb, and Philip Swihart. Adams credited them with good intentions but little else. The self-styled professionals simply did not have the requisite professional training to do the things that Adams thought most significant for constructing a viable Christian counseling model: "The study of psychology in depth coupled with a smattering of scriptural data can lead only to the grossest misstatements regarding man and the solutions to his problems."[91]

Adams did not actually charge the evangelical psychologists with heresy only because the church lacked creedal statements in the area of counseling: "When doctrine becomes creedal (e.g., the Athanasian Creed), it becomes defensible against heretics. Heresy, as well as truth, becomes identifiable. Before it takes creedal form, however almost any sort of heresy can claim a place. . . . To date, no serious theological (let alone creedal) statements have been made about the place or task of counseling in the Christian church."[92] One of the hopes Adams held for his nouthetic counseling movement was that it might spur such theological and creedal development. But though willing to fight a grassroots battle to displace and embarrass the psychologists, rather than pressing heresy charges, Adams did state his personal views frankly: "In my opinion, advocating, allowing, and practicing psychiatric and psychoanalytic dogmas within the church is every bit as pagan and heretical (and therefore perilous) as propagating the teachings of some of the most bizarre cults. The only vital difference is that the cults are less dangerous because their errors are more identifiable, since they are controverted by existing creedal statements."[93] Some of Adams's followers would be less cautious about separating personal opinion from declarative judgment.[94] But Adams had left no doubt where he stood and where pastors also ought to stand in viewing the promoters of psychotherapeutic ideas and practices. Adams's warnings against presumptive heresy proved to be one of the most compelling—and inflammatory—pieces of his rhetoric.

Adams claimed that "whenever I mention names of those who publicly propagate views I believe detrimental to pastoral counseling and the welfare of Christ's church, I want you to know that it's their opinions I am assailing, not their persons."[95] But he did not mince words:

> Because so many who have assumed places of leadership in Christian counseling have little or no training in theological thought, they have become involved in compromising the faith in various ways. Because their backgrounds are marinated with clinical psychology and psychiatry, it is not surprising to find that this is so. The shallow (and often shoddy) theological thinking exhibited in some of their books, the ease with which they slip into syncretizing, the almost total lack of exegesis (or its results) that is so apparent, are all unmistakable watermarks of the problem.[96]

Such vivid language served to warn off pastors; it hardly won him a hearing with the mental health establishment.

He named names and identified the views he found reprehensible. For example, Larry Crabb's notions of human nature were "misinformative" and "[bore] few traces" of what Adams thought the Bible taught about human nature. Adams frankly "encourage[d] anyone wishing to understand human nature as the Bible describes it to avoid such treatments of the subject."[97] The dead hand of Ellis, Adler, and Rogers lay over Crabb's theory of human personality. Similarly, Bruce Narramore's view of guilt was Freudianized: "Many of the key scriptural terms have been reworked to fit a modified Freudianism. The pigeon-holes are set up; Bible verses and terms are then tucked into them."[98] Philip Swihart's teaching on confession as a cathartic facing up to emotions—rather than as dealing with objective sin against God—was an example of a "psychological concept palmed off as God's way."[99] The widely popular James Dobson, whose views on child-rearing dominated conservative Protestant churches from the early 1970s, was guilty of child-rearing methods that represented a "near total capitulation to behaviorism." Dobson simply couched in Christian language a "cold and godless" system of manipulation, rather than giving a place for nouthetic conversations in rearing children.[100]

What was the intended effect of this final piece in Adams's polemic against psychiatry and psychotherapy? In the minds of his readers, the field would be utterly discredited, disgraced, and delegitimized. If a pastor had been to seminary, he would call into question his education in counseling. If he were a reader of popular current books, he would now view them with a deeply inculcated skepticism. Adams played the role of a master of suspicion—with the gaze of biblical revelation contemplating the products of twentieth-century secular reason—and he taught his pastors a critical epistemology and sociology that left Scripture and church as the only legitimate actors in the counseling field.

It must be noted that Adams did not expend a great deal of time, energy, and space toward criticizing those fellow religionists who presumably worked as fellow-travelers with the secular psychologists. But though his writings about the supposed compromisers were not extensive, they were

strategically placed—at the beginning of each of his four major books. He intended the demolition of the evangelical psychotherapy profession in the interests of his counseling revolution among pastors.

The psychotherapists responded quickly and often.

Chapter 7 Notes

1. Matthew 9:11–13, as translated in Jay E. Adams, *The Christian Counselor's New Testament: A New Translation in Everyday English with Notations* (USA: Presbyterian & Reformed, 1977), 26.

2. Perry London, *The Modes and Morals of Psychotherapy* (New York: Holt, Rinehart and Winston, 1964), 153.

3. Jay E. Adams, *The Christian Counselor's Manual* (USA: Presbyterian & Reformed, 1973), 9f.

4. Michael Polanyi has commented, referring to Arthur Koestler and Karen Horney respectively, "At the time when they still accepted as valid the conceptual framework of Marx or Freud—as the case may be—these writers would have regarded the all-embracing interpretative powers of this framework as evidence of its truth; only when losing faith in it did they feel that its powers were excessive and specious." Michael Polanyi, *Personal Knowledge: Towards a Post-Critical Philosophy* (Chicago: University of Chicago Press, 1958), 288. Adams's Calvinism was similarly all-embracing, but he never lost faith.

5. Jay E. Adams, "Your Place in the Counseling Revolution," in *Lectures on Counseling* (Grand Rapids: Zondervan, 1975–77), 17–18.

6. Cf., Abbott's description of how the same resources had been typically employed "to apply to problems diagnosed by others. . . . Clergy tried to invade the problems of everyday life that psychiatry had successfully defined as neuroses. . . . Clergy have accepted the diagnoses of others, but recommended treatment along religious lines." Andrew Abbott, *The System of Professions: An Essay on the Division of Expert Labor* (Chicago: University of Chicago Press, 1988), 100. Adams's jurisdictional conflict was more totalitarian, making dispute over diagnosis foundational to dispute about treatment.

7. "The power of the professions' knowledge systems, their abstracting ability to define old problems in new ways" is a "basic mechanism of interprofessional competition." Warring professions "use their abstract knowledge to reduce the work of competitors to a version of their own." Ibid., 30, 36.

8. Cf., his description of the purposes of preaching: Jay E. Adams, *Pulpit Speech: A Textbook for Use in the Classroom or Study* (USA: Presbyterian & Reformed, 1976), 42–87. The polemical streak ran so consistently through Adams's writing that he made a point of noting that his training guide for laycounselors was, uncharacteristically, "almost entirely free of polemic." Jay E. Adams, *Ready to Restore: The Layman's Guide to Christian Counseling* (Phillipsburg, N.J.: Presbyterian & Reformed, 1981), vii.

9. Jay E. Adams, "Jay Adams Response to the Congress on Christian Counseling," *Journal of Pastoral Practice* 10, no. 1 (1989): 2–4.

10. Jay E. Adams, *Competent to Counsel* (USA: Presbyterian & Reformed, 1970), 9–12, 17–19.

11. See in particular Jay E. Adams, *Change Them? . . . into What?: Counseling in America Today* (Laverock, Pa.: Christian Counseling and Educational Foundation, 1977). Reprinted as, Jay E. Adams, "Change Them . . . Into What?," *Journal of Biblical Counseling* 13, no. 2 (1995): 13–17. This address was given to faculty and students at the University Psychiatric Clinic in Vienna. Adams and Mowrer engaged in a cordial and substantive correspondence for about five years after Adams's summer in Illinois; the exchange of letters gradually tapered off as it became clear that neither was going to convince the other. Adams collaborated on one project with a secular academic: Jay E. Adams, "The Christian Approach to Schizophrenia," in *The Construction of Madness: Emerging Conceptions and Interventions into the Psychotic Process*, ed. Peter A. Magaro (New York: Pergamum Press, 1976), 133–50. This piece was similarly straightforward and informative, and did not adopt what Adams called the "preacher's stance," the authoritative persuader who called hearers to repentance and change. Jay E. Adams, *Truth Applied: Application in Preaching* (Grand Rapids: Zondervan, 1990), 21–32; Jay E. Adams, *Truth Apparent: Essays on Biblical Preaching* (Phillipsburg, N.J.: Presbyterian & Reformed, 1982), 49–52.

12. Adams detailed his own failures c. 1957 while taking a course in "Freudian" oriented counseling in his one completely autobiographical book: Jay E. Adams, *The Power of Error: Demonstrated in an Actual Counseling Case* (USA: Presbyterian & Reformed, 1978).

13. Adams, *Competent to Counsel*, xi–xvii.

14. Ibid., xi. Cf., Adams, *The Power of Error*.

15. Adams, *Competent to Counsel*, xiii.

16. Adams, *Change Them? . . . into What?*, 4, alluding to an article he had read in the *Saturday Review of Literature*, c. 1975.

17. Adams, *Competent to Counsel*, 1; from Gregory Zilboorg, *Progress in Psychotherapy*, eds. Frieda Fromm-Reichmann and J. L. Moreno (New York: Grune & Stratton, 1956), 108.

18. In Adams, *The Christian Counselor's Manual*, 9f, citing Perry London, *The Modes and Morals of Psychotherapy* (New York: Holt, Rinehart and Winston, 1964), 153–56.

19. Adams, *Competent to Counsel*, 13–15.

20. Ibid., 8.

21. Ibid., 28. Adams raised the issue of labeling over and over again in his writing. For example, "The prejudicial language of psychotherapeutic labeling is perhaps the most glaring example of language abuse that we must consider" (Jay E. Adams, *The Language of Counseling* [Phillipsburg, N.J.: Presbyterian & Reformed, 1981], 1. Cf., Jay E. Adams, "The Christian Approach to Schizophrenia," in *The Construction of Madness: Emerging Conceptions and Interventions into the Psychotic Process*, ed. Peter A. Magaro [New York: Pergamum Press, 1976], 133–50).

22. Jay E. Adams, *The Big Umbrella and Other Essays and Addresses on Christian Counseling* (USA: Presbyterian & Reformed, 1972), 3.

23. Adams, *Competent to Counsel*, 2f.

24. Adams, *The Big Umbrella*, 108. The Torrey quote was cited from "Psychiatry. It's Just Charisma," in *Medical World News* (March 26, 1971).

25. D. L. Rosenhan, "12 Admissions of Mental Error," in *Medical World News* (February 9, 1973): 17ff.

26. Adams, *Change Them? . . . into What?*, 6f. Cf., Adams, *The Christian Counselor's Manual*, 11.

27. Adams, *Competent to Counsel*, xiv–17; *The Christian Counselor's Manual*, 9–11, 71–76. Eventually, however, Adams would portray the moralists, too, as the intellectual and professional opponents they in fact were. For examples of explicit hostility to Calvinism, see, e.g., O. Hobart Mowrer, *The Crisis in Psychiatry and Religion* (Princeton: Van Nostrand, 1961), 159–61; Thomas Szasz, *Ideology and Insanity: Essays on the Psychiatric Dehumanization of Man* (Garden City, N.Y.: Doubleday, 1970), 5. And the quotation from Perry London at the head of chapter 5 hardly constitutes a plea for religious revival. From the standpoint of Adams's sectarian model, the potential for cobelligerency with advocates of other, fundamentally incompatible models was limited.

28. In one footnote Adams alluded to the differences between Mowrer, Glasser, and Szasz and gave the reader a reference. Adams, *Competent to Counsel*, 13f. He never stated the differences; his purposes were polemical, not scholarly.

29. Adams, *The Christian Counselor's Manual*, 10. Adams's terminology is often ambiguous and can engender confusion. Some statements invalidate psychiatrists, while other statements define a legitimate sphere of activity for them. Similarly, some statements validate the work of psychologists, distinguishing them from psychiatrists, while other statements lump both groups together as illegitimate. Adams's meanings are not ambiguous, however. Any activity that "competed" with pastoral ministry and theology—i.e., psychotherapy, counseling, self-help books, personality theory, ethics, etc.—he deemed illegitimate. Any activity that complemented pastoral ministry—e.g., "science" and "medicine"—was valid.

30. Abbott, *The System of Professions*, chapter 10, especially pages 280–314. Quotations are from pages 313 and 303.

31. Jay E. Adams, *Lectures on Counseling* (Grand Rapids: Zondervan, 1975–77), 7.

32. Jay E. Adams, *Counseling and the Sovereignty of God* (Philadelphia: Westminster Theological Seminary, 1975), 10.

33. Adams, *Competent to Counsel*, 12, n. 3.

34. Adams, *Counseling and the Sovereignty of God*, 12f.

35. The phrase "psychology basher" gained currency among evangelical psychotherapists circles to describe Adams and other opponents of the integration of psychology; e.g., Stanton Jones and Richard Butman, *Modern Psychotherapies: A Comprehensive Christian Appraisal* (Downers Grove, Ill.: InterVarsity Press, 1991), 30. In addition to Adams, they particularly had in mind the works of Martin and Deidre Bobgan, e.g., Martin Bobgan and Deidre Bobgan, *The Psychological Way/The Spiritual Way: Are Christianity and Psychotherapy Compatible?* (Minneapolis: Bethany House, 1979); and Dave Hunt and T. A. McMahon, *The Seduction of Christianity* (Eugene, Ore.: Harvest House, 1985). See chapters 8 and 9.

36. Adams, *Competent to Counsel*, xxi.

37. Ibid. Adams had the same view of other disciplines that might play an auxiliary role for pastoral work, e.g., sociology, law, medicine. Such disciplines might be thought provoking and informative, but Adams considered them fatal to ministry when they were allowed to set norms or to usurp pastoral practice and authority. See, e.g., Jay E. Adams, *More Than Redemption: A Theology of Christian Counseling* (Phillipsburg, N.J.: Presbyterian & Reformed, 1979), 101; Jay E. Adams, *How to Help People Change: The Four-Step Biblical Process* (Grand Rapids: Zondervan, 1986), 37–40. In Adams's worldview, theology was the queen of the sciences (and the Bible, as God's living redemptive voice, was the king).

38. See, for example, Adams, *Competent to Counsel,* xxi: "I do not wish to disregard science, but rather I welcome it as a useful adjunct for the purposes of illustrating, filling in generalizations with specifics, and challenging wrong human interpretations of the Scriptures, thereby forcing the student to restudy the Scriptures." Adams's positivistic tendencies were somewhat tempered by a "presuppositional" epistemology that paid attention to the effects of assumptions on predication in the sciences. This tempering caused him to hold "scientific findings" loosely, and, typically, to qualify any statements that depended on such findings. He alluded to this on the same page as the quotation above. Many among Adams's followers and critics were very committed to a positivistic view of scientific knowledge. See, for example, the writings of Martin and Deidre Bobgan, among Adams's followers. Among critics, numerous integrationists emphasized God's "two books" (nature and Scripture) as sources of positivistic "data" for theologizing and psychologizing respectively.

39. Jay E. Adams, *What About Nouthetic Counseling?* (Grand Rapids: Baker Book House, 1976), 31.

40. By this last phrase Adams meant a screening and redefinition process in the light of his conservative Protestant worldview. The clearest examples of the sort of cautious appropriation that met Adams's approval were seen in the medical writings of Bob Smith in the *Journal of Pastoral Practice.*

41. Adams, *How to Help People Change,* 37. Pages 33–40 constitute perhaps Adams's lengthiest description of what he saw to be the contribution of "legitimate" psychology, carefully distinguished from the "illegitimate" counseling role.

42. Adams, *What About Nouthetic Counseling?,* 31. Cf., discussions of organic problems in Adams, *Competent to Counsel, infra;* Adams, *The Christian Counselor's Manual, infra.*

43. Ibid., 384–90; Adams, "The Christian Approach to Schizophrenia."

44. Adams, *Competent to Counsel,* xxi.

45. In technical terms, it arose because "common grace" and "the noetic effects of sin on human predication" (to use the language of Adams's philosophical mentor, Cornelius Van Til) operated simultaneously. In Calvin, "In man's perverted and degenerate nature some sparks still gleam. . . . The mind of man, though fallen and perverted from its wholeness, is nevertheless clothed and ornamented with God's excellent gifts. . . . We shall neither reject the truth itself, nor despise it wherever it shall appear. . . . John Calvin, *Institutes of the Christian Religion,* trans. Ford Lewis Battles, ed. John T. McNeill, The Library of Christian Classics (Philadelphia: The Westminster Press, 1960), 12, 15.

46. Adams, *The Christian Counselor's Manual,* 76, 82f, 85f, 88, 91–93.

47. Ibid., 76.

48. Ibid., 92.

49. Adams, *Competent to Counsel,* xix.

50. Ibid. Cf., Adams, *The Christian Counselor's Manual,* 268.

51. These themes recur in Adams. Adams, *The Christian Counselor's Manual,* 71–93, offered the most sustained example of Adams's basic philosophy. These pages examine a series of psychological theorists, noting in each case elements of truth that Adams believed had been systematically distorted and hence had led to faulty conclusions.

52. Ibid., 76.

53. Adams, *The Big Umbrella,* 74–76. Cf., Adams, *The Christian Counselor's Manual,* 92f.

54. Freud, Rogers, and Skinner were more consistently skewered; Adams gave only grudging and perfunctory acknowledgment of positive features in their models (see the appropriate sections in Adams, *The Christian Counselor's Manual,* 71–93. With Mowrer and Glasser, Adams counterpoised hearty appreciation and firm criticism, especially in *Competent to Counsel.*

55. Adams, *The Christian Counselor's Manual,* 92.

56. Ibid., 34.

57. Ibid., 35.

58. Adams, *More Than Redemption,* 39.

59. Jay E. Adams, "Frankl, Victor E," in *The Encyclopedia of Christianity,* vol. 4, ed. Philip E. Hughes (Marshallton, Del.: The National Foundation for Christian Education, 1972), 244–46.

60. Adams, *The Christian Counselor's Manual,* 92, emphasis his. As noted earlier, much more appropriation of medicine took place than of psychology and other social sciences.

61. Ibid. The introductory chapters of Adams, *More Than Redemption,* ix–15, discuss these issues at some length. Also see below.

62. Cf., discussion between Adams and Bettler in David Powlison, "25 Years of Biblical Counseling: An Interview with Jay Adams and John Bettler," *Journal of Biblical Counseling* 12, no. 1 (1993): 11f. Only with respect to medicine did nouthetic counselors in fact expend much effort to "take note of, evaluate, and reclaim the truths dimly reflected."

63. The evangelical psychotherapists would find Adams's handling of the psychological schools to be as irresponsible as the identified failings of said schools. See chapter 8. To a lesser extent, even some of Adams's comrades in arms found fault with him in this regard: John Bettler, "Biblical Counseling: The Next Generation," *Journal of Pastoral Practice* 8, no. 4 (1987): 3–10. See chapter 9.

As an aside, though it was hardly his major purpose, Adams did appeal successfully to a certain number of PhD psychologists and MD psychiatrists and neurologists. Those who wrote books or articles favorable to Adams included Richard Ganz, *Psychobabble: The Failure of Modern Psychology—and the Biblical Alternative* (Wheaton, Ill.: Crossway Books, 1993) by a clinical psychologist; Edward T. Welch, *Counselor's Guide to the Brain and Its Disorders: Knowing the Difference Between Disease and Sin* (Grand Rapids: Zondervan, 1991) by a neurophysiological psychologist;

Raju Abraham, "Jay Adams: He Is Biblical Enough" *Third Way* (June 1982): 12f, by a neurologist; Martin Bobgan and Deidre Bobgan, *The Psychological Way/The Spiritual Way: Are Christianity and Psychotherapy Compatible?* (Minneapolis: Bethany House, 1979) by an educational psychologist; and Gary Almy, Carol Tharp Almy, and Jerry Jenkins, *Addicted to Recovery: Exposing the False Gospel of Psychotherapy, Escaping the Trap of Victim Mentality* (Eugene, Ore.: Harvest House Publishers, 1994) by a psychiatrist.

64. Adams, *More Than Redemption*, 14.

65. Adams, *What About Nouthetic Counseling?*, 37.

66. Ibid., 39.

67. Adams, *Competent to Counsel*, chapter 1; Mowrer, *The Crisis in Psychiatry and Religion*; and Szasz, *The Myth of Mental Illness*, discussed at length the distinctions each of these drew between a medical model and a moral model. London, *The Modes and Morals of Psychotherapy*, contrasted the "insight therapies" and the "action therapies," a distinction that covered much the same ground.

68. Mowrer had written, "There are, of course, plenty of therapists who are purportedly non-Freudian; but the majority of these . . . because they have abandoned classical Freudian technique or some minor aspect of the theory, they *call* themselves non-Freudian, or neo-Freudian, or perhaps even anti-Freudian while continuing to accept the major premises of Freud's philosophy and thought. The nondirective or client-centered type of therapy which is associated with the name of Carl Rogers will, of course, be immediately thought of by many as 'non-Freudian.' But as I am here using the term, I would say that Rogers's approach is deeply 'Freudian.'" Mowrer, *The Crisis in Psychiatry and Religion*, 164.

69. Adams, *Competent to Counsel*, 101.

70. See Ibid., 4–19. Cf., Mowrer, *The Crisis in Psychiatry and Religion*, 164f. This generic, mainstream psychodynamic psychology is described from a slightly different angle in Abbott, *System of Professions*, 306f.

71. Bettler, on the other hand, would find elements in Adlerian theory relatively good.

72. Mowrer, *The Crisis in Psychiatry and Religion*, 60.

73. Adams, *Competent to Counsel*, 17f.

74. Biopsychological theories were often criticized on an ad hoc basis, rather than included as a fourth major school.

75. Jay E. Adams, *Shepherding God's Flock: A Handbook on Pastoral Ministry, Counseling, and Leadership* (Grand Rapids: Zondervan, 1974–75), 159–71. Cf., similar comments in Adams, *Competent to Counsel*, *infra*; Adams, *The Big Umbrella*, *infra*; Adams, *The Christian Counselor's Manual*, *infra*.

76. Adams, *The Language of Counseling*, 53.

77. Adams, *The Christian Counselor's Manual*, 17.

78. Adams, *Shepherding God's Flock*, 162.

79. Adams, *The Christian Counselor's Manual*, 83f.

80. Adams also attacked particulars of numerous other theories. The moralistic (Mowrer, Glasser, and Szasz) and existentialist (Frankl) psychologists might be collocated as a loose fourth category that reappeared often in Adams's polemic. Though they stressed human responsibility and choice, and even used explicitly theological language on occasion, their theology, too, was defective, e.g., "[Mowrer] tried to use theological language as a skin to fit his humanistic beliefs." Adams, *What About Nouthetic Counsel-*

ing?, 37. Cf., Adams, *The Christian Counselor's Manual*, 34f, 73, 86–91, 268. Another popular psychological concept that Adams repeatedly criticized was the "self-esteem" teaching: e.g., Jay E. Adams, *The Biblical View of Self-Esteem, Self-Love, Self-Image* (Eugene, Ore.: Harvest House, 1986).

81. Adams, *Shepherding God's Flock*, 169.

82. Adams, *More Than Redemption*, 7.

83. Ibid., 13f.

84. Ibid., 9. This aspect of Adams's thought would naturally arouse intense, sustained opposition from evangelical psychotherapists. Adams charged them with intellectual compromise and said they had no institutional *raison-d'etre*. Presumably—this point never was discussed to my knowledge—they were by definition excluded, by their own professionalism and integrationist agenda, from the category "other Christian workers/counselors" who might function legitimately in a pastor-led context. CCEF hired a number of counselors who had acquired PhDs or MAs in psychology—along with theological education—but were committed to counsel within the nouthetic framework.

85. Jay E. Adams, "Counseling, Pastoral," in *The Encyclopedia of Christianity*, vol. 3, ed. Philip E. Hughes (Marshallton, Del.: The National Foundation for Christian Education, 1972), 188; Jay E. Adams, "Reflections on the History of Biblical Counseling," in *Practical Theology and the Ministry of the Church, 1952–1984: Essays in Honor of Edmund P. Clowney*, ed. Harvie Conn (Phillipsburg, N.J.: Presbyterian & Reformed, 1990), 206f. Adams's assessment of Boisen is similar to Andrew Abbott's, which portrayed Boisen as a "guerrilla in the psychiatric heartland" who had waged an "unsuccessful jurisdictional revolution." Abbott, *The System of Professions*, 309f. Adams's view of Boisen's successor, Seward Hiltner, was sharply at odds with Abbott's, however. Adams saw Hiltner as a compromiser (see following paragraph), whereas Abbott viewed Hiltner as carrying forward Boisen's radical program (p. 310).

86. Adams, "Reflections on the History of Biblical Counseling," 207.

87. Adams, *Competent to Counsel*, 89–93; Adams, *The Christian Counselor's Manual*, 3, 84.

88. Adams, *The Christian Counselor's Manual*, 84.

89. Adams, *Competent to Counsel*, 78–92; Adams, *The Christian Counselor's Manual*, 155. For an extended discussion of the Rogerian heyday in Protestant pastoral counseling, see E. Brooks Holifield, *A History of Pastoral Care in America: From Salvation to Self-Realization* (Nashville: Abingdon Press, 1983), 259–306.

90. Adams, *Competent to Counsel*, 92.

91. Adams, *The Christian Counselor's Manual*, 33.

92. Adams, *More Than Redemption*, xi.

93. Ibid.

94. See discussion of Martin and Deidre Bobgan in chapter 9.

95. Adams, "Jay Adams Response to the Congress on Christian Counseling," 3.

96. Adams, *More Than Redemption*, 9.

97. Ibid., 117f.

98. Ibid., 198.

99. Ibid., 218.

100. Adams, *The Christian Counselor's Manual*, 82.

CHAPTER 8

Counterinsurgency: The Response of the Environing Professions

No one who is anyone in the world of counseling respects Jay Adams.
— reported by David Goodrum, 1975[1]

[Adams's The Biblical View of Self-Esteem *is] irresponsible and vilifying garbage, like most of the rest of his stuff.*
— J. Harold Ellens, 1987[2]

More than anyone else [Adams] has attempted to develop an approach to counseling that is consistent with the truths of Scripture.
— Gary Collins, 1975[3]

A number of participants expressed the importance of Christian psychologists listening to the conservative Christian critics of integration; to fail to listen would be arrogance, and in listening we may receive correction for our errors of omission, commission, and misplaced emphasis.
— Stanton Jones, 1992[4]

We have seen that Jay Adams won adherents for his nouthetic counseling among local church-based, conservative Protestants. Among nonadherents he succeeded in creating tremendous controversy, especially in the 1970s. According to one evangelical psychologist writing in 1973, nouthetic counseling was "the [form of] Christian counseling popular today."[5] According to another, writing in 1980, "Among evangelicals, and especially evangelical pastors, Adams is perhaps the best-known and most widely heeded teacher of Christian counselors."[6] But Adams gained more opponents than followers among conservative Protestants. When the noise died down, a competing professional group, the evangelical psychotherapists, were the ones who had greatly extended and consolidated their professional authority during the 1970s and 1980s. They proved far more successful than nouthetic counselors in local churches, education, publishing, and counseling practice.[7] Adams's institutional impact proved negligible in comparison with the psychotherapists. Indeed, by the late 1980s, Adams's pastoral anti-psychotherapy was, to most observers, only a small, disagreeable voice on the periphery of an institutional development that produced a burgeoning evangelical mental health establishment.

Adams's attack forced evangelical psychologists to respond, both to clarify their self-definition and to defend their legitimacy in the eyes of their primary clientele. Adams's agenda jeopardized their intellectual validity and professional existence. This chapter will look at how evangelical mental health professionals, the ascendant cultural authorities in the personal problems jurisdiction, responded to Adams. Predictably, their response was largely negative.

The magnitude of Adams's claim, that nouthetic counseling manifested a unique and innovative fidelity to biblical truth, was mirrored by the intensity and scope of criticisms from coreligionists disappointed, dismayed, and put on the defensive by what they read. Even when critics softened their blows by noting some redeeming qualities, Adams systematically grated on their sensibilities. In the standard wisdom of the evangelical counseling world, the nouthetic counseling project, as a whole, was a monstrous miscarriage, intellectually disreputable and generally damaging to needy people. Fundamentalistic pastors and unwitting counselees might find Adams appealing, but leaders in the counseling field generally found him hard to tolerate.

Particularly the more theologically conservative criticized Adams repeatedly.[8] Numerous books and articles conducted a running debate with Adams. Indeed, an Adams citation became a stock element in introductory paragraphs or chapters of integrationist writing. His anti-psychology served as the foil against which evangelical psychology defined its intellectual and professional program. For example, Bruce Narramore routinely used Adams to get his students at Rosemead aware and aroused:

> We can turn [the attacks on psychology from other Christians] into creative challenges that stretch our students and force them to come to grips with the accusations leveled against psychology in a way that can deepen their understanding of both their Christian faith and their psychology. In fact some of the most motivating readings my students do are by . . . Jay Adams (e.g., *Competent to Counsel*).
>
> About the only readings that I assign my students that stir as strong a reaction as . . . Jay Adams are readings such as the paper that Albert Ellis (1970) delivered to the American Humanist Association some years ago entitled "The Case Against Religion"![9]

Adams was a catalyst to his opponents.

The formal views and commitments of nouthetic counselors and evangelical psychotherapists regarding theology and ethics were often remarkably similar, in all respects except two. First, what knowledge source and knowledge system primarily equipped one for competency in the counseling task? Did the Bible or modern psychology provide the critical, system-aligning ingredients? Second, who should be the counseling professionals? Did church-ordained pastors with an MDiv or DMin have the goods on human nature, and thus title to the cure of souls? Or did state-licensed clinical psychologists with an MA, PhD, or PsyD have the diagnostic insight and clinical expertise to claim the psychotherapeutic role? In other words, professional jurisdiction over the personal problems realm was continually controverted. By routine polemics, each defined itself off against the other as the true possessor of insight and expertise. Yet their core allegiances were the same: both groups assiduously sought to define themselves as distinctly evangelical, as "biblical" in contrast with the secular psychologies.

This chapter will focus on those aspects of the evangelical psychologists' knowledge system that bore on the jurisdictional conflict. I will not discuss the numerous positive, competing models of counseling that they articulated,[10] and I will not attempt a minute differentiation between their views of Adams. Rather I will explore their common arguments, generally flattening internal differences.[11] I have collected the numerous criticisms under the same six headings as Adams's positive system presented in chapters 5 through 7: the epistemological role of the "Word of God," the nature of sin, the impact of situational variables, the grace of the gospel, counseling methods and the place of the church, and the relationship between evangelical religion and secular psychology. Adams was rebutted on every distinctive. A seventh family of criticisms concerned Adams's isolationist stance and intemperate rhetoric, his "psychology-bashing." Authors across the spectrum consistently repeated the same basic criticisms. At the end of the chapter we will briefly look at the views of two audiences that only occasionally interacted with Adams: the mainline pastoral counselors and secular psychotherapists.

1. Adams's view of and use of Scripture was faulty

Parties to a public jurisdictional conflict must appeal to the values held by the constituency for which they compete. Evangelical psychotherapists, like Adams, wore their particular religious commitments openly. They frequently made a point to include a statement of faith in their defining documents. These were confessing, creedal Protestants. For example, Clyde Narramore's books and literature from his Narramore Christian Foundation often included a creed that would be unexceptionable to the vast majority of fundamentalists and evangelicals. The American Association of Christian Counselors (AACC) and the Christian Association for Psychological Studies (CAPS) both published creedal statements that affirmed standard evangelical beliefs. The Bible's

authority as an "infallible guide to faith and practice" was one cardinal doctrine in those creeds.[12]

It is not surprising, then, that when Adams and the evangelical psychotherapists squared off, their arguments frequently returned to what each side purported the Bible to say. This was a turf war between coreligionists, between "Bible-believers." Whether they acted as anti-psychotherapists or as practicing psychotherapists, they were united by a common supreme value: what did the Bible say? Among conservative Protestants, by definition, value and stigma hinged on how one's views comported with the yardstick of divinely spoken canon: "biblical" was a term of approbation and validation; "unbiblical" or "subbiblical" were terms of anathema. The commitment to a "biblical" view of problems in living and their redress infused every aspect of the turf war.

Evangelical psychotherapists openly agreed with Adams's intention to be biblical and stated their own identical commitments. Stan Jones and Richard Butman put it this way: "We agree with Christian critics of psychology such as Jay Adams who say that the counseling processes are of such a nature that they must be thoroughly reconceptualized from a biblical foundation to lay claim to the adjective 'Christian.'"[13] Gary Collins, after ruing the chaotic diversity of approaches among evangelicals, said, "To be Christian counselors we must begin with a commitment to Jesus Christ and must build our theoretical approaches on solid biblical grounds."[14] He termed Adams both "courageous and creative" for his attempt "to develop an approach to counseling that is consistent with the truths of Scripture."[15]

While Adams's evangelical critics were quick to affirm that they shared his Bible commitments, they actively disputed his interpretation of that Bible. Rosemead's John Carter spoke for the mainstream when he stated: "I am fully committed to the integrity of the Scripture as authoritative for faith and practice. Therefore, my disagreement with Adams is not over the authority of Scripture but over Adams' interpretation of it. I maintain he has misunderstood and misinterpreted the scriptural view of man and his functioning (however unintentionally) in developing his Nouthetic Counseling Theory."[16] Thus the evangelical psychotherapists took Adams to task on grounds they shared. In their eyes, Adams's model comported only more or less to scriptural teachings and exemplars. It was as remarkable for its misuse of the Bible as for its use. It was as remarkable for its lacunae, both minor and major, as for its substance. And that substance was seriously compromised by missteps, both subtle and egregious. Adams's paradigm did not win converts among those already in the counseling field—for pointedly "biblical" reasons.

The Bible was the authoritative rule for faith and practice, but Adams misused the Bible in three ways: [1] He treated it as a comprehensive counseling textbook, when the Bible itself never claimed to be such; [2] he thus denied that the secular psychologies might contribute to counseling wisdom by God's common grace; [3] he misused the Bible, by treating it as a collection of proof texts and quoting selectively. His wrong view of the Bible's purposes led him to invalidate other sources of God's truth and to use the Bible improperly. From the very earliest interactions between Adams and psychologists, the Bible was the chief point of contention.[17]

First, Adams had overstated the scope of the Bible's authoritative guidance by portraying and using it as a "textbook" for counseling. Such an approach was "erroneous . . . narrow and indefensible"[18] in one of the milder comments; according to the more biting criticisms, Adams had turned the Bible into a "celestial problem-solving manual," and "[It] reminds me that when people used [the Bible] as a textbook of geography, they concluded

that the world was flat."[19] There was no "system" of counseling to be deduced from Scripture: "I fail to find any specific counseling modality given in Scripture. . . . [Adams] eisegetically extracts from God's Word 'divine directives' which are really nothing of the kind."[20] Adams's repeated claim to be biblical actually misrepresented the Bible by treating it as a manual of information on counseling topics. Stan Jones and Richard Butman gave a tidy, comprehensive statement of the differences: "While the Bible provides us with life's most important and ultimate answers as well as the starting points for knowledge of the human condition, it is not an all-sufficient guide for the discipline of counseling. The Bible is inspired and precious, but it is also a revelation of limited scope, the main concern of which is religious in its presentation of God's redemptive plan for people and the great doctrines of the faith."[21] Contrary to Adams's assumptions, God had not revealed in the Bible all that was needed to construct a system of counseling truth and practice.[22] A system of counseling needed to be informed by Scripture, but it could only be constructed in dialogue with and by assimilation of the secular psychologies.[23] Counseling wisdom depended on the program to integrate psychology and theology into the thought and practice of professional psychotherapists.

Yet, while they consistently disagreed with Adams about whether the Bible was a counseling textbook, these psychologists could come remarkably close to his view. Bill Kirwan of Covenant Seminary, one of Adams's fiercest critics, wrote, "Even though the Bible is not a psychology textbook . . . [its] teachings contain in embryonic (and sometimes more fully developed) form all the valid teachings of modern behavioral science."[24] Gary Collins commented, "The Bible is not a counseling cookbook . . . [but it informs] a worldview that gives us a grid through which we can sift the questions of life that are not specifically addressed in

Scripture. . . . I agree with Larry Crabb that 'biblical revelation must function as the controlling guide for all our thinking about counseling,'"[25] and "the Word of God is a true standard against which all other knowledge must be tested."[26] Larry Crabb's own view of the Bible evolved to become virtually identical to Adams's, though he detected a somewhat different model of counseling emergent from the Bible.[27] Nuances of intellectual emphasis became significant chasms because professional legitimation was at stake.

The second point of dispute was a corollary to the first. If Adams made the Bible a textbook, then his "total rejection of insights from secular psychology and psychiatry"[28] followed logically. This criticism of Adams was perhaps the most common. Adams's narrow biblicism excluded both the probing insights and the caring, efficacious methods that modern psychologies had pioneered. He seemed to oppose science itself, denying God's "common grace and general revelation."[29] As Adams had overstated the scope of the Bible's contribution, so he understated the positive contribution of secular knowledge and theory: he was guilty of "theological imperialism" and had adopted a "xenophobic" stance toward culture.[30]

Adams's belief that the significant conceptual, methodological, and institutional underpinnings for counseling could be exegetically derived from the Bible had been logically wedded to his programmatic suspicion of the secular psychologies. Evangelical psychologists were more sanguine about the psychologies. To criticize particular unbiblical aspects of psychology did not mean to view the whole endeavor with suspicion. Integrationists sought to portray psychology as a source of legitimate and even necessary knowledge under the banner, "All truth is God's truth." Psychology was part of God's "second book" about human beings, supplementing and complementing Scripture.

Characteristically—again, this was a turf war among conservative Protestants—Adams's derogation of psychology was described as a biblical deficiency. Adams failed to replicate the Bible's own attitude. For example, many of the Solomonic proverbs evidenced a wide-ranging curiosity about the natural world not dependent on divine revelation: "much of the wisdom contained in *Proverbs* could have been discovered by a secular sage of the Ancient Near East or of contemporary America."[31] Adams's attempt to demean the insights of the psychologies failed to mirror what the Bible itself did. Adams was "Biblicistic not Biblical," in Vernon Grounds's words.[32]

Adams's minimizing of psychology's contribution was also a theological deficiency. Integrationists cited Jay Adams's own theological heroes—John Calvin and Cornelius Van Til—on the role of "common grace." For example, in Calvin's words, "The human mind, however much fallen and perverted from its original integrity, is still adorned and invested with admirable gifts from its Creator. . . . We will be careful . . . not to reject or condemn truth wherever it appears."[33] Adams's "Against" stance toward the psychologies was an instance of "nothing buttery," as in nothing-but-the-Bible, a sub-Christian, obscurantist point of view.[34] It attempted to locate all significant knowledge within the pages of a book intended only to give the most significant knowledge. In the large sweep, Adams had fundamentally misconstrued biblical epistemology to exclude other legitimized and necessary sources of information.

Adams had denied the contribution of legitimate science to human knowledge in the social sciences. John Carter stated that:

> [Adams's] model assumes that there is no general revelation or common grace which God has given to man which can be discovered by a non-Christian psychologist.[35]

Adams rejects common grace or general revelation for counseling by assuming the subject matter of counseling and Scripture are the same. However, he accepts common grace for medicine and presumably for other natural sciences. . . . Common grace and the problems its rejection has created for Adams' theory appears to be the "Hound of Heaven" which pursues Adams throughout his theory.[36]

Carter went so far as to charge Adams with ignoring "the data or phenomena level of psychology, e.g., the sheer observables of human functioning."[37] A few critics moderated the charge. British psychiatrist Roger Hurding noted that: "In his writings, as well as in personal conversation, Jay Adams acknowledges the existence of divine common grace. . . . [But his] seeming neglect of the biblical dimensions of general revelation and common grace *as a developed argument* is, I believe, the main root of at least some of his more disputed opinions."[38] The intellectual battle lines were drawn over the issue of the relative weight of Scripture and psychology. The degree to which arguments were developed demarcated the intellectual boundaries in this turf war. Adams spent little time studying psychology (though he agreed it had something to offer); evangelical psychotherapists spent little time exegeting Scripture (though they agreed it needed to anchor their counseling worldview). Such nuances carried vast professional implications. The turf war happened here.

Third, integrationists (along with many theologians) disagreed with the hermeneutic Adams applied to the Bible. His way of using the Bible was both atomistic and selective. Adams's frequent recourse to his concordance, to theological wordbooks and linguistic arguments, and to extensive lists of proof texts communicated a picture of the Bible as a problem-solving manual containing the necessary bits of information on any and all counseling topics. Critics believed, on the contrary, that the Bible provided general theological themes to describe human life. Not every important counseling question could be answered by looking up the appropriate word in a concordance. Adams would "cite texts without careful regard to their contexts . . . elevating out-of-context verses into revelational norms for spiritual therapy."[39]

Adams was not only atomistic but guilty of a "selective hermeneutics . . . forcing the Scriptures into his own system. Consider, for example, the assumption that behavior determines feelings, and never vice versa."[40] Such selectivity led to bending individual passages to fit preexistent meanings and excluded many things the Bible talked about: "Adams is simply subscriptural, not so much for what he asserts but for what he omits and the bias that this omission introduces."[41] While claiming to be biblical, Adams omitted the Bible's treatment of crucial aspects of human existence and wise counseling practice. Adams was a "stiff exegete" whose use of the Bible failed to relate it deeply to human experience and need, narrowing the range of permissable questions, creating simplistic answers to complex problems.[42] In his hermeneutical philosophy and exegetical practice, Adams had misused the Bible, and that misuse had extensive ramifications.

2. Adams's view of human nature was superficial and constricted

Evangelical psychotherapists agreed with Adams in principle that sin was the foundational ill of the human soul. Wheaton's David Benner asserted the standard evangelical belief about human nature: "We are now thoroughly sinful, no aspect of our personality being free from the effects of sin."[43] Many agreed that the modern psychologies were guilty of negligence by evading the problem of sin. Larry Crabb commended Adams's indictment of the psychologies: "A number of Christians—and I am among them—react strongly to any view that explains sinful behavior as the understandable consequence of psychological forces."[44] They appreciated Adams's attempt to reinject the category "sin" into discussions of problems in living:

> [Adams's] emphasis on personal responsibility is a welcome relief from those who excuse sinful behavior as unfortunate symptoms of mental disease. I read somewhere that Richard Speck's psychologist explained Speck's cold-blooded murder of eight nurses as a "psychological necessity." Skinner would have us blame environments. Freud points the accusing finger at internal psychic disturbance. Rogers empathizes with a stifled person denied his right to self-expression. In every case the person as a responsible agent is lost.[45]

A stress on human responsibility was critical to maintaining the distinctive New Testament answer to the human dilemma. Sin was necessarily the problem if the grace of God was to remain the solution. In Crabb's evaluation: "Eliminate responsibility and you do away with guilt. Do away with guilt and sin no longer exists. With the removal of sin the cross of Christ becomes a religious martyrdom rather than the basis of redemption."[46] Counselors needed to be "sensitive to the depths of selfishness resident within human nature" if they were to preserve the doctrine of substitutionary atonement as "at the heart of all Christian growth."[47]

But the psychotherapists did not like two particular aspects of Adams's view that sin caused problems in living. First, it was too shallow: Adams neglected the interior dimensions of human beings, viewing problems as largely behavioral. Second, it was too narrow: Adams excluded any causes of problems in living that were neither moral-spiritual nor physiological. We will look at these in turn.

First, there was general agreement that Adams lacked a profound, comprehensive, and sensitive grasp of human beings in their psychological complexity. "Nouthetic counselors . . . leave out the 'insides' of the behaving person"; "the most glaring weakness of nouthetic counseling theory is that . . . no theory of motivation or fundamental dynamic tendency of the person is articulated."[48] His theoretical emphases, case studies, and methodological directives focused almost exclusively on external behavioral habits: "All problems are behavioral. What else can one infer from case history after case history where, for instance, 'Mary's problem was the sin of adultery.' The bottom line is always an act or a failure to act."[49] By perseverating on his distinctives—human responsibility to moral norms and the alteration of habitual behavior—Adams precluded attention to the internal processes presumed to underlie particular acts of sinful behavior. Variations on this criticism were repeated countless times.[50] This pervasive externalism prompted intractable opposition from those committed to study, understand, and address the psyche. Nouthetic counseling appeared more behavioristic than biblical because it largely treated activities in the "heart" or "soul" as epiphenomenal to behavior.

Most of the human psychological makeup seemed to have simply been excluded from the nouthetic system. Some critic or other pointed out how every dimension of the inner life was neglected: assumption system, beliefs, attitudes, self-esteem, emotions, cognitive processes, psychological needs and desires, motives, unconscious wishes, sinful nature, inner sinful patterns, and so forth.[51] For example, like Mowrer and Glasser, Adams was a "glorifier of conscience." He failed to trace the corruptions and confusions of conscience (e.g., the identification of "false guilt") that had been one of the signal achievements of psychodynamic psychology. By taking guilt experiences at face value, guilt appeared as an unambiguous "voice of God" resident in the soul. Such a view underestimated the problems of the conscience. It correspondingly overestimated the power of the consciously rational and volitional components of the psyche, dangerously elevating the powers of the human will both as an explanation for problems in living and as the agent of positive change.[52]

This focus on conscious behavior and thoughts made Adams's counseling process rapid but superficial. His counseling, when successful, largely consisted in helping people replace identifiably ungodly habits with purportedly godly habits:

> If we locate the *source* of adjustment
> problems in specific sins of the individual
> we are likely to conceptualize responsi-
> bility as involving changing one's overt
> behavior in a relatively short period of
> time. If, in contrast, we emphasize the role
> of one's inborn sinful nature in the devel-
> opment of pathology, we are more likely to
> stress growth as a process involving insight
> into previously hidden sinful desires and
> hurts. Adams is one of the clearest expres-
> sions of the belief that the fundamental
> element in the therapy process is changed
> behavior.[53]

Adams's superficial view of the problem of sin was likely to encourage cosmetic adjustments to please the counselor during a short season of counseling sessions but unlikely to fundamentally rearrange the way a person lived.

These failings were again pointedly *biblical* and theological failings. Adams had ignored the vast amount of biblical data on the "heart" as the disordered spring of sinful behavior.[54] The degree to which Adams concentrated on behavioral renovation was abhorrent to integrationists and offended both evangelical and psychological commitments: "His view of man is thoroughly sub-Christian . . . , almost completely external and behavioral. The only thing that seemingly prevents him from being a full-fledged Skinnerian or Mowrerian is Adams' metaphysical commitment to God and the Bible."[55] Ironically, for one so committed to see sin as the problem, Adams communicated a "naive and shallow understanding" of sin.[56] In fact, by treating sin as "habit patterns of disobedience which can be broken down by the application of will power working in a process of dehabituation," he was guilty of promoting the old heresy of "Pelagianism," that overestimated the power of the human will.[57] Adams's theological forebears could again be quoted against him:

> John Calvin said that man does not know
> the thousandth part of the sin that clings to
> his soul. Luther knew that there is some-
> thing much more drastically wrong with
> man than any particular list of offenses
> which can be enumerated, confessed, and
> forgiven. . . . Yet Adams blithely asserts,
> "To have good days, one must do good
> deeds. . . ." How can Adams be so confi-
> dent in his ability to sift through the morass
> of sin in any person's life to discover the
> operant sin(s) antecedent to the person's
> bad feelings?[58]

Adams's functional theory of human nature contradicted the theology that he professed: "Jay Adams has two theologies. The one he professes is Reformed and orthodox. But his counseling model implicitly contains a second theology of conditioned habit that is Pelagian. That's what actually functions in his view of the change process."[59]

To many critics, Adams's view of the dislocation in human nature was too narrow as well as too shallow. Certain emotional and psychological dimensions of human woe did not immediately reduce to outworkings of the problem of personal sin. Inner misery, mental illness, psychological dysfunction, and social maladjustment could not always be explained either as sin or as organic dysfunction. On this issue, psychologists were divided. A few of the more theologically conservative psychologists agreed with Adams that there were fundamentally only two kinds of problems, physiological and psychospiritual.[60] But most evangelical psychologists argued that numerous aspects of problems in living needed to be categorized as emotional or psychological, rather than sinful: "the most popular [position] in contemporary Christian therapy" separated spiritual and psychological problems.[61] Most evangelicals discerned a realm of "psychological factors (like faulty learning, traumatic past experiences, internal conflicts) . . . [that] can combine to put so much pressure on an individual that he or she breaks down under stress."[62] This realm of inorganic illness or suffering was susceptible to "psychological" rather than "spiritual" treatment.[63]

3. Adams ignored the effects of interpersonal suffering

Closely related to the argument that Adams's view of the human personality was too narrow was his corresponding constriction of the role of events significantly impinging on moral responsibility. Adams and the psychotherapists agreed that human behavior did not exist in a vacuum, but that people were affected by both their bodies and their social milieu. Adams had paid close attention to medical factors, but he had been just as careful to downplay social factors that might affect counselees' responsibility: sociocultural shaping and the impact of interpersonal trauma received only superficial and anecdotal mention. The fact that Adams never systematically discussed social effects, and that he ignored the social sciences that attempted to comprehend such influences, created a major void

in his theory and practice. The psychotherapists thought that this gap caused nouthetic counseling to fall short both in insight and in compassion. In his zeal to cut off excuses for moral irresponsibility, Adams discounted the obvious: "Not only do we sin; we also are sinned against."[64]

Both the past and present social situations were neglected. Like Mowrer and Glasser, Adams dealt chiefly in the present. He had a tendency to: "stress sin and personal responsibility, to minimize the impact of being sinned against by parents and others. In minimizing the importance of the past, advocates of this viewpoint can easily underestimate the impact the sins and failures of others have on our personality development and functioning."[65] In addition to ignoring historical influences, Adams downplayed current situational pressures: "[Adams failed to account for] social influences (such as the breakup of a marriage, the loss of one's job) that . . . can combine to put so much pressure on an individual that he or she breaks down under stress."[66] Suffering, the significance of the past, the sins of others, compassion, and the pursuit of deeper personal insight all faded in the harsh light of Adams's confrontive, moral directives.

Adams was seen to embody one of two possible extreme positions regarding the interplay of individual responsibility and social influence: "The first of these is the tendency to assume that whenever a person has a problem, this is the direct result of that person's sinful thoughts or actions. From this, it follows that the only effective method of treatment is to confront the counselee with his or her sin, to help the person find forgiveness, and to challenge the individual to go and sin no more. . . . The second counseling extreme is to assume that problems all come from somebody else's sin."[67] The psychologists intended to find the balance point that Adams's extremism missed. Larry Crabb, for example, reiterated that counselees typically were both hurting and demanding, both needy and sinful. They experienced pain and disappointment at the failings of others; they selfishly demanded their own way. Adams had lost the suffering side of human nature.[68]

Some integrationists noted that Adams acknowledged in principle the impact of being sinned against. But this was another case of an undeveloped argument. When he alluded to social effects, rather than discussing and legitimating them, he hurriedly backpedaled to close off any possibility that such things would be used as excuses for moral irresponsibility: "Adams writes of both the sin nature and of being sinned against. When it actually comes down to his theory of pathology, however, he lays most of the responsibility at the feet of the individual. He writes, 'That others have done much to shape our lives, no one can deny. However, each individual must bear personal responsibility for how *he has allowed others to influence his conduct*.' Note his emphasis on *conduct* and on *allowing* others to influence."[69] The outworking of Adams's actual theory and counseling practice paid little attention to being sinned against, and in effect treated the impact of such things as negligible.

Again, Adams's failings were specifically *biblical* failings. The evangelical psychotherapists thought that Adams had almost wholly missed the point made in numerous psalms that counselees were often more sinned against than sinning. The God of the Bible cared for those who had been sinned against, and he would meet people in their sufferings just as he gave grace to them in their sins. God called those who ministered in his name to an analogous love and patience toward the oppressed, sinned against, misled. Adams was often charged with being one of "Job's counselors" in the way his confrontational model moved rapidly past suffering as somewhat irrelevant in comparison to the need to address responsible behavior.

Adams and the evangelical psychotherapists clashed over the interpretation of social effects and the consequent professional paradigm to bring to counseling. Did problems in living largely arise because people immediately sinned, hence pastors needed to provide the necessary exhortation and instruction? Or were people often more sinned against than sinning, hence therapists needed to provide the necessary context of trusting and restorative relationship?

4. Adams's approach to change was legalistic, not gracious

Evangelical psychotherapists agreed with Adams that the evangel of God's grace in Christ was the foundation of all change and the summation of all felicity. But there was a spectrum of opinions on how frankly counselors ought to evangelize. The more conservative theologically argued for the most explicit evangelism in the counseling context. For them, frank evangelism had to be part of any counseling worthy of the name "Christian." Collins wrote: "I agree with Jay Adams's position that any counseling that claims to be Christian must surely be evangelistic. . . . Critics of psychology correctly argue that Christians are failing their counselees if discussion focuses exclusively on secular methods and humanistic theories. Counseling can hardly be called Christian if counselees are helped to solve problems or cope with stress but are never made aware of their sin or told of their need for the Savior."[70] As evangelicals, they thought evangelism was appropriate and necessary because it met people in their genuine need.

Those somewhat more liberal theologically were not averse to explicit evangelism if the subject were initiated by the counselee, but they tended to emphasize how the counseling relationship itself could express God's gracious acceptance, whether or not actual words about Christ were ever stated. There was an: "implicit evangel in psychotherapy. . . . The psychotherapist does not have to state explicitly, 'Believe in the Lord Jesus and you will be saved.' . . . The message of the gospel is carried by the grace with which the therapist treats his/her client and by the implicit value system of the therapist."[71] The counseling relationship itself could incarnate wordless grace and become a vehicle of God's gracious restoration of people.

But though the psychotherapists thought that the "grace of God" had to condition counseling either explicitly or implicitly, they did not think that Adams did justice to God's grace. The most pungent, even outraged, criticisms of Adams came because his strong emphasis on changed behavior, when combined with his exhortational, didactic, and confrontive style, added up to a denial of God's gift to sinners. This was a biblical and theological criticism of Adams through and through.[72]

Nouthetic counseling had the ring of what was anathema to Protestants: "shape up your behavior, and then you'll be right with God and your conscience will be at peace." Such "legalism" was the ultimate Protestant heresy. Both Adams's content and methods seemed to deny the grace of Christ as that which mediated peace with God, balm for the conscience, and loving human relationships. Criticism of Adams on this point occurred across the spectrum: from Larry Crabb, the most conservative of the conservative Protestant psychotherapists, to Harold Ellens, the most liberal. Adams was charged with promoting and incarnating legalistic "Phariseeism" that made relationship to God a matter of self-effort, conditional upon performing religious acts.[73] He laid burdens on his counselees, pressuring them with moral demands; when they succeeded, it was joyless moralism; when they failed, he scolded them for their faults, domineering them into obedience.[74] Adams's suc-

cessful counselees, because they had only made superficial alterations in behavior, ran the danger of a "pharisaical self-righteousness."[75] His didactic and hortatory style, by focusing so heavily on the production of concrete behavioral changes, promoted a "legalistic, works-oriented system of motivation"[76] rather than an "identity morality based in Christ."[77]

Such theological errors had clinical implications. When Adams accepted the counselee's guilt feelings at face value, as denoting real guilt before God, he opened himself "to the charge of promoting (or at least not working to lessen) harsh, punitive, and even neurotic attitudes toward the self."[78] When Adams claimed that depressed counselees would begin to feel better when they began to behave better, critics were outraged. The "most serious weakness" of nouthetic counseling lay in its "assumption that the resolution of guilt feelings comes through a combination of confession of one's failures or sins and improved behavior."[79] This flew in the face of the essential conservative Protestant message: "The Bible teaches that full freedom from guilt comes solely through the forgiveness afforded us by Christ's atonement."[80] Adams's tendency to "mix changed behavior and Christ's atoning work is not new in the history of Christianity. It was the problem in the church at Galatia."[81]

Adams had reacted against the permissive, "antinomian," therapeutic ethic characteristic of both modern psychotherapy and modernist Protestant theology—the "irresponsibility ethic" per Szasz. He claimed that he emphasized a different, often neglected aspect of grace, the inworked power of grace to change practical lifestyles. But in the eyes of his critics, this high degree of attention to behavioral alteration, to getting counselees to obey God's published law, fatally ignored that the gift of grace came to sinners irrespective of their failings.

5. Adams's insistence on the primacy of the preacher-as-authoritative-counselor was problematic

Adams and the evangelical psychotherapists agreed that their churches' counseling ministries—whether pastoral or lay—had been largely unorganized, incompetent, and ineffectual. They disagreed about the solution. Nouthetic counseling offered busy pastors of local churches a rapid and directive form of counseling that promised to solve the vast majority of counseling problems in six to twelve weeks or less. Under newly competent pastoral leadership, laypeople could also be trained to help one another resolve problems in daily living. Such exclusively churchly counseling raised two sets of objections from psychotherapists. First, *how* should counseling be done? Moral confrontation was not as central as Adams made it. Adams's model, tailored to the time constraints on busy preachers and to their habits of authoritative declamation, easily degenerated into authoritarian counseling. Second, *who* should do counseling? Both halves of nouthetic counseling's dual emphasis—the pastor as the defined professional and the development of deprofessionalized laycounseling—eliminated the well-trained, licensed, evangelical mental health professional. We will look at these methodological and professional issues in turn.

First, Adams's nouthetic confrontation seemed authoritarian. This was of a piece with other criticisms noted throughout this chapter. Because Adams's entire model homed in on habitual behavioral sins, his critics thought that what he purported to be "irenically direct, biblically authoritative consultation" in fact proved aggressive, domineering, and judgmental. Psychotherapists usually agreed that timely and appropriate confrontation was one necessary tool in counseling.[82] They noted that "authoritative answers and direct advice" were appreciated in numerous societies— "Adams's nouthetic counseling approach would seem appropriate in such a culture"—though it was more problematic in American society, where "the counselor is expected to take a nonauthoritarian, nondirective, supportive role in which he relates to the counselee on a more or less egalitarian basis.[83] But Adams neither confronted the right way nor did he use many other methods appropriate to helpful counseling.

Adams's manner of confrontation was defective as a therapeutic modality. Confrontation might be an "easy method" for pastors to learn, but it was also a method easy to abuse.[84] One of the milder criticisms noted that nouthetic counseling showed "a strong similarity to legal counseling—i.e., it is directive, gives advice, and imparts information."[85] More pointedly Adams sounded "remarkably similar to a parent lecturing an adolescent."[86] The strongest reactions expressed shock: "I cannot believe that nouthetic counseling consists exclusively in the kind of legalistic confrontation and theological third degree which project themselves to the reader from the pages of *Competent to Counsel*."[87] The emphasis on pastoral authority and prophetic exhortation placed the counselor in a role that critics perceived as intrinsically authoritarian: "[It] carries a high risk of rejecting the one being counseled. . . . [It] makes it difficult for the counselor to show respect for the one being helped. . . . At the very least, the nouthetic emphasis places the counselor in a dominant position requiring the counselee to be submissive. . . . An attitude that precludes a listening ear or support as the counselee tries to come to grips with sinful behavior unduly elevates the counselor and lowers the counselee."[88] Adams's style was "coercive," and his counselees "must endure repeated authoritative confrontation."[89] The results were perceived as potentially deleterious to their mental health:

"I would imagine that those who find it difficult to change rapidly do not stay with Jay Adams in counseling and are seen by him, not as failures in his theory or method, but rather as people who are in deep rebellion or sin. It goes without saying that this may be damaging to such individuals."[90] Moralistic confrontation slid easily into tyranny in the eyes of Adams's critics.

Psychologists again mustered biblical and theological arguments to substantiate these pragmatic, therapeutic concerns. Adams had "magnified [*noutheteo*] out of its context into a catchword for condemnation."[91] When his polemic against Rogerianism explicitly denied the counselor's need to empathize with those counseled, it ran contrary both to Jesus' own example and to numerous Bible texts: "Some nouthetic teachings are difficult to reconcile with Paul's call to restore the sinner gently (Galatians 6:1)."[92] Adams's theological fathers could again be drawn into the battle. B.B. Warfield was cited for pointing out that "the emotion most often attributed to Jesus Christ is that of compassion, an internal movement of pity springing from the heart."[93]

Not only was Adams harsh in the way he confronted, but he failed to utilize the range of modalities necessary to balanced and effective counseling. Critics particularly noted the lack of emphasis on love, support, compassion, and patience. Adams's archetypal counselor seemed brisk, matter-of-fact, commanding, and impatient. This, too, was pointedly a failure against the standard of the Bible. No biblical personage either modeled or taught such an unsympathetic, businesslike authority. Adams had forced his system onto the Scriptures, running roughshod over whatever did not comport with the confrontive, didactic, behavior-oriented style that he favored. This theoretical failure led to many counseling failures. Adams failed to really understand people because he insufficiently attended to their life experiences. Nouthetic counseling practice had a moral strenuousness that could prove heartless and impatient.

The psychologists saw Scripture exemplifying a multiplicity of styles of ministry, without mandating one style. David Carlson proposed a threefold model of counseling styles—"prophetic-confrontational, pastoral-conversational, and priestly-confessional"—and described Adams as falling exclusively within the first mode.[94] Carlson was often cited by other critics for his description of the mix of styles evident in the Bible.[95] This mix corresponded to the different emphases one could observe in the psychotherapies. Adams's confrontational model exhibited the "prophetic" mode, not unlike Albert Ellis or O.H. Mowrer, whereas the Rogerian kindness and support typical of much evangelical psychotherapy expressed "priestly" forms of ministry.[96] Christian psychologists saw counseling as an activity where moral judgment and explicit guidance were secondary and occasional rather than predominant.

Criticism frequently turned on Adams's choice of the word *noutheteo* (confront, admonish, pointedly personal counsel aiming to solve a problem) rather than the word *parakaleo* (a broader semantic field, including the directiveness of *noutheteo*, but also embracing encouragement, help, and comfort) to summarize the Bible's approach to counseling.[97] While Adams's use of *noutheteo* was reasonable for some aspects of pastoral counseling, as a synopsis of counseling it ignored too much.[98] This lexical argument buttressed the charge that Adams had utterly neglected the more tender aspects of human relationship in counseling: he was all confrontation and no comfort, all directiveness and no supportiveness.[99] "At times one is 'weeping with those who weep,' 'bearing another's burden,' and at times one is confronting. Jay Adams focuses only on the latter and there is little drawing alongside to comfort and console."[100] Counseling became private preaching—and preaching with a moralistic flavor.[101] Nouthetic counselors were problem solvers and mechanics tinkering with behavior. Such "nonrelational" truth offended what psychotherapists saw in their Bibles: "change takes place when *truth is presented in relationship*."[102] The psychotherapists differentiated themselves from Adams by giving examples of what they meant in both the confrontation and the caring dimensions.[103] Adams's "monolithically directive" approach had taken one strand of biblical truth—and exaggerated it.[104] Again, integrationist psychotherapy aimed to strike the biblical balance.

Adams's biases against Carl Rogers—and for Mowrer—partly explained the imbalance in his model. Therapists often agreed with Adams's criticism of stereotypical Rogerianism: "A focus on relationship without an equally insistent focus on truth results in undirected involvement."[105] But the "therapeutic triad" popularized by Carl Rogers—accurate empathy, nonpossessive warmth, and genuineness—embodied a profound insight into interpersonal relations.[106] Whatever the failings of Rogers's overly optimistic view of human nature, Adams's reactive dismissal of therapeutic kindness had created a monstrous distortion in his counseling methodology, obviating discussion of kindness, humility, genuineness, and understanding.[107] Adaptation to the busy pastor's schedule and habits of proclamation had cost the patience needed to rebuild disintegrated lives. Nouthetic counseling was widely perceived as proceeding with a belligerent set to the counselor's jaw.

Though Adams claimed that a wide range of counselor responses was possible, his developed arguments and case studies demonstrated little if any methodological flexibility. One critic who had conversed with Adams commented, "[Adams] remarked during a course attended by one of the present authors in 1974 that the nouthetic counselor is free to be Rogerian or nondirective when he desires, or to use *any* technique not inconsis-

tent with Biblical presuppositions."[108] Critics who wished to grant Adams a certain benefit of the doubt had to rely on such hearsay: "I've heard that [Adams] overstates his case as his way of arguing, that he probably isn't as bombarding in a counseling session as the book implies."[109] But critics found little evidence of psychotherapeutic competency in Adams's books. One commented, "While I am happy to credit rumors of Adams's sensitivity and skill as a personal counselor, they do not justify the publication of such dangerous half-truths as are contained in *Competent to Counsel*."[110]

Nouthetic counselors and evangelical psychotherapists clashed over the methodological paradigm. Did strugglers primarily need truth—delivered by teaching, reproof, exhortation, and modeling—to inform and inspire new choices? Or did they primarily need love that patiently and acceptingly probed persons and their histories in pursuit of understanding? Was "counseling" largely the intrusion of counsel or the opportunity for self-exploration in a context of kindness? The divergent answers to these methodological questions mapped onto divergent definitions of the professional context appropriate for delivering cures to the soul.

Adams had insisted that problems in living could be solved by the preacher-as-counselor and by church-based laycounseling. He had pointedly excluded the "self-appointed caste of so-called professionals" by both reprofessionalizing and deprofessionalizing the counseling field. Unsurprisingly, the evangelical psychotherapists reacted strongly to Adams's attempt to invalidate their existence.

For the psychotherapists, the historical neglect, ignorance, blundering, and impotence of the pastorate comprised only part of the problem. The seminary training and professional habits of busy preachers could never suit them for competencies needed for the time-intensive probing and tolerance of face-to-face counseling. Pastors could not possibly meet counseling needs, given the magnitude and diversity of other demands on their time, and given the built-in limitations of their generalist education. Similarly, laypeople lacked the skills, time, and disinterested point of view necessary for effective psychotherapy. A more competent pastorate and a more caring church community, desirable as these were, would still necessitate a cadre of well-trained, professional psychotherapists to serve the mental health needs of the church. They had obtained the requisite specialized education in the modern psychotherapies. They possessed legitimating licensure with the state boards of the psychotherapeutic professions. Adams's assertion that "a seminary education is the best preparation for counseling skill" was laughable; after all, his own story bore witness to the contrary.

Most psychotherapists, as licensed professionals, simply disagreed with Adams's ecclesiasticism. Professional psychotherapy was simply a valid activity that had been historically neglected by evangelicals. Like medicine, counseling practice might legitimately function separate from the direct oversight of the pastoral ministry. Most psychotherapists saw sanctification and psychological healing as addressing different problems, aiming for different ends, employing different means, and facilitated by different personnel. Even psychologists who agreed with Adams diagnostically, disagreed with the professional implications Adams drew: "[There is] one basic type of problem [that counseling addresses] but . . . two separate roles in the treatment of this problem. Mental health professionals and clergy are viewed as equally valid, functionally equivalent alternative roles, both groups being appropriately involved in the treatment of the one basic problem experienced by people."[111] Adams's normative sociology of the helping professions was simply incredible.

Adams's point that pastors had the Bible's mandate for counseling ministry and, hence, that

psychotherapeutic "ministers" were extraecclesiastical irregulars, was actually never discussed directly. Fuller Seminary's James Oakland came closest, noting without comment, "Probably nowhere is this difference in mentality more evident than in Adams's insistence that it is *ministers* who are the most competent to counsel—and that by virtue of their theological training."[112] But even Oakland concentrated on the issues of competency and training, not on the issue of "ordination" and professional oversight that so preoccupied Adams as a creedal, Presbyterian ecclesiastic. In their professional self-justification, the psychotherapists could hardly cite chapter and verse from a book addressed to people in Ancient Near Eastern and Mediterranean cultures. But they did adduce a series of pragmatic arguments that contested Adams's claim that "the only legitimate career counselor is a minister."[113] First, they presented their professional credentials and the personal sincerity of their evangelical commitments. Their faith was indubitable and their achieved status was self-evident within the wider culture; that status was increasingly transferable into the evangelical churches.[114] Second, the relative incompetence of pastors provided prima facie legitimation for the expertise of state-licensed psychologists.[115] To shift responsibility from skilled specialists to unskilled generalists was unconscionable. Third, Adams's view barred women from careers in counseling because they could not generally be ordained in evangelical denominations. Adams's writing portrayed women frequently but always as the recipients of counseling, never as those doing counseling. But many psychotherapists and professors of psychology were women, as were over half the students at graduate schools in psychology, and many of these women were single career women: "Entry into the mental health field has been perceived as the most direct route toward career in ministry for women who have had no access to professional service within their conservative church bodies."[116] Adams would deny their professional existence. Fourth, Adams would bar evangelicals from the ranks of the mental health professions, as if it were an immoral profession. Such a notion represented a regression to the fundamentalistic isolation from the "worldly" environing culture.[117] Finally, Adams's proposal would prevent troubled people unwilling to come to a minister from receiving Christian counseling. Instead, the more general diffusion of evangelicals into the counseling professions would bring Christian benefits to many who might otherwise miss them.[118]

Psychotherapists not only opposed the ecclesiasticism of Adams's view of professions but also expressed concerns about the widespread deprofessionalized counseling that he, along with other "popularizers," promoted.[119] They expressed some professional anxiety about the success of popularizers untrained in psychology who offered simplistic self-help. While noting that people were often helped by informal counseling, and that community resources should complement professional practice, they argued that the psychotherapists ought to do their own popularizing, and ought to develop laycounseling models that could reflect psychological expertise. Several of the more theologically conservative psychotherapists created laycounseling programs for churches.[120] Crabb commented: "We must stop thinking of counseling as a professional activity that belongs to psychologists and psychiatrists and begin to realize that the work of counseling represents one more means through which Christians can grow and unbelievers can hear the gospel. If, as I maintain, counseling is basically the skillful application of biblical truth to individual lives, then obviously it belongs to the church."[121] Several of the widely recognized laycounseling programs were syntheses of nouthetic counseling and other

models. Nouthetic counseling could be domesticated, if stripped of its comprehensive and professional claims. Larry Crabb incorporated nouthetic counseling structurally as his midlevel counseling in churches, defining pastors as subordinate counselors. Pastors, along with elders, small-group leaders, and other Bible-trained persons, would offer teaching, exhortation, and practical advice.[122] Adams had written "a great deal of helpful material" for training such counselors.[123] Gary Collins routinely included nouthetic counseling as one approach to "people-helping," an item on a menu of options in his eclectic compendium of counseling resources for local churches.[124] Siang-Yang Tan conflated theoretical and methodological elements from Adams, Crabb, and Collins into a cognitive-behavioral approach adaptable for a counselor training program in local churches.[125] If nouthetic counseling were trimmed of its polemicism and professional claims, then pastors and laypersons might employ it to usefully strengthen the conservative Protestant churches so that only the more difficult cases needed to be treated by professional counselors.

6. Though Adams made telling criticisms, his interaction with the secular psychologies was uninformed, tendentious, and perhaps even duplicitous

Many evangelical psychotherapists appreciated Adams's criticisms of the secular psychologies, and even of their own attempts to integrate faith with those psychologies. These psychologists, like Adams, had been influenced by modern epistemologies stressing the value-laden character of psychological observation and theorizing. They were wary of those things that the culture presented as neutral and objective truth. "What we gratuitously refer to as the truths or findings of psychology are really a mixture of data and personal interpretation. . . . Psychology's findings typically represent *interpreted data* and therefore reflect to some degree a wrong set of presuppositions. . . . We must therefore move with extreme caution in accepting the conclusions of secular psychology into our Christian thinking. We may be absorbing ideas which subtly contradict our biblical position."[126] Many evangelicals besides Adams thought that "psychology has stood, in its popular form, as *the* major secular religion of our culture."[127] When closely examined, the various secular psychologies were "really alternative spiritualities" that "sound daily in our ears and bid to form us in their image," an image fundamentally at odds with the goals of reshaping people into the image of Christ.[128] Adams's "protest against psychology" was well-founded because "modern psychology has been built on presuppositions which often are in direct conflict with the fundamental assumptions of Christianity," and he was applauded "for identifying disguised religious aspects of psychological theory."[129]

Many psychologists, like Adams, noted that the entire counseling endeavor needed rehabilitation in the light of their conservative Protestant orthodoxy, that their faith might replace the "false religion of professional psychotherapy" with true religion:[130] "We agree with Christian critics of psychology such as Jay Adams who say that the counseling processes are of such a nature that they must be thoroughly reconceptualized from a biblical foundation to lay claim to the adjective 'Christian.'"[131] Indeed, such reconceptualization lay precisely at the heart of their integrationist agenda. The integrationist program of dialogue with the psychologies held out greater hope of success, for, if conducted rightly, it would provide evangelicals with:

> our own psychology, a psychology not
> derivative of the secular ones but neverthe-

less formulated explicitly in conversation with them. . . . The dialogue of Christians with psychology has been less than full because we have been held captive by the alien spirits, have not drawn with full decisiveness on the rich resources available within our tradition for understanding persons, their problems, and their well-being. And as a result we have not had much of our own to contribute to the conversation with non-Christian psychologies.[132]

A successful "conversation" with the psychologies would issue in a distinctly evangelical point of view on the soul's ailments and cures of the soul.

The sentiments quoted above represented the opinions of more theologically conservative evangelical psychologists: Collins, Crabb, and the Wheaton College psychologists (Benner, Jones, Butman, and Roberts). More moderate evangelicals tended to describe psychology and theology as more in parity. They were either two discrete disciplines that studied one or the other of "God's two books" to mutually stimulate one another (e.g., the Rosemead psychologists), or they were parallel to one another with little disciplinary overlap (some academic psychologists such as David Meyer and Malcolm Jeeves). More liberal evangelicals (e.g., Ellens of CAPS and Fuller Seminary psychologists such as Maloney and Weber) criticized statements such as those in the previous paragraphs, viewing them as recurrences of theological imperialism, overly hostile to psychology, and tending in Jay Adams's direction.[133] On the whole, however, more liberal or moderate evangelicals spoke for a small academic and professional elite. The more conservative evangelicals enjoyed greater popularity with the mass of psychotherapeutic practitioners.

The more conservative psychotherapists even expressed appreciation for Adams's criticisms of themselves, taking it as a salutary corrective to the drift toward secular psychology that they saw in their field. Christians doing integration "have deserved much of the criticism they have received from the psychology bashers."[134] Adams was right that "much of what we call Christian counseling today involves little more than taking these secular approaches and sprinkling them with a few Bible verses."[135] Such criticisms could call the integration movement back to its religious commitments: "Adams argues convincingly that this 'baptizing of secular . . . views, which has frequently characterized much that has been called Christian counseling, must be rejected. Instead, Christians must get back to these views and understand their basic antichristian presuppositions.' . . . For many the psychological cart has come before the theological horse."[136] Even more liberal evangelicals could express guarded appreciation for the attack they had received. One of the board members of CAPS commented: "When I read *Competent to Counsel* I filled it with so many red ink underlinings and marginalia that I had to buy a second copy. I disagreed with everything Adams had to say positively. But he was right about one thing. When I went into the counseling office, the fact that I was a Christian did not make much of a difference between what I did and what any secular psychotherapist did. I've tried to remedy that ever since."[137] The evangelical psychologists might have appreciated some of Adams's observations, but they certainly did not draw his conclusions. As we have seen, they found manifold defects in Adams's positive model, disqualifying it from consideration as *the* biblical approach, and they never viewed the psychotherapy professions as an illegitimate secular pastorate. Adams's attack on psychology labored under three major handicaps: it was ignorant, unfair, and unreflective.

First, Adams misunderstood the theorists he spoke about. Lacking graduate training in psychology, his analysis of psychology was burdened with ignorance. Critics noted that he had received

his PhD in speech and that he had experienced only a summer internship with Mowrer in psychiatric hospitals.[138] They also noted the absence of primary source citations of leading psychologists and Adams's recourse to secondary sources (e.g., Szasz and Mowrer) for his interpretation of Freud, Rogers, and others.[139] A few of the more theologically conservative psychologists thought him "familiar with the contemporary psychological literature," and that "for the most part Dr. Adams demonstrates a scholarly mastery of the theories and techniques of non-Christian psychiatry and psychology."[140] But the more common view was that as one untrained and unread in the field, "he betrays little appreciation and only superficial knowledge of modern schools of psychology."[141] He offered ignorant, simplistic, and distorted comments, exhibiting "naiveté" about both psychological theories and clinical realities.[142] John Carter, for example, cited Adams's reference to "Carl Rogers and other Freudians" as a particularly egregious example of Adams's ignorance.[143]

Second, Adams's use of "Freud, Rogers, and Skinner" as icons was unfair. His caricatures might prove memorable and persuasive to his intended audience, but they were maddening to those familiar with theoretical positions, who practiced different habits of discourse, who expected qualified assessments of theories. In the mildest criticism, Adams's "lack of formal training in psychology has led him to oversimplify."[144] More pointedly, he created a "gross misrepresentation" of psychologists.[145] Adams failed to communicate recognizable versions of what Sigmund Freud, Carl Rogers, and B. F. Skinner actually taught, and did gross injustice to those Christian psychologists who sought to appropriate constructive theoretical and therapeutic elements. Adams's overstated reaction against the pervading psychological culture sacrificed intellectual credibility, degenerating into posturing and belligerency.

Third, both Adams's ignorance and unfairness arose from an identifiable source. He was indebted to Mowrer far more profoundly than he acknowledged. Adams might disclaim Mowrer's influence as nothing more than clearing the ground of Freudian influences. But to critics who read Mowrer and Adams side by side, it was evident that the entire structure of Adams's therapy was Mowrerian. "*Competent to Counsel* cannot be read by those who have read Mowrer's *Crisis in Psychiatry and Religion* and *The New Group Therapy* without perceiving Mowrer's influence."[146] That influence pervaded Adams's thought: an unwarranted bias against "Freud" and "Rogers" and toward moralistic therapists; a behavioral definition of human functioning, strongly emphasizing the biological, while neglecting the psychological and social dimensions of human experience; a truncated version of both the gospel and counseling, reducing such to techniques for altering behavior by dehabituation and rehabituation; and an acceptance of guilt feelings at face value as the "voice of God" in the soul; an authoritarian style that minimized the counseling relationship; a short-term, interventive model of practice that employed standard directive techniques such as role-play, modeling, group pressure, and homework.[147] He had learned all these from Mowrer, not the Bible. He had then read the Bible in their light. For example, "Adams's strong emphasis on behavior and confrontation appears to have come directly from Mowrer and to have blinded Adams to the Scriptures' emphasis on the inner aspects of man and sin."[148]

Adams might deny Mowrer's pervasive influence, but that only made him a crypto-disciple, rather than an open disciple; he "brings secular principles through the back door."[149] The loud critic of integrationists was himself an integrationist, who simply could not or would not see and admit what was obvious to the psychologists who read him. He was guilty of the same "Christianiz-ing" or recycling of secular theories that he found so culpable in others. To accuse others of being influenced by secular psychologists, as if he alone remained biblically pure, was hypocritical.[150] In the opinion of critics, this state of affairs arose either because Adams was unreflective, genuinely unaware of his intellectual debts, or because he was dishonest, consciously concealing the origins of many of the most distinctive elements of his counseling model. In the most charitable assessments, Adams had accepted Mowrer "uncritically."[151] Somewhat more suspicious, one critic thought Adams "inadequately reflective" in that "the language and ideas of Mowrer, Glasser, and Szasz are as unconcealed as they are unacknowledged."[152] The most dubious wondered, "Is Adams duplicitous? He denies that his theory builds on Mowrer when its essential structure is Mowrer. He suggests he went to the Bible, and voilà. Does he really believe that?"[153]

The psychologists perceived the same sort of ironic affinity between Adams and a broad class of psychotherapies: moralistic, behavioral, cognitive-behavioral. They noted conceptual and methodological similarities between Adams and B. F. Skinner, William Glasser, Alfred Adler, and Albert Ellis, again correspondences Adams would not acknowledge.[154] In particular, Adams's kinship with behavioristic theories was kinship with an unpopular species of psychology. Most evangelical psychologists were critical of behavioral psychology because they found its analysis of the human condition superficial and scientistic.[155] They were typically more interested in the implications of psychodynamic, cognitive, and humanistic psychologies for understanding and helping people.

Adams might be commended for his perceptiveness and for communicating his concerns. But he was wrong to claim—in fact, to proclaim, in strident tones—that his was *the* biblical answer to a briar-patch of thorny intellectual, historical, social, and practical problems. He was wrong to announce—in fact, to pronounce, sententiously—that all others in the field were benighted. The very manner of Adams's proclamation and pronouncement generated a final set of criticisms.

7. Adams's manner was obstreperous

Adams's radical ideas and frank bid for jurisdictional authority could not help but produce controversy with the profession competing for cultural authority over conservative Protestant problems in living. But there is no doubt that his manner aggravated controversy into hostility. He would not grant the psychotherapists even a modicum of professional respect; they were interlopers, a pseudoprofession. The evangelical psychologists (and other readers, both pastors and laity) were frequently repelled by the stinging tone and totalitarian message of Adams's rhetoric. They described him in terms such as belligerent, brash, abrasive, bombastic, argumentative, strident, polarizing, angry.[156] CtC was a "nasty book. I was appalled by the hostile shots, by the way Adams blasted well-meaning Christians."[157] In the eyes of many readers, Adams's rhetoric crossed a line and became the message itself: "He confuses opinion for fact (as in his treatment of various psychologies) and derision for argument (as in his treatment of various therapies)."[158] Adams claimed that his purposes—"awakening a sleepy church to dangers all about"—warranted his style, that critics confused "clarity and conviction" with brashness.[159] But, such pleading aside, what he termed clear convictions were widely perceived as censorious, divisive, and arrogant.

Several critics found their temptation to sympathize with Adams weakened by the vehemence of his rhetoric. They thought that Adams harmed his own cause:

Unfortunately, many who could learn from Adams will not do so because his angry style which blasts clinical and counseling psychology is so distracting.[160]

Adams also has a tendency to attack psychological writers—Christian and non-Christian alike—in an unkind, name-calling manner. This undermines some of his arguments; what he says might be taken more seriously if it were presented more graciously.[161]

Even a favorable reviewer found it objectionable that Adams forced readers to choose either "for or against nouthetic counseling . . . : If accepted, Adams becomes the test for truth; if rejected, valuable knowledge and tools can be lost because the entire approach is rejected. . . . [This] does not give an acceptable choice."[162]

Several other aspects of his intellectual style compounded the offensiveness of Adams's tone. He frequently claimed novel insight while dismissing all other thinkers as benighted, being guilty of "infuriating oversimplifications and claims, as unsupported as they are arrogant."[163] He had a penchant for citing his own books: "He peppers both text and footnotes with promotional references to the many other books he has authored."[164] He offered no empirical substantiation for repeated claims of "significant and rapid success in counseling."[165] The grating effect of Adams's style compounded the offense generated by his concepts.

Some psychologists placed a psychological interpretation on Adams's mode of counseling and polemics. Sometimes the psychology they applied was common-sense: "I think Jay Adams's approach to counseling is more a reflection of Jay Adams's personality than anything else. He tends to be a somewhat confrontational type guy, and he's a confrontational counselor."[166] Other times the interpretation carried heavier theoretical freight. Anti-psychology writers (Adams was named in the context) were "living out their own personal psychology through their writings." Such conservative Protestants opposed psychodynamic psychology for psychodynamic reasons: unconscious repression, fears, and projection of unpleasant psychic contents onto perceived enemies, and so forth.[167] In this turf war, each side gave back in its own idiom: the evangelical psychotherapists acted as heretical teachers; nouthetic counselors suffered from a personality disorder.

The psychologists could give back as they had received: "The 'anti-psychology industry' is once again sharpening its knives" and was intent on "shooting the wounded" rather than helping people.[168] "Jay Adams" became iconic, a symbolic resource that served a polemical function, analogous to Adams's "Freud, Rogers, and Skinner" and "integrationist." "Adams-bashing" was a routine activity at conventions of the Christian Association for Psychological Studies and in graduate school classrooms at Rosemead, Fuller, and Wheaton.[169] Harold Ellens, who reviewed scores of books for the *Journal of Psychology and Christianity* in the 1980s, gave one of Adams's books his shortest review on record: "Irresponsible and vilifying garbage, like most of the rest of his stuff. Iconoclastic, superficial, biblicistic. Unworthy [of] a man of Reformed Tradition."[170] The temptation to intemperate language was no respecter of parties to jurisdictional conflict.

Larry Crabb, who came the closest to Adams in both perceptions and commitments, transparently alluded to Adams's nouthetic counseling in the following comment:

> One [monstrous danger] is the ongoing and strengthened tendency to treat people like dogs who can be trained to obey without offering more than the tokens of relationship. The truth of *biblical sufficiency* (a position that teaches that the answers to all of life's non-physical problems can

be found in Scripture) has been corrupted into an ugly perversion that permits us to use the Bible as a bludgeon to coerce conformity. Sin is often defined as nothing more than clear transgressions of understood rules. "Biblical" counseling, in some circles, has become a matter of looking for patterns of behavioral irresponsibility, finding passages that condemn those patterns and command better ones, and then requiring people to do what they should under threat of judgment.

> Directing hurting people to the Word of God and to prayer and to Christ, when done in this way, actually leads people away from the message of God's Word (that we are people who, because of His mercy, can enjoy a relationship with Him that will prompt obedience). This method robs prayer of its relational dimension and makes it more like filling out a form for a bureaucrat with a request for aid. It makes Christ into more a Gestapo commander than a bridegroom.

> This trend, stubbornly present in so many fundamentalist circles, is awful. . . . [It] requires us to deaden our souls, to kill all passion except anger and discipline. We become shallow, rigid people who remain, at best, warmly courteous but incapable of intimacy. . . . [It] makes too little of our hurt. . . . [It is a] dog-theology that teaches us to fetch for the master to avoid the stick and win a biscuit.[171]

This passage distills most of the leading criticisms of Adams and his disciples. With the comment on biblical sufficiency Crabb alluded to his epistemological agreement with Adams, that there were only organic and moral problems, and that Scripture addressed the latter comprehensively. But the other major charges against Adams and his kind were assembled into denunciation: the definition of sin as conscious behavior; the neglect of the counselee's experience of hurt; legalistic solutions that, abandoning the love of God, coerced behavioral compliance; a hostile and confrontive counseling style that deemphasized—because it was incapable of—loving, patient relationships; the degrading affinity with behaviorism. "Jay Adams" had become a symbolic resource, an icon. Jay Adams's followers loved him; his opponents loved to hate him.

The issues of jurisdictional conflict appeared sans ideological garb in the "Adams-bashing" that mirrored Adams's own belligerence and intransigence. Some integrationists commented on the symmetry of mutual demonization so characteristic of this no-holds-barred, our-opponents-are-quacks jurisdictional warfare among coreligionists. Eric Johnson urged readers of the *Journal of Psychology and Theology* to listen to Adams and other critics of the evangelical psychology program, despite the fact that "with their rhetoric they have helped to make dialogue with their Christian brothers and sisters very difficult." Johnson was persuaded "that we as Christian psychologists have not listened carefully enough to these critics. (Far more typical is the tendency for us to engage in 'Adams-bashing'.) This group has some legitimate concerns about contemporary psychology that we ignore to our peril."[172] Gary Collins was perhaps the most eloquent in insisting that psychologists attempt to respond peaceably to their warlike coreligionists. He thought that the purveyors of "vicious or irrational" criticism appeared to be "trouble makers and some may be troubled."[173] But Collins also thought that some psychologists responded to criticism with "the same hostility, character assassination, and cynicism." Even in an increasingly polarized environment, Collins himself attempted to avoid "endless, fruitless arguments," to learn from the "kernel of truth" in criticisms, and to respect some critics as "thoughtful, sensitive, knowledgeable, caring people whose criticisms are valid and well worth heeding."[174]

This was a head-on jurisdictional conflict, and such warfare takes many forms: conceding and preempting strong points, incorporating another's point of view as a subordinate piece of one's own more comprehensive system, blunt disagreement, iconic representation. It was an unusual interprofessional conflict, in that each group was legitimated by a different set of deep-seated cultural values, and yet both groups shared one of those sets of values. References to what the Bible was purported to teach recurred at almost every point because it was a jurisdictional conflict between evangelical coreligionists. Disagreements with Adams came in a different mode when made by nonevangelicals.

8. The response to Adams by mainline protestants

As we saw earlier, the mainline churches were decades ahead of the conservative Protestant churches in developing counseling services, in interacting with the secular psychologies, and in constructing practical theologies of counseling.[175] Mainline Protestant pastoral counselors were on occasion curious about Adams, though he posed no jurisdictional threat and thus played only a small role in their ongoing professional conversation. In assessing Adams, they largely replicated both the criticisms and guarded appreciation of Adams expressed by evangelicals, though the discussion was less detailed, the appreciation more perfunctory, the criticism more dismissive, and the overall emphasis somewhat different. That difference in emphasis arose from several characteristics of the sociocultural location that conditioned their gaze.

First, they were pastors, not evangelicals seeking legitimation as psychotherapists. Their professional existence was not at stake. In contrast, the evangelical psychotherapists had to establish and defend their very right to exist, both as psychotherapists in church settings and as evangelicals in mental health settings. Adams distinctly threatened evangelical psychotherapists in the church setting because they lacked a self-evident ground for professional existence within that biblicistic community. But as pastors, the pastoral counselors were secure in their mainline churches. In fact, pastoral theologians, through their interactions with the modern psychologies and psychological professions, had played a major role in defining the culture of mainline Protestantism throughout the twentieth century.

Second, the pastoral counselors were liberal Protestants with respect to the Bible and theology, not conservatives. Adams's biblicistic appeals represented no threat, for by definition they foreswore the "bibliolatry" of conservative Protestants. Evangelicals were vulnerable because they shared Adams's core theological commitments, and professed to operate within the same set of Bible-believing assumptions. As modernist Protestants, however, the pastoral counselors could easily dismiss Adams's starting point, as well as the system that he built upon it.

Third, the pastoral counselors existed within the ecclesiastical subculture of mainline Protestant denominations and seminaries. Adams was no social threat because there was little if any overlap of clientele. But the evangelical psychotherapists and Adams coexisted in the conservative Protestant subculture, serving the same constituency. As mainline churchmen, the pastoral counselors' social existence was untouched by the turmoil Adams produced.

Finally, the professional history of the mainline pastoral counselors contained a signal achievement. They had overcome the long-standing temptation for pastors to cast themselves in the role of moral instructor, accomplishing a radical redefinition of the pastoral role into that of therapeutic facilitator. Adams was easy to categorize and dismiss on the basis of their own history. His model was simply a recrudescence of theological and pastoral themes that had passed out of fashion over the previous century. The pastoral counselors' own defining achievement had eclipsed the point of view Adams was attempting to reassert. But at the time when Adams was ascendant the evangelical psychotherapists had yet to achieve anything distinctive, besides creating "Christianized versions of every secular therapy"[176] and gaining an uncertain foothold in educational institutions. The pastoral counseling movement, in contrast, had accomplished something that immunized it to his criticisms and proposals.

In fact, from the pastoral counselors' standpoint, the wranglings between Adams and theologically conservative psychotherapists sometimes looked like differences of emphasis within a single counseling movement among biblicistic Protestants. One pastoral theologian criticized Larry Crabb for the same failings as he had criticized Adams—a biblicism that treated the Bible as the Word of God, rather than as an errant human product with no divine inspiration.[177] In a historical review of modern pastoral counseling, Princeton Seminary's Donald Capps viewed Jay Adams and Gary Collins as initiators of a historical phase he termed "Conservative Developments."[178] In Capps's analysis, a distinctive historical phase had begun around 1970 as evangelicals sought to promote the Bible to a central role in counseling. He went on to differentiate matters among evangelicals, however, noting that Collins, Carter, Narramore, and others had not embraced Adams's program of rejecting the psychotherapies in toto, but "are now engaged in the very project that engaged many representatives of the [pastoral counseling movement in the 1940s and 1950s], which is to explore the relationships between theology and contemporary psychology."[179]

Liberal pastoral counselors and nouthetic counselors viewed one another from afar, and relations between them occurred only in print. The evangelical psychotherapists and the mainline pastoral counselors sustained a more ambiguous relationship. Evangelicals who were more conservative theologically and ethically, such as Gary Collins, criticized the pastoral counselors in much the same way as Adams.[180] But those evangelicals who were more liberal theologically and ethically (e.g., Harold Ellens, H. Newton Maloney, Samuel Southard, and Leroy Aden) cooperated with and endorsed mainline pastoral counselors, and often considered themselves part of their tradition.[181] From their side, mainline pastoral counselors could be cordial to moderate and liberal evangelicals. James Lapsley commented that "Carter's careful analysis of the many problems, both biblical and psychological, in Jay Adams's position . . . is the best dissection of Adams's work that I have seen." He looked forward to dialogue with the evangelical psychotherapists: "My hope is that soon the authors may lose their discomfort with some of the rest of us who have been struggling with these issues [the relationship between psychology and theology] for a generation. We can use their hard-nosed respect for truth as they see it."[182]

The social distance between the pastoral counseling movement and Adams was unbridgeable. This was revealed in the way the *Dictionary of Pastoral Care and Counseling*[183] handled nouthetic counseling. The editor, Rodney Hunter, discussed the factors that went into his dictionary's choice of authors. *DPCC* was "broadly inclusive of . . . neo-evangelical forms of conservative Protestantism . . . , those who have a fundamentally positive attitude toward psychology and toward the use of behavioral sciences in ministry." But Adams prompted "some of our most interesting,

challenging editorial discussions": "Where we drew the line was with others like Jay Adams who are hostile to the critical appropriation of psychology and clinical perspectives in ministry in any form and who advocate authoritarian, aggressive forms of care and counseling. Though we have articles *about* those traditions (for example, one on Adams' nouthetic counseling, another on fundamentalist pastoral care), we do not include them as authoritative voices in their own right."[184] The evangelical psychotherapists could operate inside the community of valid discourse, but Adams was outside. In this case, the demarcation registered an ecclesiastical rather than a professional conflict: sectarian and modernist Protestantism still did not mingle.

Like the evangelical psychotherapy movement, the pastoral counseling movement contained a spectrum of positions from more Bible-oriented to more psychology-oriented. Those committed to an agenda of reinjecting the Bible into pastoral care tended to say a few positive things about Adams (e.g., Donald Capps, William Oglesby, and Thomas Oden). The more traditionally liberal were only critical (e.g., Howard Clinebell, Stephen Pattison, and Rodney Hunter). Among the pastoral counselors, only Donald Capps repeatedly and extensively discussed Adams.[185] Other pastoral counselors tended to speak of (or allude to) Adams once briefly, and then never discussed him again.

The general content of both criticisms and commendations repeated many themes we have already discussed, but the flavor was distinctly different. First, pastoral counselors devoted most of their attention to things irrelevant to the evangelical psychotherapists: to the scope of Adams's pastoral program, and to the implications of Adams's conservative Protestant biblicism. Some pastoral theologians expressed carefully qualified appreciation. That Adams had attempted something vast was appreciated in some quarters. Orlo Strunk, who edited the *Journal of Pastoral Care*, commented that:

> [Attempts at a large-scale envisioning of the pastoral counseling project have] been carried out by a relatively small number of participants. Such names as Hiltner, Oates, Johnson, and Adams surface as graphic examples [of those who attempted such]. . . . The prolific works of J. Adams provide a somewhat different vision in that they focus almost exclusively on the powerful and sovereign place of the Bible in the counseling project. . . . Although this perspective has not held a central place in the mainstream pastoral counseling movement, it is surely an example of visionizing interfacing with praxis.[186]

Similarly, Thomas Oden commented that Adams was one of a handful of twentieth-century pastoral theologians who had even attempted to formulate a comprehensive model of pastoral care. But because Adams lacked an ecumenical breadth, his approach was finally inadequate, and would only prove appropriate within a narrow theological and ecclesiastical circle.[187] Adams had attempted to fill an acknowledged vacuum.

Some pastoral counselors regretted the plenum of psychology and vacuum of Bible that characterized their professional theory and practice:

> I can recall reading literally hundreds of verbatim accounts prepared by students in the seminary and ministers in parish and specialized settings. . . . Only rarely are biblical data adduced as a basis for evaluation and revision. This is not said with the intent to be critical of students and ministers. Their learning experiences have, by and large, been informed by the cultural patterns of counseling and therapy, and it is to be expected that these presupposi-

tions would be incorporated in their own attempts to be of help. Most of the widely used books in pastoral counseling are rooted in the behavioral sciences. . . . While the Bible is often cited as supporting the necessity for the cure of souls, it is rare when it is employed to inform process. An exception is the work of Jay Adams, who finds in the Greek word *nouthesia* a basis for behavior modification as the essence of the pastoral counseling task.[188]

Many of the leading mainline pastoral counselors after 1970 had a certain well-hedged appreciation for Adams's attempt to rebiblicize counseling. Their own intellectual program bore certain analogies, as a self-conscious revisionism of the "liberal consensus" of the Rogerian 1940s and 1950s: these "moderates . . . have in common the view that the Bible is more than a resource for pastoral care and counseling. For them, the Bible has a major contribution to make to the very process and goals of pastoral care and counseling."[189] Even one of Adams's sharpest critics noted: "The Bible is essential to Christianity. . . . But the contemporary literature of pastoral care . . . seems to have almost completely avoided considering the Bible. . . . Adams's work . . . corrects the tendency to completely neglect the Bible in pastoral care theory, even if it does this in rather an extreme way."[190] Adams was salutary within an extremely narrow band. He modeled a remarkably comprehensive and coherent vision—though his accomplishment was marginal to the major developments within ecumenical Protestantism. He sounded a needed call back to the Bible—but was himself too biblicistic both in worldview and hermeneutic.

Adams's extremism arose from an easily identifiable, and culpable, source: "he falls for the scripture principle hook, line, and sinker," viewing the Bible as a unique divine revelation and self-evident final authority, not a humanly produced document. Such "bibliolatry . . . chooses to imprison the work of the Spirit in a book."[191] Adams's view of the Bible was fundamentally unacceptable to mainline Protestants. Such a criticism no evangelical psychotherapist would make, by definition.

But the other criticisms of Adams repeated themes that we have already seen, though with a somewhat different emphasis. Like the evangelicals, the pastoral counselors criticized Adams's use of the Bible for being "atomistic" and purporting to find "a verse for every problem" and by constructing "alphabetical lists" of life's problems with appropriate proof texts attached.[192] But their positive alternative was to articulate a well-thought-out hermeneutical philosophy: for example, Adams's moralistic use of Proverbs failed "to take note of the much more fundamental moral vision of the book of Proverbs, its conviction that a unifying moral order inheres in the world of human experience."[193] They also criticized Adams's understanding of human nature for its shallowness. He grotesquely overemphasized behavior, both in diagnosis and treatment, and because he did not attend to the counselee's worldview and patiently reframe it, his counseling was pervasively superficial.[194] Adams's "legalism" came in for hammer blows from Howard Clinebell and others. Clinebell's *Basic Types of Pastoral Counseling* (1966) represented the apex of the genial Rogerian consensus that had dominated pastoral care in the 1940s, '50s, and '60s. In an extensively reworked second edition in 1984, Clinebell criticized Adams's moralism for returning pastoral counseling to "pre-Rogerian abuses." Adams's model chiefly signified an atavistic form of pastoral care, undoing the progress of decades of practical theological labor and casting the minister back into the role of authoritarian moralizer.[195] Adams's relationship to the psychologies also drew atten-

tion. The mainline pastoral counselors could matter-of-factly allude to Adams in mentioning "Hobart Mowrer, William Glasser, and their pastoral followers."[196] As noted above, in the discussion of the *Dictionary of Pastoral Care and Counseling*, the fact that Adams "totally rejected modern psychological theories" put him out of step with a central activity of the pastoral counselors' professional agenda. The psychologies had given both catalyst and content for their achievement of a caring and probing system of pastoral care.[197] Finally, Adams's style was duly noted: "Adams' polemical style and his tendency to misrepresent the views of those he disagrees with has caused many pastoral counselors to dismiss his ideas."[198] Like the conservative conservatives, the conservative liberals tended to view such failings calmly, attempted to listen through the polemics, and treated Adams seriously (e.g., Capps); like the liberal conservatives, the liberal liberals tended to react with a note of rancor, and dismissed Adams out of hand (e.g., Clinebell).

9. Jay Adams? The response of the secular mental health professions

The response of secular psychologists, psychiatrists, and psychotherapists to Adams is easy to summarize. Secular mental health professionals, who served across the spectrum of religious and nonreligious people, rarely ever heard of Jay Adams and nouthetic counseling. Private responses to nouthetic counselors might arise when therapists and conservative Protestant pastors happened to share a particular client, but the secular world rarely commented on biblical counseling.[199] There were no obvious professional battle lines and no structured communication.

Adams did contribute to one secular book, Peter Magaro's *The Construction of Madness*, which assembled widely varying interpretations of "schizophrenia." He earned a footnote in an article orienting mental health professionals to trends in religious counseling: Adams was an exemplar of the few who did not restrict clergy to the minor problems of day-to-day living.[200] In the Philadelphia area, psychologist and *Philadelphia Inquirer* columnist Darrell Sifford wrote a two-part article in the mid-1980s growing out of conversations with several CCEF staff members, and the article captured his strong ambivalence: "The thrust of much of what they said troubled me—not because I personally disagree with it, but because they, as counselors, seem to me to take some positions that are contrary to what generally is considered to be good counseling. One of these positions is that the Bible lays down hard-and-fast rules that are to be followed."[201] The Bible as "God's law" was simply puzzling in the counseling context.

Nowhere were emotions against Adams aroused more strongly than outside of the counseling world, in a book published by the Humanist Society. Edmund Cohen had been a Bible-believer for a short while and attended an early NANC conference before he rejected Christianity. In *The Mind of the Bible-Believer* he described Adams's nouthetic counseling as "a public health menace" and an "exploitation of the problems and vulnerabilities of counselees to bring them under mind control."[202]

Summary

The ecclesiastical location and biblicist epistemology of Adams's nouthetic counseling made it largely invisible to the wider culture, a curiosity to the mainline churches, and highly controversial within conservative Protestantism. Nouthetic counseling rarely had borders to contest outside of the conservative Protestant community because it made no professional claims on the larger culture, seeking instead to create a separate counterculture.

The counterinsurgency measures taken by evangelical psychologists proved largely successful. Their knowledge system—a combination of Scripture and psychology—and professional prestige proved to have the greater cultural currency during the 1980s. Nouthetic counseling would become increasingly isolated from the cultural centers: seminaries, colleges, universities, professional associations, book publishing, and journals where counseling ideas were debated and became influential. It became a movement largely confined within some Reformed and moderate fundamentalist churches, missionary agencies, seminaries, and Bible colleges.

Chapter 8 Notes

1. David Goodrum, "Putting Things into Perspective: An Introduction to the Writings of Jay E. Adams," *The Council of Chalcedon* 9, no. 8 (1987): 11. The full quotation captures the context: "[At] Covenant Seminary in St. Louis . . . I soon discovered that Jay Adams was a controversial figure. A rather vocal faction, among faculty and students, seemed to have little more than contempt for Jay Adams. . . . [The vice president of the seminary] said, quite vehemently, 'No one who is anyone in the world of counseling respects Jay Adams.'" Covenant Seminary served the denomination in which Adams had pastored and served as director of Home Missions during the late 1950s.

2. J. Harold Ellens, "Review of *The Biblical View of Self-esteem, Self-love, and Self-image* by Jay Adams," *Journal of Psychology and Christianity* 6, no. 3 (1987): 70.

3. Gary R. Collins, "The Pulpit and the Couch," *Christianity Today* 23 (August 1975): 1,088.

4. Stanton L. Jones, "Overview of the Rech Conference on Christian Graduate Training in Psychology and Introduction to the Collected Papers," *Journal of Psychology and Theology* 20, no. 2 (1992): 77–88. Jones was chairman of the Department of Psychological Studies at Wheaton College. The "participants" he alludes to were "academicians who provide graduate-level training in professional psychology from an explicitly Christian perspective . . . to review our past, process our present, and prepare for the future."

5. Andre Bustanoby, "Without These, Don't Start," *Christianity Today* (July 1973): 32.

6. Gary R. Collins, ed., *Helping People Grow: Practical Approaches to Christian Counseling* (Santa Ana, Calif.: Vision House, 1980), 151.

7. See the next chapter for further discussion of the historical outcome of the turf war.

8. E.g., Gary Collins (Trinity Evangelical Divinity School), Larry Crabb (Grace Theological Seminary, in the 1980s), William Kirwan (Covenant Theological Seminary), John Carter and Bruce Narramore (Rosemead Graduate School of Psychology), and Stan Jones (Wheaton College Graduate School of Psychological Studies). Critics further away on the theological spectrum made the same kinds of criticisms of Adams but made them once and then subsequently ignored him. One exception to this generalization proves the rule in a curious way. Donald Capps was a mainline pastoral theologian who taught at Princeton Theological Seminary. His intellectual mission involved reinjecting the Bible—in a manner and for purposes very different from Adams—into theologically liberal pastoral care. He, too, repeatedly came back to critique Adams.

9. Bruce Narramore, "Barriers to the Integration of Faith and Learning in Christian Graduate Training Programs in Psychology," *Journal of Psychology and Theology* 20, no. 2 (1992): 121.

10. The evangelical psychotherapists sought to "Christianize" many different psychologies. For example, Bruce Narramore adapted psychoanalytic insights and methods to his evangelical religion. Larry Crabb drew his motivation theory from humanistic psychology ("needs for significance and security") and his methodology from cognitive psychotherapy, infusing it with Jesus as the one who met psychological needs. Donald Tweedie argued for a version of Frankl's Logotherapy filled with conservative Protestant content. Stan Jones leaned toward cognitive-behavioral psychology but argued for a "principled eclecticism." Gary Collins operated in a more pragmatically eclectic manner, gathering elements from numerous approaches with little commitment to one psychological system. William Kirwan found themes from Karen Horney agreeable with his faith. Roger Bufford's theory and therapy were behavioristic. James Dobson combined a broadly humanistic motivation theory ("need for self-esteem") with a behavioristic methodology. And, as we will see later in this chapter, they viewed Jay Adams's approach as expressing significant, and significantly under acknowledged, emphases from Mowrer and Glasser.

11. I will at certain points note differences of emphasis and perspective between what might be termed conservative, moderate, and liberal evangelicals.

12. Nouthetic counseling institutions also published creeds. CCEF, NANC, and BCF had statements about the Bible almost identical to those of CAPS and AACC with the addition of one significant clause: "Counseling theory and practice are formed by the standards of Scripture." On other standard Protestant doctrines (the Trinity, the work of Christ, etc.) both groups were quite similar.

13. Stanton Jones and Richard Butman, *Modern Psychotherapies: A Comprehensive Christian Appraisal* (Downers Grove, Ill.: InterVarsity Press, 1991), 402.

14. Gary R. Collins, ed., *Case Studies in Christian Counseling*, Resources for Christian Counseling (Dallas: Word Publishing, 1991), 5.

15. Collins, "The Pulpit and the Couch," 1,088; Gary R. Collins, *How to Be a People Helper* (Santa Ana, Calif.: Vision House, 1976), 169.

16. John D. Carter, "Nouthetic Counseling Defended: A Reply to Ganz," *Journal of Psychology and Theology* 4, no. 4 (1976): 206.

Cf., Roger Hurding, *The Tree of Healing* (Grand Rapids: Zondervan, 1985), *infra*.

17. Cf., the discussions of the 1969 "Airport Meeting" and the 1979 "Krisheim Symposium" in chapters 2 and 3 respectively.

18. Gary R. Collins, *The Rebuilding of Psychology: An Integration of Psychology and Christianity* (Wheaton, Ill.: Tyndale House, 1977), 181.

19. J. Ernest Runions, "Review of *Shepherding God's Flock: Pastoral Counseling*," *Journal of the Evangelical Theological Society* 20 (March 1977): 84; Jay Van Zoeren, "Review of *Competent to Counsel*," *Reformed Review* 24, no. 3 (1971): 141.

20. Correspondence from Vernon Grounds, August 28, 1995.

21. Jones and Butman, *Modern Psychotherapies*, 27. Cf., the extended argument in Stanton L. Jones, ed., *Psychology and the Christian Faith: An Introductory Reader* (Grand Rapids: Baker Book House, 1986), 28–31.

22. Collins, *How to Be a People Helper*, 170; Robert H. Humphries, "Therapeutic Neutrality Reconsidered," *Journal of Religion and Health* 21, no. 2 (1982): 124–31; J. Oscar Jeske, "Varieties of Approaches to Psychotherapy: Options for the Christian Therapist," *Journal of Psychology and Theology* 12, no. 4 (1984): 260–69.

23. The three most significant statements of this philosophy were John D. Carter and Bruce Narramore, *The Integration of Psychology and Theology* (Grand Rapids: Zondervan, 1979); Collins, *The Rebuilding of Psychology*; Jones and Butman, *Modern Psychotherapies*.

24. William T. Kirwan, *Biblical Concepts for Christian Counseling: A Case for Integrating Psychology and Theology* (Grand Rapids: Baker Book House, 1984), 73.

25. Gary R. Collins, *The Biblical Basis of Christian Counseling for People Helpers* (Colorado Springs: NavPress, 1993), 32–34. Cf., 55f. Collins cited Lawrence J. Crabb, *Understanding People: Deep Longings for Relationship* (Grand Rapids: Zondervan, 1987), 45.

26. Gary R. Collins, *Can You Trust Psychology?: Exposing the Facts & the Fictions* (Downers Grove, Ill.: InterVarsity Press, 1988), 164.

27. Compare Lawrence J. Crabb, *Effective Biblical Counseling* (Grand Rapids: Zondervan, 1977), 47–52, with Lawrence J. Crabb, *Understanding People: Deep Longings for Relationship* (Grand Rapids: Zondervan, 1987), 35–73 (especially pp. 37–39). Crabb attacked the "two book view" of God's revelation (Scripture and nature) that characterized most integrationists.

28. Richard Winter, "Jay Adams—is he really biblical enough?," *Third Way* (April 1982): 11. Cf., James A. Oakland, et al., "An Analysis and Critique of Jay Adams's Theory of Counseling," *Journal of the American Scientific Affiliation* 28 (September 1976): 101–09.

29. James Hurley and Peter Jones, "Review of the Department of Practical Theology at Westminster Theological Seminary in California" (Westminster Theological Seminary, 1993). Their criticisms turned on the issue of common grace and the contributions of the modern psychologies. Cf., Oakland, "An Analysis and Critique of Jay Adams's Theory of Counseling," 106; Ray S. Anderson, "Isomorphic Indicators in Theological and Psychological Science,"

Journal of Psychology and Theology 17, no. 4 (1989): 373–81; Bustanoby, "Without These, Don't Start," 38f; Alice Kitchen, "Review of *Competent to Counsel*," *HIS* 33 (December 1972): 21, 31; Bob Passantino and Gretchen Passantino, "The 'Biblical Counseling' Alternative," *Christian Research Journal* 17, no. 4 (1995): 24–30.

30. Vance L. Shepperson, "Systemic Integration: A Reactive Alternative to 'The Conduct of Integration,'" *Journal of Psychology and Theology* 10, no. 4 (1982): 326; Timothy Weber, "Coincidence of Opposites: The Meeting of Psychology and Theology," in *Psychology & Theology: Prospects for Integration,* ed. H. Newton Malony (Nashville: Abingdon Press, 1978), 109. Cf., D. Russell Bishop, "Psychology and the Pastoral Ministry: Help or Hindrance," *Journal of Psychology and Theology* 17, no. 2 (1989): 153.

31. John H. Coe, *Educating the Church for Wisdom's Sake or Why Biblical Counseling Is Unbiblical* (unpublished 1991), 30.

32. Correspondence with Vernon Grounds, August 28, 1995.

33. Jones and Butman, *Modern Psychotherapies,* 27, citing Calvin's *Institutes of the Christian Religion,* 2.2.15. Cf., Kirwan, *Biblical Concepts for Christian Counseling,* 26–29; Bustanoby, "Without These, Don't Start," 32f.

34. Carter and Narramore, *The Integration of Psychology and Theology,* 76–80; Crabb, *Effective Biblical Counseling,* 40ff, 52.

35. John D. Carter, "Secular and Sacred Models of Psychology and Religion," *Journal of Psychology and Theology* 5, no. 3 (1977): 203.

36. Carter, "Nouthetic Counseling Defended: A Reply to Ganz," 207, 210.

37. Ibid., 208.

38. Roger Hurding, *The Tree of Healing* (Grand Rapids: Zondervan, 1985). Cf., Ronald P. Philipchalk, *Psychology and Christianity: An Introduction to Controversial Issues* (Lanham, Md.: University Press of America, 1987), 169: "Several popular Christian authors are known for their emphasis on the Bible, to the exclusion of psychology, as the guideline for counseling and therapy (e.g., Adams, Brandt . . .). However, probably the best known of these is Jay Adams. Jay Adams is used here as an example of a narrowly biblical approach . . . although a careful reading of his work reveals [1] an admission of truth in secular sources, [2] use of extrabiblical sources of knowledge himself, and [3] an admission that some problems have unknown causes (i.e., not either organically based or biblically defined)." Adams served as an exemplar of a Bible-only epistemology, even when a careful reading revealed otherwise. The debates over "common grace" were code for the jurisdictional conflict. In the 1970s and 1980s it provided the surest "biblical" ground to legitimize the professional identity of psychologists in the evangelical community. In the 1990s, psychologists much more often employed the rhetoric of "ministry," and, e.g., "sought to see ourselves as caring for souls rather than being technical service-deliverers." Jones, "Overview of the Rech Conference," 84.

39. Correspondence from Vernon Grounds, August 28, 1995. Cf., Runions, "Review of *Shepherding God's Flock,*" 83f; Crabb, *Understanding People,* 54–58.

40. Collins, *How to Be a People Helper,* 170f.

41. John D. Carter, "Adams' Theory of Nouthetic Counseling," *Journal of Psychology and Theology* 3, no. 3 (1975): 152.

42. Crabb, *Understanding People,* 8–10, 54–58.

43. David G. Benner, "Psychotherapies: Stalking Their Spiritual Side," *Christianity Today* (December 1981): 33.

44. Lawrence J. Crabb, *The Marriage Builder: A Blueprint for Counselors and Couples* (Grand Rapids: Zondervan, 1982, 1992), 8.

45. Crabb, *Effective Biblical Counseling,* 42.

46. Ibid.

47. Ibid., 23.

48. Ibid., 151; Carter, "Adams' Theory of Nouthetic Counseling," 154.

49. Gerald O. North in Oakland, "An Analysis and Critique of Jay Adams's Theory of Counseling," 109.

50. The following is a sampler: Anderson, "Isomorphic Indicators in Theological and Psychological Science"; Carter, "Adams' Theory of Nouthetic Counseling"; Carter, "Nouthetic Counseling Defended: A Reply to Ganz"; Robert Colton, "Review of *Essays on Counseling,*" *Criswell Theological Review* 3, no. 2 (1989): 432f; Bruce Narramore, "The Concept of Responsibility in Psychopathology and Psychotherapy," *Journal of Psychology and Theology* 13, no. 2 (1985): 91–96; Oakland, "An Analysis and Critique of Jay Adams's Theory of Counseling"; Winter, "Jay Adams—is he really biblical enough?"

51. Crabb, *Effective Biblical Counseling,* 151; Joanna McGrath and Alister McGrath, *The Dilemma of Self-Esteem: The Cross and Christian Confidence* (Wheaton, Ill.: Crossway Books, 1992); Collins, *The Rebuilding of Psychology,* 190; Crabb, *Understanding People;* Lawrence J. Crabb, *Inside Out* (Colorado Springs: NavPress, 1988), 45, 132; Kirwan, *Biblical Concepts for Christian Counseling,* 62f; Hurding, *The Tree of Healing,* 289; Narramore, "The Concept of Responsibility in Psychopathology and Psychotherapy," 91, 95.

52. Bruce Narramore, *No Condemnation: Rethinking Guilt Motivation in Counseling, Preaching, and Parenting* (Grand Rapids: Zondervan, 1984) contains a lengthy discussion of Adams's view of the conscience, *infra.* Cf., Kirwan, *Biblical Concepts for Christian Counseling,* 91; Lawrence J. Crabb, *Basic Principles of Biblical Counseling* (Grand Rapids: Zondervan, 1975), 50.

53. Narramore, "The Concept of Responsibility in Psychopathology and Psychotherapy," 95.

54. John Carter, "Nouthetic Counseling," in *Baker Encyclopedia of Psychology,* ed. David Benner (Grand Rapids: Baker Book House, 1985), 764.

55. Carter, "Adams' Theory of Nouthetic Counseling," 151.

56. David G. Benner, *Psychotherapy and the Spiritual Quest* (Grand Rapids: Baker Book House, 1988), 46. Evangelical psychologists were not Adams's only critics on this score, though they are the focus of this chapter. A pastoral theologian found his approbation of Adams tempered because Adams had "a truncated view of sin . . . [showing] little understanding of the depth and inwardness of sin." Derek J. Tidball, *Skillful Shepherds: An Introduction to Pastoral Theology* (Grand Rapids: Zondervan, 1986), 240. The next chapter will note that far more pastors found Adams unacceptable than found him acceptable.

57. Carter, "Adams' Theory of Nouthetic Counseling," 150; Carter, "Nouthetic Counseling Defended: A Reply to Ganz," 213.

Cf., Richard F. Lovelace, *Dynamics of Spiritual Life: An Evangelical Theology of Renewal* (Downers Grove, Ill.: InterVarsity Press, 1979), 220.

58. Kenneth Bowers in Oakland, "An Analysis and Critique of Jay Adams's Theory of Counseling," 107.

59. Conversation with Bruce Narramore, August 29, 1995.

60. Crabb, *Understanding People,* 46ff; David G. Benner, "Christian Counseling and Psychotherapy," in *Baker Encyclopedia of Psychology,* ed. David G. Benner (Grand Rapids: Baker Book House, 1985), 161f. They disagreed with Adams's definition of the psychospiritual, of course, as this section discusses.

61. Benner, "Christian Counseling and Psychotherapy," 162.

62. Collins, *The Rebuilding of Psychology,* 182. Cf., Kirwan, *Biblical Concepts for Christian Counseling,* 30.

63. Kitchen, "Review of *Competent to Counsel,*" 31.

64. Benner, *Psychotherapy and the Spiritual Quest,* 46.

65. Narramore, *No Condemnation,* 129.

66. Collins, *The Rebuilding of Psychology,* 182

67. Collins, *The Biblical Basis of Christian Counseling for People Helpers,* 110f.

68. This theme runs throughout Crabb's writings and dominates his *Inside Out.*

69. Narramore, "The Concept of Responsibility in Psychopathology and Psychotherapy," 93. Some pastors and pastoral theologians also thought that Adams's emphasis on personal sin understated the effect of other causes of those miseries that brought people to seek counseling. For example, "Adams does not attribute all problems and suffering to the direct sin of the one seeking counsel, as many have claimed. He recognizes that the cause of the misery may be the result of demonic activity, may have an organic basis, or that it may lie outside the individual who suffers. None the less, with the vice-like grip of a dog playing with an old slipper, he will not let go of the concept of sin as central to pastoral care." Tidball, *Skillful Shepherds,* 237.

70. Collins, *Can You Trust Psychology?,* 76.

71. Cedric B. Johnson and H. Newton Maloney *Christian Conversion: Biblical and Psychological Perspectives* (Grand Rapids: Zondervan, 1981), 151.

72. Such criticisms were not restricted only to psychologists or only to Adams's counseling books. Adams's commentary on 1 Peter was reviewed by a pastor: "The massive Gospel content of this canonical book by the apostle is almost completely obscured." Martin H. Scharlemann, "Review of *Trust and Obey,*" *Concordia Journal* 5, no. 5 (1979): 195. One theological reviewer found that in *Competent to Counsel,* "I miss a strong accent on the transforming power of the Gospel." Henry J. Eggold, "Review of *Competent to Counsel,*" *The Springfielder* 35, no. 1 (1971): 77.

73. Lawrence J. Crabb, *Men & Women: Enjoying the Difference* (Grand Rapids: Zondervan, 1991), 29.

74. This picture was a stock item in Larry Crabb's books, e.g., Crabb, *Men & Women,* 30–32, 49–52.

75. Benner, *Psychotherapy and the Spiritual Quest,* 47.

76. Narramore, *No Condemnation,* 130; cf., 128. Cf., Crabb, *Men & Women,* 52.

77. John D. Carter, "Towards a Biblical Model of Counseling," *Journal of Psychology and Theology* 8, no. 1 (1980): 47–49.

78. Narramore, *No Condemnation,* 123.

79. Ibid., 124.

80. Ibid., 125.

81. Ibid., 128.

82. David Augsburger of Fuller Seminary attempted to detail appropriate confrontation in David W. Augsburger, *Caring Enough to Confront* (Glendale, Calif.: Regal Books, 1980). Evangelical psychologists often cited his book as exemplary.

83. David J. Hesselgrave, *Counseling Cross-Culturally: An Introduction to Theory & Practice for Christians* (Grand Rapids: Baker Book House, 1984), 240; cf., Siang-Yang Tan, "Counseling Asians," in *Healing for the City,* eds. Craig Ellison and Edward Maynard (Grand Rapids: Zondervan, 1992), 110–23; Luis Villareal, "Counseling Hispanics," in *Healing for the City,* eds. Craig Ellison and Edward Maynard (Grand Rapids: Zondervan, 1992), 139–58.

84. Gary Collins, Door Interview: Dr. Gary Collins, *The Wittenburg Door* 47 (February–March 1979), 12f. Interestingly, one of Adams's chief criticisms of Rogerian methods was that they had become popular because they were so "simple, easy to learn, runs little risk, and is so immediately usable." Jay E. Adams, *The Christian Counselor's Manual* (USA: Presbyterian & Reformed, 1973), 84.

85. Carter, "Nouthetic Counseling," 763.

86. Carter, "Secular and Sacred Models of Psychology and Religion," 203.

87. Fred Donehoo, "Critique of Jay Adams's *Competent to Counsel,*" (unpublished, 1969), 5.

88. Kirwan, *Biblical Concepts for Christian Counseling,* 136f.

89. H. Newton Maloney, ed., *Wholeness and Holiness: Readings in the Psychology/Theology of Mental Health* (Grand Rapids: Baker Book House, 1983), 273f; Carter, "Adams' Theory of Nouthetic Counseling," 154.

90. Winter, "Jay Adams—is he really biblical enough?," 10.

91. Samuel Southard, "Church Discipline: Handle with Care," in *Clergy Malpractice,* eds. H. Newton Maloney, et al. (Philadelphia: Westminster Press, 1986), 180.

92. Kirwan, *Biblical Concepts for Christian Counseling,* 137; cf., 127f.

93. Ibid., 128.

94. David E. Carlson, "Jesus' Style of Relating: The Search for a Biblical View of Counseling," *Journal of Psychology and Theology* 4, no. 3 (1976): 181–92. Carlson was a professor at Trinity Evangelical Divinity School along with Gary Collins.

95. E.g., Hesselgrave, *Counseling Cross-Culturally,* 99, 106f; Siang-Yang Tan, *Lay Counseling: Equipping Christians for a Helping Ministry* (Grand Rapids: Zondervan, 1991), 45f.

96. David Carlson and Gary Collins, the Trinity Evangelical Divinity School psychologists, preferred the third style, the "pastoral" or "shepherdly" interactive friendship. They took Swiss psychiatrist and evangelical Paul Tournier as their exemplar of a gentle, conversational, mentoring style of counseling.

97. Carter, "Adams' Theory of Nouthetic Counseling," 152f; Tidball, *Skillful Shepherds,* 239; Crabb, *Effective Biblical Counseling,* 147f.; Tan, *Lay Counseling,* 45.

98. Hurding, *The Tree of Healing,* 288f, 387–406.

99. Carter and Narramore, *The Integration of Psychology and Theology*, 133; Collins, *The Rebuilding of Psychology*, 190; Jack Boghosian, "The Biblical Basis for Strategic Approaches in Pastoral Counseling," *Journal of Psychology and Theology* 11, no. 2 (1983): 99; C. Markham Berry, "Counseling in the Medical Office," *Journal of Psychology and Theology* 2, no. 3 (1974): 176–80.

100. Winter, "Jay Adams—is he really biblical enough?," 10.

101. Collins, *How to Be a People Helper*, 171ff.

102. Carter and Narramore, *The Integration of Psychology and Theology*, 133.

103. Crabb, *Effective Biblical Counseling*, 147f.

104. Stanton L. Jones, "Assertiveness Training in Christian Perspective," *Journal of Psychology and Theology* 12, no. 2 (1984): 91–99.

105. Lawrence J. Crabb and Dan B. Allender, *Encouragement: The Key to Caring* (Grand Rapids: Zondervan, 1984), 84.

106. *Toward Effective Counseling and Psychotherapy: Training and Practice* by Charles Truax and Robert Carkhuff (Chicago: Aldine Publishing, 1967) was immensely influential among evangelical psychotherapists for the thesis that such personal characteristics of the therapist were more determinative of therapy's success or failure than the theoretical model.

107. Bustanoby, "Without These, Don't Start," 38f; Kirwan, *Biblical Concepts for Christian Counseling*, 124–37.

108. Oakland, "An Analysis and Critique of Jay Adams's Theory of Counseling," 105.

109. Collins, Door Interview: Dr. Gary Collins, 13. Cf., Gerald O. North in Oakland, "An Analysis and Critique of Jay Adams's Theory of Counseling," 109, cited in section 5 of this chapter.

110. Gerald O. North in Oakland, "An Analysis and Critique of Jay Adams's Theory of Counseling, 109.

111. Benner, "Christian Counseling and Psychotherapy," 161f.

112. Oakland, "An Analysis and Critique of Jay Adams's Theory of Counseling," 104.

113. Stenberg in ibid., 105. Stenberg meant "professional with a career" not the narrow role of a "career counselor."

114. Concerns about their need for greater theological education and acumen were often mentioned, however. One refrain in integrationist writing and speaking was the lament, "We have a Ph.D. education in psychology and a Sunday school education in theology." A number of integrationists made a point of acquiring theological degrees alongside their psychological degrees: e.g., Bruce Narramore, John Carter, and Harold Ellens. The intellectual issues (redressable lack of theological education) were separated from the professional issues (whether licensure/ordination should have an ecclesiastical or a secular locus).

115. Gary R. Collins, *Excellence and Ethics in Counseling*, ed. Gary R. Collins, Resources for Christian Counseling (Dallas: Word Publishing, 1991), 32.

116. The first half of the sentence is from an interview with Bruce Narramore, August 25, 1995. Cf., Stenberg in Oakland, "An Analysis and Critique of Jay Adams's Theory of Counseling," 105. The quotation is from Jones, "Overview of the Rech Conference," 83.

117. Stenberg in Oakland, "An Analysis and Critique of Jay Adams's Theory of Counseling," 105.

118. Ibid.

119. Gary R. Collins, "Popular Christian Psychologies: Some Reflections," *Journal of Psychology and Theology* 3, no. 2 (1975): 127; Collins, *Helping People Grow*, 19.

120. Collins, *How to Be a People Helper;* Crabb and Allender, *Encouragement;* Tan, *Lay Counseling.*

121. Crabb and Allender, *Encouragement*, 133.

122. Crabb, *Effective Biblical Counseling*, 173–81; Crabb and Allender *Encouragement*, 135ff. Crabb's lower-level counseling was for laypeople and entailed learning to communicate affirmation and acceptance to others, per Carl Rogers. Crabb's upper-level counselors were those trained in his system (through intensive seminars and master's-level courses) to tackle more complex problems using a psychodynamic therapy that explored psychological "needs" and offered Jesus as the one who could fulfill them.

123. Crabb and Allender, *Encouragement*, 136.

124. Collins, *How to Be a People Helper.*

125. Tan, *Lay Counseling.*

126. Crabb, *Effective Biblical Counseling*, 37.

127. David Benner, in response to Bernie Zilbergeld, "Myths of Counseling," *Leadership* 5 (Winter 1984): 92.

128. Robert C. Roberts, *Taking the Word to Heart: Self and Others in an Age of Therapies* (Grand Rapids: William B. Eerdmans, 1993), 4, xii.

129. Gary Collins, *Psychology and Theology: Prospects for Integration*, ed. H. Newton Maloney (Nashville: Abingdon Press, 1981), 14; Roberts, *Taking the Word to Heart*, 10; Jones and Butman, *Modern Psychotherapies*, 24.

130. Crabb, *Basic Principles of Biblical Counseling*, 49.

131. Jones and Butman, *Modern Psychotherapies*, 402.

132. Roberts, *Taking the Word to Heart*, 12f.

133. See, for example, Fuller Seminary's Timothy Weber, "Optional Models for Integration," in Collins, *Psychology and Theology*, 100–109, which placed Collins and Crabb close to Adams on a scale of attitudes toward psychology. Tensions between evangelical psychotherapists could emerge openly on occasion. The *Journal of Psychology and Christianity* rarely printed letters to the editor, but Harold Ellens chose to print one that reacted to the offerings at a recent convention of the Christian Association for Psychological Studies: "We have . . . the simple (Collins), the arrogant (Crabb), the marginally heretical (Scott Peck), the worn out (Bruce Narramore and John Carter), the populist (Keith Miller and Jim Dobson). . . . Bring back Seward Hiltner [and] Vernon Grounds." Ron Johnson, Letter to the Editor, *Journal of Psychology and Christianity* 4, no. 1 (1985): 4f.

134. Jones and Butman, *Modern Psychotherapies*, 29f. Cf., Bruce Narramore, "Integrative Inquiry: How do you view our progress in integrating psychology and theology?," *Journal of Psychology and Theology* 20, no. 4 (1992): 395.

135. Collins, *How to Be a People Helper*, 168.

136. Collins, *Helping People Grow*, 328f.

137. Conversation with Leroy Aden at CAPS national convention, Chicago, 1983. Cf., Collins, *Psychology and Theology*, 53.

138. Carter, "Adams' Theory of Nouthetic Counseling," 143.

139. Carter, "Nouthetic Counseling," 764.

140. Collins, *Helping People Grow,* 16; Gerald H. O'Donnell, "Review of *The Big Umbrella,*" *Westminster Theological Journal* 35, (Spring 1973): 380.

141. Runions, "Review of *Shepherding God's Flock: Pastoral Counseling,*" 83.

142. Carter, "Adams' Theory of Nouthetic Counseling," 154.

143. Ibid.

144. Collins, *Helping People Grow,* 16; cf., Kitchen, "Review of *Competent to Counsel,*" 21.

145. Bruce Narramore, "Perspectives on the Integration of Psychology and Theology," *Journal of Psychology and Theology* 1, no. 1 (1973): 10.

146. Carter, "Nouthetic Counseling Defended: A Reply to Ganz," 211.

147. Carter, "Adams' Theory of Nouthetic Counseling," 143, 152f; Carter, "Nouthetic Counseling Defended: A Reply to Ganz," 208, 211; Narramore, *No Condemnation,* 115–30.

148. Carter, "Adams' Theory of Nouthetic Counseling," 152.

149. Collins, Door Interview: Dr. Gary Collins, 13.

150. Carter, "Nouthetic Counseling Defended: A Reply to Ganz," 208.

151. Ibid., 208, 211f.

152. Runions, "Review of *Shepherding God's Flock: Pastoral Counseling,*" 84.

153. Conversation with Bruce Narramore, August 29, 1995.

154. Collins, Door Interview: Dr. Gary Collins, 13; Paul D. Meier, Frank B. Minirth, and Frank B. Wichern, *Introduction to Psychology and Counseling: Christian Perspectives and Applications* (Grand Rapids: Baker Book House, 1991), 35, 305, 311; Runions, "Review of *Shepherding God's Flock: Pastoral Counseling,*" 83f; Winter, "Jay Adams—is he really biblical enough?," 12; Jones and Butman, *Modern Psychotherapies,* 164, 219, 241; Carter, "Nouthetic Counseling Defended: A Reply to Ganz," 212.

155. Evans and Van Leeuwen are theoretically oriented representatives of a large class of writings critical of behaviorist and empiricist premises: C. Stephen Evans, *Preserving the Person: A Look at the Human Sciences* (Grand Rapids: Baker Book House, 1977); Mary Stewart Van Leeuwen, *The Sorcerer's Apprentice: A Christian Looks at the Changing Face of Psychology* (Downers Grove, Ill.: InterVarsity Press, 1982).

156. John D. Carter, "Shallow Reflections on Crucial Issues," *Journal of Psychology and Theology* 18, no. 3 (1990): 290; Francis C. Rossow, "Review of *Preaching with Purpose,*" *Concordia Journal* 11 (May 1985): 284; David E. Carlson, "Review of *Christian Counselor's Manual,*" *Counselor's Notebook* 1, no. 8 & no. 9: 1; Collins, "The Pulpit and the Couch," 1,088; Collins, *The Biblical Basis of Christian Counseling for People Helpers,* 96; Oakland, "An Analysis and Critique of Jay Adams's Theory of Counseling," 105; Philipchalk, *Psychology and Christianity,* 169; Paul S. Otto, "Review of *What About Nouthetic Counseling?,*" *Eternity* 29 (November 1978): 47f; Waylon O. Ward, "Review of *More Than Redemption,*" *Eternity* 31 (December 1980): 43.

157. Conversation with Bruce Narramore, August 29, 1996.

158. Runions, "Review of *Shepherding God's Flock: Pastoral Counseling,*" 84.

159. Jay E. Adams, *What About Nouthetic Counseling?* (Grand Rapids: Baker Book House, 1976), 83.

160. Ward, "Review of *More Than Redemption,*" 43.

161. Collins, "The Pulpit and the Couch," 1,088.

162. Otto, "Review of *What About Nouthetic Counseling?,*" 48.

163. Runions, "Review of *Shepherding God's Flock: Pastoral Counseling,*" 83; Rossow, "Review of *Preaching with Purpose,*" 121; Thomas Van Eerden, "Review of *What About Nouthetic Counseling?,*" *Calvin Theological Journal* 12 (Fall 1977): 235f.

164. Rossow, "Review of *Essays on Biblical Preaching,*" 284; Van Eerden, "Review of *What About Nouthetic Counseling?,*" 235.

165. Carter, "Adams' Theory of Nouthetic Counseling," 153. Cf., Van Zoeren, "Review of *Competent to Counsel,*" 140.

166. Collins, Door Interview: Dr. Gary Collins, 13.

167. Narramore, "Barriers to the Integration of Faith and Learning," 119–21.

168. William Hunter, "Review of *The Useful Lie by Playfair,*" *Journal of Psychology and Theology* 20, no. 1 (1992): 67.

169. I attended a half dozen CAPS conventions during the 1980s and heard Adams regularly disparaged in an iconic manner, rather than discussed with scholarly dispassion. Conversations with attenders into the 1990s revealed the same pattern. Both current and former students at the three leading graduate schools reported the same phenomenon. I spoke with one graduate of Rosemead who subsequently had become a follower of Adams (and requested anonymity). He described how a caricature of Adams served as the foil for the evangelical psychotherapy he learned; standardized derision of Adams recurred in Rosemead's classrooms. After several years of psychotherapeutic practice, he began to contemplate a switch in allegiance. He returned to the library at Rosemead to read Adams. "In that setting, I felt like I was reading something shameful, like pornography, as if I ought to put his books in a brown paper bag so I wouldn't be seen looking at them."

170. Ellens, "Review of *The Biblical View of Self-esteem, Self-love, and Self-image* by Jay Adams," 70.

171. Larry Crabb, foreword to James Moore, *Self-Image,* ed. Tom Varney, IBC Discussion Guides (Colorado Springs: NavPress, 1992), 5, 7.

172. Eric L. Johnson, "A Place for the Bible within Psychological Science," *Journal of Psychology and Theology* 20, no. 4 (1992): 346–55. Cf., Jones and Butman, *Modern Psychotherapies,* 29f; Jones, "Overview of the Rech Conference," 81f.

173. Here he was not alluding to Adams, whom he respected, but to a new and even more strident group of anti-psychology writers who arose in the 1980s, citing Adams as their forerunner. See chapter 9.

174. Collins, *Can You Trust Psychology?,* 162f; Collins, *Excellence and Ethics in Counseling,* 166f.

175. The Emmanuel movement, c. 1910, was an abortive attempt to wed mainline Protestantism with counseling practice. In the mid-1920s, the mental hygiene movement stimulated the development of Clinical Pastoral Education. An efflorescence of mainline pastoral counseling occurred during the 1940s and 1950s. See E. Brook Holifield, *A History of Pastoral Care in America* (Nashville: Abingdon Press, 1983), *infra.*

176. Randy Timpe, "Christian Psychology," in *Baker Encyclopedia of Psychology,* ed. David G. Benner (Grand Rapids: Baker Book House, 1985), 166–71.

177. Stephen Pattison, *A Critique of Pastoral Care* (London: SCM Press, 1988), 118, 112.

178. Donald Capps, "The Bible's Role in Pastoral Care and Counseling: Four Basic Principles," in *The Church and Pastoral Care,* eds. Leroy Aden and J. Harold Ellens (Grand Rapids: Baker Book House, 1988), 7.

179. Ibid., 8.

180. Collins, *Helping People Grow,* 13–16.

181. E.g., Leroy Aden and J. Harold Ellens, eds., *Turning Points in Pastoral Care: The Legacy of Anton Boisen and Seward Hiltner* (Grand Rapids: Baker Book House, 1990); Samuel Southard, "The Current Need for 'Theological Counsel,'" *Pastoral Psychology* 32, no. 2 (1983): 89–105.

182. James N. Lapsley, "Review of *Psychology and Christianity: Integrative Readings,*" *Zygon* 18, no. 4 (1983): 465.

183. Rodney J. Hunter, ed., *Dictionary of Pastoral Care and Counseling* (Nashville: Abingdon Press, 1990).

184. Brian H. Childs, *The Dictionary of Pastoral Care and Counseling:* An Interview with Rodney J. Hunter, *Pastoral Psychology* 39, no. 2 (1990): 135f.

185. Donald Capps, "Biblical Models in Pastoral Counseling," *Pastoral Psychology* 28, no. 4 (1980): 252–64; *Biblical Approaches to Pastoral Counseling* (Philadelphia: Westminster Press, 1981); Capps, "The Bible's Role in Pastoral Care and Counseling: Four Basic Principles," in *The Church and Pastoral Care,* eds. Leroy Aden and J. Harold Ellens (Grand Rapids: Baker Book House, 1988), 41–55; Capps, "Bible, Pastoral use and interpretation of," in *Dictionary of Pastoral Care,* ed. Rodney J. Hunter (Nashville: Abingdon Press, 1990a), 82–85; Capps, *Reframing: A New Method in Pastoral Care* (Minneapolis: Fortress Press, 1990b), *infra.*

186. Orlo Strunk Jr., "The Role of Visioning in the Pastoral Counseling Movement," *Pastoral Psychology* 31, no. 1 (1982): 7, 11f.

187. Thomas C. Oden, *Pastoral Theology: Essentials of Ministry* (San Francisco: HarperCollins, 1982). Oden himself was highly critical of the dominance of the modern psychologies, and wanted to anchor counseling in the church and its theological traditions. In one of those curious and untidy ironies that arise when attempting to keep one's historical categories neat, a liberal evangelical sharply criticized Oden for being of a piece with Adams, pastorally regressive and negativistic to the psychologies. J. Harold Ellens, *God's Grace and Human Health* (Nashville: Abingdon Press, 1982), 127.

188. William Oglesby Jr., *Biblical Themes for Pastoral Care* (Nashville: Abingdon Press, 1980), 19.

189. Capps, "The Bible's Role in Pastoral Care and Counseling," 8.

190. Pattison, *A Critique of Pastoral Care,* 106, 116.

191. Ibid., 116. Cf., David C. Weiss, "Review of *The Christian Counselor's Manual,*" *Journal of Pastoral Care* 29, no. 2 (1975): 141f.

192. Chris Wigglesworth, "Bible: Pastoral Use," in *A Dictionary of Pastoral Care,* ed. Alastair V. Campbell (New York: Crossroad, 1987), 25f; Capps, "The Bible's Role in Pastoral Care and Counseling," 7.

193. Capps, *Biblical Approaches to Pastoral Counseling,* 117.

194. Capps, *Reframing: A New Method in Pastoral Care,* chapter 4.

195. Howard Clinebell, *Basic Types of Pastoral Care & Counseling: Resources for the Ministry of Healing and Growth* (Nashville: Abingdon Press, 1984, 1966), 20, 127, 163, 320, 329. See Holifield's lengthy discussion of the "revolt against moralism" that characterized the pastoral counseling movement. E. Brooks Holifield, *A History of Pastoral Care in America: From Salvation to Self-Realization* (Nashville: Abingdon Press, 1983), chapters 6–7.

196. Don S. Browning, *Religious Ethics and Pastoral Care* (Philadelphia: Fortress Press, 1983), 118.

197. Capps, *Biblical Approaches to Pastoral Counseling,* 32.

198. Ibid., 102.

199. PsycInfo and Social Sciences Citation Index searches did not yield any references to Jay Adams or nouthetic counseling.

As an aside, the border between secular mental health professionals and their evangelical counterparts was more lively, particularly regarding issues of accreditation. Fuller Seminary, Rosemead Graduate School of Psychology, and Wheaton College Graduate School of Psychological Studies each had to fight hard in the politics of accreditation. Evangelical psychologists were often concerned with their precarious status both in the world of the American Psychological Association, where they faced suspicion as religionists, and in the world of conservative Protestants, where they faced suspicion as psychologists. See, for example, Jones, "Overview of the Rech Conference," *op. cit.,* 77–88; Narramore, "Barriers to the Integration of Faith and Learning," *op. cit.,* 119–26.

200. John L. Young and Ezra E. H. Griffith, "The Development and Practice of Pastoral Counseling," *Hospital and Community Psychiatry* 40, no. 3 (1989): 274. I doubtless have missed others of this sort of brief citation of Adams in the literature.

201. Darrell Sifford, "Divorce and God's Law: Is there a compromise?," *Philadelphia Inquirer,* January 30, 1984,; Darrell Sifford, "Letting Religion Guide Your Life," *Philadelphia Inquirer,* January 29, 1984.

202. Edmund D. Cohen, *The Mind of the Bible-Believer* (Buffalo, N.Y.: Prometheus Books, 1986), 303, 52. Cohen himself aspired to become a "Feuerbach for the twentieth century," who would expose the New Testament as an unsurpassed example of "psychological acumen and artfulness" in manipulating people. Ibid., 4.

The Fortunes of War: The 1980s and Beyond

It is never wrong to ask of any claim, whether scientific, social, theological, or whatever:
Does this serve someone's interests? Does somebody lose out? Who is controlling this discourse and
for what political purposes? It strikes me that addressing these questions could throw as much light
on debates about scientific creationism and biblical hermeneutics as on the nuclear industry and
embryological experimentation. My instinct is that in many of these acrimonious feuds the cognitive claims
are routinely made the vehicle for carrying a good deal of ideological freight.

— David N. Livingstone[1]

The clergy, although generally well organized, has lost numerous jurisdictional battles . . .
where its antagonists have possessed more current cultural legitimacy.

— Andrew Abbott[2]

John Bettler and Jay Adams are the yin and yang of biblical counseling.
The real story of the history of nouthetic counseling lies in their debates and disagreements.

— George Scipione[3]

The nouthetic counseling movement entered the 1980s full of optimism. Jay Adams's "counseling revolution" had enjoyed a rapid and clamorous expansion. Adams became a best-selling author and renowned counseling authority, variously famous or infamous for his "distinctive" and "radical" point of view. The major institutions founded by Adams and John Bettler—the Christian Counseling and Educational Foundation (CCEF), the pastoral counseling program at Westminster Theological Seminary, the National Association of Nouthetic Counsel-

ors (NANC), the *Journal of Pastoral Practice (JPP)*—all initially prospered. The early success of other institutions—John Broger's Biblical Counseling Foundation (BCF) and Bill Goode and Bob Smith's Faith Baptist Counseling Ministries (FBCM)—seemed to bode well for the diffusion of nouthetic counseling.

Evangelical psychotherapists had been put on the defensive by the popularity of Adams's blunt, sweeping critique of their profession and by his biblicistic alternative. With an instinct for the jurisdictional issues, Adams had chosen to fight a logistical rather than a tactical war. He had sought to undermine the psychotherapists' support base rather than to win them to his cause. He wrote in 1976:

> I could debate, argue and try to persuade [psychotherapists to go back to their own backyards]. That, I am convinced, would in most cases be useless. . . . [Instead] by making pastors fully aware of the property given to them in a clear deed from God, I have been trying to persuade pastors to so utilize and cultivate their own backyards that such encroachments from neighbors would become unnecessary and, indeed, highly embarrassing to those who make them.
>
> This approach I believe is succeeding. The self-styled "professionals" . . . have felt the impact of thousands of pastors who have themselves begun to take seriously the work to which God called them and for which they are well equipped by their knowledge of the Scriptures.[4]

Adams may have been right that conversation with the trespassers would have proved useless, but he was wrong about the overall success of his attempt to create a pastors' revolution. Nouthetic counseling's popularity plateaued by 1980. During the decade that followed, momentum stalled, while the evangelical psychotherapists enjoyed spectacular success in capturing the mind, the respect, and the institutions of conservative Protestantism.

This chapter will look first at the results of the wider jurisdictional conflict between Adams and the psychotherapists, a conflict in which Adams and his cohorts were largely the losers. The institutional spread of nouthetic counseling was tightly contained, the fruit of its own isolationist stance and of the evangelical psychologists' successful defense of professional turf. Within wider evangelicalism, Adams remained as a cranky voice in the wilderness. The second half of this chapter will look at developments within nouthetic counseling. During the 1980s, while maintaining and slowly expanding its core of loyal pastors, several of its leading institutions withered, and internal fault lines became clear.

This chapter will be impressionistic, providing only a concise summary of events and issues. I will not attempt a close description or analysis of events, actors, and arguments; a fuller analysis of events subsequent to 1980 demands greater historical distance. This chapter is largely a probe, a description of projects that remain to be done.

Evangelical Psychotherapy: The Gainers in the Jurisdictional Conflict

Conservative Protestants interested in doing or receiving counseling often read one or two of Adams's books and, having digested and disagreed with the tone and substance of his message, no longer paid attention.[5] They no longer needed to pay attention because evangelical psychotherapists were successfully consolidating and extending their authority in higher education, in the provision of counseling services, in publishing, and in the mind of the evangelical subculture.

Psychology programs thrived in evangelical higher education during the 1980s. Numerous colleges formed or developed psychology departments; seminaries hired clinical psychologists to teach in newly formed counseling departments; new degree programs and majors in psychological fields proliferated in both colleges and seminaries. Some programs and professors were more theoretical in their orientation. For example, academic psychologists Mary Stewart van Leeuwen at Calvin College and David Myers at Hope College became particularly well known.[6] But it was in the preparation of practitioners that the greatest growth occurred.

For example, in 1980 Wheaton College (Wheaton, Ill.), one of the oldest and most respected evangelical colleges, began a master's program in psychology. A number of the faculty—David Benner, Stan Jones, and Kirk Farnsworth, along with philosophers Stephen Evans and Robert Roberts who had psychological interests—became influential in the integration movement.[7] In 1991 Jones and a colleague gave expression to Wheaton's philosophy of integrating psychotherapy in the massive *Modern Psychotherapies*. Their "responsible eclecticism" offered both a comprehensive exemplar of Wheaton's way of integrating evangelical faith with psychology, and another programmatic statement like those written by Collins and by Narramore and Carter in the late 1970s.[8]

The integrationist knowledge program busily proceeded through the 1980s. A second full-fledged journal began in 1982, as the Christian Association for Psychological Studies (CAPS) transformed its *Bulletin* into the *Journal of Psychology and Christianity,* under the editorship of Harold Ellens. The achievements of integrationist scholarship were perhaps best registered in an encyclopedia project completed in 1985 under David Benner's editorship. The *Baker Encyclopedia of Psychology*[9] was a product of the efforts of some 150 evangelical psychology professors and professionals. At the same time, after fifteen years, nouthetic counseling had no authors besides Adams who had published anything besides self-help books with small distributions. Psychologists had increasingly secured their institutional positions within Christian colleges and seminaries.

Marketplace demand and professional niches matched expanding educational production. Graduates of professional programs opened psychotherapy practices and, eventually, joined the staffs of inpatient psychiatric clinics. During the 1980s numerous independent counseling centers and psychotherapy offices opened throughout the United States. Participation in CAPS provided some measure of this growth. In the mid-1970s CAPS had 350 members; by 1988 membership approached 2,000.[10] But the most significant, even astonishing, development was the sudden emergence and explosive growth of for-profit, inpatient psychiatric services by and for evangelicals.

In the mid-1970s, Dallas Theological Seminary had hired psychiatrists Frank Minirth and Paul Meier to teach counseling to their seminarians. In 1976 the two opened Minirth-Meier Clinic, a private practice, outpatient mental health clinic, in order to supplement their income.[11] They also collaborated on a number of books and began a radio program addressing mental health topics. In 1986, they opened a second clinic. That same year, Southern Baptist psychotherapist Robert McGee founded a similar clinic, Rapha, in Houston to provide "Christ-centered Hospital and Counseling Care."[12] Unlike the nonprofit hospitals founded by Dutch and Mennonite denominations earlier in the century, these were privately owned, for-profit corporations, and they "did not take indigent or uninsured patients except on very rare occasions."[13] Both corporations rapidly expanded treatment sites, typically contracting with hospitals to take over unused floors in order to run religiously oriented psychiatric programs: inpatient, day-care, and outpatient. By 1991 both had become nationwide: Minirth-Meier operated twenty-five treatment centers, mostly outpatient, and Rapha operated thirty-two programs in seventeen hospitals.[14] The Minirth-Meier radio show appeared on some 220 radio stations across the country, and the company also marketed a line of self-help books largely targeting the problems in living addressed by its clinical services: depression, eating disorders, and recovery from abuse.[15]

Phenomenal growth continued into the mid-1990s. In 1994 Minirth-Meier merged with a third major chain, New Life Treatment Centers (owned by Steve Arterburn), that had emphasized inpatient units and was about as large as Minirth-Meier and Rapha. By 1996 the Minirth-Meier New Life Clinics (MMNL) operated some eighty clinics (twenty-five inpatient, fifty-five outpatient) and claimed that its staff had published 130 self-help books. Meanwhile, Rapha had doubled to sixty-three programs nationwide.[16] MMNL and Rapha had become two of the largest providers of private, for-profit psychiatric services in the world.

MMNL was explicitly conservative Protestant, presenting itself as a ministry that worked with "the whole person . . . the physical, psychological, and spiritual . . . integrating sound Christian counseling principles and medical strategies."[17] It included a statement of faith with its publicity materials, "beliefs which have been agreed to by the professional and support staff." This statement of faith included everything contained in CCEF's and NANC's statements of faith and appeared to be modeled on it. MMNL's statement was even more detailed and extensive, adding several articles, including one that described "humanity's rebellion and subsequent depravity." A final article spoke of psychology in terms that placed MMNL unabashedly on the conservative end of evangelical psychotherapy: "We believe that all psychological principles should be thoroughly evaluated through the grid of Scripture, and that Scripture always holds the final authority." MMNL took seriously body, soul, and spirit. It was renowned for its routine use of psychotropic medication; for its lightly Christianized adaptations of the pop psychologies, e.g., *Reclaiming Your Inner Child: A Self-discovery Workbook;* and for its prayer meetings and Bible studies.[18] Medical psychiatry, integrationist psychotherapy, creedal orthodoxy, and big business conjoined.

Proprietary psychiatric care was only the most visible evidence of the psychotherapists' success with a constituency previously unreached by the

twentieth century's therapeutic revolution. By the 1990s the evangelical psychotherapy movement was big enough and diverse enough to contain a second professional organization. In 1992 Gary Collins was invited to remake a tiny, languishing association, the American Association of Christian Counselors (AACC). The AACC set out to accomplish a different set of professional purposes than CAPS and was spectacularly successful. Like CAPS, the AACC offered professional fellowship and was not a licensing or accrediting organization. But the AACC offered three things that CAPS did not. First, whereas CAPS sought to peg its conferences and journal at an academic, scholarly level, the AACC aimed to serve the more pragmatic interests of practitioners. Second, though not outwardly hostile to CAPS—a great deal of crossover continued at national conferences—it was no secret that Collins and other theologically and ethically conservative psychologists had become troubled by developments in CAPS. Harold Ellens, the director of CAPS, had always stood at the liberal edge of the evangelical movement, open to the frankly liberal mainline pastoral counselors and openly disdainful of more conservative evangelicals. Collins was concerned that during the 1980s many in CAPS had compromised their professed Christianity by condoning immorality, by greed for status and money, by "merger with humanistic and self-centered theories," and by ignoring or denigrating the verities of simple Bible-believing.[19] The AACC stood openly for traditional doctrine and morals and for defining counseling as a straightforward form of explicitly Christian "ministry." Third, the AACC offered malpractice insurance for mental health professionals at rock-bottom rates. The attractive insurance rates both drew practitioners and put the organization on a solid financial footing.

Collins had organized two highly successful International Congresses on Christian Counseling

(Atlanta '88 and Atlanta '92), each of which drew several thousand mental health practitioners. The AACC emerged out of the momentum of these conferences. The AACC began to publish yet a third integrationist journal, *The Christian Counselor,* in 1992. This journal was distinctly for practitioners who counseled daily with troubled people, and it was distinctly for theological and ethical conservatives. It was not, like the *Journal of Psychology and Theology,* a forum for professors and graduate students to hammer out theoretical issues regarding the integration of psychology and Christianity and to publish their psychological research. It was not abstract and liberal-leaning like the *Journal of Psychology and Christianity.* The AACC and its new journal particularly fulfilled Gary Collins's vision to be both populist and professional, to be both professionally psychological and unabashedly evangelical in belief and morals. AACC proved hugely successful, a testimony to Collins's amiability and energy, to the rapidly swelling number of evangelical mental health practitioners with practical rather than highbrow concerns, and to the attractiveness of its insurance rates. By 1995 the AACC had rocketed past 17,000 members.

By the mid-1980s, "Bible-believing evangelical" had become one flesh with "professional psychotherapist," a state of affairs unimaginable twenty years earlier. Christian psychotherapy had joined the pastorate, missions, teaching, and medicine as legitimate callings for those young people who wanted to "help others" or to "go into ministry." The integration movement had accomplished two things during the 1970s and early 1980s. First, it had provided a cognitive rationale, developing intellectual habits that seemed to wed modern psychology and traditional evangelical theology successfully. Second, it had created a professional and institutional network to educate and carry into practice a professedly evangelical psycho-

therapeutic. Evangelicals could train their own in psychology, and those trained in secular settings could find their evangelicalism reinforced within religiously oriented professional associations. Almost everywhere in the United States, conservative Protestants no longer had to refer troubled members to secular therapists or to secular inpatient psychiatric units. Evangelicals trained in the modern psychologies could treat their own. A counseling revolution had occurred.

What was happening professionally was mirrored in popular evangelical culture. *Christianity Today,* the largest evangelical magazine, regularly printed articles by psychologists. In 1980 *Christianity Today* also began publishing *Leadership,* a professional journal for conservative Protestant pastors. It aimed to fill the same niche as Adams's *JPP,* founded only three years earlier. *Leadership* had much to say about problems in living experienced both by evangelical pastors and their flocks, and it had much to say about counseling ministry. But what it said about those problems and their solutions came from the evangelical psychologists' point of view, not the nouthetic view.[20] *Leadership* was noteworthy for the degree to which the social sciences framed and informed discourse. Between 1980 and 1988, an historian critical of the invasion of the therapeutic noted that, though most of the articles had to do with the various personal and counseling crises faced by pastors, "less than 1 percent of the material made any clear reference to Scripture, still less to any idea that is theological."[21] *Leadership* succeeded spectacularly. By the early 1990s it claimed more than 70,000 subscribers and 120,000 readers, three quarters of the readers being clergy.

Though Adams claimed that thousands of pastors agreed with him, it appeared that tens of thousands disagreed, finding him unsatisfactory for a variety of reasons, and esteeming the psychotherapies. While Adams's *JPP* withered, *Leadership* thrived. Pastors troubled with their own problems in living and those of parishioners often steered clear, or were steered clear, of Adams. Nouthetic counseling gained a wide reputation for being unsympathetic and dogmatic; many pastors and parishioners were afraid of "getting beat up with the Bible."[22] The following assessment—from a pastor who shared Jay Adams's theological perspective—was not uncommon: "My impressions were shaped from Jay Adams's first writings, as well as some major casualties from 'nouthetic' confrontations. In my view it was little more than behaviorism with a veneer of Bible verses."[23] Adams's attempt to cut out the support base of the professional powers-that-be had underestimated the strength of the psychotherapists, the plausibility of their ideas and practices, and the implausibility of his own proposals even among his intended audience.

Parishioners joined their pastors in embracing the therapeutic. The best-selling self-help books among evangelicals were psychologically flavored. In the early 1980s televangelist Robert Schuller's *Self-Esteem: The New Reformation*[24] had been criticized both by theologians (for his redefinition of sin into an unfulfilled need for self-esteem) and by psychologists (for the crudities of his pop psychology). But the popularity of Schuller's "possibility thinking"—Norman Vincent Peale's "positive thinking" updated—was the harbinger of a new pop-psychologized evangelicalism that swept American conservative Protestant churches in the decade that followed. Self-help books by psychotherapists—e.g., James Dobson, William Backus, Minirth and Meier, Robert McGee, Larry Crabb—dominated the religious best-seller list throughout the decade.[25] By the end of the decade Dobson's Focus on the Family radio programs was aired daily on more than 1,800 stations, bringing psychotherapists on the air as guests to discuss common life problems and to publicize their products and services.

The popular esteem of psychologists as cultural authorities on life's problems had soared. In the mid-1980s interest in the therapeutic became epidemic in the evangelical mainstream. All evangelicalism seemed to go psychodynamic—or cognitive or humanistic or twelve-step. The "recovery movement" occurring in the wider American culture was embraced widely. Pop psychology increasingly became the vernacular in which significant parts of Protestant daily life were transacted.[26] Sociologist of religion James Hunter commented on this phenomenon in its early stages: "(Their) analyses differ in degree of sophistication. At one level is the crude psychologizing of biblical language and imagery. . . . At the highest level, there is the synthesis of biblicism and humanistic or Freudian psychology. . . . Yet the substantive difference is superficial."[27] Even local church structures of caring for problems in living also shifted markedly in the late 1980s. Twelve-step "support group" programs, modeled on Alcoholics Anonymous, frequently became the small group of choice in many conservative churches, substituting for the traditional Bible study, prayer, and discipleship groups of the previous generation. Books and seminars from Lyman Coleman's Serendipity, for example, enjoyed huge popularity with their programs for instituting support groups.[28]

This mass psychological movement was not viewed uncritically by the leading evangelical psychologists, as we have seen in both this and the previous chapters. The phenomenal expansion of for-profit, inpatient psychiatry by and for evangelicals received cover story attention in *Christianity Today,* as psychotherapists tried to make sense of their profession's runaway commercial and popular success.[29] Many leaders expressed marked ambivalence about the success of the movement they had helped to bring about. For example, Gary Collins's keynote address at Atlanta '92 warned of two dangers: "Number one, that we will abandon the church. And the second danger is that our field will take over the church."[30]

One related development among the evangelical psychotherapists is worth noting. Many evangelical psychotherapists became more outspokenly conservative in their theology and ethics by the late 1980s. The most influential psychologists enthusiastically and increasingly claimed to be "biblical."[31] MMNL wore its evangelicalism openly, as we have seen. Larry Crabb came to sound quite similar to Adams in everything except his professional vision. He repudiated "integration" altogether, called for an understanding of problems in living that arose from the Bible, and aimed to return counseling to the church. Crabb became the most popular evangelical counselor during the late 1980s and into the 1990s. Gary Collins not only openly criticized some CAPS members for their drift and founded an alternative association, but he also called for explicitly "biblical" renewal of the counseling endeavor, and wrote a layman's systematic theology to that end.[32]

Professions provide services and bid for clients. Consumers vote with their feet, their time, their wallets. The huge evangelical subculture—pastors and their parishioners; publishers and those who bought their wares; counseling professionals, their clients, and their teachers—made its preferences clear. Those Adams had contemned as the "so-called professionals" were largely successful in prosecuting their professional claims among the mainstream of conservative Protestants. His own movement was confined to backwaters, with few exceptions.

This was a jurisdictional conflict in which no fundamental compromise was possible. Counseling education, licensure, professional practice, popular writing, and churchly practice would be conducted under the oversight of either psychotherapeutic or ecclesiastical professions. Each group carved out an area of uneasy domination among a sector of conservative Protestantism,

mapping roughly onto the division between fundamentalists and neoevangelicals that had characterized the previous fifty years. Nouthetic counseling tended to be more successful in fundamentalist circles and with local churches; psychotherapy predominated in evangelical circles and with the cultural gatekeepers for conservative Protestants. But borders needed continual maintenance and were easily threatened because members of both groups held so much in common.[33]

Neither Adams's continuing torrent of new books, nor books by other nouthetic authors, ever penetrated the wider counseling community.[34] Within the increasingly sectarian nouthetic community, the writings of Adams and others might play the role of "normal science," working out details and implications of their paradigm. But to the wider counseling community they were mere perseverations of an unsatisfactory paradigm. Adams became increasingly irrelevant to the psychotherapists as his jurisdictional assault was repelled and their professional prerogatives were secured. For example, in the early to mid-1980s, Rosemead's Narramore and Carter worked on what was to be a definitive book-length critique of Jay Adams. They finished eleven chapters and then lost interest, never completing or publishing the book. Adams no longer mattered enough, a judgment that reflected the increasing security of the psychotherapists' professional status.[35] The psychotherapists won most of the visible institutional high ground; nouthetic pastoral counselors won only occasional victories in the institutional hinterlands.

Internal Developments and Fault Lines in the Nouthetic Movement

Many of nouthetic counseling's leading institutions endured difficult times during the 1980s; several of them ended the decade moribund. Fault lines appeared, leading to tensions that needed continual negotiation. The movement stagnated intellectually and institutionally. Adams's distinctives were recycled, with little creative development. Both the NANC and the *JPP* sagged and by the late 1980s seemed moribund. Westminster Seminary experimented with different programs, none particularly successful in fulfilling Adams's mandate to produce "competent" pastoral counselors. Though CCEF's counseling practice grew tremendously, to many in the nouthetic movement developments at CCEF sometimes appeared to undermine nouthetic orthodoxy.

Changes of direction in Adams's career had a marked effect on the movement he started and dominated. Health problems in the mid-1970s contributed to his stepping away from regular counseling practice, seminary teaching, and a relentless travel schedule. While he continued to churn out books and articles about counseling, his period of creative development had ended. Bettler commented, "Jay Adams did a *lot* of counseling for about seven years, until 1975, but he has not developed over the past 15 years. He has a different calling. Jay didn't *love* to do counseling; he wanted to write about counseling."[36] Adams's approach to counseling was finalized with *The Christian Counselor's Manual* in 1973.

Jay Adams *did* love to preach—in print and in person. After his six-year writing sabbatical, in 1982 he moved to southern California to teach at Westminster Theological Seminary's branch campus.[37] There Adams headed up a doctor of ministry program in preaching for seven years. The preacher was returning full circle. While remaining active on the NANC and CCEF boards, and regularly speaking at their annual conferences on counseling, the problems of preaching absorbed more of his attention: he published seven books and a score of short articles on preaching over the next ten years.[38] In 1989 Adams left Westminster West and completed the circle, again becom-

ing a local church pastor. He began an Associate Reformed Presbyterian congregation outside Greenville, South Carolina. During the 1980s, while Adams gave himself to writing, and then to training preachers rather than counselors, things were not always well with the counseling institutions he had founded.

Membership in the NANC had quickly plateaued at about one hundred, where it stayed through the 1980s.[39] As an accrediting organization for pastoral counselors and for training institutions, NANC remained minuscule. Historically, clergy "do not generally have . . . associations independent of their ecclesiastical structure," and those NANC members appealed to were no exception.[40] Pastors were busy men, and however much they might be committed to nouthetic counseling in principle, they had already jumped through the significant professional hoops: theological education, ordination exams, and accountability to denominational oversight.[41] NANC's director through the mid-1980s commented, "It has always been hard to sell preachers on the idea of supervised counseling; that has been the biggest hindrance to growth."[42] The attempt to insert a certification in counseling on top of ordination largely miscarried, though a NANC membership entailed rather minimal standards: written examinations in counseling and theology, supervision of fifty hours of counseling by a NANC Fellow, and ongoing accountability to the code of ethics and statement of faith. Schools evidenced no interest in becoming approved by NANC. In the first place, few of them chose to embrace Adams's model as an ideological position. And, like pastors, educational institutions occupied an existing system of formal accreditation. A NANC "certification" was meaningless institutionally.

NANC also drifted somewhat out of favor with leaders of the other major nouthetic institutions. Concerns that the increasing professionalization of the counseling field would lead to legal restrictions on pastoral counseling had provided the impetus to create NANC: "We needed to be ahead of the game with a credible organization to legitimate us by providing institutional structure, policing, ethics, and theory. In a pluralistic society, if you want turf, you must demonstrate that you can define it and police it."[43] But for quite different reasons, John Broger and John Bettler became disaffected with NANC's mandate and performance.

Accrediting purposes had won out over Broger's desire for an organization serving fellowship purposes. He had opposed the emphasis on certifying an authoritative, professionalized clergy, preferring a loose association of Christians, both lay and clergy, who shared an interest in biblical counseling. Though Broger remained involved for the first few years, he became disillusioned by NANC's professional goals. At the annual meeting in 1983 a CCEF staff member presented a paper that Adams, Broger, and other NANC board members objected to as integrationistic. Such compromise seemed to be the product of NANC's and CCEF's aspirations to professional and intellectual credibility. Broger never again attended a NANC conference, devoting his entire attention to BCF.

Meanwhile Bettler also gradually lost both interest and confidence in NANC. It had certified several candidates whose competency he thought suspect and seemed to operate something like a "good old boys club."[44] The lack of quality control raised Bettler's fears that by certifying poor counselors and teachers, NANC would prove to be an embarrassment rather than a credit to the movement. Bettler also had little patience for sectarian posturing and polemics and feared that NANC's negativistic identity was hurting the movement. In both ways, NANC jeopardized Bettler's goal to produce an intelligentsia, a cadre of specialists in pastoral counseling, who could defend biblical counseling to the wider church. Like Broger, after

the early 1980s Bettler stepped off NANC's board and largely stopped attending annual meetings.

NANC had other troubles besides the disaffection of some leaders in the movement. Attendance at annual conferences remained flat, averaging 150 through the 1980s. There was no money to hire a director or secretarial help, let alone to do publicity. Administrative functions—grading membership exams, organizing the annual conference, refining the constitution—had been performed on a volunteer basis, with CCEF's business manager serving as executive director to handle administrative details. After NANC was let loose from CCEF, no one was willing to take on executive responsibility. Howard Eyrich, a longstanding board member, finally agreed to serve as volunteer director, a position he held until 1988. These were "the lean years," when NANC barely survived.[45] It managed to put on its annual conference and, in 1987, to begin publishing a small, occasional newsletter, *The Biblical Counselor*. Symptomatic of the general malaise, Eyrich had difficulty getting writers for the brief article that anchored each issue.

At the end of the decade, NANC gained an institutional patron that enabled it to survive. In 1988, the NANC board asked Bill Goode, the pastor of Faith Baptist Church and cofounder of FBCM, to bring NANC's administration into his church and to take over the directorship as a subset of his job description for the church. After some urging, Goode agreed. For the first time the organization had a director compensated for his time, as well as a pool of secretarial and volunteer help. A dreary decade ended with a minor revitalization.

Meanwhile, the *JPP* was similarly languishing, and it ended the 1980s moribund. Edited by Jay Adams and published by CCEF, the first five hundred subscribers came easily, and *JPP* subscriptions rose to more than one thousand in the three years after its founding in 1977. During the first two years it published biannual bound volumes. In 1979 it stepped up to a quarterly publication schedule averaging 150 pages per issue. Adams served as general editor overseeing a team of section editors each responsible for one of a wide range of pastoral topics. Counseling articles slightly predominated, but *JPP* contained regular sections on medicine, preaching, missions, and cults, along with occasional articles on law, Christian education, church finances, and evangelism. But by 1981 the journal started to lag. *JPP* dropped back to two issues a year in 1981 and 1982.

Citing rising costs and the desire to concentrate on counseling topics, the journal made a major cutback in 1983. It dropped its pretension to provide a comprehensive professional journal for pastors, abandoned its system of section editors, and put entire editorial responsibility in Adams's hands. Regular contents included only counseling, preaching, and medicine, with counseling by far predominating. Adams himself almost invariably authored the preaching section, and the medical articles were largely written by Bob Smith, the MD who had cofounded FBCM. These two largely carried the journal over the next decade. Adams contributed 30 percent of all published articles, reviews, and editorials, while Smith added 10 percent. In an attempt to get back on a regular publishing schedule, the average number of pages dropped from about 150 to 60 in 1983. For a year and a half the reduced journal was able to maintain a quarterly pace of publication. But then the pace again began to sag. During 1987–89, *JPP* was publishing only twice per year, and then it became sporadic: only one issue came out in each of 1990 and 1991.

Subscriptions tailed off throughout the decade, dropping from the peak of more than 1,000 to 450 by the early 1990s. Of these, 200 were institutional libraries, whose inertia kept the journal barely afloat. Adams could not find writers. Most of what other nouthetic counselors wrote was in the self-help genre. The pastors to whom Jay Adams appealed were practitioners, not scholars. What they did write tended to be derivative, rehearsing stock nouthetic themes. The journal failed to draw authors from the wider conservative Protestant community. Psychologist John Carter's 1980 assessment of nouthetic counseling's future proved prescient. He thought that Jay Adams had already given dogmatic answers to most of the significant counseling questions, closing off further discussion and development. The nouthetic counseling movement could do little more than rehash its founder's thoughts, and he was skeptical about the prospects:

> If CCEF and Jay seriously want to influence and relate to the larger Christian Counseling Community, [they] will have to move from a stance of hostile elite isolation into a position of dialogue and discussion. . . . [So-called] 'distinctively Christian counseling' will perish shortly after Jay's passing if it does not develop a perspective which is broader than the thoughts of one scholar and which has some root in the Christian Counseling Community outside Westminster and CCEF.[46]

Nouthetic counseling's journal, like its professional organization, was perishing even before the demise of its founder. That "Christian Counseling Community" from which Adams isolated himself was the community of evangelical psychotherapists who largely controlled discourse, education, and legitimation in the counseling field. A counseling journal—a counseling movement—by and for pastors could not sustain itself.

Adams and Bettler had quite different perspectives on the troubles that beset their journal. Adams was disappointed in CCEF. Bettler and those he had hired to teach at Westminster Seminary were supposed to provide intellectual leadership, but they evidenced little interest in the journal they published. Bettler and his CCEF staff contributed barely an article a year: only a dozen articles (out of some 250) in the twenty-five issues published during the 1980s. Adams alone published seventy-five items during that same time. Bettler's interest in *JPP,* like his interest in NANC, had waned quickly. He was disappointed in the caliber of the "intensely practical" *JPP.* Adams had encouraged generalist pastors to write, and, from Bettler's perspective, *JPP* had generated some depressingly poor quality writing and thinking. During 1980–81 Bettler explored the possibility of starting another, more scholarly journal. But plans for a second journal miscarried early when it became clear that the movement did not have enough writers, let alone scholars, to sustain even one journal. The *JPP* languished, a source of disappointment to both Adams and Bettler for their different reasons. By 1990, Adams spoke regretfully about "back when we used to have a journal."[47]

The career of *JPP* demonstrated in microcosm the professional fortunes of nouthetic counseling relative to the integrationist movement. Adams wanted to equip a pastorate to counsel from the standpoint of a distinctive knowledge system and with demonstrable competency and efficacy. *JPP* was to be an instrument to that end. Adams's programmatic editorial in 1977 had been right that conservative Protestant ministers lacked their own professional journal. But the void would be successfully filled by *Leadership,* not *JPP.* Almost 100,000 pastors read *Leadership,* which was committed to appropriate the wisdoms of the modern psychologies, not to inculcating a nouthetic counseling philosophy and practice into local churches.

Nouthetic counseling had only slightly more success in book publishing. Adams scored one publishing coup. In 1984, rights to twenty of his books were picked up by Zondervan, a major evangelical publisher, in a series that they entitled the Jay Adams Library and published under their Ministry Resources Library imprint. This location in the Zondervan product line distinctly identified Adams as an author relevant to pastors. Zondervan's main product line remained a major source of psychology and self-help books by evangelical psychotherapists. *Competent to Counsel* continued to sell a steady 7,000–10,000 copies per year through the 1980s and into the 1990s; others of his books were less successful, and a number went out of print. Only a handful of other nouthetic counselors wrote books. They gained only limited exposure to the wider evangelical church, relying on small religious publishing houses, and even self-publishing, to get their Bible-oriented self-help books into print.[48]

Higher education provided a less than friendly home for Adams's pastoral counseling. Nouthetic counseling had a difficult time establishing educational niches, even on its home ground at Westminster Seminary. The decade started out promisingly. In 1980 Bettler had gotten the program he wanted in order to "combine Harvard and Moody," intellectual rigor and ministerial practicality: a doctor of ministry in counseling that involved a year of resident course work, followed by seven hundred hours of supervised counseling and a thesis. His vision for an academically and professionally respectable version of nouthetic counseling seemed to have found an acceptable institutional vehicle, though the program was small, admitting five to ten pastors per year. But in 1986 Westminster dropped the residential DMin program because accreditors judged it too demanding in comparison to prevailing standards for DMin programs. The seminary shifted to a more standard DMin program, scaling back the requirements from a year of residency to four weeks of modular education and dropping all supervised counseling. Meanwhile, in 1984 Westminster had also initiated a two-year master's in counseling program in which CCEF taught all counseling courses. But neither program pleased Bettler. The new DMin provided little opportunity to influence students, and lacked rigor. The master's gave more time for intellectual development, but its curriculum lacked several core CCEF courses and any practicum requirements. It provided few professional prospects and was of limited use as a terminal degree. The Westminster programs bore little promise of delivering the flow of intellectually and professionally capable counselors that he desired. By the late 1980s the curriculum lacked coherence, and Bettler's "Harvard and Moody" was still a wish unfulfilled.

Nouthetic counseling made spotty headway within other schools. No broadly evangelical schools and only a few Reformed seminaries embraced it. In 1982 Westminster Theological Seminary in California (Escondido) set up an arrangement with CCEF's San Diego branch similar to the relationship between Westminster and CCEF in Philadelphia. Another seminary in the Philadelphia area, Biblical Theological Seminary (Hatfield, Pa.), began a master's program in 1984, hiring a Westminster DMin graduate to head the department. Other leading Reformed seminaries—Covenant Theological Seminary in St. Louis and Reformed Theological Seminary in Jackson, Mississippi—actively opposed Adams. Covenant's counseling professor, William Kirwan, appreciated Karen Horney's psychology and was a longtime foe of Adams. His *Biblical Concepts for Christian Counseling* (1984) conducted a running argument with Adams. Reformed's James Hurley, an advocate of family systems therapy, was less visible than Kirwan but no less critical of Adams. When invited in 1993 to evaluate the Practical Theology Department at Westminster Theological Seminary in California, three-quarters of his review involved a detailed criticism of the counseling program's commitment to Jay Adams's model and to

its neglect of the "common grace" wisdom of the psychologies.[49] Fundamentalist institutions also responded unpredictably to Adams. For example, Baptist Bible College (Clark Summit, Pa.) and Calvary Baptist Seminary (Lansdale, Pa.) taught nouthetic counseling through the 1980s. The heads of both their counseling departments had graduated from Westminster's DMin program. Jerry Falwell's Liberty University (Lynchburg, Va.) initially received nouthetic counseling favorably, also under the leadership of a trainee of Adams who had received a Westminster DMin. But when Liberty made a bid for greater intellectual respectability, they hired psychologist Gary Collins to head up the Psychology Department. Other fundamentalist institutions never embraced Adams. For example, Cedarville College (Cedarville, Ohio), where Adams had delivered his "Your Place in the Counseling Revolution" address in 1975, strongly opposed nouthetic counseling.

CCEF also struggled—and changed—during the 1980s. After Adams left, CCEF was remade into Bettler's image. I will sketch his numerous intellectual differences with Adams as well as the changes he brought to the tone and practice of counseling at CCEF. A host of specific conceptual differences played out along the fault line of the Adams-Bettler friendship and partnership. Bettler's specific criticisms of Adams were similar to those made by psychotherapists and mainline pastoral counselors (see chap. 8): misuse of the Bible, externalism, neglect of social factors, overly directive methodology, unfairness to the real views of psychologists.

First, Bettler was concerned that biblical counselors had a "tendency to twist . . . the Scripture to substantiate [their] conclusions." He indicted Adams in particular for sometimes "making the Scripture say something it never intended to say." Nouthetic counselors were at times "unfair to the text of Scripture," guilty of illegitimate proof-texting and of emphasizing some biblical themes to the neglect of others.[50] Second, like the psychotherapists, Bettler was interested in understanding the internal dimensions of human life, whereas Adams had been chiefly interested in what counselees did, not why they might have done it. Bettler's only major publication was a six-part series on self-image, an analysis of the criteria that informed the self-evaluative gaze. He also wrote about the dynamics of human desire and the structure of the functional beliefs that presumably underlay behavior.[51] Third, again like the psychotherapists, Bettler thought that the impact and influence of the social dimension on counselees was often neglected by nouthetic counselors. They could be "unfair to the enormity of problems that counselees bring,"[52] particularly problems that arose in the context of being wronged by others. He thought that Adams had been so concerned to correct secular errors that he had trivialized significant problems in living. Bettler took Adams to task—quoting Bible chapter and verse, naturally—for downplaying the effects of suffering experienced by abused counselees: "Colossians 3:21 . . . says that fathers should not embitter their children lest they become discouraged."[53] Fourth, Bettler's view of counseling methodology also led him to emphasize very different things from Adams's authoritative confrontation and directiveness. In Adams's counseling method, the counselor taught truth to the counselee who then applied it in action. Bettler was more interested in helping the counselee gain insight that would lead to change. Bettler saw counselors often playing the role of mentor or friend; Adams viewed the role as coach and pastoral authority. Bettler thought counseling was often a patient affair; Adams thought it was brisk. Finally, Bettler believed that "many biblical counselors have been unfair to their enemies," the psychologists.[54] He thought that Adams often treated psychologists unfairly, setting up straw men easy to demolish. Bettler also cultivated what had

been a subtheme in Adams: the insights of secular psychologists could be redeemed, "recycled or recast," profitably.[55]

Such intellectual differences translated into an institution quite different from the CCEF of the early 1970s. For example, over the years, CCEF's counseling became a more private and less communal affair: the average number of people in the room dropped from five to two. The number of counselees per case dropped significantly between 1970 and 1990, from 1.8 to 1.2. Increasingly counselors dealt with the problems in living of an individual rather than of a group. At the same time, the average number of counselors dropped from three (a lead counselor and two participant-observers) to one. Participant observation had grown unwieldy as the number of students increased and the demographics of the student body changed. During Adams's tenure, the counseling students were almost all male pastors or seminarians. By the late 1980s the student body was more than half female, and the percentage of pastors was under 20 percent. CCEF's educational model shifted to the academic classroom and away from the hands-on, "discipleship" style that Adams had utilized. Several other factors played into the elimination of participant observers. Bettler treated the counselor-counselee relationship differently than Adams. Adams viewed counselors as interchangeable—any competent counselor could give the necessary advice, and there was nothing special about the relationship. Bettler thought that a relationship of cultivated trust often mattered, and that nouthetic counseling needed to "strengthen the areas of love, listening, empathizing, caring, identifying, patience, understanding . . . without losing other biblical truths."[56] Finally, the reserved Bettler did not like observers sitting in, while the expansive Adams loved it.

Another striking change occurred in the typical duration of counseling. The average number of sessions per case more than doubled between 1970 and 1990. In 1970, counselees came an average of 4.7 sessions; in 1980, 7.1 sessions; in 1990, 12.4 sessions.[57]

TABLE 11

Number of Sessions of Counseling

	c. 1970	c. 1980	c. 1990
1 session	23%	16%	12%
2–3 sessions	21%	17%	21%
4–6 sessions	33%	25%	17%
7–12 sessions	19%	28%	22%
13–24 sessions	3%	11%	15%
25+ sessions	1%	3%	13%

Over the period of time since Adams had left CCEF, the percentage of people who came only one time fell from 23 percent to 12 percent. Counselees who came six times or less dropped from 77 percent to 50 percent. The number of people coming more than twelve times increased from 4 percent to 28 percent of the caseload. Nouthetic counseling at CCEF was still not long-term counseling in the vast majority of cases, but it no longer showed the rapid turnover that had characterized Adams's tightly structured, highly directive counseling.

The shift of CCEF's focus from local church pastor to pastoral counseling specialist took many forms. Most concretely, Bettler engineered marked changes in the composition of CCEF's counseling staff. In the early 1970s six of the seven counselors were experienced and practicing local church pastors (the one exception was a seminarian who subsequently became a pastor). None specialized in counseling—indeed, CCEF had no full-time employees until 1974 when Bettler returned from graduate school to become director. These pastors counseled and taught at CCEF one day a week as one aspect of their generalist ministries in local churches in the area. Already by 1980 CCEF's staffing pattern was significantly altered. Five of the twelve counselors had formerly been pastors of local churches (including Bettler, the only remaining staff member from the early years). But each had become a specialized pastoral counselor now employed by CCEF, not by a local congregation.[58] The other seven counselors—some of whom worked part time—were male, seminary graduates who had never "entered the pastorate" but who became specialized pastoral counselors directly out of seminary. By 1990, a further evolution had occurred. The professional staff consisted of thirty counselors (including twelve part-time employees). One of the part-time counselors was currently a pastor; eleven counselors were former pastors (four of these remained from 1980); eight were male nonpastors (seven seminary graduates or students; two remaining from 1980); and ten were female nonpastors (seven of whom were seminary graduates or students). The professional identity of the CCEF staff, male and female, centered in the counseling role. Adams's argument for the pastor as God's professional had excluded women from playing a professional counseling role. But when Adams wrote that "the work of counseling should be carried on preeminently by ministers and other Christians whose gifts, training and calling especially qualify and require them to pursue the work,"[59] Bettler included women among those "other Christians."[60]

During the 1980s CCEF became much more aggressive in marketing its counseling to the conservative Protestant population. Three factors registered the change: the creation of satellite counseling centers, a huge expansion of CCEF's counseling caseload, and the institution's increasing dependency on counseling fees to meet its budget. This constellation of changes raised serious philosophical questions for critics of CCEF's growing professionalism. It seemed to undercut CCEF's purported reasons for existence because CCEF's success as a freestanding counseling center presumably occurred at the expense of teaching local churches to do the job. In 1982 CCEF founded its first branch center, under George Scipione. It was located in San Diego in order to affiliate with Westminster Seminary's new California campus in Escondido.[61] Subsequently, CCEF opened four branch centers in the mid-Atlantic region (in Cherry Hill and Princeton, N. J., and in Bethlehem and Reading, Pa.), each about an hour away from the home office. In the 1980s CCEF massively expanded its caseload. The number of hours counseled yearly was 1,000 in the early 1970s. It had risen to 2,000 by 1978 and kept rising rapidly: to 4,000 in 1981 and more than 10,000 by the end of the decade. From 1979 to 1991 the hourly fee increased from fourteen dollars to fifty dollars, and the annual gross income from counseling increased from $28,000 to more than $500,000. CCEF's reliance on counseling fees to meet its budget also greatly increased. Counseling generated 12 percent of CCEF's income in 1979, 28 percent in 1984, 38 percent in 1987, and 53 percent in 1991.[62]

CCEF increasingly differed from Adams intellectually and professionally; it also differed in interprofessional relations. Bettler pursued interactions with evangelical psychologists. Adams had written them off as so-called and self-proclaimed professionals who lacked ecclesiastical credentials, but Bettler wanted to talk to the cultural gatekeepers, to field their criticisms, to win them. In 1988 CCEF sponsored a lecture series at Westminster Seminary by Roman Catholic academic psychologist Paul Vitz, a well-known critic of humanistic psychology.[63] In the mid- and late-1980s CCEF had Larry Crabb speak on three occasions; Bettler also arranged a daylong private meeting with

Crabb, intended to build understanding and to determine and debate differences. Bettler encouraged CCEF staff members to present papers at the annual meetings of the Christian Association of Psychological Studies, and CCEF was represented almost yearly between 1982 and 1989.

Nouthetic counseling always struck outsiders as monolithic because of Jay Adams's dominating and defining presence. But looked at more closely, significant fault lines ran through the movement. These became increasingly evident through the 1980s. Three tendencies within nouthetic counseling roughly expressed the differences between the three originals in nouthetic counseling's first generation: Jay Adams, John Bettler, and John Broger. The organizing concern of each man can be easily encapsulated: Adams represented generalist local church pastors, Bettler represented specialized pastoral counselors, and Broger represented laypeople.

These three found common cause in the commitment to be "biblical" in the conservative Protestant sense. Each of them brought numerous individual pastors, counseling specialists, and laypeople under his teaching but under the aspect of his dominant concern. But where those concerns pulled in opposing directions, and as institutional trajectories were established, conflicts and suspicions could and did arise. They disagreed with each other often and worried about where the others' tendencies might carry them. Adams viewed Bettler's pursuit of intellectual engagement with the evangelical psychologists as a waste of time, and the expansion of CCEF's caseload threatened to jeopardize his mission to equip pastors to do the job themselves. He was concerned that Broger's emphasis on the laity tended to lose sight of the centrality of pastor and church, and that his manual ran the danger of becoming a cookbook. Bettler did not like the narrowness and inflexibility of Broger's project; its style ran counter to his every instinct. Bettler sometimes flinched at Adams's sweeping generalizations and the lack of development in his model; the brashness and dogmatism of the movement leader could offend the self-critical academic, who did not mind decentering himself to look at things from another point of view. Broger did not like Adams's stridency toward psychologists and his tendency toward pastoral authoritarianism; he mistrusted Bettler's experimental attitude toward ideas, preferring all statements to be carefully undergirded with biblical citations.

The major institutions each bore the stamp of one or another of nouthetic counseling's three original institution builders. Adams's tendencies dominated the professional organization and journal—the NANC and the *JPP*—and were closely replicated in FBCM that took over NANC in 1988. Bettler's perspective suffused the leading educational institution, the CCEF, and struggled toward realization in Westminster Theological Seminary's curriculum. Broger's single-minded intention worked out into his training program for laycounselors through the BCF.

Broger worked in isolation from the rest of the nouthetic counseling movement after the founding years, but the other institutions were closely interwoven. Adams and Bettler negotiated their numerous differences of emphasis privately within their friendship, but institutional relationships were more tense. The many changes at CCEF produced growing mutual suspicion between CCEF and NANC through the 1980s. The adequacy and shape of the knowledge system and the definition of professional identity were both controversial. The defining intellectual question for NANC turned on whether CCEF was guilty of compromise with psychology because of its many departures from Adams's original model. CCEF seemed to define itself more by its differences from Adams than by its commonalities with him. For example, in the

1980s Bettler became so uncomfortable with the connotations of belligerency that attached to the word *nouthetic* that he stopped using it. Bettler's intellectual emphases sounded more like Alfred Adler and Larry Crabb than like Jay Adams and O. H. Mowrer. Suspicions were confirmed when several CCEF staff members presented papers at NANC during the mid- and late-1980s that were criticized as integrationistic. Fears that CCEF had tilted in Crabb's direction seemed justified, both by the repeated invitations for Crabb to speak and by the content of talks that seemed insufficiently critical of the psychologies. Bettler had his own set of intellectual concerns about NANC. He suspected that NANC was guilty of sectarian anti-intellectualism, and that it had fossilized Adams's initial version of nouthetic counseling, treating it as the standard of orthodoxy for the movement rather than as a revisable first draft. CCEF's perceived aloofness and intellectualism mirrored NANC's perceived rigidity and sectarianism.

The defining professional question for NANC concerned the implications of CCEF's shift in emphasis from pastors-who-counsel to professional pastoral counselors and laity, from the generalist in the local church to the specialist in the freestanding counseling center and the person in the pew. Meanwhile, from its point of view, CCEF worried about the quality of counseling done by those generalist pastors: counseling that was "unfair" to Scripture, motivation, suffering, relationship, and opponents would likely prove to be incompetent counseling. George Scipione, who served on both boards, reflected NANC's concerns when he said: "CCEF is biblical in content, but it's secular professional in form . . . and the pastors love it that way because they can farm out their counseling rather than having to learn to do it themselves. CCEF can say it's not a mental health center, but if it looks like a duck, and walks like a duck, and quacks like a duck, maybe it's a duck."[64]

Howard Eyrich, a CCEF employee in the 1970s and NANC's director through the mid-1980s, captured CCEF's concerns when he said that he had often been troubled by seeing in nouthetic counselors a "rigid, legalistic, exhortation orientation; advice-giving and a tendency not to listen to counselees."[65]

The two most stable institutions during the 1980s were BCF and FBCM. Each stuck successfully with one central mission, developing and replicating the model they had first learned from Jay Adams. Both avoided the financial complications of fee-for-service counseling, full-time salaried staff, capital investment in facilities, journal publishing, and administering education programs.

Broger and his fellows at BCF did not do counseling, per se. Rather, they taught a system of "discipleship" to audiences ranging in size from a score to hundreds. In effect, BCF's training consisted in an extended Bible study, intended to spur students to examine their own lives and to make appropriate changes. BCF kept to its business of refining its *Self-Confrontation: A Manual for In-Depth Discipleship.*[66] During the 1980s Broger's extensive background in missions and broadcasting opened doors for BCF all over the world, and their training course was taken to various places in Africa, Asia, and South America.

FBCM, in contrast, specifically offered professional pastoral counseling services and training. FBCM, a counseling center housed in a local church, modeled itself on the pre-1976 CCEF. Adams's goal to equip local church pastors to become competent counselors as one component of a generalist ministry found its purest expression in FBCM's training. On taking over NANC in 1988, FBCM gained a national platform. Their teachers and counselors carried condensed versions of their training to weekend and weeklong conferences across the United States, largely in fundamentalist churches and Bible colleges.

Both BCF and FBCM existed on a predictable and uncontroversial financial basis, unlike NANC and CCEF. BCF operated with extremely low overhead: its principals worked on a volunteer basis (e.g., retired government employees on pension, a wife supported by her husband, local pastors), and they used donated facilities. FBCM functioned largely within the budget and entirely on the premises of its local church; its teaching and counseling staff supported themselves doing other things (e.g., several pastors, a medical doctor, a female psychologist on the staff of a children's home). Both institutions offered their services either for free or at a nominal cost to cover administrative expenses.

Two other developments in the 1980s are worth noting. First, a new and strident polemicism, even further to the "right" than Jay Adams, emerged. For example, Martin and Deidre Bobgan and Dave Hunt commended Jay Adams for his pioneering criticisms of secular psychology in the conservative Protestant church and then intensified the polemics. The Bobgans and Hunt themselves did not do pastoral counseling but operated independent "discernment" ministries to expose errors besetting the church. They railed at "psychoheretics" who were "seducing" Christianity.[67]

Martin Bobgan (b. 1930) had received a doctorate in educational psychology and taught at a community college in California. After becoming a convert to conservative Protestantism, he became highly critical of the modern psychologies' influence on the faith. He and Adams came to know each other in the late 1970s, and an occasional collaboration began. Adams wrote an endorsement for the Bobgans' *Psychoheresy,* applauding its indictment of the integrationists' "amalgamation" of Christianity and modern psychology; they dedicated the book to him. Adams contributed a small section to another of the Bobgans' books,[68] and when Adams had difficulty finding a publisher for one of his books, the Bobgans, who had begun their own publishing house, published it.[69] Martin Bobgan spoke at a CCEF West conference in 1988 and at NANC in 1991. During that time the Bobgans increasingly suspected that CCEF and NANC harbored psychoheretical tendencies.[70] Bobgan's 1991 address warned of compromisers in the ranks. An "integrationistic" article in CCEF's newsletter in 1992 catalyzed open attack. In 1994 the Bobgans repudiated the entire biblical counseling movement and attacked CCEF, NANC, BCF, and Jay Adams himself, the fount of a corrupt and corrupting movement.[71] The Bobgans thought that any attempt to articulate a rational counseling method or to provide education in counseling was heretical, arguing that faith and a Bible were all that a Bible-believer needed: "It is entirely unnecessary to use a manual or even to discuss the problem that led the person to seek counsel. Counsel using the Scripture and empowered by the Holy Spirit is effective whether or not one even discusses the problem. . . . A believer empowered by the Holy Spirit and armed with Scripture never has and never will need a manual, method, or training program!"[72] They themselves "repented" from certain aspects of their earlier *How to Counsel from Scripture,* which they believed had erred by offering a "model or methodology . . . or technology of change."[73]

In the 1980s Adams held hopes that the Bobgans could make a constructive contribution. But even before he was attacked, he had reservations about what they were doing. First, they were "laymen," untrained theologically and operating outside the accountability structures for pastoral care. Adams was invariably cautious when masterless men bid to influence the faith and practice of the church.[74] Second, they had a "negative" ministry, criticizing others without contributing much positively: "I've tried never to knock out a window without putting a better one in its place, but

the Bobgans mainly knock out windows." Third, their positive model of counseling, such as it was, represented a regression to pietistic methods that Adams's "counseling revolution" had attempted to redress.[75] Adams thought that traditional methods of pastoral care and pastoral education had not sufficed to equip conservative Protestant pastors to solve many of the problems in living that both they and their parishioners faced. Pastoral care had lacked both a theological rationale and a practical model for engaging in a rational, intentional, and conscientious counseling process; pastoral education had lacked training in counseling. When the Bobgans' explicit anti-intellectualism and pietism led to their repudiation of "biblical counseling," they repudiated the tasks to which Adams had devoted his life.

The heresy hunters had several significant effects on the jurisdictional conflict. First, they excited and reinforced the separatist instincts of some within the nouthetic counseling movement. Second, among psychotherapists Adams's identification with the Bobgans and Hunt further reinforced the iconic image of "Jay Adams." Third, they captured popular attention and drew off attention from Adams. From the end of the 1980s on, psychotherapists devoted energies to rebutting the Bobgans and Hunt and only occasionally mentioned Adams as a historical footnote, a prototype from a previous generation. Fourth, the controversy between psychotherapists and "psychology bashers" changed the popular perception of what the counseling wars among evangelicals were all about. The dispute became increasingly identified as between evangelical psychotherapists and "anti-counseling" critics and crusaders, not between two counseling professions each making distinctive cognitive and jurisdictional claims.[76]

In a second major development, the evangelical psychotherapists and nouthetic counseling collided in one major legal case that dragged on through most of the decade. The biblical counseling move-ment was generally shielded from entanglement in the legal process under long-existing legal pro-tections and exemptions that applied to pastoral care. Its pastors and laypersons neither needed nor pursued licensure, third-party reimbursements, malpractice insurance, and so forth.[77] Nouthetic counseling never bid for the sort of legal recogni-tion that might make it subject either to legisla-tive wrangling over licensing or to vulnerability to malpractice lawsuits.[78] Most of the jurisdictional conflict occurred in the public arena, but the one court clash provided a revealing glimpse into the way evangelical psychotherapists and local church pastors were aligned against one another. *Nally v. Grace Community Church* was a very complicated clergy malpractice lawsuit in California[79] This case eventually upheld legal precedent but not before coming close to overturning a great many of the precedents that had shielded pastoral counselors and the content of their counsel.

In 1979 a depressed young man committed suicide while receiving counseling from pastors in a Los Angeles megachurch.[80] His parents filed suit, claiming clergy malpractice because their son had not been referred to psychiatric help for his problems. The case was twice dismissed at the trial level, only to be reversed each time in appeals court. In 1988 the California Supreme Court reversed the appeals court decision, ruling in favor of the church.[81] One noteworthy aspect of the trial was that four evangelical psychotherapists testi-fied for the prosecution against Grace Community Church's Bible-oriented counseling: "The case broke ground on the issue of allowing expert testi-mony on the standard of care for pastoral counsel-ors."[82] Evangelical psychotherapists were willing to line up against an evangelical church to argue for the legal incompetence of pastors to counsel, and the necessity of referral into the mental health system that licensed psychotherapists.

The Reemergence of Biblical Counseling in the 1990s

Doing contemporary history involves habits of both investigative reporting and anthropol-ogy. The people and events one describes are all midcareer. Tidy historical boundaries don't exist. Surprises happen. Trends reverse even while one is looking at them. New actors come on stage. As we have seen, the 1980s were a decade in which psychotherapists greatly expanded their jurisdictional domain while nouthetic counseling was marginalized. But around 1990, even as the therapeutic movement among evangelicals came into full flower, nouthetic counseling institutions began to grow, and doubts about psychotherapy became increasingly evident among conservative Protestants.

In 1990 attendance at the NANC conference spiked to four hundred, and in subsequent years attendance continued to climb, closing in on one thousand by the mid-1990s. Even NANC mem-bership began to edge upward after being stalled for a decade: five to ten people per year sought and acquired certification in the early 1990s, and in 1995 NANC certified a record twenty-five new members. At the same time, each of the training institutions—CCEF, FBCM, BCF—reported a spurt in student enrollments and a marked increase in churches and schools requesting their training.[83] CCEF got the program it wanted from Westminster Seminary in 1994, a four-year master of divinity in counseling that combined a full theological edu-cation and an extensive practicum in counseling. The *JPP* was also revitalized. Editorial oversight passed to CCEF from Adams in 1992, and the jour-nal came to express Bettler's emphases. The jour-nal, renamed the *Journal of Biblical Counseling* in 1992, again began publishing on a regular sched-ule; by 1995 subscriptions had increased from 450 to 2,500. Even CCEF's dilatory faculty and students finally began to publish books and articles.[84] In the first ten issues of their renamed journal, CCEF faculty and their Westminster graduates contributed 67 percent of the items, Jay Adams 8 percent. Other authors in the biblical counseling movement also began to write, producing at least twenty books in the first half of the 1990s.[85] BCF's *Self-Confrontation Manual* was picked up by a major evangelical publisher in 1994, and it was also translated into more than a dozen languages by the mid-1990s.

Several new institutions came on the scene and quickly began to play a significant role both in the nouthetic community and in the wider evangelical community. Grace Community Church and its pastor, John MacArthur, had been radicalized by the lengthy court case and the direct legal attacks on the church's ministers from evangelical psychotherapists. His book *Our Sufficiency in Christ* was sharply critical of the psychologies.[86] The Master's College and Seminary, which MacArthur had founded alongside Grace Community Church, became committed to nouthetic counseling. The college replaced its psychology department with a biblical counseling department, organized by FBCM's Bob Smith and then headed by CCEF's Wayne Mack; the church reorganized its large counseling ministry along nouthetic counseling lines, and its pastors became certified with NANC. The college and seminary faculty collaborated on a major book, *Introduction to Biblical Counseling,* that gave nouthetic counseling its first comprehensive, programmatic work since the 1970s and the first such book not authored by Jay Adams.[87]

A second institutional innovation occurred in a field contiguous to counseling. Ken Sande, a lawyer influenced by Adams and CCEF, wrote a popular book, *The Peacemaker,* and developed the Institute of Christian Conciliation (ICC) to teach and facilitate conflict resolution in evangelical churches and parachurch organizations. Sande

aimed to bypass the adversarial processes of the legal system by helping people and institutions to reconcile and resolve differences privately. Unlike the counseling field, ambitious professions were not vying to control the field of conciliation, mediation, and peacemaking by establishing cognitive dominion and rights to power, status, and financial reward. Because the ideological stakes and professional rewards were low, Sande's "peacemaking" ministry went largely unchallenged, and the ICC grew rapidly.[88] The vastly different professional ecology and Sande's amiability combined to create openings for his repackaged and nonpolemical nouthetic counseling. Sande's "conflict resolution" was welcomed into seminaries, denominations, and parachurch ministries that had resisted nouthetic counseling when it had appeared under the category "counseling" and with a reputation for belligerency. Adams endorsed *The Peacemaker,* though he was not wholly comfortable with what Sande was doing: Sande was a layman and the ICC was parachurch. But Sande became a persuasive spokesman for the biblical counseling movement.

The fault lines in the biblical counseling movement did not disappear, of course, but informal negotiation procedures were reinstated and proved reasonably successful. The alienation between CCEF and NANC, which had grown noticeable by the late 1980s, was significantly resolved in 1990 when representatives of the two institutions met to discuss their differences and commonalities. Adams was of the opinion that "a separation has been reconciled."[89] CCEF staff again began to attend NANC meetings; Bettler reappeared on the roster of keynote speakers; two of CCEF's staff members were elected to the NANC board, and CCEF hired another member of that board as an employee. Nonetheless, CCEF's teachers and writers still aroused periodic dismay for what seemed to be careless trafficking with the integrationists and with the medical model; NANC speakers still too often seemed more interested in polemics than in wrestling with hard questions. On another front, a NANC board member had become involved with BCF. Though Broger was elderly and ailing, other BCF leaders began to reappear at NANC in the 1990s after nearly a decade of absence. Here, too, historical tensions did not vanish with the warming of relations: BCF leaders were upset by the professionalistic model in some of the counseling "ministries" represented, and by the lack of biblical texts to support some of what was said in talks.[90] On the whole, cooperation increased as nouthetic counselors sought to take their own medicine and make peace, but the uneasiness did not disappear.

Whatever the internal dynamics of Adams's "counseling revolution," there is no doubt that environing cultural conditions also changed in a way that significantly shaped conservative Protestant's responses to biblical counseling in the 1990s. A significant and wide-reaching cultural shift occurred within the evangelical intelligentsia: historians, sociologists, cultural critics, pastoral theologians, apologists, reformers, and, even, psychologists. Criticism of the invasion of the therapeutic into evangelicalism became a commonplace item among the cultural gatekeepers.

Historian George Marsden noted in passing the "obviously Herculean task of integrating the largely opposed assumptions of modern psychology and evangelical theology."[91] Historical theologian David Wells commented more bitingly:

As the nostrums of the therapeutic age supplant confession, and as preaching is psychologized, the meaning of Christian faith becomes privatized. . . . The pastor seeks to embody what modernity admires and to redefine what pastoral ministry now means in light of this culture's most admired types, the manager and the psychologist.

In another age, Robert Schuller's ministry, for example, might well have been viewed not as Christian ministry at all, but as comedy. . . . Schuller is offering in easily digestible bites the therapeutic model of life through which the healing of the bruised self is found. He is by no means alone in this; he is simply the most shameless.[92]

Leading sociologists and culture critics said similar things. Even in 1983, James Hunter's evaluation of trends in evangelical publishing led him to conclude that evangelical faith was being deluged with a psychotherapeutic, narcissistic, and hedonistic preoccupation with the "sensitivities and 'needs' of modern man," and that it had lost touch with the traditional Protestant form of self-examination that was concerned with "the rule of sin in the life and the process of mortification and sanctification."[93] Os Guinness was even more impassioned, calling the modern psychologies carriers of idolatry and heresy in their social role within modern America. The therapeutic was "a substitute theology designed to replace faith in God," and "Psychology supplies us with alternative priests. Sincere counselors may bridle at this point, but there is no question that psychology itself has become an ideology—a set of ideas that serves the interests of an entire industry."[94]

During the late-1980s and 1990s a number of theological and pastoral reformers arose, who sought to bring evangelicalism back to its "roots" in historic Reformed orthodoxy: Michael Horton (Christians United for Reformation; editor of *Modern Reformation*), John Armstrong (Reformation & Revival Ministries; editor of *Reformation & Revival*), and Jay Grimstead (Coalition on Revival; editor of *Crosswinds*). Each of these made frequent reference to the way the therapeutic ethos was threatening the integrity of evangelical faith. In 1996, 150 leading evangelical scholars and pastors formed the Alliance of Confessing Evangelicals and published their "Cambridge

Declaration." This brief statement calling for theological reformation repeatedly mentioned the dangers of the therapeutic ethos: the "self-esteem gospel," the redefinition of God as the satisfier of psychological cravings and needs, the pursuit of self-fulfillment, and other "alternatives to the gospel" that arose from being "dominated by the spirit of the age."[95]

Evangelical high culture was discernibly changing in the 1990s. Many of the leading psychotherapists participated in this cultural shift, as we saw in the previous two chapters. A note of self-criticism, exhortations to listen to critics, and even malaise increasingly pervaded their reflections during the 1990s.[96] The modern psychologies that were meant to be integrated into evangelicalism posed part of the problem. Many evangelicals noted that the secular discipline on which they drew was disintegrating intellectually; microtheories predominated, symptomatic of epistemological skepticism that was inimical to fundamental progress in the pursuit of unified truth. Professionally, the secular psychological field was also increasingly disunified; professional issues and conflicts were growing in importance as confidence to pursue a coherent knowledge program waned, and postmodern skepticism and power relations increasingly claimed the field.[97] The disintegration of the "psychology" that was meant to be integrated contributed to a low-grade crisis of faith among some of the leading evangelical psychotherapists.

Their own integrationist community also seemed to be losing its creativity and vision. One leading psychologist characterized the discipline of integration as having been "in a stagnant period from 1982 to the present [1994]," after enjoying a period of vigorous model building from 1975 to 1982. Many others "expressed dissatisfaction with the disjointed direction that integrative efforts have taken."[98] A certain pall hung over the conclusions of *Modern Psychotherapies*. Jones and But-man could propose no substantial model for evangelical psychotherapy because "we do not believe that a definitive model exists and think it unlikely that it will ever exist."[99] Their final two paragraphs glanced in the direction of ecclesiasticism with a combination of unease and longing, while yet carefully guarding professional prerogatives:

> We know of several Christian psychologists who have formed accountability groups within their local churches. These groups of clergy and laypersons do not oversee or supervise their work at a specific level, but they were accountable to them at the broader level for the Christian distinctiveness and integrity of their functioning as therapists. We are impressed by their courage and openness in committing themselves to a deeper level of accountability than most of us would find "comfortable" or "convenient."[100]

The longing to act pastorally, to explicitly cure souls, to get back to theological roots and historic "spirituality" was palpable throughout the integration movement in the 1990s.[101]

The leading evangelical psychotherapists wrestled to come to terms not only with their discipline but also with the tension between the church and their highly successful professionalism. In a controversial interview in *Christianity Today*, Larry Crabb repudiated the "three-sided model that therapists are qualified to treat psychological problems, pastors spiritual problems, and doctors physical ones." He called instead for "shepherding" and "eldering" relationships in local church communities to replace "the antiseptic world of a private-practice therapist." Problems in living "belong more to the role of an elder than to an expert." But it was pointed that what Crabb meant by "elders" was "not referring to the official church position as such but to godly people." Those office-holding pastors so touted by Jay Adams were not mentioned in the interview, and Crabb defended the abiding need for mental health professionals because the "*ideal* functioning church" could never be attained.[102]

Gary Collins's AACC similarly registered the ambivalence. On the one hand, the AACC's phenomenal growth to 17,000 members in three years bore testimony to the triumph of the therapeutic. On the other hand, Collins's repeated criticisms of psychotherapeutic secularization and professionalization, and corresponding calls for "biblical" fidelity and church-oriented "ministry," gave expression to the new cultural climate within evangelicalism.

* * *

Who was competent to counsel? Some conservative Protestants thought they knew the answer. The mid-1990s found Jay Adams intransigent:

> While all Christians should counsel one another *informally,* unless called officially by God to the ministry of the Word and ordained by His church to the task, one should not take it upon himself to become a *Counselor.* . . . "My brothers, not many of you should become teachers, because you know that we teachers will receive greater judgment" (James 3:1). It is one thing to teach (or counsel); it is another to become a teac*her* or a counse*lor*. It is this lawless sort of *self*-appointment to which James addresses his words, not to the informal mutual ministry of teaching in counseling that should go on among the saints all the time. . . . To acquire and develop these skills [in understanding and applying the Word of God] takes training, time, direction, and discipline. And it requires a definitive calling from God. God's professional counselor is the pastor.[103]

Other conservative Protestants were not so sure of the answer. The mid-1990s found evangelical psychotherapists ambivalent:

> I am still haunted by the question whether the institutional existence of psychology as a context for healing does violence to the Church's healing identity. The Church should be identified as the center of healing. I feel a need for some sort of reintegration of psychological services into the fabric of church ministry, though not necessarily the clericalization of psychological services nor the elimination of independent practice. I hope for movement toward a Church having a coordinated ministry of instruction and discipleship that acts as a preventative resource in addition to its reparative healing work, a work wherein psychologists and pastoral care ministers can both be accountable to the church in their respective areas of special preparation.[104]

Competent to counsel? Two durable professional realities produced stalemate: that pastors were in fact professionally competent to understand and aid troubled and troublesome people remained dubious; that professional psychotherapists would indeed become accountable to the church for their doctrine, life, and practice remained no less dubious. Twenty-five years of controversy among conservative Protestants gave no indication that a peaceable jurisdictional settlement stood in the offing.

Chapter 9 Notes

1. David N. Livingstone, "High Tea at the Cyclotron," *Books & Culture* (January/February 1996): 23. This was a review of *A Social History of Truth* by Steven Shapin.

2. Andrew Abbott, *The System of Professions: An Essay on the Division of Expert Labor* (Chicago: University of Chicago Press, 1988), 83.

3. Conversation, October 6, 1991.

4. Jay E. Adams, *What About Nouthetic Counseling?* (Grand Rapids: Baker Book House, 1976), 45.

5. This theme emerged in conversations with, for example, Bruce Narramore, Mary Stewart Van Leeuwen, and Larry Crabb.

6. David G. Myers, *The Human Puzzle: Psychological Research and Christian Belief* (New York: Harper & Row, 1978); Myers, *The Inflated Self* (New York: Seabury, 1981); Van Leeuwen and Mary Stewart, *The Sorcerer's Apprentice: A Christian Looks at the Changing Face of Psychology* (Downers Grove, Ill.: InterVarsity Press, 1982).

7. In the mid-1990s Wheaton phased in a doctor of psychology program, joining Fuller and Rosemead in training doctoral-level psychotherapy professionals.

8. Stanton Jones and Richard Butman, *Modern Psychotherapies: A Comprehensive Christian Appraisal* (Downers Grove, Ill.: InterVarsity Press, 1991), chapter 15.

9. David G. Benner, ed., *Baker Encyclopedia of Psychology* (Grand Rapids: Baker Book House, 1985).

10. J. Harold Ellens, Editorial: "Retrospect, Prospect, and Farewell," *Journal of Psychology and Christianity* 7, no. 4 (1988): 3f.

11. Tim Stafford, "The Therapeutic Revolution," *Christianity Today* (May 17, 1993): 32.

12. From Rapha publicity materials. The name *Rapha* transliterated a Hebrew word for "healing." Robert S. McGee's best-selling book, *The Search for Significance* (Houston: Rapha Publishing, 1985), provided him with a marketing tool like the books by Minirth and Meier.

13. Tim Stafford, "Franchising Hope," *Christianity Today* (May 18, 1992): 22–26.

14. Stafford, "The Therapeutic Revolution," 32; Stafford, "Franchising Hope," 22.

15. For example, Ken Parker, *Reclaiming Your Inner Child* (Nashville: Thomas Nelson, 1993), ii, lists twenty-five titles in the Minirth-Meier Series and provides an 800 number for those seeking professional services.

16. Bob Jones IV, "Personality Splits: Minirth of Minirth-Meier fame breaks off amid controversy," *World* (March 9, 1996): 18; Steve Rabey, "Hurting Helpers: Will the Christian counseling movement live up to its promise?," *Christianity Today* (September 16, 1996): 76.

17. *A Total Approach to Life*, publicity brochure for Minirth-Meier New Life Clinics.

18. Parker, *Reclaiming Your Inner Child*; Stafford, "Franchising Hope," 22–26.

19. Gary R. Collins, "A Letter to Christian Counselors," *Journal of Psychology and Christianity* 9, no. 1 (1990): 38f.

20. Jay Adams did appear once in *Leadership* when it excerpted Bernie Zilbergeld's *The Shrinking of America: Myths of Psychological Change* and solicited the responses of four leading evangelical counselors. The others were David Benner, Gary Collins, and psychiatrist Louis McBurney. Bernie Zilbergeld, *The Shrinking of America: Myths of Psychological Change* (Boston: Little Brown, 1983).

21. David F. Wells, *No Place for Truth or Whatever Happened to Evangelical Theology* (Grand Rapids: William B. Eerdmans, 1993), 113f.

22. Comments of this sort recurred in my conversations with both pastors and laypeople.

23. From an anonymous questionnaire filled out by a conference attender.

24. Robert H. Schuller, *Self-Esteem: The New Reformation* (Waco, Tex.: Word Books, 1982).

25. William Backus and Marie Chapian, *Telling Yourself the Truth* (Minneapolis: Bethany House Publishers, 1980); Lawrence J. Crabb, *Understanding People: Deep Longings for Relationship* (Grand Rapids: Zondervan, 1987); Crabb, *Inside Out* (Colorado Springs: NavPress, 1988); Robert Hemfelt, Frank Minirth, and Paul Meier, *Love Is a Choice* (Nashville: Thomas Nelson, 1989); McGee, *The Search for Significance;* Frank Minirth and Paul Meier, *Happiness Is a Choice* (Waco, Tex.: Word Books, 1976). Several of Dobson's books from the 1970s remained in print through the 1980s. Another popular book was by a Methodist minister, David A. Seamands: *Healing of Memories* (Wheaton, Ill.: Victor Books, 1985), conflated religious ideas and practices with popular psychological concepts and sold more than half a million copies.

26. Even the secular world took notice on occasion. Wendy Kaminer's *I'm Dysfunctional, You're Dysfunctional* criticized the evangelical "recovery movement" as a subset of a culture-wide trend.

27. James Davison Hunter, *American Evangelicalism: Conservative Religion and the Quandary of Modernity* (New Brunswick, N.J.: Rutgers University Press, 1983), 95.

28. E.g., Lyman Coleman, *Small Group Training Manual* (Littleton, Colo.: Serendipity, 1991), and the multivolume Support Group Series edited by Coleman and Richard Peace.

29. Stafford, "Franchising Hope," 22–26; Stafford, "The Therapeutic Revolution," 24–32. Cf., Rabey, "Hurting Helpers," 76–78, 80, 108, 110; Robert C. Roberts, "Psychobabble: A Guide for Perplexed Christians in an Age of Therapies," *Christianity Today* (May 16, 1994): 18–24.

30. Stafford, "The Therapeutic Revolution," 25.

31. Some other psychologists took a cynical view of this "biblicizing" of psychological theories. For example, Rosemead's William Hunter commented, "Conservative Christians are much more likely to be consumers of psychology if it is sufficiently couched in the language and thought forms of theology to sound to the hearer as though it is biblically derived and not from secular psychology." Hunter himself thought people ought to take their psychology straight rather than couched so as to sound biblically derived: William F. Hunter and Marvin K. Mayers, "Psychology and Missions: Reflections on Status and Need," *Journal of Psychology and Theology* 15, no. 4 (1987): 270.

32. Gary R. Collins, *The Biblical Basis of Christian Counseling for People Helpers* (Colorado Springs: NavPress, 1993).

33. See Andrew Abbott's stimulating discussion of jurisdictional settlements and the instability of such: Abbott, *The System of Professions,* 69–79.

34. Almost every citation of Adams into the 1990s mentioned only *Competent to Counsel* (1970) and/or *The Christian Counselor's Manual* (1973). I found almost no citations of other books or of CCEF's journal.

35. Conversations with Bruce Narramore (August 29, 1995) and John Coe (July 3, 1996).

36. Conversation with John Bettler, early 1990s.

37. This seminary in Escondido, California, began as a branch campus of Westminster Theological Seminary (Philadelphia) in 1982 and soon became independent.

38. During 1970–81 counseling topics dominated Adams's publications. But counseling had always been a subset of his overriding interest in local church pastoral ministry among conservative Protestants. Preaching topics became more prominent after 1981. During 1982–91 he also published three books for counselors and another dozen books on theological and biblical topics, self-help, and other aspects of pastoral ministry. Of the three counseling books, only Jay E. Adams, *Insight & Creativity in Christian Counseling: An Antidote to Rigid and Mechanical Approaches* (Grand Rapids: Zondervan, 1982) might be considered to have broken fresh ground.

39. In 1990, NANC had 109 members. The vast majority (81) were male pastors serving in local churches (perhaps a half dozen pastors currently worked in parachurch counseling centers). The others included 18 women and 10 men; most of these worked in some parachurch capacity, either in counseling centers or as missionaries.

40. Abbott, *The System of Professions,* 8.

41. I heard this sentiment voiced often in conversations but most clearly from Paul Randolph, a pastor who completed a DMin at Westminster but never joined NANC. (Conversation, April 17, 1996).

42. Interview with Howard Eyrich, October 2, 1990. Eyrich was on the NANC board from 1976 and served as the director, 1983–88.

43. Ibid.

44. Conversation with John Bettler in the mid-1980s.

45. Conversation with Howard Eyrich, October 2, 1990.

46. Correspondence from John Carter, November 4, 1980.

47. Interview, December 4, 1990.

48. Besides Adams, the most established author was Wayne Mack (see bibliography).

49. James Hurley and Peter Jones, "Review of the Department of Practical Theology at Westminster Theological Seminary in California," unpublished, December 6, 1993.

50. John F. Bettler, "Biblical Counseling: The Next Generation," *Journal of Pastoral Practice* 8, no. 4 (1987): 6–10.

51. John F. Bettler, "When the Problem Is Sexual Sin: A Counseling Model," *Journal of Biblical Counseling* 13, no. 3 (1995): 16–18; Bettler, "Gaining an Accurate Self-Image, Part I," *Journal of Pastoral Practice* 6, no. 4 (1983): 46–52; Bettler, "Gaining an Accurate Self-Image, Part II," *Journal of Pastoral Practice* 7, no. 1 (1984a): 41–50; Bettler, "Gaining an Accurate Self-Image, Part III," *Journal of Pastoral Practice* 7, no. 2 (1984b): 52–61; Bettler, "Gaining an Accurate Self-Image, Part IV," *Journal of Pastoral Practice* 7, no. 3 (1984c): 50–58; Bettler, "Gaining an Accurate Self-Image, Part V," *Journal of Pastoral Practice* 7, no. 4 (1985): 46–55; Bettler, "Gaining an Accurate Self-Image, Conclusion," *Journal of Pastoral Practice* 8, no. 2 (1987): 24–26; Bettler, "Counseling and the Problem of the Past," *Journal of Biblical Counseling* 12, no. 2 (1994): 5–23.

52. Bettler, "Biblical Counseling: The Next Generation," 10.

53. Ibid., 9.

54. Ibid., 10; cf., 4–6.

55. David Powlison, Jay E. Adams, and John F. Bettler, "25 Years of Biblical Counseling: An Interview with Jay Adams and John Bettler," *Journal of Biblical Counseling* 12, no. 1 (1993): 11f.

56. Interview, December 13, 1990.

57. In 1970 the mean was four sessions. In 1980 it was between five and six sessions. In 1990 it was between six and seven sessions.

58. During CCEF's history no counselor counseled more than twenty hours per week; eight to fifteen hours was typical for full-time staff. Counselors who were full-time employees also carried administrative and teaching responsibilities.

59. Jay E. Adams, *Competent to Counsel* (USA: Presbyterian & Reformed, 1970), 268.

60. The other leading parachurch institutions in nouthetic counseling—CCEF West, FBCM, and BCF—also hired women on their professional staffs.

61. The difficulties of cross-country administration led to CCEF West becoming independent in 1990.

62. Educational fees and charitable donations produced the rest of the income. During the 1980s the number of counselees receiving insurance reimbursements climbed markedly. Exact figures on insurance reimbursements within these totals were unobtainable because many clients were reimbursed directly. But CCEF's director of counseling estimated that in the late 1980s as many as half of CCEF's clients were at least partially covered by third-party insurance. The realignment of the insurance industry in the early 1990s caused this figure to drop drastically, to perhaps 10 to 20 percent by the middle of the decade (conversations with Ed Welch and Chris Stroud, September 14, 1996).

63. Paul C. Vitz's book, *Psychology as Religion: The Cult of Self-Worship* (Grand Rapids: William B. Eerdmans, 1977), remained in print throughout the 1980s, and went to a second edition in 1994.

64. Interview with George Scipione, October 6, 1991. The practice of charging fees for counseling was always controversial. Adams had rationalized it because of CCEF's educational identity and the need to underwrite training. But CCEF's branch centers did not square with that rationalization. Scipione himself dropped fees from CCEF West after it became independent in the 1990s. NANC board member Lloyd Jonas voiced a common sentiment when he said that he "disagreed biblically with two trends wherein [1] nouthetic counseling becomes a 'para-church' business and [2] counselees pay to be ministered to." Interview with Lloyd Jonas, October 20, 1990.

65. Interview with Howard Eyrich, October 2, 1990.

66. This was self-published until 1994 when a major evangelical publishing house picked it up. John Broger, *Self-Confrontation: A Manual for In-Depth Discipleship* (Nashville: Thomas Nelson, 1994). By that time it had sold more than 100,000 copies over the previous fifteen years.

67. Martin Bobgan and Deidre Bobgan, *Psychoheresy: The Psychological Seduction of Christianity* (Santa Barbara, Calif.: East-Gate, 1987); Dave Hunt and T. A. McMahon, *The Seduction of Christianity* (Eugene, Ore.: Harvest House, 1985).

68. Jay E. Adams, Comments in *Prophets of Psychoheresy I,* eds. Martin Bobgan and Deidre Bobgan (Santa Barbara, Calif.: East-Gate, 1989), 105f, a critique of Larry Crabb.

69. Jay E. Adams, *The Grand Demonstration: A Biblical Study of the So-Called Problem of Evil* (Santa Barbara, Calif.: EastGate, 1991).

70. Conversation with Martin Bobgan, June 21, 1988; "Evidences of Failure of the Psychological Model," plenary address at NANC, Lafayette, Indiana, October 9, 1991.

71. Martin Bobgan and Deidre Bobgan, *Against Biblical Counseling—For the Bible* (Santa Barbara, Calif.: EastGate, 1994). Criticisms of Adams appear on pp. 54, 159–61, 167f.

72. Bobgan and Bobgan, *Against Biblical Counseling,* 167.

73. Ibid., 184.

74. Even his enthusiastic endorsement of their *How to Counsel from Scripture* pointedly stated, "Thank God for laymen like them." Martin Bobgan and Deidre Bobgan, *How to Counsel from Scripture* (Chicago: Moody Press, 1985), v.

75. Conversation with Jay Adams, December 4, 1990.

76. Rabey, "Hurting Helpers," 78, 80; William F. English, "An Integrationist's Critique of and Challenge to the Bobgans' View of Counseling and Psychotherapy," *Journal of Psychology and Theology* 18, no. 3 (1990): 228–36; James D. Foster and Mark Ledbetter, "Christian Anti-Psychology and the Scientific Method," *Journal of Psychology and Theology* 15, no. 1 (1987): 10–18; Gary R. Collins, *Excellence and Ethics in Counseling,* ed. Gary R. Collins, Resources for Christian Counseling (Dallas: Word Publishing, 1991) 166f; Ronald H. Nash, *Great Divides: Understanding the Controversies That Come Between Christians* (Colorado Springs: NavPress, 1993), 93–108.

77. CCEF was an exception, having a licensed psychologist as director of counseling and increasingly benefited from third-party reimbursements in the second half of the decade.

78. Historically, clergy malpractice suits have only been sustained when they involved violations of sexual ethics; the content and methods of clerical counsel have not been subject to review.

79. *Nally v. Grace Community Church,* 204 Cal Rptr 303 (157 Cal App 3d 912, 1984); *Nally v. Grace Community Church,* 240 Cal Rptr 215 (Cal App 2 Dist, 1987); *Nally v. Grace Community Church* (47 Cal 3d 278, 1988).

80. Grace Community Church was a nondenominational church pastored by John MacArthur.

81. A concise summary of the case can be found in John L. Young and Ezra E. H. Griffith, "The Development and Practice of Pastoral Counseling," *Hospital and Community Psychiatry* 40, no. 3 (1989): 274f. The case was one of the most written about in contemporary legal literature. See, for example, Samuel E. Ericsson, "Clergy Malpractice: Ramifications of a New Theory," in *Clergy Malpractice,* ed. H. Newton Malony, Thomas L. Needham, and Samuel Southard (Philadelphia: Westminster Press, 1986); E. Griffith and J. Young, "Pastoral Counseling and the Concept of Malpractice," *Bulletin of the American Academy of Psychiatry and the Law* 15 (1987): 257–65; Richard R. Hammar, *Pastor, Church & Law* (Matthews, N.C.: Christian Ministry Resources, 1991); H. Wayne House, *Christian Ministries and the Law* (Grand Rapids: Baker Book House, 1992).

82. Young and Griffith, "The Development and Practice of Pastoral Counseling," 275.

83. Newsletters from the three organizations in the early 1990s communicated a surprised good cheer at the doubling and tripling of enrollments and teaching opportunities.

84. Monographs included: David Powlison, *Power Encounters: Reclaiming Spiritual Warfare* (Grand Rapids: Baker Books, 1995); Gary Shogren and Edward Welch, *Running in Circles* (Grand Rapids: Baker Books, 1995); Tedd Tripp, *Shepherding a Child's Heart* (Wapwallopen, Pa.: Shepherd Press, 1995); Edward Welch and Gary Shogren, *Addictive Behavior* (Grand Rapids: Baker Books, 1995); Edward T. Welch, *Counselor's Guide to the Brain and Its Disorders: Knowing the Difference Between Disease and Sin* (Grand Rapids: Zondervan, 1991).

85. In the buoyant new climate, even Henry Brandt, Adams's erstwhile ally, emerged from a dozen years of retirement to write three new books that bluntly defined life's problems as sin and offered evangelical solutions to that problem.

86. John MacArthur, *Our Sufficiency in Christ* (Dallas: Word Publishing, 1991).

87. John MacArthur and Wayne Mack, *Introduction to Biblical Counseling: A Basic Guide to the Principles and Practice of Counseling* (Dallas: Word Publishing, 1994). One other educational development is worth noting. Trinity Theological Seminary (Newburgh, Ind.) offered programs by extension. It proved very successful in recruiting conservative Protestant students and by the mid-1990s had one of the largest seminary enrollments in the United States. Trinity hired NANC's former director, Howard Eyrich, to head up its counseling program.

88. Interview with Ken Sande, September 6, 1996.

89. Interview with Jay Adams, December 4, 1990.

90. Conversation with Bob Schneider and Shashi Smith, October 5, 1993.

91. George M. Marsden, *Reforming Fundamentalism: Fuller Seminary and the New Evangelicalism* (Grand Rapids: William B. Eerdmans, 1987), 238.

92. Wells, *No Place for Truth,* 101, 175.

93. Hunter, *American Evangelicalism,* 94, 99.

94. Os Guinness, "America's Last Men and Their Magnificent Talking Cure," in Os Guinness and John Seel, eds., *No God But God* (Chicago: Moody Press, 1992), 114, 126.

95. "The Cambridge Declaration" was released in pamphlet form by the Alliance of Confessing Evangelicals, and summarized their meeting in Cambridge, Massachusetts, on April 20, 1996.

96. These themes were woven into chapter 8, which treated the intellectual views of the evangelical psychotherapy movement synchronically rather than diachronically. These sorts of developmental nuances were largely flattened out in my earlier treatment. There is a need for an intellectual and social history of that movement to complement the study I have done of Adams's nouthetic counseling as it interacted with psychotherapists.

97. Examples of such reflections are found in John D. Carter, "Success Without Finality: The Continuing Dialogue of Faith

and Psychology," *Journal of Psychology and Christianity* 15, no. 2 (1996): 116–22; Brian E. Eck, "Integrating the Integrators: An Organizing Framework for a Multifaceted Process of Integration," *Journal of Psychology and Christianity* 15, no. 2 (1996): 101–15; Stanton L. Jones, "Reflections on the Nature and Future of the Christian Psychologies," *Journal of Psychology and Christianity* 15, no. 2 (1996): 133–42.

98. Eck, "Integrating the Integrators," 101, accesses the works mentioned in the previous two quotations.

99. Jones and Butman, *Modern Psychotherapies,* 380, 398.

100. Ibid., 416.

101. Jones, "Overview of the Rech Conference," 84; Conversation with John Coe, July 12, 1996.

102. Kevin Dale Miller, "Putting an End to Christian Psychology: Larry Crabb thinks therapy belongs back in the churches," *Christianity Today* (August 14, 1995): 16f.

103. Jay E. Adams, *Teaching to Observe: The Counselor as Teacher* (Woodruff, S.C.: Timeless Texts, 1995), 12f.

104. Jones, "Reflections on the Nature and Future of the Christian Psychologies," 141.

Postscript

In closing, let me append two personal notes that seemed more fitting as a postscript than a preface. First, if I have done my work honestly and well, then this project will have accomplished some of the things that participant-observation "field work" can do best: helping us to see other people more clearly. It is my hope that I have listened well and communicated accurately, capturing with ethnographic detail those late twentieth-century conservative Protestants who were (and are[1]) exercised about "counseling." I have sought to probe the deep rift between two professions currently engaged in a lively jurisdictional conflict, to hear both sides, and to make their views plausible. I hope that I have represented the actors in such a way that they will recognize themselves and not find their field of battle populated with men of straw. I frankly admit that I do not like icons, and that I have sought to subvert both the canonized and demonized versions of "Jay Adams" and "integrationists." But I also admit that arriving at a sympathetic understanding is a difficult task, made more difficult when the subjects are engaged in an intense conflict with one another, and when the outcome of that conflict is not something to which I am indifferent. Doubtless I have insinuated my own icons. I apologize to those I have misrepresented and request correction.

Second, Charles Bosk warned me that participant-observation left no actor untouched: I would be changed by what I observed, and my participation would change those I observed.[2] Both parts of his observation have proved true. I hope that they will continue to prove true as readers interact with what I have written. I am keenly aware that doing "live" history is difficult. Because of the lack of perspective, one cannot see how things turned out; it is easy to miss what will later seem obvious. But I want to take advantage of one unique opportunity that live history presents. Those portrayed can read and respond. I anticipate that my audience will include not only professional historians but also those about whom I have written. I am so bold as to hope that what I have written might in fact contribute constructively in the further unfolding of the history (in fact, the histories) herein portrayed. I am so bold as to hope that what I have written might in fact contribute constructively to the further unfolding of the numerous "jurisdictional conflicts" that are portrayed in some way or other.

I hope that five groups of nonhistorians might find this particular history stimulating, five groups that in different ways are locked in conflict over the cure of souls (of course subconflicts also are within each group). At one end of the spectrum are secular mental health professionals, who, perhaps because of a residual positivism, are too often unaware of what is going on in "religious" counseling and too often unaware of the fundamentally religious character of their own practice. I hope that by gazing at an alien counseling culture they might see their own culture more clearly and recognize how they unavoidably act as pastors who attempt to cure souls by offering the functional equivalents of a salvific theology and ethic.

Second, at the other end of the spectrum, I hope that "anti-counseling" polemicists might also read the story. They aim to separate the wheat and the tares unambiguously amid the rough and tumble of history. I hope that I might introduce a note of healthy ambiguity and complexity into their world.

Third, I hope that mainline pastoral counselors, who often look over the fence, might find this story about their next-door neighbors interesting. Their pastoral counseling movement in part provoked and in part was product of the division of the Protestant churches in the 1920s and '30s into "fundamentalist" and "modernist" sects—a jurisdictional conflict over the cure of souls, over the adequacy of structured knowledge systems. The ways that "fundamentalists" have engaged the modern therapeutic will doubtless resonate at many levels with the "modernists'" own history.

Fourth, this is not a history of evangelical psychotherapy—that movement is vast and complex beyond the restricted purposes of my simple telling—but it is nonetheless about those "integrationists" at almost every point. The greatest density of detail clusters along the fault line in the jurisdictional conflict between them and Adams. I think they will find the story provocative.

Finally, this is overtly the history of a conservative Protestant biblical counseling movement. I have sought to exposit their founder's knowledge system (chaps. 5–7) and to trace their history (chaps. 2–4, 8–9). I hope that my chief subjects, across the spectrum of their differences, also find that my attempt to gaze dispassionately at them provokes hard thought.

For each of these five subcultures, I hope that my portrayal will both raise and clarify questions and so will improve many conversations.

Postscript Notes

1. Rather remarkably, given the thirty-year sweep of the story, all of the actors discussed were alive in 1996. Subsequently Bill Goode and John Broger passed away.

2. Bosk is a sociologist at the University of Pennsylvania with whom I consulted about this project. He is the author of Charles L. Bosk, *Forgive and Remember: Managing Medical Failure* (Chicago: University of Chicago Press, 1979).

An Annotated Case Study of Adams's Model

Because Adams is largely unknown outside of his own conservative Protestant circles, it seemed appropriate to give readers a feel for his system by reading him in action, as it were, addressing counselees. The following contains the text of a didactic pamphlet Adams designed for counselees experiencing marital conflicts and unhappiness. I have annotated it to highlight typical Adamsian themes.

What Do You Do When Your Marriage Goes Sour?[1]
by Jay E. Adams [1]

Phil and Emily had not come for help in solving the problems in their marriage, although they had called the chaplain to ask for marriage counseling. [2]

  Actually, their minds were already made up—they had decided to get a divorce. Yet, they were Christians, and they knew that a divorce was wrong because they had no biblical grounds for it. [3] There had been no adultery, no desertion; only untold misery. [4]

Annotations

[1] This didactic brochure was designed to be given to counselees as bibliotherapeutic homework. The self-help slant—"What Do You Do When . . . ?"—typified Adams's emphasis on changing both the thinking and behavior of counselees facing particular troubles in life.

[2] Adams located counseling in church or parachurch settings. Here he envisioned a chaplain (presumably in the military) as the counseling professional.

[3] Adams envisioned professing, Bible-believing Christians as his intended counselees. God and the Bible mattered to Adams's typical counselees, even when they evaded its moral strictures or failed to live up to them.

[4] Here Adams alluded to the two grounds for divorce allowed in classic Presbyterian casuistry and distanced himself from allowing unhappiness or incompatibility as grounds for divorce.[2] For Adams, any two sinners were incompatible by definition, and the challenge of counseling was to teach skills in loving and peacemaking.[3]

If we can only get him to agree that going on in this marriage would be an impossibility, they thought, *then perhaps he will be able to show us how, in our case, God will make an exception to His law.* That was how they were reasoning inwardly when they first told their stories [5] to Chaplain Cunningham.

"So you see," Emily concluded, "there is simply nothing left to our marriage. I don't feel a thing for Phil anymore; there is nothing left to build on."

Phil ended his remarks in a similar vein: "Well, I suppose that it has been a long time since you've heard a story like that, Chaplain. And, while we don't agree on many things, I must say that Emily is absolutely correct when she claims that there is nothing left to our marriage—every drop of love that I once had for her has drained away."

They both sat back in an uneasy confidence, knowing down deep that divorce was wrong but sure that they had spoken the last word on the issue. After all, what else could the chaplain advise [6] if there was no more feeling, no more love, nothing left?

They waited, hoping that he, rather than they, would pronounce the final verdict: "If there is nothing left to your marriage, I suppose that there is nothing you can do but get a divorce."

They hoped that hearing him utter these or similar words would somehow remove the bad feelings triggered by their guilty consciences.[7]

What they really wanted was salve for their souls. [8]

"I am truly sorry to hear about your difficult times and the sorry state in which you find yourselves at present. [9] I can understand why you have come for help. When a marriage has gone sour and you find that all of your own efforts to sweeten it again fail, then you do need help. You say that there is no love and no feeling left? That's serious. If you don't love each other, there is only one thing to do. (*Here it comes,* they thought. *He will advise a divorce.*) You will have to *learn* how to love one another." [10]

"*Learn* how to love?" they retorted almost simultaneously. "What do you mean *learn* how to love?" asked Phil, as soon as he was able to regain some measure of composure.

"Yeah," offered Emily, cynically, "how can you *learn* it? You can't produce feelings out of thin air."

[5] The case study narrated in this brochure is weighted more to didactic material than verbatim reports of Adams's counseling indicate about his actual practice. Under the phrase "told their stories," he truncated what might have been an extended period of question—asking, listening, various other forms of data-gathering, and much of the exploratory give-and-take that opened the counseling process.[4]

[6] Adams believed that counselors should not duck counselees' desire for advice. He thought most counselees wanted advice, answers, workable solutions to their problems in living.[5]

[7] Contrary to theories that viewed most guilt feelings as false guilt, Adams's moral model detected a great deal of objective guilt and distinguished guilt from guilt feelings.[6]

[8] This is not something Adams would give them. He did not focus on their unhappiness but on a casuistic sorting out of specific sins—lovelessness, bitterness, selfishness, false beliefs about marriage and love—that he believed produced misery.

[9] This case study demonstrates how Adams held people responsible for their plight. He viewed this couple as reaping the consequences of sinfully self-centered lifestyles; hence, after this perfunctory consolatory word, he moved toward confrontation, in an attempt to disturb their resolve, beliefs, behavior, and hopelessness.

[10] Adams's counselor was directive and didactic about belief and morals (the "faith and practice" of Adams's Presbyterian creed)—not a stereotypically accommodating chaplain or even the wise, priestly consoler of the afflicted. He—typically he, not she—took charge of the session. The counselor acted in the mode of a teacher, coach, and cheerleader in the paragraphs that follow.

"I was not talking about feelings," said Chaplain Cunningham. "I was talking about love. The two are not identical even though Hollywood, the TV, and *Playboy* might say otherwise. [11] Love is not a feeling first. Before all else it is the determination to do good for another person because God has told you to do so. [12] Love begins, therefore, with a desire to please God. Love toward another is a willingness to give to him whatever you have that he needs because you know that God wants you to. Where true love exists, the feeling follows soon enough."

"Well, that certainly isn't what I thought you would say," Phil replied. "Nor I," echoed Emily. "As a matter of fact," she continued, "I'm dubious about the whole thing; how can you teach someone to love? And what does it mean to *learn* to love?"

"Let me begin by explaining a bit about biblical love and how it can be learned. First, notice that every-where in the Bible God *commands* us to love. You don't command people to have certain feelings do you?"

"Well . . . ?"

"For instance, if I gave the order 'Emily, be angry,' you couldn't turn on anger just like that, could you?" [13]

". . . I suppose not."

"Then listen to these verses in the Bible: *Love* the Lord your God. . . . *Love* your neighbor as yourself! Those are *commands;* God *commands* love. If love were feeling first, it could not be commanded. [14] Do you see that?"

"I think I do," said Phil. "But what does that have to do with us?"

"Everything, Phil. You see, God orders you to love your wife. Listen to what He wrote through the apostle Paul: 'Husbands, love your wives just as Christ loved the church and gave himself up for her' (Eph. 5:25). Remember, Christ died on the cross for the church." [15]

"Do you mean that I have to learn how to love Emily enough to be willing to die for her?"

"Exactly!"

"Then, forget it; I could never learn to love *her* like that."

"No, we can't forget it because God commands it. But perhaps you could begin at a lesser level. The Bible also commands, 'Love your neighbor'; she's the closest one that you've got. You eat with her, sleep with her. . . ."

[11] Such a countercultural polemic might inveigh against secular psychology in other circumstances.

[12] Adams frequently warned against "feeling-oriented" living in favor of "commandment-oriented" living that desired to please God. His counseling emphasized responsibility, fault, and action, rather than rights, desires, victimization, or feelings. Adams's God was presented as a generous King: Lawgiver, Savior, Judge, Authority to be obeyed. Numerous Bible passages are alluded to here, and in other contexts might be cited. Biblical doctrine and moral directives entered into the counseling context as an "objective" authority (here, for example, redefining the word *love*). Notice the "nouthetic confrontation" occurring here: an activistic counselor challenges the counselees' framework for self-interpretation and making decisions.

[13] The brisk, verbal sparring of this and the succeeding paragraphs exemplifies Adams's directive method—and his personality. The counselor has a clear cognitive and behavioral agenda. Adams's counseling offered a rational and ethical system, not a comfortable ambience.

[14] The counselor acted in the role of a "minister of the Word," as God's authoritative representative. This was suited to counselees who accepted a direct use of the Bible and self-consciously wanted to live believing and doing exactly what the Bible said.

[15] Sin was the perceived problem at the heart of the human dilemmas that presented in counseling (such as this "sour" marriage). God's law (here, "love spouse, neighbor, enemy") served negatively to convict of failures. The law subsequently served Adams positively as a guide for what these counselees should do instead.

"I couldn't even love her that way!"

"And I couldn't love him that way either!"

"Well, I'm sorry to hear that, but there is still hope. The Bible also insists upon love even at what for you would be the lowest level. God commands: 'Love your enemies.' You see, there is no way out. You must learn to love each other; God commands it." [16]

"Oh no!"

"No!"

"Yes. And, as a matter of fact, there is great hope since God commands love; He never commands anything of His children that He does not supply both the directions and the power to achieve." [17]

"Oh my! We came to you to help us find a way out of this miserable marriage, and you have tied us into it even more tightly. Thanks . . . for nothing!"

"Yeah, nothing."

"Hang on; I haven't finished. If you really want to get rid of the misery, I can help you do so. But you will never find a way out by breaking up the marriage. As a matter of fact, you are only heading for greater troubles if you take that route. You can't rebel against God and expect things to go well: 'The way of the transgressor is hard.' [18] You will never find peace by pursuing it or happiness by seeking it or relief from misery by trying to get out from under it. [19] These things are by-products that always elude those who chase them. They come only to those who instead focus upon pleasing God rather than themselves. If you repent of the sin that you have committed in your hearts in determining to put an end to this marriage and if you will let me help you learn how to do what God says, sooner than you have any idea, peace and joy will come. [20]

[16] Adams's theocentric moral model inevitably prompts shock, outrage, and discomfort for some readers. But there is no need to create needless reactions. In listening to Adams spring such verbal surprises on counselees, readers will most accurately envision Adams if they hear an undercurrent of robust optimism and bluff good humor, rather than envisioning a grim-faced, self-righteous moralizer. He could be loud, assertive, opinionated, provocative, humorous—but he was not rash or cantankerous, at least not with counselees. (He became cantankerous when he attacked those counselors he saw as "false prophets.")

[17] The Christian gospel—forgiveness through Christ's death and power through the Holy Spirit—was Adams's answer to people's problems in living. Because his God promised the needed help, Adams believed that selfish people could learn to love. He was optimistic about "children of God" because he believed God had changed them in some essential way and would help them continue to change.

[18] Adams brought warnings to bear based on his view that people "reap what they sow," here citing Proverbs 13:15. He interpreted much of his counselees' circumstantial and emotional misery as consequential to their beliefs, motives, and behavior. It was meant to act as a "red light on the dashboard."[7]

[19] These paragraphs hint at the four dimensions to problems that Adams discerned. *Presenting* problems typically included dysphoric feelings and other presumed consequences, either of disobedience or of being wronged—here, the misery and hardship of a "sour" marriage. *Performance* problems described sinful behaviors—here, transgression, divorce, rebellion, arguing. *Preconditioning* problems represented long-standing patterns of habitual sin—here, a false view of love, habits of not resolving problems. The *basic sinful nature* represented an underlying motivational proclivity to follow selfish desires and false beliefs rather than God's will.[8]

[20] Throughout this paragraph, Adams's counselor bluntly warned malefactors of trouble from God, and confidently promised good from God to those with ears to hear. Adams's way of change was a way of "repentance," a redirection of their lives away from pleasing themselves and toward pleasing God.

"But let me make one thing plain: you cannot do what God commands just to get rid of your misery; you must do it first and foremost to please Him." [21]

"Well, we do want to please God. As a matter of fact, that is why we came because we knew what we were planning to do was wrong. We hoped that you could make it right somehow, but I suppose that isn't possible." [22]

"No it isn't, Emily. But I do appreciate your honesty in saying what you have just said."

"But how is it possible to put a marriage as bad as ours together again? Of course we'd like to see that most of all, yet it doesn't seem realistic. Aren't you promising a lot more than you can deliver, Chaplain?"

"I know that it may sound unrealistic to you, Phil, but if you mean business with God and do as He says, I promise that within six to eight weeks you can have a marriage that sings!" [23]

"That sounds too good to be true."

"I know it does, but I've seen it happen often enough to know that it is true. But I warn you, it will not happen through talking and good resolutions alone. God will settle for no pious platitudes. He wants action; He demands change. Much of that change will be hard; you won't always like what God tells you to do. [24] But you must do it anyway—simply because He says so. You won't always understand why He tells you to do what He says, but you must do it anyway—just to please Him.

"There are concrete things to do. And the very first is to ask God's forgiveness, and then forgiveness from each other. [25] What do you say?"

"I suppose that there is no other way. . . ."

"I want to give it a try; I never really wanted our marriage to break up."

"Good. Now let me make perfectly clear to you the basic biblical dynamic of love. Love is not feeling first, we have seen. Rather, it is manifested through *giving*. Feeling is self-centered; love focuses upon another. Listen to this: 'God so loved the world that he gave his unique son that whoever believes in him shall not perish but have everlasting life' (John 3:16); He 'loved me, and gave himself for me' (Gal. 2:20) [26]; and remember the verse from Ephesians that

[21] Adams stressed the primacy of the counselees' relationship to God, with God defined as a person to know and please out of gratitude for his grace. Success in his counseling hinged on getting counselees to share this goal, as the paragraphs that follow reveal.

[22] Adams—consistent with his Reformed tradition of pastoral care—paid a great deal of attention to the various activities and problems of the conscience. Desire to obey the will of God, however ambivalent and contradictory, characterized Adams's ideal and successful counselee. Those with a different agenda would naturally resist his teaching and exhortation.

[23] Adams believed that significant change could and should occur very rapidly if counselees agreed with what the Bible said about sin and about God, and acted on it.

[24] Adams stressed hardworking engagement with specific tasks identified in counseling. He placed a heavy emphasis on habits, for good or ill, and on self-discipline in retooling mental and behavioral habits. He also placed heavy emphasis on God's authority: "God says so" was the court with no appeal.

[25] As a moral model, identification of failings, acknowledgment of specific guilt, and seeking forgiveness of God and neighbor had priority when it came to activating the change process. Also, as a moral model, counselees were faced with making a choice.

[26] Adams here cited two of the Bible verses most familiar to his conservative Protestant constituents. But he gave them an unfamiliar spin, turning formulas for evangelism and instant sanctification, respectively, into a call to more painstaking, progressive sanctification, with Christ's life as a model.

I quoted before that contains the words 'as Christ loved the church and gave himself up for her.' In every one of those vital verses concerning the love of Jesus Christ, which is the model for all love between a husband and wife, love is tied to giving, never to feeling. That is, therefore, where you must begin; you must *learn* how to *give*.

"You must give to one another all that you have that the other needs. It will not always be easy since you have developed patterns of wanting and expecting and demanding, rather than patterns of giving. [27] All of that will have to change. And you will have to learn to give even when the other party is not very loving or lovable toward you. Remember, Jesus Christ gave Himself for sinners, for rebels, for enemies. You know that you can, too, because He told us to 'do good' for our enemies. 'If your enemy hungers . . . give,' He said. He did not say, 'First, feel loving toward him, then give.' No, quite simply He said, 'Give.' If we had to wait till we felt warm and benevolent toward an enemy before giving him something to eat or drink, the chances are that he'd die of hunger or thirst waiting. We are to give; give him whatever he needs—because God says so, whether we feel like it or not."

"But doesn't that make us hypocrites if we do things for one another when we don't feel like it?" [28]

"No, Emily, again you are thinking according to a feeling-oriented view of life rather than the biblical one. Hypocrisy is not determined by whether you feel like doing something or not. In spite of what some people say today, you should do whatever God tells you to do to please Him, *whether you feel like it or not.*" [29]

"I sure don't understand that, Chaplain; you'd better fill me in."

"OK, it's like this. The very first thing that I did this morning was something that I didn't *feel* like doing, something that I did not *want* to do: I got up! Did that make me a hypocrite?"

"No, of course not."

"Neither will it make you a hypocrite to give love to another even when you don't feel like it. I would be a hypocrite only if I went about telling everyone that I enjoyed getting up when, in fact, I do not.

[27] Adams placed a great deal of emphasis on patterns and habits. He typically stressed behavior, but this passage gives a glimpse of his motivation theory. The "lusts of the flesh"—here, "patterns of wanting and expecting and demanding" and two paragraphs later, "feeling-oriented view of life"—underlay sinful behaviors, for example, the hostilities of these counselees.

[28] Again, questions of conscience are prominent, as in traditional Protestant casuistry.

[29] The italicized phrase appeared repeatedly in Adams's writing. The phrase pulled together the leading themes of his theistic moral model. First, it hinged on believing God's love and so wanting to please him. Second, it collocated behavior (do acts of love, not sin) and motive (listen to God's will rather than to what you want).

The phrase deemphasized detailed insight into motives, personal history, and so on. It frankly assailed impulse, emotion, desire, and social convention as guides to behavior, belief, and attitude.

It is not hypocrisy to do something that God commands against our feelings, so long as we don't misrepresent our true motives. The reason that I get up is because I know that to be responsible to God and to my employer I must do so. The reason you give in love basically ought to be the same—because you want to please God and thereby become a responsible husband (or wife) in His sight. [30] So long as you do not attribute your actions to false motives like, 'I am trying to please you, Honey, because you mean so much to me,' no hypocrisy is involved."

"Well, I certainly never thought about it that way before. But, you said that we would have to start with forgiveness. Suppose that I do not feel like forgiving Phil. Does the same thing hold?"

"Yes, now you are beginning to catch on. Forgiveness is not a feeling first either. It is fundamentally a promise. When you put your faith in Christ as your Savior, God promised to remember your sins against you no more. [31] That does not mean that He forgets; God never forgets anything. What it means is that He never brings up those sins to use them against you again.

"When you forgive one another, therefore, you are promising to do three things about his wrongdoings. You promise:

    1. I shall not use them against you in the future.

    2. I shall not talk to others about them.

    3. I shall not dwell on them myself. [32]

Just as the only way to begin to feel right toward another is to begin to do right toward him, so the only way to feel properly toward another—and ultimately even to forget those wrongs that he has done to you—is to keep the threefold promise that you make when you say, 'I forgive you.' You see, you don't have to feel forgiving in order to grant forgiveness; you just have to forgive. Against all feelings to the contrary, Christ told us that we must forgive a brother seven times a day if he comes saying, 'I repent' (Luke 17:4). Does that clarify things for you?"

"Whew, I'm afraid so; I'm of the opinion that it clarifies too much! I just don't think that either Emily or I have what it takes to do these things."

[30] Adams did not think such exhortations were moralistic or legalistic because he read life both *coram Deo* and under Christ's grace. Hence, for counselees to live in the sight of God was simply the "fear of the Lord that is the beginning of wisdom" (Prov. 1:7, paraphrased). Out of gratitude they should presumably want to please the one who gave his life to forgive their sins. Critics, both friendly and hostile, frequently heard this reiterated stress on obedience with only perfunctory mention of God's kindness and mercies as moralistic.

[31] The reiterated lever of moral suasion was Christ's love, meant to induce grateful obedience. Adams expected counselees to imitate what was done for them by Christ.

[32] Here is another example of how Adams sought to tutor and coach the conscience. This view of forgiveness—as a series of promises—countered arguing, gossip, and brooding, respectively, by defining them as objective sins. The counselee who said "I forgive" then became guilty if he or she later expressed hostility, talked to others, or nursed bitterness and self-pity. The cognitive changes that Adams's counseling pursued had the effect of turning more and more of life into a morally freighted endeavor. Adams envisioned a strenuous Christianity, a "Pilgrim's Progress."

"Well, it is really most encouraging to hear you say so because this is not something that you can do in your own strength, [33] yet neither is it something that you can sit around waiting for God to give you the strength to do before you do it. In that same chapter of Luke's Gospel, the disciples replied to Jesus' instructions about forgiving seven times a day with these words: 'Lord, give us more faith.' That sounded pious enough on the surface, but what it amounted to was a pious cop-out. Jesus treated it with disdain. He retorted, 'If you have faith like a mustard seed, you can say to this mountain, "Be uprooted and be planted in the sea," and it will obey you' [Luke 17:5, 6].

"Don't you see what He meant? He was saying, 'You don't need anything more. Even the faith that you have is enough to work wonders if you will only exercise it in obedience.' The same is true of you and Emily, Phil. The two of you have been saved. You have trusted in the death and resurrection of Christ and have come to know the forgiveness of sins and the assurance of eternal life. You have the very Spirit of God indwelling you. It is perfectly true that you yourselves can't obey. But you don't have to do so out of your own resources. You do not need anything more. All of God's resources are available to you already as you step out in obedience to do whatever God says in the Bible. If you genuinely, prayerfully, believingly obey God, Jesus Himself, who promised that through Him you can do all things (Phil. 4:13), will give you the strength. [34] More often than not that strength comes in the doing, so that those who disobediently sit around waiting for it, rather than moving ahead in obedient faith to do as God requires, fail to receive it. Every commandment of God should give His children hope, since, as I pointed out, God never asks His children to do anything that He does not provide both the instruction and the strength to accomplish." [35]

"Well, I can see that God has anticipated a lot more about these matters than I had thought.

"I believe that I am beginning to get some hope [36]; if the Bible gives us all of this, then perhaps it does have more to say about the solution to our other problems than I had ever dreamed."

[33] The theme of "human inability" runs throughout Calvinist theology, and in Jay Adams's hands was meant to spur optimistic reliance on God, not fatalism or despair.

[34] Promises of immediate divine aid characterized Adams's conversation with counselees. He said what he personally believed, lived, and experienced. They were without excuse if they persevered in their hostilities. He staked his counseling model on whether or not the Bible lied about God as "living and powerful, a very present help in trouble."

[35] Throughout this paragraph two constant Adamsian—Calvinistic—themes played out: the Holy Spirit who gave power and the Bible which gave instruction.

[36] Adams believed that to identify problems in living as "sin" gave people great hope because of Christ's mercy and power. He did not think that it made people feel more guilty and condemned, or that it created nervous and perfectionistic attempts to be more obedient.

"Right, Phil! Only let's be entirely clear about this matter; the Bible doesn't have merely *more* answers to your problems; it has *all* of the answers to *all* of them. [37] In His Word, God has given us '*everything pertaining to life and godliness*' (2 Pet. 1:3)."

"Well, I'm interested, too. How do we get started? Where do we go from here?"

"Good. In a few moments I'm going to lay out some homework assignments [38] for you to do during the week after you have sought full forgiveness from God and one another (and I want to talk to you about how to do this properly, too, before we finish).

"But before we go any further, there is one other matter about which I want to say a word or two. Phil, let me return to that verse in Ephesians 5:25 once more. Remember, God commands, 'Husbands, love your wives, just as Christ loved the church.' Well, throughout that section of the chapter, one thing is clear: Again and again the husband (not the wife) is commanded to love. If there is no love in your home, then it is primarily *your* fault and it is *your* responsibility to see to it that love is generated, is maintained, and grows." [39]

"Now I'm getting hope, too!"

"I'm glad about that, Emily, because there are responsibilities pertaining to you in the passage also. I shall get around to those in time. But, to continue, Paul points out that the man is the head of his home as Christ is the head of the church. That means that he is primarily responsible for seeing to it that there is love in the home. Headship has its authority, but we shall begin with its responsibilities. To sum up what God says, headship is the responsibility to take loving leadership in the home. And this leadership must follow the model provided by Christ in His loving headship over His church. In short, every married Christian has both the privilege and the obligation to exhibit the relationship between Christ and the church.

"And Phil, you know very well that it was not the church that first reached out to Christ in love. Indeed, in 1 John 4:19 we read, 'We [the church] love because He first loved us.' And, incidentally, that love was out of pure grace; there was nothing in us to commend us to God. He, of His own volition, determined to set His love upon us. [40]

[37] Adams rarely missed an occasion to inculcate in counselees his view that the Bible was God's comprehensive word on human life.

[38] Adams placed great stress on homework between counseling sessions. Typical assignments included bibliotherapy (such as reading this pamphlet), a data-gathering journal, studying the Bible, and specific behavioral tasks such as asking for forgiveness (mentioned here and earlier) and setting up a family conference table.

[39] Adams taught traditional husband-wife roles and landed hard on the husband's responsibility to love and give. He vigorously prosecuted both dictatorial, harsh husbands and neglectful, passive husbands for their failure to love well.

[40] Adams believed the traditional Calvinistic "doctrines of grace" and here alluded to total depravity and unconditional election.

So Phil, whenever you find it difficult to show love, remember that it was not easy for God either."

"I've always wanted to be the head of my home, but I've never known how to begin."

"And I've wanted him to assume the responsibilities of headship." [41]

"Well, in the assignments that I shall give you, there will be plenty for you to do that will give you a good start this week. Now Emily, while God does not require love of you as the essence of your role in the home, He does insist upon submission: 'As the church is subject to Christ, so let wives be to their own husbands in everything' (Eph. 5:24). Now let me explain what this means. I think that you are going to discover that there are some surprises connected with this command. As a matter of fact, the road to fulfillment that we hear so much about today lies in this valley. To begin with. . . ."

You have read enough to know that there is hope. Phil and Emily are just two of the thousands who this year will find help for their marriage from truly Christian counseling. [42] How about your marriage . . . has it begun to turn sour, too? There is hope. But that hope can be found nowhere but in Christ. If you do not know Christ as your Savior [43], or if you would like to learn more about biblical solutions to marriage and other life problems, contact the person who gave you this folder or write to the address imprinted in the space below. Further help may be found in the book *Christian Living in the Home* by Jay Adams.

[41] Adams could presume of his readership that these sentiments, odd-sounding as they are to many modern readers, were genuine in many of his target population of counselees. Both domineering and doormat wives faced frank challenge and instruction. He also vigorously prosecuted the egalitarian model that eliminated role distinctions. The "surprises" about wifely submission that he alludes to later in the paragraph came from his reading of Proverbs 31:10ff as a paradigm of female fulfillment.[9]

[42] A jab at evangelical psychotherapists, whom Adams saw as "Christians who counsel," not necessarily as "truly Christian counselors."

[43] Adams's counseling presumed that evangelism was an integral ingredient of counseling. According to the logic of his system, the counselor did not represent the counselee's interests in abstraction from God but represented God's interests to the counselee, which were ultimately in the counselee's best interests.

Appendix 1 Notes

1. Jay E. Adams, *What Do You Do When Your Marriage Goes Sour?* (Phillipsburg, N.J.: Presbyterian & Reformed, 1975). This sold about 350,000 copies in the next fifteen years. Reprinted by permission.

2. Jay E. Adams, *Marriage, Divorce, and Remarriage in the Bible* (Grand Rapids: Zondervan, 1980).

3. Jay E. Adams, *Christian Living in the Home* (Phillipsburg, N.J.: Presbyterian & Reformed, 1972), 10–13.

4. Jay E. Adams, *The Christian Counselor's Manual* (USA: Presbyterian & Reformed, 1973), 103–347; contains Adams's most detailed exposition of his counseling methodology.

5. Ibid., 277ff. Adams engaged in a lengthy polemic against the authorities in contemporary pastoral counseling—Carl Rogers, Seward Hiltner, Rollo May, et al.—for their nondirective therapies.

6. "Whenever I speak of 'guilt' . . . I mean 'liability to punishment,' not the unpleasant feelings that may accompany it." Jay E. Adams, *From Forgiven to Forgiving: Discover the Path to Biblical Forgiveness* (USA: Victor Books [Scripture Press], 1989), 161.

7. Jay E. Adams, *Competent to Counsel* (USA: Presbyterian & Reformed, 1970), 94.

8. Ibid., 148–51; Adams, *The Christian Counselor's Manual*, 118–24.

9. Adams, *Christian Living in the Home,* chapter 6.

APPENDIX 2

Crucial Issues
in Contemporary Biblical Counseling
(1988)

Abstract: The contemporary biblical counseling movement faces six crucial issues. One issue concerns our foundation; the other five concern how we build on that foundation. First, the "same old issues" that we always have addressed remain lively issues in the contemporary world. Second, the questions of motivation must be addressed in the same detail with which biblical counseling has addressed questions of behavior. Third, we need to clarify the ways in which human responsibility and suffering relate to one another. Fourth, many elements in the counselor-counselee relationship need to be better understood and practiced. Fifth, biblical counseling needs to interact with a wider audience. Sixth, we need to develop the nuances in our view of secular psychology.

* * *

The Christian Counseling and Educational Foundation celebrates its twentieth anniversary in 1988. CCEF's anniversary is a symbolic anniversary for the entire nouthetic-biblical counseling movement. An anniversary is a time to take stock. Where have we come from? Where are we? What issues that now face us will determine our future?

I have identified six crucial issues facing contemporary biblical counseling. These six are not the only issues. They are, however, the issues I believe merit the adjective "crucial." If we address them, we will grow in wisdom. If we neglect them, we will stagnate or even distort the counsel of God. I have attempted to look at contemporary biblical counseling (both our articulated theory and our run-of-the-mill practice) in the light of Scripture. Each issue is an issue both of theory and of practice. How do we think about people biblically? How do we counsel them biblically?

1. The "same old issues" still face us

The first issue is an old one. The problems that animated biblical counseling at its start remain live problems today. Counseling in the Christian church continues to be significantly compromised by the secular assumptions and practices of our culture's reigning psychologies and psychiatries. Biblical-nouthetic counseling was initiated to provide two things: a cogent critique of secularism and a distinctly biblical alternative. The traditional insights, strengths, and commitments of nouthetic counseling must be maintained. Biblical counseling operates within the worldview of the Bible, with the Bible in hand. It is centered on God even (especially!) when it thinks about man. It is centered on Jesus Christ, who became a man in order to save us. It is centered in the midst of Christ's people, who are called to pray for one another and to counsel one another in love.

Secular psychologies remain major competitors with the church. We face a zoo of systems united by only one thing. At best, "god" is a comforting auxiliary to the human psychic drama. At worst, he/she/it is a delusion. Lacking God, the human problem (and the power to understand and to solve that problem) is perceived to lie somewhere within or between human beings. Christ died for nothing.

The enemy was not only out there somewhere. "We have met the enemy . . . and they are us," Pogo once remarked. Secular psychological modes of thinking continue to inhabit the church of the living God. Witness the rampant self-esteem and need psychologies that bypass the man-God relationship in order to make the human psyche the place "where the action is." The living God is shriveled into an actor within an all-important psychic drama. Witness the church hiring essentially secular psychologists, referring to and deferring to their "wisdom" for solving "personal problems" and "relationship and lifestyle issues." Witness an ongoing intellectual confusion and eclecticism that pursues truth in some blend of secular psychology and biblical Christianity. We must continue to provide a distinct alternative in both the content and practice of counseling.

Biblical counseling must reaffirm and finely tune its distinctive intellectual content. We must continue to think biblically, letting biblical categories lead our understanding. We must continue to reject secular categories from a self-consciously presuppositional standpoint. The climate of schol-arly opinion has not changed drastically. The same old pattern of rehashing ideas and practices of secular psychology continues in the books, journals, schools, seminaries, and professional organizations of the Christian counseling world.

Biblical counseling must also continue to reaffirm and develop its counseling methods. We must continue to develop counseling as Christian ministry—intended to produce conviction of sin, the joyous reception of Jesus Christ, and renewal of life. Biblical counseling must continue to repudiate the notion of a "counseling profession" disconnected both structurally and intellectually from the nurture, instruction, love, discipline, authority, and friendship of the body of Christ. The patterns of professional practice have not changed drastically. Christian clones of secular methods continue to dominate the practice, no less than the literature, of the Christian counseling world.

Does this mean that nothing has changed in twenty years? I do not think so. In a number of ways 1988 is more opportune than 1968 for a message of presuppositionally consistent counseling to be heard. The intellectual climate has changed. Thomas Kuhn and other secular philosophers of science have made presuppositional modes of thought common intellectual currency among Christians and non-Christians alike. The ground has been cut away that makes psychology and psychiatry seem like neutral, objective scientific truth. Under the "all truth is God's truth" slogan, with its notion that both Science and the Bible were revelational, cartloads of undiluted secularism were hauled into the church. But now the sciences have lost much of their pretense to objectivity. Christians of various stripes also have made presuppositional styles of thinking common. Francis Schaeffer introduced the evangelical reading public to a generally presuppositional mode of thought. C. S. Lewis, G. K. Chesterton, and Harry

Blamires expounded in charming fashion the idea that we should "think Christianly." Paul Vitz and William Kirk Kilpatrick have been widely read and applauded for their crisp analyses of secular psychology's covert religious character. None of the above has articulated the biblical counseling alternatives as clearly as he has diagnosed or hinted at the failings of secularism. But all the above have plowed the ground. The message of biblical counseling, restated for contemporary hearers, may well fall on more receptive ears.

It is not redundant to call Christians to be radically biblical. Many ears still attend to the persuasive voice of secular psychology. It is not redundant to call Christians to be exegetically biblical. The Bible abounds in riches yet to be mined and applied to counseling. It is not redundant to call Christians to be biblical in practice as well as in thinking. Biblical counseling is an expression of church life. The equipping and overseeing work of the pastors and the one-anothering of the rest of the body of Christ are intrinsically counseling activities.

This first crucial issue restates where we have stood for the past twenty years. The five crucial issues that follow are newer issues. These are areas where our grasp of what it means to be biblical must be significantly extended. Issue 1: hold fast to the foundation. Issues 2, 3, 4, 5, and 6 build on that foundation.

We have had twenty years to show our strengths—and our weaknesses. An honest self-assessment reveals a number of questions, shortcomings, or growing pains we need to face as a movement. But the implications of this first crucial issue must be felt throughout the discussion that follows. Whatever changes and development need to occur within the biblical counseling movement must occur only on the foundation already laid: biblical categories of thought generating biblical methods of ministry.

2. The questions touching on human motivation must be explored and integrated more firmly within both our theory and practice

Nouthetic counseling has uniquely comprehended that the goal of counseling should be nothing less than visible obedience to the Lord. No other counseling system perceives that this is the central issue facing troubled, sinful, and suffering human beings. The counseling world around us (Christian and non-Christian alike) is agog with speculations about human motivation. Biblical counseling has rightly stressed behavior—love and good works—as the simple and accessible evidence of true change.

Biblical counseling must walk a fine line, however. There is patent "danger to the left of us." Speculative psychological systems pretend to an analytic insight into the motivations of the human heart. Biblical counseling has been rightfully suspicious of psychodynamic explanations. Purely mythical constructs like id, ego, and super ego are reified. Self-esteem or "needs" become the magic crucible from which all human life flows. My "self-talk" is invested with supreme power to determine the course of my life. Our wariness at such pseudo-explanations perhaps carries over (illegitimately) into a wariness toward the whole subject of motivation.

Those to the left forget that the dynamics of the human psyche have to do with God! Always. Without exception. There is no "psychodynamic," no motivation pattern, independent of what people are doing with God. Human psychology is theological because human beings are with-respect-to-God creatures. The prime action is in the man-God relationship, not in an encapsulated psyche whose component parts relate to one another according to some supposed pattern. What goes on in the psyche expresses and registers man-with-God dynamics, not some supposedly independent psychic structure, conflict, or need.

But we who are sensitive to danger on the left, to rank speculation about the motives and motivational structure of the human heart, often forget there is "danger to the right of us" as well. We depart from the Bible if we ignore motives and drift toward an externalistic view of man. The caricature that we are behavioristic may indeed be true more often than we would like to admit. The Bible itself tells us behavior has reasons.

Behavior flows "from within, out of men's hearts" (Mark 7:21). There is an internal cause of interpersonal conflict (James 4:1f); the varied works of the flesh express inner cravings (Gal. 5:15–21); every kind of evil roots in misplaced affections (1 Tim. 6:10). This we all know and affirm. But both our theory and practice have not given this area the attention it needs. We must become as familiar with the practical, everyday details of faith and idolatry as we are with the details of those acts of sin and righteousness, which flow, from our hearts. The changes for which biblical counseling must aim are both internal and external.

I am not saying that there is a fatal defect within existing biblical counseling. Our problem is a lack of emphasis and articulation. We already have a first approximation of the biblical view of motivation in Jay Adams's "feeling or desire orientation versus commandment orientation." He has perceptively described the two-sided, basic structure in biblical fashion. But there is a wealth of detail to fill in. Filling in that detail will make us realize that motivational issues play a far more prominent role than we have realized, both conceptually and in counseling practice.

Attending to this area will change the way we think about people and the way we counsel: nothing will be lost, but much will be gained. I believe that we will linger in areas we now rush over in our counseling. Picture to yourself an artist's rep-

resentation of a human being that is a collage of photographic snapshots and charcoal sketches. We biblical counselors have photographic likenesses, in living color, of the hands, feet, and tongue. We know the terrain in some detail, hence we feel comfortable attending to these areas in our counseling. But we have only a rough charcoal sketch of the head and heart, so we quickly run out of issues to explore and things to say.

Figure 1 portrays the structure of biblical change. Heart leads to walk. Idolatry leads to disobedience; faith leads to obedience. Change of heart leads to change of walk. Every visible sin roots in a far more massive invisible sin. What is the change biblical counseling aims for? $B \rightarrow B^*$ is rank moralism: "do's and don'ts." $AB \rightarrow A^*$ is pietism: "Let go and let God." $B \rightarrow A^*B^*$ is a subtler error. The put-off (B), put-on (B*), and faith in Jesus Christ (A*) are all present. But the structure of false faiths (A) is neglected. This is the configuration into which I fear nouthetic counselors too often drift. We fail to minister the full inner impact of the conviction of sin. Hence the desperateness of our need for Jesus Christ is weakened. Hence the renewal of mind and heart by the promises of God is practically downplayed. We become incipiently moralistic. Biblical change is $AB \rightarrow A^*B^*$. The inordinate, swarming desires of the flesh are treated in the same detail as the works of the flesh, the simple desires of the Spirit of Jesus Christ, and the fruit of the Spirit. Our instinctive orientation to inordinate desires and false beliefs yields to our orientation to Christ's mercies and wise will.

Is our current view of motivation inaccurate or unbiblical? No, but many sordid and gorgeous details must be seen and understood for the whole picture of man to take on flesh. At the very least, attending to the motivation issues will transform Adams's "presentation, performance, and preconditioning levels" of problem analysis. A fourth dimension, an enriched "desire versus

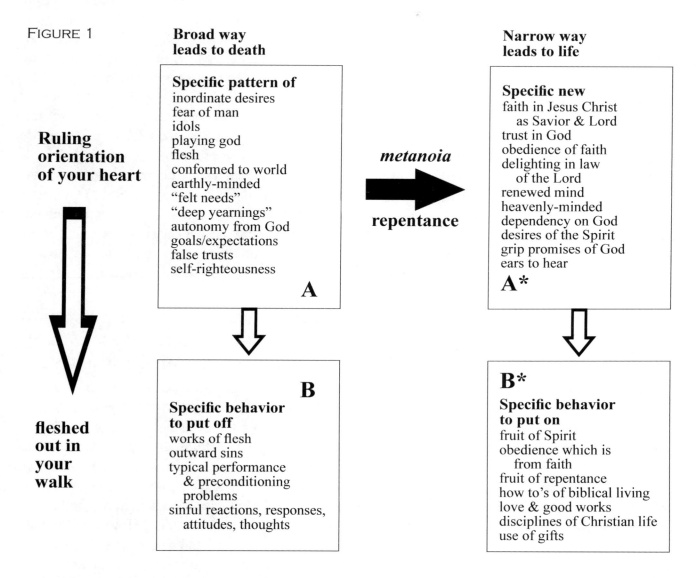

FIGURE 1

Broad way leads to death

Ruling orientation of your heart

Specific pattern of
inordinate desires
fear of man
idols
playing god
flesh
conformed to world
earthly-minded
"felt needs"
"deep yearnings"
autonomy from God
goals/expectations
false trusts
self-righteousness

A

metanoia

repentance

Narrow way leads to life

Specific new
faith in Jesus Christ
    as Savior & Lord
trust in God
obedience of faith
delighting in law
    of the Lord
renewed mind
heavenly-minded
dependency on God
desires of the Spirit
grip promises of God
ears to hear

A*

fleshed out in your walk

B

Specific behavior to put off
works of flesh
outward sins
typical performance
    & preconditioning
    problems
sinful reactions, responses,
    attitudes, thoughts

B*

Specific behavior to put on
fruit of Spirit
obedience which is
    from faith
fruit of repentance
how to's of biblical living
love & good works
disciplines of Christian life
use of gifts

commandment orientation," will be systematically woven in as fundamental to the other three.

People often present a stew of problems: anger, desires, frustrations, fears, immorality, confusion, defensiveness, cruelty, interpersonal disasters, instability, misery, substance abuse, and anxiety. These defy simple categorization on a behavioral problem list! But such a confusing stew can be tied, item after item, to organizing themes in a person's life. The Scriptures present many such themes: pride, the fear of man, mammon, the desires of the flesh, idolatry, trust in man, and so forth. Biblical counselors need to learn to think thematically about the heart. When we do not think about characteristic motivations, the counselee's "relationship with God" tends to be approached chiefly through outward disciplines: devotional life, church attendance, and the like. When we do address the motivational issues biblically, the counselee's relationship with God becomes a counseling issue we can get our hands on. "Trust in the Lord" (that most generic and abused piece of wonderful counsel!)

comes to life against the backdrop of specific false trusts. Usually "trust in the Lord" is vague and ineffectual because it is tossed like some Season-all into the stew of a person's life. Counselees in effect trust the Lord to give them their ruling desires, without ever repenting in depth of those desires. But "trust the Lord *instead of* trusting in . . ." does work because it is biblical.[1] It has the concrete two-sidedness of biblical repentance and mind renewal.

Biblical counselors can say, "Bill, you became angry at Sally, got depressed, barked at your boss, and then took drugs because you were absolutely ruled by wanting your own way—with Sally and with everything else." Counseling typically should deal in detail then with the question, What rules Bill? What particular desires, expectations, fears, and beliefs controlled his response to his life situation? His relationship with God—and with his false gods—would become the stuff of concrete counseling that tackles the heart. Counseling at this point is strongly interpretive, helping Bill to make sense out of the welter of problematic actions, words, thoughts, and attitudes that characterize his life. Conviction of sin will land him squarely before God as a repentant idolater, as well as an angry, depressed substance abuser prepared to change. As he truly understands himself and Christ's grace, the necessary behavioral changes will make sense from the inside.

We waste our breath (and precious truths) if we first talk about biblical ways to control anger, counteract depression, communicate with one's wife, show proper work attitudes, and restructure one's life to eliminate drug addiction. Those should come second as the fruit of repentance. How many times we would-be biblical counselors waste our breath because we do not deal well with motivation problems. Biblical counselors must look carefully for the "false gods" if we are to minister the first great commandment and the promises of God as concretely as we minister the second great commandment.

In conclusion, it seems to me that critics of nouthetic counseling have been right in discerning a gap, or at least relative inattention, in our treatment of motivation. Their alternatives to our lack have been so appalling that we perhaps might feel excused for not heeding their criticism. I propose that we hear their criticism, in addition to avoiding their alternatives. Or perhaps it is truer to say, I propose that we hear the Scripture. Our critics criticize in order to dismiss us. Scripture admonishes to mature us. We need not fear the biblical alternative, of course. The categories we are not yet using well are *biblical* categories.

3. The relationship between human responsibility and human suffering needs a great deal of clarification

Crucial issue 1 established our foundation for faith and practice. Crucial issue 2 made us rethink the nature of biblical change. Crucial issue 3 now challenges us to rethink our vision of the counselee and the counselee's situation. How do we see and understand the people whom we counsel? What kind of attention do we pay to the kind of world the counselee inhabits? How important are the counselee's past and present circumstances?

One of the most refreshing characteristics of nouthetic counseling has been its affirmation of human responsibility. The counseling world, Christian and non-Christian alike, concocts elaborate systems that rationalize sin by making people fundamentally victims determined by forces outside their control. Contemporary victim theories abound, whether operating under psychological, medical, sociological, or Christian aegis. All such theories rob people of moral responsibility and insert some determinism at the foundation of human life. Biblical counseling has resisted seeing people as determined—whether by heredity, the sins of others, organic imbalances, poor models, unmet needs, mental forces imposing on us as "illness," or demonic inhabitants.

In attacking notions of "man as victim," biblical counseling has reaffirmed the biblical notion of human responsibility. In most graphic terms, on the day of judgment God will ask, "What did you do?" He will not ask, "What happened to you?" Nouthetic counseling has gone on to deal forthrightly with the omnipresent human tendency to rationalize, to portray oneself as a victim whose problems and sins are someone or something else's fault. Victim theories ground our sins in our pain and our "needs." Let sins be derivative, and some other problem primary, and people will not need Jesus Christ. In Christian guise, Jesus becomes a need-meeter who makes victims feel better, not a Savior who purchases sinful men for God with his own blood.

We have been wary of any emphasis on man as victim, for every version around is tainted by sin's aversion to acknowledging sin. All this said, we still need to appreciate and clarify the many ways people are sufferers—and fully responsible— if we are to be faithful to the perfect fit between the Bible and human life. We have made a strong affirmation of human responsibility: the role of the flesh. We have not discussed as fully the impact of the world and the devil as they master and shape human life. We have mined and processed certain biblical riches; there are other riches that we have not scrutinized as closely.

There is a *biblical* view of man as a sufferer. We can say it even more plainly: There is a biblical view of man as a victim. Biblical counseling has been repeatedly misunderstood to say that all problems are a result of personal sin. Why the misunderstanding? Surely we have talked about the role of Satan, for example in Job's situation. Surely nouthetic literature and practice take seriously that people are sinned against, abused, criticized, tempted, or rejected. What about the impact of other general hardships of life: poverty, injustice, physical disabilities, allergies, sickness, and bereavement? Of course.

Because nouthetic counseling is sensitive to the Scripture, none of these areas has been wholly neglected. It at least has been implicit that man is both responsible and a sufferer. We are guilty and victims. Some of the misunderstanding of biblical counseling is caricature, from people who know all too well that "man is responsible" would undermine their whole counseling theory and practice. Some of the misunderstanding comes from people who simply do not understand that the gospel underlies biblical change. They think "man is responsible" would legitimate judging people and nagging them into change with exhortations to willpower. The gospel of Christ says, instead, that human responsibility legitimates presenting the kindness of Jesus to people and seeking the power of the Spirit to change.

But some of the misunderstanding is our fault. It highlights a problem, a crucial issue for contemporary biblical counseling. Our treatment of the victim side of the biblical portrayal of man has been anecdotal and occasional, not systematic. Under issue 2 we noted that rampant speculations about human motivation should not keep us from tackling the motivation questions biblically. Equally, rampant and systematized blameshifting should not deter us from developing the biblical view of how the things we suffer affect us.

Certainly in the biblical view sin is something we are "led into" by an enslaving master, Satan. We are blinded, powerless, led by the nose, tempted, attacked, deceived. In other words, we are victims of a slavemaster. Certainly in the biblical view sin is done to us as much as we do it to others. And sin is something we are "taught" by others, provoked to, encouraged in by the "world." In other words, we are victims of oppression. Certainly plain old hardship provides many of the chief temptations to us all. It is no accident that "temptation" and "trial" are the same Greek word, *peirasmos*. In other words, we are victims needing deliverance from suffering. We are even victims (justly) of the curse of God and delivered from his wrath by the mercy of his Christ. All this said, certainly sin is the product of the flesh, with its lusts and desires. In other words, we are fully responsible! The Bible is not embarrassed to speak of world, flesh, and Devil as coconspirators, of man as jointly responsible and victim. The Bible is not embarrassed to speak of Jesus Christ as the Savior of people who are both guilty and oppressed.

The biblical notion of man as victim is, after all, the source of much of the compassion with which our Deliverer approaches his groaning people. Our God has compassion on sufferers, who are also sinners responsible for their responses to suffering, and who even may have brought suffering on themselves.

Are nouthetic counselors needlessly skittish about hearing and entering into the counselee's suffering for fear of encouraging blameshifting? I suspect so. Yet one central avenue of approach into the life of my counselee, my friend, my fellow, is through his suffering. His body is in pain. Satan is mounting assaults on his faith. He has had a lifetime of ungodly influences that persist into the present. He is experiencing situational uncertainties: his job future and his wife's health. Such a recognition and the patience to hear it, even to pursue it, will not sabotage recognition of his responsibility. It will rather set his responsibility firmly and realistically in context. His characteristic sins were and are often forged in reaction to suffering and being sinned against.

Unbiblical views construe man-as-victim to be a reason, an excuse, a cause for our faulty and negative actions. Biblically comprehending man-as-sufferer is never meant to answer "Why do I sin?" It does answer "When? Where? With whom? Under whose influence?" It describes the situation in which one is tempted and tried. With new eyes, the situation of suffering becomes the "when, where, with whom, and against what" within which he will learn faith and obedience. We have said loudly, "responsible!" The biblical balance, "responsible amid hardship," has been more understated and assumed.

But what is understated and assumed easily becomes ineffectual. I suspect that at times we simply have been deficient in our counseling worldview; we have been subbiblical in the name of being biblical. Would anyone deny that "nouthetic" counseling practice often has been less than biblical in its sensitivity to suffering people? Biblical counselors often have worked for change in how people react to suffering without adequately attending (in word and deed) to how they experience and interpret suffering. One reason is because the biblical doctrine of "man as sufferer whom Christ delivers" has not been understood as clearly as the doctrine of "man as responsible whom Christ forgives." What we suffer powerfully influences us, even seems to rule us with an iron hand. What we suffer is then the context within which both human responsibility and Christ's power to set free operate.

We are sensitive to errors on one side of us, to the diminution of human responsibility by appeals to psychosocial trauma, situational stress, physiological causes, or demons. Are we as sensitive to the errors on the other side, to views of human responsibility that are essentially moralizing, evidencing a firm faith in willpower, self-discipline, and mind-control? There are unbiblical forms of responsibility just as destructive as unbiblical forms of victimization.

Do we subtly appeal to human willpower? Do we know how to put together the fact that counselees are often "very rebellious" and "very hurt" at the same time, without washing over the latter just because our counselees and our culture make it primary? Do we labor hard and patiently to help counselees grasp the biblical view of suffering and temptation as the context within which to understand both their responsibility and God's grace? Do we discount Satan and his attacks on people? Do we brush over discussion of situational hardships as mere blameshifting? Do we move quickly past physical or emotional pain to immediately tackle the counselee's responsibility for his reaction? Are we patient? Do counselees know we understand how they experience life? Do we pray seriously because our biblical worldview teaches us that people cannot do it by willpower but need the direct grace and power of God?

Counselees typically want to change their circumstances. Nouthetic counselors typically want to change the counselee's behavior within those circumstances. The two can lock horns needlessly. Patient and sympathetic entry into the counselee's circumstances often can open the door for biblical categories to reinterpret those circumstances. As suffering is seen through God's eyes, biblical categories then expose the lusts of the heart which seek particular circumstantial blessings rather than the Giver of gifts and promises. On such a foundation particular steps of obedience can be mapped out. The behavioral changes proposed will not be selected arbitrarily off a generic list of good things to do. Instead, the behavior appropriate for that individual (those "good works prepared in advance by God") will flow specifically from three intertwined strands of biblical understanding: the counselee's behavior, motives (issue 2), and situation (issue 3). The second and third strands need to be brought up to the level of development that the first strand has enjoyed.

Our critics' perception that our practice is often defective has been accurate, even if their alternatives are grossly misguided. The biblical alternative, another of the crucial issues in contemporary biblical counseling, is to articulate the full biblical view of both man and man's situation in all its power, realism, compassion, and subtlety. Then, by the grace of God, we must mature in wisdom to practice counseling in the light of such truth.

4. We need to press much further in understanding the biblical data about the counselor-counselee relationship

Crucial issue 1 reaffirmed our epistemological and practical foundation. Issue 2 probed the nature of change. Issue 3 reexamined our understanding of the counselee and his situation. Issue 4 asks, "What is the nature of the relationship between the counselor and counselee?"

We all know that we are to "love" those we counsel. Biblical counseling is "speaking the truth in love" (Eph. 4:15). What does this mean in practice? Nouthetic counseling has uniquely comprehended the authoritative, shepherdly, and truth-speaking elements in biblical love. We are known (perhaps notorious) for seeking to reflect the directive, confrontational, and authoritative style of counsel that the Bible repeatedly evidences.

The counseling world, Christian and non-Christian alike, abhors authority. It equates authority with authoritarian. Instead, a therapist uses a relationship of acceptance to elicit healing forces from within the counselee. Biblical counseling has rightly stressed that the lordship of Jesus Christ and the authority of his Word demand that counseling be authoritative if it is to be loving. We have avoided emphasizing the counseling relationship for fear that it smacks of transference, unconditional positive regard, and man-centeredness.

There is "danger to the left of us" in various secular constructions of the counselor-counselee relationship that zealously avoid any overt authority (covert authority is, of course, present in every counseling system). But there is also danger to the other side. The biblical view of the counseling relationship has nonauthoritative elements, in which the counselee sets the agenda, in which "the relationship" is central to constructive counseling taking place! The Scripture demands that we probe the interplay between authority and mutuality characteristic of healthy biblical relationships. We must mirror the variety of counselor-counselee configurations that the Bible portrays as vehicles for the Lord's authority.

Given the ways we historically have fought against unbiblical notions, it is perhaps no wonder that nouthetic counselors have tended even to be a bit suspicious of the counselee, have insisted on maintaining control of the agenda, have aimed for quick and obvious changes, have hesitated to appear too caring, have been leery of long-term counseling relationships. We need to rethink this. In fact, the authoritative shepherd who decisively intervenes is only one of the modes of biblical counseling. It is not even the primary mode. It is the backup mode for when the primary mode fails. The most characteristic biblical counseling relationship is a long-term friendship, consisting of mutually invited counsel, generating dependency on God and a constructive interdependency on one another. The authoritative, short-term intervention is the emergency, lifesaving measure. Is this a new message within nouthetic counseling? Far from it. There always has been a peculiar (and biblical!) tension within nouthetic counseling between short-term "restorative" counseling and ongoing "preventive" counseling.

On the one hand, nouthetic counseling has stressed the authoritative ministry of the Word. Adams has written at length about the counseling role of the pastor as "God's professional" and about the connections between remedial counseling and church discipline. His books on counseling method, in particular *The Christian Counselor's Manual* and *Ready to Restore,* set forth a model of counseling that is relatively formal, with well-defined roles. The counselor leads, sits behind the desk, sets the agenda, interprets authoritatively from the Bible, confronts, encourages, and guides. The counselee provides honest data, commits himself to counseling, and follows the remedial steps outlined.

On the other hand, from the beginning nouthetic counseling has had a peer counseling thrust which deprofessionalizes counseling. It says all wise Christians are competent to counsel one another. The laycounseling emphasis of *Competent to Counsel* implicitly and explicitly downplayed the formalized notion that counseling means a competent expert serves a needy client in a formal relationship. In fact, the daily-life normality of mutual counsel that the Bible presupposes has often become an invigorating reality in churches influenced by nouthetic counseling.[2] In this peer counseling mode, counseling moves out of the office and into all of life. Counseling verges into honest friendships, child-rearing, marriage, discipleship, small groups, and all the one-anothering that Christians do with each other.

Biblical counseling, then, has not only implied six to twelve weeks of strongly interventionist and directive counseling. It has also implied how my best friends and I ought to relate to each other over the next thirty years: as equals, honestly and mutually encouraging one another in a long-term (even lifelong!) "counseling" relationship. Such counseling occasionally requires one to confront the other. But the basis is trust, honesty about struggles, self-confrontation, mutual care, affirmation, and so forth. The "agenda" emerges only in the give and take of seeking to know and encourage one another. Adams set forth a vision in which self-counseling and informal mutual counseling create the context for formal, remedial counseling and discipline.[3]

One of the crucial issues in contemporary biblical counseling is the further articulation of the relationship between the more authoritative, frankly remedial elements of counseling and the more mutual, ongoing encouragement elements. Adams's emphasis has been on the former. This is evidenced most clearly by the relatively formal counseling model that his laycounseling book, *Ready to Restore,* presents. Adams comments, "Lay counseling must be both preventive and remedial. But in this book we shall be concerned almost exclusively with nouthetic, or remedial, counseling" (p. 10). Our goal is systematically biblical counseling, the ministry of God's truth in love. The "nouthetic" part of biblical counseling is the "fence." It is the backup mode of biblical counseling. It is for when the sheep leave the green pastures to wander out into the desert. The "paracletic" part of biblical counseling is the "field." It is the primary mode of biblical counseling, containing all the mutually edifying, encouraging, one-anothering, nourishing, praying, and loving that is the normal Christian life. It is as much a two-way street as possible. It is as egalitarian as possible. It is as *biblically* "nondirective and client-centered" as possible. The truth content and goals of counseling are invariable, fixed by Scripture. This same Scripture tells us God uses many different forms of relationships to write his Word on our hearts.

Figure 2 portrays the relationship between the authoritative fence and the mutual field in which counseling takes place. We are well known for having the fence. We are probably the only formal counseling system around that even realizes that love has a fence. There is a time to confront a counselee frankly, and biblical counseling is bounded by church discipline. But I submit that it is very important that we become equally well known for the field. Here, after all, is the place where most of the joys, changes, and constructive

FIGURE 2

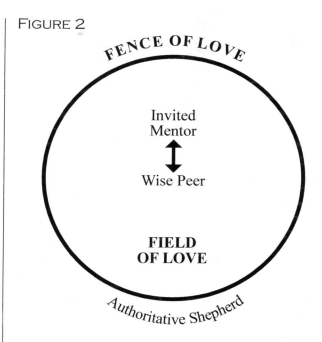

FENCE OF LOVE

Invited
Mentor

↕

Wise Peer

**FIELD
OF LOVE**

Authoritative Shepherd

counseling take place. "Preventive" is too bland to describe the field of love. Perhaps we should call the center of the circle "invited" or "wise peer" counseling.

Within the field of love there is a spectrum between invited counsel from a respected person and a more fully peer relationship. Parents, disciplers, pastors, elders, and other wise people often function in the mentor role. People seek out someone whom they respect and trust, whom they know cares for them and is wise. But full mutuality under the Lord's authority is always the desirable goal. It is, of course, unattainable in a world with children, with new converts, with great sanctification needs in old converts, with warfare and hardships. But when we are all "fully taught," this is what we shall all be like. The peer reality can be realized in part, and it ought to be fully integrated into our vision of biblical counseling's central intent. The fence is the boundary of life; the field is the life.

I see a series of benefits coming out of developing neglected elements in the counselor-counselee relationship. I will briefly sketch four benefits. First, we will gain greatly in flexibility to relate differently to different counselees. There are various ways for structuring the counseling relationship. A brief, highly structured intervention (say over six to twelve weeks) may be the appropriate strategy for helping person A at a certain stage of his life. It may be wholly inappropriate for person B, who would benefit more from ongoing accountability, friendship, and greater mutuality with a wise friend—equally biblical counseling, equally submitted to the authority of the Word.

Second, by articulating a dominant peer mode whose boundaries are the authoritative mode, we open the door wide for all Christians to counsel. Many counseling gifts are given by God to people who will rarely be called to take an authoritative position toward another. Articulating the way in which biblical counseling is a "fenced field of love" will free people to see that the very heart of biblical counseling is open to all with wisdom.

Third, biblical counseling has barely touched on many potential strengths that flow from the counseling relationship. "The relationship" is a powerful aspect of counseling. We must not let the secular emphases on transference and unconditional positive regard make us shy away from exploring a rich biblical vein. Paul continually counsels and teaches biblical truth in the context of his personal relationship with his hearers. His joys, prayers, anguish, fears, trials, needs for prayer, wonderments about his hearers, tears, memories, attitudes, plans, hopes—these and more are continually on the table. Is our relatively impersonal and objective pastoral counseling biblical here? Are we simply mirroring the professional detachment of our culture's forms of psychotherapy?

One consequence of enhanced appreciation of the relationship between the counselor and counselee is that more attention will be paid to events within the counseling process itself. Immediate data, features of the relationships between counselor, counselee, and God played out right in the room, can be particularly useful grist for the mill of biblical counseling. The counselee will not only bring outside life in, to be worked on in counseling; counselors will be attentive to the continuity between outside life and counseling. How are we treating one another? Biblical changes in attitude and actions that happen right within the friendship of counseling (from both parties!) can then ripple out into the rest of life.

Fourth, as we enrich our perspective on the biblical counseling relationship, we will change the "flavor" of much of the counseling we do. The vast bulk of biblical counseling will not look authoritative. In fact, it is desirable that a pastor aim to deemphasize the authoritative, formal, confrontive, and unilateral elements in his counseling as much as is appropriate to the case at hand. We should save the fence for when it is really needed. How many counselees have been needlessly confronted—perhaps even put on the defensive—when they would have confronted themselves if a probing and inviting question had been asked? Biblical counseling, like healthy family life, has a minimal number of confrontational and disciplinary events. Confrontation usually cuts deepest when the other forms of constructive relating create the dominant tone.

In summary, biblical counseling has always contained the seeds of two complementary visions of counseling: one relatively more authoritative and the other relatively more mutual. The former has been articulated in detail. The latter has always been more implicit, more the logical implication of the competency of wise people to help one another. These other dimensions in the counselor-counselee relationship must be articulated explicitly.

5. Biblical counseling must be contextualized to new audiences

The crucial issues of motivation, suffering, and the counseling relationship each concern our conceptual balance and the way we go about our counseling. Crucial issue 5 is a different sort of issue. It has to do with who we speak with about what we believe. Biblical counseling needs to interact with a wider audience. We have generally spoken to the conservative pastor in the trenches and to the counseling-minded layperson. We have given them tools to counsel more confidently and effectively. Our target audience has been the local church.

Biblical counseling must cultivate other audiences. We need to do so for our own edification as a truly biblical movement. We need to do so in order to edify others with what God has given us. I would like to propose one particular audience into which biblical counseling must be contextualized. We need to speak with Christian academics. We have barely begun to generate meaningful dialogue with the faculty and students in Christian colleges and seminaries.

Biblical counseling has been a grassroots movement, finding its home in healthy local church life. This is a great strength. Biblical counseling gets established in local churches because it works to transform lives. It works to transform lives because it is God's pattern for ministry: love woven through with truth. But, unfortunately, we generally have been shut out from intellectual and educational centers. We have shut ourselves out because we have not addressed that audience. Biblical counseling *does* have intellectual integrity and power, yet is not speaking to the more intellectual segments of Christian culture. Indeed, it is often dismissed as anti-intellectual and simple-minded.

How do we explain this and answer the charge? I believe the answer essentially boils down to a matter of audience analysis. Jay Adams wrote to the local church. He consciously selected his audience. He spoke the language of persuasion to that audience. Like any good preacher of the Word of God, he concealed his intellectual "bones" within vivid illustrational and practical teaching. He gave people something to respond to, believe in, and act upon. He did not dwell on qualifications, counter-instances, and nuances. He simply sought to speak clearly, simply, and persuasively. Of course he overgeneralized and oversimplified. This was not because Adams does not believe in complexities and vexed questions. It was because he does believe in the primary importance of certain central, life-changing, and essentially simple truths.

Critics have misread simple for simplistic. Biblical counseling is informed by a highly developed theological tradition. Its roots are as intellectual as they are practical. Biblical counseling is, however, like the Bible, anti-intellectual*istic*. This has generated a certain basic criticism of academia and the secular professions. The counseling world, Christian and non-Christian alike, guards its turf by creating technical vocabularies and professional structures into which would-be counselors must be initiated. Biblical counseling has rightly stressed that wisdom, lying open on the pages of Scripture, is the sole criterion for counseling. We have opposed their pretension to proprietary rights over knowledge and efficacy in the arena of counseling. We have opposed the professional elitism inherent in secular psychology, an elitism mirrored in most Christian counseling. We have opposed the notion that nonbiblical experts possess the turf of "psychological, emotional, behavioral, and interpersonal problems." We have opposed the obscurantism that substitutes technical jargon for plain talk, which confuses a label or diagnosis for true knowledge. We even have thought that academia was not the primary arena in which to discuss counseling. It is a secondary arena with well-institutionalized pretensions to primacy. So we have addressed the church because *biblical* counseling is meant for the daily lives of God's people.

The grass roots always will be and always should be the primary constituency for biblical counseling. First things first. Among counseling systems, nouthetic counseling has uniquely seen the centrality of Scripture, obedience to the Lord, human responsibility, the fence of love, and the local church ministry. But, as in the other crucial issues, we must redress imbalances. We need to reach out to the educational wing of the church of Christ. If we neglect Christian academia, the development and spread of biblical counseling will be seriously hindered.

Much of the rejection of biblical counseling in Christian academia is because of the offense of the message. We have challenged the intellectual and practical habits of secular professionalism, habits that are rampant in the educational institutions and professional organizations of Christian counseling. But I am persuaded that much of the rejection is also because we have not yet spoken their language. The offense is not the message but the medium and style. Within a context of genuine dialogue, we need to articulate the same truths in a form that is culturally hear-able.

At minimum, we want people to disagree with us intelligently, not on the basis of a caricature. Repeatedly, I have encountered gross misunderstandings of what biblical counseling was all about in people who are not as far from our basic commitments as we may think. I cannot count the number of folks from the Christian Association for Psychological Studies (CAPS), our "arch foes" when it comes to counseling, who have thought of us as crudely behavioristic, lacking even the rudiments of a view of inner life and motivation. They think Adams's comments about the sin of being "feeling oriented" meant biblical counseling discounted emotions as bad or irrelevant, just

as it discounted everything about motivation and thinking.

But feeling orientation is actually a profound motivational concept stated in street talk. It has nothing to do with whether emotions are good or bad, important or trivial. Feeling orientation is meant to communicate vividly to counselees: children or adults, illiterate or educated. Our lives get in trouble because we interpret life via unexamined subjective experience ("I feel that . . .") and because we live for what we want ("I feel like . . ."). The most profound issue in every person's life is whether he is feeling oriented or Christ oriented. Are we ruled in detail by world, flesh, devil, desires, and idols? Or are we liberated into the rule of the Lord whose truth, love, and grace we trust and delight in?

Feeling orientation often communicates well to the man in the pew or counseling office. But it bewilders scholars who wrestle to make more precise sense of human motivation and emotions. The term confuses them rather than edifies. Is that their fault? It is no more their fault than if I tried to counsel a troubled teenager by alluding to the *epithumiai tes sarkes* ("lusts of the flesh") without providing extensive translation and illustration! The solution? Analyze our audience. Contextualize our insights to the questions they are asking and the language they speak. Biblical categories have a powerful and subtle explanatory power.[4] We are not being heard through the misunderstandings of what we are saying. The responsibility to create understanding is first of all ours.

Many are alienated from our message for bad reasons, not good reasons. I have found many CAPS people who respected what we were saying once they understood it. A few loved it and have come over to become frankly committed biblical counselors. It was something they had been looking for and did not know where to find. We need to build relationships. Some people have experienced us—or imagined us—to be prickly, impolite, and unfriendly. It is our fault if we allow such an image to be perpetuated.

We need to speak a different language to target a different people group. At the simplest strategic level, we must employ the article and book that deals with theoretical questions, ambiguities, and complexities. We must have at least some non-popular writing. Our immediate goal must be to generate an extended dialogue, to listen as well as to hear. This strategy differs from the sermon, which consciously simplifies in order to immediately edify. Of course I believe that those who oppose us need the insights about psychology and biblical counseling that we have. But I also believe that we need the—many?!—potential allies and constructive critics we will find amid the current opposition.

To date we have reached thousands of Christian people with the message of biblical counseling. We need to continue to reach these same people as our primary focus. The local church people are the salt of the earth, the light of the world. But we also need to analyze a different audience and expend some legitimate effort in reaching the educational wing of Christendom. Is addressing academia simply a nice idea, to be attended to someday? I think it is a crucial issue now. The future of the *local church* is involved! Where are the church leaders and counselors of tomorrow being trained today? They are being trained in institutions where biblical counseling is dismissed with a wave of the hand.

We are on a narrow base at the moment. I am convinced with my whole heart that God has given us biblical-nouthetic counselors some outstanding and needed insights. Richard Lovelace, in summarizing the counseling needs of the church of Christ, commented, "The counseling approach which is most likely to help in congregational renewal is a tuned and adapted form of nouthetic counseling."[5] This article is in part a call for such tuning

and adapting to occur in some critical intellectual areas. But the crucial issues facing us are social as well as intellectual. I am convinced that we are shut up in a fairly narrow sector of believing Christendom, and that to spread the word more widely will bless, stimulate, and change us as much as it edifies others.

6. The relationship of biblical counseling to secular psychology needs to be publicly clarified

We need to clarify the nuances in our view of secular psychology. Our rejection of secularism has been in the headlines. The subtleties of the biblical response to secular knowledge have been in the fine print. Both halves of our view need to be developed if we are not only going to squeeze error out of the church but also going to speak cogently and persuasively to a psychologized culture.

Wait a minute, you might be thinking, *I thought you dealt with psychology when you discussed the abiding relevance of the "same old issues" that nouthetic counseling has always stressed!* Perhaps it seems a paradox, but the final crucial issue for contemporary biblical counseling is the need to define more clearly the nuances in our relationship to secular thinking. The relationship of presuppositionally consistent Christianity to secular culture is not simply one of rejection. Half of what biblical presuppositions give us is a way to discern the lie that tries to make people think about themselves as autonomous from God.

But the other half of what biblical categories do is give us a way of appreciating, redeeming, and reframing the culture of even the most godless men and women. We are, after all, even able to use the data gathered from godless counselees, reinterpreting their own perceptions back to them in biblical categories that turn their world inside out and upside down!

The critics of nouthetic counseling forget—and perhaps even those who like our opposition to secularist thought forget—that Jay Adams spoke from the beginning of a legitimate role for psychology. Right from the first chapter of *Competent to Counsel* the door was open for a properly constructed relationship between secular psychology and biblical counseling. "First, I am aware that my interpretations and applications of Scripture are not infallible. Secondly, I do not wish to disregard science, but rather I welcome it as a useful adjunct for the purposes of illustrating, filling in generalizations with specifics, and challenging wrong human interpretations of Scripture, thereby forcing the student to restudy the Scriptures."[6] Biblical counseling has never developed in any detail what that properly constructed relationship would look like or do. We have been busy establishing and defending where we stand.

I have previously spoken of secularized psychology as an enemy of biblical faith and biblical counseling practice. That stated, it is important to remember that historically Christians have done a number of different things with their enemies. There is error "to the left of us": capitulation and compromise with the world. We live in a Christian counseling world captivated by psychology. There is also error "to the right of us": running from our enemies, flatly rejecting them, perhaps fearing them, and separating ourselves. This latter temptation is the one nouthetic counseling faces. As in the previous crucial issues, there is an imbalance that needs to be corrected if we are to be more fully biblical.

Christians have not only capitulated or isolated themselves. Sometimes Christians fight with the weapons of truth and love. We are not only called to be stimulated by detailed error and to reject that error. We are also called to redeem error by placing distorted bits back within their proper biblical framework. The evangelistic and apologetic strength of biblical counseling hangs in large

degree on such an endeavor. Clear presuppositional thinking creates three strategies.

First, Christians should be stimulated by their enemies. We are forced to sort out what the Bible does say positively. Enemies are incredibly useful. In the sovereignty of God enemies act as catalysts. Unbelievers have often thought long and studied hard in areas that Christians have neglected. The close study of human beings for the purpose of changing them was one of these areas. Biblical counseling was a product of such negative prodding. Biblical presuppositions undergird a strategy of exposition provoked by questions that secular thought and practice raise for the church.

Second, Christians should oppose their enemies frankly. Knowing what we believe gives us a basis to reject what is wrong. Unbiblical concepts and practices have been understood, analyzed, and rejected as false teaching. Biblical counseling is well known for rejecting secular psychology. Secular theorists are false prophets. Those who import their ideas into the church are deceived, at best, and wolves in sheep's clothing, at worst. Biblical presuppositions undergird a strategy of negation.

Third, Christians should love and seek to convert their enemies. We have answers that are richer, truer, fuller. Our answers incorporate the very insights that non-Christians distort. We make these shine in their proper framework, proportion, and balance within the categories of biblical truth. I am proposing that we think hard about this third strategy toward our enemies. Paul used this strategy in Acts 17:22–31. His evangelistic and apologetic strategy in Athens was based on capturing three particular unbiblical thoughts (vv. 23, 28a, and 28b). He reframed them, making them function in a biblical worldview. Did he "integrate" paganism and the Word of God? No, Paul meant wholly different things from the original authors' intent. Consistent presuppositional thinking comes to fruition not only in strategies of exposition and negation. Biblical presuppositions also undergird a strategy of capture.

Presuppositional thinking has these three beauties. We have revelled in the first two but feared to look into the third. It smells dangerously of "integration." But it is not integration as that has been practiced. It is wholly different. It is a systematic reframing and reinterpreting of what secularized people see most clearly, care about most deeply, and do most skillfully. Grasping this difference is a crucial issue for contemporary biblical counseling. Beauty 1: We learn biblical categories, often through the catalyst of our enemies. Beauty 2: We attack every shred of secular thinking which would wrench human life out of context and deny God. Beauty 3: We have categories to reframe every tiny bit of secular thinking so it functions as a comprehensible part of the God-centered world. We know what they are *really* looking at.

Beauty 3 is central to the evangelistic strategy of biblical counseling. By it we redeem what was lost. We take "insights" stolen from God and distorted to work within an alien system. We presuppositional Christians need to ponder beauty 3. We have received the benefit of 1 in order to appreciate biblical truth. We have shouted out 2 in order to hold the fort against alien ideas. But beauty 3 is what a large group of Christians need to hear from us. It is what will also speak to the secular psychological world. Psychologists—Christian and non-Christian alike—are right that "biblical truth" and the rejection of error have often coexisted with massive ignorance about how in-the-flesh people really worked. They have sought to look closely . . . but they have misinterpreted what they see. Let us provide the eyeglasses that bring even error into submission to God. Beauty 3 provides the paradigm shift, the conversion experience, that changes the way familiar data looks. Beauty 3 will draw many who are currently both intellectual and psychological—Christians and non-Christians—

into useful partnership within the biblical counseling movement.

One of the ironies—whether it is bitter, humorous, or sublime I am unsure!—attending the contemporary Christian counseling world is that we, of all people, are the ones who will successfully "integrate" secular psychology. Integrationists are too impressed with psychology's insights to be able to win them to Christ or to systematically reinterpret their insights and skills. Integrationists have missed the point that the *big* question between Christians and secular psychologists is not, "What can we learn from them?" The big question is, "How can we speak into their world to turn their world upside down?" But it is also fair to say that presuppositionalists have missed that the *big* question between biblical counseling and Christian integrationists is not, "Having rejected their syncretism, how can we reject and avoid them?" The big question is, "How can we speak constructively into their world?" The key to both big questions is an ability to reframe everything that psychologists see and hold dear, and to reinterpret it into the categories of biblical truth. If we do our homework, then biblical counseling not only will be a message for the psychologized church. It will be a message for the psychologized world.

Think about this: *If* biblical counseling is true, if it is indeed biblical, then it *will* have a wide evangelistic and apologetic thrust. Is it premature to envision the conquest of the world when we are, like the French Resistance in World War II, still fighting an underground battle for our lives within our own homeland? Perhaps. But let us open our eyes to the fact that this is what we will be called to someday. And just perhaps, we are called to start now.

Is it premature? No. At minimum, there are thousands of Christians—psychologists, psychiatrists, social workers, college psychology majors, counselees drinking from a different well—who can be won by an approach that interacts with and radically reframes what enamors them about psychology. Usually what makes error enamoring is a perceived lack in their church and Bible experience. The real Bible and biblical counseling make up these lacks in ways people never have dreamed. I am not minimizing the opposition we will continue to face. Biblical counseling, by definition, treads on the toes of those whose intellectual, professional, and educational lives have been staked on the validity of secular psychology. But there are lots of Christians out there looking for a paradigm shift in which they can believe. More than we realize. Maybe there are non-Christians as well.

We must do our homework in beauty 3. We must state—and concretely illustrate—the riches of our position toward secular psychology.[7] This is one of the crucial questions facing us. Presuppositional thinking gives powerful tools we have as yet barely begun to use. We need these tools if we are to raise our sights to the possibility of doing evangelistic work at a high intellectual level with the secular psychological and psychiatric communities. If we are faithful and prayerful, the hour will come.

Conclusions

Each of the crucial issues facing contemporary biblical counseling is a test, illuminating where we are. Each delivers a challenge, calling us to where we must go. Each holds a promise, inviting us to the fresh wisdom that will come as we explore the riches of Scripture and life, and as we pursue new friendships within the body of Christ. Biblical truth is balanced, elegant, and potent to transform lives. Our exploration of neglected riches will bring biblical counseling practice into greater conformity with such truth. The way we as a movement face

these six crucial issues will determine the scope, depth, and future of our usefulness to the Lord.

In a thoughtful and thought-provoking personal letter, John Carter of Rosemead Graduate School, one of the leading critics of nouthetic counseling, commented that nouthetic counseling could only speak to audiences "who already shared Jay Adams's perspective." There was little that could be done creatively within the "radically biblical perspective" because everything such a limited perspective could say had been said already either explicitly or implicitly. As a movement we were likely to stagnate into rehashing among ourselves the thoughts of one man.[8]

Carter's words are sobering and challenging. If he is right, we are less than biblical. For the Bible portrays itself as a fountain of life, granting fresh wisdom to all who ask and dig, producing ministry that changes lives significantly. If he is right, then this article has been wrong, and it is a pathetic dream for me to lift up my eyes and see the whole world waiting. But I think Carter is wrong. Our vision has always far outstripped our attainment because it is a biblical vision. If we are indeed *biblical,* then the foundational presupposition—radically biblical counseling—will generate a dynamic of life, growth, and expansion, not stagnation. It will liberate, not limit.

Jay Adams is the only author I have ever read who has publicly and repeatedly invited colaborers to work and write in areas he barely has touched. The unexplored and undeveloped regions are more numerous than the explored. Biblical counseling's main treasure is a few big and provocative ideas. Biblical ideas. God's ideas. Seminal ideas that have implications beyond what we can even imagine:

> *The Scriptures are authoritative*
> *and sufficient for counseling;*
> *Counseling is ministry—a function of the church*
> *accomplishing sanctification.*

Many individual treasures have been already mined and refined, both exegetical riches and counseling methods. But there is much more to learn and then to say. I can do no better than to close by saying, "The subject of this paper—indeed, the subject of every section of this paper—demands at the very least a definitive book or two."

Appendix 2 Notes

1. See Proverbs 3:5–7 and Jeremiah 17:5–8 for two examples (among many) of the from-to structure of the Bible's view of motivation.

2. The vision set forth in Jay E. Adams, "Your Place in the Counseling Revolution," in *Lectures on Counseling* (Grand Rapids: Zondervan, 1986), 46f.

3. Jay E. Adams, *Handbook of Church Discipline* (Grand Rapids: Zondervan, 1986), 21–44.

4. See David Powlison, "What Do You Feel?," *Journal of Pastoral Practice* 10, no. 4 (1992): 50–61 for a discussion of the nuances in the language of "feelings."

5. Richard Lovelace, *Dynamics of Spiritual Life: An Evangelical Theology of Renewal* (Downers Grove, Ill.: InterVarsity, 1979), 218.

6. Jay E. Adams, *Competent to Counsel* (Phillipsburg, N.J.: Presbyterian & Reformed, 1976), xxi.

7. See David Powlison, "Human Defensiveness: The Third Way," *Journal of Pastoral Practice* 8, no. 1 (1985): 40–55 for one attempt to do this at a high level of generality.

8. Personal correspondence with John Carter, November 1980.

Appendix 3

Biological Psychiatry
(1999)

For about ten years, until the mid-1990s, wherever you turned in the counseling world or in a bookstore you heard that problems in living were caused by painful experiences of being used, misused, and abused by others. Unpleasant emotions and destructive behavior were energized and directed by a sense of woundedness and emptiness from bad relationships. Melody Beattie's *Codependent No More* (1987) and John Bradshaw's *Homecoming* (1990) were huge sellers. In the evangelical world, inpatient, for-profit psychiatric services prospered by offering essentially the same theory: Minirth-Meier Clinic, Rapha, and New Life Treatment Center. Evangelical psychologists and psychiatrists wrote best sellers espousing the theory that emotional pain and emptiness plays the primal, determinative role in our souls: e.g., Larry Crabb's *Inside Out* (1987) and Robert Hemfelt, Frank Minirth, and Paul Meier's *Love Is a Choice* (1989).[1]

Childhood experience was where the action was. Because our families were dysfunctional, we acted out the script of born loser and unhappy victim—until we could find intrapsychic healing and emotional filling. *"Why* do I think bad, feel bad, and act bad? I was abused. My father made me do it. Give me healing relationships and help me think healing thoughts about myself." Those were the glory days of "nurture," and thus the glory days of psychotherapy and support groups. If you were submerged within the social organism, then hanging around better people would make you better.

Then the world changed.

That needy and hurting inner self, so marked and marred by tragic experience, faded into the background. Along about the middle of the 1990s, everyone discovered that in fact our genes, hormones, and brains caused problems in living. Our bodies, not our families, were dysfunctional. Imaging technologies—PET scans and the like—let us peer into the brain to watch the neurons fire, tracing the patterns and identifying the sites where emotional states and behavioral choices occur. The Human Genome Project generates one cover story after another about the genetic underpinnings for common sins. In *It's Nobody's Fault* (1997), Harold Koplewicz says that difficult children suffer a neurotransmitter shortage, and there's nothing wrong with them as people or with the way they were brought up. In *Listening to Prozac* (1993), Peter Kramer says that we have entered the era of "cosmetic psychopharmacology." We can now tinker chemically with the brains of people who are depressed or anxious, diffident or aggressive: "Prozac can turn pessimists into optimists, turn loners into extroverts."[2] Brain chemistry and genetics become the *significant* cause of your personality, your proclivities, and your problems: a sunny or a melancholy temperament; tendencies toward violence, drunkenness, overeating, laziness, distractibility, or shyness; choices for homosexuality or promiscuity. And the *significant* cause is always the most interesting cause and the one you want to address to really change things. Or if it's an unchangeable given, hardwired, it's also the reason to accept a behavior as normal and amoral.

Because our bodies are dysfunctional, we are puppets that dance on neural strings to tunes programmed by our genes—and the right drug can smooth things out when the dancing gets spastic. *"Why* do I think bad, feel bad, and act bad? I'm miswired. My physiology made me do it. Give me healing medications to calm me down or lift me up so I can feel and function better." We are now living in the glory days of "nature," and thus the glory days of biological psychiatry. If you are a machine with malfunctioning parts, a mere organism, then whatever makes the parts work better will make you better.

Of course I've oversimplified our historical context to make a point. Things are never quite so tidy: Minirth-Meier Clinics prescribed Prozac, too, for all their wounded codependents. Fad theories may have their fifteen minutes of fame before fading from view, but they usually take a very long time to totally disappear. The concept of psychological needs and woundedness is still with us and won't vanish soon. But, have no doubt, the world did change in the mid-90s. The *action* is now in your body. It's what you got from Mom and Dad, not what they did to you. The *excitement* is about brain functions, not family dysfunctions. The *cutting edge* is in hard science medical research and psychiatry, not squishy soft, philosophy-of-life, feel-your-pain psychologies.

Psychiatry is back. Since the 1960s, psychiatrists had continually retreated from treating every-day life. In the face of numerous new psychotherapy professions, psychiatrists had stopped talking to people and had set up shop in their biological-medical heartland. But now biology is suddenly hot. Psychiatry has broken forth, a *blitzkrieg* sweeping away all opposition. The insurance companies love it because drugs seem more like "medicine," seem to be cheaper than talk, and promise more predictable results. Psychotherapy professionals are on the defensive, fearful of having to drive cabs, fretting over how to survive under "managed care," vaguely disreputable intellectually, with the golden days of the late-80s gone.

Even as biopsychiatry now plays from a position of intellectual strength, the psychologies are playing from weakness. They have been in cognitive disarray for decades, but they are now paying the price. As theories continued to proliferate, the possibility of a Grand Unified Theory of human nature became only memory, an old pipe dream from the first half of the twentieth century. There is no hope that a Freud or Adler, a Maslow or Skinner, a Kohut or Satir might actually be *right*. No one expects that a twenty-first-century genius will appear with a flair for both innovation and the grand synthesis. No one expects anyone to come up with the *true* psychology. So "eclecticism" is no longer a dirty word. Once it stood for lack of intellectual rigor and courage, for a pragmatic making do. Now, in an age of theoretical skepticism, it becomes the only honest course of thought and action: so therapists are "multimodal," and theoreticians pursue a "principled eclecticism." Microtheories and microstudies are the only things that can be offered: "grief reactions in Hispanic lesbians in their 30s" bear no theoretical relationship to "joy reactions in state champion teenage football players in Massachusetts." There is no unifying perspective. The Many devours even the possibility of the One. Postmodernism and multiculturalism pound the final nail in the coffin: since everything is only a matter of your interpretation or mine, then everything reduces to power relations. So psychotherapy professions legitimate themselves only because they have the political clout to be licensed and reimbursed, not because they possess demonstrable truth, goodness, or efficacy. "Psychology" (singular) is in fundamental trouble because no one believes there is any such thing. There are only psychologies left.

But what is true of the psychologies and psychotherapies is not true of psychiatry. The only viable candidate for a Grand Unified Theory in the whole people-helping, personal problems area is not strictly a "psychology" at all but biopsychiatry. Your "psyche" becomes a by-product of your body. Medicine is poised to claim the human personality. Sigmund Freud, a physiologist by training, dreamed of the day when the drama of human life could be comprehended biologically and cured medically. He spun his myths amid the inability of medical science to climb in behind consciousness, behavior, desire, conscience, emotion, and the rest. But Freud believed that someday science would get into the *brain* that operates within and through the id, ego, and superego. What danced in public and in semiprivate, the conscious and unconscious mind, would one day be explained by the brain. Many people now think they can put their hands on the pot of gold at the end of the rainbow. The dream of materialistic reductionism seems tantalizingly close to coming true. These days, biological psychology is the only plausible claimant (besides biblical faith) to a Grand Unified Theory of human functioning. It was idiocy and social suicide to say that everyone was a victim of abuse. It's too unpleasant to say that we are sinners against the God and Father of Jesus Christ the only Redeemer. People want to say that we are essentially bodies because then we can fix what ails us. This is the proverbial eight-hundred-pound gorilla in the theater that sits wherever it wants,

threatening to squash both psychology/psychotherapy and Christianity.[3]

For years biblical counselors have challenged the *psychologizing* of human life, arguing that human beings are fundamentally and thoroughly relational—"covenantal," to put it technically, living *coram Deo,* to put it in the language of our fathers in the faith. The grand synthesis of *all* the facts about people is . . . Christianity. Psychologized people seek to explain and fix life through some interpretation of human life that excludes God, sin, Christ, sanctification, and the rest of truth. But it is time to update our language a bit. Currently, the *biopsychologizing* of human life is having a huge effect, both in the culture and the church. We minister to an increasing number of biopsychologized people who think about themselves, their spouses, or their children as *bodies* run amuck. A recent article from *The Economist* put matters well: "Much of the new knowledge from genetics, molecular biology, and the neurosciences is esoteric. But its cultural impact is already running ahead of the science. People begin to see themselves not as wholes with a moral center but the result of the combined action of parts for which they have little responsibility."[4] The knowledge base may be overstated or underdeveloped as yet, but the ethos is clear: logically, you are not a YOU when it comes to any responsibility for what's wrong with you but only a machine whose parts aren't working.[5] Practice also tends to run far ahead of knowledge: what isn't working can be replaced, rewired, upgraded, or oiled, even if we don't totally understand the underlying mechanisms yet.

The church lags a bit behind the culture's way of thinking. But the ethos and practice of biopsychiatry are deeply affecting the church already. If it's broken, or even just not working optimally, it can be fixed from the outside by a drug: better living through chemistry. In your ministry and in your church you are probably already facing the ethos and the practices. Many people in both pew and pulpit are on mind-, mood-, and behavior-altering drugs. We all increasingly face the ideas and knowledge claims, too. The cover story in *Time* magazine starts to inform the queries and choices of Christian people in everyday life. Eventually such ideas make it into the educational system as the received wisdom of the culture with which to disciple the next generation.

This article can only go a short distance toward addressing the problem I have described in broad strokes. I'll offer two brief arguments in answering this challenge to the Faith. The first is a "presuppositional" argument, the second an "historical evidences" argument. The first is by far the most important, but I will only state it, as it has been said many times before by many other people. The second is only an auxiliary argument, but it offers the peculiar comforts of a big-picture perspective—when built upon the first argument.

First, what God has said about human nature, our problems, and the only Redeemer is true. It is True Truth. His truth is reliable. What the Bible says about people will never be destroyed by any neurological or genetic finding. The Bible is an anvil that has worn out a thousand hammers. Neurology and genetics are finding *lots* of interesting facts. New findings will enable doctors to cure a few diseases, which is a genuine good. More power to them, and we will all be the beneficiaries. But biopsychiatry cannot explain, nor will it ever explain, what we actually are. All people *are* in the image of God and depend on God, body and soul. The ability even to figure out the human genome or design a PET scan is God-given. Furthermore, all people *are* morally insane with sin, living as if we were gods, even while God restrains sin's logical outworking. That's why the implications, applications, and hopes of neurobiologists' findings combine the good with the terrifying and

perverse. Biopsychiatrists and microbiological researchers interpret their findings and determine the implications through a grid that is bent with sin. The driving assumptions and hopes of biopsychiatry are as mythological as what a Hindu peasant believes when bowing before the bloody-mouthed Kali or the perversely sexual Shiva. Biopsychiatry and Hinduism both serve fantasy views of what human life really is about. At the price of curing the few, biopsychiatrists will mislead the many. *They* do not act as their own theory ought to predict, as machines or mere organisms. They act like people made in the image of God and misdirected by sinfulness. Let God be found true and every man a liar. And they can be redeemed, personally as well as intellectually and practically. God's children are in Jesus, and learn to love Jesus, changing gradually from insanity to wisdom. That is the presuppositional argument. The Bible's presuppositions are not contrary to the facts of neurobiology, anymore than they are contrary to the facts of suffering, socialization, war, sexuality, emotions, or history. Christianity is the grand "synthesis," the unifying "theory," the truth.

That leads to my second argument against the biopsychologizing of human existence: "This, too, will pass." It is helpful to get a bit of historical perspective. Recognize that we are in the midst of the *third* major biopsychiatric wave over the past 130 years. In each case a new bit of knowledge or a new efficacy was extrapolated into vast hopes for solving the ills of humankind. In each previous case, biopsychiatry did a little bit of good and left a lot of disillusionment. The first wave lasted from after the Civil War until about 1910. New neurological knowledge—e.g., localizing certain brain functions because of the effects of head wounds received in the war—was generalized into attempts to define problems in living medically and so to treat life by medical means. "Neurasthenia" or "weak nerves" became the catch-all explanation for commonplace anxiety, depression, aimless living, irritability, and addiction to the vices. Various modes of strengthening nerves were employed: rest, diet, walks in fresh country air, working on a farm, avoiding stress, drugs. From a somewhat different angle, Ivan Pavlov's physiological psychology in the 1890s was a primitive attempt to reduce human existence to a mosaic of neuroelectrical activity in the cortex. His experiments also offered a crude demonstration that behavior and glandular function could sometimes be manipulated. Pavlov's mentor, Sechenov, had defined his materialist philosophy with the following programmatic statement that the student took to heart: "The brain secretes thought." That is an astonishing metaphor and demonstrates the force and logic of the biologizing worldview. This first biopsychological fad faded as its significant efficacies proved to be limited or little more than common sense. Its failure to cure the human condition became all too obvious, and something more attractive and comprehensive came along. Freudian psychology swept in, bringing the first "talking cure" or psychotherapy, with behaviorism and behavioral therapy following shortly thereafter. This first wave hasn't completely disappeared, however. One still occasionally meets an elderly person who mentions that so-and-so suffers from "weak nerves," an echo of that 1880s euphemism for the sins of anxiety and grumbling.

The second biological wave, during the 1940s and 1950s, was constructed on the efficacy of three newly discovered medical treatments for disturbed people: electro-convulsive therapy and lobotomy in the 1940s and the phenothiazine family of drugs in the 1950s. By using shock therapy, destroying brain cells, or administering thought-stabilizing medication, doctors could tinker with the body's electrical system, localized brain functions, and chemistry. Mood, behavior, and thought processes were all affected. But this biopsychiatric wave receded as vast hopes were dashed by intractable realities. Some symptoms were alleviated, but people weren't *really* changed . . . and the side effects were dreadful. With a rush of new psychotherapies and new psychotherapy professions in the 1960s—family systems, reality therapy, group therapy, and so on—biopsychiatry was buried from public view. ECT and the phenothiazines linger on, but no one attaches vast hopes to them anymore. They are in the dreary, use-when-nothing-else-works part of the psychiatric armamentarium.

The third wave is now upon us. It glitters with the same bright hopes as its predecessors, though of course it appears much more sophisticated. (Similarly, phenothiazines seemed very sophisticated in comparison with "rest cure" and lobotomy.) Again, the new knowledge is generated by striking new abilities to localize brain functions: now MRIs teach us, not the sequelae of bullet wounds. The new drugs don't have the disturbing and visible side effects that used to leave patients dry-mouthed, rigid, and dopey. No one pushes an ice pick in through the eye socket anymore and twists it around in the cerebral cortex (the way lobotomies were done). The brain may not be a gland secreting thought, but it *is* an electrochemical organ that produces thought, emotion, and behavior. We now hear of genetic structures, brain chemistry, and drugs designed to influence very specific neurotransmitter sites and functions. Again, there is some real and fascinating knowledge here. But it is the same *kind* of knowledge as the previous fads, shaped and blown out of proportion by similar myths. The perennial hope is that we will understand and cure what ails us by localizing brain function, greasing the neuroelectrical system, and buoying up our chemistry. Biopsychiatry will cure a few things, for which we should praise the God of common grace. But in the long run, unwanted and unforeseen side effects will combine with vast disillusionment. The gains will never live up to the promises. And the lives of countless people, whose normal life problems are now being medicated, will not be qualitatively changed and redirected. Only intelligent repentance, living faith, and tangible obedience turn the world upside down. In today's euphemisms, we say so-and-so "has" ADD or "suffers from" clinical depression or "is" bipolar. Without in any way minimizing the reality of troubling behaviors, emotions, and thought processes to which such labels are attached, we must say that such supposed diagnostic entities have the same substantiality as "weak nerves."

This third wave will also pass, though it does seem to have the potential for a decent shelf life because it has good science mixed in with fad and myth. But because there is more to human life, no biopsychology can ever satisfy as either explanation or cure. Some new theory will capture the popular fancy—probably a talking cure, a psychology, a meaning system. My guess is that it will be either something "spiritual" or something "social." Since the nineteenth century, interest in Eastern and occult religions has also come in waves like biopsychiatry, waxing and then waning. A sophisticated and learned neo-Jung might upgrade the sloppy experientialism of New Age and the sentimentality of Gaia into a spiritualized psychology. But we are also about due for a new behavioral theory and therapy, some tough-minded social psychology that pours its intellectual and practical energies into sociocultural conditioning: education, media, recreation, entertainment, family, community, and politics will be where the action is. I'm no prophet, but I am confident—both by presupposition and by historical evidences—that if we wait a few years or decades the cutting edge will no longer be biology, just as it is no longer childhood trauma or how your self-talk affects your self-esteem.

But the fad is currently in full force. The Human Genome Project has some wonderfully savvy publicists on staff who feed us all a stream of tantalizing knowledge bits charged with fantastic implications. One article I read said that we might be able to reverse the aging process and live forever! It was exhilarating stuff, accompanied by the appropriate hand-wringing about ethical implications. I can't argue with the bits of science cited, but here's what history reminds us. When the gene mapping is complete, when the folks on Prozac still can't get along with their spouses, when the fountain of youth still does not arrive in a bottle, when money and achievement fail to satisfy, and when your clone grows up to hate you . . . sinners will yet find Christ to be the one we need.

Just maybe that next new theory will be something wonderful. Think a moment more about "spirituality" and "sociality." That could be Christianity come into its own. That's worth pouring our energies toward! By the grace of God, perhaps he will enable us to bend the course of history to a vigorous revival of Christian life, thought, and practice! Just maybe that new spirituality and new community will be the body of Jesus Christ growing up into the fullness of the knowledge of Christ. Then, by the grace of the Lord, burned-out codependents, disillusioned Prozac habitués, and people who just realized they'll die anyway will grab at the hem of your clothes saying, "We want to know the Lord. Take us to Jerusalem. We are tired of fads and disappointed hopes, tired of trying to reduce life to one thing or another that cuts God out of the equation. We need real mercy and tangible hope. We want what you have." Only the Faith is able to make the grand synthesis, to make all of life hang together: physical existence, social relations, thinking, suffering, emotions, economics . . . as well as "religious" ideas, practice, and experience, both individual and corporate. Biopsychiatry? After discovering some marvels, doing a little bit of good and a lot of harm, and absorbing a lot of time, attention, money, and energy, this too will pass. But the kingdom of God will come to pass and will not pass away.

Let me close with a challenge to us all. From the starting point in 1970, biblical counselors took a position on the relationship between biopsychiatric problems and moral-spiritual problems that has stood up well over time. Probably the most common rule of thumb is "See a doctor for your body. See your pastor, other pastoral counselors, and wise friends for your heart, soul, mind, might, manner of life, and the way to handle sufferings." Jay Adams often urged pastors to work "back-to-back" with MDs. He had those he counseled get a physical checkup first thing to rule out identifiable biological problems. But he also noted that the rule of thumb was only that. It did not answer all ambiguities: "the dividing line between problems caused by organic factors and nonorganic factors is often fuzzy." And it failed to describe how counseling ministry always plays a role in addressing the biological: the Christian counselor's work "constantly involves the organic dimension" because sufferers need counsel and prayer along with whatever other forms of aid apply (James 5:13–20).[6] Doctors who have participated in the first thirty years of biblical counseling have operated on the commonsense assumption that good diagnosis can generally distinguish the truly and decidedly physiological problems from the moral-spiritual problems, whether the latter appear openly or come veiled in psychosomatic symptoms. There has always been a humility about the intricacies of this psychosomatic-whole-with-a-moral-center whom God has made. And there has always been a well-founded confidence that ministry can always give hope and direction, whether the biological problems are medically soluble or whether they remain ambiguous, insoluble, and terminal.

But what if medical doctors and medical research come to say that our emotions, behaviors, and cognitions *are* identifiably biological phenomena in their very essence? That all, or the most significant, problems in living reduce to biology? That your body determines your heart, soul, mind, and might? That a drug can really fix this or that thing that Christians call "sin"? No longer will you be able to say, "Go get a medical checkup to find out if there's a physiological cause for this anxiety, this depression, or this distorted thinking." There *will* be such a cause, by definition, in every case. A purported physiological cause for everything will mean a medical treatment for everything, a designer drug to do whatever is needed to make you feel and function in tip-top shape. There won't even be "psychosomatic" problems anymore because the emotional, motivational, behavioral, relational, and cognitive problems registering in physical symptoms will be identified as having a physical cause! They will be *somato*psychosomatic, so why bother with the intervening variable?

Biblical counselors writing about these issues have always left room for a "gray area" between the physiological and moral-spiritual. Jay Adams described organic causes, moral causes, and areas of ambiguous "other" or "combinations from both" in the causation of bizarre, "schizophrenic" patterns of thinking and behavior. Thus counseling (always indicated) and medical treatment (sometimes called for) combined flexibly and in various proportions.[7] Adams and others have always opposed promiscuous use of medications and left a certain carefully guarded place for medication to help with biologically grounded problems. Adams affirmed the strategic use of antidepressants: "The physician might uncover some of the infrequent cases of chemically caused depression and in very serious cases may help the pastor to engage in meaningful counseling by temporarily administering antidepressants."[8]

Ed Welch distinguishes those problems that may have a biological component tangled in with moral factors (e.g., some hyperactive kids and some depressions) from those things that are not biologically determined (e.g., heavy drinking and homosexuality).[9] But what happens when biopsychiatry comes and says, "Eureka! We have identified the gene for schizophrenia and bipolar. We have localized the part of the brain that produces obsessive-compulsive disorder. We have found the neurotransmitter that affects all depressive moods, and we have designed a drug that lifts all bleak moods into a realistic good cheer. We have found the genes both for homosexuality (it is a normal genetic variation) and for alcoholism (we can test for it prenatally and alter it with gene therapy)"? In such a situation, we who seek to counsel biblically need to say more. And we need to say it carefully, clearly, boldly, and persistently. When medicine seemed to mind its business in the old way, the rule of thumb worked. But when medicine takes some bits of new knowledge and operates in the imperial mode, we need a more discriminating diagnosis and prescription if we are to profit from the common-grace goods in medicine and are to resist being colonialized.

We have work to do. We need to develop our practical theology more fully in order to address the current controversies and to provide guidance for the people of God who will be beset, often confused, and sometimes misled. In many ways, it was "easier" to resist the codependency-dysfunctional family model of the late '80s or the "Rogers with a dash of Freud" of the '50s and '60s. Those were just bad psychologies that fell short when measured against the good psychology that the Faith learns from the Bible: the dynamics of human nature, the meaning of sufferings of all sorts, and so forth. But biopsychology is *medicine*, against which the Faith looks and sounds like just one more "psychology" to be bulldozed away by all-triumphant biological reductionism. When we protest, "But we can *counsel* angry and anxious people to repent and to learn faith and love," we will *sound like* we are asserting something along the lines of "Cast out that demon of cancer" or "Just believe in Jesus, and throw your eyeglasses away." When anger and anxiety are seen as treatable bodily ailments, we will sound like bizarre spiritualizers—even to people in the pews and in other pulpits. We have work to do to protect and build up the body of Christ.

Appendix 3 Notes

1. *Inside Out* is different from *Love Is a Choice* in ways that reflect favorably on Crabb. But both teach that the underlying mechanism of the soul is the same needy, wounded, longing, empty heart that has been relationally victimized and deprived.

2. Peter Kramer, *Listening to Prozac: A Psychiatrist Explores Antidepressant Drugs and the Remaking of the Self* (USA: Viking Press, 1993).

3. Interestingly, psychotherapy is now trying to legitimate itself by *appealing* to brain physiology. It turns out that talking with people changes physiology, just as drugs do! Also, a number of more mechanical-technological psychotherapy techniques are coming into use: flashing light machines and special glasses that claim to repattern the brain in order to alter behavior, emotion, and thought.

4. Alun Anderson, "Are you a machine of many parts?," in *The World in 1999, The Economist* (London: 1999), 109f.

5. It is perhaps not surprising that people usually think of themselves as machines only when things are not going well. Most people, scientists included, still take credit for their achievements, abilities, successful choices, and opinions, just as they did when dysfunctional families were the rage!

6. See Jay E. Adams, *Competent to Counsel* (USA: Presbyterian & Reformed, 1970), 37ff; Adams, *Ready to Restore* (Phillipsburg, N.J.: Presbyterian & Reformed, 1981), 32; Adams, *The Christian Counselor's Manual* (USA: Presbyterian & Reformed, 1973), 437ff. The discussion in *CCM* well captures subtleties and ambiguities in the relationship between moral and organic problems, and thus between MDs and pastors.

7. Jay E. Adams, "The Christian Approach to Schizophrenia," *Journal of Biblical Counseling* 14, no. 1 (1995): 27–33; reprinted in David Powlison, ed., *Counsel the Word* (Glenside, Pa.: Christian Counseling and Educational Foundation, 1997), 52–57. Reprint of 1976 article.

8. Jay E. Adams, "Depression," *The Encyclopedia of Christianity*, vol. 3 (Marshallton, Del.: The National Foundation for Christian Education, 1972), 362f.

9. Ed Welch, *Blame It on the Brain* (Phillipsburg, N.J.: P & R, 1999).

Cure of Souls
(and the Modern Psychotherapies)
(2007)

The epoch of a great revolution is never the eligible time to write its history. Those memorable recitals to which the opinions of ages should remain attached cannot obtain confidence or present a character of impartiality if they are undertaken in the midst of animosities and during the tumult of passions; and yet, were there to exist a man so detached from the spirit of party or so master of himself as calmly to describe the storms of which he has been a witness, we should be dissatisfied with his tranquility and should apprehend that he had not a soul capable of preserving the impressions of all the sentiments we might be desirous of receiving.[1]

The Counseling Revolution

We live in the epoch of a great revolution. Consider that in 1955, believing Protestants had *no* comprehensive models of counseling. Theological conservatives had *no* educational programs to train pastors or other Christian workers in the face-to-face cure of souls. Christian bookstores contained *no* books on the problems of everyday life and the processes of change. *No* evangelical, fundamentalist, Pentecostal, or reformed leaders were known for their skill in probing, changing, and reconciling troubled and troublesome people. Practical theology concerned itself with preaching, missions, education, evangelism, liturgical activity, church government, and administration. Good things all! Discipleship programs taught doctrine, morals, and devotional activity. Good things all! But what was the quality of corporate wisdom in comprehending the dynamics of the human heart? How rich was the human self-understanding? How well did the church analyze the destructive and practice the constructive in human relationships? What does change look like, think like, feel like, act like, talk like? How does change proceed? What sustains sufferers and converts sinners?

No systematic analysis of care for the soul grappled with the particulars of how souls needed curing and might find it. In 1955 the churches that took God at his word had little to say about "counseling." The last significant counseling work from a believing theological standpoint predated the Civil War. Without a well-developed practical theology of change and counseling—and without the institutions, books, and practitioners to embody and communicate such—churchly resources were reduced to religious forms in abstraction from systematic understanding: a prayer, a Bible verse, a worship service, a banished demon, a creed, a testimony, an exhortation, a commitment. Should these fail, there were no options but referral out to the secular experts.[2]

The counseling vacuum among evangelicals was inversely proportional to the counseling plenum in the surrounding culture. The twentieth century had witnessed the birth and proliferation of the modern secular psychologies, and of those mental health professions that mediated such theories into lives. Secular institutions teamed with the mainline churches, the latter being part product and part coauthor of the emerging therapeutic culture. Modern forms of self-knowledge were psychological or social or somatic or psychosocial or psycho-somatic or psycho-social-somatic, per se. In other words, intrapsychic, interpersonal, and bodily phenomena pointedly did not operate vis-à-vis God. Religious beliefs, practices, and experiences might be privately engaging and meaningful, but the God of the Bible was insignificant for objectively explaining and addressing the human condition.

We humans were not made and sustained; our diverse sufferings did not exist in a context of meaningfulness; we were not accountable, observed, and evaluated; we were not condemned; we were not pursued and redeemed. "God" was an objectively weightless concept with respect to the human psyche; the weighty things in our souls had to do with other things. Evangelicals might object to the secularity of the modern and modernist worldview, but they were not doing more than a rudimentary job in offering an alternate analysis and cure. Knowledge and skill to conduct patient, probing, remedial conversation became the province of secularists and liberals.[3]

The Revolutionaries

But a revolution has occurred in the past fifty years, a counseling revolution. Evangelicals have begun to counsel, to write about counseling, and to educate counselors. They have written best sellers and have founded thriving graduate programs and counseling centers. Everyone agrees that a serious defect needs serious repair: confused, suffering, and wayward people need more than a verse and a prayer. But as in most revolutions, those who agree heartily about the need for change disagree profoundly about the changes needed. Countless gradations and variations exist, but in broad strokes there have been two parties within this counseling revolution.

One group has developed in the footsteps of Clyde Narramore and along the lines of Fuller Seminary's Graduate School of Psychology. Its core intellectual agenda can be characterized this way: wise counseling requires that evangelical faith be carefully integrated with the theories, therapeutic methods, and professional roles of the modern psychologies. An "evangelical psychotherapy" movement has arisen to tackle this intellectual and educational task, and has set out to address the counseling needs of the church with the specific goods of psychology.

The other group has developed in the footsteps of Jay Adams and along the lines of the Christian Counseling and Educational Foundation's pastoral training at Westminster Seminary. The core intellectual agenda can be characterized this way: wise counseling recognizes that the Bible mandates development of a comprehensive pastoral theology distinctly different from prevailing cultural paradigms. A "biblical counseling" movement has arisen to tackle this intellectual and educational task and has set out to address the counseling needs of the church with the specific goods of Scripture.[4]

During the tumult of passions, serene impartiality is impossible, even suspect and undesirable. How can a thoughtful person remain indifferent when the issues at stake are so momentous? The well-being, self-understanding, and practice of real people, the people of God, both corporate and individual, are at stake. Our ability to love and address those outside of Christ is at stake. God's glory in this therapeutic culture is at stake. How can we know and do what we need to know and do in order to cure souls?

This essay is no attempt at dispassionate history. My commitments and convictions will be obvious in what follows. I believe that the church needs above all else a comprehensive and case-wise pastoral theology, something worthy of the name *systematic biblical counseling*. But I am no triumphalist. I am as interested in the remaining agenda as in the extant accomplishments of those whom I think are fundamentally on the right track. And I am no sectarian. I am keenly sympathetic to many of the concerns and intentions that energize those with whom I must fundamentally disagree. No one in the body of Christ will "arrive" until we all arrive. And arriving is not only a matter of asserting the bare truth of a systematic model. Truth, love, skill, and institutional structure must all grow to the same stature. That is our Lord's call to his children in Ephesians 4.

Finding a Workable Taxonomy

Christ's call to walk and talk worthy of his calling creates an immediate problem of terminology for all of us. Participants in the counseling revolution sharply disagree about how things ought to be run. This is not merely bickering between ideologues over inconsequential matters. None of us should be indifferent to the existence of vastly disparate conceptions of the faith and practice of Christ's people. People have staked education,

career, reputation, institutions, and ministries on significantly differing points of view about what is true and necessary for the health of the church. But how do we talk about the conflict constructively? How can we fairly characterize the different "sides" in the current "counseling wars," so that matters are clarified not muddied? How do we speak the truth in love in pursuit of a just peace, rather than exacerbating quarrels and perpetuating self-serving caricatures? At the most basic level, what terminology best describes the parties, so that the issues at stake can be seen and discussed without prejudice?

Psychology Bashers Versus Psychoheretics? Unfortunately, when so-called psychology bashers and so-called psychoheretics square off, it produces the edification effect of loud static in the public address system. Sneering obliterates all discussion of profound issues. God's children are rarely edified by scathing words. When we look at each group through the worst of the other's language, both groups appear shamefully disreputable. Reckless and factious words fail the test of constructive, gracious, gentle speech to which God binds us and by which he will examine us (Matt. 7:1–5; Eph. 4:15, 29; 2 Tim. 2:24f). In fact, there are some true bashers and heretics around. But provocative language and sweeping generalizations usually serve to provoke, nurture, and justify the worst tendencies in human nature, not the further outworking of our redemption. It is always good policy to interact with the best representatives of a point of view, not the worst representatives. We feel self-righteous when we pose and posture next to our caricatures. We must listen, think, and argue well when we engage a thoughtful disputant.[5]

I suspect that most of us are brothers and sisters to be dealt with gently. We ought to sympathetically appreciate the other's honest description of shaping experiences. We ought to acknowledge the valid insights and concerns, even if we end

271

up disagreeing with the conclusions. All of us are more or less ignorant and wayward, beset with weakness (Heb. 5:2). Many well-intended believers on both sides of the debate are more clumsy than perverse. Our sin makes us clumsy thinkers, clumsy practitioners, clumsy theologians, clumsy exegetes, clumsy cultural analysts. We all get pigheaded, shortsighted, particularly stuck in those forms of error that contain partial truths. Yes, all error has a perverse logic, but we may hold to errors and semitruths without being wholly perverted people. May God make us deft—together.

Here is the inescapable fact that we have in common: throughout the twentieth century and into the twenty-first, the Bible-believing church has been woefully weak in the cure and care of souls.[6] And Christ would have us do some serious maturing in individual and collective wisdom. Maturing is hard, slow work, made the slower because the issues at stake are momentous. No doubt, the sower of discord and falsehood is always active in hindering the church from growing up toward real wisdom regarding both the ailment and the redemption of our humanity. But the Sower of love and truth seems willing to work amid the tumult of passions over the long haul: over decades, lifetimes, and centuries. Biblical wisdom does not spring full grown from the head of Zeus. It is born small and grows through many trials and missteps, by the sustaining grace of God, toward the fullness of the mind of Christ.

So-called psychology bashers—those who believe in the sufficiency of Scripture for generating a comprehensive counseling model—do fundamentally disbelieve the modern psychologies, taking them to be systematic counterfeits and pretenders in the final analysis. They believe that the Bible fiercely resists syncretism. But they still claim that something can be learned from the psychologies: wrong does not mean stupid; error must borrow elements of truth to be plausible; God often

allows observant and persuasive error to expose lacunae, crudities, and distortions in his own children's thinking and practice. That Scripture is "sufficient" to transform us never means that the Bible is "exhaustive." It does not mean that the Bible's message for us is accessed and communicated only through proof-texts. All application of Scripture demands that we engage in a theological and interpretive task. Good, true, faithful theology is closely grounded in the text but often says a somewhat different thing than the text says because it is speaks to a different set of questions.[7] Face-to-face ministry must use the Bible in the same way; ministry is not simply a matter of inserting proof-texts into conversation. All ministry demands sensitivity and flexibility to the varying conditions of those to whom one ministers.[8]

Though one might find some exceptions, most supposed psychology bashers are not anticounseling. Most work to develop and practice loving and effective cure of souls as the alternative to secular or quasisecular psychotherapy. The debate is not whether to counsel; the debate is about what sort of counsel to believe, what sort of counseling to do, what sort of cure to offer.

So-called psychoheretics—those who believe that Scripture does not intend to be sufficient for generating a comprehensive counseling model—do see an essential role for the secular psychologies. Psychological disciplines offer some sort of necessary truth; psychological professions offer some sort of necessary and valid practice. But the so-called psychoheretics still claim that the Bible must provide the final authority. That Scripture is not sufficient does not mean the Bible is irrelevant or that it ought to be subordinated to secular psychologies, but that the Bible itself mandates looking and learning from outside. The Bible itself resists biblicism.

Though one can find exceptions, most supposed psychoheretics are not out to swallow the camel of secularity and foist it on an unsuspecting church. Many work to critique the secularity of the modern psychologies and to screen out what seems to fail the test of Scripture. Why do they become psychologists? Glaring defects in the church's current understanding and practice are the main reason they expend time and effort to do hard study of human beings. In this culture, that often means to study psychology. Where else is one permitted and disciplined to gaze steadily into the complications and miseries of the soul? Where else do defective relationships come under scrutiny? Where else can one be taught to probe the details of life lived, and then to offer timely and patient aid? Theological and pastoral training typically does not look closely enough or get hands-on enough to engender case wisdom and a patiently probing counseling process.[9]

Theologizers Versus Psychologizers? Polemical language tends to subvert understanding and godliness by superheating the conversation.

Perhaps we could describe the "bashers" and "heretics" more calmly by alluding to the practice of different intellectual disciplines, as theologizers and psychologizers respectively. These terms, too, quickly become misleading. In reality, both parties claim to be in the same business. Both claim to think theologically about psychological matters, and both claim to do Christian ministry with those who experience problems in living.

Those who pursue a systematic pastoral theology specifically discuss psychological experience through the lens of explicitly biblical categories. They seek to interpret the case-study realities of life lived. Their view of theology is that it is about the interior and horizontal dimensions no less than the vertical. Good theology interprets psychological phenomenon, and good pastoral practice addresses psychological and interpersonal problems. As a God-centered theory of human personality, biblical counseling claims to offer a psychology that systematically differs from the various secular personality theories. As a gospel-centered approach to helping people, biblical counseling claims to offer a psychotherapy qualitatively different from the various secular psychotherapies.

On the other side, those who pursue an integration of or dialogue between Christianity and psychological theory specifically claim to do theology. They seek to unfold the implications of the doctrine of God's common grace with respect to intrapersonal and interpersonal problems, and regarding the methods of skillfully addressing such problems. There is solid theological rationale for viewing secular disciplines as fit subjects for hard study. The stuff of psychology does not necessarily wholly overlap the Bible. They frequently view their counseling practice as a communication of God's grace to people whose church experiences have often fed legalism and dishonesty. Where the church has been brusque, they aim to offer an incarnation of grace, a generous and accepting attitude in which trust and honest conversation can flourish. In sum, both parties claim to be both theological and psychological.

Pastoral Counselors Versus Psychologists? How about using occupational categories to characterize the contemporary debate? Is this simply a turf war between pastors and psychotherapists? It is clear that the pastoral counselors strongly value explicit ministry of the Word and see the crucial significance of the local church where God works through both authoritative and mutual counsel. They think that counseling theories and practices should operate under theological accountability. It is equally clear that the psychologists strongly value state licensure for professional identity and because it makes possible insurance reimbursements as a fiscal underpinning. They resist coming under ecclesiastical jurisdiction for their ideas and their practice. But one cannot draw lines in the sand regarding occupational title or the educational background that qualifies for an occupation.

On one side, the "biblical counseling" group includes many people with training, experience, and credentials in social science and mental health fields: psychologists of various sorts, psychiatrists, neurologists, psychiatric nurses, social workers, MD general practitioners, graduate students, former psychology majors.[10] They know the psychologies from the inside. They usually appreciate the observational detail and credit the intention to be helpful. But they think the theories are pervasively flawed and the therapies finally impotent. The Bible and theology probe the human heart far more graphically, make better sense of life lived, and bring the living power of Christ to turn lives upside down.

On the other side, the "psychologist" group includes many people with theological training, experience, and credentials: pastors, elders, deacons, seminary graduates and professors, laycounselors, graduates of pastoral counseling programs, members in good standing of local churches. They know and believe their Christian faith from the inside. But they find the operative faith and practice of their ecclesiastical training and setting all too often ignorant, peremptory, and pat. Psychology, despite obviously bumbling the closer it gets to ultimate issues, validates neglected dimensions of human experience, prompts intellectual curiosity, and encourages the patient pursuit of both self-knowledge and case wisdom. In sum, neither mental health nor ecclesiastical experience offers a predictable guide to the issues at stake.

Biblical Counseling or Christian Counseling? What about the names the groups have largely adopted as self-designations: biblical counseling (as in *Journal of Biblical Counseling*) and Christian counseling (as in American Association of Christian Counselors [AACC])? Each group finds the other's self-designation objectionable. The label *biblical counseling* seems to presume that whatever advocates believe and do comes with the full authority of the Bible, further implying that anything else is unbiblical. What if what they teach and do falls short of offering wise biblical help for strugglers? Similarly, the label *Christian counseling* seems to presume that what advocates believe and do is distinctly Christian. What if what they teach and do is at odds with their professed faith? In both cases, the reality beneath the label is a complex maybe/maybe-not. The terms *biblical* and *Christian* are precisely what is at stake and up for debate in the present tumults.

Here is further dilemma in coming up with accurate terminology. In the landscape of Christians-who-counsel, it has become harder to keep the parties straight because they seem to have moved closer together in the past twenty years. There have been significant developments on both sides.

The psychologists became more explicitly biblically oriented in the 1990s than they were in the 1970s and 1980s. Larry Crabb and the AACC are only the most visible exemplars of how the *evangelical* part of the evangelical psychotherapists' dual identity is no longer an embarrassment to professional identity. A more holistic view of human nature has emerged among many evangelical psychotherapists. Some still attempt to sector off "spiritual" problems from "psychological, emotional, relational, mental" problems, attempting to validate their professional existence and activity as something qualitatively different from cure of souls. But many at the leading edge of the profession see that the divide between "spiritual" and "psychological" problems is artificial and problematic. Advocates have been won to John Calvin's foundational insight that true self-knowledge and knowledge of the true God are interchangeable perspectives. This more holistic gaze has affected professional self-image. Increasingly, Christian counselors seek to express an explicitly Christian identity by defining their work of counseling as care for the soul, or eldering, or ministry for Christ that must be more closely linked to the church. The psychotherapists have come to sound more like the pastoral counselors and pastoral theologians who followed Jay Adams.

Meanwhile, the "biblical counselors" have also changed. Their writing now evidences a broader scope of concerns and concepts than they had in the early 1970s. They have supplemented, developed, or even altered aspects of Adams's initial model. They are paying a great deal of attention to (1) intrapersonal dynamics such as motivation theory, self-evaluation, belief, and self-deception; (2) the impact of and response to varieties of suffering and socialization; (3) the compassionate, flexible, probing, and patient aspects of counseling methodology; (4) nuances in the interaction between Christian faith and the modern psychologies; (5) the practicalities of marital and familial communication; and (6) the cause and treatment of so-called addictions.[11] The model of biblical counseling is now more detailed and comprehensive about any number of "psychological" matters.

So, the psychologists seem more biblical and the biblical counselors seem more psychological. What does this apparent convergence mean? Are the parties heading toward a rapprochement or toward a more profound collision? Or are they moving toward an as yet unimagined realignment?

I believe that the two visions are still fundamentally incompatible. But I also believe that our current situation is ripe for a fresh articulation of the issues. Half-truths and good intentions—all too easily corrupted by posturing, tunnel vision, and parochial ignorance—can appear in a very different light when they are reframed within a more comprehensive call and truth. I hope that we, the body of Christ, can identify where ideas and practices are fundamentally incongruent. Such incongruities ought to be openly stated and debated, so that the church can evaluate positions and choose wisely. We may also find places of unexpected agreement that bid us to cross or realign current party lines. Some apparent differences may prove to be either the same thing stated in different words or complementary things that can be accounted for within a common model. After all, we serve the living God who masters history to his glory and our welfare. He will not leave his children bedraggled by ignorance, incompetence, quarrels, and confusion. In the rough-and-tumble of our gropings after him, in our uneven hearing and partial seeing, he manages to triumph in and through us.

So what taxonomy should we use? I suggest that we use language that is minimally prejudicial and maximally descriptive of the sticking point. The core question turns on the intent and scope of Scripture, the nature of pastoral theological work, and the degree of significance attached to what the church can appropriate from the world. In short, is the engine of counseling theory and practice external or internal to the Faith?

VITEX or COMPIN?

I will speak of two fundamentally different tendencies, two incompatible organizing centers, using the acronyms VITEX and COMPIN. Acronyms are dull? All the better! Though these sound like creatures from Jurassic Park, I hope the very oddity and connotative flatness of the terms will aid discussion by damping the excesses of passion.

VITEX believes that secular psychologies must make a *VITal EXternal contribution* in the construction of a Christian model of personality, change, and counseling. While biblical faith gives us certain controls to evaluate outside input, it does not give enough detail to enable us to constitute and develop a model. The operating premise of VITEX, whether explicit or implicit, is that Christian truths must be "integrated" with the observations, personality theories, psychotherapies, and professional roles of the mental health world. Modern psychologies are the engine producing insights, theories, and practices. In an essential way, the counseling that Christians do will orient to and take its cues from outside sources. The fascinating, exciting, relevant, and important developments are taking place external to Christian faith and practice. Biblical truth is static in comparison.

In contrast, COMPIN believes that the Christian faith contains *COMPrehensive INternal resources* to enable us to construct a Christian model of personality, change, and counseling. While the modern psychologies will stimulate and inform, they do not play a constitutive role in building a robust model. The operating premise of COMPIN is that the Faith's psychology offers a take on the human condition essentially different from any of the other contemporary psychologies. The living Christ working in his people through his Word is the engine producing depth of insight, accurate theory, and effective practice. The counseling that Christians do must orient to and take its cues from our own source. Practical theological development is the cutting edge. The modern psychologies and psychotherapies are relatively dull, shallow, and misleading in comparison.[12]

The three sections that follow pose questions whose answers over the coming years will define the intellectual, methodological, and institutional characteristics of evangelical counseling. Those characteristics will ultimately be shaped by either a VITEX or a COMPIN vision. We will examine three essential questions, around which a host of subquestions cluster. The first has to do with epistemology. What knowledge most matters for understanding and helping people? The second has to do with motivation theory. How do we fundamentally understand people? The third has to do with social structure. How should we educate, license, and oversee counselors in order to deliver the goods?

1. Epistemological priorities

What knowledge really matters for understanding and helping people? Evangelical counselors have apparently been deeply divided over formal epistemology. On the one hand, VITEX is interested in "integrating" Christianity and psychology because secular psychological theories, therapies, and professional roles will make a vital contribution to Christian counseling. Christians can learn constitutive things from what the world has to offer in the social and behavioral sciences. Christians can participate in psychological research and in the mental health professions. But as honest evangelicals, VITEX advocates want Scripture to exert final and functional authority.

On the other hand, COMPIN is interested in the sufficiency of Scripture for informing and defining counseling ministry because resources internal to the Christian faith are comprehensively about what counseling is about. Scripture is sufficient, not in that it is exhaustive, containing all valid knowledge, but in that it rightly aligns a coherent and comprehensive system of counseling that is radically at odds with every a-theistic model. Christians can offer a distinct alternative to what the world has to offer. Christians can revitalize their own distinctive shepherdly and mutual ministries. But as honest observers and thinkers, COMPIN advocates want to gain what knowledge they can, both theoretical and applied, from the social sciences and other fields.

But both sides tend to talk past each other. VITEX discredits itself to COMPIN ears by sounding epistemologically naïve and syncretistic. "All truth is God's truth" is an epistemological truism, without bottom-line value, exactly like "All lies are the devil's lies." The real question is how you tell the difference, which throws us back into the crucible: we need to define the sources and criteria of significant and reliable knowledge. Furthermore, the actual products of VITEX thinking—in the name of "general revelation" and "common grace"—have usually been, self-admittedly, rewarmed and baptized versions of secular theory. As much as thoughtful VITEX would like to dissociate itself from the egregious offenses of Christianized pop psychology, they tend to sound like birds of a feather.

On the other side, COMPIN discredits itself to VITEX ears by sounding biblicistic, obscurantist, and anti-intellectual. "Sufficiency of Scripture" stumbles too easily into pat answer, legalism, pietism, or triumphal separatism.

What anyone says the Bible says is not self-evident and must be subjected to serious scrutiny and criticism. "The Bible says" ought to engender hard thought, close observation, and careful discussion—not freeze our minds, end the conversation, and close our eyes to life lived. Furthermore, in the name of biblical authority, the actual products of COMPIN thinking have too often been, self-admittedly, reversions to moralism, pietism, and exorcism.[13] As much as thoughtful COMPIN would like to dissociate itself from the egregious offenses of biblicistic quick fixes and ranting, they can sound like birds of a feather.

The church's counseling has been locked in epistemological stalemate. Both sides say we can learn something from psychology; both sides say the Bible gets final say. The debates usually sputter into fruitless generalities about common grace and biblical authority. How can we break through to fresh ground? To break the stalemate, I propose that we significantly reframe the epistemological debate. We should ask ourselves about epistemological priorities, and then show how our answers concretely work out. This priority question has a double reference. First, what epistemological priorities are expressed by the Bible itself? Second, what priorities do we need in our time and place, both for the church's welfare and to engage the therapeutic culture to which the church is called to bear witness? I believe that both the example of Scripture and the need of our times yield the same answer:

- Our first priority must be to articulate positive biblical truth, a systematic practical theology of those things that our culture labels "counseling issues." A systematic theology of care and cure for souls will wed conceptual, methodological, and institutional elements.

- Our second priority must be to expose, debunk, and reinterpret alternative models, whether secular or religious. Personality theories and counseling models assert different "gazes," different interpretations of human life. Our point of view radically critiques other points of view, and invites them to a thoughtful conversion.

- Our third priority must be to learn what we can from defective models. We will always be stimulated, challenged, and informed by those with whom we disagree and whom we aim to convert. Articulating our own model (1st) and critiquing other models (2nd) frees us to learn from others without being counterconverted or becoming syncretistic. Such learning also enables us to enter the frame of reference of those we hope to persuade.

If we keep these priorities in their proper order, the church will thrive, both in our ministries to each other and as light to the world.

The Bible's Priorities

Does the Bible itself model this particular ordering of priorities? Yes. This is one of those questions whose answer suffers from an embarrassing abundance of supporting material.

The first priority: articulating biblical truth and developing our systematic theology of care for the soul. Biblical confirmation of this first priority is unmistakable. God's primary revelatory purposes are neither to criticize nor to adopt what floods the cultural surround. He is different, holy. He aims to proclaim, teach, and model something distinctive. The Bible's positive message both *is* counseling and *is about* counseling. In content, method, and institutional locus the Bible overflows with counseling instructions and implications, not only in proof-texts but in the whole body of Scripture.

From the outset, Scripture redefines how we tend to define "counseling." Counseling is not fundamentally a professional helping activity, where an identifiably competent party intentionally offers aid to an identifiably distressed party in a formalized structure (such as weekly one-hour sessions on a fee-for-service basis). Given the culture's professionalized definition, the Bible seems relatively insufficient—even utterly silent—on the subject of counseling. But if counseling is about the tongue, and wise or foolish companions, and master-disciple relationships, and one-anothering influences for good or bad, and the truth or lie that speaks in the heart, and ministry of the Word of life . . . then the Bible brims. Relatively formal, private counseling ought only to apply and extend the practical truth and knowledgeable love that ought to characterize both informal relationships and public ministry. Counseling, whatever its formal or informal status, is either foolish (reorienting us away from God and toward our own self-trust) or wise (reorienting us to God). We need, first and foremost, to learn our own paradigm for understanding and transforming human nature, and that is exactly the Bible's major focus in revealing God on the stage of human life.

The second priority: exposing, debunking, and reinterpreting alternative models. The Bible conducts a running border war with multiform error. Idolatries and lies, false teachers and "the world" are like viral pathogens that endlessly mutate. Every book of the Bible has a backdrop, those formal systems or merely idiosyncratic tendencies that would lead us away. Falsehood is always new and creative, yet it always plays variations on the same old themes. Sinful human beings instinctively think about life as if there were no living God, no weighing of our lives in his eyes, and no need for a divine Savior. Human beings assiduously construct God-substitutes and truth-substitutes, other meanings of life, other ways of making life work. Theories about our lives are like our lives, embodying the instinct for evading reality.

Sin exerts a systematic distorting effect on thought and practice. The Bible teaches us how to see and expose sin and error. Most ungodliness is not unusually vile. It is so utterly commonplace that we miss it. In our day, it includes the deep assumptions every secular psychology makes about what transpires in the human heart. Secular psychologists can't help the godlessness of their view of the psyche and relationships. A secular psychology is the cultural product of a God-less person and will reflect and express that. Theories systematize and rationalize the unbelief of those who create and embrace those theories. Because the wisdom of the world has always been foolishness with God, the Bible always conducts a secondary polemic in order to defend and clarify the truth and to protect people from plausible falsehoods. This running argument arises from redemptive intention, not paranoid irascibility. The Redeemer is conducting an invasion, and he critiques other theories in order to convert people to his indestructible truth. The Bible's demonstrated second priority, criticizing untruths, is one logical implication of the demonstrated first priority, revealing truth.

The third priority: learning what we can from other models. We can learn from everything around us. Saying that God himself "learns" from ancient Near Eastern societies is inaccurate. But there is no doubt that God's prophets and apostles learn from everything around them. God adapts his message to time, place, language, culture, and people. The Bible freely co-opts surrounding cultures as one aspect of God's redemptive, transformative working. God's servants work with what is around them linguistically, politically, religiously, economically, artistically, educationally, agriculturally, and militarily. Committed to knowing the truth and critiquing error, they then appropriate lots of things. Redemption works with what is at hand, the "human documents," both individual and social, and the cultural products.

From the standpoint of fundamental model building, such learning plays a distinctly tertiary role. But this third priority is not unimportant. Because we ourselves are both limited by finitude and tainted by sin, God often uses "perceptive error" to reprove his people. It's part of how he makes us work to refine our understanding and application of his truth. Others may be seeing things we aren't seeing, doing things we aren't doing, asking questions we aren't asking. God's redemptive revelation is constitutive, but even counterbiblical theories may be provocative. And extrabiblical knowledge—of ourselves and our world—is always the grist with which biblical truth works continually to extend the range and depth of understanding. We learn, critique, reinterpret, convert, apply. We are able to traffic in the extrabiblical constructively when we know what we ought to know that reorients and controls our gaze (the first and second priorities).

This is God's world, so everything, even if it intends to efface God, bears witness to God— understood and reinterpreted through biblical eyeglasses. The Bible freely traffics in the extrabiblical, in the creation, in fallen cultural products, in the terminology of the very contemporary falsehoods that God is attacking. But God always interprets or reinterprets. He is imperial. Biblical truth is a corrective gaze. For example, the formal structure of Deuteronomy was modeled on ancient Near Eastern political treaties, but what God appropriates he radically reworks. Some proverbs are formally identical to older Egyptian sayings. But they mean something fundamentally different when embedded in the context of Yahweh-fearing proverbs from what they meant when embedded in a context of superstition, animism, idolatry, and self-trust.

The Bible never fears secular education. Moses was educated in all the learning of the Egyptians (Acts 7:22); God gave Daniel and his friends knowledge and intelligence in every branch of Chaldean literature and wisdom (Dan. 1:17); Paul was a man of great learning (Acts 22:3; 26:24). But Moses, Daniel, and Paul interpreted life through God's redemptive grid. Paul could quote with favor an "anthropologist" who studied life in Crete (Titus 1:12), and he could weave the words of Greek literati into his argument in Athens (Acts 17:28). Where the living, speaking, seeing, acting God rules, his servants move freely into the culture of their time and place. The Bible gives no warrant for Christians to be intellectual isolationists, to be biblicistic, cut off from culture, speaking a private language to our own kind.

Fallen though it is, this world is God's stage of redemption. But notice how the appropriation of culture is always subordinated, first to a clear-eyed grasp of God's truth, and second to keen-eyed skepticism about fallen alternatives. Paul had obviously learned a great deal from his culture. But he did not learn the living, systematic truth he proclaimed from those sterile and deviant substitutes. And the truth he proclaimed radically reworked those substitutes.[14]

The Needs of the Hour

The Bible itself models these primary, secondary, and tertiary priorities. What then are the needs of our time and place regarding the modern secular psychologies and psychotherapies? I believe the same priorities apply to how we engage them. First, both the confused church and the benighted culture need, more than anything else, positive biblical truth pointedly applied. We need to understand and practice our own distinctive psychology. We need to understand and practice our own distinctive care for souls. If we do not know well the peculiar wisdom of our own truth, we act not as light in the current darkness but as second-rate disciples of that darkness. Truth is the best thing we can offer.

Second, we need a penetrating critique of contemporary sources of confusion and darkness. Secular alternatives for understanding and caring for souls need careful exposure and pointed challenge. Priorities one and two will enable us to build up and protect the people of God. They will also enable a telling and timely proclamation of Christian truth into a psychologized culture. We believe differently and do differently from the world around us. We have depth where they are shallow. We have riches where they are impoverished. We see where they are blind.

Third, we will develop our model through interacting with contemporary models. Their successes can certainly reprove us and help us see more clearly places where we are inept and ignorant—as long as we do not counterconvert.

Their observations of what makes human life go and not go can inform us—if we radically reinterpret them from within our worldview. At every point, the first priority must be first, the second second, the third third.

Getting priorities sorted out generates a host of implications and applications. I will briefly flag three: the task of psychological research, the ability of the church to evangelize psychologized people, and the appropriation of historical theology.

First, the necessity of reordering our priorities does not mean that it is wrong to closely study psychological, relational, and counseling processes. Exactly the opposite. Psychological study that submits itself to God's truth becomes part of the joyous outworking of the church's first priority. When we believe in the sufficiency of Scripture, we enter into a vast practical-theological task, not a concordance search for the proof-text for every problem. Adopting a frankly biblical worldview, we should get about the business of hard, fruitful study, in subordination to the mind of Christ.

For example, Jonathan Edwards's *Treatise Concerning Religious Affections* is a model of empirical study constrained by biblical presuppositions. His was not positivist science pretending to neutrality; it was not narrow biblicism closing its eyes to the very phenomena that need study and interpretation; it was not a borrowing of secular thinking, thinly glossed with Christian words. Rather, it was a theological labor to develop systematic biblical understanding. But Edwards looked at only one (significant) slice of human life. Who will do the equivalent work regarding the multitude of significant counseling issues we face today? A hundred Edwardses could write a hundred equally masterful books, and a systematic practical theology of counseling would not yet be finished. There is no reason that study and a treatise on the "affections" in general—desires, emotions, attitudes, motives—cannot be done from frank Christian convictions about the nature of the human heart. It will not be a need theory, instinct theory, drive theory, or self-esteem theory. It will understand human experience with God in view.[15]

The Bible itself invites systematic inquiry, by the very generality and universality of God's revelation. The writers of the Bible intend to provide eyeglasses that enable all seeing, not an encyclopedia that contains all facts. For example, Galatians 5:19–21 says that the manifest lifestyle of sin is "obvious." Paul then gives fifteen representative examples, closing with "and the like." That provides an inexhaustible research agenda. Of course, Paul does not pretend to be methodologically and theoretically neutral. Those "works of the flesh" are sinful; they arise causally from various "lusts of the flesh"; both desire and doing will be morally evaluated by God, with inescapable consequences. We know à priori that loveless behaviors are not fundamentally products of enculturation, psychosocial trauma, unmet needs, a DSM-IV syndrome, or a somatic disease process. Each of the items on the Galatians 5 list—"interpersonal conflict," "substance abuse," "dysphoric emotions," and "sexual disorders"—invites extensive research to flesh out biblical understanding.

What about problems, like those labeled "eating disorders" or "obsessive-compulsive disorders," that do not appear on the representative list in Galatians 5? "Obvious" (and close study will unpack the details to show the how and why of those works of the flesh).[16] Fear and anxiety are not on the list? "Obvious." The countless faces and voices of self- and other-deception? The many forms of self-righteousness, self-pity, self-serving bias, self-exoneration? The psychological and interpersonal complexities of people-pleasing? "And the like." There is work to be done in cultivating a biblical gaze; a biblical gaze then cultivates wide-ranging knowledge.

Our doctrine must control our study, and our study must flesh out our doctrine. Careful "psychological" study is one direct implication of the sufficiency of Scripture and of getting our first priority straight. We best study human psychology not by submitting ourselves to the world's deviant psychologies but by looking at the world through the gaze of our own systematic biblical understanding. If we want to understand people so that we can truly help them, we undertake a task in practical theology.

Second, powerful, relevant evangelism to psychologized people is another direct implication of getting priorities straight. Contemporary secular psychological models are observationally rich, but they fundamentally misconstrue what people are like. If we are their beggars, they will never see their need. But if we have the true riches of accurate interpretation, and a corresponding critique of their poverty, we have something they will want.

I believe that several aspects of the contemporary psychological culture make the time ripe for the church to display its goods. In this post-Kuhnian, postmodern climate, confidence in positivistic scientific methodology for the social sciences has waned. The underpinnings of "psychology" as neutral truth have been kicked out. The age of confident model building, of the Grand Unified Theory (GUT), has faded. Microtheories and eclecticism are the order of the day. Despite the brave face psychologists attempt to put on it, these tendencies in fact register epistemological skepticism and despair. All this creates an opportunity for the church to get about business and stand up with our own counseling model.

We have the GUT—the work-in-progress of a systematic practical theology of counseling. As the mental health professions increasingly rationalize themselves by their licensed control over turf, rather than by defensible truth or efficacy, the church will doubtless suffer intimidation, lawsuits, legal restrictions, and so forth. But the fundamentally nonprofessional character of biblical wisdom shines with particular poignancy in such a world of brazen self-interest. We need not care much about licensure, accreditation, and third-party reimbursement schemes. The state does not license the church to believe and do what we need to believe and do, and it cannot stop us.

Counseling is not primarily a profession according to our GUT. Instead, it is a lifestyle. It is a matter of character, wisdom, every word out of our mouths, walking worthy of our calling. It is serving up the message of life to the ignorant and wayward, to the afflicted and dying, to the redeemable, to ourselves.

As Christians get our priorities straight, wonderful things happen. We become distinctively wise, able to help our own with our own resources. We begin to shine into a world in which people realize, when they are honest, that the mental health professions are groping in the dark. We have something positive to offer our world: truth, love, and power, in the exact areas in which people are most concerned and most confused. Our critique becomes more than sectarian intransigence. Our message becomes more than religious mumbo-jumbo for and from religious people. It's about life as it is *actually* lived, experienced, motivated, and evaluated—for every human being.

Third, our labors will result in something the world has not yet seen. We can appreciate the achievements of theologians, philosophers, and pastors who have alerted us to the historic resources of the Christian faith: e.g., Thomas Oden's series *Classical Pastoral Care,* Robert Roberts's *Taking the Word to Heart,* Tim Keller's "Puritan Resources for Biblical Counseling," Paul Griffiths's "Metaphysics and Personality Theory," Dennis Okholm's "To Vent or Not to Vent?"[17] The intellectual revival of long-departed practical theologians offers a healthy corrective to the subjection of evangelical faith to various contemporary psychologies, and it reasserts positive Christian

wisdom about the nature of persons, relationships, and the activities we call counseling.

But we must not forget the call to do fresh theological work. It is not enough to recover what has been long forgotten or obscured regarding human nature and counseling; it is not enough to appropriate the fruits of historical theology for present edification. Yes, Augustine's *Confessions* is a marvel of insight into the myriad ways that sin disorders our loves and grace reorders us. Yes, Edwards's *Treatise Concerning Religious Affections* is a masterpiece of empirical study conducted under the authority of Scripture. Yes, Gregory the Great and William Baxter collated vast practical wisdom. But the questions those books address are only partly universal; they are also significantly dated. Our generation must—and will—break new ground. The positive formulations of fresh theological work will enable us to criticize our Christian past discerningly. Not all earlier practical theologies were created equal. Not all are equally worth resurrecting. We must appropriate the best and forsake the worst, and that demands fresh criteria for judgment. Our task is always fresh: "A theology that does not build on the past ignores our debt to history and naively overlooks the fact that the present is conditioned by history. A theology that relies on the past evades the demands of the present."[18]

None of our forebears hammered out fidelity to Christ in a culture with a knowledge explosion in the social sciences, and with an omnipresent mental health establishment that attempts to define and meliorate human nature. The church's cure of souls has never before faced such stiff, organized, and persuasive competition. This has arisen in the sovereignty of God, that we might expect and pursue fresh wisdom.

Robert Roberts was hesitant to suggest that we expect a radically Christian counseling model to emerge internally, from within the Christian faith: "A Christian psychology would not have to be pursued in dialogue with secular psychology—at least not if the psychologist in question were Augustine or Kierkegaard or Saint John of the Cross. But I can think of two reasons why we more ordinary Christian thinkers are well advised to do our psychology in dialogue with important secular psychologists."[19] Perhaps Roberts rightly fears presumption and incompetence, our lack of intellectual and practical stature. I grant that our own psychology will emerge in interaction with the environing psychologies—and with everything else we experience culturally. But such dialogue should not be seen as a matter of constitutive necessity. That dialogue with secularity has so far been largely unprofitable in the VITEX tradition. It has resulted in counseling models that are recapitulations of and capitulations to secular forms of thinking and practice. A biblically guided dialogue will certainly contribute in a tertiary way, but our primary call is to the dialogue between the Bible and lives lived, as COMPIN asserts. Let us work explicitly from our own foundation.

Roberts may be right that no solitary and extraordinary genius will arise among us. Perhaps since care and counseling are fundamentally tasks of corporate wisdom, our Lord will be pleased to raise up something better, a corporate Augustine, a hundred Augustines, a hundred thousand Augustines, for the task that faces us. Perhaps many Christians will tackle the same massive intellectual and practical project: to construct "systematic biblical counseling" for the beginning of the third millennium anno Domini. After all, the Bible offers unique and superior wisdom, not only for extraordinary people but also for ordinary people (see Ps. 119:98–100; 1 Cor. 1—2). Our problem is not so much a matter of talent but a matter of corporate vision and will.

If our counseling model arises from Scripture, it will explicitly cohere with long-formulated Chris-tian orthodoxy and orthopraxy. It has often been said regarding the relationship of Old Covenant to New Covenant that "The new is in the old concealed; the old is in the new revealed." The same is true of theological progress. A systematic pastoral theology for the twenty-first century will cohere with historic orthodoxy, yet will break open new light and new power. Our concepts will probe the depths of the human heart and map the diversity of individual and cultural differences. Our methods will deliver the goods that comfort the disturbed and disturb the comfortable, converting all into the image of Jesus. Our institutional structures will be ecclesiastically rooted, vehicles of the ministry of the Word, combining wise pastoral authority and mutual encouragement.

Systematic biblical counseling—the Faith's psychology—will break fresh ground theologically, practically, and institutionally. For example, our understanding of the Christian life will be radically transformed as we deliver progressive sanctification out of its religious closet—a sector of religiously colored experiences, doctrines, morals, and activities—and work out the renovation of our humanity in daily life and in our social existence. We might barely recognize the radical new forms that church, ministry, and piety will take when Ephesians 4 and Hebrews 3:12–14; 4:12–16; and 10:19–25 come into their own—and yet they will be utterly familiar.

Disordered Priorities

We have looked at three implications of getting our priorities straight. But what happens when our priorities get tangled? "The dialogue of Christians with psychology has been less than full because we have been held captive by the alien spirits. . . . As a result, we have not had much of our own to contribute to the conversation with non-Christian psychologists."[20] Those who elevate the tertiary

283

priority—learning from defective models—to the first priority, find themselves subtly or overtly psychologized. Those who overweigh the significance of secular psychology "learn" more than they bargained for. They tend to undergo a wrong-way conversion, becoming anesthetized to the God-centered realities actually playing out in the human psyche. They begin to reason godlessly about behavior, mood, relationships, motives, cognition, and so on. They promulgate faulty reasoning and practice through the body of Christ.

Consider the popularity of "psychological need theories" (needs for self-esteem, achievement, love) since the 1980s. Consider the uncritical acceptance of DSM-IV categories as normative and explanatory, rather than as merely descriptive and as both biased and blinkered by faulty assumptions about human nature. Consider the fascination with psychotropic medication. Such distortions of human life occur when the scope of Christian faith is constricted, its significance restricted to a "spiritual" sector. However unwittingly, Christians allow conceptual categories from personality theory or self-help or medicine, the authority of the latest research study, the well-socialized and tacit assumptions of the mental health professional, and the necessities of licensure and accreditation to permeate thought and practice. All of this works in concert to unnerve faith. The Bible becomes an ancillary and supportive text, a source of prooftexts in the worst sense. Christian faith and biblical citation are pressed to rationalize ideas intrinsically alien to the mind of God. Only when our first priority is first will we truly think and act in ways that transform our culture, those we counsel, and ourselves.

Those who major in the secondary priority—exposing and debunking alternative models—create a different problem for the body of Christ. Criticism without the rich, growing edge of the first priority is unpalatable and unedifying. If we major in criticism, we become polemicists, rather than agents of redemption.

Often polemicists excuse their loveless rough edges by the demands of truth. But they lose more than they realize. In fact, when love and the growth of positive truth are lost, truth is also lost. Biblical truth loses its scope, balance, depth, applicability, savor, and growing edge when the second priority seizes center stage. The positive theological task that is the need of our age gets obscured. Caricatures of truth and discernment replace the realities. Words that are not constructive, timely, and grace giving are rotten and nonnutritive, whatever their formal likeness to Christian content (Eph. 4:29). To lose charity, tenderheartedness, sympathy, and generosity is always to simultaneously pervert the redemptive nature of biblical revelation. Narrowed "truth" may bristle enough to defend one city wall, but it is not good enough to conquer the world.[21] Only when our first priority is first do we Christians have a robust, radiant, and sensible alternative in our hearts and in our mouths, something good to offer those we critique, those we counsel, and ourselves.

The church must transcend the misplaced priorities and fruitless posturing of much current debate between VITEX and COMPIN. The tertiary priority must be submitted to the call to pursue the primary and secondary priorities.

The secondary must be submitted to the primary, and then the implications of the tertiary spelled out. We must get our priorities straight. Such shifts will invigorate both the secondary and the tertiary to function as they ought and will produce a buoyant intellectual and practical confidence for both counseling ministry and evangelism. Our ability to understand ourselves, to counsel our own, and to reach the world with our own distinctive truth is at stake.

2. Our theory of motivation

The first crucial question dealt with epistemology. This second question deals with human motivation, with personality theory. Why do people do what they do? What is wrong with people and how can we make it right?

At the center of every view of human nature is a theory of motivation, and the logical end of every theory of motivation is a cure. The various answers to the question, "Why do we do what we do?" provide synopses of the various schools of thought. Each definition of the core problem is then a signpost to the cure of soul that the respective theory proposes. Everyone agrees that something is wrong with us. The big questions are always *Why?* and *What can be done about it?*

- If your brain chemistry is unhinged, then you need chemical reengineering.
- If you are fixated somewhere on the hierarchy of needs, then you need particular needs met.
- If your drives have been conditioned in unacceptable directions, then you need to be redirected and reconditioned.
- If your spirit is dead while your soulishness is too lively, then you need God's Spirit to release your spirit to master your soul.
- If you are wounded, then you need healing.
- If you search for meaning while believing and doing meaningless things, then you need the courage to embrace something meaningful.
- If this is a bad-star day for those born under your zodiac sign, then stay home today.
- If you feel bad about yourself, then you need reasons for more self-confidence.
- If you were born in a miserable existence because of previous karma, then you need to work it off in hopes of something better next time around.

- If your self-talk is self-defeating, then you need a motivational speech and a dose of stoic philosophy.
- If you are mentally ill, then find the right medicine to make you well.
- If you are lazy, then you need more self-discipline.
- If it's just a guy-thing or a girl-thing, then affirm the quirks that make you hard to live with.
- If you've been oppressed by society, then you need to stand up for your rights.
- If you are in flight from acknowledging unacceptable impulses, then you need to stop and look in the mirror.
- If a demon of anger has staked out turf in your soul, then someone must eject it.
- If you have psychic voids created by disappointing object relations, then you need to find ways to understand your personal history and redirect your longings.
- If you are compensating for your inferiority complex, then learn to accept yourself realistically and do something worthwhile.

And so forth.

Everyone in the supermarket of ideas knows that something is wrong with people.

What is it? Everyone in the supermarket of cures wants to do something to make it better. What gives the life that is life indeed? Different views of the soul's ailments will logically propose different cures for the soul. Wrong views of any disease always bring with them wrong views of the remedy. The right view brings the right remedy.

So what is the problem? The three-word description that Christians have harvested from the Bible is "sin and misery." The remedy for our disorientation and suffering? The two-word solution that Scripture sows into our lives is "Jesus Christ." The seven-word version of the solution, encompassing our response, is "Christ's grace enabling repentance, faith, and obedience." God is in the business of turning folly and misery into wisdom and felicity. How is such theological shorthand relevant to the problems that counselors of all stripes address daily? How do basic Christian diagnostic categories map onto the details of such things as interpersonal conflicts, unpleasant emotions, misdirected lives, twisted cognitions, chaotic cravings, compulsively escapist behaviors, sufferings at the hands of others, somatic afflictions, devilish temptations, sociocultural lies? That last sentence simply offers a twenty-five-word elaboration of "sin and misery." One could further elaborate any topic or subtopic into book length without ever needing to slip into another set of categories. Similarly, the wise felicity of grace—God's solution—can, must, and will be elaborated, tailored, and nuanced as it is worked into our lives.

The holy grail after which counseling theories finally aspire is redemption from what ails us, a cure for the diagnosed problem. In the Bible's comprehensive view, this must engage both inward and outward aspects of the person, and it must engage both the individual and the community. The renewing of our hearts (fructifying cognitive, emotional, and volitional processes), the renewing of our manner of life (transforming individual behavior), the renewing of our community (transforming corporate relationships), and the renewing of our bodies (resurrection from the dead) go together. In biblical language, such comprehensive renewal is "wisdom and felicity." It is the goal of God's counseling.

The writers of the Bible portray and intend to create such wisdom at every turn. For example, we are taught and shown a tremendous amount about the psychology of Jesus. This is the centerpiece for understanding. We know how he thought, felt, chose, acted, and spoke. We know not only how he related interpersonally but also how he related individual identity to community. We know how he interpreted and responded to sufferings and how he located individual life in the larger flow of history. In what terms did his psychic life transpire? How did he interpret what he saw? What did he want? How did he understand himself? We learn how the human soul is intended to work, hence we learn the standard from which to make diagnoses of defection and distortion.

We witness the psychology of Jesus not only in the Gospels but also in Psalms, Proverbs, the books of History, and the Prophets. Every revelation of the ways of God and the ways of godliness give expression to how Jesus worked both intrapsychically and interpersonally. What emerges as the central drama and pivot of human existence? What threads through every emotion, cognition, action, relationship, suffering?

Our souls play out a drama of evil and good. Sin and righteousness, fall and redemption, false and true, misery and felicity, folly and wisdom, deafness and hearing, stupor and wakefulness, death and life—these are playing in the theatre of life lived. Every life. We play out this drama vis-à-vis God, at every moment, in every choice, in every nuance of cognition, emotion, and volition, in every detail of lifestyle. Every aspect of our existence plays out on the stage of God's history, with a day of reckoning coming.

We also learn about psychopathology, the madness in our hearts. From the biblical point of view, one of the leading characteristics of sin's psychopathology is that we repress awareness of these moral, theological, social, and historical terms in which the drama of our psyches is cast. Psalms 10, 14, and 36 are but a few examples of how the thought processes of the sinful psyche are analyzed as attempts to elude reality. The repression of God and of our historical embeddedness and accountability are prominent themes. Only a biblical psychology reveals how significant this is;

fallen psychologies manifest the repression. This is a stunning psychology. Other psychologies repress awareness, participating in the universal psychopathology of fallen human nature. People with problems in living, and people who seem to function in healthy ways, and psychological models that attempt to make sense of human behavior are only differently sick (Eccles. 9:3). They all repress the truth.

The psychology that Jesus teaches us is multifaceted. The psalmist is simultaneously sinner and sufferer, par excellence. The proverbist is simultaneously wise and keenly aware of remnant folly, par excellence. The prophet lives simultaneously in his moment and in the larger flow of history, par excellence. And in each case, individual identity and community identity interweave. What cure is there for what ails us? The steadfast love of Yahweh is the only hope for deliverance from both sin and suffering. We all know this. These things lie on the surface of Scripture; they constitute the depths of Scripture. They deconstruct and reconstruct the human soul. They are so familiar and so "religious" that we barely hear them. We barely hear their shocking implications for our conceptual and applied psychology.

What does this mean for our model of counseling? Jesus owned the Psalms, Proverbs, and Prophets as the voice of his experience and emotion, the content of his cognitive process, and the framework of his action.[22] They articulate what human life is really about. The fully honest, fully human person thinks, feels, and reacts in these ways. These things record the categories of consciousness and action for the only fully conscious and seeing man whoever lived. They record the categories through which the gaze of the Searcher of hearts ransacks our lives. One sees in the Bible the normatively wise human psychology; it is so radically God-centered that we can barely see it as a psychology and as the true psychology. It sounds like theology, not psychology. But the Bible portrays the nitty-gritty of human psychology as pervasively theological.

One also sees in the Bible many portrayals of the normally foolish human psychology. This is utterly familiar stuff—dysfunctions and eufunctions of relationship, emotion, cognition; the Lego pieces with which every false psychological theory plays; the descriptive case study data. It all looks shockingly different seen through biblical gaze, seen against the diagnostic backdrop of the normative psychology of God-fearing. Jesus experienced life as he counseled others to experience life: the issues of life lived are specifically about sin and misery, specifically about gracious deliverance, and specifically about the felicitous wisdom of repentance, faith, love, and obedience. There is no "religious" sector of life. Such sectoring is one of the commonplace machinations of sin's logic that flies in the face of reality.

Why belabor this? I wish I could belabor it better, less impressionistically, more radically! What the Bible communicates to us about God's gaze on the psyche and relationships is so "odd" that even to glimpse it turns our whole notion of psychology and counseling inside out, upside down, and backward. God gives a radically "other" explanation and agenda. Contemporary counseling models—including "Christianized" models—do an extremely poor job of reflecting and communicating what life is really about. They are weakest where they claim to be strongest. We are immersed in decidedly bad psychologies, in gross misinterpretations of human existence.

The Christian subjects modern psychological models to thorough critique not because they are some bogeyman called "Psychology," but because they are specifically faulty psychologies. By definition, a personality theory ought to help counselor and counselee alike accurately understand what's going on within and between persons. By definition, a counseling model claims to help us reorient to reality, to know what to do to fix things. But what should we make of models that essentially and consistently evade reality? That misdefine the basic problem? That suppress the major Player in human psychological, relational, and somatic existence? That suppress the historical conditions—past, present, future—that qualify human existence? That redefine the dynamics of our God-dealing hearts by expunging God? That redefine the basic solution, so it is no longer a Person? That redefine the desired human response that is so radically interpersonal? A model that does not move within the categories of human experience that Jesus himself moved in, and by which God himself looks at life, will fundamentally disorient and misguide those who embrace it. Every counseling model offers a map of reality, an interpretive framework. The Bible's reality map sets the goal of all valid counseling lived in the consciousness and lifestyle of Jesus. We witness and listen in on the normative subjectivity and intersubjectivity.

This has huge implications for our theory of motivation. First of all, the dynamics of human intention and desire cannot be defined in purely psychological terms (or psycho-social terms, or psycho-social-somatic terms). Motivational dynamics do not simply operate within or between persons. The human heart has to do with God. So when the Bible describes the desires that obviously play within our souls and rule our lives, it does not portray them as hard-wired psychological or physiological givens: as needs, instincts, drives, longings, wishes. It speaks of them as morally freighted vis-à-vis God, as moral-covenantal choices: we are ruled either by cravings of the flesh or by repentance-faith-obedience to God's desires. Our desires are tilted one way or the other, either toward the true God or toward the host of idols we fabricate both collectively and idiosyncratically. Our mastering desires are relationally and morally qualified.

Similarly, when the Bible describes the beliefs, assumptions, and inward conversations that so obviously play within our souls and shape our lives, it does not portray them in neutral fashion, as mere cognitive functions: as self-talk, schemata, conscious or unconscious contents, memory, attitude, imagination, worldview, and the like. Our functional beliefs not only occur *coram Deo;* they actually have to do directly with God. Our actual mental life transpires either for or against God. Lies and unbelief contend with truth and faith. In the Bible, people whose self-talk talks as if there were no God—and hence no ongoing and eventual moral evaluation by God—are described in vividly moral terms: they are foolish, wicked, proud. People who talk in their hearts in the light of God are also described in vividly moral terms: wise, righteous, after God's own heart. Our mastering beliefs are relationally and morally qualified.

In the same way, when the Bible describes the self-evaluating capacities that play within our souls and so powerfully determine us, it does not portray them as merely intrapsychic entities: self-esteem, self-image, self-worth, self-love, self-confidence, inferiority complex, and identity. Our evaluative and self-knowing capacity registers human-before-God realities. The conscience or "eyes" by which we weigh ourselves either expresses self-will ("in my own eyes," pride) and subjection to the opinions of others ("in others' eyes," fear of man), or it expresses and is informed by God's evaluative criteria ("in God's eyes," *coram Deo,* the fear of the Lord). Self-evaluation is not intrinsically an autonomous, intrapsychic function. It only acts that way when sin operates to suppress God-awareness. Our mastering conscience is relationally and morally qualified.

In sum, the human heart—the answer to why we do what we do—must be understood as an active-verb-with-respect-to-God. Climb inside any emotional reaction, any behavioral choice or habit, any cognitive content, any reaction pattern to suffering, and you are meant to hear and see active verbs working out. Love God or anything else. Fear God or anything else. Want God or anything else. Need God or anything else. Hope in God or anything else. Take refuge in God or anything else. Obey God or anything else. Trust God or anything else. Seek God or anything else. Serve God or anything else. The Bible's motivation theory shouts from every page—but it does not look like a motivation theory to those whose gaze has been bent and blinded by sin's intellectual logic. How can we learn to think and see psyche and behavior in the moral-covenantal terms in which life actually transpires?

Consider this analogy. The Bible's psychology is like a hyper-psychosocial theory. Psychosocial theories embed psychic functions in social realities. The Bible's motivation theory is a psychosocial theory in three dimensions. A covenantal-relational analysis of the human heart adds a pervasive and determinative dimension to which both encapsulated psyche theories and interhumanly psychosocial theories are utterly oblivious. No secular theory can say this because no secular theory can see this because no secular theory wants to see this. But this is what explains human behavior. No one else in the modern world is able or willing to say what the church can and must say: human beings are radically sin sick. The cure of souls must cure this ailment, or else it is prescribing painkillers for cancer. Other cures whistle in the dark while a deadly, unseen corruption festers and an imminent, unrecognized destruction approaches.

Christ cures sin-sickness. Where sin abounds, grace superabounds. One small, but significant, part of the cure is that he reveals his own psychology to us and demonstrates exactly how these are in fact the realities transpiring in our souls. When we get straight how the active heart works vis-à-vis God, then the grace of Jesus maps straight onto human need. The good news of Jesus refuses to be relegated to a religious sector of life. It is the explicit need of the psychologically honest and the clear seeing. All other psychologies—whether formulated into personality theories or merely lived out in the workings of individual idiosyncrasy—traffic in myth, lie, false consciousness, and perverse speculation.

The Bible locates the core motivational dynamic as existing in covenantal space, not merely in psychological, physiological, or psychosocial space. What God sees in us mocks the paradigm and contents of the encapsulated psyche that most of the older psychologies posited. It mocks the social psyche of many of the newer psychologies. It mocks the epiphenomenal psyche of the empty organism posited by behaviorists, medicalists, and sociobiologists. The intricacies of behavior, emotion, forgetting and remembering, attitude, and cognitive processes specifically come out of the God-relational heart. This is not simply a vague, religiously toned generalization. What people do with the living God plays out into the details. In other words, our core psychological problem is sin, and the core resolution is awakening faith. Sin operates specifically here and now, not somewhere in the background in general.

Difficulties in Understanding the Heart from God's Point of View

Sin is the problem, but people find it difficult to make the core of Jesus' gaze useful in developing a counseling model. Several common distortions in the working definition of sin make us unable to trace the psychological logic of sin.[23]

First, people tend to think of sins in the plural as consciously willed acts where one was aware of and chose not to do the righteous alternative. Sin, in this popular understanding, refers to matters of conscious volitional awareness of wrongdoing and the ability to do otherwise. This instinctive view of sin infects many Christians and almost all non-Christians. It has a long legacy in the church under the label *Pelagianism,* one of the oldest and most instinctive heresies. The Bible's view of sin certainly includes the high-handed sins where evil approaches full volitional awareness. But sin also includes what we simply are and the perverse ways we think, want, remember, and react.

Most sin is invisible to the sinner because it is simply how the sinner works, how the sinner perceives, wants, and interprets things. Once we see sin for what it really is—madness and evil intentions in our hearts, absence of any fear of God, slavery to various passions (Gen. 6:5; Ps. 36:1; Eccles. 9:3; Titus 3:3)—then it becomes easier to see how sin is the immediate and specific problem all counseling deals with at every moment, not a general and remote problem. The core insanity of the human heart is that we violate the first great commandment. We will love anything, except God, unless our madness is checked by grace.

People do not tend to see sin as applying to relatively unconscious problems, to the deep, interesting, and bedeviling stuff in our hearts. But God's descriptions of sin often highlight the unconscious aspect. Sin—the desires we pursue, the beliefs we hold, the habits we obey as second nature—is intrinsically deceitful. If we knew we were deceived, we would not be deceived. But we are deceived, unless awakened through God's truth and Spirit. Sin is a darkened mind, drunkenness, animal-like instinct and compulsion, madness, slavery, ignorance, stupor. People often think that to define sin as unconscious removes human responsibility. How can we be culpable for what we did not sit down and choose to do? But the Bible takes the opposite tack. The unconscious and semiconscious nature

of much sin simply testifies to the fact that we are steeped in it. Sinners think, want, and act sinlike by nature, nurture, and practice. We instinctively return evil for evil. All psychological processes are sin-kinked. That is the most interesting and significant thing about them diagnostically.

The tendency to only see sin as behavioral and fully volitional carries enormous implications for counseling. When people see sin only as willed actions, then they must invent other categories to cover the blind chaos, insanity, confusion, compulsion, impulsivity, bondage, and fog that beset the struggling human soul. A few people, the consciously bad people, can then be usefully described as sinners. Everybody else might commit a few sins: "Of course, we're all sinners." But that is a weightless comment. The weighty action typically occurs elsewhere in the person, going on beneath or beside those occasional, undefined, generic sins. If sin is only conscious badness, then the person grappling with the chaos of the human condition must suffer something else: emotional or psychological problems, demons, mental illness, addiction, inner wounding, unmet needs and longings, adjustment reactions, or some other DSM-IV syndrome.

If a certain problem happens on occasion, and presumably under conscious control, then it might be sin. But if the problem happens a lot, and is driven by blind compulsion, then it is presumably something else and only remotely sin. When the deacon gets drunk and sleeps with his secretary, he sins. But when the drunkard and pornography habitué succumbs, he suffers alcoholism and sexual addiction. When a normal mother feels some anxiety about her children and pressures them, she ought to repent of her worry and domineering and learn to trust God. But when someone is a walking nervous breakdown, feels wracking anxiety about everything and manipulates everyone, then she suffers neurosis or codependency or borderline personality or an adjustment reaction. Such thinking swings a wrecking ball into the church's ability to think about counseling the way Jesus thinks about it. A psychologically astute gaze will discern how sin plays out in people's problems—and in the things they do not think are problems. False psychologies obscure what the true psychology sees.

The modern psychologies are primarily wrong about psychology itself. Of course, their descriptive acuity about certain features of human existence is challenging and informative. We should listen and learn. But the theoretical gaze always blinkers out the most significant data. It necessarily distorts the very things seen most acutely and cared about most intensely. It always fabricates significant data because what is seen is an artifact of the way of seeing. Sin blinds, while preserving the illusion of seeing.

As far as secular psychologists know themselves, they want to understand and help people. But they are committed to defining the core, causal problem as *anything* except sin. Imagine a group of detectives examining a murder scene. The criminal has left countless clues. An hour before the crime he had been heard in a restaurant making loud threats. He dropped his business card at the scene of the crime. He stood in front of a surveillance camera that took pictures every three seconds. He left fingerprints everywhere, including the gun, which lay beside the body and which he had purchased three days earlier. He made a credit card call on the victim's telephone moments after the crime. He was collared running away from the scene wearing blood-spattered clothes. Under questioning he is extremely agitated, alternating between contradictory excuses and sharp cries of remorse. But imagine further that the detectives are committed to find some other culprit, any other culprit, because they themselves are accomplices. All the evidence will be processed through a grid of intentions that forbids the truth. Secularity cannot help noticing the clues screaming out "sin," even as it cannot help rationalizing away the true interpretation.

A further problem almost invariably accompanies this defective view of sin. When people think of naming problems as "sin," they tend to react in one of two ways. One reaction is to punish sin. They become moralistic and condemning, morbidly curious about others' failings, morbidly depressed about their own failings. So when someone assumes a punitive stance toward sin, and assumes that others do the same, then calling something "sin" necessarily involves attitudes of condemnation of self or others. We all know, however, both by Scripture and instinct, that those who would help others need to love them, and those who would find help need to know love. In the interest, then, of bringing sweet necessities—grace, kindness, gentleness, patience, acceptance, tender solicitude, and sympathetic understanding—it seems that we must come up with other categories besides sin. The unexamined and ultimately bizarre logic assumes that we can be Christlike toward people and ourselves only if a problem is defined as something other than sin—as a psychological problem, mental illness, or addiction.

People who would understand a problem as "sin" must presumably be punitive. But how curious it is that Jesus, whose gaze was, and is, utterly conditioned by the sin analytic, brought grace and kindness! In fact, to be conscious of how sin is the problem is the only way to experience grace for oneself and then to really love as Jesus loved. When we know ourselves accurately, we become recipients of spectacular grace, which we are able to give away freely and patiently. Because they knew their own sins and God's grace, the high priests were able to "deal gently even with the ignorant and wayward" (Heb. 5:2 ESV; cf., 4:12—5:8). May we learn to know and do likewise.

The second reaction is to excuse sin. People euphemize, whitewash, relabel, evade, rationalize, and blame other things. They get defensive about themselves and so try to excuse others. As we have said above, this strategy is at work throughout the modern psychologies. It is part of their allure that they pretend to present deep and determinative knowledge about the human soul, yet they evade the essential problem of the human soul. But when we know grace, we have no reason not to look frankly in the mirror at ourselves, and no reason not to help others look in the mirror. Indeed, we look in the mirror so that our hearts might be remade with shouts of exultation.

The Bible is crystal clear about all these things. This is Theology 101 applied remedially to contemporary bad psychologies in the interests of forming a sound psychology. These are the ABCs of a biblical theory of why we do what we do and what we should do about it. These concepts appear nowhere in any secular model and rarely with any profundity in Christian counseling models. Instead, one finds counterfeits, abstractions of human existence ripped out of their true theistic context.

Let me pose a series of questions to the VITEX community, the community of people who believe that secular psychological models must make a vital external contribution to the construction of a Christian model of personality, change process, and counseling method.

- Why do the models of Christian counseling that have been proposed over the past fifty years not teach the biblical view?
- Why does one or another secular theory of human motivation almost inevitably control the theory at the punch line, where counseling engages the details of life lived?
- In particular, why have "need" theories that define significance, love, and self-esteem as the standard needs been so prominent, when this is so alien to the gaze of God and to the psychological experience of Jesus?
- Why has the most typical, and apparently the most vital, external contribution of psychology been secular motivation theory, the very thing that wrenches human life out of its true context and drains psychological experience of its essential characteristics?
- Why do integrationist theories not take seriously the specific, omnipresent nature of sin as the chief and immediate problem in the hearts and lives of those we counsel?

VITEX paid lip service to sin as a general concept inhabiting the remote background. But where is the hard work and clear thinking that shows exactly how sin in specific, here-and-now, underlies those dysfunctions and dysphorias that plague those we counsel? Why do current Christian counseling models have such a hard time portraying the gospel of a sin-bearing and wisdom-giving Savior as intrinsic to all cure, as vivid, logical, and immediately relevant? Why do Christian counselors so often override the biblical view of the active heart by considering suffering (socialization, trauma, unmet needs, biochemistry, and genetics) to be determinative and finally causative? Why do Christian counseling models fail to recognize, mention, and make clear God's immediate and sovereign purposes in such sufferings? Why do they treat sin so vaguely, while other factors are considered deeper, more significant, and more interesting for both theory development and therapeutic attention? Why aren't counselors who would call sin "sin" credited with bearing such mercy and grace, both personally and from Christ?

The conservative church has often been touched by Pelagian and semi-Pelagian tendencies. In some circles, that has fed moralism and tendencies toward punitive harshness. In other circles, that has fed a flight to other explanations for what is deep in the human heart. But the comprehensive

Bible, and a faithful, systematic practical theology for curing souls, surely corrects all such defects by bringing amazing grace to sin-sick souls.

3. Educating, licensing, and overseeing counselors

How should help be organized? As we have just seen, when we get our epistemological priorities straight, then our understanding of diagnosis and cure radically changes. Those same reordered priorities also bring radical implications for institutional structure. So far in this essay I have concentrated on epistemological and conceptual concerns. But some readers will have noticed that a concern about social structure has been simmering on the back burner. For example, in describing the VITEX position, I described not only a vital external contribution of theory and knowledge from secular disciplines but also incorporation of the mental health professions into overall Christian ministry. This easy segue from epistemology to the sociology of professional practice needs to be analyzed, rather than assumed to be self-evident. Institutional structure is not the same thing as epistemology.

Evangelicals' earliest rationalization for psychotherapeutic professionalism utilized trichotomist anthropology. If human nature can be divided into body, spirit, and soul, then we need the doctor to treat the body, the pastor to treat the spirit, and the psychologist to treat the soul. Though highly dubious both theologically and logically, some Christians still buy the argument. Subsequent rationalizations for professional practice have more often tended to use theoretical epistemology. If we can learn something about people from secular intellectual disciplines, then mental health professions can provide leadership in cure of souls. That is equally dubious both theologically and logically—an intellectual sleight of hand—but it has been frequently assumed without examination.

We need to ponder and discuss two sets of questions. The first set of questions asks: What ought to be the social structure of counseling if we are to please the Shepherd of sheep? How should the cure of souls be organized? What institutional structures ought to be in place to equip and oversee those who do face-to-face ministry? How should grassroots counseling be delivered? What credentials and characteristics define leadership or professionalism, in the cure of souls? How should the faith and practice, the concepts and methods, of our counseling be both enriched and regulated so that we grow and stay faithful to God?

The second set of questions asks: What is the viability and validity of our current institutional arrangements? What are the implications for the church of Christ when its designated or presumed experts in the cure of souls are state-licensed, fee-for-service, mental health professionals without any organic linkage to ecclesiastical oversight? What are the implications for the church of Christ of its current lack of many crucial institutional structures that are necessary for caring for souls?

These questions are structural. They are matters of the sociology of pastoral care, of biblical ecclesiology, of the role and function of professions and social institutions. Our epistemological foundation, the Bible, addresses not only ideas and practices but also social structure. Does the Holy Spirit intend that we develop a normative social institution for curing souls? The answer is yes. The church—as the Bible defines it—contains an exquisite blending of leadership roles and mutuality, of specialized roles and the general calling. It is the ideal and desirable institution to fix what ails us.

During the past fifty years, a new ministry role has emerged in the body of Christ, claiming legitimacy: the professional psychotherapist. In the 1950s, there were perhaps six main categories of full-time Christian workers: pastors, missionaries, chaplains, school teachers, parachurch evangelism and discipleship workers, and medical personnel. *Christian psychotherapist* would have been an oxymoron, rather like *Christian Mormon,* for reasons that had to do both with conceptual framework and social structure. But in recent decades, the vocation of state-licensed psychotherapist has become viable and popular for Christians who want to help people. Christian psychotherapists have rapidly become a seventh category of full-time Christian work—sort of. The relationship between church and this autonomous, state-accredited, fee-for-service profession remains uneasy; it will always be uneasy. That uneasiness arises from structural contradictions that cannot be effaced.

I am not saying, by the way, that there is no place for various sorts of Christian workers besides pastors, missionaries, and the rest. I am not saying that there is no place for institutional innovation in church and parachurch structures and for development of specialized ministries, including counseling ministries. I am not saying that there is no place for people with particular gifts, training, and experience in caring for and curing souls. What I am saying is that state-licensed professionalization of care for souls is not a desirable direction. A care-for-souls profession operating autonomously from the church is an anomaly.

When VITEX advocates offer an explicit intellectual rationale for integrating secular psychology with Christian faith, they most often make epistemological arguments: secular science can make a constitutive contribution to Christian thinking about human nature and change.[24] But the social effect of importing psychotherapeutic professions has been at least as significant as the intellectual effect of importing secular personality theory. The VITEX community has historically ignored efforts to bring this question up for discussion. For example, Jay Adams repeatedly challenged the evangelical

psychotherapy community on ecclesiological and professional grounds, but he was repeatedly rebutted by psychologists on epistemological grounds. When psychologists ritually charged Adams with adopting an against-psychology position epistemologically, denying common grace and general revelation, they skirted the fact that Adams was most often exercised about sociology of professions, not epistemology.[25]

In fact, Adams's formal epistemology is a rather typically reformed, transformationist position toward the observations and ideas of secular disciplines. He denied their necessity for constructing a systematic pastoral theology but affirmed their potential usefulness when appropriated through Christian eyes. Epistemologically, Adams is a radical Christianizer of secularity, not a biblicistic xenophobe. He is no triumphalist, believing that Christian faith has already arrived at the sum of all wisdom, but believes that secular disciplines can both challenge and inform us.[26] But Adams was sharply against psychology when it came to dubious theoretical models and when it came to giving state-licensed, secularly trained mental health professions the reins to the face-to-face care of souls.[27]

The evangelical counseling community has only apparently been locked in an epistemological stalemate between VITEX and COMPIN positions. The underlying reality is more complicated—and social. I suggest that "common grace" has often served as a symbolic resource by VITEX to evade discussion of the implications of professionalization. I also suggest that rhetoric about "the church" has often served as a symbolic resource by COMPIN to evade discussion of the actual state of the church regarding cure of souls. We must look at and address both what ought to be and what is, bringing the two together to design solutions.

What *ought* to be? The church is in trouble when its designated experts in the cure of souls are mental health professionals who owe their legitimacy to the state. Cure of souls is a decidedly *pastoral* function, in the broadest and deepest sense of the word. It is deeply problematic to operate as if the Word of God is useful, necessary, and sufficient for public ministry—preaching, teaching, worship, sacraments—but that training and credentialing in secular psychology are necessary for private ministry. In the Bible, the same truths that address crowds address individuals. A preacher no more needs a PhD in public speaking than a counselor needs a PhD or PsyD in clinical psychology. Graduates of psychology programs should not have rights and honors to teach the church about the human condition. Fee-for-service psychotherapeutic professions should not have the rights and honors to practice the cure of souls. They have the wrong knowledge base, the wrong credentials, the wrong financial and professional structure.

According to the Bible, caring for souls—sustaining sufferers and transforming sinners—is a component of the total ministry of the church, however poorly the contemporary church may be doing the job. There is no legitimate place for a semi-Christian counseling profession to operate in autonomy from ecclesiastical jurisdiction and in subordination to state jurisdiction.[28] The Lord whose gaze and will the Bible reveals lays claim to the cure of souls. If counseling is indeed about understanding the human condition, if it deals with the real problems of real people, if it ever mentions the name of Jesus Christ (or should mention, but doesn't), then it traffics in theology and cure of souls; it ought to express and come under the church's authority and orthodoxy.[29]

Psychotherapists are "ordained" by the state, not by the church. From the church's standpoint, they are laypersons, not professionals. They attempt exceedingly significant and delicate work in people's lives in a dangerously autonomous way, without guidance or checks from the church

that has responsibility for those people's lives. If the books and articles are any guide to what is actually done in counseling, then they often mediate falsehoods. But however sincere the beliefs and intentions of individual practitioners and however close particular individuals may be to biblical thinking, the problem is structural. A hugely influential profession is operating by claiming title to the most personally intimate and weighty aspects of the cure of souls: addressing identity confusion, disordered motivation, distortions of functional beliefs, broken relationships, responses to suffering, compulsive sins, and the like. In effect, functional authority over the souls of Christ's sheep is being granted to a semisecular, unaccountable parapastorate. This invites trouble.

Christian counseling is currently out of control doctrinally. It lacks regulative ideas and regulative structures, though the Bible clearly gives both. The integration of psychology has provided a carte blanche for "every man did what was right in his own eyes" (Judg. 21:25 ESV). One can arise as a leader in the Christian counseling world with little more than an apparently sincere profession of faith, an advanced secular degree, and authorship of a popular book.

We must face the question of professionalism, of the social structure for delivering counseling care. Creedal standards must also be formulated to guide and constrain the content, the theory, of private counseling. For example, a counselor's motivation theory will align the entire interpretive endeavor toward truth or error. The spectrum of Christian counselors currently mediates any and every motivation theory, however contradictory to Scripture. Nothing besides the good faith and reputation of individuals currently protects the evangelical psychotherapy professions (and pastoral counselors, too) from importing serious error into the church regarding cure of souls. Sadly, the flimsiness of current protections shows. The mind of the church about counseling is being shaped, and largely misshaped, by Christians of presumably good intentions who have their primary education and their professional identity outside of the church they claim to serve.

Psychotherapeutic professionalism is a defective institutional structure for cure of souls. Some leaders have expressed hope that they might eventually form a Christian version of state licensing boards, in order that Christians might qualify and accredit fellow Christian psychotherapists. But that would only bump the problem back a step. Those who claim expertise to teach and counsel others will still not be significantly accountable to the church and to orthodoxy for their faith and practice. To replicate an inherently defective social structure within the body of Christ is no solution.

We have looked at what ought to be and the failure of mental health professions to match up to the structures enjoined by the Bible. What is the state of the church itself regarding cure of souls? It is not enough for those who believe in COMPIN to proclaim "the church, the church, the church!" That sounds good in theory. The Bible does locate care and cure in the body of Christ. But the church in reality does not currently have institutional structures in place to deliver the goods. Functional autonomy and potential for confusion and error are not only problems of mental health professionalism. Within the church herself, cure of souls operates in almost identical autonomy, with almost identical potential for theological and practical trouble.

Let me give a concrete example of the problem. I am part of the Presbyterian Church in America (PCA). One of the leaders in our congregation, AJ, is pursuing ordination. In order to be ordained in the PCA, to be recognized as competent to lead the people of God pastorally, AJ will be tested in many significant areas. His personal character must match the requirements for Christian maturity and seasoned fidelity to Christ. He must sustain examinations in Bible knowledge, in theology proper (view of God), in soteriology (view of salvation), in exegesis (his ability to get at what the Bible says), in church history (how we got where we are), in church government (how the machinery works), and in preaching (his ability to talk to a crowd).

But what about the cure of souls and counseling? AJ will not be examined on what he believes and how he practices ministry to individuals. He will present no case study of a disintegrating marriage or of a woman who binges and purges. There is no tradition of wisdom for the cure of souls into which AJ has himself been systematically discipled. There is no institutional system—creedal, educational, qualifying, and supervisory—to help him think as biblically about counseling as he does about preaching and evangelism. His views on counseling will be matters of opinion and conscience. He can believe what he wants about counseling, as long as he is able to profess the right answer to the technical theological question about sanctification.

Imagine, then, that AJ must deal with Roger, a troubled church member. Roger is emotionally volatile, given to fits of rage, bouts of depression, and restlessly pervasive anxiety. His relationships with others are estranged, and his work history is spotty. As a pastor in the PCA, AJ could take any of many fundamentally different approaches toward Roger. Perhaps Roger could be sent to a Meier New Life Clinic, put on a course of Prozac, and taught the principles of *Love Is a Choice*. Perhaps AJ could counsel Roger according to Larry Crabb's *Inside Out* model, teaching him to explore his pain and disappointment at primary care-givers, in order to refocus his deep longings for relationship onto the Lord. Roger could be sent to a secular psychiatrist to get Prozac to level his moods.

AJ could attempt to identify and cast out demons of anger. Roger could be referred to a secular psychologist for cognitive-behavioral retooling that would inculcate stoic rationalism rather than a relationship with the living Savior. AJ could give Roger a course of study in basic Christian doctrines or a concentrated dose of a particular doctrine or a Navigators 2:7 study. AJ need not believe in counseling at all but might assert that sitting under the preaching of the Word, participating in corporate worship, and cultivating a more consistent devotional life will be sufficient to cure what ails Roger. Or AJ might seek to understand and counsel Roger according to the thought forms and practices of biblical counseling, as best he understood things (which might include components from the various options mentioned above). In any case it is his choice what Roger will receive. AJ will not be taught, questioned, supervised, or disciplined about that choice.

How can this problem be remedied? Let me identify five needs. First, the church needs to *become wise in the face-to-face care of souls.* We cannot practice, teach, or regulate what we do not know how to do or think. Much of the plausibility of the VITEX position does not arise from its intellectual plausibility but from the practical reality that the church has been poor in understanding and enabling the processes of change. We must articulate wisdom conceptually, we must become wise methodologically, and we must incarnate wisdom institutionally. Let us highlight the institutional. When people are troubled or troublesome, who will help them? Where is the social location of that aid? How long will it last? What forms of help are offered? Because all ministry costs money, how will help be funded? I believe that the COMPIN position will sound increasingly plausible as mature biblical counseling characterizes the grassroots practice and structures of the church of Jesus Christ.

Second, we need *creedal standards* for the care and cure of souls, or at least a widely recognized corpus of practical theological writing. A system of practical theology is something to which we can subscribe, toward which we can aim educationally, on the basis of which we can be supervised and challenged regarding our faith and practice. Currently, the requisite "faith and practice" does not include views of counseling (except by extension and application from historical formulations that generalize about the nature of ministry, human nature, and progressive sanctification). Our faith and practice need to be extended to include personality theory, counseling methodology, dynamics of change, and delivery systems for the care of souls.

Third, we need *educational institutions* committed to the Bible's distinctive model of understanding persons and change. For many years seminaries taught virtually nothing substantive about progressive sanctification and the particulars of hands-on, case-wise, heart-searching, life-rearranging care for souls. Since the mid-1960s there has been a massive effort to create counseling programs and departments, but the results are very spotty in terms of consistent biblical thinking. Christian colleges typically contain a psychology department. But, typically, neither seminary nor college teaches things that significantly differ from what a secular institution would teach. Most institutions give a junior version of secular theory and methods or prepare students for graduate education in mental health professions or make students "ordainable" with those state-licensed professions. Few teach how to understand and counsel people in ways harmonious with the Bible's vision for the cure of souls.

Fourth, we need cure of souls to become part of the church's *qualifying procedures* that recognize fit candidates for ministry. Licensure, ordination, and accreditation usually occur on two levels. One level qualifies the pastoral leadership, ordination, per se. Skill in counseling individuals, couples, and families must become as important as doctrinal fidelity and as skill in speaking to crowds. The second level qualifies members of local churches to function in grassroots ministry under the authority of pastor and elders. Here is where most skilled counseling, whether formal or informal, will occur. Most psychotherapists are laypersons—not professionals—ecclesiastically, whatever their secular credentials. Are they willing to submit their theories, methods, and structures to the church's professional oversight, to subscribe to a distinctly Christian model of persons and change?[30]

Fifth, we need ecclesiastically grounded *supervisory structures* for cure of souls. The secular mental health professions usually offer continuing education, case supervision, and discipline for morals offenses (breach of trust in sexual, financial, or confidentiality matters). The church has often offered continuing education in the form of books, seminars, and doctor of ministry programs. The church has often disciplined for morals or doctrinal offenses. But cure of souls tends to drop through the cracks; it is an optional activity with optional beliefs and practices. Case supervision and case discussion are clear needs within local churches. Ecclesiastical supervision ought to be extensive over the faith and practice of cure of souls, both in local churches and at higher ecclesiastical levels. It matters what theories and ideas are being mediated to counselees. A secular psychotherapist can freely adopt any of many theoretical orientations—behavioral, cognitive, psychodynamic, existential, somatic, and so on—or can hold theory loosely and function multimodally. The church does not believe in such theoretical diversity but aims to refine its doctrine to cohere with the gaze of God revealed in the Bible.

Current ecclesiastical structures, functions, standards, and competencies are far removed from what I am proposing. Perhaps it sounds ludicrous even to propose that the church get a grip on cure of souls. Counseling is renegade from God and truth within the culture; counseling is largely a runaway from the church even within the church. But without such wisdoms of truth, practice, and social structure, we as the people of God court trouble. In the previous section we considered the prevalence of secular motivation theories in the cure of souls. Such ideas would not last five minutes if they were examined in a decent systematic theology class on human nature. But the shoe fits on the other foot, too. The current state of most ecclesiastical structures, theoretical development, and definitions of ministry for the cure of souls would not last five minutes in a secular counseling class on how to go deep and hang in for the long haul with a troubled person. In the pages of the Bible we have a social model the secular world can only dream about. The Bible's vision seamlessly joins specialized competency with community and peer resources. It animates both nurturing and remedial functions. It comforts those who suffer; it transforms those whose lives are misformed; and it does both at the same time. But in the practice of the extant church, both the defined specialists in curing soul and the community of care often fall woefully short of biblical understanding and competency.

Those who rightly tout the centrality of the church face a dilemma because the church has few structures that facilitate and regulate the hands-on cure of souls. What if the conceptual and structural defects of secularity among psychotherapists are mirrored by the intellectual and structural defects of religiosity among pastors and other Christian workers? It is fine to call Christians to practice and seek cure of souls in submission to the local church. But the church needs to become a far better place to come under.

The intellectual leading edge of VITEX— What things can we adopt from the disciplines of psychology?—has masked a serious defect in the social structure for delivering counsel. To orient face-to-face cure of souls toward the mental health professions is fundamentally, even disastrously, wrong-headed. At the same time, the commitments of COMPIN—my own commitments—toward church-oriented counseling ministry are years and decades from significant institutional realization.

What must we do now? Jesus calls us to row our boat in the right direction, however far away the destination seems. He is committed to complete us together in the maturity of his wisdom. Ephesians 4 both gives our modus operandi and our goal. I hope this very article serves as one small "speaking the truth in love" (Eph. 4:15 ESV) in the direction of perfecting the collective wisdom, love, and power of the people of God. We must each labor to disassemble autonomous professionalism rather than to further assembling it. We must each labor to make our professed loyalty to the church a significant reality rather than a hollow profession of good intentions.

Conclusion

I am firmly committed to that point of view I have labeled COMPIN. I do not think that the VITEX epistemological priorities can equip us to understand and help people. We need our own robust, comprehensive theory—our own paradigm—to guide our interaction with the "human documents" entrusted to our care. We need our own paradigm to guide interaction with the secular models that "read" and attempt to "edit" those documents in ways significantly different from God's reading and editing. We need our own paradigm to become incarnate institutionally. We need a fresh practical theology of the cure of souls. This is a corporate work-in-progress, an agenda, a presuppositional gaze that seeks to be faithful to the Word of our Redeemer. It coheres with orthodox theology about God, about persons, and about the in-working and outworking of grace. It is distinctly different conceptually and structurally from the world's counseling models. It recognizes historical and current defects in the Bible-believing church's understanding of human nature and proposed remedies but does not let that recognition rationalize a flight from biblical resources.

I propose no return to pietism, moralism, or exorcism, let alone sacerdotalism, doctrinalism, or any other reassertion of a "spiritual" sector of life. I am not inviting counselors to inhabit some windowless, sectarian hovel. I have sought to describe a large house with wide-open doors and with picture windows gazing on all life, a habitation in which all God's people can thrive. I hold no bias against Christians who happen to have mental health education and credentials, but they must grasp that there is no inherent bias in their favor, either. They must recognize that their education and credentials have not prepared them to cure and care for souls but for offering a different cure and care, a different wisdom.[31] When it comes to cure of souls, the question for Christian mental health professionals, just as for Christians who have ecclesiastical credentials and education, is: Do you think and practice in fidelity to the mind of God? Whether in a local church or at higher ecclesiastical levels, whether in a parachurch or even "secular settings," only biblically wise people should qualify to counsel other people.

Counseling, when it comes into its own, will cohere intellectually and structurally with every other form of the church's ministry: worship, preaching, teaching, discipleship, child-rearing, friendship, evangelism, mercy works, missions, and pastoral leadership. Counseling ought to operate within the same worldview and with the same agenda that all ministry for Christ must have. I hope that what I have proposed, general as it is, merits the adjectives *biblical* and *Christian*. My recommendations are a creation forged from the Word of God for our time and place, for our questions, for our tumults. I have attempted to sketch faithful answers to burning contemporary questions. The church stands at a crossroads regarding these questions. We cannot go just any way, or both ways, or every which way, except to our harm. We could go bad ways, lurching either into sectarianism or into syncretism. But I hope that I have mapped the good way forward. I hope that I have described for our times one essential part of the "building up of the body of Christ, until we all attain to the unity of the faith, and of the knowledge of the Son of God" (Eph. 4:12f).

This essay began with a comment about the difficulty of finding and keeping one's bearings amid the tumults and animosities that gust through times of great revolution. It is worth closing on the note of clear confidence with which Paul closes 1 Thessalonians. One day we who love Christ will be collectively conformed to final wisdom: "May the God of peace himself sanctify you completely. . . . He who calls you is faithful; he will surely do it" (1 Thess. 5:23f ESV).

Appendix 4 Notes

1. William Duane, an American historian writing in 1798 about the French Revolution even as events continued to unfold, cited in Richard N. Rosenfeld, *American Aurora* (New York: St. Martin's, 1997), 11.

2. I am not implying that the living God does not sustain and transform his chosen people through times when our ability to systematically articulate his ways is weak. The grassroots wisdom of godly people often far exceeds what is written in both secular and Christian counseling books. The Holy Spirit often works despite our ignorance in articulating his ways. Plain folks, without a whisper of counseling training, will often size up others insightfully and communicate to them the honey and light of timely biblical wisdom. They will read a best-selling counseling book and comment, "I liked xyz, but abc didn't seem right to me." Their discernment—not analysis but instinct—is frequently profound. God does sustain his own, but where our articulated understanding of truth is defective we become vulnerable to deviant and distracting theories, for which we pay a price in confusion and harm. A well-systematized biblical counseling model will not transcend grassroots wisdom but will express, encourage, and defend such wisdom.

3. For a description of how liberal-psychological pastoral theology eclipsed conservative-soteriological pastoral theology, see E. Brooks Holifield, *A History of Pastoral Care in America: From Salvation to Self-Realization* (Nashville: Abingdon Press, 1983). For a description of how secular mental health professions subordinated mainline pastoral care, see Andrew Abbott, *The System of Professions: An Essay on the Division of Expert Labor* (Chicago: University of Chicago Press, 1988).

4. Brief descriptions of this revolution among evangelical believers—from varying points of view—can be found in Jay Adams, *Lectures on Counseling* (Grand Rapids: Zondervan, 1975–77); Donald Capps, "The Bible's Role in Pastoral Care and Counseling: Four Basic Principles," *Journal of Theology and Christianity* 3, no. 4 (1984): 5–15; George M. Marsden, *Reforming Fundamentalism: Fuller Seminary and the New Evangelicalism* (Grand Rapids: William B. Eerdmans, 1987). An extended description of the issues raised in the last two paragraphs is found in David Powlison, "Competent to Counsel?: The History of a Conservative Protestant Biblical Counseling Movement" (PhD diss., University of Pennsylvania, 1996, 2nd ed., 2006).

5. Eric L. Johnson, "A Place for the Bible in Psychological Science," *Journal of Psychology and Theology* 20 (1992): 346–55. Johnson comments insightfully on the communication breakdown caused by posturing, polemics, and disparaging labels. Of course, we must generalize if we are to speak in any context wider than private conversation, and I will generalize in this essay. But I hope to do so in a constructive way.

6. "Cure of souls" refers to the transformation of individual lives and communal life into the image of Jesus Christ. "Care of souls" refers to the pastoral processes aiming to bring about such changes in others. The former is the goal; the latter is the method. As is always so in the dynamic of the gospel, those being cured learn how to care.

7. A good summary of the difference between biblicism and *sola scriptura* can be found in John Frame, "In Defense of Something Close to Biblicism: Reflections on *Sola Scriptura* and History in Theological Method," *Westminster Theological Journal* 59 (1997): 269–91.

8. At the most rudimentary level, the Bible itself teaches us that ministry does not always lead out with a Bible verse. We read in Acts 13:14–41 that Paul cited and applied specific "chapter and verse" with a timeliness that created an uproar of interest in his hearers. In Acts 14:8–18 we see that he gained entry by a loving action, vigorously identified with his hearers and then discussed everyday human experiences, weaving in biblical truth without specific citation. In Acts 17:16–34 we read that Paul began by talking about some observations that had given him pause. He went on to cite their own poets and philosophers—the psychologists and psychotherapists of that day—co-opting their words to proclaim Jesus, to call to a change of mind, and to awaken lively concern about the day when our lives will be weighed in the balance. How did Paul know the difference? Case-wisdom. He had come to know people through his diverse experience in applying the singular message of the Bible.

9. The introductory chapters of Stanton L. Jones and Richard Butman, *Modern Psychotherapies: A Comprehensive Christian Appraisal* (Downers Grove, IL: InterVarsity Press, 1991) and of David Powlison, *Seeing with New Eyes: Counseling and the Human Condition Through the Lens of Scripture* (Phillipsburg, N.J.: P & R, 2003) capture the differences in emphasis from the insufficiency and sufficiency points of view, respectively.

10. I am among this number. I majored in psychology as an undergraduate, then worked for four years in psychiatric hospitals, intending to go on to graduate school in clinical psychology. My conversion to Christ rerouted me to seminary.

11. Articles, reviews, and bibliographies in the *Journal of Biblical Counseling* provide an entry point into the literature. In my view, one regrettable aspect of the debates in print is that evangelical psychologists continue to cite only Jay Adams's earliest works, *Competent to Counsel* (1970) and *The Christian Counselor's Manual* (1973), seemingly unaware of thirty-five years of development. One introduction to further developments is David Powlison, "Crucial Issues in Contemporary Biblical Counseling," *Journal of Biblical Counseling* 9, no. 3 (1988): 53–78.

12. Though a sharp social divide has existed between integrationist psychologists (approximately VITEX) and biblical counselors (approximately COMPIN), my definition muddies that divide a bit, adding some immediate twists and nuances. For example, coming out of Wheaton College, Stan Jones and Richard Butman's *Modern Psychotherapies* is a classic articulation of VITEX, but Robert Roberts, *Taking the Word to Heart: Self and Others in an Age of Therapies* (Grand Rapids: William B. Eerdmans, 1993), comes within a millimeter of COMPIN. Intending to "mitigate the Christian captivity to psychology," Roberts says that "A Christian psychology would not *have* to be pursued in dialogue with secular psychology" (p. 14).

Clearer categories help focus discussion but never solve all vexed questions. For example, the adjectives *vital* and *comprehensive* contain ambiguities. The concrete implications need to be fleshed out.

Furthermore, clearer definition does not answer whether the actual products (theory and practice) live up to a person's stated commitments. For example, most COMPIN advocates, myself included, disagree with the motivation theories and views of personhood proposed by Larry Crabb and John Eldredge. Crabb and Eldredge voice COMPIN commitments, as I do. But what any of us thinks the Bible teaches is fair game for evaluation. Part III of this extended article bears on the particular question of motivation theory.

As a similar example from the VITEX position, Jones and Butman have said that "too much of what passes for integration today is anemic theologically or biblically and tends to be little more than a spiritualized rehashing of mainstream mental health thought" (p. 415; cf., pp. 29ff). They are articulately critical of the many lightly Christianized pop psychologies.

13. In fact, Jay Adams opened *Competent to Counsel* not by criticizing psychology but by criticizing the Bible-believing church's impoverishment in what it thought was biblical counseling. He did not consider "read the Bible, pray, yield, or cast out a demon" to be adequate either as a reflection of Scripture or as a way to meet human need. His *Insight and Creativity in Christian Counseling* (Grand Rapids: Zondervan, 1982) was an extended critique of the tendency of biblical counselors to fall into a cookbook mentality. I critiqued the demon-deliverance movement as a reversion to superstition and animism in the name of biblical counseling in David Powlison, *Power Encounters: Reclaiming Spiritual Warfare* (Grand Rapids: Baker Book House, 1995).

14. All that I have said about appropriating, working with, and learning from what is around us is no less true of what is within us. We make our own experience normative to our peril. Experience is not autonomous, self-interpreting, or self-interpreted (except in sin's delusion). The truth of the mind of Christ (priority one) critiques us (priority two) and remakes us, folding and reinterpreting all of life's particular learning and experience (priority three) into God's pattern and story (priority one).

15. The next section of this essay offers a sketch of how God explains and interprets human motivation—and he gets both first say and final say on how people tick! The second half of my *Seeing with New Eyes* (Phillipsburg, N.J.: P & R, 2003) is a collection of essays on these topics.

16. See, for example, Mike Emlet, "Obsessions and Compulsions: Breaking Free of the Tyranny," *Journal of Biblical Counseling* 22, no. 2 (2004): 15–26, and David Powlison, "Is the 'Adonis Complex' in Your Bible?," *Journal of Biblical Counseling* 22, no. 4 (2004): 42–58.

17. Paul J. Griffiths, "Metaphysics and Personality Theory" in *Limning the Psyche: Explorations in Christian Psychology*, eds. Robert C. Roberts and Mark R. Talbot (Grand Rapids: William B. Eerdmans, 1997), 41–57; Timothy J. Keller, "Puritan Resources for Biblical Counseling," *Journal of Pastoral Practice* 9, no. 3 (1988): 11–44; Thomas C. Oden, *Classical Pastoral Care*, vol. 3, *Pastoral Counsel* (Grand Rapids: Baker Book House, 1987); Roberts, *Taking the Word to Heart*; Dennis Kohl, "To Vent or Not to Vent?," in *Care for the Soul: Exploring the Intersection of Psychology and Theology*, eds. Mark McMinn and Timothy Phillips (Downers Grove, Ill.: InterVarsity Press, 2001).

18. John Murray, *Collected Writings* (Edinburgh: Banner of Truth, 1982), 9.

19. Roberts, *Taking the Word to Heart*, 14. His two reasons are consistent with COMPIN: (1) the fact that psychology is part of our cultural surround and (2) the fact that we can learn some things, while maintaining our distinctive point of view.

20. Robert Roberts, "Psychology and the Life of the Spirit," *Journal of Biblical Counseling* 15, no. 1 (1996): 26–31.

21. See John Frame, "Scripture and the Apologetic Task," *Journal of Biblical Counseling* 13, no. 2 (1995): 9–12, for a stimulating discussion of matter and manner in defending the faith.

22. Of course, the sinless Lamb of God was not himself a sinner. But he entered the experience of temptation, immediately experiencing the dynamics of choice between light and darkness. And he entered the plight of sinners by identification, fully bearing the due wrath.

23. Sin's very logic produces these distortions in the view of sin, for sin is elusive and evasive. As an aside, if I were to add another section to this article, I would discuss the interplay of situational variables with our sins in a cursed, redeemable world.

The Bible is clear how God's sovereign and immediate purposes play out in our reactions to being sinned against, diverse somatic problems, sociocultural conditioning, the devil, suffering, misery, temptation, and so forth. There are many fine Christian books on suffering and on God's purposes within suffering (things about which the psychologies are ignorant); I will leave the reader to those sources.

24. COMPIN only drops the word *constitutive* from that last sentence, and adds that because science is not neutral and objective; its findings must always be evaluated and reinterpreted by Christian presuppositions.

25. Roger Hurding, *The Tree of Healing* (Grand Rapids: Zondervan, 1985) is an exception to the ritual charge that Adams is against "psychology." He recognized Adams's principal willingness to learn from and interact with secular psychological knowledge and theory but accurately observed that this was not a "developed argument" in Adams's overall writing and practice (285).

26. See Jay E. Adams, *The Christian Counselor's Manual* (USA: Presbyterian & Reformed, 1973), 71–93; and Jay E. Adams, *Lectures on Counseling* (Grand Rapids: Zondervan, 1976), 31f. See extended discussion of Adams's views of psychology in chapter 7 of this publication. Adams's transformationist attitude toward culture is most apparent in his attitudes toward medicine. He is less interested in and more suspicious of the social sciences but never denies that things can be learned from anyone and everywhere. In *The Christian Counselor's Manual* (p. 80), he even cited a swami favorably! Adams's willingness to appropriate and rework insights from secular theorists is most evident in his discussions of moralistic therapies (e.g., Mowrer and Glasser) and existentialists (e.g., Frankl). No doubt, if Aaron Beck's cognitive-behavioral therapy had been prominent in the early 1970s when Adams wrote in this vein, Beck would have come in for treatment similar to what was extended to the moralists and existentialists. Adams rarely demonstrated the same sort of carefully critical appreciation when discussing psychodynamic and humanistic psychologists, which in my view is a weakness in how he applied what he believed. The playing field is level, and none of the secular psychologies are either uniquely privileged or uniquely hobbled in comparison to each other.

27. Jay E. Adams, *More Than Redemption: A Theology of Christian Counseling* (Phillipsburg, N.J.: Presbyterian & Reformed,

1979), ix–15; Jay E. Adams, "Counseling and the Sovereignty of God," *Journal of Biblical Counseling* 11, no. 2 (1993): 4–9.

28. It is not necessarily wrong for Christians to work within the secular mental health system, if they can do so without being forced to communicate false ideas, diagnostically and prescriptively, to those they counsel. Sometimes in God's common grace, Christians are given great freedom within an ostensibly secular setting. But Christians in such settings must realize that when they are barred from mentioning sin and Christ, then they can only describe problems, but they cannot accurately diagnose them; they can only suggest the outward shell of solutions, but they cannot get to the deep issues that plague the heart. Christians in such settings are still free to love people, to know them, and to provide various outward mercies, but they are limited to being relatively superficial and moralistic in the content of their counsel. Unfortunately, in my observation, well-meaning Christians in mental health settings typically are far more profoundly socialized and enculturated than they realize. They fail to recognize that they are working in a radioactive zone, and they absorb faulty diagnostic, explanatory, and treatment models without knowing that they have done so.

29. I do not mean that there is not a carefully circumscribed place for parachurch, specialized ministries. They can often serve useful auxiliary roles with a scope beyond what a particular local church might be able to do. But they need to remember they are valuable but barely legitimate and only ought to exist when they genuinely and consciously serve the interests of the community whose mature functioning will put them out of business. Autonomous psychotherapeutic professionalism competes with, rather than serves, those interests.

30. The typical professional self-image of Christian mental health personnel is that they are at the top of the pyramid of wisdom, competency, and legitimacy; that pastors are at the midlevel; and that laypersons are at the bottom. The biblical image has true pastors at the top of the pyramid, with laypersons of all sorts functioning under their oversight. This biblical image must define our corporate task. Psychotherapeutic professionalism works at odds to that task, and each increment of progress in that task will mean a further repudiating and abandoning of professionalistic social structures as defective, redundant, and counterproductive.

31. Robert Roberts's *Taking the Word to Heart* is provocative in this regard.

Note on Sources

Since this is a history of a largely undocumented movement, I have worked almost entirely with primary sources: writings, interviews, transcriptions, and case records. The following pages describe the sources available to me.

The primary writings in nouthetic counseling consist of approximately one hundred books and pamphlets published since 1970 and some five hundred articles and editorials published chiefly in the *Journal of Pastoral Practice* (since 1977).[1] Jay Adams was by far the dominant writer, both in quantity and in magisterial authority. He published about sixty books and scores of short pieces. Until the 1990s, most other authors were fundamentally derivative, filling in details where Adams either had painted in broad strokes or had merely gestured in a direction that he thought needed further work.

Let me orient the reader to the pre-1995 biblical counseling literature.* It can be divided into six genres: (1) programmatic articulations of Adams's philosophy of counseling and the basics of his methodology; (2) supplemental counseling issues, treating particular topics of interest to counselors; (3) practical, didactic helps and self-helps for counselees, directly applying the counseling method to particular problems in living; (4) instructions on preaching, targeting the public ministry of preaching as complementary to the private ministry of counseling; (5) general pastoring, treating varied aspects of "shepherding God's flock" besides counseling and preaching; and (6) doctrinal expositions of classic theological issues.

First, Adams considered four of his books to provide a fundamental, programmatic orientation to nouthetic counseling.[2] *Competent to Counsel* sounded the call to reject the medical model and various psychotherapeutic systems. It reconceptualized counseling as a fundamentally pastoral activity addressing the problems in living as fundamentally moral problems. Adams thought that behavior, belief, meaning, values, attitudes, purposes, desires, and the like could be rationally categorized, assessed, and addressed in explicitly biblical-theological terms. *The Christian Counselor's Manual* restated and further developed Adams's basic philosophy and outlined in some detail the methods of Adams's directive counseling model. *Lectures on Counseling* brought together five shorter essays. Three of these sought to win potential followers among seminary and college students, by proclaiming Adams's interpretation of the warfare for jurisdiction over the tasks of

---

* I have not attempted to update the bibliography beyond the time frame of this project.

explaining and addressing sin and misery. *More Than Redemption* sought to ground counseling in the systematic theology of historic Reformed orthodoxy: the doctrine of God, the doctrine of human nature, the doctrine of sanctification. Adams gave traditional doctrines a counseling slant. Andrew Abbott has written of how crucial redefinition of problems is in interprofessional jurisdictional conflict.[3] Adams's strategy provides an unusual example of this process. He submitted his redefinitions not to the mental health community, as a set of interpretations competing in the wider marketplace. Rather much of his work aimed at redefining or extending the scope of meaning and relevancy of theological terms that were familiar to his primary audience—pastors—but had not been applied to counseling.[4]

Second, Adams and others wrote numerous books and articles on specialized topics intended to inform and train counselors. This category includes Adams's translation of the New Testament and his books on marriage counseling, creativity in counseling, divorce, self-esteem, crisis counseling, training counselors, and case studies. Other authors wrote on topics ranging from interpersonal reconciliation to anti-psychology polemics to neurophysiology.[5] Most articles in the *Journal of Pastoral Practice* consisted of such topical studies.

Third, Adams and others wrote many short, popular pieces intended to offer direct help to counselees who struggled with particular problems: suffering, marital and other interpersonal conflict, fear, worry, depression, child-rearing, and the like. The self-help genre included pamphlets, tracts, workbooks, Bible studies, and other expositions of what might be termed "practical Christian living."

Fourth, Adams wrote a dozen books on preaching. This is neither incidental nor coincidental to his attempt to inspire a counseling revolution. Defining a conceptual coherence between the content and goals of preaching and counseling lay at the heart of his strategy to convince conservative Protestants to embrace his counseling system. He conceived of counseling as private ministry of the Word and connected counseling intellectually and methodologically to the public ministry of the Word from the pulpit.

Fifth, Adams wrote a number of books and articles on what might be termed topics in general pastoring: church discipline, Christian education, visitation, missions, and a miscellany of other topics. His two pieces on education—*Back to the Blackboard* dealing with primary and secondary education, and "Design for a Theological Seminary"—articulated his concern that educational philosophy in Christian institutions was largely impractical. He contended that much of the weakness of pastors in counseling derived from inadequacies in preparation. Seminary graduates could spot and rebut a nineteenth-century German liberal theologian—should they ever happen to meet one—but did not know how to put a marriage back together or help someone who was depressed.[6]

Sixth, Adams and others affiliated with the biblical counseling movement wrote a number of books and tracts on traditional theological topics: baptism, eschatology, the problem of evil, the sovereignty of God, limited atonement. Most of these books were written early in the authors' careers, before they focused the bulk of their attention on counseling and other aspects of practical theology.

The many critics of nouthetic counseling also wrote frequently in response. Adams stirred up a tempest among conservative Christians in the counseling professions. These many responses provided a second trove of primary source material on the jurisdictional conflict, and figured significantly in chapter 8. Adams was frequently discussed in monographs that would devote anywhere from a paragraph to a page to a chapter to him. He was the subject of scores of book reviews (particularly in the 1970s) and a number of dissertations. He was cautiously commended by some and sharply criticized by many. Adams and his critics met face-to-face on several occasions, and I gained access to detailed records—notes or transcripts—from two forums (1969 and 1979) where Adams and his critics debated at length.

Interviews and case records filled out the primary sources that I used. In addition to reading their publications, I was able to interview many of the founders, developers, and leaders of nouthetic counseling. I was also able to interview or correspond with a number of Adams's opponents. Face-to-face conversation added depth and texture to my impressions, corrected numerous misimpressions, and filled in areas of outright ignorance.

I also was granted access to the case files at the Christian Counseling and Educational Foundation (CCEF) from 1968 to the present. Adams had founded CCEF primarily in order to offer a site where pastors and seminarians could be trained through participant observation in counseling. The CCEF archives contained more than 10,000 files for individual, marital, and family counseling. I analyzed some 600 files, taken at random from each of three time periods. I took the first set of cases from 1968–74, when nouthetic counseling was being created by Jay Adams, and he was the primary counselor at CCEF. The second set of cases was taken from 1979–81, when a second generation of counselors began practicing at CCEF. The third set of cases was taken from 1990–91. I had two chief purposes in analyzing the case records. The first purpose was to map the demographics of the clientele. Who sought out this sort of counseling? What were the lines of referral? What were the characteristics of counselees: religious background and commitment,

marital and socioeconomic status, gender, age, constellation of presenting problems, counselee expectations of counseling, and so forth. By taking samples at ten-year intervals, I also sought to find whether there were changes in the counselee population over time. The second, and secondary, purpose was to gain a subjective feel for the methods and emphases of counselors. The case records were a rich source of demographic detail but did not easily yield quantifiable data on matters of counseling process or outcome. They abounded, however, in the sort of information that added texture, color, and detail to the books describing counseling method.

Sources Notes

1. This journal was renamed the *Journal of Biblical Counseling* in 1992.

2. Jay E. Adams, *Ready to Restore: The Layman's Guide to Christian Counseling* (Phillipsburg, N.J.: Presbyterian & Reformed, 1981), vii. These four books were Adams, *Competent to Counsel;* Adams, *The Christian Counselor's Manual* (USA: Presbyterian & Reformed, 1973); Adams, *Lectures on Counseling* (Grand Rapids: Zondervan, 1975–77); Adams, *More Than Redemption: A Theology of Christian Counseling* (Phillipsburg, N.J.: Presbyterian & Reformed, 1979).

3. Andrew Abbott, *The System of Professions: An Essay on the Division of Expert Labor* (Chicago: University of Chicago Press, 1988), 36–44, 98.

4. Books by other authors that might be considered programmatic are Martin Bobgan and Deidre Bobgan, *How to Counsel from Scripture* (Chicago: Moody Press, 1985); Michael W. Bobick, *From Slavery to Sonship: A Biblical Psychology for Pastoral Counseling* (USA: Michael W. Bobick, 1989); John MacArthur and Wayne Mack, *Introduction to Biblical Counseling: A Basic Guide to the Principles and Practice of Counseling* (Dallas: Word Publishing, 1994).

5. For example, Richard Ganz, *Psychobabble: The Failure of Modern Psychology—and the Biblical Alternative* (Wheaton, Ill.: Crossway Books, 1993); Ken Sande, *The Peacemaker: A Biblical Guide to Resolving Personal Conflict* (Grand Rapids: Baker Book House, 1991); Edward T. Welch, *Counselor's Guide to the Brain and Its Disorders: Knowing the Difference Between Disease and Sin* (Grand Rapids: Zondervan, 1991).

6. Jay E. Adams, "Design for a Theological Seminary," *Journal of Pastoral Practice* 3, no. 2 (1979): 1–10; Adams, *Back to the Blackboard: Design for a Biblical Christian School* (Phillipsburg, N.J.: Presbyterian & Reformed, 1982).

Bibliography

Abbott, Andrew. *The System of Professions: An Essay on the Division of Expert Labor*. Chicago: University of Chicago Press, 1988.

Abraham, Raju. "Jay Adams: He Is Biblical Enough." *Third Way* (June 1982): 12f.

Adams, Jay E. "An Open Letter to Former United Presbyterians." *Bible Presbyterian Record* (January 1959a): 15.

———. *Realized Millennialism: A Study in Biblical Eschatology*. St. Louis: Jay Edward Adams, 1959b.

———. *The Time Is at Hand*. Greenville, S.C.: A Press, 1966.

———. "Behind the Study Door." Part 1. *The Presbyterian Guardian* (April 1968): 39f.

———. *Competent to Counsel*. USA: Presbyterian & Reformed, 1970.

———. *Christ and Your Problems*. Nutley, N.J.: Presbyterian & Reformed, 1971a.

———. "Group Therapy—or Slander?" *The Presbyterian Guardian* (February 1971b): 25–27.

———. *The Big Umbrella and Other Essays and Addresses on Christian Counseling*. USA: Presbyterian and Reformed, 1972a.

———. *Christian Living in the Home*. Phillipsburg, N.J.: Presbyterian & Reformed, 1972b.

———. "Counseling, Pastoral." In *The Encyclopedia of Christianity*, vol. 3, edited by Philip E. Hughes, 188–90. Marshallton, Del.: The National Foundation for Christian Education, 1972c.

———. "Victor E. Frankl." In *The Encyclopedia of Christianity*, vol. 4, edited by Philip E. Hughes, 244–46. Marshallton, Del.: The National Foundation for Christian Education, 1972d.

———. *Godliness through Discipline*. Phillipsburg, N.J.: Presbyterian & Reformed, 1972e.

———. *The Christian Counselor's Manual*. USA: Presbyterian & Reformed, 1973.

———. "The Pastoral Life." In *Shepherding God's Flock Series: A Handbook on Pastoral Ministry, Counseling, and Leadership*. USA: Presbyterian & Reformed, 1974.

———. *Shepherding God's Flock Series: A Handbook on Pastoral Ministry, Counseling, and Leadership*. Grand Rapids: Zondervan, 1974–75.

———. *Counseling and the Sovereignty of God*. Philadelphia: Westminster Theological Seminary, 1975a.

———. *The Meaning and Mode of Baptism*. Phillipsburg, N.J.: Presbyterian & Reformed, 1975b.

———. *Studies in Preaching*. Vol. 3, *The Homiletical Innovations of Andrew W. Blackwood*. USA: Presbyterian & Reformed, 1975c.

———. *What Do You Do When Anger Gets the Upper Hand?* Phillipsburg, N.J.: Presbyterian & Reformed, 1975d.

———. *What Do You Do When Fear Overcomes You?* Phillipsburg, N.J: Presbyterian & Reformed, 1975e.

———. *What Do You Do When You Become Depressed?* Phillipsburg, N.J.: Presbyterian & Reformed, 1975f.

———. *What Do You Do When You Know That You're Hooked?* Phillipsburg, N.J.: Presbyterian & Reformed, 1975g.

———. *What Do You Do When You Worry All the Time?* Phillipsburg, N.J.: Presbyterian & Reformed, 1975h.

———. *What Do You Do When Your Marriage Goes Sour?* Phillipsburg, N.J.: Presbyterian & Reformed, 1975i.

———. *Your Place in the Counseling Revolution.* Nutley, N.J.: Presbyterian & Reformed, 1975j.

———. *Lectures on Counseling.* Grand Rapids: Zondervan, 1975–77.

———. "The Christian Approach to Schizophrenia." In *The Construction of Madness: Emerging Conceptions and Interventions into the Psychotic Process,* edited by Peter A. Magaro, 133–50. New York: Pergamon Press, 1976a.

———. *Coping with Counseling Crises: First Aid for Christian Counselors.* USA: Presbyterian & Reformed, 1976b.

———. *Pulpit Speech: A Textbook for Use in the Classroom or Study.* USA: Presbyterian & Reformed, 1976c.

———. *Studies in Preaching.* Vol. 2, *Audience Adaptation in the Sermons and Speeches of Paul.* USA: Presbyterian & Reformed, 1976d.

———. *What About Nouthetic Counseling?* Grand Rapids, Michigan: Baker Book House, 1976e.

———. *Change Them?. . . into What?: Counseling in America Today.* Laverock, Pa.: Christian Counseling and Educational Foundation, 1977a.

———. *The Christian Counselor's New Testament: A New Translation in Everyday English with Notations, Marginal References, and Supplemental Helps.* USA: Presbyterian & Reformed, 1977b.

———. Editorial. *Journal of Pastoral Practice* 1 (1): 1f (1977c).

———. *How to Overcome Evil.* Nutley, N.J.: Presbyterian & Reformed, 1977d.

———. *Four Weeks with God and Your Neighbor: A Devotional Workbook for Counselees and Others.* USA: Presbyterian & Reformed, 1978a.

———. *The Power of Error: Demonstrated in an Actual Counseling Case.* USA: Presbyterian & Reformed, 1978b.

———. "Design for a Theological Seminary." *Journal of Pastoral Practice* 3 (2): 1–10 (1979a).

———. *More Than Redemption: A Theology of Christian Counseling.* Phillipsburg, N.J.: Presbyterian & Reformed, 1979b.

———. *Prayers for Troubled Times.* Grand Rapids: Baker Book House, 1979c.

———. *A Theology of Christian Counseling: More Than Redemption.* Grand Rapids: Zondervan, 1979d.

———. *Marriage, Divorce, and Remarriage in the Bible.* Grand Rapids: Zondervan, 1980a.

———. *What to Do about Worry.* Phillipsburg, N.J.: Presbyterian & Reformed, 1980b.

———. *The Christian Counselor's Workbook: A Primer of Nouthetic Counseling.* Phillipsburg, N.J.: Presbyterian & Reformed, 1981a.

———. *Counseling and the Five Points of Calvinism.* Phillipsburg, N.J.: Presbyterian & Reformed, 1981b.

———. *The Language of Counseling.* Phillipsburg, N.J.: Presbyterian & Reformed, 1981c.

———. *Ready to Restore: The Layman's Guide to Christian Counseling.* Phillipsburg, N.J.: Presbyterian & Reformed, 1981d.

———. *Back to the Blackboard: Design for a Biblical Christian School.* Phillipsburg, N.J.: Presbyterian & Reformed, 1982a.

———. *How to Handle Trouble: God's Way.* Phillipsburg, N.J.: Presbyterian & Reformed, 1982b.

———. *Insight & Creativity in Christian Counseling: An Antidote to Rigid and Mechanical Approaches.* Grand Rapids: Zondervan, 1982c.

————. *Preaching with Purpose: A Comprehensive Textbook on Biblical Preaching.* Phillipsburg, N.J.: Presbyterian & Reformed, 1982d.

————. *Truth Apparent: Essays on Biblical Preaching.* Phillipsburg, N.J.: Presbyterian & Reformed, 1982e.

————. *What to Do on Thursday: A Layman's Guide to the Practical Use of the Scriptures.* Phillipsburg, N.J.: Presbyterian & Reformed, 1982f.

————. *Solving Marriage Problems: Biblical Solutions for Christian Counselors.* Phillipsburg, N.J.: Presbyterian & Reformed, 1983.

————. *The Biblical View of Self-Esteem, Self-Love, Self-Image.* Eugene, Ore.: Harvest House, 1986a.

————. *Handbook of Church Discipline.* Grand Rapids: Zondervan, 1986b.

————. *How to Help People Change: The Four-Step Biblical Process.* Grand Rapids: Zondervan, 1986c.

————. "What about Emotional Abuse?" *Journal of Pastoral Practice* 8 (3): 1–10 (1986d).

————. "A Reply to the Response." *Journal of Pastoral Practice* 9 (1): 1–5 (1987a).

————. "What Are/Is Christian Ethics?" *Journal of Biblical Ethics in Medicine* 1 (2): 20f (1987b).

————. *Sibling Rivalry in the Household of God.* Denver, Colo.: Accent, 1988.

————. "Comments." In *Prophets of Psychoheresy I,* edited by Martin Bobgan and Deidre Bobgan, 105f. Santa Barbara: EastGate Publishers, 1989a.

————. *From Forgiven to Forgiving: Discover the Path to Biblical Forgiveness.* USA: Victor Books (Scripture Press), 1989b.

————. "Jay Adams' Response to the Congress on Christian Counseling." *Journal of Pastoral Practice* 10 (1): 2–4 (1989c).

————. "The Physician, the Pastor, Psychotherapy, and Counseling." *Journal of Biblical Ethics in Medicine* 3 (2): 21–26 (1989d).

————. *The War Within: A Biblical Strategy for Spiritual Warfare.* Eugene, Ore.: Harvest House, 1989e.

————. "Reflections on the History of Biblical Counseling." In *Practical Theology and the Ministry of the Church, 1952–1984: Essays in Honor of Edmund P. Clowney,* edited by Harvie Conn, 203–17. Phillipsburg, N.J.: Presbyterian and Reformed, 1990a.

————. *Truth Applied: Application in Preaching.* Grand Rapids: Zondervan, 1990b.

————. *The Grand Demonstration: A Biblical Study of the So-Called Problem of Evil.* Santa Barbara: EastGate Publishers, 1991.

————. "Christian Counsel: An Interview with Jay Adams." *New Horizons in the Orthodox Presbyterian Church* 14 (3): 3–5 (1993a).

————. "Counseling and the Sovereignty of God." *Journal of Biblical Counseling* 11 (2): 4–9 (1993b).

————. *The Christian Counselor's Commentary: I & II Corinthians.* Hackettstown, N.J.: Timeless Texts, 1994.

————. "Change Them . . . into What?" *Journal of Biblical Counseling* 13 (2): 13–17 (1995a).

————. *The Christian Counselor's Commentary: Romans, Philippians, and I & II Thessalonians.* Hackettstown, N.J.: Timeless Texts, 1995b.

————. *Teaching to Observe: The Counselor as Teacher.* Woodruff, S.C.: Timeless Texts, 1995c.

————. *The Christian Counselor's Commentary: Hebrews, James, I & II Peter, and Jude.* Woodruff, S.C.: Timeless Texts, 1996.

Aden, Leroy, and Harold Ellens., eds. *Turning Points in Pastoral Care: The Legacy of Anton Boisen and Seward Hiltner.* Grand Rapids: Baker Book House, 1990.

Almy, Gary, Carol Tharp Almy, and Jerry Jenkins. *Addicted to Recovery: Exposing the False Gospel of Psychotherapy: Escaping the Trap of Victim Mentality.* Eugene, Ore.: Harvest House, 1994.

Anderson, Jack, and Les Whitten. "Military Radio Mismanagement Cited." *The Washington Post,* 13 January 1977.

Anderson, Ray S. "Isomorphic Indicators in Theological and Psychological Science." *Journal of Psychology and Theology* 17 (4): 373–81 (1989).

Augsburger, David W. *Caring Enough to Confront*. Glendale, Calif.: Regal Books, 1980.

Backus, William, and Marie Chapian. *Telling Yourself the Truth*. Minneapolis, Minn.: Bethany House Publishers, 1980.

Ben-David, Joseph. "Professions in the Class System of Present Day Societies." *Current Sociology* 12: 247–98 (1963).

Benner, David G. "Psychotherapies: Stalking Their Spiritual Side." *Christianity Today* (December 1981): 32f.

———. ed. *Baker Encyclopedia of Psychology*. Grand Rapids: Baker Book House, 1985a.

———. "Christian Counseling and Psychotherapy." In *Baker Encyclopedia of Psychology*, edited by David G. Benner. Grand Rapids: Baker Book House, 1985b.

———. *Psychotherapy and the Spiritual Quest*. Grand Rapids: Baker Book House, 1988.

Berry, C. Markham. "Counseling in the Medical Office." *Journal of Psychology and Theology* 2 (3): 174–81 (1974).

Bettler, John F. "Gaining an Accurate Self-Image, Part I." *Journal of Pastoral Practice* 6 (4): 46–52 (1983).

———. "Gaining an Accurate Self-Image, Part II." *Journal of Pastoral Practice* 7 (1): 41–50 (1984a).

———. "Gaining an Accurate Self-Image, Part III." *Journal of Pastoral Practice* 7 (2): 52–61 (1984b).

———. "Gaining an Accurate Self-Image, Part IV." *Journal of Pastoral Practice* 7 (3): 50–58 (1984c).

———. "Gaining an Accurate Self-Image, Part V." *Journal of Pastoral Practice* 7 (4): 46–55 (1985).

———. "Gaining an Accurate Self-Image, Conclusion." *Journal of Pastoral Practice* 8 (2): 24–26 (1987a).

———. "Biblical Counseling: The Next Generation." *Journal of Pastoral Practice* 8 (4): 3–10 (1987b).

———. "CCEF: The Beginning." *Journal of Pastoral Practice* 9 (3): 45–51 (1988).

———. "Counseling and the Problem of the Past." *Journal of Biblical Counseling* 12 (2): 5–23 (1994).

———. "When the Problem Is Sexual Sin: A Counseling Model." *Journal of Biblical Counseling* 13 (3): 16–18 (1995).

Bishop, D. Russell. "Psychology and the Pastoral Ministry: Help or Hindrance." *Journal of Psychology and Theology* 17 (2): 151–56 (1989).

Bobgan, Martin, and Deidre Bobgan. *The Psychological Way/The Spiritual Way: Are Christianity and Psychotherapy Compatible?* Minneapolis: Bethany House, 1979.

———. *How to Counsel from Scripture*. Chicago: Moody Press, 1985.

———. *Psychoheresy: The Psychological Seduction of Christianity*. Santa Barbara, Calif.: EastGate Publishers, 1987.

———. *Against "Biblical Counseling": For the Bible*. Santa Barbara, Calif.: EastGate Publishers, 1994.

Bobick, Michael W. "A Biblical Alternative to Inner Healing." *Journal of Pastoral Practice* 6 (4): 25–45 (1983).

Boghosian, Jack. "The Biblical Basis for Strategic Approaches in Pastoral Counseling." *Journal of Psychology and Theology* 11 (2): 99–107 (1983).

Boisen, Anton T. *The Exploration of the Inner World: A Study of Mental Disorder and Religious Experience*. New York: Harper Publishing, 1936.

Bosk, Charles L. *Forgive and Remember: Managing Medical Failure*. Chicago: University of Chicago Press, 1979.

Broger, John. *Self-Confrontation: A Manual for In-Depth Discipleship*. Nashville: Thomas Nelson, 1994.

Browning, Don S. *The Moral Context of Pastoral Care*. Philadelphia: Westminster Press, 1976.

———. *Religious Ethics and Pastoral Care*. Philadelphia: Fortress Press, 1983.

————. *Religious Thought and the Modern Psychologies: A Critical Conversation in the Theology of Culture.* Philadelphia: Fortress Press, 1987.

Bustanoby, Andre. "Without These, Don't Start." *Christianity Today* (July 1973): 32f.

Calvin, John. *Institutes of the Christian Religion.* Translated by Ford Lewis Battles. Edited by John T. McNeill. The Library of Christian Classics. Philadelphia: Westminster Press, 1960.

Capps, Donald. "Biblical Models in Pastoral Counseling." *Pastoral Psychology* 28 (4): 252–64 (1980).

————. *Biblical Approaches to Pastoral Counseling.* Philadelphia: Westminster Press, 1981.

————. "The Bible's Role in Pastoral Care and Counseling: Four Basic Principles." *Journal of Psychology and Christianity* 3 (4): 5–15 (1984).

————. "The Bible's Role in Pastoral Care and Counseling: Four Basic Principles." In *The Church and Pastoral Care,* edited by Leroy Aden and J. Harold Ellens, 41–55. Grand Rapids: Baker Book House, 1988.

————. "Pastoral Use and Interpretation of the Bible." In *Dictionary of Pastoral Care,* edited by Rodney J. Hunter, 82–85. Nashville: Abingdon Press, 1990a.

————. *Reframing: A New Method in Pastoral Care.* Minneapolis: Fortress Press, 1990b.

Carlson, David E. "Review of *Christian Counselor's Manual.*" *Counselor's Notebook* 1 (8, 9): (1974).

————. "Jesus' Style of Relating: The Search for a Biblical View of Counseling." *Journal of Psychology and Theology* 4 (3): 181–92 (1976).

Carter, John. "Nouthetic Counseling." In *Baker Encyclopedia of Psychology,* edited by David Benner, 762–65. Grand Rapids: Baker Book House, 1985.

————. "Adams' Theory of Nouthetic Counseling." *Journal of Psychology and Theology* 3 (3): 143–55 (1975).

————. "Nouthetic Counseling Defended: A Reply to Ganz." *Journal of Psychology and Theology* 4 (4): 206–16 (1976).

————. "Secular and Sacred Models of Psychology and Religion." *Journal of Psychology and Theology* 5 (3): 197–208 (1977).

————. "Towards a Biblical Model of Counseling." *Journal of Psychology and Theology* 8 (1): 45–52 (1980).

————. "Shallow Reflections on Crucial Issues." *Journal of Psychology and Theology* 18 (3): 289f (1990).

————. "Success without Finality: The Continuing Dialogue of Faith and Psychology." *Journal of Psychology and Christianity* 15 (2): 116–22 (1996).

Carter, John, and Bruce Narramore. *The Integration of Psychology and Theology.* Grand Rapids: Zondervan, 1979.

Childs, Brian H. "'The Dictionary of Pastoral Care and Counseling:' An Interview with Rodney J. Hunter." *Pastoral Psychology* 39 (2): 131–39 (1990).

Clinebell, Howard. *Basic Types of Pastoral Counseling.* Nashville: Abingdon Press, 1966.

————. *Basic Types of Pastoral Care & Counseling: Resources for the Ministry of Healing and Growth.* Nashville: Abingdon Press, 1966, 1984.

Coe, John H. *Educating the Church for Wisdom's Sake or Why Biblical Counseling Is Unbiblical.* unpublished, 1991.

Cohen, Edmund D. *The Mind of the Bible-Believer.* Buffalo, N.Y.: Prometheus Books, 1986.

Coleman, Lyman. *Small Group Training Manual.* Littleton, Colo.: Serendipity, 1991.

Collins, Gary R. "Popular Christian Psychologies: Some Reflections." *Journal of Psychology and Theology* 3 (2): 127–32 (1975a).

————. "The Pulpit and the Couch." *Christianity Today* (August 29, 1975b): 5–9.

————. *How to Be a People Helper.* Santa Ana, Calif.: Vision House, 1976.

————. *The Rebuilding of Psychology: An Integration of Psychology and Christianity.* Wheaton, Ill.: Tyndale House, 1977.

————. "Door Interview: Dr. Gary Collins." *The Wittenburg Door* 47 (February–March, 1979).

————, ed. *Helping People Grow: Practical Approaches to Christian Counseling*. Santa Ana, Calif.: Vision House, 1980.

————. *Psychology and Theology: Prospects for Integration*. Edited by H. Newton Maloney. Nashville: Abingdon Press, 1981.

————. "Moving through the Jungle: A Decade of Integration." *Journal of Psychology and Theology* 11 (1): 2–7 (1983).

————. *Can You Trust Psychology?: Exposing the Facts and the Fictions*. Downers Grove, Ill.: InterVarsity Press, 1988.

————. "A Letter to Christian Counselors." *Journal of Psychology and Christianity* 9 (1): 37–39 (1990).

————, ed. *Case Studies in Christian Counseling*. Resources for Christian Counseling, ed. Gary R. Collins. Dallas: Word Publishing, 1991a.

————. *Excellence and Ethics in Counseling*. Resources for Christian Counseling, ed. Gary R. Collins. Dallas: Word Publishing, 1991b.

————. *The Biblical Basis of Christian Counseling for People Helpers*. Colorado Springs: NavPress, 1993.

Colton, Robert. "Review of *Essays on Counseling*." *Criswell Theological Review* 3 (2): 432f (1989).

Corsini, Raymond J. et al. *Current Psychotherapies*. Itasca, Ill.: F.E. Peacock, 1973.

Crabb, Lawrence J. *Basic Principles of Biblical Counseling*. Grand Rapids: Zondervan, 1975.

————. *Effective Biblical Counseling*. Grand Rapids: Zondervan, 1977.

————. *The Marriage Builder: A Blueprint for Counselors and Couples*. Grand Rapids: Zondervan, 1982, 1992.

————. *Understanding People: Deep Longings for Relationship*. Grand Rapids: Zondervan, 1987.

————. *Inside Out*. Colorado Springs: NavPress, 1988.

————. *Men and Women: Enjoying the Difference*. Grand Rapids: Zondervan, 1991.

Crabb, Lawrence J., and Dan B. Allender. *Encouragement: The Key to Caring*. Grand Rapids: Zondervan, 1984.

Dobson, James. *The New Dare to Discipline*. Wheaton, Ill.: Tyndale House, 1992.

Donehoo, Fred. "Critique of Jay Adams's *Competent to Counsel*." unpublished, 1969.

Early Days of the Biblical Counseling Foundation: A Brief History. Rancho Mirage, Calif.: Biblical Counseling Foundation, 1993.

Eck, Brian E. "Integrating the Integrators: An Organizing Framework for a Multifaceted Process of Integration." *Journal of Psychology and Christianity* 15 (2): 101–15 (1996).

Eggold, Henry J. "Review of *Competent to Counsel*." *The Springfielder* 35 (1): 76f (1971).

Ellens, J. Harold. *God's Grace and Human Health*. Nashville: Abingdon Press, 1982.

————. "Review of *The Biblical View of Self-Esteem, Self-Love, and Self-Image* by Jay Adams." *Journal of Psychology and Christianity* 6 (3): 70 (1987).

————. Editorial: "Retrospect, Prospect, and Farewell." *Journal of Psychology and Christianity* 7 (4): 3f (1988).

English, William F. "An Integrationist's Critique of and Challenge to the Bobgans' View of Counseling and Psychotherapy." *Journal of Psychology and Theology* 18 (3): 228–36 (1990).

Ericsson, Samuel E. "Clergy Malpractice: Ramifications of a New Theory." In *Clergy Malpractice*, edited by H. Newton Malony, Thomas L. Needham, and Samuel Southard. Philadelphia: Westminster Press, 1986.

Evans, C. Stephen. *Preserving the Person: A Look at the Human Sciences*. Grand Rapids: Baker Book House, 1977.

Eyrich, Howard A., ed. *What to Do When*. Phillipsburg, N.J.: Presbyterian & Reformed, 1978.

————. *Three to Get Ready: A Christian Premarital Counselor's Manual*. Grand Rapids: Baker Book House, 1978, 1991.

Eysenk, H. J. "The Effects of Psychotherapy." In *Handbook of Abnormal Psychology*, edited by H. J. Eysenk. New York: Basic Books, 1961.

Fitzpatrick, Elyse. "Helping Overeaters." *Journal of Pastoral Practice* 11 (1): 51–56 (1992).

———. "Helping Bulimics." *Journal of Biblical Counseling* 11 (2): 16–20 (1993).

———. "Helping Anorexics." *Journal of Biblical Counseling* 11 (3): 19–23 (1993).

———. "Disorderly Eating . . . for the Rest of Us." *Journal of Biblical Counseling* 12 (1): 20–23 (1993).

Foster, James D., and Scot A. Bolsinger. "Prominent Themes in Evangelical Integration Literature." *Journal of Psychology and Theology* 18 (1): 3–12 (1990).

Foster, James D., Debra A. Horn, and Steve Watson. "The Popularity of Integration Models, 1980–1985." *Journal of Psychology and Theology* 16 (1): 3–14 (1988).

Foster, James D., and Mark Ledbetter. "Christian Anti-Psychology and the Scientific Method." *Journal of Psychology and Theology* 15 (1): 10–18 (1987).

Foucault, Michel. *Madness and Civilization: A History of Insanity in the Age of Reason.* Translated by Richard Howard. New York: Pantheon Books, 1965.

Frame, John M. "Proposal for a New Seminary." *Journal of Pastoral Practice* 2 (1): 10–17 (1978).

Freidson, Eliot. *Professional Powers: A Study of the Institutionalization of Formal Knowledge.* Chicago: University of Chicago Press, 1986.

Ganz, Richard. *Psychobabble: The Failure of Modern Psychology—and the Biblical Alternative.* Wheaton, Ill.: Crossway Books, 1993.

Gevitz, Norman, ed. *Other Healers: Unorthodox Medicine in America.* Baltimore: Johns Hopkins University Press, 1988.

Glasser, William. *Reality Therapy: A New Approach to Psychiatry.* New York: Harper and Row, 1965.

Goffman, Erving. *Asylums: Essays on the Social Situation of Mental Patients and Other Inmates.* Garden City, N.Y.: Anchor Books, 1961.

———. *Stigma.* Englewood Cliffs, N.J.: Prentice-Hall, 1963.

Goldenberg, Irene, and Herbert Goldenberg. *Family Therapy: An Overview.* Pacific Grove, Calif.: Brooks/Cole Publishing, 1985.

Goodrum, David. "Putting Things into Perspective: An Introduction to the Writings of Jay E. Adams." *The Council of Chalcedon* 9 (8): 10–12 (1987).

Griffith, E., and J. Young. "Pastoral Counseling and the Concept of Malpractice." *Bulletin of the American Academy of Psychiatry and the Law* 15: 257–65 (1987).

Grob, Gerald N. *Mental Illness and American Society, 1875–1940.* Princeton: Princeton University Press, 1983.

Guinness, Os, and John Seel, eds. *No God but God.* Chicago: Moody Press, 1992.

Hammar, Richard R. *Pastor, Church & Law.* Matthews, N.C.: Christian Ministry Resources, 1991.

Harris, Ronald T. "Entering Zion with Singing." *Journal of Pastoral Practice* 9 (2): 35–57 (1988).

Hart, D. G. *Defending the Faith: J. Gresham Machen and the Crisis of Conservative Protestantism in Modern America.* Baltimore: Johns Hopkins University Press, 1994.

Hemfelt, Robert, Frank Minirth, and Paul Meier. *Love Is a Choice.* Nashville: Thomas Nelson, 1989.

Henry, Carl. *The Uneasy Conscience of Modern Fundamentalism.* Grand Rapids: William B. Eerdmans, 1947.

Hesselgrave, David J. *Counseling Cross-Culturally: An Introduction to Theory & Practice for Christians.* Grand Rapids: Baker Book House, 1984.

Hofstadter, Richard. *Anti-Intellectualism in American Life.* New York: Random House, 1962.

———. *The Paranoid Style in American Politics, and Other Essays.* New York: Random House, 1963.

Holifield, E. Brooks. *A History of Pastoral Care in America: From Salvation to Self-Realization.* Nashville: Abingdon Press, 1983.

House, H. Wayne. *Christian Ministries and the Law*. Grand Rapids: Baker Book House, 1992.

Hughes, Everett C., and Agostino DeBaggis. "Systems of Theological Education in the United States." In *Education for the Professions of Medicine, Law, Theology, and Social Welfare*, edited by Everett C. Hughes et al. 169–200. New York: McGraw-Hill, 1973.

Humphries, Robert H. "Therapeutic Neutrality Reconsidered." *Journal of Religion and Health* 21 (2): 124–31 (1982).

Hunt, Dave, and T. A. McMahon. *The Seduction of Christianity*. Eugene, Ore.: Harvest House, 1985.

Hunter, James Davison. *American Evangelicalism: Conservative Religion and the Quandary of Modernity*. New Brunswick, N.J.: Rutgers University Press, 1983.

Hunter, Rodney J., ed. *Dictionary of Pastoral Care and Counseling*. Nashville: Abingdon Press, 1990.

Hunter, William. "Review of *The Useful Lie* by Playfair." *Journal of Psychology and Theology* 20 (1): 63–69 (1992).

———. "Review of *Clinical Handbook of Pastoral Counseling*." *Journal of Psychology and Theology* 21 (4): 328f (1993).

Hunter, William F., and Marvin K. Mayers. "Psychology and Missions: Reflections on Status and Need." *Journal of Psychology and Theology* 15 (4): 269–73 (1987).

Hurding, Roger. *The Tree of Healing*. Grand Rapids: Zondervan, 1985.

Hurley, James, and Peter Jones. "Review of the Department of Practical Theology at Westminster Theological Seminary in California." Escondido, Calif.: Westminster Theological Seminary, 1993.

Hutchinson, George P. *The History Behind the Reformed Presbyterian Church, Evangelical Synod*. Cherry Hill, N.J.: Mack Publishing, 1974.

Jeske, J. Oscar. "Varieties of Approaches to Psychotherapy: Options for the Christian Therapist." *Journal of Psychology and Theology* 12 (4): 260–69 (1984).

Johnson, Cedric B., and H. Newton Maloney. *Christian Conversion: Biblical and Psychological Perspectives*. Grand Rapids: Zondervan, 1981.

Johnson, Eric L. "A Place for the Bible within Psychological Science." *Journal of Psychology and Theology* 20 (4): 346–55 (1992).

Johnson, Ron. Letter to Editor. *Journal of Psychology and Christianity* 4 (1): 4f. (1985).

Jones IV, Bob. "Personality Splits: Minirth of Minirth-Meier fame breaks off amid controversy." *World,* 19 March 1996, 18f.

Jones, Stanton L. "Assertiveness Training in Christian Perspective." *Journal of Psychology and Theology* 12 (2): 91–99 (1984).

———, ed. *Psychology and the Christian Faith: An Introductory Reader*. Grand Rapids: Baker Book House, 1986.

———. "Overview of the Rech Conference on Christian Graduate Training in Psychology and Introduction to the Collected Papers." *Journal of Psychology and Theology* 20 (2): 77–88 (1992).

———. "Reflections on the Nature and Future of the Christian Psychologies." *Journal of Psychology and Christianity* 15 (2): 133–42 (1996).

Jones, Stanton L., and Richard Butman. *Modern Psychotherapies: A Comprehensive Christian Appraisal*. Downers Grove, Ill.: InterVarsity Press, 1991.

King, Steven D. "Fundamentalist Pastoral Care." In *Dictionary of Pastoral Care and Counseling*, edited by Rodney J. Hunter, 448–50. Nashville: Abingdon Press, 1990.

Kirwan, William T. *Biblical Concepts for Christian Counseling: A Case for Integrating Psychology and Theology*. Grand Rapids: Baker Book House, 1984.

Kitchen, Alice. "Review of *Competent to Counsel*." *HIS* 33 (1972): 21, 31.

Kovel, Joel. *A Complete Guide to Therapy: From Psychoanalysis to Behavior Modification*. New York: Pantheon Books, 1976.

Kubler-Ross, Elizabeth. *On Death and Dying.* New York: Macmillan, 1969.

Kuhn, Thomas S. *The Essential Tension: Selected Studies in Scientific Tradition and Change.* Chicago: University of Chicago Press, 1977.

Lapsley, James N. "Review of *Psychology and Christianity: Integrative Readings.*" *Zygon* 18 (4): 464f (1983).

Livingstone, David N. "High Tea at the Cyclotron." *Books & Culture* (January/February 1996): 22f.

London, Perry. *The Modes and Morals of Psychotherapy.* New York: Holt, Rinehart and Winston, 1964.

Lovelace, Richard F. *Dynamics of Spiritual Life: An Evangelical Theology of Renewal.* Downers Grove, Ill.: InterVarsity Press, 1979.

MacArthur, John. *Our Sufficiency in Christ.* Dallas: Word Publishing, 1991.

MacArthur, John, and Wayne Mack. *Introduction to Biblical Counseling: A Basic Guide to the Principles and Practice of Counseling.* Dallas: Word Publishing, 1994.

Mack, Wayne A. *How to Develop Deep Unity in the Marriage Relationship: A How To Manual for Christian Growth and Development.* USA: Presbyterian & Reformed, 1977a.

———. *How to Pray Effectively: A How To Manual for Christian Growth and Development.* USA: Presbyterian & Reformed, 1977b.

———. *How to Read the Bible: A How To Manual for Christian Growth and Development.* USA: Presbyterian & Reformed, 1977c.

———. *Homework Manual for Biblical Counseling.* Vol. 2, *Family and Marital Problems.* USA: Presbyterian & Reformed, 1980.

———. *Your Family God's Way: Developing and Sustaining Relationships in the Home.* USA: Presbyterian & Reformed, 1991.

Mack, Wayne A., and Nathan A. Mack. *Preparing for Marriage God's Way.* Tulsa, Okla.: Virgil W. Hensley, 1986.

Malony, H. Newton, ed. *Psychology and Faith: The Christian Experience of Eighteen Psychologists.* Washington, D.C.: University Press of America, 1978.

———, ed. *Wholeness and Holiness: Readings in the Psychology/Theology of Mental Health.* Grand Rapids: Baker Book House, 1983.

Malony, H. Newton et al., eds. *Clergy Malpractice.* Philadelphia: Westminster Press, 1986.

Marsden, George M. *Fundamentalism and American Culture: The Shaping of Twentieth-Century Evangelicalism, 1870–1925.* New York: Oxford University Press, 1980.

———, ed. *Evangelicalism and Modern America.* Grand Rapids: William B. Eerdmans, 1984.

———. *Reforming Fundamentalism: Fuller Seminary and the New Evangelicalism.* Grand Rapids: William B. Eerdmans, 1987.

———. *Understanding Fundamentalism and Evangelicalism.* Grand Rapids: William B. Eerdmans, 1991.

Martin, Steven C. "'The Only Truly Scientific Method of Healing': Chiropractic and American Science, 1895–1990." *Isis* 85 (2): 206–27 (1994).

Marty, Martin. *Modern American Religion.* Chicago: University of Chicago Press, 1986ff.

Marty, Martin, and R. Scott Appleby, eds. *Fundamentalisms Observed.* The Fundamentalism Project. Chicago: University of Chicago Press, 1991.

———, eds. *Fundamentalisms and Society: Reclaiming the Sciences, the Family, and Education.* Chicago: University of Chicago Press, 1993.

McGee, Robert S. *The Search for Significance.* Houston: Rapha Publishing, 1985.

McGrath, Joanna and Alister McGrath. *The Dilemma of Self-Esteem: The Cross and Christian Confidence.* Wheaton, Ill.: Crossway Books, 1992.

McMillen, S. I. *None of These Diseases.* Westwood, N.J.: Spire Books, 1963.

Meier, Paul D., Frank B. Minirth, and Frank B. Wichern. *Introduction to Psychology and Counseling: Christian Perspectives and*

Applications. Grand Rapids: Baker Book House, 1991.

Meyer, Donald. *The Positive Thinkers: Popular Religious Psychology from Mary Baker Eddy to Norman Vincent Peale and Ronald Reagan*. Middletown, Conn.: Wesleyan University Press, 1988.

Miller, Kevin Dale. "Putting an End to Christian Psychology: Larry Crabb thinks therapy belongs back in the churches." *Christianity Today* (August 14, 1995): 16f.

Minirth, Frank, and Paul Meier. *Happiness Is a Choice*. Waco, Tex.: Word Books.

Moody, Raymond. *Life after Life*. New York: Bantam Books, 1975.

Moore, James "Trip". *Self-Image*. Edited by Tom Varney. IBC Discussion Guides. Colorado Springs: NavPress, 1992.

Mowrer, O. Hobart. *The Crisis in Psychiatry and Religion*. Princeton: Van Nostrand Co., 1961.

———. *Abnormal Reactions or Actions? (An Autobiographical Answer)*. Dubuque: William C. Brown Co., 1966.

Myers, David G. *The Human Puzzle: Psychological Research and Christian Belief*. New York: Harper & Row, 1978.

———. *The Inflated Self*. New York: Seabury, 1981.

Narramore, Bruce. "Perspectives on the Integration of Psychology and Theology." *Journal of Psychology and Theology* 1 (1): 3–18 (1973).

———. *No Condemnation: Rethinking Guilt Motivation in Counseling, Preaching, and Parenting*. Grand Rapids: Zondervan, 1984.

———. "The Concept of Responsibility in Psychopathology and Psychotherapy." *Journal of Psychology and Theology* 13 (2): 91–96 (1985).

———. "Barriers to the Integration of Faith and Learning in Christian Graduate Training Programs in Psychology." *Journal of Psychology and Theology* 20 (2): 119–26 (1992a).

———. "Integrative Inquiry: How do you view our progress in integrating psychology and theology?" *Journal of Psychology and Theology* 20 (4): 395–97 (1992b).

Nash, Ronald H. *Great Divides: Understanding the Controversies That Come Between Christians*. Colorado Springs: NavPress, 1993.

Neufeld, Vernon H. *If We Can Love: The Mennonite Mental Health Story*. Newton, Kans.: Faith and Life Press, 1983.

Noll, Mark A. *The Scandal of the Evangelical Mind*. Grand Rapids: William B. Eerdmans, 1994.

Numbers, Ronald L. *The Creationists*. New York: Alfred A. Knopf, 1992.

O'Donnell, Gerald H. "Review of *The Big Umbrella*." *Westminster Theological Journal* 35 (Spring 1973): 378–81.

Oakland, James A. et al. "An Analysis and Critique of Jay Adams's Theory of Counseling." *Journal of the American Scientific Affiliation* 28 (September 1976): 101–109.

Oden, Thomas C. *Pastoral Theology: Essentials of Ministry*. San Francisco: HarperCollins, 1982.

———. *Pastoral Counsel*. Vol. 3. *Classical Pastoral Care*. Grand Rapids: Baker Book House, 1987.

Oglesby, William Jr. *Biblical Themes for Pastoral Care*. Nashville: Abingdon Press, 1980.

Otto, Paul S. "Review of *What About Nouthetic Counseling?*" *Eternity* 29 (November 1978): 47f.

Outler, Albert. *Psychotherapy and the Christian Message*. New York: Harper & Row, 1954.

Parker, Ken. *Reclaiming Your Inner Child*. Nashville: Thomas Nelson, 1993.

Passantino, Bob, and Gretchen Passantino. "The 'Biblical Counseling' Alternative." *Christian Research Journal* 17 (4): 24–30 (1995).

Pattison, Stephen. *A Critique of Pastoral Care*. London: SCM Press, 1988.

Philipchalk, Ronald P. *Psychology and Christianity: An Introduction to Controversial Issues*. Lanham, Md.: University Press of America, 1987.

Polanyi, Michael. *Personal Knowledge: Towards a Post-Critical Philosophy*. Chicago: University of Chicago, 1958.

Popper, Karl R. *Conjectures and Refutations: The Growth of Scientific Knowledge*. New York: Harper & Row, 1963, 1965.

Powlison, David. "Human Defensiveness: The Third Way." *Journal of Pastoral Practice* 8 (1): 40–55 (1985).

———. "Crucial Issues in Contemporary Biblical Counseling." *Journal of Pastoral Practice* 9 (3): 53–78 (1988).

———. "Idols of the Heart and 'Vanity Fair.'" *Areopagus* 2 (1): 2–21 (1991).

———. "Integration or Inundation?" In *Power Religion*, edited by Michael Horton, 191–218. Chicago: Moody Press, 1992.

———. *Power Encounters: Reclaiming Spiritual Warfare*. Grand Rapids: Baker Book House, 1995.

Powlison, David, Jay E. Adams, and John F. Bettler. "25 Years of Biblical Counseling: An Interview with Jay Adams and John Bettler." *Journal of Biblical Counseling* 12 (1): 8–13 (1993).

Rabey, Steve. "Hurting Helpers: Will the Christian counseling movement live up to its promise?" *Christianity Today* (September 16, 1996): 76–78, 80, 108, 110.

Rieff, Philip. *The Triumph of the Therapeutic: Uses of Faith after Freud*. Chicago: University of Chicago Press, 1987.

Roberts, Robert C. *Taking the Word to Heart: Self and Other in an Age of Therapies*. Grand Rapids: William B. Eerdmans, 1993.

———. "Psychobabble: A Guide for Perplexed Christians in an Age of Therapies." *Christianity Today* (May 16, 1994): 18–24.

Rogers, Carl R. *Counseling and Psychotherapy*. Boston: Houghton Mifflin, 1942.

———. *On Becoming a Person: A Therapist's View of Psychotherapy*. Boston: Houghton Mifflin, 1961.

Rosenberg, Charles E. "The Crisis in Psychiatric Legitimacy: Reflections on Psychiatry, Medicine, and Public Policy." In *American Psychiatry Past, Present, and Future*, edited by George Kriegman et al. 135–48. Charlottesville, Va.: University Press of Virginia, 1975.

———. *Explaining Epidemics and Other Studies in the History of Medicine*. New York: Cambridge University Press, 1992.

Rosenhan, D. L. "12 Admissions of Mental Error." *Medical World News* (February 9, 1973): 17ff.

Rossow, Francis C. "Review of *Preaching with Purpose*." *Concordia Journal* 11: 121 (1985).

———. "Review of *Essays on Biblical Preaching*." *Concordia Journal* 13 (3): 284f (1987).

Runions, J. Ernest. "Review of *Shepherding God's Flock: Pastoral Counseling*." *Journal of the Evangelical Theological Society* 20: 83f (March 1977).

Sande, Ken. *The Peacemaker: A Biblical Guide to Resolving Personal Conflict*. Grand Rapids: Baker, 1991.

Scharlemann, Martin H. "Review of *Trust and Obey*." *Concordia Journal* 5 (5): 194f (1979).

Schuller, Robert H. *Self-Esteem: The New Reformation*. Waco, Tex.: Word Books, 1982.

Scipione, George C. *Timothy, Titus, and You: A Workbook for Church Leaders*. Phillipsburg, N.J.: Pilgrim Publishing Co., 1975.

———. "The Limits of Confidentiality in Counseling." *Journal of Pastoral Practice* 7 (2): 29–34 (1984).

Scull, Andrew. *Museums of Madness: The Social Organization of Insanity in Nineteenth-Century England*. New York: St. Martin's Press, 1979.

———, ed. *Madhouses, Mad-Doctors, and Madmen: The Social History of Psychiatry in the Victorian Era*. Philadelphia: University of Pennsylvania Press, 1981.

Seamands, David A. *Healing of Memories*. Wheaton, Ill.: Victor Books, 1985.

Shepperson, Vance L. "Systemic Integration: A Reactive Alternative to 'The Conduct of Integration.'" *Journal of Psychology and Theology* 10 (4): 326–28 (1982).

Shogren, Gary, and Edward Welch. *Running in Circles*. Grand Rapids: Baker Book House, 1995.

Showalter, Elaine. *The Female Malady: Women, Madness, and English Culture, 1830–1980.* New York: Penguin Books, 1985.

Sifford, Darrell. "Divorce and God's law: Is there a compromise?" *Philadelphia Inquirer,* 30 January 1984: 8-E.

———. "Letting Religion Guide Your Life." *Philadelphia Inquirer,* 29 January 1984: 1-G, 6-G.

Slosser, Gaius J., ed. *They Seek a Country: The American Presbyterians, Some Aspects.* New York: Macmillan, 1955.

Smith, Robert D. "Illness and a Life View." *Journal of Pastoral Practice* 1 (1): 80–84 (1977).

———. "A Physician Looks at Counseling: Depression." *Journal of Pastoral Practice* 1 (1): 85–87 (1977).

———. "A Physician Looks at Counseling: Symptoms." *Journal of Pastoral Practice* 1 (1): 88–90 (1977).

———. "A Look at Psychosomatic Relationships." *Journal of Pastoral Practice* 1 (2): 81–87 (1977).

———. "Psychosomatics in the Bible." *Journal of Pastoral Practice* 1 (2): 88f (1977).

———. "It's Not What You Eat, It's What Eats You." *Journal of Pastoral Practice* 8 (1): 1–10 (1985).

———. "Fearfully and Wonderfully Made." *Journal of Pastoral Practice* 8 (2): 2–12 (1986a).

———. "God's Word and Your Health." *Journal of Pastoral Practice* 8 (3): 11–27 (1986b).

———. "What to Do When Illness Strikes." *Journal of Pastoral Practice* 8 (4): 11–18 (1987).

Somerville, Robert B. *Help for Hotliners: A Manual for Christian Telephone Crisis Counselors.* USA: Presbyterian & Reformed, 1978.

Southard, Samuel. "The Current Need for 'Theological Counsel.'" *Pastoral Psychology* 32 (2): 89–105 (1983).

Spalink, Larry. "Warning: This Office Bugged by the Holy Spirit." *Journal of Biblical Counseling* 3 (3): 56–62 (1979).

Stafford, Tim. "Franchising Hope." *Christianity Today* (May 18, 1992): 22–26.

———. "The Therapeutic Revolution." *Christianity Today* (May 17, 1993): 24–32.

Strunk, Orlo, Jr. "The Role of Visioning in the Pastoral Counseling Movement." *Pastoral Psychology* 31 (1): 7–18 (1982).

Szasz, Thomas. *The Myth of Mental Illness: Foundations of a Theory of Personal Conduct.* New York: Harper and Row, 1961

———. *Ideology and Insanity: Essays on the Psychiatric Dehumanization of Man.* Garden City, N.Y.: Doubleday, 1970.

———. "Mental Illness Is Still a Myth." *Society* 31 (4): 34–39 (1995).

Tan, Siang-Yang. *Lay Counseling: Equipping Christians for a Helping Ministry.* Grand Rapids: Zondervan, 1991.

———. "Counseling Asians." In *Healing for the City,* edited by Craig Ellison and Edward Maynard, 110–23. Grand Rapids: Zondervan, 1992.

Tidball, Derek J. *Skillful Shepherds: An Introduction to Pastoral Theology.* Grand Rapids: Zondervan, 1986.

Timpe, Randy. "Christian Psychology." In *Baker Encyclopedia of Psychology,* edited by David G. Benner, 166–71. Grand Rapids: Baker Book House, 1985.

Tripp, Tedd. *Shepherding a Child's Heart.* Wapwallopen, Pa.: Shepherd Press, 1995.

Truax, Charles B., and Robert R. Carkhuff. *Toward Effective Counseling and Psychotherapy: Training and Practice.* Chicago: Aldine Publishing, 1967.

Van Eerden, Thomas. "Review of *What About Nouthetic Counseling?*" *Calvin Theological Journal* 12 (fall 1977): 235f.

Van Leeuwen, Mary Stewart. *The Sorcerer's Apprentice: A Christian Looks at the Changing Face of Psychology.* Downers Grove, Ill.: InterVarsity Press, 1982.

Van Zoeren, Jay. "Review of *Competent to Counsel.*" *Reformed Review* 24 (3): 140f (1971).

Vandegriff, John. *In the Arena of the Mind: Philippians 4:8.* Howell, N.J.: Ask, Seek, and Knock Publishing, 1992.

Viars, Steve. "Counseling in the Local Church—A Working Model." DMin diss., Westminster Theological Seminary, 1988.

Villareal, Luis. "Counseling Hispanics." In *Healing for the City*, edited by Craig Ellison and Edward Maynard, 139–58. Grand Rapids: Zondervan, 1992.

Vitz, Paul C. *Psychology as Religion: The Cult of Self-Worship*. Grand Rapids: William B. Eerdmans, 1977.

Ward, Waylon O. "Review of *More Than Redemption*." *Eternity* 31 (December 1980): 42f.

Warner, John Harley. "Medical Sectarianism, Therapeutic Conflict, and the Shaping of Orthodox Professional Identity in Antebellum American Medicine." In *Medical Fringe and Medical Orthodoxy, 1750–1850*, edited by W. F. Bynum and Roy Porter, 234–60. London: Croom Helm, 1987.

Weber, Timothy. "Coincidence of Opposites: The Meeting of Psychology and Theology." In *Psychology & Theology: Prospects for Integration*, edited by H. Newton Malony, 100–09. Nashville: Abingdon Press, 1978.

Weiss, David C. "Review of *The Christian Counselor's Manual*." *Journal of Pastoral Care* 29 (2): 141f (1975).

Welch, Edward T. *Counselor's Guide to the Brain and Its Disorders: Knowing the Difference Between Disease and Sin*. Grand Rapids: Zondervan, 1991.

Welch, Edward T., and Gary Shogren. *Addictive Behavior*. Grand Rapids: Baker Book House, 1995.

Wells, David F. *No Place for Truth or Whatever Happened to Evangelical Theology*. Grand Rapids: William B. Eerdmans, 1993.

Wigglesworth, Chris. "Bible: Pastoral Use." In *A Dictionary of Pastoral Care*, edited by Alastair V. Campbell, 25f. New York: Crossroad, 1987.

Winter, Richard. "Jay Adams—is he really biblical enough?" *Third Way* (April 1982): 9–12.

Young, John L., and Ezra E. H. Griffith. "The Development and Practice of Pastoral Counseling." *Hospital and Community Psychiatry* 40 (3): 271–76 (1989).

Zilbergeld, Bernie. *The Shrinking of America: Myths of Psychological Change*. Boston: Little Brown, 1983.

———. "Myths of Counseling." *Leadership* (Winter 1984): 87–94.

Zilboorg, Gregory. "Rediscovery of the Patient: An Historical Note." In *Progress in Psychotherapy*, edited by Frieda Fromm-Reichmann and J. L. Moreno. New York: Grune & Stratton, 1956.

Index